# IFIP Advances in Information and Communication Technology 380

Editor-in-Chief

*A. Joe Turner, Seneca, SC, USA*

Editorial Board

Foundations of Computer Science
*Mike Hinchey, Lero, Limerick, Ireland*
Software: Theory and Practice
*Michael Goedicke, University of Duisburg-Essen, Germany*
Education
*Arthur Tatnall, Victoria University, Melbourne, Australia*
Information Technology Applications
*Ronald Waxman, EDA Standards Consulting, Beachwood, OH, USA*
Communication Systems
*Guy Leduc, Université de Liège, Belgium*
System Modeling and Optimization
*Jacques Henry, Université de Bordeaux, France*
Information Systems
*Jan Pries-Heje, Roskilde University, Denmark*
ICT and Society
*Jackie Phahlamohlaka, CSIR, Pretoria, South Africa*
Computer Systems Technology
*Paolo Prinetto, Politecnico di Torino, Italy*
Security and Privacy Protection in Information Processing Systems
*Kai Rannenberg, Goethe University Frankfurt, Germany*
Artificial Intelligence
*Tharam Dillon, Curtin University, Bentley, Australia*
Human-Computer Interaction
*Annelise Mark Pejtersen, Center of Cognitive Systems Engineering, Denmark*
Entertainment Computing
*Ryohei Nakatsu, National University of Singapore*

# IFIP – The International Federation for Information Processing

IFIP was founded in 1960 under the auspices of UNESCO, following the First World Computer Congress held in Paris the previous year. An umbrella organization for societies working in information processing, IFIP's aim is two-fold: to support information processing within ist member countries and to encourage technology transfer to developing nations. As ist mission statement clearly states,

> *IFIP's mission is to be the leading, truly international, apolitical organization which encourages and assists in the development, exploitation and application of information technology for the benefit of all people.*

IFIP is a non-profitmaking organization, run almost solely by 2500 volunteers. It operates through a number of technical committees, which organize events and publications. IFIP's events range from an international congress to local seminars, but the most important are:

- The IFIP World Computer Congress, held every second year;
- Open conferences;
- Working conferences.

The flagship event is the IFIP World Computer Congress, at which both invited and contributed papers are presented. Contributed papers are rigorously refereed and the rejection rate is high.

As with the Congress, participation in the open conferences is open to all and papers may be invited or submitted. Again, submitted papers are stringently refereed.

The working conferences are structured differently. They are usually run by a working group and attendance is small and by invitation only. Their purpose is to create an atmosphere conducive to innovation and development. Refereeing is less rigorous and papers are subjected to extensive group discussion.

Publications arising from IFIP events vary. The papers presented at the IFIP World Computer Congress and at open conferences are published as conference proceedings, while the results of the working conferences are often published as collections of selected and edited papers.

Any national society whose primary activity is in information may apply to become a full member of IFIP, although full membership is restricted to one society per country. Full members are entitled to vote at the annual General Assembly, National societies preferring a less committed involvement may apply for associate or corresponding membership. Associate members enjoy the same benefits as full members, but without voting rights. Corresponding members are not represented in IFIP bodies. Affiliated membership is open to non-national societies, and individual and honorary membership schemes are also offered.

Luis M. Camarinha-Matos   Lai Xu
Hamideh Afsarmanesh (Eds.)

# Collaborative Networks in the Internet of Services

13th IFIP WG 5.5 Working Conference
on Virtual Enterprises, PRO-VE 2012
Bournemouth, UK, October 1-3, 2012
Proceedings

 Springer

Volume Editors

Luis M. Camarinha-Matos
Universidade Nova de Lisboa
Campus de Caparica, 2829-516, Monte Caparica, Portugal
E-mail: cam@uninova.pt

Lai Xu
Bournemouth University
Poole House, Talbot Campus, Poole, Dorset, BH12 5BB, UK
E-mail: lxu@bournemouth.ac.uk

Hamideh Afsarmanesh
University of Amsterdam
Science Park 904, 1098 XH Amsterdam, The Netherlands
E-mail: h.afsarmanesh@uva.nl

ISSN 1868-4238                 e-ISSN 1868-422X
ISBN 978-3-642-42949-1      ISBN 978-3-642-32775-9 (eBook)
DOI 10.1007/978-3-642-32775-9
Springer Heidelberg Dordrecht London New York

CR Subject Classification (1998): H.5.3, C.2, H.4, J.1, D.2, H.3.4-5, K.6.3, K.6.5

© IFIP International Federation for Information Processing 2012
Softcover reprint of the hardcover 1st edition 2012
This work is subject to copyright. All rights are reserved, whether the whole or part of the material is
concerned, specifically the rights of translation, reprinting, re-use of illustrations, recitation, broadcasting,
reproduction on microfilms or in any other way, and storage in data banks. Duplication of this publication
or parts thereof is permitted only under the provisions of the German Copyright Law of September 9, 1965,
in ist current version, and permission for use must always be obtained from Springer. Violations are liable
to prosecution under the German Copyright Law.
The use of general descriptive names, registered names, trademarks, etc. in this publication does not imply,
even in the absence of a specific statement, that such names are exempt from the relevant protective laws
and regulations and therefore free for general use.

*Typesetting:* Camera-ready by author, data conversion by Scientific Publishing Services, Chennai, India

Printed on acid-free paper

Springer is part of Springer Science+Business Media (www.springer.com)

# Preface

## Collaborative Networks in the Internet of Services

Recent developments under the umbrella of the Future Internet offer new concepts and mechanisms to support a new generation of advanced collaborative networks. Particularly relevant is the consolidation of the Internet of Services and its associated infrastructures and related concepts such as service ecologies and service parks. Complementarily, recent progress on cyber physical systems has induced new virtualization possibilities for resources and capabilities, leading to notions of Industrial Internet, Sensing Enterprise, Internet of Events, etc.

Moving from services provided by a single entity to more complex or integrated multi-stakeholder services requires new approaches in dynamic service composition and thus the effective consideration of the "collaboration" perspective. This is a fundamental step in reducing the gap between the notions of software service and business service.

Collaborative networks naturally benefit from such new possibilities, but they also bring important elements to the future Internet at various levels, including structural and behavioral models, value systems and value creation, and the business perspective. On the other hand, development of the so-called services science adds clarification to the semantics of the service concept in which context synergies with collaborative networks need to be further explored.

The accumulated body of empiric knowledge and the size of the research community involved in collaborative networks provide the basis for leveraging the potential of new concepts and mechanisms in addressing big societal challenges and consolidating the scientific discipline in "collaborative networks." Such discipline is strongly multidisciplinary and thus the PRO-VE Working Conference is designed to offer a major opportunity to mix contributions from computer science, engineering, economics, management or socio-human communities. The main theme of PRO-VE 2012 focused thus on crucial aspects to empower collaborative networks as a main actor of change in society.

PRO-VE 2012, held in Bournemouth, UK, was the 13th event in a series of successful conferences, including PRO-VE 1999 (Porto, Portugal), PRO-VE 2000 (Florianopolis, Brazil), PRO-VE 2002 (Sesimbra, Portugal), PRO-VE 2003 (Lugano, Switzerland), PRO-VE 2004 (Toulouse, France), PRO-VE 2005 (Valencia, Spain), PRO-VE 2006 (Helsinki, Finland), PRO-VE2007 (Guimarães, Portugal), PRO-VE 2008 (Poznan, Poland), PRO-VE 2009 (Thessaloniki, Greece), PRO-VE 2010 (St. Etienne, France), and PRO-VE 2011 (São Paulo, Brazil).

This book includes a number of selected papers from the PRO-VE 2012 Conference, providing a comprehensive overview of identified challenges and recent advances in various collaborative network domains and their applications, with a particular focus on the Internet of Services. With this focus, this edition of the conference specifically emphasizes collaborative network topics related to:

- Service-enhanced products
- Service design
- Service composition
- Collaborative ecosystems
- Platforms for service-oriented collaborative networks
- Cloud-based support to collaborative networks
- Collaborative business frameworks
- e-Governance
- Collaboration motivators
- Collaboration spaces
- Virtual organization breeding environments
- Collaboration in traditional sectors
- Design of collaborative networks
- Cost, benefit, and performance analysis
- Identification of collaboration patterns
- Collaborative behavior models
- Risk, governance, and trust

We would like to thank all the authors both from academia/research and industry for their contributions. We hope this collection of papers represents a valuable tool for those interested in research advances, emerging applications, and future challenges for R&D in collaborative networks. We also appreciate the dedication of the PRO-VE Program Committee members who helped with the selection of articles and contributed with their valuable comments to help authors in improving the quality of their work.

July 2012

Luis M. Camarinha-Matos
Lai Xu
Hamideh Afsarmanesh

# Organization

**PRO-VE 2012 – 13<sup>th</sup> IFIP Working Conference on VIRTUAL ENTERPRISES**
Bournemouth, UK, October 1–3, 2012

## Program Committee Chair

Luis M. Camarinha-Matos (Portugal)

## Organizing Committee

### Chair
Lai Xu (UK)

### Co-chair
Keith Phalp (UK)

## Chairs

### Associated Workshops Chairs
Jeremy Bryans (UK)
Antonio Volpentesta (Italy)

### Applied Developments Track Chair(s)
Paul de Vrieze (UK)
Myrna Flores (Switzerland)
David Romero (Mexico)

### Systems Demonstration Chairs
Alok Choudry (UK)
A. Luis Osorio (Portugal)

### Special Journal Issues
Xavier Boucher (France)
Hamideh Afsarmanesh (The Netherlands)

## Publicity/Dissemination Chairs

Xavier Boucher (France)
Dmitri Ivanov (Germany)
Lai Xu (UK)

## Awards and Recognitions Chairs

Paulo Novais (Portugal)
Iraklis Paraskakis (Greece)

## Panel Chairs

Willy Picard (Poland)
Jens Eschenbaecher (Germany)
Joseba Arana (Spain)

# Program Committee

Antonio Abreu (Portugal)
Hamideh Afsarmanesh
 (The Netherlands)
Cesar Analide (Portugal)
Dario Antonelli (Italy)
Américo Azevedo (Portugal)
Panagiotis Bamidis (Greece)
Alain Bernard (France)
Peter Bertok (Australia)
Xavier Boucher (France)
Jean Pierre Bourey (France)
Carlos Bremer (Brazil)
Jeremy Bryans (UK)
Luis M. Camarinha-Matos (Portugal)
Tiago Cardoso (Portugal)
Val Casey (Ireland)
Wojciech Cellary (Poland)
Alok Choudhary (UK)
Paul de Vrieze (UK)
Rob Dekkers (UK)
Alexandre Dolgui (France)
Schahram Dustdar (Austria)
Jens Eschenbaecher (Germany)
Elsa Estevez (Argentina)
Erastos Filos (Belgium)
Myrna Flores (Switzerland)
Rosanna Fornasiero (Italy)
Cesar Garita (Costa Rica)

Virginie Goepp (France)
Ted Goranson (USA)
Paul Grefen (The Netherlands)
Jairo Gutierrez (Colombia)
Tarek Hassan (UK)
Dmitri Ivanov (Germany)
Tomasz Janowski (Macau)
Nan Jiang (UK)
Toshiya Kaihara (Japan)
Eleni Kaldoudi (Greece)
Iris Karvonen (Finland)
Kurt Kosanke (Germany)
Adamantios Koumpis (Greece)
George Kovacs (Hungary)
Antonio Lucas Soares (Portugal)
Patricia Macedo (Portugal)
István Mézgar (Hungary)
Paulo E. Miyagi (Brazil)
Arturo Molina (Mexico)
Benoit Montreuil (Canada)
David Newell (UK)
Ovidiu Noran (Australia)
Paulo Novais (Portugal)
Eugénio Oliveira (Portugal)
Martin Ollus (Finland)
Angel Ortiz (Spain)
A. Luis Osório (Portugal)
Hervé Panetto (France)

Iraklis Paraskakis (Greece)  
Alexandra Pereira-Klen (Brazil)  
Keith Phalp (UK)  
Willy Picard (Poland)  
Ricardo Rabelo (Brazil)  
João Rosas (Portugal)  
Hans Schaffers (The Netherlands)  
Jens Schütze (Germany)  

Weiming Shen (Canada)  
Jens Schütze (Germany)  
Chrysostomos Stylios (Greece)  
Klaus-Dieter Thoben (Germany)  
Lorna Uden (UK)  
Antonio Volpentesta (Italy)  
Lai Xu (UK)  
Peter Weiß (Germany)  

## Technical Sponsors

IFIP WG 5.5 COVE  
Co-Operation Infrastructure for Virtual Enterprises  
and Electronic Business

Society of Collaborative Networks

## Organizational Co-sponsors

**Bournemouth University**

New University  
of Lisbon

University  
of Amsterdam

# Table of Contents

## Service Composition II

## Collaborative Ecosystems

## Platform Requirements

## Cloud-Based Support

## Collaborative Business Frameworks I

## Collaborative Business Frameworks II

## Services Design

## e-Governance

## Collaboration in Traditional Sectors

## Collaboration Motivators I

# Collaboration Motivators II

# Virtual Organization Breeding Environments

# Collaboration Spaces

# Designing Collaborative Networks

## Cost, Benefits and Performance

## Identification of Patterns

## Co-innovation and Competitiveness

## Collaborative Behavior Models

## Risk, Governance, Trust

# 1

## Introduction

# A Service Science for Collaborative Enterprises – Observations and Theses on Future Developments

Kyrill Meyer

Universität Leipzig, Business Information Systems, Johannisgasse 26,
04103 Leipzig, Germany
meyer@informatik.uni-leipzig.de

**Abstract.** The evolution of the global economy can be characterized through ever shorter life cycles for products and services while, at the same time, development costs increase and the time to bring a new idea into the market reduces. Collaboration has introduced itself as a promising approach to address various challenges enterprises are faced with in such a context. The paper presents a number of observations and theses that point towards future developments. In doing so, the role of services and their development as a major element for successful long-term cooperation in value networks or as a basis for the collaborative enterprise is presented. Instead of providing a clear outline, we will present a number of theses that point towards future developments.

**Keywords:** Service Science, Service Economy, Collaboration in Services.

## 1    Introduction

The evolution of the global economy can be characterized through ever shorter life cycles for products and services while, at the same time, development costs increase and the time to bring a new idea into the market reduces [1]. In the struggle to be innovative and competitive in the market, new products and solutions are increasingly developed in collaborative settings within value networks or entire value chains that involve more than one company or institution [2]. Collaboration has introduced itself as a promising approach to address various challenges enterprises are faced with in a knowledge driven society [3]. Thus, expert knowledge can be transferred, resource limitations overcome and expertise included that is not covered by one company itself, which is of high interest especially for small and medium sized enterprises (SME) [4].

In this paper we present a number of observations that the careful bystander will be able to note looking at this development and the background in the market against which they occur. We argue on the role of services and their development as a major element for successful long-term cooperation in value networks or as a basis for the collaborative enterprises. Instead of providing a clear outline, we will present a number of theses that point towards future developments.

L.M. Camarinha-Matos, L. Xu, and H. Afsarmanesh (Eds.): PRO-VE 2012, IFIP AICT 380, pp. 3–10, 2012.
© IFIP International Federation for Information Processing 2012

## 2    Observations

*Observation I: The service economy is a reality.*

The importance of services in modern economies has been continuously rising during the past decades. Today, about two thirds of the GDP in the EU Member States and in other western economies can be directly accounted to services [5]. Given the statistic frameworks such as the NACE nomenclature of economic activities this information is derived from, one needs to consider that the real significance of services will potentially be even higher. For example, if an industrial company provides services such as maintenance or a remote service for a machine it produces, this will most likely not be captured as service activity. Services are everywhere in the market and in many cases they are the real differentiating factor between competitors. Current studies show that many enterprises recognize the importance of services for their business and expect growth to come especially from new or improved service offerings [6]. For quite a number of companies services have taken a system leadership, meaning that not a specific product or offering is core of the business approach, but customer-oriented service solutions drive the company efforts [7, 8]. Such enterprises have adopted a view that is scientifically called the "service-dominant-logic" [9-11]. However, even with the given economic importance of services, many companies still act product-centered and the role and significance of services is neglected.

*Observation II: Service markets and demands change*

The economy and also the service sector undergo changes with their development. Along with the growing economic importance of services during the years the competition has intensified and the markets can be characterized as highly dynamic. Main factors of this development include:

- Deregulation and internationalization
- Market saturation and excess capacities
- Merging and emerging markets with the entry of new competitors
- Multiplication of successful service concepts

In this environment, companies offering services cannot be successful just through being cost-effective or with their marketing image. Long-term success is based on offering innovative solutions. These need to be based on an understanding for the needs of the customers, integrated into a holistic high-quality offering and provided with efficiency and productivity. A company needs to continuously improve their service portfolio and provide such service offerings faster than the competition. It might be that the company offering such service solutions needs to re-adjust their own view of services and organizational as well as management changes need to be implemented.

*Observation III: Technological infusion is a major driver for new services*

The service economy is closely linked with the management of knowledge and information. With the possibility to collect and share information through networks such as the internet, new business and collaboration models arise that are mostly offered as services. Also existing services profit from the support through information technology because they can be provided in new forms (e.g. a remote service instead of a maintenance on location), with better efficiency or based in better connection to customer information.

Trends in this respect are the notions of "cyber-physical systems" or the "internet-of-things". They refer to hard- and software that is embedded in goods, machines, buildings, means of transportation, logistic chains or manufacturing equipment. Such hard- and software collects information and data through sensors or interactions with users, processes them and is able to distribute and interact through interfaces in communication networks. In areas such as health, environment, transportation, logistics and communication the information acquired through such systems will be needed to manage complexity, but can only harvested to any benefit if their development is embedded in collaboration and service structures.

*Observation IV: Service Research is not coherent and clearly focused*

Given the significance of services, the market demands and the possibilities that arise from technology one could assume that major efforts and activities exist in the area of service research. In fact, there are scientific efforts to analyze, create and manage the socio-technical systems that produce services on the background of the technological, managerial, theoretical and design aspects involved. In doing so, service research is a highly multidisciplinary field [12] that is not yet clearly defined. Most research work conducted is part of the respective field such as sociology, anthropology, ergonomics, system science, computer science, marketing and business administration. Currently, the working areas of service research are part of the scientific discussion [12-14] and the viewpoint taken may differ. For example, some researchers argue from the viewpoint of an optimal service for the customer, while others have the focus of their work on the systematic engineering of the service delivery. While those differing perspectives are not adjacent to each other, they make it harder to form a common understanding of a service science. Also, one has to take into account that the contributing fields itself have varying background in respect to their own history and development.

# 3    Theses

*Thesis I: Services will be High-Tech/Smart in the future*

Looking at the potential development of the broad service field, one has to ask the question where innovation in services can take place. Research in the field of service innovation has identified three main areas for service innovation [15]: the concept of the service system itself, the way interaction within the service system takes place or the way the service is delivered through the service system. Interestingly, they are connected through a fourth field, the technological options (see figure 1).

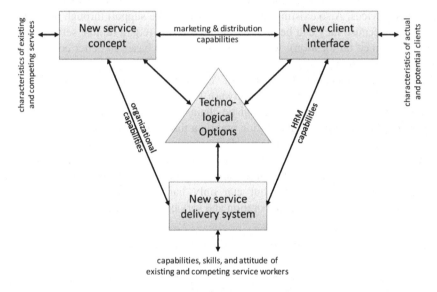

**Fig. 1.** The 4-D-Model of Service Innovation [15]

The model illustrates the high significance technology plays for future services. Many of the challenges modern societies are faced with can be addressed properly only if there is a proper technology support in the field (e.g. questions of health, mobility, energy security). Therefore, one can conclude that services need to be developed further into complex service systems that provide solutions that are high-tech-based or can be called Smart Services because they incorporate technology that is helpful in the application field. On the other hand, if technology is not embedded properly within the service system, the potential it provides is lost (e.g. what good is a smart meter for water if there is no service connected with it).

*Thesis II: Managing system complexity will be core*

Service research has a long tradition in arguing about the key elements of a service and its characteristics [13]. Respectively, a general service definition will have to be generic. Currently, such approaches to define services focus on the elements service provider, service consumer and the service object/subject that is operated upon [16]. Those elements form a socio-technical service system, where the different elements form actors and resources and the service itself is a change of configuration of the service system. Those systems will be increasingly complex and the real challenge is not only to see in understanding the system, but also in managing its complexity. If for example, mobility services have to be switched away from fossil fuels, it is not only the question of where the batteries come from. Complex infrastructures have to be changed and entire value changes need to be restructured or built anew. So in the long run, if a company provides integrated solutions for questions or is able to contribute in a complex service system, this will be the key factor for success. For this, services need to be not only consumer oriented (whatever makes the customer happy), but need to be engineering. Here, the service engineering [17] is a valid approach that also focusses on identifying service components[18] and, by doing so, mange complexity through the division of the problem in manageable parts.

*Thesis III: Collaboration will be key*

The trigger for innovation in general can be divided into two streams: technology push and demand pull [19]. Technology push means that research gives rise to new technologies or applications that are thereafter applied to create new solutions. Demand pull means that the market signals a need for a solution to a particular problem which is then solved in the innovation process. The 1970s debate about the impact and importance of each of the triggers came to the conclusion that a separated view would be leading nowhere. In practice, innovation is a coupling and matching process where interaction and collaboration is essential. Successful innovation requires the interaction between (technology) "push" and (demand) "pull" actors. A strong potential lies, therefore, in the collaboration between typical push actors such public research institutions and typical pull actors such as small and medium sized enterprises[4]. It is also a very practical approach as it shows that in many cases companies that start technology driven do not become market leader in their respective technology but in the end are able to provided high-quality and dedicated services within a value chain or network. Overall to focus on collaboration as key for successful service development develops different aspects that for a single company will be hard to achieve by itself:

- cooperative R&D activities and pooling of innovation stakeholders,
- reducing resources disadvantage,
- enabling a bottom-up information flow (demand driven) and combining it with top-down approaches (technology or result driven).
- successful establishment of value chain networks with dedicated and specialized actors that provide services to others
- network-structures with benefits to all participating actors and the creation of innovative milieus [19]

*Thesis IV: We need a Service Science*

Even though the service sector is the most important and fastest growing business sector of developed countries, we currently have no integrated service research or academic community. With the field developing, the lack of conceptual foundation [20] and the problems arising from the fact that there is no holistic research agenda for services become more and more apparent. For this reason, scientists call out for an academic discipline they call service science and put forward research agendas or plans to sharpen the understanding of services [8, 20, 21]. Service science is understood by many as a multidisciplinary field, focusing on the combination of fundamental science and engineering theories, models, and applications, aiming at enhancing and improving service innovation and giving insights on how to design, build and manage service systems [21-23].

To successful establish such a service science that provides applicable research results for the business world, service research needs a strong theoretical foundation but must also provide methods, procedures and tools that can be used to build and manage actuals service systems. Therefore, knowledge-focused basic research such as empirical studies and observations has to be combined and interlinked with application-focused approaches in cumulative and innovative ways [24].

A service science cannot be a merely academic effort. The phenomenological variety and the high significance of services for economic success and everyday life concerns many different knowledge and decision stakeholders from science, business and politics [24].

To harvest the potential such a service science brings to the service world we suggest building centers of service excellence at a number of research centers around the world, where theoretical work from the different contributing fields is combined with the possibility to design, engineer, test, measure and simulate services. Such service centers could be the core of an innovative milieu that stimulates cooperation and networking.

## 4    Conclusions

Research in the field of service, dealing with the engineering, design and management of increasingly complex socio-technical systems to provide services and solutions is a highly significant field, which has not yet reached is full potential. Being a collection of contributions from various fields at the moment, is remains to see whether an integrated service science will be able to form. Such a service science will have to focus on a systematic technology driven service systems engineering and management. It seems clear that collaboration structures and technology support play an important part in future service systems and for the companies providing those solutions. With its help, it will be easier to address the social, environmental and economic challenges of our societies. Due to their complexity it will be necessary to form collaboration structures in which different stakeholders, knowledge and solution providers can work together and provide services to each other that in the larger context define an overall service system.

## References

1. Ball, D.A.: International business: the challenge of global competition. McGraw-Hill Irwin, Boston (2010)
2. Cases, M., Bodner, D.A., Mutnury, B.: Architecture of Service Organizations. In: Salvendy, G., Karwowski, W. (eds.) Introduction to Service Engineering, pp. 109–137. John Wiley and Sons, Hoboken (2010)

3. Camarinha-Matos, L.M., Afsarmanesh, H.: Collaborative Networks - Value creation in a knowledge society. In: Wang, K., Kovacs, G.L., Wozny, M., Fang, M. (eds.) IFIP TC5 International Conference on Knowledge Enterprise: Intelligent Strategies in Product Design, Manufacturing, and Management; Proceedings of PROLAMAT 2006, Shanghai, China, June 15-17, vol. 207, pp. 26–40 (2006)
4. Thieme, M., Meyer, K.: Innovation through Collaboration: A Case-Study Based Strategy to Connect Research Institutions and Enterprises. In: Annual (SRII) Global Conference, SRII, pp. 622–629 (2011)
5. OECD: Evolution of Value Added by Activity. In: OECD Factbook 2010: Economic, Environmental and Social Statistics. OECD Publishing (2010)
6. Edvardsson, B., Meiren, T., Schäfer, A., Witell, L.: New Service Development in Europe – Results from an empirical study. In: AMA SERVSIG International Service Research Conference, Porto, Portugal (2010)
7. Vandermerwe, S., Rada, J.: Servitization of business: Adding value by adding services. European Management Journal 6, 314–324 (1988)
8. Rust, R.T., Miu, C.: What academic research tells us about service. Commun. ACM 49, 49–54 (2006)
9. Vargo, S.L., Lusch, R.F.: Evolving to a New Dominant Logic for Marketing. Journal of Marketing 68, 1–17 (2004)
10. Vargo, S.L., Lusch, R.F.: From goods to service(s): Divergences and convergences of logics. Industrial Marketing Management 37, 254–259 (2008)
11. Vargo, S., Lusch, R.: Service-dominant logic: continuing the evolution. Journal of the Academy of Marketing Science 36, 1–10 (2008)
12. Fisk, R.P., Grove, S.J.: Broadening Service Marketing: Building a Multidisciplinary Field. In: Spath, D., Ganz, W. (eds.) Teh Future of Services, pp. 233–244. Carl-Hanser-Verlag, München (2008)
13. Edvardsson, B., Gustafsson, A., Roos, I.: Service portraits in service research: a critical review. International Journal of Service Industry Management 16, 107–121 (2005)
14. Edvardsson, B.: Development of Service Research in Europe against the background of Global economic Change: Experiences, Challenges and Trends. In: Streich, D., Wahl, D. (eds.) Moderne Dienstleistungen, pp. 23–26. Campus, Frankfurt/Main (2006)
15. Hertog, P.d.: Knowledge-intensive business services as co-producers of innovation. International Journal of Innovation Management 4, 491–528 (2000)
16. Araujo, L., Spring, M.: Services, products, and the institutional structure of production. Industrial Marketing Management 35, 797–805 (2006)
17. Bullinger, H.-J., Fähnrich, K.-P., Meiren, T.: Service Engineering – methodical development of new service products. International Journal of Production Economics 85, 275–287 (2003)
18. Böttcher, M., Klingner, S.: Providing a Method for Composing Modular B2B-Services. Journal of Business and Industrial Marketing 26, 320–331 (2011)
19. Marinova, D., Phillimore, J.: Models of Innovation. In: Shavinina, L.V. (ed.) The International Handbook on Innovation, pp. 44–53. Pergamon, Amsterdam (2007)
20. Chesbrough, H., Spohrer, J.: A research manifesto for services science. Commun. ACM 49, 35–40 (2006)
21. Ostrom, A.L., Bitner, M.J., Brown, S.W., Burkhard, K.A., Goul, M., Smith-Daniels, V., Demirkan, H., Rabinovich, E.: Moving Forward and Making a Difference: Research Priorities for the Science of Service. Journal of Service Research (2010)

22. Paton, R.A., McLaughlin, S.: The Services Science and Innovation Series. European Management Journal 26, 75–76 (2008)
23. Paulson, L.D.: Services Science: A New Field for Today's Economy, vol. 39, pp. 18–21 (2006)
24. Ganz, W., Tombeil, A.-S.: Institutionalisation in the context of new forms of knowledge production. In: Spath, D., Ganz, W. (eds.) The Future of Services: Trends and Perspectives. Carl-Hanser-Verlag, München (2009)

**2**

## Service Enhanced Products

# Collaborative Business Scenarios in a Service-Enhanced Products Ecosystem

Luis M. Camarinha-Matos[1], Patricia Macedo[1,2], Filipa Ferrada[1],
and Ana Inês Oliveira[1]

[1] Universidade Nova de Lisboa, Faculty of Sciences and Technology and UNINOVA Institute
Campus de Caparica, 2829-516 Monte Caparica, Portugal
cam@uninova.pt
[2] EST Setúbal, Instituto Politécnico de Setúbal, Setúbal, Portugal

**Abstract.** Effective support to highly customized and service-enhanced products along their life cycle requires new organizational structures, involving the manufacturers, customers and local suppliers in a process of co-creation and co-innovation. In order to properly develop supporting infrastructures, tools and governance models, it is necessary to first identify representative business scenarios which enable individual requirements to be viewed in relation to one another in the context of the overall use case / target domain. In this context, a set of relevant business scenarios derived from the requirements of the solar energy domain are identified and discussed.

**Keywords:** Collaborative networks, Services ecosystem, Business scenarios.

## 1 Introduction

The notion of service-enhanced product and the associated idea of service-enhanced manufacturing represent a growing trend, particularly in the context of complex products. The motivation is that buyers of manufactured products increasingly want more than the physical product itself, they might want finance options to buy it, insurance to protect it, expertise to install it, support to maintain it fully operational during its life cycle, advice on how to maximize returns from it, expertise to manage it, etc. [1], [2].

This has led to the idea of bundling products and services together in customized packages for clients. For the case of complex products, e.g. solar energy plants or intelligent buildings, services are increasingly necessary to ensure that sophisticated component sub-systems can be designed, integrated, operated and maintained as final complex products. In this context, the distinction between delivery of products and services has become less distinct or blurred. As a result, the term "servitization" is also used when referring to provision of services to clients of manufacturing firms [3].

ICT and particularly Internet technologies developments also led to putting greater focus on knowledge and high value added when it comes to design such services. This requires not only a shift from 'goods dominant logic' to 'service dominant logic', but

L.M. Camarinha-Matos, L. Xu, and H. Afsarmanesh (Eds.): PRO-VE 2012, IFIP AICT 380, pp. 13–25, 2012.
© IFIP International Federation for Information Processing 2012

also associated changes in the organizational structures and business models. Provision of integrated services along the life cycle of complex products requires collaboration among multiple stakeholders. More than a shift from product-oriented enterprise to customer-oriented enterprise, a shift to a 'community or ecosystem oriented' model is needed.

On the other hand, despite the developments in ICT and the globalization of the economy, proximity is becoming increasingly important for innovation and growth. In fact, easy interconnectivity is now just a pre-requisite rather than a differentiator in achieving competitive advantage. Therefore, the notion of *glocal* enterprise emerged to represent the idea of thinking and acting globally, while being aware and responding adequately to local specificities, namely in collaboration with local stakeholders and customers.

This paper presents preliminary results of the GloNet project in this direction.

## 2      The GloNet Project

GloNet aims at designing, developing, and deploying an agile virtual enterprise environment for networks of SMEs involved in highly customized and service-enhanced products through end-to-end collaboration with customers and local suppliers (co-creation) [4]. The notion of *glocal* enterprise is implemented in GloNet with value creation from global networked operations and involving global supply chain management, product-service linkage, and management of distributed production units.

Further to service-based enhancement, there is a growing trend in manufacturing to move towards highly customized products, ultimately one-of-a-kind, which is reflected in the term *mass customization*. In fact, mass customization refers to a customer co-design process of products and services which meet the needs/choices of each individual customer with regard to the variety of different product features. Important challenges in such manufacturing contexts can be elicited from the requirements of complex technical infrastructures, solar energy parks, intelligent buildings, etc.

The guiding use case in GloNet is focused on the production and life cycle support of **solar energy parks**. The norm of operation in this industry is that of one-of-a-kind production. The results (products and services) are typically delivered through complementary competences shared between different project participants. A key challenge is the design and delivery of multi-stakeholder complex services along the product life cycle (typically 20 years). Focused issues: (i) Information / knowledge representation (product catalogue, processes descriptions, best practices, company profiles, brochures, etc.); (ii) User-customized interfaces, dynamically adjusted to assist different stakeholders (smart enterprise approach); (iii) Services provision through cloud; (iv) Broker-customer interaction support: from order to (product/service) design (open innovation approach); (v) Negotiation support; (vi) Workflow for negotiated order solution & its monitoring; and (vii) Forecast risks & suggest prevention measures.

The GloNet project started in Sep 2011 with a planned duration of 3 years, and involves the following partners: CAS (Germany), UNINOVA (Portugal), University of Amsterdam (Netherlands), iPLON (Germany), SKILL (Spain), Steinbeis (Germany), KOMIX (Czech Republic), and PROLON (Denmark).

## 3    Use Case Characteristics

The development of business scenarios is an important technique that helps in better characterizing requirements, identifying and understanding business needs, and thus provides important inputs for the next phase of GloNet when a system's architecture has to be designed.

Although the concept is not precisely defined in the literature, the adopted notion here is that a **business scenario** represents a **significant business need or problem** in the target domain. In other words, it provides a reasonably extensive description of a business problem, which enables individual requirements to be viewed in relation to one another in the context of the overall use case / target domain [5].

In order to identify the set of relevant business scenarios for GloNet the following **method** is adopted (as illustrated in Fig. 1):

1) Start with the guiding use case of GloNet (solar energy plants) and identify its main abstract characteristics, leading to an <u>abstract use case</u>.
2) Analyze the needs of the abstract use case and suggest a set of <u>relevant</u> business scenarios.

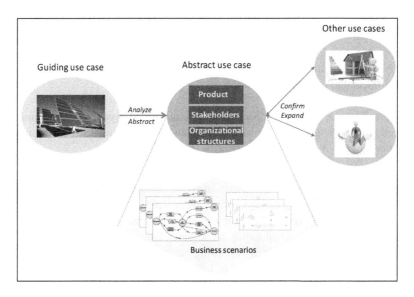

**Fig. 1.** Identification of relevant business scenarios

3) Confirm the relevance of the scenarios in the context of other use cases. Possible iterations with phase 2 are included here.
4) Develop detailed descriptions of the selected business scenarios.
5) Confirm the details and refine descriptions in consultation with end-users representative of the use cases / application domains.

As mentioned before, the guiding use case is the solar plants domain, with particular emphasis on the maintenance and operation of the power plants. The other two use cases, which share similar abstract characteristics, are the building automation and the physical incubator facilities for enterprises.

The main characteristics of the target business cases can be summarized by:

a. *Product characteristics*
– Complex (physical) product, involving several sub-systems
– Long life-cycle, but having components with different life-cycles
– Need for business services provision along the life-cycle (service-enhanced product); new services are likely to be demanded
– Integrated business services typically combine contributions from multiple stakeholders
– Mass customization, nearly one-of-a-kind product (and properly adapted services).

b. *Stakeholders characteristics.* The manufacturing and service provision for such products involve a large diversity of stakeholders performing a number of roles:
– Product / project designers
– Product manufacturers, including sub-systems / components providers
– Service providers
– Support entities, including financial, insurance, training, cloud infrastructure provision, regulator entities, etc.
– Customers and users differentiation.

c. *Organizational structures.* Stakeholders can appear organized in a number of networked structures that reflect a variety of relationships, some sense of community, and different levels of collaboration maturity. These include:

– Long-term strategic alliances - which typically involve product / project designers, manufacturers, service providers, and some support entities, configuring a kind of virtual organizations breeding environment (VBE) [6], [7]. A VBE represents an association of organizations and a number of related supporting institutions, adhering to a base long term (formal or informal) cooperation agreement, and adopting common operating principles and infrastructures, with the main goal of increasing their preparedness towards rapid configuration of goal-oriented networks (Virtual Organizations/Virtual Enterprises - VO/VE).

- Customer related communities - involving, besides the customer, local non-critical components suppliers, services providers, and a variety of support entities. Although this group might not be well organized and structured, it shares some minimal bonds like geographical vicinity, culture, business environment, legal regulations, etc.
- Goal-oriented networks - in which intense and well focused cooperation and/or collaboration (towards a common goal or a set of compatible goals) is practiced among their partners. Two inter-related cases are foreseen:
    - Product development network - a dynamic (temporary) VE involved in the development of the physical product and design of associated services.
    - Product servicing network - a long-term VE organized to provide integrated (multi-stakeholder) business services along the product life-cycle.

A product servicing VE might have (a few) members in common with the product development VE, but typically corresponds to a different organizational structure. A mechanism of inheritance between the product development VE and product servicing VE needs to be established. The recruitment base (constituency) for these networks include, preferentially, the manufacturers VBE and the customer related community, but it might also include outside entities (see Fig. 2).

These networked structures need to cope with a variety of membership levels. Instead of a binary "member / not member" situation, multiple degrees of membership have to be considered (e.g. core members, regular members, associated members, etc.) with different levels of rights and responsibilities. The degree of membership might not even be a constant parameter for each entity but rather vary with the context or perspective of analysis, which leads to different geometries of the networks. These networks need to interact and may span over a wide geographical distribution.

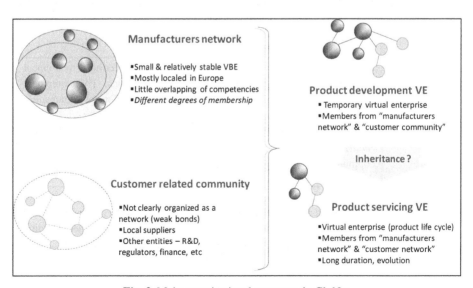

**Fig. 2.** Main organizational structures in GloNet

**Table 1.** Mapping to the solar plant use case

| Abstract elements | | Solar plant use case |
|---|---|---|
| Product | Complex (physical) product | Power plant itself. |
| | Long life-cycle | Typically 20~25 years for the power plant; many components / subsystems have shorter lives and need to be periodically replaced. |
| | Business services | Examples include: Plant operation & management, Panel cleaning & preventive maintenance, Training, Diagnosis, Performance improvement support, etc. |
| | Mass customization | Although sharing some general characteristics, each solar plant is a distinct case (one-of-a-kind product) depending on power requirements, geographical and environmental characteristics, local regulations, etc. |
| Stakeholders | Product/project designers | Project development companies, Procurement & Construction (EPC) companies, Consultants |
| | Product manufacturers | Photo Voltaic (PV) equipment manufacturers, EPC, Construction & Commissioning companies, Monitoring & Control companies |
| | Service providers | Operation & maintenance companies, Monitoring & Control companies, etc. |
| | Support entities | Lending organizations (banks), Insurance companies, Government agencies |
| | Customers and users | Customer (owner), Utility companies |
| Organizational structures | Strategic alliance / Manufacturers VBE | Project development firms, Engineering, Procurement & Construction (EPC) companies, PV equipment manufacturers, Monitoring & Control companies, Construction & Commissioning companies |
| | Customer *related* community | Customer (owner), Utility company, Lending organization, Government agencies, Insurance companies, Operation & maintenance companies, other suppliers, etc. |
| | Product development VE | Project development companies, EPC, PV equipment manufacturers, Construction & Commissioning companies, Monitoring & Control companies, Lending organization, Insurance company, … |
| | Product servicing VE | Operation & maintenance companies, Monitoring & Control companies, Utility company, etc. |

# 4      Relevant Business Scenarios

*Identification of Relevant Business Scenarios.* When addressing the issue of identifying and selecting relevant business scenarios in GloNet it is important to consider the specificities of a research project and its defined goals. As such, the relevance of business scenarios cannot be determined by the current operational business practices of single companies, but rather by their contribution to identify the "backbone" (models, infrastructure, tools, and processes) for a new way of doing business in a collaborative networked environment. In other words, the selected scenarios should help in creating the conditions to get prepared to effectively doing business in a different way.

Under this perspective, it is also important to consider the need for some base or "enabling" scenarios, which just create the proper conditions for the development of other scenarios that are more directly appealing to an end-user. For instance, while for end-user companies it might be relevant to have a scenario focused on the formation of goal-oriented networks (in response to a business opportunity), it is also clear that the agility of the consortium formation process very much depends on the existence of a long-term strategic network that promotes the preparedness of its members for collaboration. Therefore, the effectiveness of the mentioned scenario depends on the consideration of an "enabler" scenario focused on the management of long-term networks or business ecosystems.

In this context, and after extensive consultation with end-users and system developers, the following business scenarios are considered in the GloNet environment:

1. *Management of Long-term Collaborative Network* - Management of the strategic long-term alliance of product designers & manufacturers
2. *Formation of Goal-oriented Collaborative Network* - Consortia formation for virtual enterprises: product development VE, Product servicing VE
3. *Co-design and Co-innovation* - Environment and processes to support collaboration with customers and local suppliers (co-creation)
4. *Base Operation and Management of Product Servicing* - Handling the "trivial" processes of operation and maintenance of the product
5. *Advanced Supervision Services for the Collaborative Network* - Handling advanced processes / functionalities of operation and maintenance and network coordination
6. *Shared Resources Repository Management* - Management of the shared repository of community resources: general sharable information / knowledge (e.g. processes), software tools, lessons learned, etc.
7. *Product Portfolio Management* - Management of all information related to products: product catalog, product model, historic data on the product (sensorial data, product updates / changes, etc.) ... single 'access point' along the product life-cycle.

8. *Semi-automated Learning-based Decision Support* - to assess the feasibility of building semi-automated learning-based decision making support system for complex products.

In terms of **representation of business scenarios**, the following main elements are considered: (i) Description and purpose, (ii) Goals, outcomes and main features, (iii) Environment and actors, (iv) Details on actors, roles and responsibilities, (v) Business processes, and (vi) Required software services.

In addition to tables and textual descriptions, the following formalisms are adopted to help characterizing the business scenarios: i* (i-star) - to describe actors, individual and common goals, tasks, and their inter-relationships; and BPMN – to represent business processes.

***Examples.*** As an illustration, let us consider the following scenarios:

**E1. *Management of Long-term Collaborative Network*.** A Long-term Collaborative Network is a strategic alliance of organizations adhering to a base long term cooperation agreement while also adopting common operating principles and infrastructure, thus a kind of VBE (Virtual Organizations Breeding Environment). In this case the Solar Plants VBE alliance brings together and supports collaboration among otherwise independent and mostly small organizations which are currently involved in solar plants industry. As such, through the formation of energy-related VBE alliances for instance, collaboration among their stakeholders increase, since they can join their efforts, capabilities, and capacities, to better fulfill the emerged opportunities in the market. A system to support the management of this kind of network provides services to manage member's profiles and VBE's ontology, to support performance management and to manage trust among VBE member.

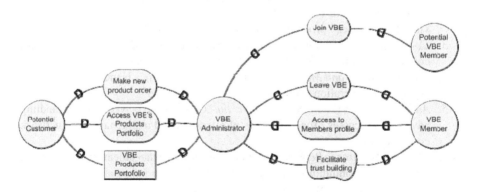

**Fig. 3.** i* Strategic Dependency model for Long-term Collaborative Network

Strategic goals for this scenario include: Manage admission and withdrawal of members in the VBE; Ensure that complete information about member's profile and competencies are available; Ensure secure access to VBE members; Promote trust among VBE's members; Promote the adoption of a common ontology.

Fig.3 (in i* notation) shows the main actors as well as their inter-dependencies in terms of (hard) goals (e.g. Join VBE), soft goals (e.g. Members trust), and resources (e.g. VBE ontology).

A more detailed description is shown in Fig. 4, where a zoom in is made on the VBE Coordinator actor.

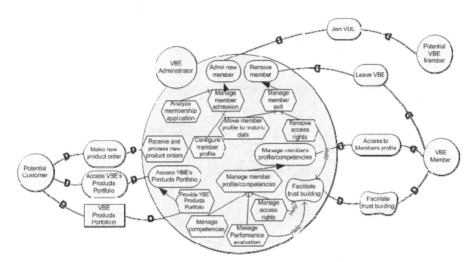

**Fig. 4.** i* Partial Strategic Rational Model for Long-term Collaborative Network scenario

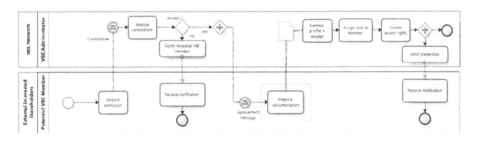

**Fig. 5.** Partial BPMN process for admission of new VBE member

Examples of required software services: VBE Member Admission Service, VBE Member Withdrawal Service, Membership Level Access Management Service, Ontology Management Service.

**E2. *Co-design and Co-innovation.*** This scenario aims at providing an environment that supports and promotes the collaborative design and development of products and services as well as the emergence of innovative solutions. It thus includes the aspects of mass customization as well as the emergence of new products / new solutions to identified needs, through collaboration between manufacturers and the customer and members of the customer's community.

Strategic goals for this scenario include: Co-design and co-development of products, Provide co-innovation support, and Guarantee customer satisfaction & VO partners satisfaction. Fig. 6 shows the main actors and their inter-dependencies for this scenario.

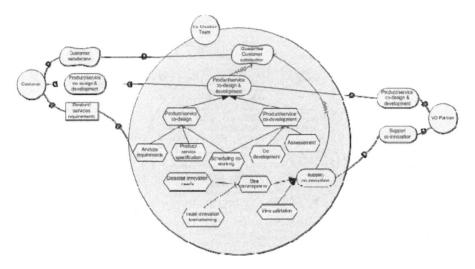

**Fig. 6.** i* Strategic Rational model for Co-design and Co-innovation

Fig. 7 shows an example of business process for the case of co-innovation.

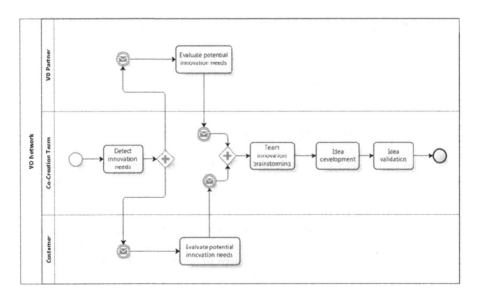

**Fig. 7.** BPMN diagram of the Co-innovation Process

## 5    Implementation Issues

GloNet adopts a cloud-based approach [4] for the development of its ICT environment so that its supporting services can dynamically upgrade without influencing the nodes and stakeholders in the environment. Regarding the base platform the following main characteristics are planned:

- Cloud-based infrastructure, based on open-source technologies, adopting relevant standards and based on OSGi.
- Incremental pool of services, knowledge, and other resources (scalability characteristic).
- Supporting the notion of extended or service-enhanced product - combination of physical product with a set of linked support services (e.g. maintenance, remote diagnosis, remote user assistance, training, insurance services, etc.). A product model will become available in a *Business Services Provision Space* as a single entry point for product-related information and services along its life cycle. The product servicing virtual enterprise (see Fig. 2) will naturally be linked to this product model.
- Besides the cloud-based platform, the environment includes two main (virtual) spaces: (i) *Collaborative solution space* - where new products and services are designed, developed / customized (co-creation/mass customization) through the interplay of the various stakeholders (product development virtual enterprise); (ii) *Business services provision space* - where models of products and associated services are kept along the product life cycle, supported by the product support virtual enterprise.

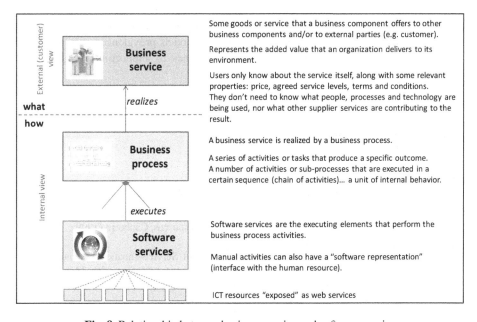

**Fig. 8.** Relationship between business service and software service

The GloNet platform being developed is aimed to provide not only the mechanisms to compose software services via business processes, but also to model business services and bundle them together with the product.

Since the term 'service' is used by both the business and software communities, it is important to clarify the corresponding meanings and inter-relationships. Fig. 8 summarizes the adopted interpretation.As illustrated, the concept of *business service* corresponds to an external (i.e. client-oriented) view while the *software service* is one of the mechanisms to materialize a business service.

# 6      Conclusions

Effective development and exploitation of complex products require that the physical product is enhanced with a number of associated (business) services. These services are likely to integrate contributions from multiple stakeholders and thus require a collaboration environment. Furthermore, the involvement of the customer, and other local stakeholders associated to the customer, in the process of design, development and delivery are important in a context of mass customization and to leverage the 'proximity' factor.

GloNet is developing an environment to support such co-design and co-innovation processes for complex and long-life cycle service-enhanced products.

One of the open issues is to assess the adequacy of a cloud computing implementation approach and determine which business models are needed for that approach. Although the advantages of cloud computing for SMEs have been extensively discussed, there are a number of critical issues that remain, namely the lack of interoperability among cloud providers, which raises the issue of risk of business continuity, particularly acute when we address products with a long life cycle, such as the solar energy plants. The business models prevalent in current cloud computing solutions also seem limited when it comes to supporting collaborative networks environments.

**Acknowledgments.** This work was funded in part by the European Commission through the GloNet project (FP7 programme). The authors also thank the contributions from their partners in this project.

# References

1. Marceau, J., Manley, K.: Service enhanced manufacturing in the building and construction product system. Department of Industry, Science and Resources, Canberra (1999), http://eprints.qut.edu.au/41286/
2. Shen, Q.: Research on Organization Mode Selection of Service-enhanced Manufacturing Enterprise. In: Proceedings of 3rd International Conference on Information Management, Innovation Management and Industrial Engineering, Kunming, China, November 26-28, pp. 358–361. IEEE Computer Society (2010)

3. Tether, B., Bascavusoglu-Moreau, E.: Servitization: The extent and motivations for service provision amongst UK manufacturers. In: Proceedings of DRUID 2012 - Innovation and Competitiveness: Dynamics of Organizations, Industries, Systems and Regions, Copenhagen, Denmark, June 19-21 (to appear, 2012)
4. Camarinha-Matos, L.M., Afsarmanesh, H., Koelmel, B.: Collaborative Networks in Support of Service-Enhanced Products. In: Camarinha-Matos, L.M., Pereira-Klen, A., Afsarmanesh, H. (eds.) PRO-VE 2011. IFIP AICT, vol. 362, pp. 95–104. Springer, Heidelberg (2011)
5. OpenGroup, Business Scenarios (2001),
   `http://www.opengroup.org/architecture/`
   `togaf7-doc/arch/p4/bus_scen/bus_scen.html` (accessed April 5, 2012)
6. Afsarmanesh, H., Camarinha-Matos, L.M., Msanjila, S.S.: Models, Methodologies, and Tools Supporting Establishment and Management of Second-Generation VBEs. IEEE Transactions on Systems, Man and Cybernetics – C 41(5), 692–710 (2011)
7. Camarinha-Matos, L.M., Afsarmanesh, H.: Collaborative Networks: Reference Modeling. Springer, New York (2008) ISBN 978-0-387-79425-9

# Economic and Organizational Transition towards Product/Service Systems: The Case of French SMEs

Xavier Boucher

Ecole Nationale Supérieure des Mines de Saint Etienne, Fayol-EMSE
F-42023 Saint Etienne, France
Boucher@emse.fr

**Abstract.** The French ANR Project ServINNOV intends to analyze the transition of industrial SMEs towards the integration of service activities and the production of PSS Systems. Based on the first results of a qualitative analysis of a set of 8 case studies, the paper discusses key factors influencing such organizational transitions.

**Keywords:** Product-Service Systems, Servicization, Transition of business model.

## 1    Introduction

This paper presents a research approach developed by the French ANR project ServINNOV "Sustainable Industrial Innovation via Servicization", and some first results. This project studied the economic and organizational transition of industrial Small and Medium Enterprises (SMEs) towards a service economy, or more precisely towards a functional economy [1]. This transition to the progressive integration of service activities in industrial firms together with their more traditional manufacturing oriented activities induces [3] a profound makeover of enterprise models: a transformation of both business and organizational models, called servicization [4]. Servicization deals with the development of integrated product/service offers, also called PSS (Product Service Systems). Currently, such new enterprise models are emerging within the international economy.

Integrated product/service offers brings new research questions for collaboration: (i) internal collaboration problems emerges at along the frontier among manufacturing-oriented and service-oriented business processes ; (ii) external collaboration is also strongly necessary, because such integrated offers require at their heart, value creation collaborative firm networks. As a first stage of research in this new innovative domain, our paper will only focus on better understanding product/service coupling mechanisms within the context of SMEs, with the following objectives: (1) the identification of various coupling modes between product oriented and service oriented business processes, and (2) the identification of transition drivers

L.M. Camarinha-Matos, L. Xu, and H. Afsarmanesh (Eds.): PRO-VE 2012, IFIP AICT 380, pp. 26–34, 2012.
© IFIP International Federation for Information Processing 2012

and influence factors to be considered by managers when building integrated product/service offers. Section 2 introduces the notion of product/service coupling with a state of the art which underlines the variety of potential coupling modes. Section 3 explains the organization of the research program and presents several case studies used to generate the results discussed in this paper. Section 4 presents some first results concerning distinct modes of product/service coupling, then influencing factors considered by SME managers when developing product/service market offers.

## 2    State of the Art: Variety of Coupling Modes between Manufacturing-oriented and Service-oriented Business Processes

This research work attempts to better understand the dependency between product-oriented and service-oriented business processes within a single enterprise. That means that, as a hypothesis, our work centers on companies which intend to develop internally both 'service-oriented' and 'manufacturing-oriented' activities. Such organizational coupling brings new questions on collaboration: internal cooperation between various entities of a company, and external alliances among companies. The study, strives to identify the mutual influences among material production processes and immaterial service offers, along the path of development and innovation in a company.

Academic literature provides various typologies which can be used as basis to manage such complexity. Balin [5] provides a large state of the art on typologies which directly concentrate on the service concept. The author distinguishes 3 main orientations : (1) economic oriented typologies (classification criteria are linked to the nature of the economic activity); ( 2) marketing oriented typologies, where the classification criteria concern marketing features of the service offers, customer implication level, or delivery modes; and, finally, (3) typologies directly based on the client implication, where criteria are linked to the volume and variety of the market as well as customization level which are eventually used jointly with other criteria linked to the type of service production process.

Although they are mainly centered on services, such typologies cannot completely ignore the product: either because a material product is the concrete object of the service (for instance maintenance service), or because the material product is directly one of the components of the offer (for instance a service offering the access to use specific equipment). For example, the service typology provided by Fitzimmons [6] uses a criteria 'Process object' by distinguishing 'Material oriented', 'Information oriented' and 'Person oriented' services separately. Giard has elaborated an interesting synthesis [7] which proposed a classification which integrates the link among products and services, both of final consumer oriented services (B to C) and business oriented services (B to B). The main classification criteria is the object of the service offer, consider as a 'Product use offer', 'Information use offer' or a 'Resource state transformation'.

Beyond service classifications, whose aim is to manage the complexity of these notions, several academic publications are more directly interested in the process dependency among product manufacturing and service production. In the field of industrial strategy, the framework of Johansson & Ohlager [8]   analyses the pertinence and consistency of various coupling alternatives. Their framework is based on a criterion of demand level for both the product and service activities, then on a criterion for the process control level (on one side for the manufacturing processes and on the other side for the processes needed to produce the services).

Complementary to such a strategic vision, other authors only focus on classifying the nature of the PSS offer. Hockerts [ 9], Manzini [8], Tukker [10] or more recently Baines [1] have progressively converged towards a widely accepted typology :

- *Product Oriented PSS:* the product is sent in an ordinary fashion, but the sales contract includes services deployed along the product life-cycle.
- *Use oriented PSS:* the provider only contracts an access or a utilization of a product, without product purchase for the customer.
- *Result oriented PSS:* Independently of any pre-defined product, the provider guaranties to answer specific customer needs, with a contracted engagement on the final result/performance.

# 3      Research Approach

## 3.1      Overview on the Research Program

In a regional context of industrial SMEs, the objective of these research efforts is to identify and understand various product/service coupling forms. This paper only delineates a first step of the research, anterior to the scientific formalisation, which consists in structuring consistent information collected to be deployed in industrial companies, and to extract the first, non-formalized, comprehension of the product/service coupling mechanisms under study.

The research approach is standard, and based on three separate but complementary objectives:

1. *Analysis of the academic literature.* The scientific literature is analyzed following two tracks: first the PSS systems, to identify coupling parameters between service and manufacturing oriented activities which are induced by the PSS offer; second the Service Oriented Enterprise (SOE), to identify strategic and organisational characteristics of such SMEs. The objective is to analyze the correspondence among the PSS system characteristics and the features of the associated productive system.

2. *Diagnosis tool building.* Two tools have been built, to be used as a support later diagnostics.  First, an interview guide (Semi-structured information collection), structuring the information to be gathered by interviewing top managers of SMEs. And second, a modelling referential, which is capable of modelling structurally, enterprise practices used to manage client/customer relationships.

3. *Analysis of cases studies*. As we will further develop below, 8 case studies of regional SMEs made from various interviews with general and industrial managers are used to try and analyse the variety of coupling modes among product and services as well as the advances of the companies towards this integration.

## 3.2    Analysis of Case Studies

The qualitative study is based on a collection of 8 case studies (table 1). The objective is to follow a qualitative analysis approach adapted to a reduced set of case studies. The nearby SMEs have been selected via the fact that they incorporate both internal manufacturing activities and service-oriented initiatives. However, one additional criterion must be considered: all the case studies are in the field of B to B. This ensures higher coherence of the analysis, since B to B or B to C present significant differences as to servicization. In table 1, some descriptive features are presented.

In qualitative research, case studies are used to understand and model emerging phenomenon, confront hypotheses with reality, and provide a clearer and better comprehension of the reality under study [12]. These case studies have been constituted following a so-called 'narrative' approach: during each interview, top managers are asked to make explicit the company history highlighting on the key moments of change, which underline significant strategic decisions. This narrative approach can make explicit firm transformational processes. It is based on a rather detailed account of a change process, through organization description, analysis of activity or complementary dialogs. In the current work, the interview directly concerned top managers of SMEs to be able to address the strategic trajectory of the company.

**Table 1.** Eight Case Studies

| Firm | Business sector | Size | Contact |
|------|-----------------|------|---------|
| A | Mechanics industry Design/Manufacturing | 10 | Top Manager |
| B | Medical Products Design/Manufacturing/Sales | 100 | Top Manager |
| C | Metal spring Supply Chains Subcontractor Design/Manufacturing | 30 | Top Manager |
| D | Surface processing. Service offers. Design and manufacturing of industrial processes | 1200 | R&D business sector manager |
| E | Production of machining centers. Design/Manufacturing/After Sales Integrator of subsystems. | 150 | Top Manager |
| F | Tooling Industry. Design/Manufacturing/Tool sharpening Subcontractor | 70 | Top Manager |
| G | Industrial machines and processes Design/Production/industrialization of new processes | 60 | Top Manager |
| H | Medical material and products Design/Manufacturing/Sales | 1400 | Industrial Manager |

Our objective was to try and understand the mechanisms of change driving the progressive integration of services in manufacturing companies. Through the company story, it was necessary to make explicit the origin of the evolution on the way to services, progressive transformation of its industrial strategy, and renovation of the organization modes as well as collective competencies. The semi-structured interview guide consisted mainly of open questions. Thus, giving the managers an the opportunity of a spontaneous expression, before going deeper on some key points. Among the various chapters of information collected, we insisted notably on product-service offers, the internal development of a service culture, transformation of customer relation ship, as well as the innovations on production modes and their impacts on internal proficiency.

# 4      First Synthesis of Results

## 4.1      Variety of Product/Service Coupling Modes

All the case studies concern SMEs with an industrial history and culture, oriented on design and/or manufacturing of products. In all the companies, the notion of services has emerged progressively, always with a strong link to production activities. The study shows that the managers have very diverse perceptions and comprehensions of the notion of service. We identified 3 distinct visions of the integration of services in industrial activities, illustrated by some examples in table 2.

**Table 2.** Diversity of the integration of services within industrial activities

|  | Firm A | Firm H | Firm F | Firm G |
|---|---|---|---|---|
| Providing quality of service | Client orientation & integrated offer | Development and Management of Quality of Service | Client orientation & Quality of service | Client orientation & integrated offer |
| Offering differentiated services | / | Specific business sector : 'customized products' | Tool sharpening | Sales of technical Competencies |
| Developing PSS offers | Transition towards a global capacity offer | / | Servicization model under study | / |

- *Providing quality of service associated to the product.* Historically, all the SMEs analyzed have first tried to increase systematically the "quality of services" in producing and delivering their industrial products. The orientation towards customers turns out to be re-enforced, new service-oriented competences emerge together with a new vision of the product offer.
- *Offering differentiated services.* Complementary to product sells, new service-oriented business area is developed. These first service offers are directly linked to the product life cycle. Specific service oriented competences have to be

developed. The manufacturing processes and service production processes remain separated, only linked by the product life-cycle and the competencies required.

- *Developing PSS offers.* Here, the selling products and services are both integrated in a unique economic and contractual relationship with the customer. The economic model is profoundly transformed. Depending on the context, the various forms of PSS underlined in section 2.1can appear.

Depending on the context of each case study, the product-service coupling strategies remain very specific to each form. The progressive development of services in industrial SMEs appears to depend on several influencing factors (see section 4.4). The study emphasized both (i) a necessity of internal coherence among these various influencing factors, shared by all the companies, but also (ii) a clear differentiation of strategic positioning and decisions for each particular case. This induces that the 3 visions of service integration mentioned in table 2 could not be assigned to generic types of SMEs; however there is certainly genericity in the influencing factors to consider and decision process to ensure internal coherence among these factors.

The various case studies also put forth that this transition towards services is a progressive process over time. The development of services appears as systematically linked to intentional changes of vision in the company history. These changing points also induce a transformation in internal proficiencies, which requires integration and learning periods. Afterwards, such transitions can generate new opportunities.

However, in spite of this temporal factor, the 3 visions of table 2 can not be considered as progressive maturity levels towards services. For all the case studies, *Providing quality of service associated to the product* was a shared starting point of the strategic progress. However the transition towards PSS does not require *offering differentiated services* previously. Furthermore, several of these 3 visions can co-exist in a same SME (in various business areas).

The interviews have underlined 3 main types of managerial drivers for the transition towards product/service coupling: (i) re-enforcement of firm core competencies, (ii) long term vision of maintaining both industrial and service capabilities and (iii) need for innovation. Due to a lack of available place, they can not be discussed in this paper, but the reader can refer to [14].

## 4.2    Influence Factors to Build Product/Service Offers

### 4.2.1    Complexity

Three distinct forms of complexity, influencing the strategic choices of SMES managers can be underlined:

- *Product technological complexity:* the increase of product complexity is linked to need of differentiating product added-value. Higher product complexity can generate higher potential of product-associated services. The integration of multiple know-how and competences in complex products offers new opportunities for offers of specific services.
- *The client/provider relationship complexity*: in B to B relationships, there is a transformation of the client/provider relation towards a demand of providing

complex integrated functions, with a significant adaptation to the specific requirements of each customer. A large part of the complexity of project management of integrated product/services is transferred from the client in the direction of the provider.

- *Usage complexity*: linked to the other forms of complexity, the complexity of B to B product life-cycle management also increases. Depending on the degree of complexity, internal skills of the clients and other life-cycle actors, as well as on the competencies of the provider, the product-life cycle can generate service offers opportunities.

As influencing factors, which correspond to the needs of service offers associated with a product and its life-cycle, these 3 forms of complexity should be considered by the managers when determining their broad product-service market offers.

### 4.2.2 Internal Competences

Several mechanisms of mutual adjustment appear, among available competencies on one side and services offers on the other one. They underline a dynamic process of co-evolution among internal competencies and offers of product-service systems.

- All the SMEs' managers underline t*he need to develop a collective firm competency, oriented on 'service' culture.* This includes: capability to better perceive the customer needs and ability to answer, even proactively, to the variety of the demand, beyond the direct technical need. This collective service-oriented culture induces a transformation of individual competencies as well as re-enforced integration mechanisms among Marketing, Innovation and Production.
- The *development of a service offer remains under the constraint of the competencies required* to ensure this service. This constraint is both qualitative (which ones are necessary?) and quantitative (a full network required to cover the territory). This appears as a strong constraint for SMES, however partnership strategies afford potential organizational answers (see the section that follows).
- The *internal integration of new competencies also opens innovative opportunities of service offers.* A two-directional interaction appears between integrating new competencies and innovation in services. In several cases, the internal acquisition of new differentiating competencies required for a first service offer, generates afterwards additional opportunities of service innovations.
- Additionally, SMEs managers put forth that *the development of product/service offers leads to the emergence of a new strategic collective competence.* In fact, service deployment is based on a close proximity to the customers. As a consequence, service production becomes crucial in customer relationships. Thus, it can become a key source of innovation. Such new strategic competence takes distinct forms depending on which case study considered.

A more systematic analysis of the link between competencies and service offers would be interesting to better understand this dynamic process of co-evolution.

### 4.2.3 Partnership Strategies

Of course, strategies of external alliances have been developed for long time by most SMES. However, in the context of emergence of service/product coupling, partnerships become a deliberate managing lever, notably (i) because the complexity increase induce the need of integrating multiple know-how and (ii) because ensuring service of a large territory requires a full service network. The service infrastructure is often built on partnership, so as to share the investment…and the risks. Such partnerships induce strong added-value sharing risks. Currently the approaches for servicization risk management appear to be unique to each context. There is a clear need to better adapt risk managing solutions.

### 4.2.4 Investment and Innovation Policies

The study underlines that investment and innovation policies strongly influence the development of product/service coupling. For the 8 case studies, innovation of service systematically responds to a need of new sources of value creation. As mentioned before, service production can be transformed into a strong driver of innovation. However, most of the time, SMEs are confronted with an intense need for both the human and technical investment required for service production. Internal financing limits as well as French difficulties to get access correctly or easily to institutional or bank funding support can become very limiting (Case A, D, F, G).

## 5    Conclusion

Only partial results of the case studies developed for the SPOS project have been presented within the limit of this paper. The various forms of product-service coupling, as well as crucial factors which influence managers when determining their strategies of integrated product-service offers were focused upon. Four key influencing factors have been emphasized: all of them are correspond to internal managerial aspects. Additionally external factors of innovation strategy have also to be considered as changes in PSS offers, customer behaviors, technological progress changes,….Such factors will be developed in further publications. Beyond the academic knowledge generated by the study, a future perspective will be to build diagnosis methods and tools to help managers to manage the economic and organizational transition towards product-service coupling.

**Acknowledgement**. the authors wish to thank Chris Yukna for his help in proofreading.

## References

1. DuTertre, C.: Modèle industriel "et" modèle serviciel de performance. In: XVIIth International Conference of RESER, Tampere, Finlande, Septembre 13-15 (2007)
2. Baines, T.S., Lightfoot, H.W., Evans, S., et al.: State-of-the-art in product-service systems. In: Proceedings of the Institution of Mechanical Engineers, Part B: Journal of Engineering Manufacture, pp. 1543–1552 (2007)

3. Baines, T.S., Lightfoot, H.W.: Towards an Operations Strategy for the infusion of Product-Centric Services into Manufacturing, into Service Systems Implementation. In: Demirkan, H., Spohrer, J.C., Krishna, V. (eds.) Springer (2011)
4. Balin, S.: Amélioration de processus de production de services par la simulation. PhD thesis, University Paris Dauphine (2007)
5. Fitzsimmons, M.J.: Service Management. McGraw Hill, New York (2004)
6. Giard, V.: Ingénierie de Services. Economica, Paris (2005)
7. Johansson, P., Olhager, J.: Linking product–process matrices for manufacturing and industrial service operations. Int. J. Production Economics 104, 615–624 (2006)
8. Manzini, E., Vezzoli, C.: A strategic desaign approach to develop sustainable product service systems: examples taken from the 'environmentally friendly innovation' Italian prize. Journal of Cleaner Production 11, 852–857 (2003)
9. Hockerts, K.: Eco-Efficient Service Innovation: Increasing Business-Ecological efficiency of Products and Services. In: Charter, M. (ed.) Greener Marketing: A Global Perspective on Greener Marketing Practice, pp. 95–108. Gereenleaf Pub., Sheffield (1999)
10. Tukker, A., Van Halen, C.: Innovation Scan for Product Service Systems; A manual for the development of new product-service systems for companies and intermediaries for the SME sector. TNO, PriceWaterhouseCoopers, Delft/Utrecht (2003)
11. Mucchielli, A.: Les méthodes qualitatives. Presses Universitaires de France, Paris (1991) (Que sais-je 3, 2591)
12. Weick, K.E.: Sensemaking in Organizations. Sage, Thousand Oaks (1995)

# GPS: An Architecture to Help Firms Running from a Product to a PSS Offer

Sophie Peillon, Sarra Dahmani, and Xavier Boucher

Institut Henri Fayol, Ecole nationale supérieure des mines
158 cours Fauriel 42100 Saint-Etienne, France
{peillon,dahmani,boucher}@emse.fr

**Abstract.** For many reasons (differentiation, duration of the relationship with the customers…) a lot of firms, especially SMEs, are moving from an offer of product to an offer of a product-service. From this point of view, firms need to implement new management rules, in terms of skills and control. In this paper, we propose a framework with three levels of modeling, which aims at providing guidelines to firms that enter in this new paradigm. This framework is based on theoretical investigations on the service concept, and on real SMEs cases.

**Keywords:** Product-service system, process, modeling, skills, decision-making.

## 1  Introduction

For the past recent years, we observe that manufacturers of capital goods rely increasingly on services: for much of their corporate profits and revenues, services are compensating the pure activity of manufacturing often delocalized in low cost countries. For many companies, particularly for SMEs whose business is often based on a technological know-how, the move towards a more service-oriented activity remains problematic. In this paper, we propose a process model of the customer-supplier relationship that aims at assisting companies in their efforts towards a servitization strategy. In section 2, we present our approach; in section 3, we propose an analysis of the servitization drivers and we expose a three levels modeling (Generic/Partial/Specific) and finally we present a case study in section 4.

## 2  General Framework

### 2.1  PSS and Servitization

The subjects "functional economy", "servitization" or "PSS" were first developed in 1988 [1]. Since then, there was an increasing production of scientific documents from U.S. and Western Europe that appear primarily in management literature and business practice, with authors who tend to differentiate concepts of operations, services and their activity areas [2]. In the "servitization of manufacturing" [1], firms begin to define themselves as specialist in goods or service production, then they focus on

L.M. Camarinha-Matos, L. Xu, and H. Afsarmanesh (Eds.): PRO-VE 2012, IFIP AICT 380, pp. 35–42, 2012.
© IFIP International Federation for Information Processing 2012

supplying associated and closely related services, and finally they take a middle position as offering a "package" which consists of combinations directed to a targeted customer segment, of goods, services, support, self-service and knowledge. Manufacturing companies were always interacting on the services market. However, traditionally, managers tend to see services as necessary to product support in the context of marketing strategies. The main part of value creation was seen as a consequence attached mainly to physical goods and services were taken purely as an «add-on» to product [3]. Since then, there has been a radical change in service production and marketing ways in manufacturing firms. Service delivery is now transformed into explicit strategy with ambition to transform services to a primary differentiating factor in integrated products / services offers [4], [5]. In industries where excellence is based on design and manufacture, originality remains linked to product basically, then, in this case, the PSS developing operation can lead to a path loss rather than gain in innovation terms. Thus, companies must carefully evaluate their capacity to face competition while ensuring their PSS sale [6].

## 2.2 Approach and Aims

We focus on the organizational consequences of implementing a service-oriented strategy, and especially on the changes in the productive system and development of skills related to this transition. The study described in this paper aims at answering this question by mobilizing an approach not only based on literature, but through an exploratory empirical analysis, using examples from the field. We have analyzed the approaches deployed by different companies, and tried to model the concatenation taken, within a common framework (cf. paragraph 3). For this modeling, we focus on customer-supplier relationship. In fact, what distinguishes a product oriented approach from a product-service approach is how to manage the customer-supplier relationship, especially over time. In the first case, relationship is qualified as "punctual" related to the exchange moment of ownership of product, at least in case of a "pure" product approach. In the second case, the customer-supplier relationship grows over time, so it will be necessarily deployed on a number of processes, and these processes' quality will lead service quality (cf. paragraph 4).

## 3      The Servitization Drivers

From both a literature review and our field experience, we identified several key determinants in the company's transition to a service-oriented strategy, which we name "servitization drivers". The transition to services can't be understood with considering only the company itself, but relationship between company and client. Within this relationship, several factors might be considered potentially as service generating. We therefore consider here the customer-supplier relationship, where service-oriented supplier (SOS noted later) is the provider of a PSS. The different cases of SOS that we could study show that several elements are crucial in the transition from a pure product offer (or where the service is marginal), to a real product-service offer.

## 3.1 Product Use Complexity (UC)

The first servitization driver is related to the product's characteristics offered by the SOS and specifically, to its use complexity. Indeed, this complexity of use can potentially generate a customer's need of services, concerning its installation, handling, maintenance, etc. We notice this aspect particularly in companies whose main businesses are in special machines design and supply, the complexity is related to the technology embodied in the product (i.e. the special machine) or to the production process of the customer who uses a special machine. The technological complexity of some special machines could generate such needs of fine adjustments, which are not generally mastered by client and provided by SOS. SOS then moves from a product supplier position (selling special machines only) to a product-service offer (in this case special machine + regular settings).

## 3.2 Product Criticality in Customer Process (PC)

Criticality occurs when the product sold is an intermediate good that client will use in its production process. Thus, it can be either a technically simple element with low added value to final product, but whose quality is essential to final product functioning, or, a more complex product whose quality is essential to client's production process functioning. In both cases, the criticality will generate a need for service, particularly in terms of monitoring, tracking, or logistics. An example related to customer's process is about supplying cutting tools for automotive and aerospace industries. The concerned company intends to move towards service finding that cutting tool is critical in its client's process. Indeed, the poor quality of cutting tool can cause interruption of the customer production chain, which is unexpected. This criticality thus, makes customers aware about necessity of monitoring quality level (especially sharpening) of cutting tool.

## 3.3 Potential Aggregate Supply (AS)

Given current trend towards multiple product offerings available on market, it becomes increasingly difficult to manage efficiently (turnover, inventory levels ...) the diversity of these offers especially for distributors. A product provider will be able to offer its distributors to manage a more comprehensive service offering by combining essential product with complementary ones. The proposed service can range from simple suggestions to full support of management and ranges evolution on trade and logistics aspects. For example, a crockery supplier may propose services that fit tables. There is emergence of "trade integration" services as in previous decades there were an emergence of industrial integration activities and for the same reasons of reducing subsets complexity management by customer.

## 3.4 Customer's Nature (CN)

Which seems essential is the nature of direct customer of the company. Indeed, several types of direct customers seem to be generating services, especially when direct customer is a reseller, service needs may come from the dealer's need to showcase the product and / or optimize its layout in store or warehouse and logistics supply. In this case, the key skills of supplier can move from product to service and then decline on other similar products. When direct customer is a prescriber, he may need services related to adapting product to his customers, and/or training services. For instance, in medical / paramedical domains (orthotics, prosthetics...), the supplier may incorporate into its product offering a service based on a detailed understanding of users end customers to provide a customized product or bespoke.

### 3.5  Customer's Capabilities and Skills (CS)

The last servitization driver lies in the customer's capabilities or skills availability regarding the use and management of the product sold. Actually, to remain viable, service offering must represent source of specific competitive advantage. If customer doesn't have in-house necessary skills for proper use and management, then SOS may have a competitive advantage to offer the service. Conversely, this means that if the service is easily imitated, competitive advantage is not sustainable. For example, a company initially providing special machines for automotive industry has decided to change its customer segment by targeting food industry. Indeed, in automotive sector, the skills required for mechanical and automatic maintenance are typically owned in-house, while in food industry, customers have little in-house expertise about these skills (the core business is mainly focused on process control). In other words, if competences mastered by customer-company are similar to those mastered by provider, this will threaten the service orientation plan, while the lack of similar skills can be an engine to SOS.

From these five characteristics and their possible combination, stems a more or less important "service potential". The servitization of the supplier company will therefore partly depend on these characteristics.

## 4      A Three Level Modeling of the SOS

### 4.1  The Modeling Framework and Principles

The Service-Oriented Architecture (SOA) framework includes several modeling approaches, but all of them keep focused on IT services [7], [8]. As we aim at modeling other types of services, we will use a less IT service focused approach: the blueprint one, based on three level architecture [9]. This approach is particularly interesting because it makes it possible to show all the components of the service delivery, especially the customer and the SOS internal actors and processes.

The modeling purpose of this work does not consist in creating any new modeling language or methodology. On the contrary we re-use a rather standard modeling method and language, by adapting their use to the servitization focus. Concerning the modeling methodology we refer to the Model Driven Architecture [10], by using the 3 following modeling levels : CIM (Computation-Independent Model); PIM (Platform-Independent Model); PSM (Platform-Specific Model). Concerning the modeling language we use the Business Process Modeling Language [11] available on the Adonis modeling platform, and compatible with BMN. On the CIM level, we suggest a generic model focused on the relationship between the SOS and its customers. This level aims at being generic, that is at being able to modelize every case of customer/supplier relationship. The PIM level describes the same relationship, but from a more particular point of view. Indeed, we assume here that the processes that would have to be achieved by the SOS would be different depending on the main servitization driver. Finally, the PSM level describes the activities that a specific firm has to perform in order to carry out the sub-processes defined PIM level.

The GPS architecture relies on these three modeling levels, named Generic/Partial/Specific. The first two levels are modelized through processes and sub-processes; the last one is built upon an activity model.

**The G-Level.** This level aims at describing all the processes required in the customer/supplier relationship in order to deliver a PSS. Its building is mainly based on the literature analysis. We have organized this model in three areas that show the sub-processes that each actor has in charge along the PSS life-cycle (Figure 1).

The top area is the customer one. It shows all the processes needed, in the customer firm, within the framework of a PSS delivery relationship. The down area is the SOS one, showing the internal processes needed within the framework of a PSS delivery relationship. The middle part is the coordination area. In a classic product offer, this coordination area is a classic market area, where the offer and the demand meet each other. In the case of a PSS offer, this classic market area is no more relevant, and a collaborative area is needed, because the PSS has to be co-created with the customer(s). The collaborative area includes three main processes: the customer's needs analysis; the PSS solution delivery; and the follow-up of the PSS performance.

**The P-Level.** This level aims at precising the G one. The idea here is that each generical process defined on the G-level could be implemented in a different way according the servitization driver of the SOS, because every servitization driver will lead to specific modeling constraints. For instance, in a servitization driver of a PC type, the servitization lies mainly in the criticality of the product within the customer's activity. This means that traceability mechanisms will be of a great importance, and should be offered through the services added to the product, in particular through IT devices and through an information system. The P-level is of particular usefulness for the SOS, because it can help the company's head and managers in organizing their approach to the new servitization strategy.

**The S-Level.** The last level shows the activities that the SOS has to perform for its PSS strategy. We can consider this level as the most useful one for the SOS's head and managers, because it aims at helping them solving the operational difficulties they face, and handling their approach of the PSS offer development. Two main difficulties can be highlighted here. The first one lies in the implementation of the PSS strategy which generally leads to the implementation of a new organization, including new activities and new skills. The SOS has then to well identify these new activities and new skills, and then to choose either to develop them internally (through training and/or hiring) or to find them externally (external growth and/or partnerships). The second one lies in the pricing of the new PSS offer. If the SOS might know quite well the costs covered by its product offer, the evaluation of the costs and then of the price of the added services is much more difficult. Here the S-level could be of a great support for the SOS management, as it enables to identify the activities needed, then to better know the costs involved, and to define a price. We have used this GPS approach to modelize an industrial case, which is described below.

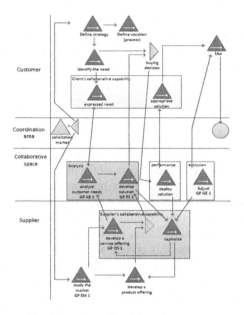

**Fig. 1.** The overall collaborative process

## 4.2 A Case Modeling: The LDN Company

LDN is a small manufacturer of house facilities accessories. These accessories are manly sold in DIY superstores. In 2010, LDN undertook a strategic reflection which led to identify the PSS strategy as a possible way of growth. The service drivers that have been detected lie mainly on the customer's (i.e. the DIY superstore) behavior and needs. We are here within a B2B relationship, between a supplier (LDN) and a retailer (the DIY superstore). The customer's needs identified lie mainly in the optimization of its offer to the final customer (the DIY shopper). In order to increase the whole accessories department turnover, the DIY superstore is interested in having a comprehensive offer, including logistics aspects. Therefore, the supplier has to offer not only a single product but a whole solution, which includes a range of complementary accessories on the one hand, and complementary services like the follow-up and the delivery logistics on the other hand.

More precisely, LDN undergoes several constraints from its customer, because the distribution process includes two actors with specific goals: the purchasing service of the DIY superstore, and the accessories department chief. LDN has to convince the first one that its global PSS offer is relevant and competitive, and to negotiate with him the quantities, the prices, and the supplying modes. For this negotiation, our S-level modeling can be of a great usefulness. The second actor is a more operational one. He would be mainly interested in the selling performance of the range of accessories, i.e. in the turnover per linear meter. Then, he would like added services such as the setting-up of the range of accessories within the shelves, including advertising aspects, the follow-up and the continued supply.

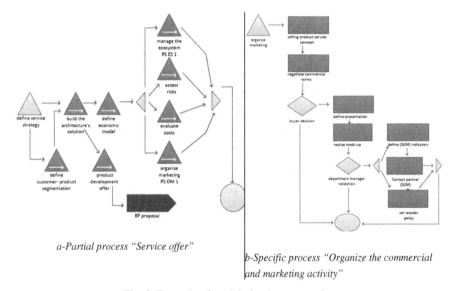

*a-Partial process "Service offer"*

*b-Specific process "Organize the commercial and marketing activity"*

**Fig. 2.** Example of models for the case study

We have thus considered that the servitization driver is mainly of a NC type. The Figure 2.a shows the sub-process "Create a service offer", which stems from the collaborative area "Collaborative capability of the supplier" of the G-level model. The Figure 2.b shows the activities needed by LDN to achieve the process "Organize the commercial and marketing activity", and highlights the constraints stemming from the customer and stated above.

This modeling approach can be used to help LDN in analyzing the processes and skills needed to achieve its PSS offer. Then the company could identify the in-house skills and the skills that must be developed (by hiring or co-contracting).

## 5    Conclusion

Looking for competition factors which could help them to maintain their industrial capabilities, many SMEs are currently developing innovative strategies of product/service coupling. This rather new type of market offer constitute a quite drastic economical and organizational transition for small firms: which kind of service offers should be developed? How should the organization and internal competencies change to provide the adequate quality of service level? To address such issues, this paper has emphasized 2 contributions: first, the identification of the key factors to be considered when developing the servitization potentiality of a SME; second, a 3 levels Modeling Architecture to be used as a support to implement new product-service offer. This research is a work in progress: we currently work at enlarging the panel of firm under study, so as to later improve the conceptual approach and the modeling framework.

# References

1. Vandermerwe, S., Rada, J.F.: Servitization of business: Adding Value by adding services. European Management Journal 6(4), 314–324 (1988)
2. Baines, T.S., Lightfoot, H.W., Benedettini, O., Kay, J.M.: The servitization of manufacturing: A review of literature and reflection on future challenges. Journal of Manufacturing Technology Management 20(5), 547–567 (2009)
3. Gebauer, H., Fleisch, E., Friedli, T.: Overcoming the service paradox in manufacturing companies. European Management Journal 23(1), 14–26 (2005)
4. Oliva, R., Kallenberg, R.: Managing the transition from products to services. International Journal of Service Industry Management 14(2), 160–172 (2003)
5. Baines, T.S., et al.: State of the art in product service system. Engineering Manufacture 221(10), 1543–1552 (2007)
6. Tukker, A., Tischner, U.: Product-service as a research field: past, present and future. Journal of Cleaner Production 14, 1552–1556 (2006)
7. Arsanjani, A.: Service-oriented modeling and architecture (2004),
   http://www.ibm.com/developerworks/library/ws-soa-design1/
8. OASIS, Reference Model for service oriented architecture 1.0 (2006),
   http://www.oasis-open.org/committees/
   download.php/19679/soa-rm-cs.pdf
9. Shostack, G.L.: How to design a service. European Journal of Marketing 16(1), 49–63 (1982)
10. OMG, Mda guide version 1.0.1, volume omg/2003-06-01 (2003)
11. Karagiannis, D., Junginger, S., Strobl, R.: Introduction to Business Process Management System Concepts. In: Scholz-Reiter, B., Stickel, E. (eds.) Business Process Modeling, pp. 81–106. Springer, Berlin (1996)

# Using the Product Life Cycle as a Basis
# for a Product-Service Strategy Model

David Walters and Jyotirmoyee Bhattacharjya

Institute of Transport and Logistics Studies, The University of Sydney, Sydney,
NSW 2006, Australia
{david.walters,jyotirmoyee.bhattacharjya}@sydney.edu.au

**Abstract.** The recent financial problems of the 2008/10 GFC and the likelihood
of similar events occurring in 2012/13 has 'spooked' business and consumer
confidence and has resulted in fierce competition in both B2C and in the
derived demand companies in B2B markets. The problems are exacerbated by
the very slow recovery response of developed economy business organizations,
many facing competition from Asian companies whose business models have
become sophisticated and are moving rapidly away from their traditional *"high
volume/low value"* manufacturing expertise towards a *"low volume/high value"*
value proposition thereby threatening well established traditional western
companies; some are moving away from tangible/hardware products towards
becoming *solution providers*.

**Keywords:** Innovation, Imitation, Commoditization, Value migration, the
PRODUCT-service life cycle, the product-SERVICE life cycle.

## 1 Introduction

Today the engine for growth is Asia and the model has shifted from a business owing
all of the production assets to managing partners in supply chains to even more
complex relationships. While the focus on Asia by western organizations was
originally about lowering costs in the supply chain; as these resource markets
expanded they have become massive consumer markets in their own rights such that
now China is the world's fastest growing market. More recently the Indian
automotive market has been expanding rapidly. This has been accompanied by market
led product and manufacturing process designs that call into question whether the
"global products and platforms" that many manufacturers have strived for are really
just extensions of Western requirements. The launch of the Nano (small automobile)
by Tata, for example, identified a need for product and service design to reflect local
requirements and capabilities. General Electric and Panasonic have introduced
'reverse/frugal' innovation into Asian markets based upon a policy that reflects
"meeting local needs with local resources". It follows that the competitive strategy of
western/traditional business models needs to be adapted to changing market
circumstances.

L.M. Camarinha-Matos, L. Xu, and H. Afsarmanesh (Eds.): PRO-VE 2012, IFIP AICT 380, pp. 43–50, 2012.
© IFIP International Federation for Information Processing 2012

## 2      Asian Innovation and Competition: An Issue for the 21st Century

There is no shortage of examples demonstrating the innovative ideas emerging from Asia. Much of this success is based upon *open innovation,* the use of external sources to enhance a company's internal research processes. These external sources may be other individuals in the same industry, not technically related to the company, professionals, entrepreneurs, or even ordinary consumers (crowd sourcing) that have a mind for innovation. Open innovation accepts the fact that knowledge is everywhere; companies benefit from the influx of externally sourced knowledge, and this ensures they keep from stagnating in their internal research and development. Many of the most important innovations consist of incremental improvements to products and processes aimed at the middle or the bottom of the income pyramid "Frugal" or "constraint-based" innovation takes the needs of poor consumers as a starting point and working backwards stripping the products down to their bare essentials. India's *Mahindra & Mahindra* sells lots of small tractors to American hobby farmers, filling John Deere with fear. China's *Haier* has undercut Western competitors in a wide range of products, from air conditioners and washing machines to wine coolers. *Godrej & Boyce Manufacturing* has developed a battery powered $70 fridge. *Li & Fung* (HK) and *Chingquing Lifan Group* (China) can use their huge supply chains to produce fashion items or motorcycles in response to demand. *Aravind Eye Care System* that makes high-quality eye care accessible to low income customers. Its founder, Dr. G. Venkataswamy, is applying the principles of McDonald's that led him to creative ideas about efficient, high-quality care that have had untold impact on the lives of hundreds of thousands of the poor of South India

Western organizations are responding to the imitation and reverse/frugal innovation that are becoming dominant forms of competition. *GE and Smith & Nephew's* emerging market strategies, for example, also include mechanisms for deploying "reverse innovation" back to mature Western markets to widen the impact of its investments. In this way, the work they do within emerging markets benefits their key developed markets as well. There are powerful messages here for western based organizations. Thus it follows that if the western business model is to survive there are a few strategic considerations to be considered. One is to follow the merger and acquisition and strategic alliance route that companies such as *GE, Pfizer, Abbot Laboratories, ABB* and others are pursuing. Another is to study market development trends very closely and watch and time the strategies being implemented by the "new competition"; these being, imitation, commoditization, and reverse innovation. We suggest the product-life cycle model offers a useful starting place.

## 3      Revisiting the Product Life Cycle

It is not only the shift towards the more intangible aspects of value delivery that are undergoing change; so too is the notion of the product life cycle (PLC); a concept that continues to appear in marketing texts (and sadly in boardroom thinking despite the fact that the original concept, in many instances, is older than many of the directors!). The PLC concept has been influenced by developments in the management of knowledge, technology, processes and relationships management. In the context of this discussion academic and corporate analysis should consider the planned transformation of the "product" delivered benefits into "service" benefits. This process is influenced by changing, or evolving customer expectations, and the improved business model delivery of competitors. This suggests a fresh look at the concept will be useful to this discussion.

Kotler [1] suggested the value of the product life cycle is "... that it provides insights into a product's competitive dynamics. At the same time the concept can prove misleading if not carefully used". He suggested further: "The product life cycle portrays *distinct stages* in the *sales history* of a product, corresponding to these stages are distinct opportunities and problems with respect to marketing strategy and profit potential. By identifying the stage that a product is in, or may be headed toward, companies can formulate better marketing plans". Kotler's words of caution were reinforced by comments concerning the level of aggregation used to apply the life cycle theory. He used an illustration based on the work of Page (unpublished) which suggested three levels of analysis. Page produced evidence to suggest that we should consider product category, product form and brand, and used alcohol beverages as an example. Page's case example suggested that over time, depending on which level the analysis is conducted, the 'stage' of the product life cycle might differ from the life cycle stages at other levels. Furthermore, as Kotler ably demonstrated, there are many shapes that product life cycles may adopt. This raises an issue concerning the reliability of the PLC for planning purposes.

It has been argued that the product life cycle was not as reliable a model as might have been hoped for, particularly if large investment is required. Doyle [2] proposed that if there is no predictable life cycle and similarly no standard pattern of market evolution, alternatives are required. He suggested there are common processes that shape markets and consequently that by analyzing these managers can anticipate new markets and how competition will develop, and in so doing determine the likely shape of market volumes. This "... can develop strategies both to capitalize on these changes and to influence those forces of change". The forces—or common processes—he identified are *customers, competition, new entrants, substitute products and technologies, and supply relationships*; in the fifteen years that have passed these effects have become increasingly dynamic and often unpredictable.

Prior to this, Ansoff [3] had revised the product-life-cycle model, offering a more realistic and current view. Ansoff argued that *demand life cycle* for a product-service is ongoing – in other words end-user 'product application needs' (the desired value) remain unchanged – we continue to 'count and calculate', and undertake many other activities; what has changed is the ways and means of achieving the outcomes. Technological development has accelerated and introduces the notion of the *DTLC (demand technology life cycles)*. We suggest technological development is not the only influence; knowledge management, relationship management, and process management have had influence to a greater or lesser degree. The scope of a business may be defined as being a combination of customer needs, functions, customer groups/segments and technologies in a viable market cell within which the business can focus its capabilities and capacities to service customer needs and segments within the current technology base. Ansoff identified space created within the *demand technology cycle* as a *strategic business area (SBA)* and utilizes this idea for strategic market planning decisions.

If the *demand technology cycle* provides the *strategic business area* within which the firm is to apply its capabilities and capacities; then *applications cycles* create *operational business areas.* It is within these that a range of product applications appear using the technology of the demand technology cycle. Thus each *strategic business area* potentially offers a number of *product application technology* opportunities within which *organizational product life cycles, individual product-service offers,* describe the product variants possible *within the available technology* and are offered by competing organizations. Examples can be seen in the computer industry with competing notebook products, tablets and ultra-thin note books, each representing competitive activity in an *applications cycle.* Within this cycle manufacturers' individual brands are offered. The approach is essentially customer/market led and linked with research and development activities which identify emerging customer needs and technological feasibility.

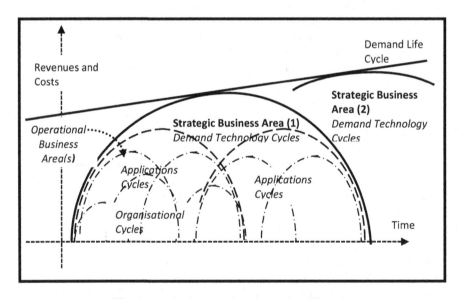

**Fig. 1.** A revised approach to the product life cycle

Figure one depicts ongoing *demand life cycle* as a growth trend (simplified to be a straight line) and servicing the demand are a series of *demand technology cycles* (within which two *applications cycles* can be observed). It is within the *organization lifecycles* that individual companies (and network structures) compete. At a *macro level* the strategic planning cycles (within strategic business areas) are *selective competitive responses* to meet imitation, commoditization, and value migration with strategies based upon *reverse innovation, asset management,* and, *solution provision.* At a *micro level* operational planning (within applications cycles) product-service variations are based upon the technology prescribed by the application (for example in computer hardware we currently have a cluster of 'tablet' products); within the applications cycles organizational cycles appear offering specific brand based value propositions. See Fig. 1.

# 4     Product-Service Life Cycle Strategy

Johnson [4] describes how **Hilti** (a leading hand-power tool manufacturer) realized that its value proposition with its emphasis on being a premium brand had lost its visibility with major customers. The product became "commoditized"; users began to regard it as disposable and after-use care was ignored. This suggests a transformation of the product life cycle model one that reflects what appears to be a move towards a business model that has emphasis on "asset management and cash flow performance"; suggesting a *"PRODUCT-service"* as being a predominantly tangible product providing "hardware" solutions to a customer problem and is clearly applicable to both business-to-business and business-to-consumer market sectors and as competition intensifies the service content of the package can become a critical factor in vendor/customer relationships and at a particular time (or situation) in the relationship the *PRODUCT-service* becomes a *product-SERVICE.* The 'solutions' response approach by organizations such as IBM, Rolls Royce Engines, and Boeing) is to deliver "value–based" service products. IBM's recently announced financial results suggest their 'solutions' business model is considerably more successful than the tangible product computer hardware business model. We suggest in this paper that the somewhat neglected *product-life-cycle model* can provide a structured approach to the construction of a workable business model by focusing on *strategic pathways* over time.

Recent Capgemini [5] research demonstrates the increasing importance of integrating service into product strategy 'packages'. It adds emphasis to the notion of the *PRODUCT-service/product-SERVICE* concept whereby as customer attitudes shift the *PRODUCT-service* 'package' moves through a life cycle and emphasis is placed upon *product-SERVICE.* Capgemini's research suggests that post-2000 a number of issues became important in the vendor-customer equation. These include; increasing costs, reduced margins (for both vendor and customer), rapid commoditization (particularly noticeable in computer hardware), and changing customer expectations. See also Capgemini [6] for a review of companies' approaches to creating competitive advantage by planning their product-SERVICE strategies.

Successful businesses plan response strategies that manage the migration of their PRODUCT-Service *value* proposition towards one based upon a product-SERVICE offer. Katz [7] suggests this may explain the problems currently being experienced by the Japanese electronics industry; rather than compete with Samsung (and others) all having the advantage of low cost capital and superior (and more efficient) manufacturing processes.   An immediate response was to look for synergy and economies of scales from mergers. **Elpida**, a manufacturer of DRAM chips, was one such attempt by merging the relevant activities of **Hitachi, NEC**, and **Mitsubishi**. Elpida filed for bankruptcy in February 2012.   See figure two.

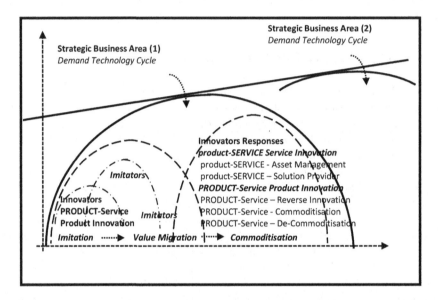

**Fig. 2.** Plotting competitive strategy in a revised product-service life cycle

A *"PRODUCT-service"* is a predominantly tangible product that provides a "hardware" solution to a customer problem and is clearly applicable to both B2B and B2C market sectors.  As competition intensifies the service content of the package can become a critical factor in vendor/customer relationships and at a particular time (as for Hilti) in the relationship the *PRODUCT-service* may become a *product-SERVICE* to maintain competitive advantage.

Maintaining *customer performance management* is vital; it is indisputable that the growth rates in the emerging markets exceeds that of the older, traditional markets, so much so that a number of large, global, capital equipment manufacturers are locating their production facilities in these markets; this is not simply for operational outsourcing benefits but is more a strategic outsourcing move to create strategic alliances in the emerging market to ensure *'market viability and longevity'* by establishing a business model that offers a locally produced relevant, 'fit for purpose' product-service value propositions to local end-user customers at competitive prices. The "reverse innovation" or "frugal innovation" activities of **GE** and **Panasonic** to re-engineer their product-services to meet specific 'local' requirements (affordable healthcare and a comfortable living environment) are reflecting "a service-dominant view in which intangibility, exchange processes, and relationships are central". [8]

The model presented in figure two is being used by a number of *Innovator* organizations as response to the territorial expansion from Asian organizations.

Examples of organizations using a *PRODUCT-service* /product-SERVICE strategy successfully include: *Asset Management;* **Boeing** is offering users a global routine service facility; working with its airline customers it can position parts inventories in locations where aircraft service requirements become due, this may relieve the customer of planning both flight and servicing schedules so that they coincide. **Caterpillar, Rolls Royce Engines** provide early indication of impending product failure enabling service personnel to put into motion product component replacement responses as a failure occurs. *Solution Provider* strategies are being pursued by **IBM, Dell,** and **Cisco; IBM** and **Cisco** accumulate knowledge and refine their skills through their research activities and their experiential learning as they help clients implement innovations. Working with multiple clients creates learning effect economies and provides opportunity to engage in repeated application of skills, which helps them address problems and enhance their ability to recognize cause-and-effect relationships. *Value migration* occurs as both economic and shareholder value flows away from obsolescent (and obsolete) business models. Slywotzky [9] argued that new models offer the same benefits to customers but at lower cost by changing the model structure. This change often results in a restructuring of profit sharing throughout the business model. An example of value migration as a response to customer expectations that have changed is **Dell's** adjustment to its business model and its value proposition; Dell now focuses on what it calls a "segmented supply chain," offering solutions to various groups of customers depending as much on what they need as what they're willing to pay for. *Reverse/frugal innovation* is being practiced by a number of global organizations (manufacturers of capital goods) have found difficulties in marketing their products in emerging markets. They have worked with local users, manufacturers, and distributors to produce a *feasible* (meets user requirements) and *viable* (within cost and profit margin budgets) series of health care products. The more innovative among them consider "reverse innovation" or "frugal innovation" opportunities to re-engineer their product-services to meet specific 'local' requirements as a sound strategy for growth. **General Electric** and **Panasonic** have been notably successful in this approach. *"Commoditization"*; **Dell Computers** commenced selling laptop computers through retail outlets such as **Wal-Mart** in the USA in 2010 marking a significant change in distribution strategy. The product offers characteristics that allow basic applications to be used; they have in fact become *commodity products* that meet and offer limited user expectations and are made available in convenient locations patronized by the target market. *De-commoditization* examples include mineral water pack-size differentiation to meet convenience and location availability, FMCG internet shopping and home delivery. [10].

## 5    Concluding Comments

This paper has explored recent additions (and proposals) to the product-life-cycle concept that has conceptual and practical interests to academics and practitioners. Earlier the changing nature of the product-service life cycle was discussed; one of the topics raised in the discussion was that of commoditization and its implications.

Developing an understanding of the impact on current customers' business models of downstream changes in *their* expectations (and *their customers'* expectations) and the implications these may have on the supplier organisation's strategic and operational decisions: do they require short-term adjustments to the organisation's positioning in *Operational Business Areas* or do they present longer-term concerns for strategic positioning in the *Strategic Business Area?* An ongoing examination of the changes in cost structures (fixed and variable) and the implications these have on customer expectations, network partners, and stakeholder partners. Clearly there is a changing role for an integrated and coordinated role of; marketing, research, design and development, operations and finance and with partner organisations if the *Product-Service-Life-Cycle* based business model is to be effective.

# References

1. Kotler, P.: Marketing Management, 8th edn. Prentice Hall, New York (1994)
2. Doyle, P.: Marketing Management and Strategy. Prentice Hall, London (1994)
3. Ansoff, H.I.: Implanting Strategic Management. Prentice Hall, New York (1984)
4. Johnson, M.: Seizing the White Space. Harvard Business Press, Boston (2010)
5. Capgemini: Service as a Strategy, http://www.capgemini.com/m/en/tl/tl_Service_as_a_Strategy.pdf
6. Capgemini: Making the Shift to Service Management, http://www.capgemini.com/insights-and-resources/by-publication/making-the-shift-to-service-management/
7. Katz, R.: What's Killing Japanese Electronics? Wall Street Journal (March 23, 2012)
8. Vargo, S., Lusch, R.: Evolving to a new dominant logic for marketing. J. of Marketing 68, 1–17 (2004)
9. Slywotzky, A.J., Morrison, D.J.: The Profit Zone. Wiley, New York (1997)
10. Schumpeter: Frugal ideas are spreading from East to West. Economist (May 24, 2012)

# 3

## Service Composition I

# A Formal Model-Based Approach to Engineering Systems-of-Systems

John Fitzgerald, Jeremy Bryans, and Richard Payne

Centre for Software Reliability, Newcastle University,
Newcastle upon Tyne NE1 7RU, United Kingdom
{John.Fitzgerald,Jeremy.Bryans,Richard.Payne}@ncl.ac.uk

**Abstract.** Systems-of-systems (SoS) are network-enabled synergistic collaborations between systems that are operationally and managerially independent, distributed, evolve dynamically and exhibit emergence. The design of dependable SoS requires model-based approaches that permit description of contracts between constituent systems at interfaces in a SoS architecture, including functionality and interaction behaviour, and that permit verification of global behaviours. We describe an approach to formal model-based SoS engineering using complementary notations for functional, interaction and architectural aspects. A case study in modelling information flow in an emergency response SoS demonstrates the viability of the proposed approach and highlights a need for common semantic foundations.

**Keywords:** Systems-of-systems, Information flow, SysML, CSP, VDM, Analysis, Verification.

## 1    Introduction

Systems-of-systems (SoS) are network-enabled integrations of heterogeneous systems, delivering capabilities and services which cannot be achieved by the constituent systems alone. Examples include enterprise information systems, integrated manufacturing systems, and emergency response collaborations. SoS technology enables the provision of holistic services such as more efficient management and control, more agile response or efficient energy management.

SoS are distinguished from large monolithic systems by several characteristics [1]. The **managerial and operational independence** of the constituent systems means that it may be impossible to exercise centralised control over operation, or to ensure that goals are respected. SoS must cope with **evolution** caused by changes in the purposes and identity of constituent systems. Their geographically **distributed** character leads to a reliance on network/Internet technologies to ensure communication between constituents. **Emergence** is central to their functioning in that the SoS delivers a purpose that is not explicitly present in the constituent systems.

SoS can be viewed as Collaborative Network Organisations (CNOs) in the terms of the ARCON reference modelling framework [2]. SoS are classed as *Virtual*,

L.M. Camarinha-Matos, L. Xu, and H. Afsarmanesh (Eds.): PRO-VE 2012, IFIP AICT 380, pp. 53–62, 2012.
© IFIP International Federation for Information Processing 2012

*Collaborative, Acknowledged* or *Directed* [3,1] based on the strength of explicit acknowledgement and subordination to centralized control. They thus exhibit a range of levels of joint endeavour [2], from simply networking to maintaining a joint identity.

The engineering of SoS is challenging because of the complexity of interactions of constituent systems, and the need for effective communication among diverse stakeholders. A consistent theme of SoS research has been the role of model-based techniques [4,5] as it has been for CNOs in general [6]. A precise model of SoS architecture, constituent systems, infrastructure and environment allows early exploration of design alternatives and the contracts that exist between constituent systems. This makes it possible to validate global properties such as resilience to faults or attacks, liveness, safety and security, that affect the reliance that can be placed on a SoS. If models are defined using languages with formal semantics, it becomes possible to perform machine-assisted analysis of global properties, providing early identification and elimination of errors. Formal methods thus offer a way to manage risk.

Although formal methods can be challenging to apply [6], advances in their automation have increased their viability, notably in software development [7]. However, these techniques have been applied only experimentally in SoS Engineering (e.g. [8]). The goal of our work, supported by the COMPASS project[1], is to develop modelling languages that are expressive enough to model the architecture and behaviour of candidate SoS structures, and sufficiently rigorously defined to permit trustworthy machine-assisted analysis of global properties.

This paper proposes an approach to formal model-based SoS engineering using complementary formalisms to describe functional and behavioural aspects of constituent systems, and verify global properties of the SoS. In Section 2 we describe this approach, and in Section 3 we describe its pilot application to a study of an emergency response SoS. Section 4 describes future research towards our goal.

## 2    A Formal Model-Based Approach to SoS

Model-based engineering approaches are challenged by several characteristics of SoS. Independence means that there can only be limited knowledge about, and control over, constituent systems. This suggests that models should support the recording of contracts that bound constituents' behaviour without defining it completely and deterministically. Geographical distribution implies a need to model concurrency in terms of message passing between constituents. The need to manage evolution and structural change requires the ability to model architectural structures and particularly interfaces between constituents. The central role of emergence in SoS makes it imperative to support the verification of SoS-level properties. In addition to these requirements, experience in industry deployment of formal methods teaches us that it

[1] Comprehensive Modelling for Advanced Systems-of-Systems, EC FP7 Project 287829, http://www.compass-research.eu

is necessary to provide strong links to an accepted architectural notation, and to have robust tools that support both simulation and static analysis [7].

No single formalism meets all of the demanding requirements. As the ECOLEAD project concluded, there is no "universal language" for modelling problems for CNOs in general [2]. We therefore aim to define combinations of interoperable modelling techniques and extend them for SoS development to allow trade-off analysis and verification of SoS-level properties.

Many formal languages have been developed for expressing and analysing particular system characteristics [9, 10, 11]. However, for a SoS, we need to cover functionality, concurrency, communication, inheritance, time, sharing, and mobility. Some languages cover a few of these features, and there are integrations of formalisms that cater for data, concurrency, and time [12, 13, 14, 15, 16]. The verification of global properties in design also suggests a need for a theory that covers refinement.

Given the requirements above, our baseline technologies are SysML for architectural description, CSP [10] for describing concurrency and communication and VDM [17] for data and functionality. We extend SysML [18] with the ability to express rigorous interface contracts [19], giving SoS engineers the ability to experiment with consequences of different architectural design decisions. SoS engineers may also define expected interfaces of the constituent systems, which may in turn be provided to developers/operators of constituent systems, or used as a basis of their assessment, providing greater confidence that constituent systems adhere to the expected properties on interfaces. We aim to allow engineers to operate either at the SysML graphical level or at the textual level, or at a combination of these, since there will be support for moving between these views. In Section 3, we explore the feasibility of this combination of formalisms for model-based SoS engineering via a case study.

## 3    A Case Study in Emergency Service Co-ordination

In this section we present a study in emergency coordination in order to evaluate the modelling approach proposed in Section 2. Our study is based on the London Emergency Services Major Incident Procedure Manual [20] which documents the process for identifying a major incident, initiating appropriate services (fire, police, ambulance etc.), and the roles and responsibilities of service members involved. The coalition of services forms a SoS: the constituent systems are normally independent services; there is mobility and geographic distribution, and a need to evolve rapidly as goals or volatile conditions change. Ultimately, the SoS must provide an emergent service to stakeholders ranging from people involved in the incident to the media and authorities. This coalition was previously explored using the Event-B formalism [21]. However, that model does not address interaction between participants, and does not provide an accessible representation of the SoS architecture.

We first introduce the application and then the formalisms SysML, CSP and VDM. We present models of the complementary architectural, behavioural and functional aspects of the SoS (Sections 3.1-3.3). For brevity, we omit some details of the formal models, but give a flavour of them. In Section 4, we draw conclusions about the research required to develop a more integrated modelling and analytic framework.

The response to all major incidents follows a broadly similar structure. Members of each service attending the scene form *Bronze* (operational) command. For more severe incidents, a *Silver* (tactical) command is formed containing representatives of all the services involved. For long-running incidents, a *Gold* (strategic) command may be formed at a geographically distant point. Each service has members working at each level, e.g. *Silver Police*. Each level and service has different responsibilities.

There is a strict information flow policy in the Bronze/Silver/Gold structure, illustrated in Figure 1. The members of the coalition in a given service and level are permitted to communicate with other members and the same level, for example Bronze Police may communicate with other Bronze officers. The services also have their own communication structure which may be used between adjacent levels. For example, Bronze Police may communicate with Silver Police, but not directly with Gold Police. Communication with the media is (in this example) the sole responsibility of Gold Police.

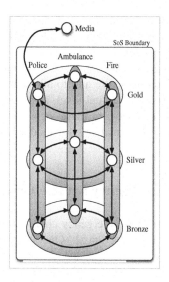

**Fig. 1.** Permitted information flows between coalition members of different levels

We focus on the rules [20,22] for releasing casualty information to the media, and the requirements that these rules place on the interfaces between the emergency services (constituent systems). Confusion can arise if the media aggregate casualty figures from multiple sources ("double-counting"), leading to overestimation of the incident's severity. To avoid this, all casualty details must be given to Gold command, which is then responsible for producing a more reliable estimate and passing this to the media. The previous Event-B study [21] considered the passage of information through the emergency response system, and sought to ensure that information was not released to the media without first being cleared by Gold.

## 3.1    Architectural Model in SysML

SysML [18] is a profile for UML 2.0, developed for system engineering, but also supporting the modelling of SoS architectural definitions. It has wide industrial support and a sound tool base. SysML provides several diagram types, with "precise natural language" semantics, to support the description of SoS architectural structure, behaviour and requirements.

A detailed SysML architectural definition of the case study is given in [22]. For brevity, we omit the general SoS structure. However, Figure 2, a SysML Internal Block Diagram, details the points of interaction between the SoS constituent systems relevant to casualty information clearance. Contracts between constituent systems are given as provided and required interfaces, containing collections of operation signatures. For example, in Figure 2, the `order_to_collect_info` interface is provided by Bronze officers and required by Gold command. The interface contains a single operation (given in the full interface definition [22], with the signature `collectCasualtyDetails(loc:Location)`, where location is an abstract data type) to order Bronze officers to collect casualty information. The inclusion of pre/postconditions on operations is optional in SysML, and rarely used in practice. However, in order to accommodate interface specifications rich enough for formal analysis of SoS, extensions to interfaces have been proposed, including more rigorous operation definitions, state machine diagrams defining communication protocols, and the means to record the rationale for contract agreement between interfaces [19].

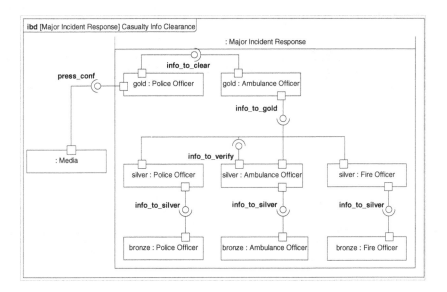

**Fig. 2.** SysML Internal Block Diagram of Major Incident Response connections

Given a SysML architectural model, complementary CSP and VDM models may be defined covering the interaction behaviour and data and functionality aspects respectively. The SysML model provides a basis for ensuring consistency between the defined SoS internal structure and the interface definitions.

### 3.2    Modelling Interaction behaviour Using CSP

The CSP [10] formalism allows the interaction behaviour of the SoS to be modelled as a set of processes. A process is made up of sequences of actions (or *events*). Process combinators make explicit the events shared between processes. An abstract model serves to specify the permitted SoS behaviours; more concrete models include communication and structural detail, and may be checked for conformance with the abstract model.

In the abstract specification, the passage of information through the SoS is modelled as a process INFO(i). The variable i is parameterised over the set of all information Inf. A process INFO(i) is made up of three events: each information item i can first be learned, then cleared, and finally released to the media. No further activity is then possible for that process. The specification ACOAL is the combination (|||) of these processes for all possible values of parameter i. The interleaving combinator (|||) indicates that the individual processes INFO(i) do not interact with each other.

```
INFO(i) = learn.i -> clear.i -> release.i -> STOP
ACOAL = ||| i:Inf @ INFO(i)
```

The more concrete model below identifies the coalition levels and the communication events between them. The Bronze process BR(i) begins by learning the information item i and then describes the passing of i to Silver. The synchronisation event bscomm.i describes the passing of information item i along the channel bscomm. The Silver process SI(i) begins with the synchronisation event bscomm.i, through which it learns about information item i. Silver then passes the item to Gold, which clears and releases the item.

```
BR(i) = learn.i -> bscomm.i -> STOP
BRONZE = ||| i:Inf @ BR(i)
SI(i) =  bscomm.i -> sgcomm.i ->   STOP
SILVER = ||| i:Inf @ SI(i)
GD(i) = sgcomm.i -> clear.i -> release.i -> STOP
GOLD = ||| i:Inf @ GD(i)
```

The three processes are combined in the concrete specification as CCOAL, communicating on the events bscomm and sgcomm.

```
CCOAL = BRONZE [|{|bscomm|}|] (SILVER [|{|sgcomm|}|] GOLD)
          \ {| bscomm, sgcomm |}
```

A model checker such as FDR can be used to check that this concrete SoS description admits only behaviours permitted by the abstract specification. The next step is to decompose GOLD into processes representing the emergency services. For example:

```
P(i) = sgcomm.i -> pclear.i -> release.i -> STOP
Police = ||| i:Inf @ P(i)
```

The distributed GOLD command is the combination of these processes:

```
GOLDdist = ((Police [|{| sgcomm, release |}|] Fire)
            [|{| sgcomm, release |}|] Amb)
```

The distributed SoS combines the distributed GOLD with the previous processes.

```
COALdist = (BRONZE [| {|bscomm|} |] SILVER)
           [| {|sgcomm|} |] GOLDdist
           \ {|bscomm, sgcomm, pclear, fclear, aclear|}
```

The requirement that the distributed coalition model (`COALdist`) respects (denoted by "`[T=`") the behavioural constraints specified in the abstract model (`ACOAL`) can be asserted formally as follows and checked with tool support:

```
assert ACOAL \ {|clear|} [T= COALdist
```

### 3.3   Modelling Functionality Using VDM

The VDM formal method [17] supports the description of functionality in terms of executable code or in terms of abstract contracts. Tool support is particularly strong for simulation, and there is an established coupling to UML.

A model of the emergency response SoS is given in this section. The model contains two model-specific data types: `Info` is an abstract token type and `CType` is an enumerated type representing the coalition levels (Bronze, Silver, and Gold). The model focuses on recording its state in terms of the information in each state (`known`, `cleared` or `released`), and the level at which that information is known (`coal_known`). A data type *invariant* records consistency restrictions on the allowable state. In this model, the invariant ensures that released information must have been cleared (`released subset cleared`), and all known information is known by allowed coalition levels (`dom coal_known = coalition`).

```
types
Info = token;
CType = <Bronze> | <Silver> | <Gold>

state Coal of
      known: set of Info
      cleared: set of Info
      released: set of Info
      coalition: set of CType
      coal_known: map CType to set of Info
inv mk_Coal(-,cleared, released, coalition, coal_known) ==
      released subset cleared and
      dom coal_known = coalition
```

State-changing functionality is defined in terms of operations that are specified contractually by means of preconditions and postconditions. Consider, for example, Gold command's `clear` and `release` events, the interaction behaviours of which are specified in CSP in process `GD(i)` in Section 3.2. In VDM, the functionality is specified as operations parameterised over information `i:Info`. The `ClearGold` operation assumes in the precondition, `pre i in set coal_known(<Gold>)`, that `i` is known to Gold command. If this assumption is satisfied, the operation guarantees in the postcondition, `post cleared = cleared~ union {i}`, to add it to the cleared set (where `cleared~` refers to the initial value of the `cleared` state variable). The `ReleaseGold` operation is similar.

```
ClearGold(i:Info)
pre i in set coal_known(<Gold>)
post cleared = cleared~ union {i};

ReleaseGold(i:Info)
pre i in set coal_known(<Gold>) and
    i in set cleared
post released = released~ union {i};
```

Both operations give rise to proof obligations to ensure preservation of the state invariant, including that of ensuring that released information must have previously been cleared, and that both operations preserve this. Such obligations can be generated automatically, and may be discharged by inspection, testing or formal proof.

**Comments on the Case Study.** Compared to Bryans et al.'s model in Event-B [21], this multi-paradigm approach more clearly shows the interfaces between constituent systems, and hence the points at which structural change is possible, as well as the interaction behaviour, which is here explicit in the CSP rather than "hidden" in event guards. Most importantly, it permits the verification of SoS-level properties that cut across multiple aspects. For example, extending the model to encompass communications errors entails alterations to interaction behaviour (in CSP) and functionality (recording "lost" messages) in the VDM model. Adding redundancy to manage such error would require a modification to the architectural model as well.

Although Bryans et al.'s previous model is less transparent with respect to the SoS architecture and interaction behaviour, it does benefit from the specialist automated verification tools that can be developed for a single formalism. Currently our multiple formalisms do not benefit from a completely consistent semantic base, so that we are not yet able to automate analysis to the same extent.

# 4   Conclusions and Future Work

We have proposed a multi-paradigm modelling approach to address the particular challenges of SoS engineering, using baseline formalisms that cover architectural modelling, communication and concurrency, data and functionality. Our case study suggests that it is possible to produce consistent models in such formalisms that describe features of a SoS sufficient to verify global properties of interest.

Although multiple modelling techniques are required to cover the full range of aspects of a SoS, we note that researchers and practitioners in CNO modelling tend to stick with one approach even though it might not be the most appropriate for all or a part of the modelling effort [6]. We aim to develop a unified framework that integrates architectural, behavioural and functional models. Semantic interoperability between models is needed for verification of properties that cross aspects. A promising starting point is Hoare & He's Unifying Theories of Programming [23]. This will be developed in a series of definitions starting with basic modelling features and extending these with time and object-orientation.

While formal model-based methods are valuable in describing and verifying the properties of SoS configurations, the capacity exists to restructure or reconfigure during operation in response to faults or attacks. Indeed, a SoS architecture has been proposed to manage such reconfiguration [24]. The semantics and pragmatics of policy languages for dynamic reconfiguration remain open, including the definition and acquisition of metadata, and the expression and verification of policies [25].

Feedback from practice is required in any attempt to develop any formal modelling framework. In the COMPASS project, our emerging methods will be evaluated through several industry case studies. For example, in a home audio-video ecosystem, networked systems such as TV, home cinema, DVD and MP3 players deliver digital content from internal or external sources to multiple users. Providers and integrators of constituent systems require the ability to verify overall performance and that the SoS will respect digital rights management (DRM) contracts on the content. A second example is dynamic coordination of healthcare services in response to an accident (call management, dispatching, triage, hospital management systems, etc.). As with the audio-video ecosystem, global properties such as confidentiality need to be analysed. In both cases, the ability to perform such verification is complicated by the need to cope with failures in infrastructure or constituents.

In spite of the emerging potential of formal techniques, there naturally remains a gap between the formal "supply-side" models of SoS compositions and the users' "demand-side" experience [26]. As with collaborative networked organisations more generally, the development of dependable SoS requires a wide range of disciplines and skills, both socio-technical and formal.

## References

1. Maier, M.W.: Architecting Principles for Systems-of-Systems. Systems Engineering 1(4), 267–284 (1998)
2. Camarinha-Matos, L.M., Afsarmanesh, H. (eds.): Collaborative Networks: Reference Modeling. Springer (2008)
3. Dahmann, J.S., Rebovich, G., Lane, J.A.: Systems Engineering for Capabilities. CrossTalk Journal 21(11), 4–9 (2008)
4. Maier, M.W.: Research Challenges for Systems-of-Systems. In: IEEE Intl. Conf. on Systems, Man and Cybernetics (2005)
5. Valerdi, R., Axelbrand, E., Baehren, T., Boehm, B., et al.: A Research Agenda for System-of-Systems Architecting. Intl. Jnl. System of Systems Engineering 1(1–2), 171–188 (2008)

6. Camarinha-Matos, L.M., Afsarmanesh, H.: A comprehensive modelling framework for collaborative networked organizations. J. Intell. Manuf. 18, 529–542 (2007)
7. Woodcock, J.C.P., Larsen, P.G., Bicarregui, J.C., Fitzgerald, J.S.: Formal Methods: Practice and Experience. ACM Computing Surveys 41(4), 1–36 (2009)
8. Caffall, D.S., Michael, J.B.: Formal methods in a system-of-systems development. In: IEEE Intl. Conf. Systems, Man and Cybernetics, pp. 1856–1863 (2005)
9. Woodcock, J.C.P., Davies, J.: Using Z Specification, Refinement, and Proof. Prentice-Hall (1996)
10. Hoare, C.A.R.: Communicating Sequential Processes, 1st edn. Prentice Hall Intl. (1985); New edn. Davies, J. (ed.) (2004)
11. Pnueli, A.: The temporal logic of programs. In: 18th IEEE Symp. Foundations of Computer Science, pp. 46–57 (1977)
12. Treharne, H., Schneider, S.: Using a process algebra to control B Operations. In: 1st International Conference on Integrated Formal Methods, IFM 1999. LNCS, pp. 437–457. Springer (1999)
13. Fischer, C.: Combination and Implementation of Processes and Data: from CSP-OZ to Java. PhD thesis, Fachbereich Informatik Universität Oldenburg (2000)
14. Dong, J.S., Hao, P., Qin, S.C., Sun, J., Yi, W.: Timed Patterns: TCOZ to Timed Automata. In: Davies, J., Schulte, W., Barnett, M. (eds.) ICFEM 2004. LNCS, vol. 3308, pp. 483–498. Springer, Heidelberg (2004)
15. Leavens, G.T., Leino, K.R.M., Poll, E., Ruby, C., Jacobs, B.: JML: notations and tools supporting detailed design in Java. In: OOPSLA 2000, pp. 105–106 (2000)
16. Beckert, B., Hähnle, R., Schmitt, P.H. (eds.): Verification of Object-Oriented Software. LNCS (LNAI), vol. 4334. Springer, Heidelberg (2007)
17. Fitzgerald, J.S., Larsen, P.G., Mukherjee, P.P., Verhoef, N.M.: Validated Designs for Object-oriented Systems. Springer (2005)
18. Object Management Group: OMG Systems Modeling Language (OMG SysML) v1.2, OMG Document Reference: formal/2010-06-02 (2010)
19. Payne, R.J., Fitzgerald, J.S.: Interface Contracts for Architectural Specification and Assessment: a SysML Extension. In: Proc. Workshop on Dependable Systems of Systems, WDSoS 2011, University of York, UK (2011)
20. London Emergency Services Liaison Panel: Major Incident Procedure Manual, 7th edn., TSO (The Stationery Office) (2007)
21. Bryans, J.W., Fitzgerald, J.S., McCutcheon, T.: Refinement-Based Techniques in the Analysis of Information Flow Policies for Dynamic Virtual Organisations. In: Camarinha-Matos, L.M., Pereira-Klen, A., Afsarmanesh, H. (eds.) PRO-VE 2011. IFIP AICT, vol. 362, pp. 314–321. Springer, Heidelberg (2011)
22. Payne, R.J., Bryans, J.W.: Modelling the Major Incident Procedure Manual: A Systems of Systems Case Study. Tech. Rep. CS-TR-1320, School of Computing Science, Newcastle University, UK (2012)
23. Hoare, C.A.R., He, J.: Unifying Theories of Programming. Prentice-Hall (1998)
24. Calinescu, R., Kwiatkowska, M.: Software Engineering Techniques for the Development of Systems of Systems. In: Choppy, C., Sokolsky, O. (eds.) Monterey Workshop 2008. LNCS, vol. 6028, pp. 59–82. Springer, Heidelberg (2010)
25. Payne, R.J.: Verifiable Resilience in Architectural Reconfiguration. PhD Thesis, School of Computing Science, Newcastle University, UK (2012)
26. Cohen, B., Boxer, P.: Why Critical Systems Need Help to Evolve. IEEE Computer 43(3), 56–63 (2010)

# A Framework for Automated Service Composition in Collaborative Networks

Hamideh Afsarmanesh, Mahdi Sargolzaei, and Mahdieh Shadi

University of Amsterdam, Informatics Institute,FCN group,
Science Park 107, 1098 XG Amsterdam, The Netherlands
{H.afsarmanesh,M.sargolzaei1,M.shadi}@uva.nl

**Abstract.** This paper proposes a novel framework for automated software service composition that can significantly support and enhance collaboration among enterprises in service provision industry, such as in tourism insurance and e-commerce collaborative networks (CNs). Our proposed framework is founded on service oriented architecture (SOA) paradigm, in which software services implementing on-line business services that are provided by different enterprises, will be formally defined, using an extended BPMN notation to capture their *semantics and behavior*, as well as the WSDL notation to capture their *syntax*. Furthermore, with registering the *syntax, semantics and behavior* of these software services in a service repository at the CN, the task of service discovery in this framework can go far beyond the current practice, which comprise of service search by name, to the possibility of discovering by service behavior. The paper addresses enhancement of automated software service integration in CNs, through the application of the Reo coordination language, which is used to formalize interaction among the composed services. The main reason for using Reo in this context is that it supports separating the computations needed by software components in an integrated system from their interactions. The suggested framework provides more flexibility, adaptability, as well as cost-effectiveness in service composition, when supported in collaborative networks.

**Keywords:** Software service composition, service discovery, business process modeling, business service, collaborative network, coordination language.

## 1 Introduction

Nowadays, in a number of application areas such as tourism and e-commerce, an increasing number of SME organizations are formalizing the definition of their provided *business services*. This formal definition is usually provided as business processes (BPs), e.g. a BP is defined to represent the reservation of a hotel room or an airline ticket, and they usually apply certain standards such as BPMN or UML for this definition. The resulted sets of BPs at the SME are then used by software developers that implement them as software services. For a large number of service industries such as the tourism, insurance, banking, etc. most of their business services provided to the customers are now accessible on line (through Internet), i.e. developed as *web*

L.M. Camarinha-Matos, L. Xu, and H. Afsarmanesh (Eds.): PRO-VE 2012, IFIP AICT 380, pp. 63–73, 2012.
© IFIP International Federation for Information Processing 2012

*services,* e.g. the on-line hotel reservation web service. These web services are typically accessible by customers through user-friendly interfaces, which automate the execution of their requested transactions e.g. making a hotel or airline reservation, at the local SME sites.

But SME organizations are increasingly interested in working together and joining their knowledge, skills, resources, capabilities, and capacities, and in establishing collaborative networks (CNs) [1]. One form of CNs, the so called Virtual Organization (VO), is usually established for one of the following two purposes. One purpose is to target one specific emerged opportunity in the market or society, for which a number of organizations would be selected by the VO broker and invited to accept the joint responsibility of fulfilling tasks needed to achieve the common goal of the VO. A second purpose is for innovation, when usually a VO broker identities a potential opportunity that can be fulfilled through merging abilities, resources, capacities, etc. of a number of SMEs who get invited to the VO [2].

In order for VOs to compete in the market and society with real large existing organizations, the base for collaboration among its partner SMEs must also be pre-established before the VOs can operate. For this purpose, usually another form of CN, the so called Virtual organizations Breeding Environment (VBE) [3] is established as an association/community of SMEs in a sector, who have general common and/or compatible interests, who are interested in involvement in VOs, and who are also willing to work and share their potentials and competencies with other organizations. Since VBEs on one hand gather and organize large amount of information/knowledge about their member organizations, and on the other hand establish the base for common/uniform interoperation among their member organizations, they represent valuable communities, and therefore usually they do not dissolve [4]. But sometimes VBEs metamorphose either through expansion with another related area of activity, or narrowing down and focusing on a subset of the original activities.

Formation of a VBE is typically aimed at bringing the following set of advantages to its member organizations [5]:

(i)   Capturing more opportunities and bigger market, and thus making more profits through sharing their customers.
(ii)  Reducing individual costs through focusing/applying only their core competence, while benefiting from the existence of complementary expertise in the network.
(iii) Increasing the ability to take risks, through sharing and distribution of potential losses, while agreeing to share their profits.

Focusing on the service industry, which is the main emphasis of this paper, in order to join others and collaborate effectively, SMEs in a VO must together act as a single entity, and therefore they must share their business services and software systems with each other as if they all belong to and co-work within one single real organization. But to share software services, they must be formally and uniformly defined. Such unification in definition format can occur at the VBE level. As such, once in a VO, other SME partners will be able to share them, e.g. to integrate them with each other and/or together create new value-added services and innovate in this industry.

For example, consider the case of one SME (SME-S1) in a VBE (V1) planning to simply create an integrated tourism package, including the reservation of flight-ticket, hotel-room, day-trip and dinner at restaurants, and assume that these business services are all already implemented by several different SMEs at the VBE as web-services by different other SMEs in this VBE. In fact once SME-S1 identifies the most-fit SMEs to work with for creating this package as an integrated service, SME-S1 (as the VO broker) can start forming a VO together with these other SMEs. However, today due to the lack of uniformity in full and formal definition of implemented business services at SMEs, the creation of such an integrated single tourism package and providing it as an on-line service to the customer is quite challenging. In this paper we aim to address this challenge and define an approach and architecture that can in fact support the semi-automation of this challenging task.

Today, even without any automation, for developing such an integrated service, the following steps are needed to be taken:

(a) SME-S1 must first identify any and all potentially relevant web-services shared by other SMEs in the V1. But clearly to identify relevant web-services for this purpose, it is not enough for SME-S1 to only have access to the syntax information of these web-services, e.g. their names, and the name/type of their input and output. This is due to the fact that "names" for web-services and their input/output are not even necessarily mnemonic and/or using any common standards. On the contrary, these names are usually selected and assigned by different software developers and usually represent only their personal preferences.

(b) Beside the naming challenges, also the semantics of the web-services and each of their input and output elements are not uniformly provided. There is a need for common ontological definitions to clarify the actual intention of the software developer behind these elements.

(c) Furthermore, for the purpose of developing a new integrated web-service, through composition of other existing web-services, although SME-S1 (as the developer of this new integrated service) does not need to know and fully understand the exact code and how each of the existing component services are implemented, SME-S1 must in fact have a very good understanding of the functionality and interaction (namely the behavior) of each component service, in order to integrate it with the others. In some cases in fact SME-S1 needs to adapt the behavior of some of these services in order to make them match the others and become compatible.

But considering the real practice, it should be first noted that the SMEs in the VBE are fully independent and autonomous, therefore unlike the case of software service integration within one large enterprise, or through outsourcing, in the case of SMEs in service industry, there are no common base for definition of service syntax and semantics, and no standards is observed when developing their software services. Therefore, as a first step to support collaboration among such service providing SMEs in a VBE, it is necessary to establish a framework for their service interoperability.

This interoperability framework shall create the common understanding about the existing services in the VBE and thus requires a common frame and meta-data to formally express the syntax, semantics, and behavior of software services.

The structure of this paper is as follows. Section 2, address the application of SOA to the collaborative networks. In Section 4 we address the implemented architecture for the approach and introduce its 4 aspects of service modeling, service registering, service discovery, and service integration. Finally in Section 4, some conclusive remarks are drawn.

## 2     Applying SOA to Collaborative Networks

From the ICT perspective of a CN, supporting its agility, cost-effectiveness, and adaptability need designing more advanced infrastructures. The SOA and service utility paradigms [6] as prominent ICT approaches provide the strong required architecture for a system in which there are components interacting with each other, while their functionalities are viewed as software modules called services [7]. In service industry, software service accessibility by each enterprise in the collaborative network, in support of service interoperability, results in reinforcing its collaboration with others and decreasing its service development and hosting costs. In the SOA context, SaaS (Software-as- a-Service) [8] is a powerful model that can benefit the CNs. As clients, remote access to services can be supported for CN members, who can for instance pay per use, based on the contractual rules specified in SLAs (Service Level Agreement) [9]. As such, it does not matter where the services providers are located, and how the services have been deployed [10].

Using SaaS, CN members (as clients) can search among existing services, build and register their own new services, compose existing services, or adapt the accessed services according to their needs. In this sense, both common representation of software services as well as formal modeling and coordination of their interactions are fundamental issues which assist flexible and better service discovery and service composition. We focus and discuss these two aspects in the following paragraphs.

Currently there are several notations and graphical modeling tools used for modeling of business processes, such as the Business Process Modeling Notation (BPMN) and the Unified Modeling Language (UML) Activity Diagram, the Event-driven Process Chains (EPC), and the Role Activity Diagrams (RADs) [11]. BPMN and UML Activity Diagrams are currently considered as the two most suitable and popular ones. While these standards are largely overlapping, BPMN is slightly stronger and more expressive [12], so we have choose BPMN as the basic notation for modeling business processes in the proposed platform. Despite its popularity, the BPMN notation is too abstract to convey sufficient details required to represent the syntax, semantics, and operational behavior properties of software services, necessary for service composition/integration. Interface, data types and structures of each service are represented by its syntax. Web Service Definition Language (WSDL) is the most popular language for syntactical representation of software services [13].

Most web service models and languages such as Simple Object Access Protocol (SOAP) [14], and Universal Description Discovery Integration (UDDI) [15] are also used at the syntactic level. These technologies support interoperability between different services through common standards, but human interaction is still needed to search for appropriate services and for composing them in a reasonable manner. The intervention of human is however in contrast to the strategic goals of SOA, such as the scalability, agility, etc. [16]. Therefore, it is necessary to automate main tasks of SOA such as service discovery, composition and adaptation to the extent possible. To achieve this goal, besides the syntax, we should also consider more conceptual properties of services that are known as *semantics*. The semantics represent conceptual aspects of services, using explicit and machine-interpretable descriptions.

Further to syntax and semantics, *behavioral properties* of a service must also be formally defined. These properties address the set of operations involved in a service and indicate the order of invocations of these operations. Composition and integration of web services lie at the heart of our framework and they cannot be successful without behavioral specification of software services. BPMN may also be used to define the behavior of a service, but, there are some drawbacks and ambiguities in this aspect of BPMN [17]. Therefore, developing service ontology is required to specify service semantics and disambiguate current BPMN process specification of services.

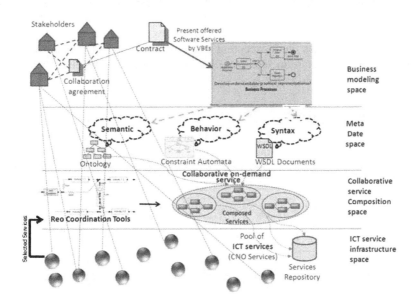

**Fig. 1.** A new SOA-based platform for a CN

We propose a new SOA based platform for a CN, as shown in Figure 1. This architecture is composed of four layers including *business modeling space, meta data space, service composition space* and *IT infrastructure space*. As Figure 1 illustrates, members/stakeholders of a CN share their software services according to their contracts in *business modeling space*. These services shall be represented as extended

BPMN diagrams, from which Meta Data (as represented in *meta data space*) is extracted, to derive their syntactical, semantics and behavioral descriptions. Software Services are designed to support interoperable machine-to-machine interaction over a network using two basic standards including WSDL which describes the interface in a machine-interpretable format, and SOAP [13] which is used to format the exchanged messages. For documenting syntactical information of software services, we need to parse the XML-based documents generated by WSDL and Soap, to extract the syntax of operations and messages of web services. We also use the formal notation of constraint automaton [18] for specification of the (external) behavior of a service. In this formalism, a web service is represented as a sequence of operations in which there are some constraints defined on operations' invocation order [19]. In the next section, we discuss requirements and the needed architecture to implement this platform, considering the mentioned Meta Data.

# 3     Implementation Architecture and Requirements

Our proposed framework for implementation of composition of software services within collaborative networks consists of four components, which are implemented as modules,   to address: (i) modeling business processes and obtaining their formal meta-data (on syntax, semantics, and behavior), (ii) registering the extracted metadata in corresponding repositories, (iii) discovering, matching and adapting appropriate services (needed for their composition into a new integrated service), and (iv) coordinating, integrating, and executing composed services. Thus, the complete implementation architecture includes four modules, labeled as: modeling, registering, discovery, and integration.

## 3.1     Modeling of Services

This module supports the formal definition of the software services to be shared with the community of enterprises at the CN.

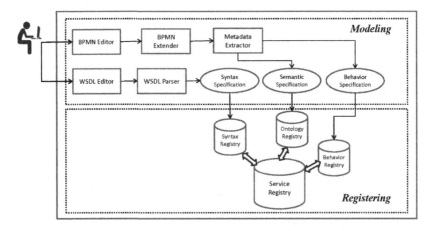

**Fig. 2.** Architecture of *Service Provision* in the platform

See Figure 2 that represents the general architecture for *service provision* with two of its modules, modeling and registering. From the end users point of view at each enterprise, their shared business services are required be defined. At first, user presents the complete flow of his every business process as a BPMN diagram or BPD (Business Process Diagram) using the BPMN editor. Each diagram should be further extended to define the syntax, semantic and behavior of its corresponding software service. Such enrichments, which is represented in the box labeled as "BPMN Extender", consist of three parts: adding new descriptions, refining ambiguities, and annotating to facilitate extraction of these metadata. The task of extracting elements needed to register the behavior and semantics metadata of the service in appropriate repositories has been presented with the box labeled "Metadata Extractor". To obtain Syntactical metadata, besides some basic syntactical meta-data derived from the primary BPMN diagram, we need to load and parse WSDL documents of web services, which are represented in the boxes labeled as "WSDL Loader" and "WSDL Parser". These steps are shown within the *Business Modeling Space* and *Meta Data Space* in Figure 1.

## 3.2     Registering of Services

As mentioned in Section 3.1, we formalize the externally observable behavior of the software services in terms of constraint automata. There is therefore, a constraint automaton generated for each service which should be captured within the behavior registry. The data structure of this registry is formed of state tables which store current state, next state, ports (operation names) and data constraints of constraint automaton [19]. Behavior registry of services is needed to generate final executable code for integrated services, as described in the next subsections. Also the syntactical metadata for services need to be captured in syntax registry. Most activities in the framework e.g. discovery, integration and execution of services, refer to this registry.

The services meta-data is improved by using OWL-S, a rich description language for representing semantics. Service semantics are then captured within the ontology registry, which describes "individual" services, together with the set of their "property assertions" relating individual services to each other [20].

Obviously beside the three metadata registries addressed above, the framework also needs a service registry, such as UDDI which contains all shared services with their syntactic metadata. But in addition to syntactic information, we also keep the ontological and behavioral metadata associated with each published service synchronized in the service registry. Figure 2 illustrates the required operations for registering new services by the service provider in the platform. This task uses the BPMN for modeling the behavior and semantic of the services and the WSDL for specification of their syntax. We will describe in the next section how we use these registries to compose existing services into an integrated service. All mentioned registries are considered as *Service Repository* within the *ICT Service Infrastructure Space* in Figure 1.

## 3.3    Discovery of Services

Figure 3 represents the general architecture for *service composition* in our framework, where its four different aspects of modeling, registering, discovery, and integration are also indicated. We will of course in this subsection focus on describing the Discovery aspects of this architecture. Let us consider the example provided in Section 1, where the user in SME-S1 intends to create a new integrated tourism service composed of a number of other services (i.e. reservation of flight ticket, reservation of accommodation, etc.). This user will then need to first specify this integrated business process and its components through the BPMN editor. The task of decomposing the integrated service into its component services is represented in the box labeled as "Decomposer". The step after this decomposition is the performed by the service search engine, which starts to match as much as possible the description of the component services defined by the user against the services existing at the service registry, to be offered as alternatives to the user. As such, the role of Service search engine is the discovery of potential required services among the existing shared services. The Service search engine has to search the syntax and ontology service registries simultaneously, for matching the syntactic and semantic aspects of the registered services against the decomposed components. The report of all the partially matched services, as well as those that are not found will be sent to the user, where he can apply his/her preferences in selecting among the alternatives.

Nevertheless standardizing the service definitions does not remove the need for service adaptation. Usually the discovered services, do not fully, but only partially match the requirements and context of the desired service component (decomposed tasks). In this case, in case such a service is selected by the user, the service adapter modifies it in order to make it compatible with the user's desired service. This adaptation provides semi-automated support for identification and resolution of interface-level mismatch between the intended and the discovered services[21]. As Figure 1 shows, the dashed lines connecting the *Composed Services* to the *Service Repository* indicate the process of service discovery.

## 3.4    Integration of Services

We apply the Reo [18] circuits to model the coordination aspects related to the interactions among software services. As such, the user at SME-S1 will use the Extensible Coordination Tools (ECT) [22], which is a collection of Eclipse plug-ins, to design these interaction circuits, using a drag-and-drop graphical interface. But, some essential activities like communication between web services and the Reo circuits, and generating executable code from a circuit diagram cannot be done by ECT. Therefore, we need a wrapper to connect web services to the boundary nodes of Reo circuits as Reo components, to communicate with web services and exchange data via SOAP message, and also translate Reo circuits to java code [19]. Using wrapper provides interaction among the running software services in a way coordinated by the Reo circuits and also dynamic and automatic service invocation. For these purposes, the Reo compiler produces the glue-code among the individual services involved in the integrated service, and the Proxy generator produces the proxies for each involved service. Furthermore, to generate final executable code for a composed service, we need its syntactic metadata and behavioral properties of selected services. We have described more details about the design and the current implementation of this wrapper in another paper [19]. As shown in Figure 1, the *Selected Services* would be integrated by *Reo Coordination Tools* within the *Collaborative Service Composition Space*.

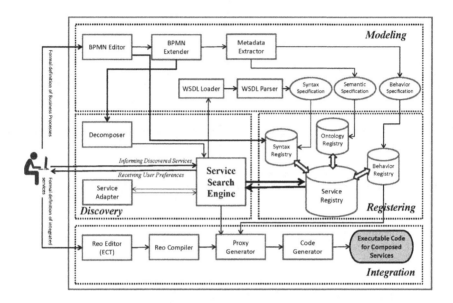

**Fig. 3.** Architecture of *Service Composition* in the platform

## 4    Conclusion

This paper addresses the design of a framework to assist service providers in a collaborative network, e.g. the SMEs involved in a tourism or insurance VBE, to uniformly create the formal definition of their services, so that they can be understood and shared with others. For this purpose, the paper proposes a novel SOA-based Collaborative Business ICT framework to support CNs in service provision industry with their effective collaboration through sharing and composition of their web services. This approach supports the organizations involved in a service industry CN with a platform-independent, easy-to-use, on-demand, and pay-per-use ICT service interoperability infrastructure. From the technical point of view, this is a web-based integrated platform devoted to the CNs, for providing value-added business services, via service composition. The platform improves software service discovery and service integration using variant metadata, as well as concrete formal machine readable definitions. Moreover, it uses Reo circuits as coordination models, used to coordinate the complex interaction protocols among enterprise business processes, which is one of the most challenging issues in modeling and executing business processes in CNs.

**Acknowledgements.** The work on this paper is partially supported by the FP7 project GLONET, funded by the European Commission.

# References

1. Camarinha-Matos, L.M., Afsarmanesh, H.: A comprehensive modeling framework for collaborative networked organizations. In the Journal of Intelligent Manufacturing 18(5), 527–615 (2007)
2. Kaletas, E.C., Afsarmanesh, H., Anastasiou, M., Camarinha-Matos, L.M.: Emerging technologies and standards. In: Virtual Organizations: Systems and Practices, ch. 2.2, pp. 105–132. Springer (2005) ISBN 0-387-23755-0
3. Afsarmanesh, H., Camarinha-Matos, L.M.: On the classification and management of Virtual organisation Breeding Environments. IJITM 8(3), 234–259 (2009)
4. Camarinha-Matos, L.M., Afsarmanesh, H.: A framework for virtual organization creation in a breeding environment. Annual Reviews in Control 31(1), 119–135 (2007)
5. Afsarmanesh, H., Camarinha-Matos, L.M., Msanjila, S.S.: On Management of 2nd Generation Virtual organizations Breeding Environments. In the Journal of Annual Reviews in Control 33(2), 209–219 (2009)
6. Framing the future of the Service Oriented Economy (2006),
   http://www.nessi-europe.com/documents/
   NESSI_SRA_VOL_1_20060213.pdf
7. Singh, M., Huhns, M.: Service Oriented Computing. Wiley, Chichester (2005)
8. Software as a Service: Strategic Backgrounder (2001),
   http://www.siia.net/estore/ssb-01.pdf
9. Web Service Level Agreement (WSLA) Language Specification. V 1.0 (2003),
   http://www.research.ibm.com/wsla/WSLASpecV1-20030128.pdf
10. Ma, D.: The Business Model of Software-As-A-Service. In: IEEE International Conference on Services Computing, SCC 2007, pp. 701–706 (2007)
11. Ko, R.K.L., Lee, S.S.G., Wah Lee, E.: Business process management (BPM) standards: a survey. Business Process Management Journal 15(5), 744–791 (2009)
12. Wohed, P., van der Aalst, W.M.P., Dumas, M., ter Hofstede, A.H.M., Russell, N.: On the Suitability of BPMN for Business Process Modelling. In: Dustdar, S., Fiadeiro, J.L., Sheth, A.P. (eds.) BPM 2006. LNCS, vol. 4102, pp. 161–176. Springer, Heidelberg (2006)
13. Web Service Description Language, http://www.w3.org/TR/wsdl
14. Simple Object Access Protocol, http://www.w3.org/2000/xp/Group/soap
15. UDDI Version 3.0.2, http://uddi.org/pubs/uddi_v3.html
16. Thomas, E.: SOA Principles of Service Design, p. 608. Prentice-Hall (2008)
17. Kokash, N., Arbab, F.: Formal Behavioral Modeling and Compliance Analysis for Service-Oriented Systems. In: de Boer, F.S., Bonsangue, M.M., Madelaine, E. (eds.) FMCO 2008. LNCS, vol. 5751, pp. 21–41. Springer, Heidelberg (2009)
18. Christel, B., Sirjani, M., Arbab, F., Rutten, J.: Modeling Component Connectors in Reo by Constraint Automata. Science of Computer Programming 61(2), 75–113 (2006)

19. Jongmans1, S.T.Q., Santini, F., Sargolzaei, M., Arbab, F., Afsarmanesh, H.: Automatic Code Generation for the Orchestration of Web Services with Reo. Submitted to European Conference on Service-Oriented and Cloud Computing, Italy (to appear, 2012)
20. Sirin, E., Parsia, B.: Bringing Semantics to Web Services with OWL-S (2007)
21. Motahari Nezhad, H., Benatallah, B., Martens, A., Curbera, F., Casati, F.: Semi-automated adaptation of service interactions. In: Proceedings of the 16th International Conference on World Wide Web (2007)
22. Arbab, F., Krause, C., Maraikar, Z., Moon, Y., Proenca, J.: Modeling, Testing and Executing Reo Connectors with the Eclipse Coordination Tools. In: Proceedings of the International Workshop on Formal Aspects of Component Software, FACS, Malaga, pp. 10–12 (2008)

# Open Ecosystems, Collaborative Networks and Service Entities Integrated Modeling Approach

Rubén Darío Franco, Angel Ortiz Bas, Pedro Gómez-Gasquet, and Raúl Rodriguez Rodriguez

Research Centre on Production Management and Engineering, Ciudad Politécnica de la Innovación, Edificio 8B, Acceso L, Pta 2 46022 Valencia, Spain
{dfranco,aortiz,pgomez,raurodro}@cigip.upv.es

**Abstract.** This paper introduces an integrated modeling approach that has been used to design and implement the ColNet platform. ColNet is the result of creating an integrated system, supporting distributed business processes design and execution in a Collaborative Network (CN) belonging to an Open Ecosystem (VBE). The work has been carried out as a part of the FP7 REMPLANET European Project, which aims at providing methods and tools for better decision-making in non-hierarchical collaborative networks. The functional alignment of Open Service Ecosystems, Collaborative Networks and Services Entities lifecycles is adopted as main functional requirements for the platform design and implementation while, at the same time, they raise an integrated modeling need. Both constitute the underlying approach followed when designing and implementing ColNet and are briefly described here.

**Keywords:** VBE modeling, CN Management System, Service Entities.

## 1 Introduction

The scientific community related to Collaborative Networked Organizations (CNO) research has agreed on the usefulness and convenience of considering Virtual organizations Breeding Environments (VBE) as fertile spaces where CN lifecycle takes place, from its creation to its final dissolution. Similar considerations have been stated for Open Service Ecosystems [1]. In this work, both terms are used interchangeably as in [1].

Broadly speaking, VBE are expected to establish normative rules, define reference processes and to host a set of registered nodes which, in turn, will be selected to arrange, setup and launching a new CN.

Two research streams have been heavily developed, and contributed, in the past, from both VBE and CN management perspectives. Moreover, in the ECOLEAD project [2], VBE [3] and CN [4] management systems were characterized and functionally described but interactions among both systems were just briefly mentioned.

Based on such previous works, what this paper addresses:

L.M. Camarinha-Matos, L. Xu, and H. Afsarmanesh (Eds.): PRO-VE 2012, IFIP AICT 380, pp. 74–83, 2012.
© IFIP International Federation for Information Processing 2012

**Is it possible to design and implement a single IT system managing, in an integrated way, both VBE and CN operations? If so, which architectural principles must be considered?**

Service Entities have been proposed [5], [6] as a third component of the model which would play a main role in supporting the engineering and operating of those CN in a VBE, based on a service-oriented approach.

This paper aims at contributing in that integration by means of two mechanisms:

- The functional alignment of the three main lifecycles, namely Ecosystem (or VBE), CN and Service Entities respectively, and
- The definition and identification of the corresponding modeling perspectives as architectural support of an integrated management system.

The rest of the paper has been structured as follows: Section 2 introduces a set of background concepts that are needed for better understanding the focus of this contribution. In Section 3, main processes of the above mentioned three lifecycles will briefly described. Section 4 discusses on the functional integration of those lifecycles and Section 5 shows how the integration is proposed from the alignment of their corresponding modeling views perspective. Finally, in Section 6, some conclusions and next actions are introduced.

## 2    Related Concepts

### 2.1    Virtual Breeding Environments and Collaborative Networks

Collaboration between partners is a preferred way to ensure optimal resource balance and to get perdurable benefits [7]. Time of preparation and difficulty of launching a CN will increase in the same proportion of the number of potential partners and complexity of collaborative processes to be carried out.

Virtual Breeding Environments [8] are aimed to harmonize the preparedness level of involved organizations while, at the same time, a collaborative infrastructure is deployed in order to deal with interoperability problems at different levels: communications, data, services, processes or business [9].

In VBEs, the main goal is to restrict the number of potential participants by drawing a border to the open universe and allowing some partners to come inside. Those partners have to agree on common operating principles: business semantics, strategies or goals, distributed business processes management practices or even common ICT tools. Rapidness and flexibility in CN preparation and launching are requirements that any VBE management system must accomplish.

### 2.2    Service Entities

Service Entities (SE) are proposed as modeling constructs for CNOs, for both the Structural and Functional dimensions. As they have been defined, a Service Entity [5] is the result of logically tying together:

- A finite set of business services – understood as functional capabilities that a service provider may offer to third parties by means of public interfaces – which jointly define the expected behavior of these entities and,
- A finite set of attributes which allow characterize and distinguish among them.

There exist two different types of SE: Abstract Service Entities (ASE) and Concrete Service Entity (CSE).

- An Abstract Service Entity is a generic building block used to represent different 'types' of entities that are present in the problem domain, mainly at Ecosystem level. ASEs are not linked to any specific instance of entities they are defining. They only represent the abstract definition of the attributes and also the specifications of the business service interfaces being defined for them.
- Concrete Service Entity: CSE are expected to be real entities of the problem domain, CSE are instances of actual ASE. Instantiating an ASE means to provide meaningful values to its attributes and specific implementation for its service interfaces (i.e. bank account validation and account balance sheet). At modeling level, this means to create an open repository where CSEs can be searched, discovered and used to create and launch CN instances.

# 3    Functional Lifecycle Integration

The synergies of an integrated approach for VBE and CN management have been raised by Romero et al in [10]. In that work, a common framework for VBE and CN is proposed. Along the respective lifecycles, the authors introduce a set of business processes which provide the expected functional linkage between VBE and CN roles.

Despite this process-centric contribution, building an integrated system for VBE and CN will still require additional elements in order to achieve a truly operational status for managing extended business process involving also the nodes.

As a complement, this work takes advantage of the SE approach in order to realize the integration as expected. Next sections describe how this approach is also integrated with those already mentioned.

## 3.1    Ecosystem Lifecycle

The Ecosystem Manager is in charge of managing the creation; operation and dissolution of ecosystems (see Fig. 1).

First stage is aimed at setting up and running all the technical tasks supporting the creation of the ecosystem. In the ColNet platform, this task mostly deals with the initialization of databases, creation of empty repositories and main roles assignment.

Main processes of the operational phase are also represented in Fig. 1. For this work, most relevant ones are:.

- **Service Entities Management:** this task is related to the profiling of generic nodes (ASE) that later on will exist inside the ecosystem.

- **Reference Process modeling:** refers to the design of business processes that include ASE as its main actors and their services as functional blocks to be included in the process model.
- **Business Documents and messages:** aimed at defining the actual business documents and message schemas that may rule the information exchanges and co-ordination patterns inside the ecosystem.
- **Collaborative Networks Management:** includes the creation of CN and supervising some activities related to their lifecycle.

The final stage is aimed at supporting the ecosystem dissolution that will consist of a set of activities collecting the knowledge gathered from its operational phase.

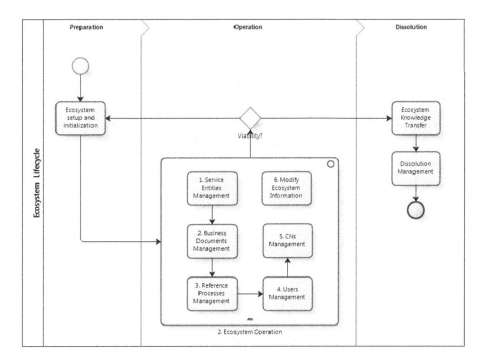

**Fig. 1.** Main processes at each stage of the ecosystem's lifecycle

### 3.2    CN Lifecycle

As depicted in Fig. 2, CN are created, operated and dissolved. For creating a new Cn, the CN manager will request its approval to the ecosystem manager of the VBE to which the CN will belong to. Once approved, the CN configuration can be started.

During the operational stage of the CN, the manager will have several duties to accomplish. Among them, it is possible to mention the management of:

- **Network structure:** this task implies to decide which available resources of the network will be invited to join the network for future transactions.

- **Concrete nodes management:** interested nodes may request joining a CN as preferred partners. Other nodes will be invited to join the CN.
- **Network business documents and messages:** actual XML schemas that are used for both information exchange and co-ordination purposes in the CN.
- **Network processes:** aimed at creating the collaborative processes that will represent the operational perspective of the CN.
- **Network monitoring:** ColNet also provides managers with simple monitoring tools intended to monitor main CN parameters.

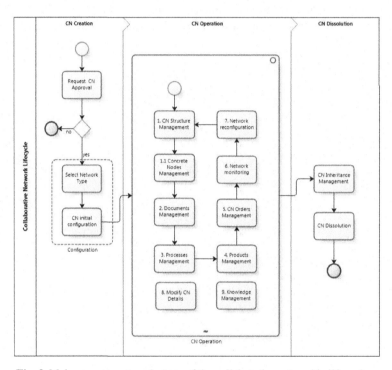

**Fig. 2.** Main processes at each stage of the collaborative network's lifecycle

After the CN has met its business goals, the manager may decide on keep it operational or proceed to its dissolution. In this case, proper mechanisms will be needed to support both the inheritance management and the final repositories disposal.

### 3.3 Service Entities Lifecycle

Each Ecosystem member is represented by a CSE instance. This role can be played by any organizational or physical resource (for instance, a whole company, a single department of that company, a person of that department, a truck of that company, etc.) being able to provide functional capabilities, from a service-oriented perspective, that will be contributing to the extended business process execution.

As shown in Fig. 3, the Service Entities (SE) lifecycle is composed of three main stages: preparation, operation and dissolution.

At the preparation stage, the node manager will need to register it into the ecosystem. That means to identify which generic node (ASE) better describes the node being registered and creating a concrete instance (CSE) of it.

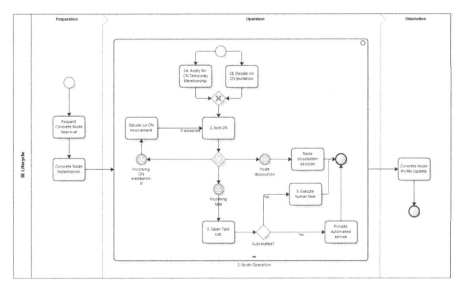

**Fig. 3.** Main processes at each stage of the Concrete Service Entity's lifecycle

Once they are operative, nodes may perform some specific tasks:

- Decide on invitations received from different collaborative networks. If some invitation is accepted, the node becomes part of the network and it can receive different requests from the CN in terms of functional contributions or transactions.
- Send an application to be considered a potential member of a CN. This mechanism goes in the opposite direction than the previous one. Here, the node offers its capabilities and services to some specific network. If accepted, it can start interacting with that network.
- Receive, accept and perform all the tasks coming from the network

## 4    Integrated Functional Approach

In the previous section, three lifecycles were introduced. This section will briefly explain how them are linked together in order to build up the integrated approach proposed here. Main blocks of the Fig. 4 are schematic representations of the above-described lifecycles. For better comprehension, only main processes linkage is shown.

Since the ecosystem is considered the main enabler, during its operational phase, other two lifecycles will take place:

- Service Entities: where incoming members are registered on it, and, later on, they will be ready to join future collaborative networks opportunities.
- Collaborative Networks: network managers may request the creation of a new collaborative network to the ecosystem manager by selecting the initial members from those entities already registered into it.

After the open ecosystem is created and configured, its management phase is launched. This comprises, among many others, two main activities: memberships' management and collaborative network management support.

When the creation of a new CN is decided, network managers will request its approval to the ecosystem manager. Once approved, the CN will be operative.

The operational phase of the network has many activities. For illustrating this approach, just two main processes have been included: managing the network topology, i.e. nodes being part of it; and also defining the business processes or current networked operations.

While at the same time, organizations have also started their registration process into the ecosystem. Once it is completed, they become full members of the ecosystem and they move to the network participation phase.

At this functional level, the management of the network topology is aligned with the process of organizational adhesion to a single CN. This interaction may occur as many times as the company is either invited to join a CN or offering its services to it.

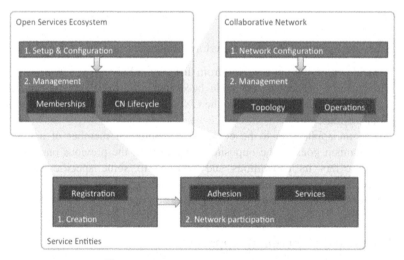

**Fig. 4.** Functional integration of lifecycles

Finally, when the CN is operative, single organizations are asked to provide their services, either manual or automated, in order to realise different extended business process instances.

The approach proposed here considers that such expected integration can only be achieved if also the involved entities – ecosystems, collaborative networks and organizations – share a common integrated modelling framework.

## 5    Integrated Modeling Views

In the previous section, the integrated approach has been illustrated from a functional perspective. This section now describes how such integration will be realized by means of an integrated modeling framework where all the corresponding modeling views for VBE, CN and SE are properly aligned.

In the ARCON [11] reference modelling framework for CN, a set of modelling perspectives has been proposed for their modelling.

Moreover, a modelling framework for service-based ecosystems, which identified a set of common modelling perspectives for both VBE and CN has been also proposed in [12]. The considered set of modelling perspectives includes: Processes, Services, Information/Data, Resources, Organization and Performance (see Fig. 5).

The proposed integrated approach aligns VBE/Ecosystem and CN modeling views while it also shows how Service Entities, either abstract or concrete ones, are used as integration mechanism providing consistence to VBE and CN modeling activities.

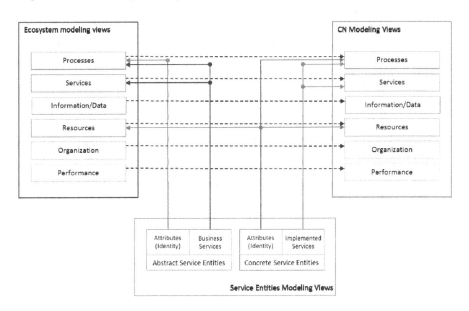

**Fig. 5.** Integration of modeling perspectives for Ecosystems, CN and Service Entities

### 5.1    Using Abstract Service Entities in the Integrated Modeling Approach

Abstract Service Entities are composed of two integrated sets that define their structure: a defined set of attributes and a set of business service interfaces.

Attributes will be used to univocally distinguish among all its corresponding instances created while the ecosystem is operating. For the integration purposes stated here, these attributes will include, for instance, a unique name for them. This attribute will allow CN modellers to use it as actors of reference processes of the ecosystem.

As it, the ecosystem would include a set of reference processes which later on can be used to be instantiated for creating different CN. Those processes would use generic references to nodes (actors) as ASE allows. Then, a reference process may include a Manufacturer, Component Supplier and Raw Material Supplier as actors of those generic processes.

When a reference process is imported into a specific CN, the ASE can be replaced by actual CSE belonging to that CN and which have been created by instantiating the corresponding ASE.

On the other hand, business services interfaces represent functional capabilities that each SE is able to provide to compose business processes. In the case of ASE, service interfaces must be considered as service specifications that, later on, concrete nodes will provide to a CN. When used at ecosystem level, service interfaces can be used as functional parts of the reference processes. Once reference processes are instantiated into specific CNs, these business services will be implemented by actual CSE to realize process instances.

In this way, all the services defined for the ASEs are grouped into the corresponding Ecosystem y CN Service modeling view.

### 5.2    Using Concrete Service Entities in the Integrated Modeling Approach

Concrete Service Entities are instances of actual ASE defined at the ecosystem level. From the integrated modelling approach introduced here, CSE are integrated as described.

- Ecosystem/Resources: once instantiated, CSE become resources of the ecosystem. The attributes will characterize each single entity inside the ecosystem.
- CN/Resources: all the CSE registered at the ecosystem become potential nodes of a CN. The network manager will decide on the final CN structure and actual CSE will be picked up to create a new CN.
- CN/Processes: CSE become actors of actual CN processes. Moreover, concrete services (implemented ones) will allow realizing actual extended processes instances inside the CN.
- CN/Services: this view is formed from all the services provided by the current CSE belonging to a specific CN.

## 6    Conclusions

This paper has introduced an approach for integrating the modeling needs arising when a functional alignment of VBE or Open Ecosystems, Collaborative Networks and Services Entities is expected.

The proposal is based on two main pillars: a) the functional alignment of the corresponding lifecycles and their adoption as main functional requirements to design and implement an integrated management system for them, and b) the identification and alignment of their corresponding modeling perspectives by including the Service Entities approach as a main enabler of such integration.

Thus, the ColNet platform, not focus of this work, is the result of creating an integrated system, supporting distributed business processes design and execution in collaborative networks in the context of a service-based open ecosystem.

The ColNet prototype can be accessed at www.spr.upv.es/ColNet and next research steps will include additional use cases for fully validating the overall approach.

## References

[1] Osório, A.L., Afsarmanesh, H., Camarinha-Matos, L.M.: Open Services Ecosystem Supporting Collaborative Networks. In: Ortiz, Á., Franco, R.D., Gasquet, P.G. (eds.) BASYS 2010. IFIP AICT, vol. 322, pp. 80–91. Springer, Heidelberg (2010)

[2] Camarinha-Matos, L.M., Afsarmanesh, H., Ollus, M.: Ecolead: A Holistic Approach to Creation and Management of Dynamic Virtual Organizations. In: Collaborative Networks and Their Breeding Environments, pp. 3–16 (2005)

[3] ECOLEAD D22.1, ECOLEAD D22.1 VBE Management System (VMS) Requirements and Architecture Design. ECOLEAD Project WP2 (2005)

[4] ECOLEAD D23.1, Requirements and mechanisms for VO planning and launching (2005)

[5] Franco, R., Bas, Á.O., Lario Esteban, F.: Modeling extended manufacturing processes with service-oriented entities. Service Business 3(1), 31–50 (2009)

[6] Franco, R.D., Bas, Á.O., Prats, G., Varela, R.N.: Supporting Structural and Functional Collaborative Networked Organizations Modeling with Service Entities. In: Camarinha-Matos, L.M., Paraskakis, I., Afsarmanesh, H. (eds.) PRO-VE 2009. IFIP AICT, vol. 307, pp. 547–554. Springer, Heidelberg (2009)

[7] Jagdev, H.S., Thoben, K.-D.: Anatomy of enterprise collaborations. Production Planning & Control 12(5), 437–451 (2001)

[8] Camarinha-Matos, L.M., Afsarmanesh, H.: Collaborative networks: a new scientific discipline. Journal of Intelligent Manufacturing 16(4), 439–452 (2005)

[9] Ruggaber, R.: ATHENA-Advanced Technologies for Interoperability of Heterogeneous Enterprise Networks and their Applications. Interoperability of Enterprise Software and Applications (2006)

[10] Romero, D., Molina, A.: VO breeding environments & virtual organizations integral business process management framework. Information Systems Frontiers 11(5), 569–597 (2009)

[11] Camarinha-Matos, L.M., Afsarmanesh, H.: Towards a Reference Model for Collaborative Networked Organizations. In: Shen, W. (ed.) Information Technology For Balanced Manufacturing Systems. IFIP, vol. 220, pp. 193–202. Springer, Boston (2006)

[12] Franco, R.D., Ortiz, Á.O., Gómez-Gasquet, P., Varela, R.N.: Towards a Modeling Framework for Service-Oriented Digital Ecosystems. In: Camarinha-Matos, L.M., Boucher, X., Afsarmanesh, H. (eds.) PRO-VE 2010. IFIP AICT, vol. 336, pp. 486–493. Springer, Heidelberg (2010)

**4**

---

**Service Composition II**

# Quality Driven Web Service Composition Modeling Framework

Georgiana Stegaru, Cristian Danila, Ioan Stefan Sacala,
Mihnea Moisescu, and Aurelian Mihai Stanescu

University Politehnica of Bucharest, Splaiul Independentei 313,
Bucharest, 060042, Romania
{georgiana_stegaru,sacalaioan,amstanescu}@yahoo.com,
{danila.cristian.84,mamihnea}@gmail.com

**Abstract.** Software as a Service (SaaS) has become the new paradigm in software development. Ecosystems of Web Services can be flexibly and dynamically composed to suit user specific needs. Quality is essential to the success of service based applications. The process of service composition has a major impact on the quality of the final product. We propose a dynamic and flexible Quality of Service Composition (QoSC) model for the composed service and a conceptual framework for the service composition process.

**Keywords:** Service Composition, Quality of Service, Internet of Services.

## 1    Introduction

Rapidly changing Information technology (IT) is bringing radical changes and new opportunities in different aspects of our lives: economic, social and political. The Internet has evolved from a source of information to a critical infrastructure representing the ideal medium for the development of new services.

One area of research for Future Internet is Internet of Services where everything (e.g. information, software, platform and infrastructure) is available as a service. Software as a Service (SaaS) has become increasingly significant in the past few years due to the popularity growth of Service Oriented Architecture (SOA). SOA provides key concepts for Future Internet Enterprise Systems (FInES) such as service composability and reusability. Using today's broadband Internet connection Web-based Information Systems providers can develop complex, cross-organizational business solutions through Web Service compositions. In order to increase market share, organizations will need to develop competitive services that would differentiate themselves through high availability, flexibility, performance, more exactly through high quality. Quality assurance becomes a key factor to provide the desired end-to-end quality of distributed services. This requires not just an agreement on quality attributes, but also monitoring and control during runtime.

While much focus has been recently spent on services and service composition specifications, little research has been done in the area of service composition

L.M. Camarinha-Matos, L. Xu, and H. Afsarmanesh (Eds.): PRO-VE 2012, IFIP AICT 380, pp. 87–95, 2012.
© IFIP International Federation for Information Processing 2012

validation and verification. The ability to correctly assemble new systems based on existing services strongly relies on the quality of each service and on the quality of the assembly. Research in this area has been mostly focused on Quality of Service (QoS) attributes that describe non-functional requirements, while functional specifications are supposed to be tested in-house by service providers.

A quality driven service composition should address quality from both the final product and process points of views. In this paper we propose a QoSC (Quality of Service Composition) model for the quality of the composed service and a framework for the service composition process. Section 2 presents an overview of related work concerning the evaluation of the quality of service composition. In section 3 we present the QoSC model and section 4 describes conceptually the framework for a quality driven service composition. We conclude and present our future developments in section 5.

## 2    Related Work

Innovative services are created by composing existing Web Services (WS). Web Service composition implies two important aspects: the specification by means of a composition language and the execution by means of an appropriate runtime. In the area of specification there are several existing process-oriented composition languages widely accepted by the industry and the researchers. [1]

Research in the service composition area recently shifted its focus from service composition tools and techniques to validation and verification of composed services. Verification of composed services borrowed testing principles from software testing and adapted them to SOA [2]. Strategies for testing services in isolation or in composition have been developed similar to the ones used in component-based systems. One approach for service composition unit and integration testing argues that choreography-based or orchestration-based testing must be done, according to the service view [3]. Dedicated tools are used for the validation of functional requirements for Web Services. One example is TGSE (Test Generation, Simulation and Emulation), a testing tool using a black-box approach for testing WS composition described in BPEL [4].

Most QoS driven service composition approaches focus on selection methods. The authors of [5] present such an approach, where the main features consist in a WS quality model and a quality driven service selection method. The WS quality model takes into consideration WS non-functional properties: execution duration, execution price, availability and reliability. Service selection is formulated as an optimization problem where linear methods are used to compute optimal service execution plans. Global optimization techniques and local selection methods can be used to find the best combination of services [6].

Other researchers consider a different approach that is more user-oriented [7]. They propose a framework for Quality of Experience aware service composition for Future Internet that allows users to compose service templates and coordinate network and computing resources in order to meet user requirements.

Another field of research is concerning the composition of services using Service Level Agreements (SLAs). A SLA driven approach proposes a model-based framework that autonomously builds services with a guaranteed level of quality [8]. There are also a number of works focused on QoS management of Web Services which can be classified by the methods used for monitoring and controlling the QoS properties of services: policies [9], [10], contracts [11], agents [12], [13].

State of the art approaches address quality only from the point of view of the final product i.e. the composed service. The focus is set, in most cases, on the selection of different services based on their non-functional properties. But there are process related quality indicators that have an impact on the final product, such as interoperability or adaptability. Also most approaches are context-dependent and cannot be applied to different business scenarios. They consider a certain domain where the services are running, or a certain specific language of the service composition (e.g. BPEL). We argue that there is a need for a Quality of Service Composition model that addresses both product and process quality and we present it in the following section.

## 3    Quality of Service Compositions Model

The Quality of a Service Composition (QoSC) is a key factor to the success of a business process. State of the art approaches focus mostly on non-functional requirements of Web Services. A reliable service composition also requires service interoperability and adaptability as services are heterogeneous in nature. Therefore, there is a need for quality assessment models that not only evaluate the performance of the composite service but also cover important aspects such as: interoperability, adaptability and security. We propose a hierarchical model for quality driven service composition that takes into consideration all these factors.

The model has three quality dimensions which assess the composed service from a certain point of view: business, operational or systemic. Each quality dimension is composed of one or more quality aspects. For each aspect we consider one or more quality items, which are tightly coupled with service characteristics and can be measured based on a quality criteria. The measurement can be either qualitative or quantitative. The three quality dimensions are: Business, Operational and System as represented in figure 1. The business quality dimension describes quality aspects that belong to the business value of service compositions. The operational quality dimension describes quality aspects related to interactions between services while the system dimension includes quality aspects that apply to the entire service composition.

Business quality dimension contains the following quality items: reputation (service provider reputation and service reputation), service affordability, service discoverability, service penalty and incentive, service usability and governance. These items can be qualitatively evaluated based on a history of the service usage experience and user feedback.

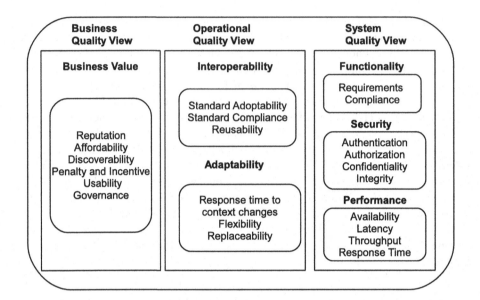

**Fig. 1.** Quality of Service Composition Model

Operational quality model includes service interoperability and service adaptability quality aspects. Interoperability quality aspect is concerned with the evaluation of the compatibility level between Web Services. Although WS technologies have been standardized, Web Services are still developed on different platforms and according to different specifications. Standards adoptability and standard compliance are quality items that evaluate the message exchangeability and conformity to a certain standard in order to make the composition inter-operable. Reusability defines the extent to which a Web Service can be used in another composition. Adaptability quality aspect evaluates the ability of a service to respond to external stimuli. Adaptability implies three abilities: the ability to recognize an environmental change, the ability to determine the change to be applied to the service and the ability to effect the change. These abilities reflect a Web Service's flexibility and replaceability. Based on metrics defined in [14], we can evaluate the adaptability of a Web Service.

System quality model evaluates the composite service compliance with user defined requirements both functional and non-functional. It contains the following quality aspects: service functionality, service security and performance. The quality of the security incorporated into the service has the following quality items: authentication, authorization, encryption, non-repudiation, audit and integrity. The performance quality aspect of the composite service can be composed of quality items like: response time, throughput, availability, accessibility, latency, accuracy. Metrics for security and performance evaluation have been discussed in [15], [16].

The list of quality items is not exhaustive, but only describes most common quality features desired in a Web Service. The QoSC model includes not only product related QoS characteristics but also process specific QoS attributes. The quality model can be easily extended with more quality items according to the context of the service composition. Domain-depended quality items can be added for complex domain specific service based applications.

In the following section we present a conceptual framework to achieve quality driven service composition based on the QoSC model proposed earlier.

## 4    Framework for Quality Driven Service Composition

Technological, social and behavioral factors are driving businesses on the online market. Web-based Information Systems (WIS) are at the core of the networked devices, organizations and people. Adaptable WIS must support high service customization in order to be accepted by any user. Consumers must choose from an increasing number of services providing similar functionalities. Quality of Service Composition has a great impact on the composed service; therefore we need to address not only the quality of the final service but also the quality of the service composition process.

Based on the analysis on different service composition methods presented in [17], we identified the main phases of a service composition process. In figure 2 we present the model of a generic service composition process, developed using the business process modeling standard, Business Process Model and Notation, BPMN.

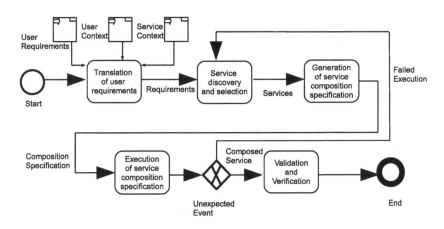

**Fig. 2.** Quality driven Service Composition Process in BPMN

### 4.1    Translation of User Requirements

First requirements are collected from the service request initiated by a user. A configurator based on dynamic questions should be used to capture user preferences. Then the user's requirements and preferences should be mapped to QoS properties, both functional and non-functional. At this phase we must also consider user context (e.g. location, request scope and purpose of usage, software and hardware capabilities) and service context (e.g. provider, availability, location, description,

SLA). By analyzing these inputs we identify the quality aspects and quality items at the business, operational and system levels based on the QoSC model in section 3. The result is the service selection specification which includes QoS properties, both functional and non-functional. The QoS properties can be explicit, stated by the user, and implicit, derived from the context.

## 4.2     Service Discovery and Selection

Service discovery and selection processes are based on the QoS criteria identified at the previous phase. Service registries are queried to identify services with required functionalities. To select the best matching service accordingly to QoS specification, each candidate service should be verified to ensure that it matches both functional and non-functional requirements (e.g. performance, security). The candidate services should be kept into a sorted list according to the probability for their selection.

In order to prevent possible issues at the execution phase, interoperability and adaptability of services involved in the composition must be assessed. The proposed QoSC model captures these requirements in the operational quality dimension. An approach to measure service interoperability is to verify the degree of adoptability and compliance to industry interoperability standards and guidelines. Service adaptability is necessary in pervasive environment where devices come and go, but also when a significant mismatch occurs between the supply and demand of a resource: such as network problems, service disconnection, change of service, new service available, or change in user requirements. Adaptability for a service can be calculated as the division between the number of dimensions where the service is capable to detect and react to a change and the total number of dimensions taken into account.

## 4.3     Generation of Service Composition Specification

After having identified the services that match the user requirements, both explicit and implicit, as captured in the first phase, the specification of the service composition must be developed.

The service composition specification depends on the composition method. The most common are service orchestration and service choreography. Service orchestration describes interactions at the message level in a service composition using a central coordinator. In contrast, service choreography describes from a global perspective the interactions between services participating in a business process. Service composition requires collaboration between services involved in the composition, thus interoperability and adaptability at the service level is needed. To prevent mismatching service interfaces or lack of compatibility between messages exchanged in the execution phase, we address these requirements at the service selection phase.

## 4.4     Execution of the Service Composition Specification

Finally the builder executes the service composition specification and produces an implementation corresponding to the required composite service. Depending on the service composition language, the WS-CDL specification or WS-BPEL is executed.

The SLA of the composite service is also produced during this step. The SLA of the composite service will specify the agreed levels of quality for the composite service. In case of a possible infrastructure/service problem the system returns to step 2: Service discovery and selection, and replaces the affected service with the next available service from the list. Steps 3 and 4 are executed again.

### 4.5    Verification and Validation of the Composed Service

Verification and validation should be realized during the entire process, from user requirements gathering and service selection to execution of the service composition. Checkpoints must be implemented at each phase to verify if it is successfully completed, before going to the next one. Fail-safe mechanisms need to be established in case of failure during the execution phase.

The new value-added service must be verified to ensure its correct functioning according to its specification. In the literature there have been several approaches to verification of service composition, either service orchestration [18] or service choreography [19].

Monitoring capabilities should be employed during the entire service composition process, from the requirements gathering phase to the execution of the service composition specification. However the service should be monitored also during its functioning to ensure that it runs in the desired parameters specified in the SLA.

## 5    Conclusions

Software as a Service has become the new paradigm in software development allowing organizations to achieve their business goals in a flexible manner that only requires a connection to the Internet. This new paradigm brings benefits but also new challenges regarding the Quality of Services and Service Compositions. Different quality aspects were covered in the literature, but there isn't a standard quality model for service compositions.

The proposed QoSC model addresses quality from a business, operational and systemic view, including both functional and non-functional requirements. However, our approach considers the quality of the final product (the composed service) and also the quality of the service composition process. We provide a framework to achieve quality driven service composition, independent of the composition language or platform. The framework addresses issues that might have an impact on the quality of the composed service, from user requirements gathering to execution of the service composition specification. Using state of the art technologies and techniques, the proposed QoSC model and framework can be adapted to different service composition types in different domains, such as Semantic Web or Artificial Intelligence.

Future work consists in the implementation of the framework on a real business use case in order to validate the proposed QoSC model.

**Acknowledgments**. The work has been funded through the European Social Fund, Sectoral Operational Programme Human Resources Development 2007-2013 of the Romanian Ministry of Labour, Family and Social Protection, Financial Agreement POSDRU/107/1.5/S/76813.

# References

1. Baryannis, G., Danylevych, O., Karastoyanova, D., Kritikos, K., Leitner, P., Rosenberg, F., Wetzstein, B.: Service Composition. In: Papazoglou, M., et al. (eds.) Service Research Challenges and Solutions for the Future Internet. LNCS, vol. 6500, pp. 55–84. Springer, Heidelberg (2010)
2. Harris, T.: SOA Test Methodology (2007), http://www.thbs.com/soa4
3. Bucchiarone, A., Megratti, H., Severoni, F.: Testing Service Composition. In: Proceedings of ASSE 2007, Mar del Plata, Argentina (2007)
4. Cao, T.D., Patrick, F., Castanet, R., Berrada, I.: Testing Service Composition Using TGSE tool. In: IEEE 3rd International Workshop on Web Services Testing. IEEE Press, Los Angeles (2009)
5. Zeng, L., Benatallah, B., Dumas, M.: Quality Driven Web Services Composition. In: Proceedings of the 12th International Conference on World Wide Web, WWW 2003. ACM Press, New York (2003)
6. Alrifai, M., Risse, T.: Efficient QoS-aware Service Composition. In: Proceedings of the 18th International Conference on World Wide Web, WWW 2009, New York, USA (2009)
7. Park, J., Lee, H.Y., Yi, D., Kim, J.: QoE Dynamic Service Composition for Immersive Media-oriented Services. In: Proceedings of 3rd International Conference on Future Internet Technologies, New York, USA (2008)
8. Di Marco, A., Sabetta, A.: Model-based dynamic QoS-driven service composition. In: Proceedings of QUASOSS@MODELS (2010)
9. Badidi, E.: A Scalable framework for Policy-based QoS management in SOA Environments. Journal of Software 6(4) (2011)
10. Farroha, B.S., Farroha, D.L.: Policy-based QoS Requirements in a SOA Enterprise Framework – An Investigative Analysis. In: Proceedings of 3rd Annual IEEE Systems Conference. IEEE Press, Vancouver (2009)
11. Gwyduk, Y., Tsai, W.-T., Bai, X., Min, D.: Design of a Contract-based Web Services QoS Management System. In: Proceedings of 29th IEEE ICDCS Workshop. IEEE Press, Washington (2009)
12. Nyguen, X.T., Kowalczyk, R.: Agent-Based QoS Conflict Mediation for Web Service Compositions. In: Proceedings of the IEEE/WIC/ACM, IAT 2006, Washington, USA (2006)
13. Malak, J.S., Mohsenzadeh, M., Seyyedi, M.A.: Web Service QoS Prediction Based on Multi Agents. In: Proceedings of ICCTD 2009, Kota Kinabalu, Malaysia (2009)
14. Chung, L., Subramanian, N.: Process-Oriented Metrics for Software Architecture Adaptability. In: Proceedings of 5th International Symposium on Requirements Engineering, pp. 310–320. IEEE Press, Toronto (2001)
15. Ran, S.: A model for Web Service Discovery with QoS. In: ACM SIGecom Exchange, vol. 4(1), ACM Press, New York (2003)
16. Gollmann, D., Massacci, F., Yautsiukhin, A.: Quality of Protection: Security measurement And Metrics. In: Gollmann, D., Massacci, F., Yautsiukhin, A. (eds.) AIS, vol. 23. Springer, Heidelberg (2006)

17. Kapitsaki, G., Kateros, D.A., Foukarakis, I.E., Prezerakos, G.N., Karlamani, D.I., Venieris, I.S.: Service Composition: State of the art and future challenges (2007),
    http://www.cin.ufpe.br/~redis/intranet/bibliography/
    middleware/kapitsaki-composition07.pdf
18. Wang, Y., Wang, L., Dai, G.: A Web Service Orchestration Model Based on Concurrent Transaction Logic. In: Proceedings of 7th International Conference on Grid and Cooperative Computing, GCC 2008, pp. 475–482. IEEE Press (2008)
19. Zhou, L., Xiao, H., Ping, J., Pu, G., Zhang, H.: Simulation and validation of Web services choreography. In: Proceedings of IEEE International Conference on Service-Oriented Computing and Applications, SOCA. IEEE Press (2009)

# An Efficient QoS Preference Oriented Recommendation Scheme for the Internet of Services

Le Xin, Yushun Fan, and Hongbo Lai

Tsinghua National Laboratory for Information Science and Technology
Department of Automation, Tsinghua University, Beijing 100084, China
xin-l09@mails.tsinghua.edu.cn, fanyus@tsinghua.edu.cn,
laihongbo_001@163.com

**Abstract.** Internet of services provides the services capabilities to interact and collaborate. Users are able to create, share and access services by means of heterogeneous devices and interaction channels, in extremely personalized ways. However, in the dynamic and ever-growing scenario, lacks of customization and flexibility have become more and more crucial. In this paper, a QoS preference oriented service recommendation scheme is proposed. First, the customer's preference is well described by a matrix model, which can be updated dynamically with customer's feedback evaluation. Entropy evaluation method is introduced to measure the weight coefficient of each QoS attribute. Furthermore, ant colony optimization algorithm is used to seek optimal service compositions. This recommending procedure will be repeated until the customer's requirement is satisfied, also can be restarted whenever the service process is blocked in execution. Theoretical analysis and numerical simulation indicate that the proposed scheme can satisfy the customer's requirements effectively and flexibly.

**Keywords:** Service recommendation, Customer's preference, Internet of Service.

## 1    Introduction

Internet of Services (IoS)[1, 2] is a relatively new paradigm, enabling the operation and reorganization of business services, in which the enterprises package their business units into business modules and provide services on users' demand. The services, either IT or business, are arranged under standard protocol [3]. Because of the unified ports of service units, the services can be used as "plug and play" mode on customers' demand [4], supported by the technologies as cloud computing [5]. The business collaboration is achieved by providing and consuming services, which are managed according to the service level agreement between users and providers.

Based on this environment, complex business application can be dynamically composed by existing service components from different providers. The composite services may have different performances with the same functionalities, such as price, response time, availability, reputation, security level and so on. These quality-of-service

L.M. Camarinha-Matos, L. Xu, and H. Afsarmanesh (Eds.): PRO-VE 2012, IFIP AICT 380, pp. 96–104, 2012.
© IFIP International Federation for Information Processing 2012

(QoS) factors, as the measurements of non-functional features, are important to the service selection and composition. After functional matching based on UDDI, users can compare candidate services from the respects of QoS. However, for both single task service discovery and aggregative service composition, requesters still lack an efficient method to solve the global optimization because of the following reasons.

1) Different users value different characters of services. For example, patients require fast medical services, while banks need stable data services. The researches on service selection mostly handle different QoS factors equally [6, 7], which lead to absence of customization in service selection. How to differ and determine the importance of each QoS attributes, dynamically corresponding with user's online feedback is still a weakness to identify and satisfy requesters' demand in IoS.

2) Under the users' global constraints to QoS [8], searching the optimal composition has been proved to be an NP-hard problem [9]. Exhaustive and evolutionary algorithms are two kinds of approaches of QoS-based optimization computation. Some algoritms must restart from the initial state when interrupted by unavailable services, which leads to lack of flexibility [10, 11].

In IoS, personalized service recommendation has become more and more crucial. Considering the large number of services, requesters also need flexible and effective composition. In this paper, we study an efficient service recommendation method based on customer's preferences of QoS. First, the degree of customer's preference to each QoS attribute is well described by a value similar to membership in fuzzy space. Then services' matching level can be computed by customer's preference and QoS value of service. On these bases, services are recommended dynamically to customer, and customer's feedback evaluations of the services are obtained. Preference matrix is re-computed, and then goes to the next iteration. The ant colony optimization algorithm is used to optimize the searching in service selection.

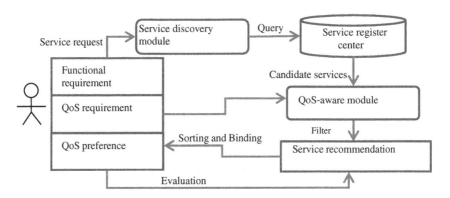

**Fig. 1.** QoS preference Oriented recommendation model

## 2    QoS Preference Oriented Service Recommendation Model

In this section we designed a service selection method through a process as illustrated in Fig.1. When customer raises request in IoS, service discovery is carried out.

Through querying in register center, the candidate services which fit functional requirement can be obtained. Then customer's restrict to QoS is checked to filter out those not matching constraints, detailed computation method of which can refer to Huang [6]. After these, the list of services can be sorted and recommended, at the same time, customer's preference to QoS can be perceived by his evaluation to services on line. With these feedbacks, service recommendation result is able to be optimized closer and closer to customer's requirements. In the following models, Section 2.1 pays attention to measure customer's preference and sort the services by match degree.

## 2.1    Customer's Preference Model

In the model proposed above, it is difficult to measure customers' preference, which leads to lack of customization. In this section, we give the QoS model and customers' preference model based on fuzzy logic matrix first. Entropy evaluation method is introduced to measure the weight coefficient of each QoS attribute. And then services' matching level can be calculated by these models.

After normalization, the $i$ th QoS factor can be divided into $n$ level, e.g. if $n = 5$, it means {very high, high, medium, low, very low}. For each level there is a median value $\{m_{i1}, m_{i2}, m_{i3}, \cdots, m_{in}\}$, and $1 \geq m_{i1} \geq m_{i2} \geq m_{i3} \geq \cdots \geq m_{in} \geq 0$. For $q_i{}'$, euclidean distance is used to determine which level it belongs to.

$D_{ij} = |q_i{}' - m_{ij}|$ , if $D_{ik} = \min\limits_{1 \leq j \leq n}\{D_{ij}\}$, then the $i$ th QoS factor belongs to the $k$ th level.

**Definition 1.** Quality of service is denoted by a $m \times n$ matrix $Y$. The matrix element is $y_{ij} = \begin{cases} 0, & \text{if } q_i{}' \text{ does not belong to the } j\text{th level} \\ 1, & \text{if } q_i{}' \text{ belongs to the } j\text{th level} \end{cases}$ .

**Definition 2.** Customers' evaluation is denoted by $a$, and $a \in [0,1]$. The greater $a$ is, the higher evaluation is.

**Definition 3.** Customers' preference is denoted by a $m \times n$ matrix $P$. The element of which is $p_{ij}( i = 1, 2, \cdots m; j = 1, 2, \cdots n) \in [0,1]$ is the customer preference degree to $i$ th QoS factor belongs to $j$ th level, and $\sum_{j=1}^{n} p_{ij} = 1$.

Customer's preference can be obtained by records of evaluation. After N times judging on the services, preference matrix is, $P(N) = (1/N)\sum_{k=1}^{N} a_k Y_k$ . In the following section, it will be proved that $\lim\limits_{N \to \infty} P(N) = \lim\limits_{N \to \infty}(1/N)\sum_{k=1}^{N} a_k Y_k = E(a \cdot Y)$ can present the customer's true preference consistently.

**Definition 4.** Match degree between customer's preference and quality of service can be calculated as $M = m^{-1}\sum_{i=1}^{m} c_i \sum_{j=1}^{n} y_{ij} p_{ij}$ , Where $c_i$ is the weight coefficient corresponding to the $i$ th QoS attribute, and $c_i \in [0,1]$, $\sum_{i=1}^{m} c_i = 1$.

To determine the weight of each attribute, entropy evaluation method can be used. Shannon entropy [12] is a measure of the average information content. The entropy H of a discrete random variable $Y_i$ with possible values $\{y_{i1}, \cdots, y_{in}\}$ and probability mass function $p_{ij}(j = 1, \cdots, n)$ is denoted as, $H(Y_i) = E(I(Y_i)) = k \sum_{j=1}^{n} p(y_{ij}) I(y_{ij})$

$$= k \sum_{j=1}^{n} p(y_{ij}) \ln[p(y_{ij})]^{-1} = -k \sum_{j=1}^{n} p_{ij} \ln p_{ij} .$$

The entropy H should be normalized to $H \in [0,1]$. This indicates that $k = (\ln n)^{-1}$.

In the information system, entropy is a measure of disorder, or more precisely unpredictability. The higher entropy means the lower utility value. Hence we use $1 - H(Y_i)$ to measure the weight coefficient of the $i$ th QoS attribute. After normalization, it can be denoted as $c_i = [1 - H(Y_i)]/\sum_{i=1}^{m}(1 - H(Y_i))$ ,

$$M = m^{-1} \cdot \sum_{i=1}^{m} \{[1 + (\ln n)^{-1} \sum_{j=1}^{n} p_{ij} \ln p_{ij}]/\sum_{i=1}^{m} (1 + (\ln n)^{-1} \sum_{j=1}^{n} p_{ij} \ln p_{ij})\} \cdot \sum_{j=1}^{n} y_{ij} p_{ij}$$

Here, if an element of the preference matrix is $p_{uv} = 0$, to avoid $\ln p_{uv} = -\infty$, let $p_{uv} = 10^{-\lambda} \min_{1 \le j \le n, j \ne v} \{p_{uj}\}$, $p_{uj} > 0$, where $\lambda$ is a positive integer.

For a given service, the values of QoS attributes are fixed. The customer's evaluation to services can be found in the historical information register and transferred to preference matrix. So the match degree between customer's preference and quality of service can be obtained, which is the basis for sorting of recommending services.

## 3    QoS Preference Based ACO Algorithm

The ant colony optimization algorithm (ACO) is a bionics probabilistic technique for solving optimization problems which can be transferred to finding good paths through graphs, initially proposed by M. Dorigo in 1992 [13]. The Convergence of ACO algorithm has been proved [14], which means it is able to find the global optimum in finite time, though difficult to estimate the theoretical speed of convergence.

In the service recommendation scheme, ACO can be used to optimize the service selection for each task node. The service composition based on process model is illustrated in Fig. 2.

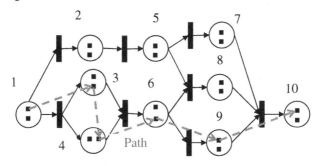

**Fig. 2.** An example of service composition

When service process is aggregated, there are several services for a task to choose. From the start to the end, it can be presented as a path, e.g. Path 1 is an executing sequence, which can be denoted as a linked list, liking the node presented by $(taskNo, serviceNo)$. Thus service selection problem can be transferred to seeking an optimal path in the directed digraph. In this example, No. 2 and No. 3 tasks are in parallel split pattern, while No. 5 and No. 6 mean exclusive choice. As shown in the Fig. 2, we handle the parallel task as sequence pattern to seek the path, so as to guarantee them being executed both; however, the aggregative QoS value is still calculated as parallel pattern.

The ACO algorithm is suitable for service composition selection because of its flexibility. Seeking an optimal path can starts from any task node. Thus if service process is interrupted by an unavailable service, the optimization algorithm can be restarted immediately.

## 3.1    The Algorithm for Service Recommendation Oriented to QoS Preference

**Algorithm 1.** QoS preference oriented ACO algorithm for service recommendation

1) Initialization: set iteration count $N_s = 0$ , the max iteration count $N_{s\,max}$ , customer's preference matrix $P(N_{eva})$ , initially $N_{eva} = 0$ , and pheromone $\tau_{ij}(0)$ . Put $M$ ants in the start task node, the initial number of ant is $k = 1$ ;

2) The iteration count $N_s = N_s + 1$ ;

3) The ant number $k = k + 1$ ;

4) When the $k$ th ant is in the *taskNo* th task, update the $\{allowed\}$ list, which contains the services in next task node able to link directly to the *taskNo* th ant;

5) Choose the next service according to the state transition rule. The ant staying in service $i$ moves to service $j$ .

If $q \le Q_0$ , $j$ is determined by $\zeta_{ij}(t) = Max(\tau_{ij}(t)^\alpha * \eta_{ij}^{\ \beta})$ , $j \in \{allowed\}$

Else if $q > Q_0$ , the probability to select service $j$ is defined by

$$p_{ij}(t) = \begin{cases} \tau_{ij}(t)^\alpha * \eta_{ij}^{\ \beta} / (\sum_{u \in allowed} \tau_{iu}(t)^\alpha * \eta_{iu}^{\ \beta}), j \in \{allowed\} \\ 0, otherwise \end{cases}$$

Where $q$ is a uniform distribution random number in $[0,1]$; $Q_0 \in [0,1]$ is a predefined parameter which determine the probability of following the optimal result; $\zeta_{ij}(t)$ is transition rule from service $i$ to service $j$ ; $\tau_{ij}(t)$ denotes the density of pheromone; $\alpha$ presents the importance of pheromone while $\beta$ stands for importance of expected heuristic information; $\{allowed\}$ means the collection of services in the task node which can be moved to at next step.

$\eta_{ij}$ is the local expected factor, presenting the heuristic information in QoS-based service selection, and measuring the short term benefit, which has the same function with match degree of service $j$ , thereby, $\eta_{ij} = M (service\ j, P(N_{eva}))$

To avoid the probability to select service $j$ being 0 when $q \geq Q_0$, the initial pheromone $\tau_{ij}(0)$ should not be 0. Thus it can be defined as the average local expected factor, $\tau_{ij}(0) = \sum_{i=0}^{N-1} \sum_{j=0}^{N-1} \eta_{ij} / 2$.

6) If there is no service can be searched, go to 4) and move to another task node. Otherwise, go to 7);

7) If $k < M$, update the allowed list and go to 3), otherwise, go to 8);

8) Update the global pheromone.

During $\Delta t$, M ants have completed food seeking, so called an iteration. Thus the pheromone between service $i$ and service $j$ is updated as,

$$\tau_{ij}(t + \Delta t) = R \cdot \tau_{ij}(t) + \Delta \tau_{ij}(\Delta t)$$

$R \in [0,1]$, and $(1 - R)$ means the evaporation rate of pheromone over time, aiming to reduce the influence of previous cases.

Here $\Delta \tau_{ij}(\Delta t) = \sum_{k=1}^{M} \Delta \tau_{ij}^k(\Delta t)$, and $\Delta \tau_{ij}^k(\Delta t)$ means in this iteration, the increment of pheromone left by the $k$ th ant, qualified by,

$$\Delta \tau_{ij}^k(\Delta t) = \begin{cases} Q / L_k, & \text{if ant } k \text{ go through } i \text{ and } j \\ 0, & \text{otherwise} \end{cases}$$

$Q$ is a constant. $L_k$ means the length of path ant $k$ go through, which is the measurement of difficulty to find food. Thus in service recommendation, let $L_k = 1 / M(\text{comp } k, P(N_{eva}))$

$M(\text{comp } k, P(N_{eva}))$ denotes the match degree between customer's preference and service composition presented by the path of ant $k$ in this iteration.

9) Recommend the service compositions sorted by $M(\text{comp } k, P(N_{eva}))$ to customer;

10) If customer doesn't evaluate any services or compositions, go to 11);

Otherwise, when the customer evaluate $N_k$ new services or compositions, the preference matrix is recalculated as,

$$P(N_{eva} + N_k) = (1 / (N_{eva} + N_k)) \sum_{k=1}^{N_{eva} + N_k} a_k Y_k = P(N_{eva}) + N_k (P(N_k) - P(N_{eva})) / (N_{eva} + N_k)$$

Where $P(N_k)$ denotes the average evaluation to the new $N_k$ services.

$$P(N_k) = (1 / N_k) \sum_{k=N_{eva}+1}^{N_{eva} + N_k} a_k Y_k. \text{ Then let } N_{eva} = N_{eva} + N_k ;$$

11) If customer's requirement is satisfied, or $N_s > N_{s\max}$, stop. Otherwise, go to 2).

## 4    Experiment and Analysis

To evaluate the performance of proposed service composition recommendation method from the convergence rate and computation complexity, experiments have been conducted in the example process model illustrated as Fig.2. For each task there are 100 candidate services. Every service has 3 QoS attributes which are generated randomly in $[0,1]$ according to uniform distribution. Each attribute has 5 levels. Thus we can skip the normalization steps and calculate the QoS matrix directly. The parameters are set as follows: the amount of ants $M = 100$, pheromone factor $\alpha = 0.9$, expected heuristic factor $\beta = 1$.

### 4.1    The Influence of Pheromone Persistence Factor

The pheromone evaporation rate $(1-R)$ determines the global search ability and convergence rate. If the pheromone evaporates too quickly, the initial pheromone trails never been searched will decrease almost to zero, which reduces the global search ability and stochastic property. However, if the evaporate rate is too low, the convergence rate will be lessened. Figure 3 describes the variances of $R$ and iteration times. The number is average value of 10 experiment results. The stop rule of iterations is that difference between the last two maximum match degree values is less than 0.0001.

These results indicate that 0.7~0.9 is a proper scope of $R$. In this scope, the performance of algorithm is stable, and it gains balance in convergence and global optimization.

### 4.2    The Process of Recommendation Optimization

According to the result above, let $R = 0.8$, which means the evaporation rate of pheromone is 0.2. Services' QoS values are generated randomly. Figure 4 describes the variances of match degree and iteration times, which are the average values of 10 experiment results.

Figure 4 shows that based on ACO algorithm, the match degree value of service composition increases rapidly and gets to the optimal value, which means ACO algorithm has good global convergence property. This recommending method can improve the agility and flexibility of service composition, even if the process is complex.

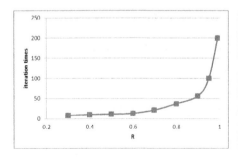
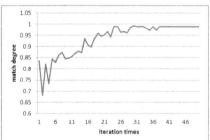

**Fig. 3.** Variances of R and iteration times    **Fig. 4.** Variances of iteration times and match degree

# 5    Conclusion

In this paper, a QoS preference oriented service recommendation method is proposed. Ant colony optimization algorithm is used to optimize the service composition selection. Supported by the matrix model, customer's preference to QoS can be obtained and expressed dynamically. Furthermore, ant colony optimization algorithm is used to seek the optimal service compositions. After each iteration, several compositions are recommended according to the match degree with customer's requirement. During this period, with customer's evaluation feedback of services, the preference matrix will be recalculated and updated. The recommendation results are optimized gradually with the ACO algorithm iterating. This recommending procedure will be repeated until the customer's requirement is satisfied. If the service process is stopped in execution by some unavailable services, the recommendation procedure can restart immediately to search from the blocked task node. Theoretical analysis and numerical simulation indicate that the service composition recommendation algorithm proposed in this paper can satisfy the customer's requirements effectively and flexibly.

**Acknowledgments.** This work is supported by National Natural Science Foundation of China under grant No. 61033005 and 61174169, National Key Technology R&D Program under Grant No. 2010BAH56B01.

# References

1. Schroth, C., Janner, T.: Web 2.0 and SOA: Converging concepts enabling the internet of services. IT Professional 9, 36–41 (2007)
2. European Commission ICT Research in FP7,
   http://cordis.europa.eu/fp7/ict/home_en.html
3. Lijun, M., Chan, W.K., Tse, T.H.: An Adaptive Service Selection Approach to Service Composition. In: IEEE International Conference on Web Services, ICWS 2008, pp. 70–77 (2008)
4. Ying, L., Fangyan, R., Ying, C., Dong, L., Li, T.: Services ecosystem: towards a resilient infrastructure for on demand services provisioning in grid. In: IEEE International Conference on Web Services, ICWS 2004, pp. 394–401 (2004)
5. Armbrust, M., Fox, A., Griffith, R., Joseph, A.D., Katz, R., Konwinski, A., Lee, G., Patterson, D., Rabkin, A., Stoica, I., Zaharia, M.: A view of cloud computing. Commun. ACM 53, 50–58 (2010)
6. Huang, A., Lan, C.W., Yang, S.: An optimal QoS-based Web service selection scheme. Inform. Sciences 179, 3309–3322 (2009)
7. Fan, X.Q., Fang, X.W., Jiang, C.J.: Research on Web service selection based on cooperative evolution. Expert Syst. Appl. 38, 9736–9743 (2011)
8. Chen, Z., Liang-Tien, C., Bu-Sung, L.: DAML-QoS ontology for Web services. In: Proceedings IEEE International Conference on Web Services, pp. 472–479 (2004)
9. Canfora, G., Di Penta, M., Esposito, R., Villani, M.L.: A Lightweight Approach For QoS-aware Service Composition. In: IEEE International Conference on Service-Oriented Computing, ICSOC 2004 (2004)

10. Liu, S.L., Liu, Y.X., Zhang, F., Tang, G.F., Jing, N.: A dynamic web service selection algorithm with qos glabal optimal in web services composition. Journal of Software 18, 646–656
11. Zhang, C.W., Su, S., Chen, J.L.: Genetic Algorithm on Web Services Selection Supporting QoS. Chinese Journal of Computer 29, 1029–1037 (2006)
12. Shannon, C.E.: A Mathematical Theory of Communication (1948)
13. Dorigo, M.: Optimization, learning and natural algorithms. Ph. D. Thesis, Politecnico di Milano, Italy (1992)
14. Zlochin, M., Birattari, M., Meuleau, N., Dorigo, M.: Model-based search for combinatorial optimization: A critical survey. Ann. Oper. Res. 131, 373–395 (2004)

# Meta-model for Data Harmonization and Business Process Compliance in Service Procurement

Maik Herfurth[1], Thomas Schuster[1], and Peter Weiß[2]

[1] FZI Forschungszentrum Informatik, Karlsruhe, Germany
[2] ISS International School of Services, Hamburg, Germany
{herfurth,schuster}@fzi.de
weiss@iss-hamburg.de

**Abstract.** Diminished transaction costs, increased transparency and shortened procurement times entail increased importance of service e-procurement compared to traditional service procurement. Due to proprietary data exchange formats and individual business processes, data harmonization and business process compliance are shortcoming. In this paper a meta-model to formulate requirements of service procurement collaborations with a combined view on information and control flow is presented. Our focus is on two constituent elements of the model: collaborative business processes and service objects. Both elements define features which are characteristic for investigated value constellations. Challenge at hand is to implement standardized interfaces easing seamless exchange of information between business partners. Existing procurement systems need enhanced process-awareness and compliance with service-dominant-logic. The meta-model also serves as reference framework which identifies and correlates typical entities of service procurement collaborations. Furthermore a domain specific meta-model extension for industrial service procurement is derived. This extension serves as basis for data harmonization of service procurement data and enacts compliance of business processes in industrial service procurement collaborations.

**Keywords:** Collaborative business processes, service procurement, business process compliance, data harmonization, meta-modeling, reference-modeling.

## 1    Introduction

Service procurement collaborations in service chain networks are gaining more attention since industrial services contribute progressively more to value creation of organizations. Industrial services present more than 40 percent of revenues in the industrial sector [13]. Especially in the sector of the machine and plant manufacturing, the relevance of e-business for services especially of service procurement is seen as a decisive factor for the long term success in a competitive environment [7]. Capital goods producer and service providers are organized locally. Therefore complex value chains evolve from industrial service chain network structures. The paper focuses on industrial services, especially product-related services.

L.M. Camarinha-Matos, L. Xu, and H. Afsarmanesh (Eds.): PRO-VE 2012, IFIP AICT 380, pp. 105–113, 2012.
© IFIP International Federation for Information Processing 2012

## 2     Challenges of Service Procurement

The collaboration of service providers and requesters poses challenges for the definition of business processes and data for service procurement [18]. An integrated perspective of goods and services is in focus of industrial service procurement [1]. Industrial service procurement is source of high cost because underlying business processes are error prone in most companies. Errors and failures occur foremost at the interface between buyer and supplier. This can be explained through the absence of coherent e-business standards and reference frameworks offering meta-models of processes, data objects and interaction patterns. Although, a variety of e-business standards and frameworks is available, they typically cover solely parts and phases of business processes, and causing numerous media breaks as well as require manual error and exception handling. Service procurement meets challenges based on the characteristic attributes of services [16]. These characteristics influence business processes and data structures. Business processes and data structures for service procurement collaborations aren't harmonized yet. Harmonization is defined as combined term of integration, standardization, consolidation, synchronization and coordination [15]. Business processes must support interaction and communication between service suppliers and requesters [12] [10]. Process compliance addresses the need of harmonized business processes in order to ensure and facilitate compliance with regulations. For the harmonization of business processes, different approaches like process integration [3], process orientation [5], process patterns [6] or reference process models [4] can be utilized [14]. Data harmonization enables integration of information systems for service procurement orders. For data harmonization identical objects with different syntax must be adapted. Data structures must support complex industrial services descriptions as well as service transaction document types [9] [10]. Therefore the creation of new collaborations hampers the business relations by increasing integration and transaction costs, offline communication and procurement times; also resulting in less transparency and low quality of processes and data [8]. Information systems have to be aware of business processes and related document flows. Systems that execute business processes control relevant tasks as well as coordinate complex flow of information and documents between organizations [11].

## 3     Meta-model for Service Procurement

In order to improve harmonization of business processes and data structures for the design and development of information systems in service procurement, a MOF-compliant meta-model is developed. This meta-model defines requirements for business processes and data structures of service chain collaborations. Relevant entities are associated with each other. The meta-model serves as a conceptual model for developing further concrete models such as a reference of process object models. This information is gathered in the meta-models. The meta-model documents elicited requirements concerning types of business interactions in the domain of industrial services. It is focused on four perspectives: *(1) collaboration, (2) organization and resources, (3) business processes* and *(4) data*. As information model, the meta-model enables the definition and evaluation of requirements and serves as a basis for development of information systems. The modeling is motivated by the design of business processes and data structures. Due to a harmonization of data exchange, the collaboration of service suppliers and service requesters can be improved by the development of common or new e-business standards. The meta-model is presented with Unified Modeling Language (UML) class diagrams.

## 3.1   Requirements

For the development of the meta-model, general requirements are formulated.

- **Formal and graphical representation:** To apply a precise and formal modeling notation to represent relevant entities.
- **Consistency:** To provide a consistent composition to avoid redundancies. A consistent modeling approach improves the perpetuity of model elements.
- **Distribution and independence:** Collaborative use and distribution for different involved parties. Use of a neutral representation and graphical notation ensures further development for software services and applications.
- **Principles of proper modeling:** Principles of proper modeling [2] encompass design recommendations concerning syntactic and semantic correctness, relevance, economic efficiency, clearness and comparability.

Furthermore context specific requirements are the refinement of choreography and collaboration aspects. The choreography defines a certain perspective of collaboration and describes the interaction of the two collaboration parties via document- and/or message-oriented inter-organizational processes. Thus relevant interrelations between entities in service chain collaborations should be described.

## 3.2   Model Perspectives

The meta-model is described by different model perspectives: collaboration model, organization and resources model, data model and business process model. The collaboration and organizational and resource model perspective are presented below.

**Collaboration Model Perspective.** The class `CollaborativeBusinessProcess` defines instances of collaborative business processes. `ServiceChainProcess` is a specialization of `CollaborativeBusinessProcess` and possesses additional attributes representing the specificities of service processes. Bilateral and multilateral collaborations can be differentiated. The class `ChoreographyActivity` represents choreography activities. The choreography defines the order of collaborative activities by message exchanges. The classes `ReceiveActivity` and `SendActivity` are sub classes of `ProcessActivity` for sending and receiving messages. The class `Legal-Terms` defines contractual agreements of collaborations.

**Organization and Resource Model Perspective.** For tasks and business processes, roles are defined and assigned to collaboration participants. The class Role defines role concepts and builds a super class of CollaborationParticipantRole. The class CollaborationParticipantRole defines roles participating in a collaboration. The class OrganizationalUnit defines organization units. A role of the class CollaborationParticipantRole is assigned to an instance of the class CollaborationParticipant. The super class Role as well as the sub class OrganizationUnit and colalborationParticipantRole are connected with the sub class HumanResource. Each role is completed by a human resource. Further subclasses of resource are information systems or organizations. The complete meta-model is shown in Fig. 1.

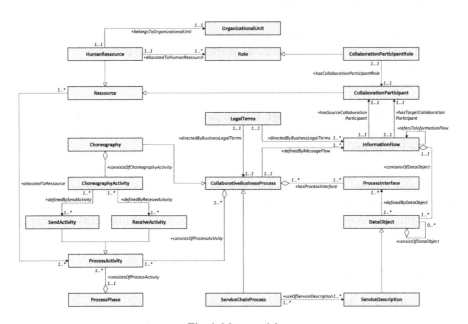

**Fig. 1.** Meta-model

## 4    Meta-model Extension for Industrial Service Procurement

For the support of information system design, the meta-model is extended concerning for requirements of bilateral industrial service procurement collaborations. Based on the meta-model extensions, domain specific models can be derived. The extensions of the meta-model are also additionally described by the model perspectives outlined above.

## 4.1     Requirements for the Meta-model Extension

Context specific requirements for the meta-model extensions are focus on the data model and process model perspective:

- **Data model perspective (service design):** The design of service descriptions should consider specificities and properties of services. For the flexible design of service descriptions, modularization, standardization and variant definitions should be possible. Main factors of industrial services (resources) need to be described including the external factor of a service. Specifically for industrial services, the interaction place must be included in the service description. Electronic classification of services supports the grouping and coherent description offering a standardized coding system to be referenced by all business partners.
- **Process model perspective (process structures and modularization):** Process modularization and structuring improves the understanding of collaborative business processes and reduces complexity. Business processes can be subdivided into partial processes and allow for the building variants for business process models.

## 4.2     Model Perspectives

Extensions of the *data model* and *process model* perspectives are outlined below.

**Data Model.** The classes `DataObject` and `ServiceDescription` are extended by adding specializations of these classes. The class `BusinessTransactionDocument` defines an abstract super class of specific transaction document types for service procurement (Fig. 2).

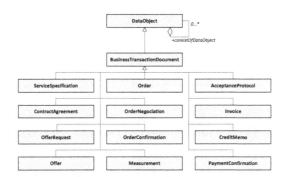

**Fig. 2.** Extensions of `DataObjects`

The class `ServiceDescription` is extended by specific specialization of classes for the description of industrial services (Fig. 3). An industrial service description is a composite construct of `ServicePosition`, `MaterialPosition` and `MachinePosition`. The `RelatedObject` describes the external factor and is a sub class of `MachinePosition`. All these classes are connected with the class `Classification`. The class `Classification` assigns codes to groups of industrial services with similar attributes using a classification scheme (ClassificationScheme) and features (Features).

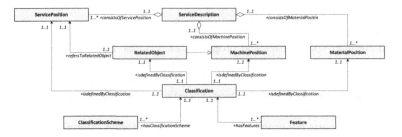

**Fig. 3.** Extension of ServiceDescription

**Process Model.** The classes CollaborativeBusinessProcess and Process-Phase are associated with specialization classes possessing additional attributes and special behavior. A collaborative business process can be capsulated by process modules. A capsulated process of a process module is executed by one collaboration partner. Process modules are defined by the class CollaborativeProcessModule. Service procurement processes consist of different process phases. Business processes are assigned to one or more of respective process phases. The class ProcessPhase defines specific process phases of service procurement. The extended process phases are Predefinition, Request, Offer, Order, Execution, Measurement, Acceptance and Accounting (Fig. 4).

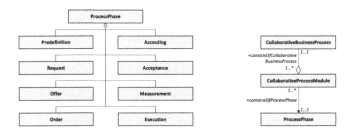

**Fig. 4.** Extensions of ProcessPhase and CollaborativeBusinessProcess

## 5    Meta-model Instance of Data Model Extension

The extended meta-model represents relevant entities and dependencies of business processes and information flows for industrial service procurement in a structured manner. The meta-model requirements have been defined and evaluated in several use cases [10, 11]. Based on the meta-model, existing e-business standards can be extended and new standards can be developed in order to fulfill the logic dependencies (related to service-dominant-logic [19]). Meta-model instances define data objects for information systems. Generated meta-model instances provide standardized semantics of descriptions with common understanding to improve the information exchange in service procurement collaborations. So far standardized semantics are not available due to a variety of heterogeneous data formats. The given example is related to the service object *order* referencing service descriptions agreed between buyer and supplier in a respective frame contract. *Order* is a document type and represents a typical model instance of the data model perspective. In Fig. 5, the meta-model instance of an *order document* and also an example of a runtime data object *order* is shown. An order document type consists of a header and a body part. The header describes meta-data like the ID of an order, the date, the `ContractID` reference and the `ServiceSpecificationID` reference. The header part includes information about the service requester and Service provider with their IDs and their addresses. The body part lists the industrial service description as service positions. As a runtime example, an UML object diagram of the relationship between a body element and three service description positions is shown.

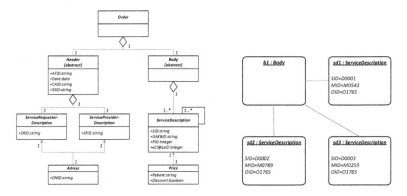

**Fig. 5.** Meta-model instance *order* of data model perspective and runtime example

## 6    Conclusion and Outlook

In this paper, a meta-model for business process compliance and data harmonization for service procurement collaborations was presented. It offers an integrated view on business processes and respective information flows. Furthermore a domain specific meta-model extension could be derived. The meta-models are information models supporting the design of process-aware information systems meeting the requirements of the flow of XML documents and the control flow of the underlying business process. Presented results have been applied and validated within the development of e-business standard concepts (based on the meta-model extension). Developed e-business standard concepts are currently being implemented in practice [11]. The meta-model was designed in conformity with hands-on requirements which could be elicited from real-life case-studies [10]. Next step foresees to elaborate further on the reference process model using a formal description language for modeling (such as Petri nets) and applying an integrated modeling approach enclosing various views and levels. Process and data model perspective were combined with the aim to design an abstract reference process model for service procurement. The meta-model extension also serves as reference system which captures best practices in industry. Furthermore it allows identifying and referencing relevant data objects by business partners using a shared framework.

# References

1. Aurich, J.C., Schweitzer, E., Siener, M., Wolf, N.: Lebenszyklusorientierte Konfiguration investiver Produkt-Service-Systeme. Zeitschrift für wirtschaftlichen Fabrikbetrieb (ZWF) 102(12), 820–824 (2007)
2. Becker, J., Rosemann, M., Schütte, R.: Grundsätze ordnungsgemäßer Modellierung. In: Wirtschaftsinformatik, vol. 37(5), pp. 435–445. Vieweg+Teubner (1995)
3. Bullinger, H.-J., Fröschle H.-P., Brettreich-Teichmann, W.: Informations- und Kommunikationsinfrastruktur für innovative Unternehmen. Zeitschrift Führung und Organisation (4), 225–233 (1993)
4. Fettke, P., Loos, P.: Methoden zur Wiederverwendung von Referenzmodellen – Übersicht und Taxonomie. In: Becker, J., Knackstedt, R. (eds.) Referenzmodellierung - Methoden, Modelle, Erfahrungen. Arbeitsbericht No. 90 des Institut für Wirtschaftsinformatik, pp. 9–30. Westfälische Wilhelms-Universität Münster (2002)
5. Fließ, S.: Prozessorganisation in Dienstleistungsunternehmen, Stuttgart (2006)
6. Fowler, M.: Analysis Patterns: Reusable Objects Models. Addison-Wesley (1996)
7. Gebauer, H., Hildenbrand, K., Fleisch, E.: Servicestrategien für die Industrie. Harvard Business Manager 28(5), 47–55 (2006)
8. Meier, A., Stormer, H.: eBusiness & eCommerce: Management der digitalen Wertschöpfungskette. Springer, Berlin (2008)
9. Herfurth, M., Weiß, P., Rudolf, C., Kern, R.: Reducing Complexity of Services. In: Böhmann, T., Leimeister, J.M. (eds.) Proceedings Teilkonferenz: Integration von Produkt und Dienstleistung: Hybride Wertschöpfung, Multikonferenz Wirtschaftsinformatik MKWI 2010 (2010)
10. Weiß, P., Herfurth, M., Schumacher, J.: Leverage Productivity Potentials in Service-oriented Procurement Transactions: E-Standards in Service Procurement. In: Proceedings of RESER 2011 (2011)
11. Österle, H.: Geschäftsmodell des Informationszeitalters. In: Österle, H., Winter, R. (eds.) Business Engineering – Auf dem Weg zum Unternehmen des Informationszeitalters, Springer, Berlin (2003)
12. eBusInstand – Einsatz von Standards in der industriellenInstandhaltung, Research transfer project funded by Federal Ministry of Economics and Technology (2011), http://www.ebusinstand.de
13. Rai, A., Sambamurthy, V.: Editorial Notes – The Growth of Interest in Service Management: Opportunities for Information Systems Scholars. Information Systems Research 17(4), 327–331 (2006)
14. Rinderle-Ma, S., Ly, L., Dadam, P.: Business Process Compliance. In: EMISA Forum, pp. 24–29 (2008)
15. Schuh, G., Schmidt, C.: Prozess. In: Schuh, G. (Hrsg.): Produktionsplanung und steuerung. Grundlagen, Gestaltung und Konzepte, pp. 108–194. Springer (2006)

16. Smeltzer, L.R., Ogden, J.A.: Purchasing Professionals Perceived Differences between Purchasing materials and Purchasing Services. Journal of Supply Chain Management 38(19), 54–70 (2002)
17. Vargo, S.L., Lusch, R.F.: Evolving to a New Dominant Logic for Marketing. Journal of Marketing 68, 1–17 (2004)
18. Winkelmann, K.: Prospektive Bewertung der kooperativen Erbringung industrieller Dienstleistungen im Maschinenbau durch Simulation mit Petri-Netzen. Shaker Verlag (2007)

**5**

## Collaborative Ecosystems

# A Collaborative Services Ecosystem
# for Ambient Assisted Living

Luis M. Camarinha-Matos, João Rosas, Ana Inês Oliveira, and Filipa Ferrada

Universidade Nova de Lisboa, Faculty of Sciences and Technology
Campus de Caparica, 2829-516 Monte Caparica, Portugal
`cam@uninova.pt`

**Abstract.** A conceptual architecture for ambient assisted living is introduced as a contribution to the development of an ecosystem of products and services supporting active ageing. In order to facilitate understanding and better inter-relate concepts, a 3-layered model is adopted: Infrastructure layer, Care and assistance services layer, and AAL ecosystem layer. A holistic perspective of ambient assisted living, namely considering four important life settings is adopted: (i) Independent living; (ii) Health and care in life; (iii) Occupation in life; and (iv) Recreation in life.

**Keywords:** Collaborative networks, Services ecosystem, ICT and Ageing.

## 1    Introduction

The severe demographic changes faced by most developed countries, leading to a rapid increase of the percentage of aged population, raises tough challenges to our society. In this context there is an urgent need to find effective and affordable solutions to provide care and assistance to elderly.

Technology, and particularly high-speed pervasive broadband connectivity, cloud-computing and web-based technologies, offer new opportunities to provide care and assistance, as well as new ways of working, facilitate social interaction, and reduce limitations imposed by location and time. Many research projects and pilot experiments have focused on ICT and ageing (see, for instance, [1], [2], [3], [4]).

But many good ideas and promising pilot cases fail to scale because the adopted approaches have been excessively techno-centric. A purely technology centered approach, without consideration of the socio-organizational aspects is likely to add only marginal value, not getting accepted by users, or not finding a sustainable business approach for wider deployment.   Therefore, while designing a new conceptual architecture for ICT and Ageing it is fundamental to also address the need for organizational and cultural change.

On the other hand, the frequent association of senior citizens with a dependent stage of life does no longer match the reality. The adoption of the concept of "**active ageing**" provides a more appropriate understanding of the later phases of life [5]. Furthermore, the notion of "**productive ageing**" [6] has opened new perspectives for a change in the way society often perceives older people. Thus supporting the active

L.M. Camarinha-Matos, L. Xu, and H. Afsarmanesh (Eds.): PRO-VE 2012, IFIP AICT 380, pp. 117–127, 2012.
© IFIP International Federation for Information Processing 2012

ageing process is not only about creating an environment exclusively focused on providing healthcare and assistance but rather a more comprehensive one, in which the elderly citizens do not feel excluded, and have a chance to use their knowledge and expertise in a fruitful way, by making a valued contribution to the communities in which they live [7], [8], [9].

Aiming at providing a contribution to the ICT and Ageing area, the Portuguese AAL4ALL project is focused on the development of an ecosystem of products and services for Ambient Assisted Living (AAL), complemented with an adequate business model for this ecosystem. The ALL4ALL consortium involves 32 partners from industry, service providers, and academia, associated to the Health Cluster Portugal.

The underlying assumption in this project is that the creation of effective support environments for the ageing citizens requires the involvement and effective coordination of multiple stakeholders, from diverse sectors and distinct backgrounds. Hence, before addressing specific (technical) implementation approaches and technologies, it is important to consolidate concepts in order to mobilize and align all the needed stakeholders. As such, one of the initial results of the project was the establishment of a **conceptual architecture** for AAL, which is summarized in this paper. The aim is not simply to support the development of (complex) technological artifacts, but rather conceive systems to support the formation and operation of sustainable AAL ecosystems.

## 2    Trends in Elderly Care Services

Past research and developments in elderly care services as well as current market offers are characterized by some fragmentation. The focus has been predominately put on the development of isolated services - e.g. monitoring of some health related parameter, fall detection, agenda reminder, alarm button, etc. - each one typically provided by a single organization, and often showing an excessive techno-centric flavor. A current trend is to move from fragmented services to progressively more **integrated care services** [9], [10], which are likely to be provided by multiple stakeholders through well-elaborated collaboration mechanisms. Furthermore, the importance of the role of communities and other forms of collaborative networks involving all stakeholders, operating as an ecosystem, is being recognized.

At this point, we should note that a term frequently causing misunderstandings is what refers to the concept of **service**, which is used with different meanings by different communities. Therefore, we distinguish two types of *services*:

- **Software services** – basically software functionalities that are (remotely) accessible or callable (e.g. web services). This concept corresponds to the view of service typically adopted by ICT experts.
- **Care and Assistance Services** – which correspond to the services provided to the end users (senior citizens, in this case). This notion is equivalent to what is usually called business services. A care and assistance service may involve a number of software services and human intervention. The actual structure of such service also depends on the interaction between the provider and the user, and may ultimately (and dynamically) vary according to the flow of that interaction.

Associated to the notion of service – either software service or care and assistance service – there is the notion of service provider. Since a provider might offer more than one service, it is convenient to introduce the concept of **service entity** – an encapsulation of the various services provided by the same entity; in other words, a representation of a service provider [9], [10]. For instance, a device used in AAL can be represented (modeled) as a service entity that provides several software services (the software functionalities of the device). Similarly, a care institution can be represented by a service entity encapsulating all care and assistance services provided by that institution.

On the other hand, developments in this area should not be exclusively focused on ICT (and related technologies, e.g. sensors, intelligent home appliances, service robotics), but need to also consider the design and launching of adequate policy actions in order to guarantee the success of any such development. Complementarily, training actions, not only for the senior citizens, but for all the other stakeholders, are a condition for success.

This trend was clearly confirmed by the BRAID roadmapping project [11], [12]. This European initiative went through an extensive consultation of stakeholders in the AAL area towards identifying the most relevant research actions in this sector for the next decade.

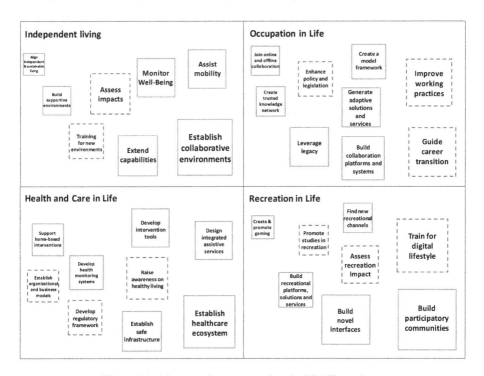

**Fig. 1.** Prioritization of research actions in BRAID roadmap

When asked to prioritize the identified actions, participants in the roadmapping process clearly privileged actions such as:

- Establishment of collaborative environments for independent living
- Establishment of healthcare ecosystems
- Building collaboration platforms and systems for occupation in life
- Building participatory communities for recreation in life
- etc.

These priorities confirm the mentioned trend towards integrated services provided through collaborative ecosystems. Fig. 1 shows these findings of BRAID. Each square represents one (needed) R&D action; the area of the squares is proportional to the number of votes given by participating stakeholders. In addition to the technology-oriented development actions, BRAID also identified the need to develop, at the same time, a number of policy related actions (dashed boxes in Fig. 1).

# 3    A Conceptual Architecture

AAL4ALL takes into account the findings and recommendations of BRAID roadmap, while adapting them to a national context. As an important element to facilitate the creation of synergies among stakeholders, a conceptual architecture was designed. This architecture aims at structuring the developments for AAL by defining a unified terminology, and describing the functionality and roles of components.

A services ecosystem model is considered in which the basic idea is to have an environment that facilitates rapid composition of (eventually multi-stakeholder) services, forming integrated care and assistance services (analogous to consortia formation). This requires that services and their providers are prepared to collaborate with each other. While designing this architecture, a socio-technical approach was followed, since socio-organizational aspects are vital to realize the potential benefits of technology in support of the ageing population. Similar to a virtual organizations breeding environment (VBE), we can consider in this environment the existence of supporting entities that take care of issues such as quality of service, billing, etc.

In order to facilitate understanding and better inter-relate the involved concepts, a 3-layered model is adopted for the AAL4ALL conceptual architecture, as illustrated in Fig. 2. Each layer is focused on specific aspects of the intended ambient assisted living environment, and a logical hierarchical structure is established among these layers.

The lowest level - the **Support Infrastructure** - represents a facilitator (providing support) for the development and delivery of care and assistance services. Such infrastructure should provide, among other functionalities, channels and mechanisms for safe communications and information sharing and exchange among the members of a given AAL ecosystem. As a "support" component, the infrastructure is neutral regarding any specific set of care and assistance services, or any specific organizational model of the ecosystem. The infrastructure comprises two sub-layers (Fig. 3): (1) Local infrastructure, corresponding to the support infrastructure located in a specific "location", e.g. user's home, care center. (2) Global infrastructure, supporting the network of "spaces" (or local environments) "inhabited" by the various stakeholders. This division is justified both by the different technical specificities of each sub-layer and (possibly) different business models associated to each one.

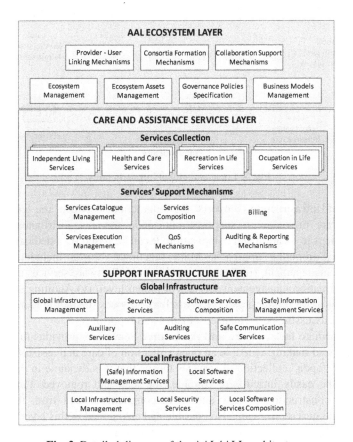

**Fig. 2.** Detailed diagram of the AAL4ALL architecture

The local infrastructure provides support for the user care services in his/her current location. It should allow the installation of sensors and actuators through adequate network standards. Examples of locals are the senior's home, senior hotels, care-center, senior in movement outside, and intelligent built environments.

The local infrastructure supports critical services, processes and data, requiring high level security. It will manage multiple networked sensors and actuators of several kinds, including implantable/wearable devices, as well as automation and robotic mechanisms. All these devices are modeled / wrapped as software service entities. In this sense, the local (physical) infrastructure is transformed into a software services ecosystem (which is distinct from the concept of AAL ecosystem). Main functional blocks at this level include: (i) Local Infrastructure management, (ii) Local security services, (iii) Local software services composition, (iv) Safe information management services, and (v) Local software services.

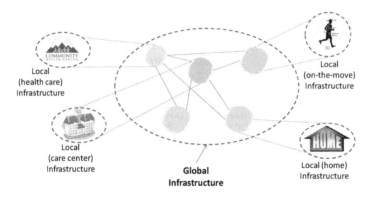

**Fig. 3.** Local and global infrastructures

The global infrastructure supports the interaction between the entities/nodes engaged in care provision. It supports multi-node services, distributed processes, software services invocation and composition. It can be based on a dedicated portal or on a Cloud Computing approach. Main functional blocks include: (i) Global infrastructure management, (ii) Security services, (iii) Software services composition, (iv) Safe information management services at global level, (v) Auditing services, (vi) Safe communication services, and (vii) Auxiliary services (including identification of critical issues, assessing performance, statistics and reporting).

The intermediate layer - **Care and Assistance Services** - provides functionalities for managing and making available an open collection of care and assistance services. The notion of "open" collection of services means that it is dynamic in the sense that services can be easily introduced, editable, replaced and removed. Functionalities allowing the construction of new and more complex services from the available elementary (atomic) services are also possible and envisioned in this layer.

In AAL4ALL a number of demonstrative services are being developed, addressing relevant needs as identified through scenarios analysis, complemented with requirements derived from an extensive set of questionnaires used to identify user needs.

This layer is logically split in two sub-layers: Services collection and Services' Support Mechanisms. The higher level represents the open care and assistance services collection. To facilitate the organization and management of the collection, care and assistance services are divided into four groups according to the four life settings of:

- *Independent living* - how technology can assist in normal daily life activities e.g. tasks at home, mobility, safety, agenda management (memory help), etc.
- *Health and care in life* - how technology can assist in health monitoring, disease prevention, and compensation for disabilities.

– *Occupation in life* - how technology can support the continuation of professional activities along the ageing process.

– *Recreation in life* - how technology can facilitate socialization and participation in leisure activities.

The lower level layer comprises a set of support mechanisms for the management of the services. Main functional elements include: (i) Services catalog management, (ii) Services composition mechanisms, (iii) Billing, (iv) Services execution management, (v) QoS Mechanisms, and (vi) Auditing and reporting mechanisms.

The top layer of the architecture - **AAL Ecosystem** - provides organization, governance, and collaboration support for the AAL multi-stakeholders from a socio-technical perspective.

An AAL ecosystem can involve, in addition to the senior citizens, a combination of formal care and informal care networks, as illustrated in Fig. 4.

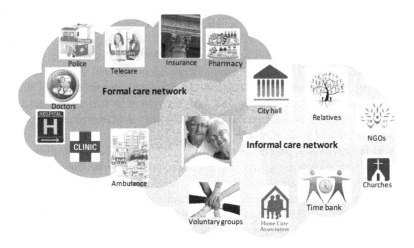

**Fig. 4.** Example of AAL ecosystem

The purposes of the AAL Ecosystem can only be achieved if adequate functionalities for modeling and management are provided. Such functionalities should then give support to organize and structure dynamic organizations; defining and enforcing governance policies; defining profiles, roles, business models, launching collaborative processes, and supporting links between providers and clients/users. Main functional elements of this layer include:

(i)     *Ecosystem Management* - To provide effective management of the AAL Ecosystem in terms of service providers, users, regulators, and support entities. Functionalities for membership and roles management; profiles and competencies management (providers); user profiles management; other stakeholders management, and management of interaction with external entities. It also includes a model of the organizational structure.

(ii) *Assets Management* - To provide mechanisms that allow the management of all AAL Ecosystem assets: products, services, shared knowledge, etc. It includes modeling of assets, and their ownership and access rights as well as mechanisms for sharing of assets, as well as market gap analysis.

(iii) *Governance Policies Specification* - To provide mechanisms that allow the specification of the governance policies of the AAL Ecosystem, including collaboration agreements. It includes definition of governance policies through instantiation of templates, rules / clauses, etc., as well as definition of rights and duties and identification of performance indicators.

(iv) *Business Models Management* - To provide means for identification, characterization and management of specific business models adopted by the AAL Ecosystem and its members. Such mechanisms include: the specification of the business models, contracting, accounting services, specific business plans, support mechanisms, etc. Associated to the business models, value systems are also modeled. Models for assignment of responsibilities / liabilities and benefits distribution are included. This element also includes the definition of service packages tailored to each user / class of users.

(v) *Providers - Users Linking Mechanisms* - To provide mechanisms to support links between AAL services or products providers and end users of the AAL Ecosystem. In other words, offering mechanisms to promote usage of the care and assistance services offered by the AAL ecosystem. A variety of mechanisms can be considered in each ecosystem, including: e-Marketplace, Brokerage, Dissemination and marketing, etc.

(vi) *Consortia Formation Mechanisms* - To provide mechanisms that allow (rapid) consortia formation among AAL providers, including external entities if needed, in order to deliver integrated services. It also includes consortia formation mechanisms in response to emergency situations, selection criteria specific to each ecosystem and involving elements such as stakeholders' profiles / offered services, past record of QoS, availability, collaboration readiness, costs, etc.

(vii) *Collaboration Support Mechanisms* - To provide mechanisms to support cooperation and/or collaboration among the AAL Ecosystem members. A collaboration platform allowing multiple collaboration processes, involving different subsets of stakeholders. Therefore, different virtual collaboration spaces should be allowed.

## 4      Implementation Issues

**Implementation Architectures.** As mentioned above, the purpose for the AAL4ALL conceptual architecture is to provide a kind of reference framework for the various stakeholders in the sector. Particular implementations will require the derivation / instantiation of implementation architectures that detail the intended systems and give guidance on how to implement them. In order to validate the conceptual framework, which was already the result of wide consultation among stakeholders, AAL4ALL is currently implementing a number of pilot cases (large scale trial), covering an extensive set of scenarios.

The feasibility of sustainable AAL ecosystems supported by an environment developed according to the concepts of the proposed architecture depends on the elaboration of appropriate business models that go "hand-in-hand" with the techno-organizational developments. Therefore, a number of critical questions related to the business models are also being addressed: Who pays for / who owns the infrastructure? Which business model for implementations based on cloud computing? Which service billing criteria? Which value systems and benefits distribution model? Etc.

**AAL Ecosystem: Regional or national?** One of the characteristics of Internet and computer networks in general is to allow some independence from geographical barriers. This characteristic allows remote delivery of care and assistance services, what could suggest the possibility of building an AAL ecosystem at national (if not European) level. On the other hand we cannot ignore the reality of existing organizational structures - many entities operate on a regional / local basis, e.g. care centers, health care centers, city hall related entities, etc. Furthermore, the importance of local communities in the process of supporting social inclusion of senior citizens is well recognized. Therefore, it seems more realistic to focus on regional / local AAL ecosystems. Even within one (small) geographical area we might foresee the emergence of different AAL ecosystems based on different criteria (e.g. cultural, interests, economic level).

Certainly there are major stakeholders (e.g. infrastructure operators, special service providers, insurance companies, etc.) that operate at national (or international) level. But this fact is not an obstacle for a model based on local ecosystems, since such stakeholders might participate in several local ecosystems.

The notion of local ecosystem, although associated to a community present in a given geographical area, is not strictly bounded by geographical borders. For instance, relatives of senior citizens might be living in different geographical regions and still be part (mostly through remote access) of a local ecosystem where their senior relatives live.

Nevertheless, although AAL4ALL can foresee a future scenario in which care and assistance to elderly is provided through a multiplicity of local ecosystems, there are clear advantages, from a perspective of economy of scale that all these local ecosystems are built following a common conceptual architecture (a kind of reference architecture at national level). Some form of **federation of** those **ecosystems** would also be useful to allow more affordable access to some specific services (e.g. very specialized health care services) and also to guarantee continuity of services when users travel from one region to another (a kind of "*roaming* between ecosystems").

## 5    Conclusions

ICT combined with new collaborative organizational structures represent a promising contribution to face the challenges of providing care and assistance services to a rapidly growing percentage of aged population. In this direction, many efforts have been carried out during last decade, but most of them were focused on the development of single, non-integrated services. Current trends point to the need of more integrated services, which are likely to result from contributions of various stakeholders.

In this context, the AAL4ALL project has developed a conceptual architecture to support an ecosystem of integrated (collaborative) services. The architecture follows a holistic socio-technical approach, which is reflected in the ecosystem notion, in opposition to more traditional techno-centric solutions. This proposal is aimed at acting as a facilitator for the necessary "convergence" of stakeholders and effective support for their collaboration. Having a technology-independent conceptual architecture facilitates evolution and coping with emerging technologies. The set of technology / service developers that adhere to a common conceptual architecture can more easily collaborate in specific ecosystems (shorter adaptation time), which represents a competitive advantage in comparison with outsiders.

**Acknowledgments.** This work was funded in part by the Project AAL4ALL (QREN 13852), co-financed by the European Community Fund through COMPETE - Programa Operacional Factores de Competitividade. Partial support was also obtained from the European Commission through the BRAID project (FP7 programme). The authors also thank the contributions from their partners in these projects.

# References

1. Aguilar, J.M., Cantos, J., Exposito, G., Gómez, P.: The improvement of the quality of life for elderly and relatives through two tele-assistance services: The TeleCARE approach. In: Proceedings of TELECARE 2004 Workshop – Tele-Care and Collaborative Virtual Communities, pp. 73–85. INSTICC Press, Porto (2004)
2. Camarinha-Matos, L.M., Rosas, J., Oliveira, A.: A mobile agents platform for telecare and teleassistance. In: Proceedings of TELECARE 2004 – Int. Workshop on Tele-Care and Collaborative Virtual Communities in Elderly Care, pp. 37–48. INSTICC Press, Porto (2004)
3. Costa, R., Novais, P., Costa, Â., Neves, J.: Memory Support in Ambient Assisted Living. In: Camarinha-Matos, L.M., Paraskakis, I., Afsarmanesh, H. (eds.) PRO-VE 2009. IFIP AICT, vol. 307, pp. 745–752. Springer, Heidelberg (2009)
4. Vontas, A., Protogeros, N., Moumtzi, V.: Practices and Services for Enabling the Independent Living of Elderly Population. In: Camarinha-Matos, L.M., Paraskakis, I., Afsarmanesh, H. (eds.) PRO-VE 2009. IFIP AICT, vol. 307, pp. 753–758. Springer, Heidelberg (2009)
5. USDHHS, Active Aging: A Shift in the Paradigm – Denver Summit of Eight (Industrial Countries). U.S. Department of Health and Human Services (May 1997),
   http://aspe.hhs.gov/daltcp/reports/actaging.pdf
6. Garlick, S., Soar, J.: Human capital, innovation and the productive ageing: Growth and senior aged health in the regional community through engaged higher education. In: Annual AUCEA Conference, Alice Springs, Australia, July 2-4 (2007)
7. Llmarinen, J.: Aging and Work Life Balance in the EU (June 2006)

8. HSBC Insurance, The future of retirement – The new old age (May 2007),
   `http://www.hsbc.com/1/PA_1_1_S5/content/assets/retirement/`
   `gender_perspective_eurasia_africa_1.pdf`
9. Franco, R.D., Bas, Á.O., Prats, G., Varela, R.N.: Supporting Structural and Functional Collaborative Networked Organizations Modeling with Service Entities. In: Camarinha-Matos, L.M., Paraskakis, I., Afsarmanesh, H. (eds.) PRO-VE 2009. IFIP AICT, vol. 307, pp. 547–554. Springer, Heidelberg (2009)
10. Cardoso, T., Camarinha-Matos, L.M.: Pro-activity in Collaborative Service Ecosystems. In: Camarinha-Matos, L.M., Pereira-Klen, A., Afsarmanesh, H. (eds.) PRO-VE 2011. IFIP AICT, vol. 362, pp. 377–387. Springer, Heidelberg (2011)
11. Camarinha-Matos, L.M., Afsarmanesh, H.: Collaborative Ecosystems in Ageing Support. In: Camarinha-Matos, L.M., Pereira-Klen, A., Afsarmanesh, H. (eds.) PRO-VE 2011. IFIP AICT, vol. 362, pp. 177–188. Springer, Heidelberg (2011)
12. Camarinha-Matos, L.M., Ferrada, F., Oliveira, A.I., Rosas, J.: Consolidated roadmap for ICT and Ageing, Deliverable D6.21, BRAID project (October 2011),
   `http://www.braidproject.eu/`

# Evaluating Collaboration Effectiveness
# of Patient-to-Doctor Interaction in a Healthcare
# Territorial Network

Dario Antonelli[1], Dario Bellomo[2], Giulia Bruno[1], and Agostino Villa[1]

[1] Politecnico di Torino, Dept. Industrial Engineering and Production
Corso Duca degli Abruzzi, 24 10129 Torino, Italy
[2] Azienda Sanitaria Locale ASL-AT
Via Conte Verde, 125 14100 Asti, Italy

**Abstract.** The emerging crucial point of healthcare organizations is to involve patients in autonomous monitoring their own health status by using personal ICT-based systems to manage data, and to ask for an effective cooperation with the doctor, if necessary. Two motivations urge this innovation: the growing costs of healthcare services, and the need to promote patients' education. Therefore, the objective of this paper is to outline a Patient Guidance System (PGS) architecture to allow the patients an ubiquitous and secure management of personal health data and an easy call to the doctor in case of a critical or suspicious health situation. The PGS architecture will support an effective cooperation between the patient and the doctor in such a way to assure to the patient – either at home, or moving and/or being monitored by wearable devices – a clear interaction to get an easily understandable healthcare service.

**Keywords:** Healthcare network, Patient-to-Doctor interaction, Collaboration.

## 1 Introduction

Almost everywhere in Europe healthcare systems are organized at the regional level, in the form of territorial networks of different types of service centers, including hospitals, local consulting and health status testing centers, and mainly family doctors and specialists. Referring to the Italian organization, the territorial healthcare management unit is the Local Healthcare Agency – LHA (i.e. Agenzia Sanitaria Locale – ASL), which is referred to a territory whose population and whose extension are usually corresponding to a province. All LHAs located in a same region depend on the Regional Government, which coordinates the healthcare services in terms of political plans and attribution of an annual budget.

In any country, unless relevant adjustments will be applied to the healthcare systems, incidence of the care costs is going to become explosive [1,2]. New methods and procedures for the performance evaluation of the services and for controlling their costs are going to be studied and sometimes applied, but a reasonable compromise between the necessity of reducing costs and the healthcare system scope of assuring to any person a sufficient health status, is far from being found and tested.

L.M. Camarinha-Matos, L. Xu, and H. Afsarmanesh (Eds.): PRO-VE 2012, IFIP AICT 380, pp. 128–136, 2012.
© IFIP International Federation for Information Processing 2012

Experience of the authors in analyzing the care system of the LHA in the Asti province, North-West Italy, in recent research projects (www.codesnet.polito.it and www.lep.polito.it/prinsalute), shown that a real key of the health care quality is the improvement of the cooperation between the patients and the family doctors: these last ones are the basic stones of the healthcare system, because they operate at the same time as patient's consultant – by acquiring symptoms and selecting therapies – and as "drivers" of patients flows among the LHA service centers. Then, an effective collaborative interaction between a patient and his/her doctor becomes the crucial step for improving the LHA quality of services.

Based on these concepts, the *Patient Guidance System (PGS) Architecture* here outlined has two complementary goals. First, to allow the patient an ubiquitous and secure management of his/her personal health data and, in case either of not being able to recognize the health status, or of a critical health situation, to call the doctor for help by supporting an effective cooperation between the patient and the doctor (the two "actors" of the healthcare system).

As it will be shown in the following, the PGS Architecture could also support some innovative collaborative actions. Since the remote patients are persons frequently not expert of the LHA service network operations neither of the devices for self-monitoring their health status, patients and doctors must be equipped with a proper connection with a Data Maintenance and Securitization Centre (usually located at the regional healthcare government centre), managing data and information for the whole PGS Architecture, and equipped with a connection with the Network Maintenance Resources devoted to assure the efficiency of the whole connecting network. Furthermore, Distributed Telemedicine Network, already existing, will make possible to remote or moving patients to activate the connection with their Personal Health Records (PHR) by operating on data and information of various type and nature (monitored, vocal, images).

The described project is currently at a design stage, but a real application to an Italian LHA is under consideration.

## 2    The PGS Architecture

Based on the above introduced scope of the PGS Architecture, the effective cooperation between the patient and the doctor must be obtained through an IT infrastructure suitable for applying the following actions/controls.

- To enable the patient to contact his/her Personal Health Record (PHR), stored in a secure digital repository, by using a *PHR Consultation Facilitator*, that is a new original communication system assuring the effective interaction between patients and their own PHRs;
- To support the patient in monitoring his/her own PHR by using a Digital Library of simple and comprehensive patient's health status models (ontology) and an original set of patients-dedicated rules to analyze PHR (semantics), all organized into a *Patient Consultation Support Base* such to be used also by unskilled persons;

- To enable the patient to call a doctor for help, by using a *Patient-To-Doctor (P2D) Interaction Facilitator* which makes as cooperative and as easy as possible the communication between the two actors;
- To facilitate remote or moving patients in activating connection with either their family doctor or any other healthcare service centre through a *Distributed Telemedicine Network (DTN)*, to transfer physiologic data and health information of various type and nature and to ask for immediate and understandable support.

The following sub-sections will give a detailed presentation of the above listed PGS components.

## 2.1    The PGS Infrastructure

The basic scheme of the PGS Architecture is the infrastructure illustrated in Figure 1. In schematic terms, it will be obtained by the functional integration of (i) the PHR Intelligent Management System (*PHR-IMS*), devoted to Patient-To-Doctor collaborative communication, (ii) the IT network connecting patients whose health status is continuously monitored by portable devices with their PHR Digital Repository, and (iii) the Communication Support System between the PGS and the coordination centre (usually located at the regional level), to support all users of the PGS Architecture in front of unexpected events, either due to connection problems or due to exceptional situation of the patient's health status.

The basic functionalities of the PGS Architecture will be the following:

- To facilitate the patient in the consultation of his/her Personal Health Record (PHR), such to apply a personal monitoring of the health status as well as of safety alert parameters;
- To facilitate the patients mobility in three forms: *Mobility of a patient inside the area* managed by the Local Healthcare Agency where patient is residing, from his/her family doctor to other doctors, specialists and other health care centres; *Mobility of a patient outside*, i.e. towards sanitary centres of other Territorial Healthcare Agencies; *Mobility of a patient to another country*, with a different language.
- To facilitate the interaction between a patient and the doctor such that the former could receive help in understanding his/her own health status, and should be supported in giving an as clear as possible presentation of his/her symptoms;
- To support on one hand the request of new sanitary information by the doctor to the public (or private) Regional Agency managing healthcare services (also disseminating information on new products, new protocols, etc.), on the other, to help doctors in detecting potential patient mistakes in contacting them or wrong or unwilling choice made by non-expert patients, using P2D.

In addition, assurance of the necessary data security and privacy protection requires that a common management of data, as well maintenance of both data and system effectiveness, must be guaranteed by a Regional Healthcare Agency which must have at disposal both the complete data base of PHRs, such to make analyses of the population health, and the most recent information on new drugs, new protocols and treatments, and be able to support demands from doctors and also disseminate information, such as to integrate latest available medical knowledge.

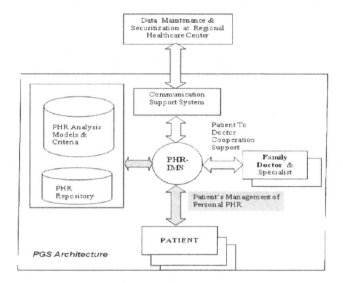

**Fig. 1.** Scheme of the PGS Architecture

## 2.2    Conceptual Model of the PHR Intelligent Management System

Figure 2 gives a sketch of the Intelligent Management System to be made at disposal of the patient in order to make a consultation of the personal PHR and, in case of critical situations, to ask the doctor for help.

The basic components of the PHR-IMS are described in the following (numbers are referred to the PHR-IMS components and the data/information flows illustrated in the Figure 2).

1.  Data generated from the patient monitoring system (portable device, wearable computing, etc.)
2.  Data & information from a contact call by the patient ( patient's inputting data using a Web form, phone call with a health care centre operator, etc.)
3.  Ontology with patient medical and social models as well as rules concerning healthcare services that could be obtained (e.g. administrative norms established for the considered region, country, etc.), generated by formalizing existing and newly defined models, as well as by integrating/extending existing standards, taxonomies, etc.

4. Semantic rules to guide the calling patient to analyze his/her own PHR and making a personal "diagnosis" of the proper health status such as to recognize if a call to doctor is necessary, owing to unclear vision of the health status or to physical problems;

5. *Facilitator* of the patient interaction with the system (input), exploiting medical and social models to tailor the PHR monitoring process to the patient's characteristics, attitudes, etc. ("interact to understand"), and *Generator* of a snapshot of patient health status to be stored (by descriptive model based on measured parameters, historical data, models & thresholds), by verifying each time the patient's clinical parameters and adjusting their thresholds to the current conditions of the calling/monitored patient;

6. Patient instance (PHR) in the Digital Repository;

7. Patient profiling (models, thresholds, history, etc., mining literature and analogies), doctor profiling, Patient-To-Doctor matchmaking and guide to read of patient history (e.g. augmented reading, variation in patient health status), description of the rules for diagnosis to the calling patient (reasoning, procedures and prescriptions), update of the Digital Repository with the outcomes of the Patient-To-Doctor cooperation process.

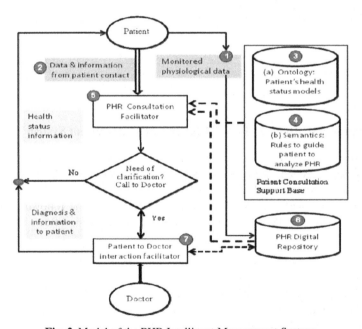

**Fig. 2.** Model of the PHR Intelligent Management System

It must be remembered indeed that the remote patients are persons frequently not expert of the connecting network operations neither of the devices for monitoring their health status. Then, the two blocks N° 5 and N° 7, that are the PHR Consultation Facilitator and the Patient-to-Doctor Interaction Facilitator must be equipped with a proper connection with the Data Maintenance and Securitization Centre (usually located at the regional healthcare government centre), managing data and information for the whole PGS Architecture, and have also to be equipped with a connection with the Network Maintenance Resources devoted to assure the efficiency of the whole connecting network. The above mentioned connections play the role of Communication Support System among patient, doctor and the Data Maintenance and Securitization Centre.

# 3    Short Survey of the State-of-the-Art

In order to evaluate the innovation contained in the proposed PGS Architecture, as well as of its potential application, two types of existing systems in the healthcare sector, with special reference to the patient support and the interactions between patients and doctors have been analysed: (i) systems already in operation, and (ii) recently published results.

Referring to existing systems for PHS analysis already in operation, the following two examples have been analyzed. The Microsoft HealthVault[1] allows for the creation of a personal repository of health information a citizen can "bring" with him/her and access when needed. The HealthVault can be populated by either uploading data from health/fitness devices, by digitizing paper records or by connecting to pharmacies and labs online. Google Health[2] is designed to allow citizen to organize, track, monitor, and act on their health information. Specifically, its users can manage their health history online, set personal health and wellness goals and track and monitor their progress through both embedded and third-party services.

By comparing the two examples with the main features of the on-going PGS Architecture, it can be seen that Microsoft HealthVault and Google Health are strongly oriented to the citizen/patient, with lazy connections with the healthcare system, but they are not specifically designed for collaborative analysis and diagnosis. In general, their functionalities depends on third-party applications developed upon the PHR infrastructure.

Along with the two above products, Dossia[3] is one of the largest PHR deployments in the world, based on Open Source software. The Dossia system enables individuals to gather copies of their own medical data and to create and utilize their own personal, private and portable electronic health records. In practice, Dossia is an information management system. No specific facilitation of the patient-to-doctor interaction is considered.

By the MHO – Management Health Online system[4], a healthcare organization can have a complete informatics system, reliable and adapted to the needs with a

---

[1] http://www.healthvault.com/personal/index.aspx.

[2] https://www.google.com/accounts/ServiceLogin?service=health &nui=1&continue=https://health.google.com/health/p/&followup= https://health.google.com/health/p/&rm=hide

[3] www.dossia.org.

[4] www.mhc.com.ar

reasonable cost of ownership. MHO connects patients and the sanitary structure in a town or a province or a region, through a unique internet-based system, thus managing the patient history and current information in terms of hospitalization, analysis, pharmacy, and make statistics and reports. However, MHO operates as a data base management system with multiple users, the patients; no specific module will support the patients in their understanding of the personal PHR, and no module is providing a cooperative integration of patients with doctors, till now.

Recent years revealed a wide diffusion of papers and, sometime, also books, on the aspects of healthcare when the patient-centered approach is considered. Research and analysis efforts have been developed mainly in the medical area with attention to the potential use of new ICTs, according to two lines.

On one hand, some authors and research centers move to analyze the potentiality of wireless body area sensors, to be used as basic connecting elements in a patient-to-service interaction system. This is the case of [3], where the idea is that a number of tiny wireless sensors, strategically placed on the human body, create a wireless body area network that can monitor various vital signs, providing real-time feedback to the user and medical personnel. In a recent paper with similar approach [4], the authors discuss and map the main findings resulting from the development of a series of four Wireless Sensor Network (WSN) health monitoring prototypes, under the generic name of MoteCare. It devised a generic framework that can be adapted for healthcare monitoring, both at a patient's home or in a care facility is proposed. Other works dealing real-time and mobile physiological data analysis can be found in [5,6].

Whereas the first generation of patient-centred e-health studies have been focused largely on discussing how to assure a good tracking of patients, in a recent paper [7] it is proposed that the next generation of e-health research begin to better address the questions of why, how, and for whom the e-health interventions across a variety of health domains could work. This paper discusses some design and analytic approaches for determining what components of e-health programming work, how they work, and for whom. Intuitively, this paper has the ambition of being normative. It gave interesting suggestions for the PGS Architecture here outlined.

One of the most diffused book [8] on the patient-centred healthcare approaches shows how the adoption of a user-centered design (UCD) focus has immensely enriched the health industry, because the application of UCD concepts are key to successful development of e-services, including e-health. Then, it confirms that Patient-Centered E-Health presents the perspective of a distinct form of e-health that is patient-focused, patient-aware, patient-empowered, and patient-active. These same concepts have been considered the basic ones for the PGS Architecture.

# 4    Application in Living Laboratories

The Local Healthcare Agency of the Province of Asti (ASL-AT) is a typical public institution to manage, control and financing the healthcare service units located in the province territory and the hospitals located in the towns of Asti and Nizza Monferrato. The ASL-AT operations consist of the organization of all territorial services, and a special attention is dedicated to the dissemination of healthcare service opportunities over the territory, directly to patients at their home, to avoid spare time and costs for patients and sanitary operators in the healthcare centres. To perform such operations and to monitor the services supplied to patients, the ASL-AT collects detailed information on the patients' calls as well as on the doctors' contacts. A very large data base, ranging over the last four years, has been made  at disposal for analyzing the patient's needs of both information on their own personal healthcare status (that means, the patient history stored in the PHR), and the actual patients' utilizations of the healthcare centres even in case of no real necessity (then, when the use of a remote facilitated connection with a PHR repository could satisfy this type of information need) [9]. The contribution of ASL-AT to the present on-going research will allow to give a complete evaluation of the potentials of the proposed PGS Architecture in a region where the actual healthcare service is centred on the doctor and the patient is still considered a "client" of the service network. Indeed, the evolution of any healthcare organization must be towards a patient-centred system: this is the expected evolution also of the new Italian Minister of Health for the ASLs innovated operations. Then, the on-going evolution of the PGS research line will move along the following two directions. On one hand, to complete the definition of the health status models, the ontology and the semantics by analyzing actual healthcare prescriptions and devising their translation into easy/usual language. On the other, to analyze the actual patients' needs, by using the ASL-AT data base with about 8.7 million prescriptions per year, for about 215.000 persons, among which 48% contact doctors and/or healthcare service centres for a number of times ranging from 20 (healthy person) to 350 (with chronic disease) per year,  all registered in the ASL data base,  and with about 200 doctors providing sanitary services.

# References

1. Villa, A., Antonelli, D., Bellomo, D.: Transferring industrial concepts to helthcare service network management. In: 21st Int. Conf. on Production Research (2011)
2. Antonelli, D., Villa, A., MacCarthy, B., Bellomo, D.: Transferability of Industrial Management Concepts to Healthcare Networks. In: Camarinha-Matos, L.M., Paraskakis, I., Afsarmanesh, H. (eds.) PRO-VE 2009. IFIP AICT, vol. 307, pp. 266–273. Springer, Heidelberg (2009)
3. Otto, C., Milenkovic, A., Sanders, C., Jovanov, E.: System Architecture of a Wireless Body Area Sensor Network for Ubiquitous Health Monitoring. J. of Mobile Multimedia 1(4), 307–326 (2006)
4. Navarro, F., Lawrence, E.: WSN (Wireless Sensor Network) Applications in Personal Healthcare Monitoring Systems: A Heterogeneous Framework. In: 2nd Intl. Conference eHealth, Telemedicine, and Social Medicine, ETELEMED 2010, St. Maarten (2010)
5. Varshney, U.: Pervasive healthcare and wireless health monitoring. Mob. Netw. Appl. 12(2), 113–127 (2007)
6. Apiletti, D., Baralis, E., Bruno, G., Cerquitelli, T., Fiori, A.: Real-time and Mobile Physiological Data Analysis. Information Discovery on Electronic Health Records, pp. 227–249. Chapman & Hall/CRC (2009)

7. Resnicow, K., et al.: Methodologic and Design Issues in Patient-Centered e-Health Research. Am. J. Prev. Med. 38(1), 98–102 (2010)
8. Vance Wilson, E.: Patient-centered e-Health. Medical Information Science Reference, New York (2008)
9. Villa, A., Bellomo, D.: Design of performance evaluation and management systems for territorial healthcare networks of services. In: Cultural Factors in Systems Design – Decision Making and Action, pp. 199–217. CRC Press, Taylor & Francis Group, Boca Raton, FL (2012)

# Modeling of Digital Ecosystems:
# Challenges and Opportunities

John Krogstie

IDI, NTNU, Trondheim, Norway
krogstie@idi.ntnu.no

**Abstract.** 'Digital ecosystems' is a metaphor inspired by natural ecosystems which describes a set of distributed, adaptive, and open socio-technical systems. Being parts of such ecosystems, individual persons, public and private organisations are becoming increasingly dependent on each other. When such cooperation moves beyond simple buying and selling of goods and well-defined services, there is a need for a flexible infrastructure that supports not only information exchange, but also collaborative knowledge creation, evolution and sharing across a number of cooperation and collaborative networks that traditionally work in a bottom-up and rather improvised way. We will in this paper look at how techniques and approaches to modelling used e.g. for enterprise architecture and collaborative networks should evolve to support the development, support and evolution of digital ecosystems.

## 1 Introduction

All organizations are dependent on an application systems portfolio supporting its current and future tasks, and newcomers in any area are dependent on establishing a similar application portfolio quickly in a way that can evolve with changed business needs, technological affordances and expectations among co-operators, competitors and customers. An increasing fraction of the value creation in modern society comes from knowledge work using ICT. Such knowledge work is vital to meeting the grand challenges of today. As stated in the Digital Agenda for Europe [1], "*Smart use of technology and exploitation of information will help us to address the challenges facing society like supporting an ageing society, climate change, reducing energy consumption, improving transportation efficiency and mobility, empowering patients and ensuring the inclusion of persons with disabilities*".

The current organization of knowledge work result in a waste of ideas, knowledge, and solutions, which are not put into use where they are developed, and not exploited by others. An approach to address this is using 'open innovation' [2]. Open innovation will have to rely heavily on ICT, facilitating virtual communities of nomadic, human/ organizational actors, co-working on partially shared digital artefacts [3]. The term *digital ecosystem* has recently been used to generalize such communities, with focus on that their actors constantly interact and cooperate with other actors in both local and remote ecosystems. Examples of digital ecosystems are communities for Creative

L.M. Camarinha-Matos, L. Xu, and H. Afsarmanesh (Eds.): PRO-VE 2012, IFIP AICT 380, pp. 137–145, 2012.
© IFIP International Federation for Information Processing 2012

Commons and Open Source (OSS), social media networks as in Facebook, blogs and around computer games, virtual organizations, or voluntary groups of citizen. Note that we use the term in a wider context than what is termed business ecosystem in the collaborative networks literature [4] (a cluster or industry district).

A number of needs can be identified for supporting digital ecosystems. We will in this article discuss these issues highlighting the application and possible changed role of *modelling techniques*. In section 2 we describe the role of modelling in information systems development in general. In section 3 some traits of digital ecosystems are described, and section 4 describes a vision of the role of modelling in this landscape.

## 2    The Role of Modeling and Quality of Models

Information system modelling in general and modelling of collaborative networked organizations [5] is usually done in some organizational setting. One can look upon organizations and their information systems abstractly to be in a certain state (the current state, often represented as a descriptive 'as-is' model) that are to be evolved to some future wanted state (often represented as a prescriptive 'to be' model). These states are often modelled, and the state of the organization is perceived (differently) by different persons through these models. This open up for different usage areas of conceptual models as described e.g. in [6, 7].

1. Human sense-making: The model of the current state can be useful for people to make sense of and learn about the current situation as it is perceived.
2. Communication between people [8].
3. Computer-assisted analysis: To gain knowledge about the situation through simulation or deduction, often by comparing a model of the current state and a model of a future, potentially improved state.
4. Model deployment and activation: To integrate the model of the future state in an information system directly. Models can be activated in three ways:
   a. Through people, where the system offers no active support.
   b. Automatically, where the system plays an active role, as in an automated workflow system.
   c. Interactively, the computer and the users co-operate on the process [9].
5. To give the context for a traditional system development project, without being directly activated.
6. Achieve acceptance of solution due to acting as a common ground
7. Quality assurance, ensuring that e.g. an organization acts according to a certified process achieved for instance through an ISO-certification process.

SEQUAL (Semiotic Quality Framework) is a generic framework for assessing quality of models [10, 11]. The framework has earlier been used for evaluation of modelling and modelling languages of a large number of perspectives, including data, object, process, enterprise, and goal-oriented modelling. Quality has been defined referring to the correspondence between statements belonging to the following sets:

- *G,* the goals of modelling.
- *L,* the language extension, i.e., the set of all statements that are possible to make according to the rules of the modelling languages used.
- *D,* the domain, i.e., the set of all statements that can be stated about the situation.
- *M,* the externalized model itself.
- *K,* the explicit knowledge relevant to the domain of the audience.
- *I,* the social actor interpretation, i.e., the set of all statements that the audience interprets that an externalized model consists of.
- *T*, the technical actor interpretation, i.e., the model as 'interpreted' by tools.

The main quality types are:

- The deontic quality of a model relates to that all statements in the model *M* contribute to fulfilling one or more of the goals of modelling *G*, and that all the goals of modelling *G* are addressed through the model *M*. In particular, one include under deontic quality the extent that the participants after interpreting the model learn based on the model (increase *K*) and that the audience are able to change the domain *D* if this is beneficially to achieve the goals of modelling.
- The goal defined for social quality is agreement among social actor's interpretations.
- Perceived semantic quality is the similar correspondence between the social actor interpretation *I* of a model *M* and his or hers current knowledge *K* of domain *D*.
- Pragmatic quality is the correspondence between the model *M* and the actor interpretation (*I* and *T*). One differentiates between social pragmatic quality (to what extent people understand the models) and technical pragmatic quality (to what extent tools can be made that can interpret the models).
- Semantic quality is the correspondence between the model *M* and the domain *D*. This includes validity and completeness.
- Syntactic quality is the correspondence between the model *M* and *L*.
- Empirical quality deals with comprehensibility and predictable error frequencies when a model *M* is read or written by different social actors.
- Physical quality: The main goal is that the externalized model *M* is physically available to the relevant social and technical actors for interpretation (*I* and *T*).

# 3     Characteristics of Digital Ecosystems

The long-term trend in ICT has been towards IT-systems being developed and evolved further and further away from the users of the system [12]. We see a development in the direction of systems to a larger degree being supported by virtual communities of nomadic, human/organizational actors, co-working on partially shared digital artefacts [13]. The term *'digital ecosystem'* has recently been used to generalize such communities. Such systems are characterized by self-organization, scalability and sustainability, providing both economic and social value. Digital ecosystems are part of an even larger area called digital ecologies [14].

However, the existing digital ecosystems have limited scope, various degree of transparency, insufficient support for search and evaluation of useful quality artefacts, and none does fully support a wide range of shared artefacts from a wide range of actors. There are two main variants of digital ecosystems; *content ecosystem and software ecosystems.*

*Content ecosystems* are networks that deal with creation and sharing of artistic and intellectual artefacts. ICT have increasing impact on participative and democratic processes, and this impact will continue to grow with the increasing personalization, witnessed through the increase of social networking and user generated content and services. Internet already allows highly visual and multimodal interactions, and these interactions will become represented through richer means.

*Software ecosystems* are *"a set of businesses functioning as a unit and interacting with a shared market for software and services, together with relationships among them. These relationships are frequently underpinned by a common technological platform and operate through the exchange of information, resources, and artefacts"* [15]. See also work on software ecosystems for product families [13], more general software systems [16], and guidelines for using such ecosystems [15]. For instance within open source systems (OSS) a large number of co-evolved software components are freely available. The quality is variable and often poorly documented. Yet, many organizations now integrate OSS components into their own applications, and some also contribute back [17]. Traditional customers - like municipalities - cooperate to provide improved e-services for their inhabitants. And end-users - even kids - are becoming their own developers.

To address combined digital content and software ecosystems, there must be substantial and concerted improvements of the state-of-the-art in three traditionally unrelated and partially isolated research areas. Enterprise architecture and enterprise modelling, new business models and data management.

# 4    Modeling of Digital Ecosystems

The kind of modelling we are looking on in our work in particular applies to the first two areas above, i.e. enterprise and business modelling. Organizations are becoming less self-sufficient and increasingly dependent on partners and other actors, e.g. by outsourcing non-core activities. However, when such cooperation moves beyond simple buying and selling of goods and well-defined services, there is a need for a flexible infrastructure that supports both information exchange, knowledge creation, evolution and sharing across the different collaborative networks that tend to work in a bottom-up and rather improvised way. Within many organizations, it has become customary to develop enterprise architectures [18]. Ecosystem architecture takes the ideas of enterprise architecture to a higher level of abstraction, looking upon the support of a more fluid landscape of business actors providing and consuming services for information systems support in an organizational setting. In this way it extends the process perspective in BPM-in-the-Large [19] to a wider setting. In also extend work in collaborative networks, such as ARCON [5]. ARCON offers an approach to model collaborative networks (CN), including: the CN life cycle dimension, the CN environmental perspectives dimension, and the CN modelling intent dimension.

A new approach to enterprise integration is needed. User-initiated software applications and enterprise mash-ups should be based on active knowledge modelling (AKM) and supports learning [20]. For this to function, one must support more open business models. In this, one must consider financial success, sustainability, competition, copyright and licensing, and the impact on work processes, leadership, internal coordination, work processes, strategy and planning. The *open innovation* approach [2] is often chosen as a basic cooperation mechanism. Companies should allow freer ("open") import and export of ideas and knowledge concerning products, processes and business models that flow between organization and their environments. Indeed, more openness will provide a larger set of possible business opportunities. Problems connected to IP and revenue sharing must be considered. Furthermore, an open innovation strategy must be reflected not only in the business models, but also by revised behaviour (process practice) and in new thinking patterns. The SEM modelling language [15] attempts to analyze the business along customer-supplier lines. Furthermore, the $E^3$value model [21] describes value-generation and value-exchange among partners in a value network. Other relevant approaches are BMO [22] and ARCON [5].

There are two main scenarios for the future use of modelling in this setting. What we term the steady state scenario, where modelling continues to be a somewhat esoteric activity for a limited number of experts is of course one possibility. The more optimistic scenario in our view is that abstraction techniques such as modelling are taken into use in an increasing number of areas, to make it possible to at all be able to manage this development. One striking aspect is that the number and variety of stakeholders that will need to relate to models of some sort will increase. Given the increased educational level in most countries, it is not unlikely that also more people will be able to relate to these types of abstractions.

Using the sets in SEQUAL, we predict the following under this scenario (in Fig. 1, the areas we foresee large changes are shown with stippled lines):

- G: The same list of goals and applications of modelling that is described in Section 2 will still be relevant, but emphasis on less formal, interactive approaches will increase to be able to support the more federated landscape needed to address digital ecosystems.
- D: The range of relevant domains is increasing given that systems to an increasing degree ranges across and is expected to integrate a number of areas. Business aspects must to a larger degree be integrated with more traditional enterprise aspects such as goals, processes, products, systems and data.
- K: One need to deal with a more varied set of stakeholders, with a more varied set of skills and knowledge. Not only do you need to align IT-experts with business-experts, but also people across a large range of expertise, and across organizations, being used to express their knowledge in different notations.
- L: Using domain specific modelling, the possibilities of tailoring the language to fit the domain, and the knowledge of the stakeholders have increased. To bring

more people into (semi-) formal modelling these possibilities will have to be exploited to a larger degree. Thus rather than having a consolidation of modelling languages like the one done in object-oriented design with UML, there will be an increasing number of variants of modelling languages. We will also see a mix of richer media components being integrated with the more traditional "box and arrow"-conceptual modelling notations, thus supporting also richer meta-meta models defining and limiting the type of constructs to include in models.

- T: An increasing number of tools will be available to extract model information from raw data, e.g. in the area of process mining and semantic web. In addition, tools for meta-meta modelling and meta-modelling will be more common.
- M: Models will be pervasively available being coordinated in a federated manner. Models will be across meta-levels in an increasing degree (compared to the models in traditional software engineering being primarily on the type level). Models, in particular interactive models [9] will have a larger value in themselves, acting to a larger extend as knowledge commons and open models (http://www.openmodels.at/).

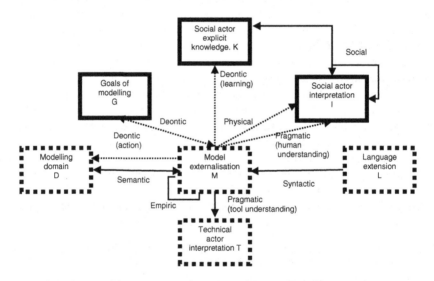

**Fig. 1.** SEQUAL with areas that is changing when modelling digital ecosystems

We believe the core dimensions of SEQUAL will be relevant for discussing also models used in digital ecosystems. On the other hand, a number of specializations might be envisaged. We will briefly discuss some main aspects here.

- Deontic quality: Models will be more important, due to increased dependencies across traditional organizational boundaries and needs to be handled in a more professional manner [8].
- Social quality: This will be important in smaller communities, and in interfaces between communities, but less needed across federation. Note on the other hand

that since different stakeholder groups might see different views of the overall model, possible visualized in radically different ways, the effort to assure that they comprehend the models equally will potentially have to increase [23].

- Pragmatic quality: Given that more types of stakeholders are involved, this is of increasing importance. Different techniques can be used for different types of stakeholder, supporting multiple views for different stakeholder types on the same model to ensure individual comprehension.
- Semantic quality: The federated approach needed for modelling will bring new challenges as for how we look upon the semantic quality of the overall model. Whereas semantic quality in smaller domains would be followed up much as before (i.e. looking at the feasible (perceived) completeness and validity), one would to a larger degree need to be able to live with inconsistencies across federations. In connection to this, it would be important to be able to identify those aspects of the models across domains that need to be consistent.
- Syntactic quality: Syntactic quality can be looked upon as trivial in a sense, since adherence can be enforced. On the other hand, one often sees that one extend languages with new aspects in an (not always conscious) attempt to turn semantic problems into syntactic problems. New tools based on meta-modelling makes this easier to do, and then makes in even more important to do right in the sense that one do not end up with too restricted languages.
- Empirical quality: Support for empirical quality will be more built in, e.g. in tools that build up models from raw data in process mining, thus integrating information visualization tools and modelling tool. Different meta-meta models can necessitate rethinking guidelines for achieving empirical quality [6].
- Physical quality: Rather than being based on central repositories, more distributed, federated storage of model fragments must be available, utilizing standard interchange formats and supporting model mash-ups. What part of the total model that should be available for each partner must be addressed.

## 5    Concluding Remarks

From the above descriptions, we see that the technical challenges and opportunities with digital ecosystems give new challenges and opportunities for model-based techniques. In a way many of the core problems are not new. Even if the use of modelling needs to be extended and improved, general categories underlying discussions on quality of models as described in [10] remains relevant, although need to be adapted to e.g. quality of interactive models [9,20,24]. We plan to pursue this work by working on case studies in selected domains including public sector, smartgrids and the petroleum industry to investigate more concretely how to extend the techniques described in section 4 for modelling of digital ecosystems.

**Acknowledgements.** This work is part of ongoing cross-disciplinary work on this area. I would in particular like to thank my colleagues Letizia Jaccheri, Jon Atle Gulla, Reidar Conradi, Tonje Osmundsen, Per Morten Schiefloe, Guttorm Sindre, Kjetil Nørvaag, Martha Molinas, and Alf Inge Wang in this regard.

# References

1. European Commission, A Digital Agenda for Europe, COM, Brussels (2010)
2. Chesbrough, H.: Open Services Innovation. Rethinking your Business to Growth and Compete in a New Era. Jossey-Bass, San Francisco (2011)
3. Ali Babar, M., Dingsøyr, T., Lago, P., van Vliet, H. (eds.): Software Architecture Knowledge Management - Theory and Practice. Springer (2009)
4. Camarinha-Matos, L.M.: Taxonomy of Collaborative Networks Forms, FInES (2012)
5. Afsarmanesh, H., Camarinha-Matos, L.M.: The ARCON modeling framework. Springer, New York (2008)
6. Nossum, A., Krogstie, J.: Integrated Quality of Models and Quality of Maps. In: Halpin, T., Krogstie, J., Nurcan, S., Proper, E., Schmidt, R., Soffer, P., Ukor, R. (eds.) Enterprise, Business-Process and Information Systems Modeling. LNBIP, vol. 29, pp. 264–276. Springer, Heidelberg (2009)
7. Krogstie, J.: Model-Based Development and Evolution of Information Systems: A Quality Approach. Springer, London (2012)
8. Wesenberg, H.: Enterprise Modeling in an Agile World. In: Johannesson, P., Krogstie, J., Opdahl, A.L. (eds.) PoEM 2011. LNBIP, vol. 92, pp. 126–130. Springer, Heidelberg (2011)
9. Krogstie, J., Jørgensen, H.D.: Quality of Interactive Models. Paper Presented at the First International Workshop on Conceptual Modelling Quality, IWCMQ 2002 (2002)
10. Krogstie, J., Sindre, G., Jørgensen, H.D.: Process Models as Knowledge for Action: A Revised Quality Framework. EJIS 15(1), 91–102 (2006)
11. Krogstie, J., Sølvberg, A.: Information systems engineering - Conceptual modeling in a quality perspective. Kompendiumforlaget, Trondheim (2003)
12. Davidsen, M.K., Krogstie, J.: A longitudinal study of development and maintenance. Information and Software Technology 52, 707–719 (2010)
13. Bosch, J.: Architecture Challenges for Software Ecosystems. In: Proc. Fourth European Conference on Software Architecture, ECSA - Companion Volume, Copenhagen, Denmark, August 23-26, pp. 93-95. ACM Press (2010)
14. Vyatkin, V., Zhabelova, G., Ulieru, M., McComas, D.: Toward Digital Ecologies: Intelligent Agent Networks Controlling Interdependent Infrastructure. In: IEEE Conference on Smart Grid Communications, Gaithersburg (October 2010)
15. Jansen, S., Finkelstein, A., Brinkkemper, S.: A sense of community: A research agenda for software ecosystems. In: Proc. 31st International Conference on Software Engineering, ICSE, Vancouver, Canada, May 16-24, pp. 187–190 (2009)
16. Hunink, I., van Erk, R., Jansen, S., Brinkkemper, S.: Industry taxonomy engineering: the case of the European software ecosystem. Proc. In: Fourth European ECSA - Companion Volume, Copenhagen, Denmark, Aug. 23-26, pp. 111–118. ACM Press (2010)
17. Hauge, Ø., Ayala, C., Conradi, R.: Adoption of Open Source Software in Software-Intensive Industry - A Systematic Literature Review. Information and Software Technology 52(11), 1133–1154 (2010)
18. Lankhorst, M.: Enterprise Architecture at Work. Springer (2009)
19. Houy, C., Fettke, P., Loos, P., van der Aalst, W.M.P., Krogstie, J.: BPM-in-the-Large – Towards a Higher Level of Abstraction in Business Process Management. In: Janssen, M., Lamersdorf, W., Pries-Heje, J., Rosemann, M. (eds.) EGES 2010 and GISP 2010. IFIP Advances in Information and Communication Technology, vol. 334, pp. 233–244. Springer, Heidelberg (2010)
20. Lillehagen, F., Krogstie, J.: Active Knowledge Modeling of Enterprises. Springer (2008)

21. Gordijn, J., Yu, E., van der Raadt, B.: E-service design using i* and e³value modeling. IEEE Software 23(3) (2006)
22. Osterwalder, A., Pigneur, Y., Smith, A.: Business Model Generation. Wiley (2010)
23. Krogstie, J., Dalberg, V., Jensen, S.M.: Process modeling value framework. In: Manolopoulos, Y., Filipe, J., Constantopoulos, P., Cordeiro, J. (eds.) ICEIS 2006. LNBIP, vol. 3, pp. 309–321. Springer, Berlin (2008)
24. Krogstie, J., Jørgensen, H.D.: Interactive Models for Supporting Networked Organisations. In: Persson, A., Stirna, J. (eds.) CAiSE 2004. LNCS, vol. 3084, pp. 550–563. Springer, Heidelberg (2004)

# 6

## Platform Requirements

# ICT Requirements Analysis for Enterprise Networks Supporting Solar Power Plants

Hamideh Afsarmanesh[1] and Victor Thamburaj[2]

[1] University of Amsterdam, Informatics Institute, FCN group,
Science Park 107, 1098 XG Amsterdam, The Netherlands
h.afsarmanesh@uva.nl
[2] iPLON GmbH, The Infranet Company, Karl-Kurz-Str. 36,
D- 74523 Schwaebisch Hall, Germany
victor.thamburaj@iplon.de

**Abstract.** Establishing solar power plants are being accepted worldwide as a source of renewable energy. The Total Life Cycle (TLC) of these plants [1] lasts a few decades and includes the three main stages of (i) *design and engineering, (ii) construction and commissioning,* and the long term *(iii) operation and maintenance.* A number of different stakeholders are typically involved and contracted that together produce, parameterize, operate, and maintain these plants. Each solar plant is then developed as a complex, one-of-a-kind, massively customized product, which is enhanced by a large number of varied services, either provided as software systems or as business services supported by humans and/or robots. ICT support for the TLC of the solar power plants is challenging. We propose to establish enterprise networks in form of long term alliances, in order to enhance the functionality effectiveness for co-working and co-innovation among the involved stakeholders in this area. This network establishes the common ICT platform and the tools supporting interoperability and secure sharing and exchange of distributed data. The paper provides results from early stages of our goal-oriented requirements engineering [2], mostly focused on domain analysis, requirement elicitation, and stakeholders' verification/agreement. It identifies the high level ICT requirements for this environment, through analyzing its life cycle stages, main entities, stakeholders, and base functionality. This paper concludes with the synthesis of our findings into five classes of ICT requirements.

**Keywords:** Solar power plants, ICT requirement analysis, collaborative networks, Virtual organizations breeding environments, virtual organizations.

## 1 Introduction

Three major factors have been driving the growth in renewable energy generation in the last decade: (i) The main source of energy, fossil fuel, has been depleting fast, but the demand for energy has been growing at tremendous pace, (ii) The burning of fossil fuels has resulted in the emission of huge volumes of Green House Gases (GHG) including $CO_2$, which is widely accepted to be the cause of global warming,

L.M. Camarinha-Matos, L. Xu, and H. Afsarmanesh (Eds.): PRO-VE 2012, IFIP AICT 380, pp. 149–157, 2012.
© IFIP International Federation for Information Processing 2012

climate change and environmental disasters, and (iii) The political turmoil in countries that are major producers of fossil fuels.

Renewable energy is increasingly considered as a solution to the above problems. Next to the solar panels, a number of other equipment are necessary for construction of solar plants, such as the tables, DC junction Boxes, Inverters, Transformers, electrical switchgear, and grid power connection. But besides the emergy generation related equipment, other fundamental equipment for the solar plants include the monitoring and control equipment which are used by a number of software systems and for performing certain business services. These include systems for control of the operation, management, and maintenance, to ensure smooth production and efficiency of power generation, as well as preserving the legality and security aspects of the solar plants that clearly differ from region to region and country to country.

The primary aim behind the domain analysis phase of our solar plant requirements engineering approach [2] and [3], was to identify the variety of high level ICT requirements for solutions to smoothen collaboration among involved enterprises and stakeholders in the industry, and improving the TLC management of solar plant installations. In this direction, the elicitation process focused on addressing the needed co-innovation, co-creation, and mass customization of service-enhanced products and software systems to meet the stakeholders' needs.

In the remaining of this paper, first in Section 2 we briefly describe the general description of solar power plant environment. This is done along the *three phases* of its life cycle, as the base for our requirements elicitation purposes. We then address and exemplify in Section 3, the identified stakeholders in this environment, and in Section 4 the need for collaborative development of advanced functionality within this young industry. Section 5 provides a synthesis of the main identified high level ICT requirements for solar power plants, and Section 6 concludes the paper.

## 2    Development Phases of Solar Power Plants

This paper considers the scope of large ground mounted solar power plants (between 1 MWp to 40 MWp). The Total Life Cycle (TLC) of large power plants consists of three main phases: (a) The *phase-1* constitutes *design and engineering*, typically lasting 3 to 6 months; (b) The *phase-2* constitutes *construction and commissioning*, typically lasting 3 to 6 months; and (c) The *phase-3* constitutes *Operation and Maintenance* of the plant, typically lasting 20 to 25 years.

Development phase-1:  **Design and Engineering**
This phase is complex and involves various categories of stakeholders. Besides supporting their requirements, the ICT requirement analysis also needs to focus on the needed functionality in this environment, e.g. through a set of business services and software systems. This phase is typically divided into the following three steps:

   a) **Project Assessment.** This step includes a complete analysis of the site and its technical assessment, including: (i) Connection to power GRID (power evacuation point), (ii) Technical stability (due diligence) in the area, and (iii) Land field stability (e.g. slopes).

**b) Project Design.** This step focuses on early engineering, assessment, and selection of technology, including: (i) Pre-engineering (e.g. simulation of distance between tables of solar panels, and arrangement and angels of panels), (ii) Evaluation/selection of solar power technology equipment, and (iii) Selection of inverters (to invert DC from panel to AC for grid).

**c) Project Implementation. This step establishes all needed technical connections** (e.g. to the Utility company). Furthermore, it finalizes the technology selection and engineering, and the procurement of the needed: equipment, support business services, and software systems, which cover the needed monitoring and control services, as well as the operation and maintenance services for the plant.

Development phase-2: **Construction and Commissioning**
During this phase, the solar plant equipment is installed at the site and put into operation. This process is split into two steps of construction and commissioning.

**a) Construction.** During this step equipment will arrive at the site, and the construction of plant is achieved by different enterprises, ranging from pulling electric cables to installing the monitoring and control equipment. These multi-stakeholder activities need to be carefully coordinated, using project management software.

**b) Commissioning.** This step deals with testing, adjusting and tuning all control devices and ICT systems, and continues with trouble shooting until the solar plant is successfully started and operational.

Development phase-3: **Operation and Maintenance**
The operation and maintenance steps of the solar power plant are intertwined, and focused on efficient generation of electricity, and its transmission to the utility companies, through the evacuation points at the plant. A number of software systems and business services enhance the performance of power plants and assist/guarantee their proper operation [3]. Two main categories of software systems are typically required, namely: (i) the *monitoring and control software systems*, and (ii) the *operational management software systems*. The main aim of monitoring a plant is to determine its performance, and weak points, e.g. a malfunctioning device, in which case a flag is raised for maintenance. Furthermore, several software systems at the plant need to interact and exchange information, to coordinate their inter-related functions.

# 3    Stakeholders in Solar Energy Industry

Various stakeholders are identified in the solar plant environments, who are either impacted and/or have impact on this area [4]. Many of these stakeholders need to join effort and co-work, while some others have only interest in receiving information about certain features of the plants, e.g. configuration,  performance, etc. The categories of identified stakeholders include: *Project developing firms, EPC*

(Engineering, Procurement, and Construction) *contractors, Lending organizations, Government agencies, Insurance companies, Owner investing firms, Utility companies, equipment manufacturers, Software system developers, Business service providing companies, etc.* These stakeholders are typically involved in more than one solar plant, and the plants are often located in different geographical regions. At the same time, at each plant, equipment and devices, the monitoring and control systems, business services, etc. are provided by different specialized enterprises, which frequently need to work jointly. For example, several solar plants in India are now being designed and engineered in Germany [5]. As such clearly the mentioned processes in Section 2 become quite challenging and may involve collaboration among very large number of supporting SME organizations, from different locations, what calls for establishing collaborative network, as addressed in Section 7.

## 4      Need for Collaborative Development of Advanced Functionality

Solar energy is a young industry, in which supporting enterprises, e.g. developers of operation and maintenance systems, must continuously innovate and propose new services in response to the identified needs and/or raised problems by different stakeholders. Therefore, as a part of our requirements analysis [6], besides the general ICT requirements mentioned above, we identify and analyze the need for provision of advanced services and functionality in this industry. These are mostly related to *co-creation, co-innovation,* and *mass-customization* functionality, while involving customers. This section addresses a real case example, to demonstrate the need for *innovation through co-development* within collaborative networks. The case is about a solar plant built by German companies in the desert in Gujarat, India [5]. The customer at this plant raised the problem that the solar panels are frequently covered with dust, hence hindering their effective electric power generation capabilities. Among the main challenges were: finding necessary clean water in the desert, and training the local staff at the site to safely clean the panels (which generates 1000 V DC) while avoiding electric shock. To find an innovative solution needed a group of companies partly in Germany and partly in India to collaborate in designing a novel semi-automatic cleaning system. The required expertise for this innovation included: (i) Mechanical cleaning tools, with brushes and clamps, (ii) Sensitive chemicals to not damage the panels or environment, (iii) Collecting used water from different sources, (iv) Recycling used water, (v) Control systems for measurement of dust before and after cleaning, (vi) Safety checking device for humans cleaning panels, and (vii) Developing multimedia training tools (with audio, video, and text). The designed approach uses waste-water from close-by homes and industries to be recycled for cleaning dusty panels, and design of a new specialized equipment.

Once this semi-automatic cleaning system is developed and tested at different sites ,with varied requirements, it will be provided in the market with *mass customization* features to fit the requirements at different plants. This means that in future customers can buy this cleaning equipment, and remotely download the customization software needed to parameterize/tailor/configure the cleaning system to fit their specific needs and preferences, and become a part of their operation and maintenance services.

## 5    Analysis and Synthesis of Main Identified Requirements

The solar power plant domain embeds many complexities that can benefit from ICT-based developments. Our main identified requirements are analyzed and classified below into *four requirement classes,* addressed below. These synthesized requirements are verified/validated by experts in the field of solar power plants [5].

**<u>Requirement Class 1 – Networking among Involved Stakeholder Organizations</u>**
Considering the variety of involved stakeholders, and their needed interactions and information sharing/exchange, establishment of formal long term strategic alliance networks is required to serve as the base infrastructure for their collaboration. Some forms of informal networking already exists in this industry, but it is necessary to establish a so-called ***VBEs (Virtual organizations Breeding Environments)*** [7] in support of collaborative activities in this industry. The VBE alliance brings together and supports collaboration among otherwise independent and mostly small organizations, e.g. those providing the needed equipment, business services, and software systems, etc. with decision makers, and even customers when they are included within innovation loops. At present, these stakeholders need to collaborate on different tasks, from simple service delivery to co-construction, and even to increasing the potential of turning a customer need into innovation. Within such a VBE, a number of goal-oriented Virtual Organizations (VOs) can be dynamically established, each aimed to fulfill specific joint task by a group of enterprises, e.g. a joint construction or commissioning task, or certain co-creation/co-innovation activity. Fig. 1 represents different involved stakeholders and, their relation with EPC, plus our proposed high level networking interrelations through the VBE and VOs.

Through establishing VBEs [7], its member stakeholders can together: (i) capture bigger market, and more opportunities, (ii) reduce individual costs, by each focusing only on its core competencies, and (iii) increase individual abilities to take risks, through distribution and sharing of their profits and losses.

Research on VBEs has so far addressed a number of ICT supporting tools. Among them, the base functionality that are identified as required for the solar energy domain includes the following: *(i) Catalog of member profiles [8] identifying who is who in the VBE & what are their competencies, (ii) Performance-based trust establishment [9] among the VBE stakeholders, (iii) A glossary and/or ontology of terms/concepts [10] to define the common terminology related to the energy area, and (iv) Common set of basic tools for goal-oriented collaboration among VBE members including: the Most-fit partner selection tool, for establishing the so called opportunity-based **VOs (Virtual Organizations)** [11], and  the Negotiation tool, to record agreements on responsibilities, liabilities, and distribution of the profits and losses.* For the case of service-enhanced complex products, every one of the above mentioned functionality are needed to be carefully researched and developed.

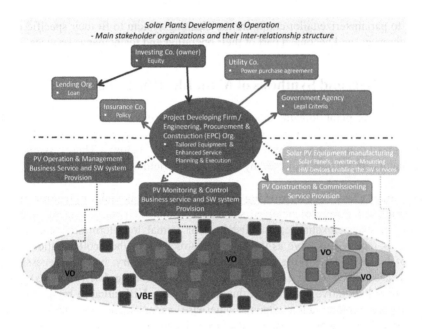

**Fig. 1.** Main Stakeholders & Enterprise Networks

## Requirement Class 2 – Infrastructure for Co-working & Co-development

Currently ICT is used minimally for collaboration in energy area. The needed collaboration is rendered through simple means of communication, such as telephone, fax, and email. And although greatly needed, there is no common ICT framework where the needed sharing and collaboration can be supported, i.e. a framework where joint services can be developed, provided, channeled, and offered as a complete solution to customer. For this purpose, a supportive ICT infrastructure is required to be developed and tailored to the identified needs. The infrastructure shall preferably be based on *de-facto standards*, providing a base sharing platform and tools through which the information/knowledge, as well as software systems, can be easily provided and effectively retrieved and accessed by any authorized user at any geographic location. Our analysis of identified requirements has revealed that *cloud computing* infrastructure can serve as the base communication and sharing infrastructure [12] for this domain, the *service oriented architecture* [13] can serve as the foundation for ICT developments, while *web services* can support the uniform creation, aggregation, and delivery of data/knowledge through the web to all the stakeholders.

Following are the main requirements for this needed sharing infrastructure and its support tools: *(i) Communication infrastructure shall provide: cost effective solution, preserving security/privacy, access by authorized users, ease of use by different stakeholders, timely transfer of sensored data (in pseudo real time); (ii) Interoperability infrastructure shall support: sharing/integration of information/knowledge, discovery and composition of software components in support of developing integrated business services; (iii) Multi-media based infrastructure shall support multi-user co-design.*

**Requirement Class 3 – Shared Information/Knowledge and Software System Assets (within the VBEs)**

Once operational, the energy-related VBEs gradually build up a large set of information/knowledge assets, during the operation/maintenance phase of their life cycles. we have identified ten main such entities about which their information / knowledge need to be stored and shared with the VBE, that constitute a virtual Bag Of Information/Knowledge Assets (BOIKA). These entities include: equipment, support services, stakeholders, orders history, brochures, products, historic sensored data, generated knowledge - represented as processes (e.g. best practice, lessons learned, etc.), product-based VBE network, and the VO networks. Besides the BOIKA, this domain generated innovative software systems that can be shared and integrated into more value added solutions. But for sharing purposes, innovate approaches need to be developed to formalize the syntax, semantics, and behavior of the software modules – e.g. applying formalisms such as the UML for semantics[14], WSDL for syntax [15], and constraint automata for behavior [16], in order to make them machine readable, needed for their discovery and potentially their semi-automated composition into integrated systems. Such system are in principle applied to: *(i) enhancing the abilities and performance of different equipment in the plant (e.g. advanced monitoring systems enhancing the camera equipment), and (ii) managing the operation of the plants (e.g. event handling systems).*

Further to the requirement for an information system to organize and storage these information/knowledge assets in the VBE, in order for them to be shared within the community, other mechanisms and ICT tools with user-friendly interfaces and editors are required to support: *(i) Search, retrieve, and update of assets; (ii) Protecting the privacy of community assets, while providing authorized shared access; and (iii) Developing incentives for contribution to the sharable bag of community assets and supporting their providers.*

**Requirement Class 4 – Semi-automated Learning-Based Decision Support Tools Assisting Stakeholders**

Continuous collecting, monitoring, and analysis of the vast amount of historic information and knowledge, and sensored data is required in the plants. It is necessary to build tools to assist users with their complex decision making tasks in this environment, and aiming to partially automate decision making. Stakeholders in this domain express uncertainty and need to use intuition and/or partial information when making some decisions in this domain. Simultaneously, large amount of historic data exists at plants with many relevant parameters that if processed, can assist with making accurate decisions. Development of the following two machine-learning based systems are identified as required to assist stakeholders: *(i) Semi-automated assisting tool for power plant **product configuration** – learning based techniques to gradually learn from analysis of data related to establishment of past power plants; (ii) Semi-automated assisting tool for power plant **performance enhancement & fault prognosis** – learning from data about past repair reports and discovering their relationships to past collected sensored/ monitored performance data at the plant. For instance to identify potentially malfunctioning components in the plan or* *forecasting needed repair, before the actual break down of such components; thus using the techniques for prognosis of faults at the power plant.*

# 6    Concluding Remarks

This paper presents the ICT requirements analysis results performed within the solar power plant area. It describes the main stages of solar power plants life cycle and identifies the main roles of various stakeholders in this domain. It also discusses the need to support challenging functionality in this domain, e.g. co-innovation among geographically dispersed organizations. The main identified ICT requirements are then analyzed and synthesized, which is validated by experts in the field.

**Acknowledgements.** The work on this paper is partially supported by the FP7 project GLONET, funded by the European Commission. We also thank the members of the GLONET consortium for the fruitful discussion on service enhanced products, such as solar power plants.

# References

1. Methodology Guidelines on Life Cycle Assessment of Photovoltaic Electricity,
   http://www.clca.columbia.edu/IEA_Task12_LCA_Guidelines_
   12_1_11_Latest.pdf
2. Ross, D., Schoman, K.: Structured Analysis for Requirements Definition. IEEE Transactions on Software Engineering 3(1), 6–15 (1977)
3. Addressing Solar Photovoltaic Operations and Maintanance Challenges (2010),
   http://www.smartgridnews.com/artman/uploads/1/
   1021496AddressingPVOaMChallenges7-2010_1_.pdf
4. Nuseibeh, B., Easterbrook, S.: Requirements Engineering: A Roadmap. In: Proc. Conference on the Future of Software Engineering, Ireland, pp. 279–289 (2000)
5. Afsarmanesh, H., Thamburaj, V.: Detailed Requirements for GloNet use case and Domain Glossary. EU Project GloNet (285273) - Deliverable 1.1, Global enterprise network focucing on customer-centric collaboration (2012)
6. Zave, P.: Classification of Research Efforts in Requirements Engineering. ACM Computing Surveys 29(4), 315–321 (1997)
7. Afsarmanesh, H., Camarinha-Matos, L.M., Msanjila, S.S.: Models, Methodologies, and Tools Supporting Establishment and Management of Second-Generation VBEs. IEEE Transactions on Systems, Man, and Cybernetics, Part C: Applications and Reviews 41(5), 692–710 (2011)
8. Afsarmanesh, H., Ermilova, E.: Competency modeling targeted on boosting configuration of Virtual Organizations. International Journal of Production Planning & Control, special issue on Engagement in Collaborative Networks 21(2), 103–118 (2010)
9. Msanjila, S.S., Afsarmanesh, H.: FETR: A Framework to Establish Trust Relationships among Organizations in VBEs. Journal of Intelligent Manufacturing 21(3), 251–265 (2010)

10. Afsarmanesh, H., Ermilova, E.: The Management of Ontologies in the VO Breeding Environments Domain. International Journal of Services and Operations Management - IJSOM, Special Issue on Modelling and Management of Knowledge in Collaborative Networks 6(3), 257–292 (2010)
11. Camarinha-Matos, L.M., Afsarmanesh, H.: Collaborative networks: A new scientific discipline. Intelligent Manufacturing 16, 439–452 (2005)
12. Eight ways that cloud computing will change business (2009),
    `http://www.zdnet.com/blog/hinchcliffe/`
    `eight-ways-that-cloud-computing-will-change-business/488`
13. Arbab, F.: Will the Real Service Oriented Computing Please Stand Up? In: Barbosa, L.S., Lunpe, M. (eds.) FACS 2010. LNCS, vol. 6921, pp. 277–285. Springer, Heidelberg (2012)
14. Unified Modeling Language (UML), `http://www.uml.org/`
15. Web Service Description Language (WSDL), `http://www.w3.org/TR/wsdl`
16. Constraint automata,
    `http://reo.project.cwi.nl/`
    `cgi-bin/trac.cgi/reo/wiki/ConstraintAutomata`

# Enterprise Architecture Management-Based Framework for Integration of SME into a Collaborative Network

Igor Polyantchikov[1], Anoop Bangalore Srinivasa[2], Guruprakash Veerana Naikod[2], Tarvi Tara[1], Taivo Kangilaski[1], and Eduard Shevtshenko[1]

[1] Tallinn University of Technology, Estonia
[2] Linköping University, Sweden

**Abstract.** In current research it is suggested to use the Enterprise Architecture (EA) management approach, which enables to decrease the duration and to improve the efficiency of IS integration process. Developed framework for business process implementation is adapted to the requirements of the Virtual Collaborative Network of Enterprises. The key business processes should be described internally based on common standard for all collaborative partners and it is suggested to use the ISO 9000 Quality Management standard as a base. This process is followed by analysis of inter-organizational business processes and possible process modeling solutions are also outlined in the paper. The implementation and management of collaborative business processes decrease the risks for the new potential customers and partners on the way to successful collaboration. After the collaborative business process is described it is possible to proceed with the implementation of collaborative IS.

**Keywords:** ARIS, ISO 9001, Business Process Modeling.

## 1    Introduction

Under the new business conditions and increased market competitiveness, the companies often need to integrate their business processes with other company's business processes. It is considered as a Virtual Enterprise or a temporary coalition of enterprises that co-operate to fulfill common goals. Such cooperation can be successfully supported by data received directly from Information Systems (IS) of partner enterprises, but the implementation of such systems as Enterprise Resource Planning (ERP) is time and resources consuming process. There is the need to start the implementation in the cost efficient way, due to the reason that usually small companies do not need the full functionality of ERP from the beginning.

In current research it is suggested to use the Enterprise Architecture (EA) management approach, which enables to decrease the duration and to improve the efficiency of ERP system implementation process. It is suggested that key business processes should be described internally based on common standard. The implementation and integration of enterprise IS with the collaborative partners should be started from the integration of business processes. The implementation and management of collaborative processes will decrease the risks for the new potential customers and partners on the way to successful cooperation.

L.M. Camarinha-Matos, L. Xu, and H. Afsarmanesh (Eds.): PRO-VE 2012, IFIP AICT 380, pp. 158–165, 2012.
© IFIP International Federation for Information Processing 2012

# 2    Background

In global market the standalone companies are not able to stay competitive and provide the full spectrum of products and services to satisfy today's customer requirements. To face those challenges organizations should be flexible, adaptable, and prepared for the collaboration. It could be achieved through integration of Business Processes (BP) followed by efficient implementation of ERP systems and integration into the Collaborative Network It is suggested to use ISO standards and EA management for the better integration of collaborative partners. The collaborative networks enable partners to concentrate on core professional skills and capabilities [1].

## 2.1    ISO Standards

ISO 9000 is a family of standards developed to provide framework for implementation of an effective and operative quality management system in organizations. The most recent ISO 9001: 2008 standard QMS clearly emphasizes on the process approach for realizing the quality within the organization. The advantage of process based approach is that, it helps organizations to identify the necessary process required to achieve the product or services [2]. Also, the interaction of these processes within the organization can be visualized and the expected outcome of the process can be measured against the real outcome of the process. Organizations within the collaboration network are required to have ISO 9001:2008 QMS for understanding each other's major process. However, some of the major limitations of ISO 9001: 2008 QMS are, it is time consuming process for implementation and certification, difficulties in interpreting and adapting standard [3].

## 2.2    ERP Systems

Over the past decade, several vendors have successfully offered configurable off-the-shelf software that functions as a tool for building enterprise IS-s, known as ERP system [4]. ERP systems do central work of running, tracking and reporting on business data processing. Even when data is efficiently captured and stored in ERP systems, it may remain relatively useless for reporting and decision making purposes. [5]. The ERP systems are mainly focused on transactions and insufficient for VE requirements. Despite of ERP systems popularity, the failure rate of the ERP implementation still remains high [6]. The majority of the ERP implementations made in SME's fail to deliver the expected results [7]. In PRODNET project it was proposed to use internal module and cooperation layer in order to achieve the software interoperability [8]. Moreover the important critical failure factors are poor top management support, ERP software misfit, poor knowledge transfer, poor IT infrastructure and unclear conception for the use of ERP system from the users' perspective [9]. Finally, it can be seen that the major problems which occur in the ERP projects is due to not considering the non-technical aspects like people [10].

## 2.3    Collaborative Networks and Virtual Enterprises

Collaboration starts with a shared objective. In a collaborative process, participants need to assume certain roles and responsibilities; they share information, take sequence of actions to accomplish the same goal [11]. (Highly) customized According to Stephan Alter, setting-up a collaborative network requires integration of partners on five subsequent levels, see Fig 1. [12].

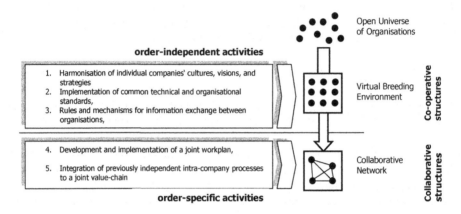

**Fig. 1.** Five steps in implementing collaborative networks [12]

## 2.4    Enterprise Architecture Management

In today's business environment organizations move towards business process oriented architectures like defined with the three-tier architecture of business process excellence [13].

When a business Process is executed by a VE parts of the decomposition of this Business Process (BP) are assigned to different enterprises, becoming a distributed business process (DBP). Several languages and formalisms have been used for BP modeling. Examples are IDEF3, MANIFOLD, UML, PIF and workflow definition languages [14]. In production area problems can appear in any of the basic elements. [15]. Still, there is a lack of adequate concepts and tools for ensuring effectiveness of integrating potential partners in collaborative networks. To improve the manufacturing activities (quality, cost, time) is necessary to find the sources of enterprise problems.

# 3    Framework for Collaborative Business Process Implementation

## 3.1    Importance of ISO Implementation for Virtual Enterprise and CN

In case of the collaborative networks faith and integrity between partners has overcome the need of quality standards. However, organizations that are collaborative network partners, have obligation to measure or control the quality of the other organization's processes [16]. ISO 9001 QMS will provide the environment for a network partners who tries to integrate their core competences of their processes for a specific period of time in order to fulfill the customer's requirements in the best possible way. Also, by combining the core competences of all the organizational members in the collaborative network, a value chain can be created where customer requirements will act as a link between core competences of each of the organizational member in the CN.

## 3.2    Framework for Inter-organizational Business Processes

Developed framework for business process integration is adapted to the requirements of Virtual Collaborative Network of Enterprises. It is suggested to start from the analysis of inter-organizational business processes, prior to implementation of IS and possible process modeling solution is outlined in the current paper, see Fig. 2.

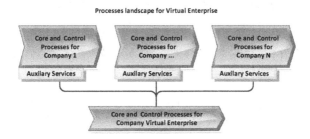

**Fig. 2.** Framework for the business processes integration within Virtual Enterprise

The prerequisite is that both the customer and vendor enterprise processes are described accordingly to the ISO 9001 recommendations, because it will guarantee the discipline, control of repeatability, traceability and conforms to the product quality. We suggest using the Event-Driven Process Chain (EPC) methodology for description of business processes and ARIS Express 2.3 software for this purpose. The partners in the CN share their core processes and selected supporting processes.

When the processes of partner enterprises are described, the structure of collaborative business process will be described in the same way. The following steps are to be performed prior to the successful implementation of collaboration, see Fig 3.

1. The business processes of the customer enterprise are described as the sequence of events and activities based on ISO 9001 standard.
2. The business processes of the vendor enterprise are described based on the same standard as in the customer enterprise.
3. The audit of vendor enterprise business processes is performed by customer followed by recommendations of what should be improved before the cooperation.
4. The collaborative business process is described. During this process the inputs and outputs of collaborative process are clarified, which is used as input for the integration of enterprises.

5. The plan for the collaboration establishment is developed. During this step the list of activities to be performed prior to establishment of the cooperation is created.
6. The required changes are implemented in the IS of customer and vendor enterprise.

**Fig. 3.** Six steps of successful implementation of collaboration

### 3.3     Framework for the Forming of Virtual Enterprise

Virtual Enterprise (VE) is usually formed based on existing requirements. In current paper we developed different topologies of VE see Fig.4. In First Use Case the VE is formed between the Customers and Collaborative Network which include Manuf.1 and 2 partners; In second Use Case the VE is formed between the Manufactures and Collaborative network which include Customer 1 and 2; In third Use Case the VE is formed between the Customers 1 and 2, Manuf. 2 and CN which include Manuf.1.

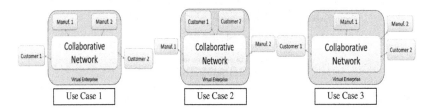

**Fig. 4.** Virtual Enterprise forming Use Cases

### 3.4     Data Exchange

After the data required for the collaboration is known it is analyzed from which informational sources it could be received. One way to exchange data is import-export through Microsoft Excel or point to point integration see Fig 5.

Next option is CN solution when both customers and manufacturers have their own ERP systems. In order to exchange and transform the data the mapping of data within existing functionality of ERP system is done. Usually no changes are required from the customer side in this case. Most of the today's ERP can share data through Web Services. With proper authentication and authorization, external systems like Collaborative Network, can read and write data on pages and call code units as XML Web services. If the ERP system is not implemented the analysis will heal to agree on priorities of modules implementation. Last option is to use the Web module to provide the EPR system service for the CN participant enterprise [17].

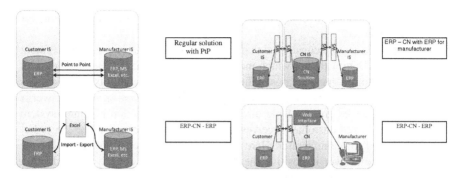

**Fig. 5.** Integration of Customer and Vendor business

# 4    Case Study APL Production-Densel Baltic OÜ

In current case study we consider how EA management based framework can be used for the integration of business processes of collaborative partners, see Fig 6.

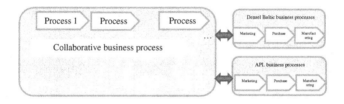

**Fig. 6.** Integration of Customer and Vendor business processes

In order to prepare for collaborative solution implementation the Marketing, Purchase and Manufacturing business processes of Densel Baltic and APL are described in ARIS express based on ISO 9001 standard. The major activities of marketing process are discussion and order confirmation. The confirmation of order in marketing process is recorded in the web of collaborative network. The next process 'purchasing' is initiated; the main activities of this process are placing purchase order and receiving it in to the warehouse. The quality of the goods received in this process is ensured by the collaborative partner. This is seen as advantage of collaborative network, where it is easier to find the trusted partner.

Finally, the manufacturing process is initiated by the last activity of purchase when it is updated in the web of collaborative network. Main activities of this process includes, getting drawings from web of CN, planning the production and execution. The execution process is updated on the web of CN. Hence, it is easier for the customer to check the status of the order.

The next step on the way to collaboration is to design the future CN system. In designed CN web environment we are going to use the basic ERP functionality for small manufacturers that enables the integration of several web based applications for production management.

In current case study it is considered that the customer APL has a signed agreement with manufacturer Densel Baltic, which includes the fixed price list. Before the order is placed the customer has the possibility to check the availability of resources directly from collaborative network, see Fig 7. Collaborative network will discover if manufacturing resources are available directly from the production planning system of Densel Baltic. When customer receives this information he will place the order, which is forwarded to Manufacturer. Here we have also additional possibility for the credit check. If the answer is positive the order is forwarded directly to production planning operation, if not the corresponding answer will be received by customer.

Current solution will enhance the collaborative work and it will be also possible easily to add more customers and manufactures in future.

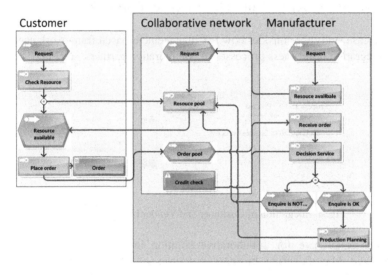

**Fig. 7.** The integration of collaborative network business processes with manufacturer and customer

# 5     Conclusion

Developed framework for business process implementation is adapted to the requirements of Virtual Collaborative Network of Enterprises. It is suggested to start from the analysis of inter-organizational business processes, prior to implementation of IS which is followed by collaborative business process development. Consensus within the project team has to be established while deciding what should and should not be included in process documentation. Finally, project team has to be realistic in deciding resource implication and training activities for staff.

After the collaborative business process is described the framework suggests using the existing legacy software for communication. The data exchange can be done from

Web Server of main enterprise or the Web Server of subcontractor can be used instead. This research paper is intended for use by partner enterprises that are looking forward to enhancement of collaborative business processes.

**Acknowledgments.** Authors of this paper would like to acknowledge financial funding from Estonian Ministry of Education and Research for targeted financing scheme SF0140113Bs08, Grant ETF9460 and DoRa.

# References

1. Patrick, S., Falk, G., Marcus, S.: Partner profiling to support the initiation of collaborative networks. EJOV 20 (2007)
2. Carmignani, G.: Process-based management: A structured approach to provide the best answers to the ISO 9001 requirements. Business Process Management Journal 14, 803–812 (2008)
3. Gamboa, A.J., Melão, N.F.: The impacts and success factors of ISO 9001 in education: Experiences from Portuguese vocational schools. International Journal of Quality & Reliability Management 29, 384–401 (2012)
4. Zheng, L., Dölken, P.: Strategic production networks. Springer (2002)
5. http://www2.enel.ucalgary.ca/People/far/
6. Chen, C.C., Law, C., Yang, S.C.: Managing ERP implementation failure: a project management perspective. IEEE Transactions on Engineering Management 56(1), 157–170 (2009)
7. Wang, E.T.G., et al.: Improving enterprise resource planning (ERP) fit to organizational process through knowledge transfer. International Journal of Information Management 27(3), 200–212 (2007)
8. Msanjila, S., Afsarmanesh, H.: Network-Centric collaboration and Supporting Fireworks. IFIP, vol. 224, pp. 161–172 (2006)
9. Ganesh, L., Arpita, M.: Critical Failure Factors in Enterprise Resource Planning Implementation at Indian SMEs. Asian J. Managm Research 1(1), 44–57 (2010)
10. Botta-Genoulaz, V., Millet, P.: An investigation into the use of ERP systems in the service sector. Intern. J. of Production Economics 99(1-2), 202–221 (2006)
11. Camarinha-Matos, L.M., Afsarmanesh, H.: Collaborative Networked Organizations – A research agenda foremerging business models, A framework for management of virtual organization breeding environments. Kluwer Academic Publishers (2004)
12. Alter, S.: Information Systems – The Foundations of e-Business. Prentice Hall Publishing, Upper Saddle River (2001)
13. Jost, W., Scheer, A.-W.: Business process management: a core task for any company organization. In: Business Process Excellence- ARIS in Practice, Berlin, pp. 33–43 (2002)
14. Camarinha-Matos, L.M., Pantoja-Lima, C.: Supporting Business Process Management and Coordination in a Virtual Enterprise. In: Advances in Networked Enterprises Virtual Organizations, Balanced Automation, and Systems Integration (2000) ISBN 0-7923-7958-6
15. Branzei, O., Vertinsky, I.: Strategic pathways to product innovation capabilities in SMEs. Journal of Business Venturing 21(1), 75–105 (2006)
16. Polyantchikov, I., Shevtshenko, E.: Collaborative framework for Virtual organization. In: Proceedings of 7th International DAAAM Baltic Conference "INDUSTRIAL ENGINEERING", Tallinn, Estonia, April 22-24 (2010)
17. http://docs.oracle.com/cd/B31017_01/core.1013/b28938/intro.htm

# Towards CPS Based Aircraft MRO

Kai Mertins, Thomas Knothe, and Pavel Gocev

Fraunhofer IPK, Pascalstr. 8-9, 10587 Berlin, Germany
{kai.mertins,thomas.knothe,pavel.gocev}@ipk.fraunhofer.de

**Abstract.** Cyber Physical Systems (CPS) receiving more and more industrial reality. In this paper a concept for the application of CPS for Aircraft maintenance repair and overhaul, sketched with airline partners, will be given. Based on industrial needs and requirements as well as the current state of the art the concept is describing a direct assignment of MRO-tasks to mechanic, tools and spare parts in order improve aircraft availability. The planning will be supported through simulation based generation of contextual MRO-tasks.

**Keywords:** Cyber Physical Systems for MRO, modelling and simulation, MRO Planning and Control.

## 1 Introduction

**Availability and reliability** of aircrafts are essential factors in the global competition of the airlines. Beside the operative execution of Maintenance, Repair and Overhaul (MRO) the planning and control of the MRO processes impacts the aircraft availability too. This emerges directly from the configuration complexities of IT-Systems, variety of tools and spare parts as well as numerous locations with their qualified specialists. At present the planning and control processes are carried out sequentially including unnecessary loops, redundancies and interfaces using different media and various structures from the MRO demand until the aircraft serviceable. The complexity is even higher due to the mixture of the planned and unforeseen MRO work. The improvement potential is estimated on 1 to 3% of availability increase yielding an amount of two-digit EUR Millions per mid-sized airline.

There is a necessity for a novel solution that will eliminate **current problems** emerging from the above described situation:

- Changes of flight plans or unforeseen technical problems extend the Aircraft on Ground (AOG) time due to unavailable MRO-Resources.
- MRO-Process landscape causes long through put time on operational and administrative level.
- Diagnosis systems do not consider the all necessary and available data for prediction of possible malfunctions and failures.
- Large C- and D-Checks are carried out as separate projects, but not broken into small work packages (Single Running Tasks) that can be executed during the daily checks of the aircrafts.

L.M. Camarinha-Matos, L. Xu, and H. Afsarmanesh (Eds.): PRO-VE 2012, IFIP AICT 380, pp. 166–173, 2012.
© IFIP International Federation for Information Processing 2012

- The response data and information from the MRO-Processes are not promptly used by the suppliers, either for design and development of components, nor for the modernisation and further improvement.

In order to answer on these challenges in this paper a solution is proposed based on deployment of Cyber Physical Systems (CPS) for context-sensitive planning, control and realisation of aircraft MRO-Processes. CPS is defined by Broy (1) as a narrow connection of embedded systems with the global digital networks with the goal of monitoring and control of physical occurrences using sensors and actuators as well as communication equipment. The goal of the below described solution concept is to reduce the complexity in the execution of MRO-Processes and to shorten administrative process parts. The aircrafts will carry CPS-Components that will be networked in one Platform and will be able to take decisions based on the particular situation. Therewith the aircrafts will issue an MRO-Order directly to the MRO-Operation under consideration of the available time, resources and spare parts. The solution will generate Single Running Task for MRO that will be released in a flexible way reducing the through put time and AOG time, increasing the availability of the aircrafts. The paper will give an overview of the challenges and will describe the concept for a solution as well as the necessary steps towards the solution realisation in this complex environment.

## 2    Industrial Challenges, Requirements and Needs

The improvement potential as mentioned in chapter 1 is currently limited by the complexity of planning and control of frequent as well as unscheduled MRO events for different stations in accordance to the individual work demand for each aircraft. Cost intensive spare parts, specific tools and equipment as well as special qualified personal are only available in selected stations. For unforeseen events expensive maintenance flights are required or deletions have to be taken. In order to prevent flight deletions reserve aircrafts have to been foreseen. As consequence the utilization of the entire fleet will be reducing. Unsatisfied customers and additional effort for aircraft operations are additional consequences.

TOP Level Business Requirements for Aircraft MRO-Provider:

- Realization of direct and consequently free of loop processes for maintenance planning and control. This would reduce the current process duration drastically.
- Improvement of reactivity of the MRO-provider regarding sudden required maintenance and repair activities. It has to be implemented that mechanic-resources, spare parts, tools at locations will be provided in accordance to flight-plan, diagnostic data by optimal use of maintenance slots.
- Optimize the implementation of the concept of "Single Running Tasks". This means, that a small maintenance step of complex C- and D-Checks can be

applied during regularly daily line checks and enable the reduction of the normally long duration of these C- and D-Checks. Currently this improvement cannot be applied, because of the complexity of planning and control procedures.

- Correct estimation of "out of order" cases and integration into the maintenance planning and control. Through this the number of sudden cases will be reduced, which cannot be planned in beforehand. The time of "Aircraft on Ground" has to be reduced and the availability improved.
- For Aircraft and Aircraft Equipment Provider:
  - A fast feedback of specific flight and maintenance data for improved support of aircraft modernisation, which is performed sometimes annually. This leads to enhanced agility and customer orientation.
  - Direct data integration of maintenance related feedback from aircraft operations and maintenance into the IT-Systems for aircraft development and modernisation.

Similar requirements and needs are relevant in other industries like rail.

## 3     State of the Art

The demand on solution can be deducted from the viewpoint of the MRO-Service provider and from aircraft producers. Usually the process of MRO planning and control in air traffic is supported by specific IT-Applications as TRAX, or similar (2). These systems consider diagnosis data as well as operative aircraft information. Typical for these solutions is a redundancy of acquisition of data and information, data management. Moreover there are information gaps along the information process chain that impact the realization of the process in negative manner. Furthermore the long planning chain from MRO demand to the MRO operation by the mechanic requires too much time and implies a lot of inefficient loops (Fig. 1).

Related to the planning and control Sampigethaya (3) describes on a conceptual level the functionality of a direct communication between aircrafts and one Cyber Physical System (CPS). Thereby a focus is put on security of networks and communication infrastructures and a distributed planning and control as well as integration of CPS in the MRO-Processes is not mentioned at all.

The interface between the diagnosis and the predicted MRO is considered by Lee (4) already for more than 10 years but the suggested solution cannot answer on the challenges to cope with the specific dependencies within the MRO in the context of complex circumstances as for example the holistic air traffic systems.

The aircraft producer Boeing developed in the last years the so called "Boeing e-Enabled Solution" on a base of a reference architecture which should enable a strategic connection and integration of business processes, human resources, aircrafts, information and knowledge. The optimized and transformed processes through direct Ordering of Mechanic personnel and their response for the accomplished work are not foreseen with this solution and therewith there is no simplification of the MRO planning and control processes. For the feedback aim between MRO and the producer there are various additional systems which besides the partial data integration are dependent on manual efforts (4).

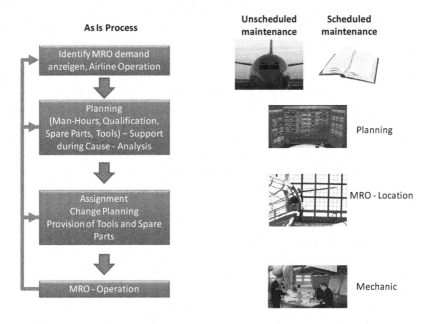

**Fig. 1.** AS-IS Process of Aircraft Maintenance Planning and Control

In the domain of services exist also reference models (6), like those which facilitate simulation of planning and control processes for MRO (7). The specific situation and the complexity of aircraft maintenance is only limited considered in the models. Methods for handling the complexity in integrated models are not inside these reference models. A suitable method would be a contextual integration of product and process models (8). The market is also supported by Integrated Product-Service Systems (IPS Systems) through contracting and material ordering up to response on carried out MRO work (9). In this case the MRO orders and responses need manual inputs of the MRO order progress status. IPS-Systems generate MRO-plans on the base of the available information and under deployment of rigid and predefined rules. These rules are usually operational charts, procedural conditions and are not flexible and not context sensitive. Routings are usually created manually and can be hardly adapted to the emerging situation. All these constrains and restrains the overall agility of the realization of MRO processes. The results from the research project SoPro (10; 11) is worth to contribute to the intelligent planning and control of MRO activities through self-organized production. In the SoPro project small computational unit eGrains have been developed which can be assembled on the MRO assets, transportation means, processing resources, tools and fixtures and that are equipped with agent based software and radio communication. Therewith through combination of negotiation of the agents the best optimal routing can be suggested and carried out, so a technical foundation for support of MRO processes is given. The German national project ARAMiS (12) is developing a concept for multiprocessors which offer new functionalities in the air traffic. Although there is no direct relation between to MRO, these processors can be utilized into CPS due to their efficiency and stability in order to enable direct assignment of the mechanical personnel by the system.

In general, the technological base for CPS extended aircraft avionic and MRO processes is available but there are numerous constraints which have to be adopted, integrated in the practical MRO environment. The mechanisms for system-integrated assignment, calculation, planning and control of MRO orders are still in an early phase and not applicable yet. The conditions for overall and comprehensive deployment of integrated MRO systems are still not available. The feedback from the MRO domain to the product design with the purpose of product improvement occurs at present only when corrective action and measures have to be taken or based on statistic evaluation. A direct context-sensitive feedback to the suppliers does not exist and therewith the improvement of processes and products are cost and effort-intensive.

## 4     Solution Concept

The above described challenges were addressed by Fraunhofer IPK considering an aircraft MRO-process chain form aircraft component supplier, aircraft OEM up to airline and MRO service provider. The solution is related to a context-sensitive planning, control and realization of aircraft MRO-Processes based on deployment of Cyber Physical Systems (CPS) with the goal to reduce the complexity in the execution of MRO-Processes and to shorten the administrative part. The aircrafts and their components will carry CPS-Components that will be networked in one solution platform and will be able to take decisions based on the particular situation, and consequently will issue an MRO-Order directly to the MRO-Operation under consideration of the available time, resources and spare parts. The solution will generate Single Running Task for MRO that will be released in a flexible way reducing the through put time and Aircraft-on-Ground (AOG) time, increasing the availability of the aircrafts. The goal is to deploy and utilize the solution of Cyber-Physical Systems within the MRO-processes. Moreover the depending processes like product design, production planning and control, as well as ergonomics will be considered.

Due to the complexity of the whole concept, the solution will be developed on the basis of one or more use cases that will prepare the challenges and requirements for a solution from the industrial and business point of view. This will support the formal description of the necessary objects within the MRO domain, as well as their transformations along the MRO-Processes. In particularly the specifics of processes, resources, technologies, products and practices of MRO will be considered and their nature and features will be analyzed. The relations and dependencies between the objects (aircrafts, components and MRO-resources) within the MRO-processes will be described in one extended process model that will keep all relevant aspects and the respective interdependencies.

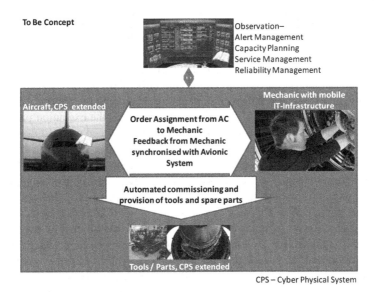

**Fig. 2.** TO-BE Concept of direct task assignment from Aircraft to mechanic, tools and parts

The solution will utilize the definition and description of the MRO-processes and activities that have to be performed to each aircraft component according to the defined plan or checks. This will include a list of activities to be carried out and necessary resources for each activity. The challenge is to cope with the real situation at the airlines. On one side the aircrafts are changing their geographical position with the time and on the other side the MRO-resources are spatially scattered in more locations. As not every MRO-location offers every MRO-service the solution will offer an execution of the MRO-processes (checks) in one optimal way. The aircrafts and their components that are a subject of MRO will be integrated into the MRO-planning and control system in the way that they can be pro-active and react on the environment. This will be enabled through equipment the aircraft components with CPS-objects like sensors, actuators, RFID, respectively "small computers" that are able not only to read and write data and information but to process them and pro-actively to cooperate in one CPS based MRO system. In that way each aircraft component will carry with itself the information about the MRO-demand and necessary MRO-processes to be carried out. Moreover the aircraft component will be "aware" about the required MRO-resources that will be capable to perform the MRO-process. In regard to the current location of the aircraft and considering the flight plan each aircraft or component can match the MRO-process to be realized with the available resources at the same location. Matching the all criteria relevant for performing the MRO-process the aircraft or the component will be able to take a decision, to select a single running task to be realized, to generate a MRO-order for selected MRO-resource and to assign the MRO-work to the resources. All that will happen locally via direct communication between the aircraft or its component and the MRO-location and its resources.

The personnel responsible for accomplishing the MRO-work will get the work instruction and all necessary information including the history values about the aircraft or component directly from the CPS-object carried by the aircraft or component. In a similar way the realized MRO-work and the findings as well as the performed changes and the information about the built spare parts can be sent to the CPS-object directly to the aircraft or component and therewith the history values will be updated in a very direct way of communication between the execution participant of the MRO-work and the aircraft or component that experienced the MRO-process.

The impact of the proposed solution can be multiple regarding the better performance of the MRO-Processes, improved utilization and sustainability of the systems, bringing together various information sources for better planning and control. Moreover this will foster the further development of the CPS-components and open the perspectives for new applications of CPS in other domains. One example is the railway sector with similar business conditions to synchronize overnight short maintenance, regular long lasting maintenance projects, timetable oriented operation and many maintenance locations as well as expensive equipment and parts. The new paradigm will drive the R&D community for new solutions that will improve the efficiency of the systems and will enable an accomplishment of complex challenges with the final goal of improvement of the economic well-being.

## 5    Outlook and Further Steps

Besides the opportunities of the described concept, the longterm aircraft product live cycle will be a barrier of the implementation of CPS based aircraft and CPS based aircraft maintenance. Nevertheless there are two midterm steps to go on the modernization way:

- Start with the implementation according to software updates for the aircraft avionic, because the infrastructure (e.g. wireless LAN on airports) and the technology (e.g. Boeing avionic) is currently available.
- Enhance the flight bag system (tablet PC for pilots, contain routes, maps and calculators, e.g. for fuel consumption estimation) with reading interface to aircraft data bus system. A communication system to the maintenance planning and control integrated on the flight bag system can support the direct processes from aircraft to maintenance staff. The improvement of the flight bag system is independent from aircraft design changes; the interface to the aircraft data bus already exists.
- Implement auto-id systems for expensive parts and tool as well as insure the data integration into maintenance planning and control system.

The solution approach affects a number of standards, especially aircraft architecture like ATA42 chapter „Aviation Industry Standards for Digital Information Security", MRO-Standards, regarding MRO-operations from EASA, Part-145, Part-66, Part-M. In the near future these standards need to be checked and if necessary revised in order to allow CPS based aircraft maintenance. E.g. the part-145 is currently very much element oriented and on a status like ISO 9001 was in 1994. Here a process orientation is required, because the interaction of most of the elements of part-145 (e.g. staff qualification and repair procedure) have to be defined and implemented in their process context.

# References

1. Broy, M.: Cyber-Physical Systems: Innovation durch softwareintensive eingebettete Systeme. In: Manfred Broy, C. (ed.). Springer, Acatech Diskutiert (2010)
2. TRAX, http://www.trax.aero/index_main.htm
3. Sampigethaya, E.A., Sampigethaya, K., Poovendran, R., Shetty, S., Davis, T., Royalty, C.: Future e-enabled aircraft communications and security: The next twenty years and beyond. In: Proceedings of the IEEE, Special issue on Aerospace Communications and Networking in the Next Two Decades (December 2011) (accepted)
4. Lee, E.: Intelligent Maintenance Systems: The Next Five Years and Beyond - Transforming Condition-based Maintenance to Productivity and Service Innovation. Asset Management and Maintenance Journal, 6–13 (July 2010)
5. Aircraft Commerce. Integrating maintenance & engineering IT systems with the OEMs. Aircraft Commerce (36), 25-34 (2004)
6. Fettke, P., Loos, P., Zwicker, J.: Business Process Reference Models: Survey and Classification. In: Kindler, E., Nüttgens, M. (Hrsg.) Business Process Reference Models. Proceedings of the Workshop on Business Process Reference Models (BPRM 2005), Satellite Workshop of the Third International Conference on Business Process Management (BPM), pp. 1–15 (2005)
7. Knothe, T.: Referenzmodell Auftragsdurchlauf für Dienstleistung und Verwaltung. In: Wenzel, S. (Hrsg.) Referenzmodelle für die Simulation in Produktion und Logistik, SCS Verlag, Delft (2000)
8. Girod, M., Schramm, A., Schultz, R., Wintrich, N.: Integrierte Produkt- und Prozessmodellierung. In: ZWF Zeitschrift für wirtschaftlichen Fabrikbetrieb, pp. 454–457 (June 2011)
9. MacInnes, R.L., Pearce, S.L.: Strategic MRO–A Roadmap for Transforming Assets into Competitive Advantages, pp. 253–278. Productivity Press (2003)
10. Hohwieler, E.: Die Fabrik der Zukunft steuert sich selbst / The factory of the future will steer itself. Industrial Insight, pp. 11–15 (2010)
11. Mertins, K., Rabe, M., Schallock, B.: Innovative production control based on decentralized intelligence. In: Marco, T., et al. (Hrsg.) Proceedings International Conference on Advanced Production Management Systems, Poliscript (2010)
12. ARAMIS, http://www.kit.edu/downloads/pi/PI_2011_179_Neue_Computersys teme_fuer_Auto_Bahn_und_Flugzeuge.pdf

# 7

## Cloud-Based Support

# A Cloud Based Data Integration Framework

Nan Jiang[1], Lai Xu[1], Paul de Vrieze[1], Mian-Guan Lim[2], and Oscar Jarabo[1]

[1] Software Systems Research Centre, School of Design, Engineering and Computing,
Bournemouth University, United Kingdom
{njiang,lxu,pdvrieze}@bournemouth.ac.uk,
ojarabo@gmail.com
[2] Future Computing Group, School of Computing
University of Kent, United Kingdom
m.g.lim@kent.ac.uk

**Abstract.** Virtual enterprise (VE) relies on resource sharing and collaboration across geographically dispersed and dynamically allied businesses in order to better respond to market opportunities. It is generally considered that effective data integration and management is crucial to realise the value of VE. This paper describes a cloud-based data integration framework that can be used for supporting VE to discover, explore and respond more emerging business opportunities that require instant and easy resource access and flexible on-demand development in a customer-centric approach. Motivated by a case study discussing power incident management in the Spanish Electricity System, an effective on-demand application is also implemented to demonstrate how to use this framework to solve real world problems.

**Keywords:** Cloud computing, Situational application, Mashup, Virtual enterprise, Data as a Service.

## 1 Introduction

Virtual enterprise (VE) is a temporarily and dynamically formed alliance of businesses where these organisations collaborate and share their skills, core-competency and resources in order to better respond to market opportunities [1]. It is commonly understood that the success of VE relies on the flexibility and agility of resource sharing across its member organisations in the virtual network (VN) [2]. Therefore, the key to actualise this lies in the effective data integration and management of each autonomous organisation in the network. VE is intended to meet a market opportunity that cannot normally be answered by individual organisations. However, the current financial and economic situation creates a highly competitive market condition where market opportunities are often unpredictable, short-lived and fast-changing in a wide social context which calls for the development and fast adoption of new information and communication technology (ICT) [8]. Thus, new challenges of maintaining sustained competencies have been brought to enterprises and VE [7]. In this paper, we propose a cloud based data integration framework which allows VE to better respond these market opportunities and customer needs that

L.M. Camarinha-Matos, L. Xu, and H. Afsarmanesh (Eds.): PRO-VE 2012, IFIP AICT 380, pp. 177–185, 2012.
© IFIP International Federation for Information Processing 2012

require instant and easy access to resources with fast and flexible development in a customer-centric approach. Motivated by a case study focusing on a real world problem, the implementation of this framework is also discussed where an effective on-demand application is actualised to tackle real-time power incident management in the Spanish Electricity System.

First, a motivational case is described in the Section 2. Next, the requirements of implementation are analysed in Section 3. A proposed cloud-base framework is then described in Section 4 followed by the presentation of application in Section 5. Last, the conclusion and the future work are drawn.

## 2   A Motivational Case Study

A national electricity system is formed with a high-voltage electric power transmission network and grid connecting power stations and substations to transport electricity from where it is generated to where it is needed in the country. In an industrial perspective, there are three key stakeholder areas in the system: generators, distributors and suppliers [3]. When an incident occurs in the system, effective communications from these stakeholders to clients become crucial. However, this is not normally well managed for various reasons which results in negative impacts on all stakeholders in the system and the community.

### 2.1   The Spanish Electricity System and Key Stakeholders

As shown in Fig. 1, Act 9(1) in Law 17/2007 defines six key stakeholder areas in the nation's electricity system: generators, distributors, system operator, market operator, suppliers and end users [4]. In practice, a utility company commonly plays multiple roles in the system. For example, Endesa (E), Iberdrola (I) and Gas Natural Fenosa (GNF) are the three major energy companies in Spain. They are not only the main suppliers but also the principle generators as well as distributors. Red Electrica De España (REE) is the system operator and carrier for operating the nation's power transmission system and electricity grid and Compañía Operadora del Mercado Español de Electricidad (OMEL) is the market operator dealing with electricity wholesales. End users include industrial users and domestic users where the former is often connected to the high voltage network directly.

The electricity transmission starts from power stations where energy is generated from various sources. The production is later transformed to a high-voltage and transported to REE, the system operator, through the transmission network. After that, it is transmitted from power substations, through an output line substation, to a transforming centre and is finally transformed to the needed voltage level for different consumption needs. Since electricity cannot be stored in large quantities, the whole process must work continuously without any interruptions. Moreover, it also needs to consider balancing the system to make sure that demand is met by supply. Consider Spain is the fourth biggest wind power producer. With intermittent generation, it is becoming even more difficult.

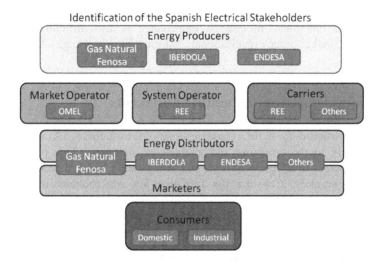

**Fig. 1.** The Spanish Electricity System in a market perspective

## 2.2    Incidents and the Situational Environment

The whole system is complex. Thus, several incidents can occur during the process to transport electricity from energy production plants to customers. These incidents will affect energy supply, lead to power cut and eventually generate negative impact to some stakeholders and the community. A 2007 blackout on 23rd July 2007 in Spain affecting 323,337 customers living in Barcelona area for more than 56 hours is seen as a prime example which resulted in huge fines, severe punishments and supplier switch [5].

Incidents have to be coordinated at a system level, typically involves the system operator REE and all energy distributors in the system where REE works as a coordinator to provide knowledge of problem to all distributing companies. This is because distributing companies may use each other's substations to provide services to their own clients in others' serviced areas and regions. Industrial users who are usually connected to the high voltage are also informed for the incidents by their suppliers bound to an "interruptibility" contract (ITC 2370/2007) but domestic customers are often ignored. As a result, call centres could be overwhelmed with an unprecedented number of calls in the event of an incident, leading to customer dissatisfaction. Therefore, following a customer-centric approach, all customers, rather than only the important ones, must be actively informed with the incidents and progress. However, energy suppliers show little interest in doing this due to technical difficulties and cost issues.

A misunderstanding is that informing clients should not be a difficult task for suppliers who also work as distributors in the system. The problem is that energy distribution and supply are operated as separate businesses due to strongly different market focus so the inter-connection between them does not exist. In addition, for a business where scattered information systems are normally used for different operations and functions, information interchange is also difficult. These issues subsequently make inter-organisational information exchange become more complicated.

## 3   Business Opportunities and Requirements

Business opportunities lie in the enterprise situational awareness (SA) which relies on a fast response to the emerging and/or changing situations. This requires instant access to resources of different systems and owners and rapid and flexible customer-oriented development. Consider the fact that key stakeholders in the Spanish Electricity System use different information systems for supporting their operations and activities. The following requirements for implementing an effective incident management application have been formed:

1.  A list of affected streets should be obtained from a distributor.
2.  A list of the affected customers should be obtained from suppliers.
3.  Customers must be effectively informed with the problem, the forecast and the progress through available communication channels provided by both suppliers and distributor.

In addition, the key requirement of situational driven enterprise applications is that their initial development until in a working stage is reasonably simple and cheap, which means that little time must be spent in the development [7].

## 4   Cloud-Based Data Integration Framework

As shown in Fig. 2, a cloud based data integration framework using a DaaS (Data as a service) model [9][10][11] is proposed. From the bottom up, it includes three different parts. First, *enterprise data*, which is supplied by different VE partners, is wrapped from the owners' different information systems and served as services embedded into an open/private cloud. Second, *a cloud infrastructure* is adopted to include all different functional services which can be later used to process data or can be composed for different data processes. Third, *mashups* are used to specify situational demands in the real business environment. Implemented mashups are also served as services within the cloud infrastructure.

*First Part: Data Wrapped as Services:* An organisation's master data are normally stored in different information systems and business applications used by the organisation. Such data are often shared and exchanged intra-organisationally to support the organisation's business functions and activities. With a number of appropriate processes such as data integration and MDM, some data can be extracted as individual services directly and made available in the virtual network (e.g., *Service A, B* and *C*). Since data access is controlled through the data services, it tends to improve data quality in an end-user perspective.

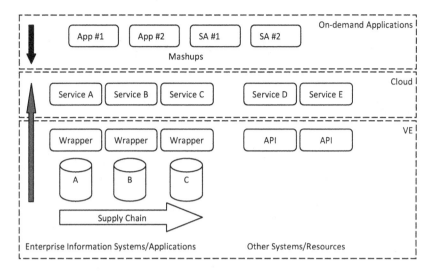

**Fig. 2.** The cloud-based data integration framework for VE

Sometimes the data services can be provided in a more convenient way with the integration of third-party applications. For example, Web mapping applications (e.g., Google Maps [6]) have been widely used by organisations to provide location-based services. Therefore, organisations may also consider creating their service in an open architecture through the support of third-party APIs (e.g., *Service D* and *Service E*) with business mashups.

*Second Part: Cloud as Service Infrastructure:* Cloud is considered as the service hosting infrastructure for VN to address two common limitations of VE: maintainability and flexibility [1]. First, a virtual network (VN) is a temporary collaborative network where participating organisations are dynamically allied in a customer-centric approach. This brings challenges to the long-term maintenance of the network as participants can stay, join or leave the network at any time. The loose-coupling feature of cloud makes changing the presentation layer of the virtual network is very cost-effective and much more feasible. Second, although VE is highly flexible as it optimises supply chain in a wider context, it aims to provide value-added services over existing services/activities rather than creating new services. This means that a traditional VE is not highly flexible to respond emerging business opportunities that require instant access of different resources. A cloud empowered VN can provide good agility due to the simplicity of the data access without the need for extensive knowledge of the underlying data. Additionally, cloud also makes it possible to merge VEs to enter a new market as long as data access can be maintained at the presentation layer of the new cloud.

*Third Part: Mashups as Interface:* Mashups are used to manage inter-organisational data communications/activities. With common data access protocols provided by mashups, organisations and customers can access all available services on the cloud and create applications on-demand through the mix-n-match of different services that represent different business opportunities [12]. Moreover, mashups remove the internal boundaries in a dynamic supply chain formed in the VE so that any member organisation in the virtual network can access any available services from anywhere and form its own customised applications.

## 5   Implementation

In this section, we demonstrate how the proposed framework can facilitate on-demand applications, which actualises effective incident management for the Spanish Electricity System in the case described in the Section 3. In Section 5.1 we explain different data sources which related to the applications. Final implementation of the applications can be found from Section 5.2.

### 5.1   Data Sources

A distributor typically operates two distinct information systems, named SGC (*Sistema de Gestión y Control*) and BDI (*Base de datos integrada*). SGC is a management and control system containing a list of transformer centres (CT) where each associates with customers and a supplier. This allows the distributor to charge a supplier directly for the energy consumed by its customers and in turn allows a supplier to charge their customers with this information. BDI is an integrated database containing substation detail where each substation includes a list of positions inside a substation in which a CT list is attached to each position. As shown in Fig. 3, a substation-customer service can be created and published through data extraction and integration from SGC and BDI.

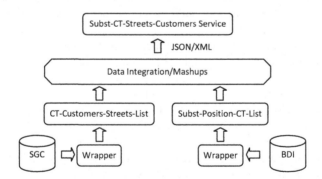

**Fig. 3.** Distributor's service integration for substation-customer

Incidents are normally discovered through a distributor's SCADA system which can also be extracted as a situation service trigger as shown in Fig. 4.

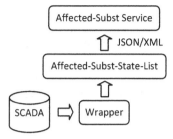

**Fig. 4.** Distributor's service integration for substation incident triggers

Supplier stores information about their customers and marketing offers etc in its CRM, which can be extracted to form a customer notification service in conjunction with supplier's existing communication channels as shown in Fig. 5.

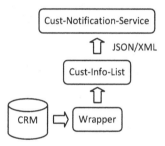

**Fig. 5.** Supplier's customer notification service

## 5.2    On-Demand Application

Situational application [1]can be created by using mashups to mix-n-match the above services to notify customers and report progress when an incident occurs (Fig. 6).

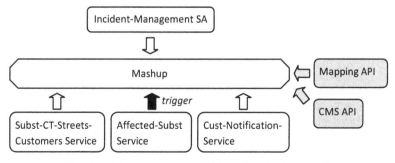

**Fig. 6.** Incident management SA based on the framework

---

[1] A working demo of the SA using this framework has been developed through the use of a public service cloud hosting and IBM Mashup Center 2.0.

A better application can be further actualised in conjunction with third-party services. For example, a CMS API can be integrated to provide incident information on all suppliers' websites and a mapping API can be integrated to provide interactive location-based views of incidents and progress. Additionally, the situational application can extend its communication channels through the integration of other social Web service APIs (e.g., twitter/facebook updates).

## 6   Conclusion

The core concept of the framework is that it uses DaaSs and mashups to help VE member organisations respond to immediate customer needs that require instant and easy resource access and rapid and flexible on-demand development. The case study has demonstrated how the framework facilitates in solving a real world problem effectively. Whilst it is based on the Spanish Electricity System but it can also be applied to other electrical systems especially for the European Union countries in compliance with Act 17/2007. Moreover, the situational application shown in the case study focuses on power incident management which can also be extended to other emerging application areas and industrial sectors where immediate communications to clients are needed.

**Acknowledgments.** This work is made possible by the support of the Natural Science Foundation of China (NSFC) under Grant No.61150110484, ESSENTIAL: Enterprise Service deSign based on ExistiNg software Architectural knowLedge.

## References

1. Martinez, M.T., Fouletier, P., Park, K.H., Favrel, J.: Virtual Enterprise – Organisation, Evolution and Control. Intern. Journal of Production Economics 74(1-3), 225–238 (2001)
2. Camarinha-Matos, L.M., Afsarmanesh, H.: A Comprehensive Modeling Framework for Collaborative Networked Organizations. The Journal of Intelligent Manufacturing 18(5), 527–615 (2007)
3. National Grid, http://www.nationalgrid.com
4. Red Eléctrica de España, http://www.ree.es
5. Barcelona blackout may last weeks for 80,000, http://www.msnbc.msn.com/id/19921787/ns/world_news-europe/t/barcelona-blackout-may-last-weeks
6. Google Maps API, https://developers.google.com/maps
7. de Vrieze, P.T., Xu, L., Xie, L.: Situational Enterprise Services. In: Encyclopedia of E-Business Development and Management in the Digital Economy, pp. 892–890. Idea Group Publishing, Hershey (2010)
8. O'Reilly, C.A., Harreld, J.B., Tushman, M.L.: Organizational ambidexterity: IBM and Emerging Business Opportunities. California Management Review 51(4), 75–99 (2009)
9. Mateljan, V., Cisic, D., Ogrizovic, D.: Cloud Database-as-a-Service (DaaS) – ROI. In: 33rd International Convention on MIPRO, pp. 1185–1188. IEEE Press, New York (2010)

10. Wang, L., von Laszewski, G., Younge, A., He, X., Kunze, M., Tao, J., Cheng, F.: Cloud Computing: a Perspective Study. New Generation Computing 28(2), 137–146 (2010)
11. Youseff, L., Butrico, M., Da Silva, D.: Towards a Unified Ontology of Cloud Computing. In: Grid Computing Environments Workshop (2008)
12. de Vrieze, P.T., Xu, L., Bouguettaya, A., Yang, J., Chen, J.: Building Enterprise Mashups. Future Generation Computer Systems 27(5), 637–642 (2011)

# SMEs' Perception of Cloud Computing: Potential and Security

Reza Sahandi[1], Adel Alkhalil[2], and Justice Opara-Martins[2]

[1] Head of Creative Technology
[2] School of Design, Engineering & Computing,
Bournemouth University, Bournemouth, UK
{rsahandi,aalkhalil}@bournemouth.ac.uk

**Abstract.** Cloud computing is a new paradigm for emerging technology in the computing and IT industries. Cloud computing offers a new pathway for business agility and supports a faster time to market by offering ready-to-consume cloud-based IT services. SMEs can wisely take advantage of the cloud computing services, without the need for upfront costs. The perception of cloud computing from an SME stance is explored. The potential and concerns surrounding the adoption of cloud computing are discussed. A survey of SMEs conducted in the UK by the authors shows SMEs interests in exploiting the cloud computing services, but there are still some concerns with regards to security and vendor lock-in. This could have affected the speed of cloud computing being adopted.

**Keywords:** Cloud computing security, cloud computing services, SMEs.

## 1 Introduction

The dynamic force in the contemporary business market is rapidly eroding competitiveness, thereby causing products and skills to become obsolete [1]. Organisations are under pressure to find and implement new strategic ideas at an even faster pace to gain the competitive edge over their rivals within the global market. In order to increase competitiveness, organisations need to rationalise output to reduce costs, enhance process innovation and incorporate new technologies. Organisations in search of this competitive edge are continually putting pressure on their IT departments to provide new solutions that are deemed to be more flexible, efficient and cost-effective, enabling even faster time to market. This process is often referred to as realising "business agility". A flexible IT infrastructure can remove some of the barriers to global competition and allow smaller businesses to be efficient, competitive and also provide a degree of flexibility. Cloud computing has the potential to play a major role in addressing inefficiencies and make a fundamental contribution to the growth and competitiveness of organisations.

Small and Medium-sized Enterprises (SMEs) play a vital role in the European economy by fostering competitiveness and employment. SMEs are often confronted

L.M. Camarinha-Matos, L. Xu, and H. Afsarmanesh (Eds.): PRO-VE 2012, IFIP AICT 380, pp. 186–195, 2012.
© IFIP International Federation for Information Processing 2012

with difficulties in obtaining capital for the early start-up phases due to their small size [2] which may restrict their access to new technologies or innovations. By adopting cloud computing service models, SMEs will be able to avoid large up-front costs on IT resources for their production needs and business model of innovation.

Much of the research on cloud computing has concentrated on two broad issues: i) business agility and ii) catalysts for more innovation. However, difficulties still exist in deciding on the approach for implementing cloud computing service offerings for SMEs. To assist SMEs to adopt cloud computing services, this study aims to answer the research question: "How do SMEs perceive 'Cloud Computing'?". The findings of this research are expected to assist smaller companies in their adoption of cloud computing services; they may also inform service providers with respect to end-users' concerns. A survey of SMEs was conducted to explore the views and concerns they had for the adoption of cloud computing and results analysed (see section 3). This is followed by some discussion on how to rectify the shortcomings and concerns, particularly in the areas of security and vendor lock-in.

The paper is organized as follows. Section 2 presents the concept of cloud computing in a wider context. Section 3 presents a survey that explored the views and concerns of cloud computing services. Section 4 discusses the main issues hindering cloud computing adoption. The conclusions drawn from the research and survey analysis are presented in Section 5.

## 2      The Concept of Cloud Computing

Cloud computing is an all-embracing and rapidly evolving concept; hence the understanding of cloud computing by SMEs can assist in their approaches for cloud computing services utilisation [3]. The idea behind cloud computing is based on a set of many pre-existing and well researched concepts such as distributed and grid computing and virtualization. Although many of the concepts do not appear to be new, the real innovation of cloud computing lies in the way it provides computing services to customers [4]. The National Institute of Standards and Technology (NIST) has provided a commonly agreed definition of cloud computing that is "a model for enabling convenient, on-demand network access to a shared pool of configurable computing resources that can be rapidly provisioned and released with minimal management effort or service provider interaction" [5].

However, organisations and enterprises are often being confronted by conflicting and exaggerated claims of how cloud computing will dramatically transform their industries. Therefore, it should be mentioned that the marketing hype and meagre analyses from many vendors, IT analysts and users have an impact on the obscurity of the cloud capability and incumbent issues. Nevertheless according to the survey conducted in this paper (see section 3), just over half of the surveyed SMEs (51.5%) claimed to know what cloud computing is, whereas 25.1% were not sure about its term and 23.4% have no knowledge about it. A survey conducted by ACCA [6] also paints a similar picture with just over 50% of respondents saying that SMEs have very limited or no understanding of cloud computing.

In spite of the ambiguity of understanding of the cloud computing concept, industry research giants including Gartner, Forrester and other industry research analysts predicted that a substantial number of the world's top enterprises would have migrated their IT needs to the cloud offerings by 2011 [7]. Moreover, a recent study conducted by Craig shows that there is an increase of 14% of SMEs in understanding cloud computing [8].

# 3    Cloud Computing from SMEs Perspective (The Survey)

The survey attempted to explore the requirements of SMEs and their concerns in respect of cloud computing services. The study investigated the driving factors that encouraged SMEs to move to cloud computing services or hindering their adoption. The methodology employed was based on a quantitative online survey questionnaire approach. The target population consisted of SMEs situated within the United Kingdom. Participants varied between IT decision-makers and managers within their respective business enterprise. The group incorporated participants from organisations of different sizes and from diverse industry sectors.    300 SMEs were invited to participate in the survey. A total of 169 SMEs responded by completing the questionnaire. This gives a satisfactory response rate of 56% for this type of survey where response rates below 15% become questionable [9]. Table 1 provides a socio-demographic profile of the organisations and participates in the survey. The sample was slightly dominated by SMEs sized between 51 to 250 employees.

**Table 1.** Socio-Demographic Profile of Participant Organisation

| Organisation Size | Percentage |
|---|---|
| 1 – 24 | 20.5% |
| 25 – 50 | 19.3% |
| 51 – 250 | 41.0% |
| More than 250 | 19.3% |
| Total: | 100% |
| Organization Sector | Percentage |
| Manufacturing and industrial market | 15.6% |
| Financial services | 3.0% |
| Public sector & healthcare | 11.6% |
| Business sector | 22.3% |
| ICT services | 15.0% |
| Trading sector | 7.8% |
| Other | 24.7% |
| Total: | 100% |

## 3.1    Why Should SMEs Adopt Cloud Computing Services?

Cloud computing offers a new pathway to business agility and supports a faster time to market by offering ready-to-consume cloud enabled resources such as IT infrastructure as a service, software platforms, and business applications. These services can all be accessed on-demand and provide support to new business requirement far faster than acquiring, installing, configuring and operating IT resources in house [10]. Clearly, this is an attractive proposition to the organisations where upfront spending for Information and Communication Technology (ICT) is an issue, especially SMEs.

Business agility is the key to commercial success and the current economic downturn has heightened its importance for SMEs. To survive, SMEs need to decrease time-to-market. Therefore, if "the cloud" is used appropriately within an overall IT strategy, it can provide a real competitive advantage, improve business performance and control the cost of IT resources for the organisation [11]. Cloud computing can also provide the IT resources required for a scalable business growth. The cloud is capable of providing a degree of flexibility for IT resources which would allow organisations to adapt to changing demands of their business needs. In addition, the cloud comes with high speed of implementation and ease of upgrading. Cloud services would also eliminate the need for expensive equipments to be located at the company's site. Furthermore, cloud computing can enable SMEs to focus on innovation and creation of new business, thereby enhancing productivity without requiring frequent updates of IT resources, servers and software licenses.

In order to observe the motivations of SMEs for adopting cloud-based services, the survey raised the question of "what were the reasons behind using cloud computing?". Figure 1 shows the analysis of the reasons that the SMEs provided.

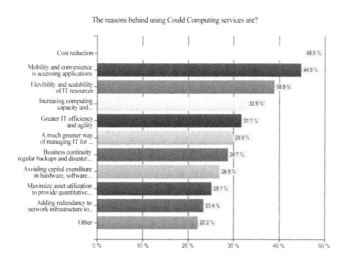

**Fig. 1.** Drivers for Cloud Computing Adoption by UK SMEs

As can be seen in Figure 1, cost reduction (45.5%), mobility and convenience in accessing applications (44.9%) appear to be the key reasons behind SMEs adopting cloud computing services. This signifies that SMEs find cloud computing a strategic idea for reducing the cost of IT infrastructures and operation. In agreement with this finding, a recent study conducted by Craig [8] concluded that cost reduction is still the top priority for SMEs. The ability for cloud users gaining convenient access from anywhere and at any time were also found to be a key reason for adopting cloud computing. This indicates that SMEs are interested in access to applications and data from anywhere, on-demand, through cloud computing. Therefore, the cloud is remarkably an ideal IT solution for businesses whose employees require on-demand remote access to tools and data.

SMEs find ubiquity and flexibility in the cloud fascinating too (38.9%). This indicates the need for innovative solutions that would enable SMEs to gain the competitive advantage over their rivals. Increasing computing capacity and providing greater IT efficiency were also found to be important reasons for using Cloud computing services (32.9%) and (31.7%) respectively.

## 3.2     Concerns for Adopting Cloud Computing

Despite the enormous advantages that the cloud can offer, cloud computing adoption has been at a slower rate from what had been expected [12]. In order to determine which issues mostly affect the adoption of cloud computing, the study further explored SMEs' concerns of cloud-based services. Figure 2 illustrates issues raised by participants hindering the cloud computing adoption rate. Security and vender lock-in were raised by SMEs as their major concerns. Moreover, SMEs have also shown concern of other aspects regarding the adoption of cloud computing. These concerns were not found as significant as security and vender lock-in; therefore they are not included in the discussion.

Figure 2 shows that 54.6% (the second largest percentage response to any question asked in the research) of the surveyed SMEs indicated data protection and privacy as the number one reason for not considering cloud-based IT as a service. In contrast to the traditional provision of onsite IT resources, the multi-tenant nature of cloud computing usually raises the question in respect of privacy, confidentiality and data integrity. Cloud computing presents its own set of security issues coupled with the risk and threats inherent in traditional IT computing. The fact that consumers can tap into cloud services using Web browsers, shows the benefits of mobility and convenience on the one hand, but on the other, it has raised issues concerning data privacy and security.

Moreover, about half of the surveyed SMEs consider vender lock-in as a major concern for adopting cloud computing. Cloud computing users are concerned about losing control of their data that could be locked-in by a cloud provider. Although the cloud providers implement up-to-time and a secure IT infrastructure; consumers continue suffering from the loss of control and lack of trust problems [13]. To further substantiate on this matter in agreement with StarUK [14], "for many people, the issue is one of control: many IT managers believe that if something is not under their direct oversight, then they cannot know if it is secure until it has been compromised: which is sometimes the hallmark of a put upon, reactive, service-based culture". The subsequent section provides further considerations with respect to these key issues.

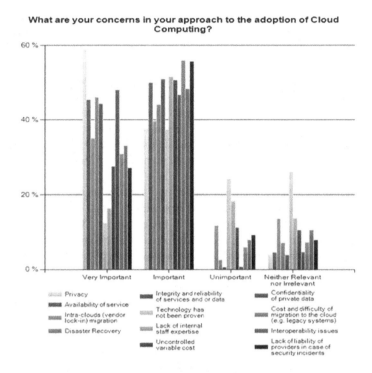

**Fig. 2.** Barriers to Cloud Computing Adoption in UK

# 4    Discussion of the Main Issues

## 4.1    Security and Data Privacy

Security and data privacy are often presented as the key risks when outsourcing IT services that may include critical data. These risks have made data privacy and security the main issues delaying cloud computing adoption [15]. The fact that before data can get into the cloud, it has to progress outside a company's firewall via an access network and can be prone to attacks. For example, the most common way of accessing the cloud is through a web browser. Therefore, cloud services may share much vulnerability as any website, such as SQL injection or cross-site scripting (XSS) [16]. The cloud also relies on virtual machines (VMs), which mean any compromises in the set up of the software used could cause unauthorised access to sensitive data.

Normally, cloud computing providers have multiple data centres at different geographical locations in order to optimally serve consumers' needs around the world. In most cloud service scenarios, consumers have no idea of where there data is stored. Therefore, legal and regulatory issues arise which require careful consideration because the physical location of data centres determines the set of laws that can govern the management of data.

Cloud computing comprises of different deployment models, nevertheless each service comes with its own security issues. Thus, to guarantee the security of corporate data in the cloud is difficult, if not impossible [17]. In Infrastructure as a Service (IaaS) model, for example, the security responsibility of the underlying infrastructure and abstraction layers belong to the cloud service provider, while the remainder of the stack is the consumer's responsibility. Organisations, before moving applications outside their corporate firewalls, should be aware of the data intrusion risks associated with such an environment. IaaS cloud models are prone to attacks like XML Signature Element Wrapping [18] – this is a well-known attack on protocols using XML Signature such as SOAP (that stands for Simple Object Access Protocol) messages. These protocols are used to provide authentication for messaging through the web.

With Platform as a Service (PaaS) model, the security of the platform used for development is the service provider's responsibility, but the security of the applications developed is the responsibility of the consumers. Concerns about cloud service integrity and binding issues with PaaS' cloud models should be given further consideration. PaaS models are prone to cloud malware injection attacks and metadata spoofing attack as described by Jensen [19].

In Software-as-a-Service (SaaS) model, the service provider is responsible for not only providing physical and environmental security capabilities, but also the security control for the infrastructure, applications and data. According to a Forrester research, security concerns are the most commonly cited reason why enterprises are not interested in SaaS [20]. A major concern of SaaS is unauthorised access due to data being transferred to a remote server thought the internet. This might allow adversaries to obtain passwords, inspect data, and modify or damage the data. This would be more harmful in case of unauthorised access to sensitive information such as payments details and information on human resources. Denial of service attacks and network failure present the availability concern of SaaS.

There are a number of security measures which can be developed and implemented to tackle the above security issues. For example, implementing a robust authentication mechanism, encrypted protocols, secure backup applications and secure physical resources could improve security. Access control can be enhanced by incorporating security measures to the network layers. Web Services Security (WSS) is a security technique that can be incorporated to SOAP messages to assure the integrity and confidentiality by signing and encrypting their context [21]. The confidentiality and integrity can also be improved by incorporating cryptographic protocols such as (TLS) Transport Layer Security, and (SSL) Secure Socket Layer to the transport layer. Moreover, it is highly recommended that cloud providers protect the integrity of consumers' data by complying with relevant standards including Payment Card Industry – Data Security Standards [22]. In [23] it is also recommended to adopt the standards for identifying and accessing management such as SPML, SAML, OAuth, and XACML. These standards could increase the security of the identity federation among different cloud platforms. Securing Virtual Machines (VMs) is critically important to avoid unauthorised access, so it is vital to consider security practices that may include enabling perimeter defence on VMs. Other security practises may be considered such as implementing file integrity checks and maintaining backups. On the other hand, SMEs should ensure the security aspects of their side that include firewall configurations, reliable and high bandwidth internet connections, and upgrading their software.

### 4.2    Vendor Lock-In

The lack of standards in cloud computing may raise interoperability and manageability issues inside and between cloud providers, with possible economic impacts. Interoperability is concerned with the migration and integration of applications and data between different vendor's clouds. Whereas standardisation strives to support applications by different service vendors to interoperate with one another, exchange traffic and cooperatively interact with data, as well as protocols, for joint coordination and control [24].

In the absence of standardisation, SMEs willing to outsource and combine the range of services from different cloud providers to achieve maximum efficiency, will experience difficulty when trying to get their in-house (legacy) systems to interact with the cloud providers system. Likewise, the lack of standardization may also bring disadvantages, when migration, integration, or exchanges of resources are required. The main negative aspect is the necessity of factoring applications to comply with other cloud Application Programming Interfaces (APIs), which can possibly lead to higher costs, delays and risks, thus opposing agility, efficiency, and low costs [25]. In the aforementioned, reconfiguration of systems and applications to achieve interoperability are time consuming and thus, require a considerable amount of expertise, which could be challenging for SMEs. Further, interoperability and portability will give rise to standard reusability, which in turn will lead to faster cloud deployment [26].

## 5    Conclusion

The concept of cloud computing was briefly discussed. A survey of 300 SMEs showed their motivations and concerns for adopting cloud computing services. The results of the survey show that SMEs are highly interested in cloud computing enabling them to reduce costs, improve accessibility, flexibility and scalability. These benefits are seen by SMEs as key driving factors in adopting cloud computing services. However, the rapid increase in corporate data, placed in the cloud, has raised issues concerning security, vendor lock-in, and complications with data privacy and data protection. Consequently, this resulted in the slow growth of cloud computing adoption.

In order to convince more SMEs to migrate their systems to the cloud, these issues need to be addressed. The privacy challenge for cloud-based software architects, demands the design of a service were security risks are reduced, whilst ensuring legal compliance. In other words, safety of data should be placed at the front and in the centre of the design process of any cloud service. Security can be enhanced by developing existing security measures such as perimeter defence on VMs, data encryption, backups, incorporating cryptographic protocols such as TLS, SSL, and WSS. Furthermore, implementing a standardised framework for cloud services will support seamless cloud service integration between different vendor platforms. This would allow cloud users to switch from one provider to another.

Cloud computing is still a new technological venture for SMEs, but it takes good business sense and appropriate steps to fully reap its benefits. Whenever security, data privacy, interpretability, and portability standards ameliorate, cloud computing adoption will proliferate.

# References

1. Pauly, M.: T-Systems Cloud-Based Solutions for Business Applications. In: Buyya, R., Broberg, J., Goscinski, A. (eds.) Cloud Computing: Principles and Paradigms. John Wiley & Sons, Inc., Hoboken (2011)
2. European Commission: The New SME Definition: User Guide and Model Declaration (2005),
   http://ec.europa.eu/enterprise/policies/sme/files/
   sme_definition/sme_user_guide_en.pdf (accessed on May 1, 2005)
3. David, W.C.: Cloud computing Key Initiative Overview (2010),
   http://www.gartner.com/it/initiatives/pdf/
   KeyInitiativeOverview_CloudComputing.pdf (accessed on May 1, 2010)
4. Leimeister, S., Christoph, R., Markus, B., Helmut, K.: The Business Perspective of Cloud Computing: Actors, Roles and Value Networks. In: European Conference on Information Systems (2010)
5. Mell,P., Grance,T.: The NIST Definition of Cloud Computing (2011),
   http://csrc.nist.gov/publications/nistpubs/
   800-145/SP800-145.pdf (accessed on May 1, 2012)
6. Association of Chartered Certified Accountants, ACCA: A Digital agenda for European SMEs (2011),
   http://www.acca.co.uk/pubs/general/activities/library/
   small_business/sb_pubs/pol-afb-adaf.pdf (accessed on May 1, 2011)
7. Mohan, T.S.: Migrating into a Cloud, in Cloud Computing: Principles and Paradigms. In: Buyya, R., Broberg, J., Goscinski, A. (eds.) John Wiley& Sons, Inc., Hoboken (2011)
8. Craig, D.: How Are SMBs Viewing the Cloud? (2012),
   http://www.constructioncloudcomputing.com/2012/02/16/
   how-are-smbs-viewing-the-cloud/ (accessed on May 1, 2012)
9. Perry, C., Cavaye, A., Coote, L.: Technical and social bonds within business-to-business relationships. Journal of Business & Industrial Marketing 17(1), 75–88 (2002)
10. Lozano, B., Marks, A.E.: Executive's Guide to Cloud Computing. John Wiley & Sons (2010)
11. Brookbanks, M.: More Clouds Coming. IT Now Magazine, 16–19 (2010)
12. GoGrid : Cloud computing adoption slower than expected (2012),
    http://www.gogrid.com/news/2012/02/22/cloud-computing-
    adoption-slower-than-expected (accessed on May 1, 2012)

13. Almorsy, M., Grundy, J., Ibrahim, A.: Collaboration-Based Cloud Computing Security Management Framework. In: IEEE 4th International Conference on Cloud Computing (2011)

14. Star UK: Can Cloud Computing give you the freedom to be more strategic? – UK businesses' attitudes to Cloud Computing revealed. White paper (2009), http://www.montal.com/newsletters/Jan10/STAR_041209.pdf (accessed on May 1, 2012)

15. Sabahi, F.: Cloud Computing Security Threats and Responses (2011), http://ieeexplore.ieee.org/stamp/stamp.jsp?arnumber=06014715 (accessed on May 1, 2012)

16. Devine, S.D.: Flying too Close to the Sun Can be a Risky Business. Business Technology E-Magazine (2011), http://www.lyonsdown.co.uk/publications/2011/infosec.pdf (accessed on May 1, 2012)

17. Kandukuri, B.R., Paturi, V.R., Rakshit, A.: Cloud Security Issues. In: IEEE International Conference on Services Computing, pp. 517–520 (2009)

18. McIntosh, M., Austel, P.: XML Signature Element Wrapping Attacks and Countermeasures. In: SWS 2005: Preceedings of the 2005 Workshop on Secure Web Services, pp. 20–27. ACM Press (2005)

19. Jensen, M., Gruschka, N., Iacono, L.: On Technical Security Issues in Cloud Computing. In: IEEE International Conference on Cloud Computing, pp. 109–116 (2009)

20. Forrester Research: Top Corporate Software Priority Is Modernizing Legacy Applications. Press release (2009)

21. National institute of Standards and technology: Guide to secure web services (2007), http://csrc.nist.gov/publications/nistpubs/800-95/ SP800-95.pdf (accessed on May 1, 2012)

22. Jansen, W., Grance, T.: Guidelines on Security and Privacy in Public Cloud Computing. NIST Draft Special Publication 800-144 (2011)

23. Al Morsy, M., Grundy, J., Müller, I.: An Analysis of The Cloud Computing Security Problem. In: Proceedings of APSEC 2010 Cloud Workshop, Sydney, Australia (2010)

24. Yoo, C.S.: Cloud Computing: Architectural and Policy Implications. Prepared for the October 22, 2010 Conference on Antitrust and Dynamics of Competition in "New Economy" Industries (2010), http://techpolicyinstitute.org/files/yoo%20architectural_and _policy_implications.pdf (accessed on May 1, 2012)

25. Machado,G.S., Hausheer,D., Stiller,B.: Considerations on the Interoperability of and between Cloud Computing Standards (2009), http://citeseerx.ist.psu.edu/viewdoc/ summary?doi=10.1.1.155.51 (accessed on May 1, 2012)

26. Craig, D.: Constructing cloud computing (2010), http://www.constructioncloudcomputing.com/2010/08/25/ can-we-talk-interoperability-and-portability-hold-the-keys/ (accessed on May 1, 2012)

# Software Co-development in the Era of Cloud Application Platforms and Ecosystems: The Case of CAST

Dimitrios Kourtesis, Konstantinos Bratanis, Dimitris Bibikas, and Iraklis Paraskakis

South-East European Research Centre,
International Faculty, The University of Sheffield
Thessaloniki, Greece
{dkourtesis,kobratanis,dbibikas,iparaskakis}@seerc.org

**Abstract.** Interest around cloud computing has been growing quite rapidly during the past few years, and the model of cloud computing is evolving into an indispensable component of innovation strategy across the software industry. We are witnessing a paradigm shift that will have a profound impact on software platforms and ecosystems and will give rise to new forms of software co-development. In this paper we make a first attempt to discuss the evolution of the relationship between software co-development, platforms and ecosystems in the era of cloud computing, and the role of cloud application platforms. We present the case of a cloud application platform designed to support advanced forms of software co-development, and to foster the emergence of a novel type of software ecosystem. As demonstrated, cloud application platforms can be designed in a way that facilitates the emergence of new forms of hierarchical cloud-centric software ecosystems.

**Keywords:** Co-development, Software Ecosystems, Cloud Application Platforms, Platform as a Service; PaaS.

## 1    Introduction

Software co-development represents a form of collaborative product development [1, 2] that has been gaining more and more attention. For many years, vendors have been practicing the development of commercial software products in relative isolation from others in the same industry. At some point however, they started realising the benefits of partnerships beyond their obvious role for software distribution, and started opening their products to co-development. Large-scale software products (e.g. operating systems) started to transform from single-vendor projects into platforms for co-development and software ecosystems [3, 4].

As a term, software co-development is used rather loosely to refer to several different models of collaboration in creating software—ranging from limited outsourcing partnerships to large-scale networks for open innovation. In this paper we appeal to a notion that is closer to the latter, and examine how co-development as a practice is affected by the advent of cloud application platforms.

L.M. Camarinha-Matos, L. Xu, and H. Afsarmanesh (Eds.): PRO-VE 2012, IFIP AICT 380, pp. 196–204, 2012.
© IFIP International Federation for Information Processing 2012

The contribution of this paper is twofold. First, we discuss the concept of software co-development in relation to software platforms and software ecosystems, and provide our view on how the relationship between these concepts evolves in the era of cloud computing, giving contemporary examples of major cloud-platform-centric environments for software co-development. Second, we present the case of a cloud application platform that was designed with the objective of supporting advanced forms of software co-development [5]. We place emphasis on the features of the platform that are particularly aimed at making this possible, and discuss implications with respect to the future of co-development on cloud application platforms.

## 2    Software Co-development and Software Ecosystems

In the past, software products were largely created by vendors in relative isolation from their wider community [6]. At some point, however, software companies started becoming aware of the benefits of external collaborations and networked operations [7]. Software vendors realised that by bringing more partners into their development process (and by being involved into others' supply chains), they could gain increased functionality and keep customers loyal with less capital investments [8]. The previously "fixed" supply chain model of collaboration in the software industry started giving way to a fuzzy partnership approach, where virtually infinite numbers of partners could add value upon a central product [9]. Large-scale software products started to transform from single-vendor projects into platforms for co-development and software ecosystems.

In this new context, the platform provides a central coordination mechanism for software development. Irrespective of the degree of separation between the platform core and each member of the network, there can be many advantages for everyone involved: decreased software and business development costs, quicker time-to-market, improved focus, reduced complexity, and of course, economic profit [6]. In some cases a software platform is open for all interested partners to commit their resources - as in free and open source projects like Apache, Linux, etc. In other cases, a platform is closed and owned by a central partner who controls access levels and/or contributions by third parties (e.g. Facebook/Apps, iPhone/Appstore, etc). As long as there can be benefits to the network [7], individual developers and companies will continue to incorporate their contributions to the platform core, making them available for further use by other parties. Open collaboration between companies in the software industry is evolving into a standard practice.

## 3    Software Co-development in the Context of Cloud Computing

The models of Software as a Service (SaaS), Platform as a Service (PaaS), and Infrastructure as a Service (IaaS), represent new ways of thinking about the delivery of computing capabilities within the emerging paradigm of cloud computing. In all its different forms, cloud computing has been gaining more and more attention during the past few years, and is rapidly evolving into an indispensable component of innovation strategy across the software industry. We are witnessing a paradigm shift that will have a profound impact on software platforms and ecosystems as we know them, and will give rise to new forms of software co-development. A predominantly important trend is the rise of cloud application platforms.

### 3.1    Cloud Application Platforms

Cloud application platforms offer a combination of some form of computing infrastructure that is made accessible over the internet, and a set of tools and services which allow developers to create applications and have them deployed and executed over that infrastructure. They are often referred to as *aPaaS* (application-Platform-as-a-Service) [12], so as to avoid confusion with other types of PaaS offerings which have different objectives, such as *iPaaS* (integration-Platform-as-a-Service) or *bPaaS* (business-process-Platform-as-a-Service) [11].

For companies interested in creating new applications and making them commercially available in the form of SaaS offerings, adopting a cloud application platform carries many benefits. Development of applications against a platform of this kind allows a significant portion of the effort traditionally required for engineering, distributing and maintaining web applications to be shifted to the provider of the platform. This in turn allows application developers to concentrate on what they know best, i.e. on their domain-specific problems and solutions, rather than the setup and operation of a supporting infrastructure.

Seen from a platform provider's perspective the value proposition of the aPaaS model is different. Most importantly, it allows software vendors to realise new models of partnership and co-development while leveraging their potentially existing partner networks. In many cases, the goal for vendors engaging in this model is to transform one of their core products into a platform that fosters the emergence of a software ecosystem. In other cases the goal is to create an ecosystem for software co-development that doesn't revolve around a central product or application domain.

Results from recent surveys suggest that the market around this cloud computing model is still immature and fast-changing [12]. However, it is anticipated that the vendors who will succeed in creating ecosystems with a critical mass of developers will also attract a large community of users, particularly those who, in addition to richness of software features, also seek safety in numbers [11].

### 3.2    Cloud-Platform-Centric Software Ecosystems

In the following paragraphs we provide an overview of some examples of software ecosystems centred on the platform offerings of major cloud service providers.

Force.com is a cloud application platform offered by Salesforce.com – presently the leading SaaS vendor in the domain of Customer Relationship Management (CRM). Force.com supports the development of custom applications by providing a comprehensive stack of database, integration, logic and user interface capabilities on top of the core technology used in the CRM environment of Salesforce.com. The custom applications can be used either independently or as extensions of the core

CRM. A developer can publish their application to the AppExchange application marketplace, allowing end-users to find it and buy it. The form of co-development enabled by Force.com is the creation of custom applications by third-parties which introduce new features to the platform provider's core CRM product.

In 2010 Salesforce.com acquired Heroku, the dominant cloud platform for developing applications in the Ruby programming language. Except for Ruby, Heroku supports several other technologies such as Java, Python, and Scala. Heroku offers an add-on provider program for third-party Independent Software Vendors (ISVs). Third-party ISVs can use a self-service portal and development kit in order to offer their services as add-ons to the Heroku platform. As such, the Heroku platform is co-developed by being continuously extended with more features (services) that other developers can use for creating new applications on the platform.

Google Apps is another popular software ecosystem. Google Apps provide APIs to ease the integration between third-party applications with the core Google Apps (e.g., Google Docs, Google Calendar and others). The third-party applications can be either provisioned by a third-party infrastructure, or developed against the Google Apps Engine. The Google Apps Engine is a cloud platform for developing applications in various programming languages, such as Java, Python and Go. Third-party ISVs can make their applications available in the Google Apps ecosystem by publishing them to the Google Apps Marketplace. In short, the form of co-development is allowing third-party ISVs to build solutions that interact with one or more of Google's core products, and are mostly hosted and executing outside Google.

Windows Azure is a cloud application platform for developing software applications using the .NET Framework. An integral part of the platform is the Windows Azure Marketplace. Windows Azure offers a third-party ISVs scheme which aims to help ISVs bring SaaS solutions to the market faster. Publishing their SaaS applications and datasets in the marketplace allows ISVs to reach a global market of customers using an integrated environment that provides comprehensive management of their services (e.g., self-service on-boarding, creation of terms of use and trial offers). In this co-development model, third-party ISVs partner-up with the Windows Azure platform to co-develop new SaaS products.

## 4    The CAST Platform

The CAST project was a collaborative EU-supported research effort that begun in 2009 and finished in 2011[1]. It was set up to investigate the engineering challenges associated with realising a cloud application platform that enables the development and delivery of on-demand (SaaS) business applications. One of the central requirements for the CAST platform's design was to ensure that the way in which development and delivery will be carried out will promote positive network effects [14] and will foster the emergence of a software ecosystem around the platform.

---

[1] CAST: Enabling Customisation of SaaS Applications by Third parties (www.cast-project.eu)

Instrumental in achieving this design goal was to employ an appropriate model of software co-development that maximises collaboration and reuse of resources.

## 4.1    CAST Concepts and Terminology

Before discussing the model of software co-development employed in the CAST platform, it is necessary to introduce some key concepts and terminology.

**CAST Platform Solutions.** A *solution* is defined as a complete enterprise software application that targets a specific application domain or market niche (e.g. customer relationship management for French insurance companies, or event management for Greek exhibition centres). It is deployed on the CAST platform and made available to end-users as on-demand software (SaaS). A solution is not manifest as executable artefacts – there are no code binaries in a solution, just metadata. This is because a solution is effectively a logical bundle of finer-grained components which provide the actual functionality.

**CAST Platform Apps.** The finer-grained components that solutions are composed of are called *apps*. Each app within a solution provides a highly-specialized function. An app can be data-centric or process-centric. A data-centric app provides the implementation for creating, viewing, editing and storing a custom-built data object (for example, an employee's record, or a project's timesheet). A process-driven app provides the implementation for supporting an end-user in carrying out a sequence of tasks (for instance, supporting a sales employee for mass-importing customer addresses from a spreadsheet file). Apps can (albeit are not required to) affect all of the platform's runtime layers. That is, an app may define new data object types on the data layer, new business operations on the business logic layer, and new user interface elements on the presentation layer. An app's behaviour can be extended by creating so called app extensions which interface with the app at designated extension points. An app extension is therefore not a standalone component, but functions as a plug-in to one or more apps.

**External Services.** Apps and app extensions may rely on external services to deliver part of their functionality. By external services we refer to systems that are deployed and executing outside the platform and are accessible over the Web, through a programmatic interface (i.e. REST and SOAP Web services). The ability to use Web services enables the developers of solutions to leverage already existing (and tried) solutions for particular specialized tasks within their apps. For example, an app or app extension for contact management could invoke an external service to perform email address validation for a particular contact, or to obtain stock quote information for a contact's company.

## 4.2    Development and Delivery on the CAST Platform

The platform constructs presented above represent a generic model of abstraction that can be applied to a wide range of cloud application platforms. But how do these constructs map to specific roles in a cloud platform ecosystem? Who creates and who extends those constructs in the context of co-development?

Figure 1 illustrates the mapping between platform constructs and the different ecosystem roles through an abstract example.

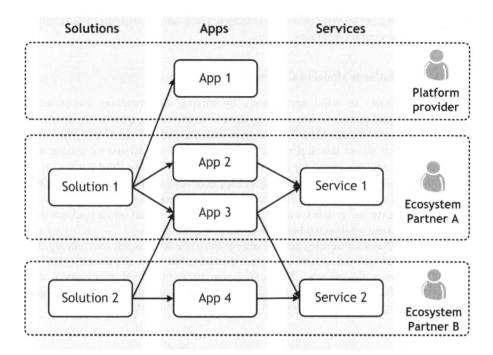

**Fig. 1.** Example mapping of platform constructs to ecosystem roles

Apps and app extensions may be built both by the platform provider and by third-parties (ecosystem partners A and B). In order to help developers to bootstrap their work, the platform provider may build a number of apps that target functionality that is rather common in business applications, such as document management (App 1). Any partner that needs to use a built-in app is allowed to configure it for the needs of a particular solution (Solution 1). Alternatively, apps and app extensions can be developed from the ground-up by an ecosystem partner (Apps 2, 3, 4). Optionally, those apps can depend on external services (Apps 2, 3, 4) which may not necessarily be owned by the same ecosystem partner (App 3, Service 2). In any case, as soon as a third-party app, app extension, or external service is added to the platform it can be made available for other partners to reuse in their own works (opting-out of reuse could theoretically be offered as an option).

Composing built-in and third-party apps (and app extensions) into solutions is the responsibility of ecosystem partners (Solution 1, 2). In creating a solution package ecosystem partners are also specifying how the appearance and behaviour of the included apps should be customised (at run-time) for the particular solution at hand.

This is done by defining solution-specific constraints on the apps. Since an app can be part of more than one solution (App 3), different constraints can be active for a particular app depending on the execution context. A typical constraint is a domain-specific restriction of the allowed range of values for some field (which may be unbounded in the general data model for an app). For example, data validation rules for fields such as a postal code or a vehicle license plate can be customized differently depending on the country a solution targets.

## 4.3    CAST Platform Model of Co-development

Enabling developers to build applications by mixing and matching components contributed by third parties within an ecosystem is an increasing trend in the space of cloud application platforms [15]. A distinctive characteristic of the CAST platform, however, is that it allows developers to create applications (solutions) by reusing not only low-level services offered by the provider of the platform or third-parties, as is usually the case, but also entire applications (apps) developed and deployed by third-parties. The third-party apps to be reused can be customised to fit new needs, integrated with external systems via Web services, and combined into a package that is resold as a distinct on-demand business application (solution).

This model allows co-development relationships to be formed not only among the platform provider and individual ecosystem partners, but most importantly, among ecosystem partners themselves. This gives rise to a model of many-many co-development relationships, as opposed to the traditional model of one-to-one collaboration. Figure 2 provides an illustration of the two alternative models.

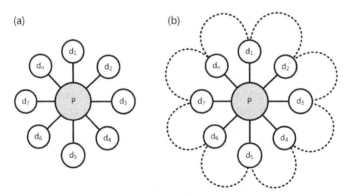

**Fig. 2.** Alternative models of software co-development: one-to-one (a) vs. many-to-many (b) co-development relationships (P=platform; $d_i$=developer)

The model of co-development that CAST employs allows members of a software ecosystem to be linked not only to the central platform provider, but to each distinct partner. Each partner can be directly associated with other ecosystem members and can become a centre around which others develop their own work, resulting in a multi-centric co-development environment. This approach allows for fundamentally new forms of collaboration within a cloud-centric software ecosystem.

# 5 Conclusions

In this paper we attempted a first discussion on how the relationship between co-development, platforms and ecosystems evolves in the era of cloud computing, and specifically how cloud application platforms contribute in shaping the future of software co-development. We have also presented the model of co-development employed by CAST—a cloud application platform designed with the objective of supporting collaboration between a PaaS provider and an ecosystem of SaaS developers.

As we have demonstrated, cloud application platforms have some novel characteristics that are of great interest in relation to software co-development. Firstly, cloud application platforms embody both the core software artefact on which co-development is centred—i.e. the core software product that partners extend and/or out of which new products materialize, but also the central mechanism for coordinating the ecosystem and the software co-development process. Secondly, as demonstrated by the case of CAST, cloud application platforms can be designed in a way that allows co-development relationships to be formed not only among the platform provider and individual ecosystem partners, but most importantly, among ecosystem partners themselves. The combination of those two characteristics with the agility intrinsic in the cloud computing paradigm has far reaching implications for software co-development. Most notably, it allows ecosystems to be rapidly formed not only around the platform core, but also around contributions by third-parties, thus giving rise to new forms of hierarchical cloud-platform-centric software ecosystems.

# References

1. Chesbrough, H., Schwartz, K.: Innovating Business Models with Co-Development Partnerships. Research Technology Management 50(1), 55–59 (2007)
2. Buyukozkana, G., Arsenyanb, J.: Collaborative product development: a literature overview. Production Planning & Control: The Management of Operations 23(1), 47–66 (2012)
3. Meyer, M.H., Seliger, R.: Product Platforms in Software Development. Sloan Management Review 40(1), 61–74 (1998)
4. Evans, D.S., Hagiu, A., Schmalensee, R.: A Survey of the Economic Role of Software Platforms in Computer-based Industries. CESifo Economic Studies 51(2), 189–224 (2005)
5. Kourtesis, D., Kuttruff, V., Paraskakis, I.: Optimising Development and Deployment of Enterprise Software Applications on PaaS: The CAST Project. In: Cezon, M., Wolfsthal, Y. (eds.) ServiceWave 2010 Workshops. LNCS, vol. 6569, pp. 14–25. Springer, Heidelberg (2011)
6. Enabling Open Collaboration with Development Partners. CollabNet (2007)
7. Parker, G., Van Alstyne, M.: Managing Platform Ecosystems. In: Proceedings of the 29th International Conference on Information Systems, pp. 1–24 (2008)
8. Bosch, J.: From software product lines to software ecosystems. In: Proceedings of the 13th International Software Product Line Conference, pp. 119–119. Springer (2009), http://dl.acm.org.eresources.shef.ac.uk/citation.cfm?id=1753235.1753251

9. Messerschmitt, D.G., Szyperski, C.: Software Ecosystems, Understanding an Indespensable Technology and Industry. The MIT Press, Cambridge (2003)

10. Pezzini, M., Lheureux, B.J.: Integration Platform as a Service: Moving Integration to the Cloud. Gartner Research (2011)

11. Natis, Y.V., Lheureux, B.J., Pezzini, M., Cearley, D.W., Knipp, E., Plummer, D.C.: PaaS Road Map: A Continent Emerging. Gartner Research (2011)

12. Rymer, J.R., Ried, S.: The Forrester Wave: Platform-as-a-Service for App Dev and Delivery Professionals, Q2 2011. Forrester Research (2011)

13. Evans, D.S., Hagiu, A., Schmalensee, R.: Invisible Engines: How Software Platforms Drive Innovation and Transform Industries. MIT Press (2006)

14. Chou, D.C.: Rise of the Cloud Ecosystems. MSDN Blogs, March 16 (2011)

**8**

## Collaborative Business Frameworks I

# The Service Dominant Strategy Canvas:
# Towards Networked Business Models

Egon Lüftenegger[1], Paul Grefen[1], and Caren Weisleder[2]

[1] School of Industrial Engineering at Eindhoven University of Technology
P.O Box 513, 5600 MB Eindhoven, The Netherlands
{e.r.luftenegger,p.w.p.j.grefen}@tue.nl
[2] De Lage Landen International B.V.
P.O Box 652, 5600 AR, Eindhoven, The Netherlands
{c.weisleder}@delagelanden.com

**Abstract.** Service orientation, customer focus and collaboration between firms are profoundly changing the way of doing business. Marketing scholars are the first academics to conceptualize these changes under a new mindset, known as the Service Dominant Logic. However, management constructs are needed to apply this mindset to the business environment. Therefore, we have developed a new conceptual model of a Service Dominant Strategy with a visual representation in the form of a canvas. Our model is constructed by integrating current definitions of a Service Dominant strategy and by confronting them with traditional strategies. The model facilitates the design of Service Dominant strategies by answering the questions associated with fifteen elements. Experimental application of our approach in several industry domains shows the importance of both strategic level design and Service Dominant thinking.

**Keywords:** service dominant strategy, service dominant logic, business canvas, strategy model, service science.

## 1    Introduction

Service Science is an interdisciplinary area of study addressing the challenge to become more systematic about innovating in services. There is a strong industry and academic shift in interest towards services. However, most academics and industry professionals are still working under the manufacturing paradigm rather than the service paradigm [1]. This slow change has a negative impact on service innovation. The ability to change is constrained by the dominant logic of manufacturing, which is Goods Dominant. This issue that prevents the adoption of new ways of doing business is known as the dominant logic trap: the prevailing dominant logic act as a filter in a funnel that prevents the ideation and adoption of business concepts that do not fit with the current dominant logic [2], [3].

A new innovative mindset that addresses this change towards a service dominant economy focused at the network level is known as the Service Dominant Logic (SDL) [4]. This theoretical foundation has been developed by marketing scholars and

L.M. Camarinha-Matos, L. Xu, and H. Afsarmanesh (Eds.): PRO-VE 2012, IFIP AICT 380, pp. 207–215, 2012.
© IFIP International Federation for Information Processing 2012

recognized as a key theory for the advancement of Service Science. However, this theory as originally stated is difficult to understand and communicate [5]. Management constructs are needed to drive businesses development under the SDL. We need to focus on the organizational change and business models that will make service-oriented technologies and collaborative networks the main drivers to solve business problems. Hence, the strategy is the first management construct that we need to communicate this dominant logic change to decision makers. Nowadays, there is a lack of management tools developed specifically to design service dominant strategies. Current tools, like the Balanced Scorecard [6], have been constructed by using the manufacturing mindset in which improving the efficiency of the firm from an internal perspective is desired [7]. In today's complex and dynamic business environment, we need management tools that emphasize service orientation and networked collaboration from a service dominant perspective on doing business.

In this paper, we focus on a management tool that facilitates the design of strategies for the Service Dominant landscape. We have developed this conceptual model by reviewing existing research on SDL at the strategic level and by confronting it with traditional business strategies developed by business and marketing scholars. This approach has been chosen to have traditional strategic concepts acting as a bridge between the current dominant mindset and the new Service Dominant mindset. Our conceptual model takes the canvas approach as a visual representation to communicate and design. This approach has emerged from the Information Systems domain in academia and currently has been widely accepted in industry [8].

This paper is structured as follows: In Section 2, we identify and analyze the background research on SDL at the strategic level. In section 3, we establish a strategic bridge with traditional strategies to identify the elements of a Service Dominant strategy. In Section 4, we visualize the Service Dominant strategy and discuss the results of prototype application of the canvas in several industrial settings. We end this paper with conclusions.

## 2    Analysis of Background Research on SDL

In this section we study the literature in which a strategic view on the SDL is developed. We select the research by tracking the original authors of the SDL, and by searching Google Scholar using the keywords "service dominant strategy" and "service dominant strategic".

Firstly, the *"competing through service" research* argues that to compete effectively through service, the entire organization should view the market and itself with a SDL [9]. In this research, the SDL authors define derived propositions from the original foundational premises of the SDL as strategy. One of these derived proposition is "Firms can compete more effectively through the adoption of collaboratively developed, risk-based pricing value propositions".

Secondly, the *"strategic service orientation" research* is focused on the interactions with the customer [10]. The author defines his strategic approach on service by interactions. One of these interactions is stated as "Individuated interaction with an emphasis on understanding individual customers".

Finally, the *"constructing a service dominant strategy"* research complements the previous approaches by bringing the perspective of economics [11]. In this work the authors develop a Service Dominant strategy with a start-up company as real case scenario. In this research, the strategy is presented as goods dominant versus service dominant defined by statements like: "rigid versus flexible organizational boundaries". For our purposes, we take the service dominant aspect only: flexible organizational boundaries.

We identify as Service Dominant strategic statements the derived propositions of the SDL defined in the "strategic service orientation" research, the interactions defined in the "strategic service orientation" research and the service dominant aspects of "constructing a service dominant strategy" research. In Section 3, we use the background research to identify the elements of a Service Dominant Strategy. The complete list on the Service Dominant strategic statements is presented in [12].

# 3    Bridging Service Dominant and Traditional Strategies

In this section, we identify a conceptual bridge between traditional strategies and the Service Dominant research efforts discussed in Section 2. This conceptual bridge aims to facilitate the communication of a Service Dominant strategy by using traditional strategic concepts. The conceptual bridge is being developed by analyzing five traditional strategies identified and classified in [13] as being developed from business and marketing scholars. Firstly, within the strategies developed by business scholars we can distinguish: industry-based, competence-based and resource-based. Secondly, within the strategies developed by marketing scholars we can distinguish: market-oriented and relational marketing [13].

We establish a conceptual bridge with three of the five traditional strategies. Firstly, we discuss why we discard the industry-based and market-oriented strategies. Secondly, we explain the how we establish a strategic bridge between the service dominant strategy and the competence-based, relational marketing and resource-based strategies.

Firstly, we discard the industry-based strategy as a strategic bridge; because Porter's approach is more suitable for the manufacturing mindset with the value chain approach rather the Service Dominant mindset and its value network focus [19]. Secondly, we discard the market-oriented strategy as strategic bridge, because the Service Dominant mindset focuses on the individual relationship with "the customer" rather than the market as a whole.

We establish below a strategic bridge with three traditional strategies: competence-base, relational marketing and resource-based. The strategic bridge is being developed by conceptualizing the Service Dominant strategy as business competences, market relationships and business resources elements. These elements are identified from the background research on the SDL depicted in Section 2. We illustrate with an example our line of reasoning on how we identify the elements for each strategic bridge. However, the identification process for all the elements is presented in [12].

**Business Competences.** The competence-based strategic view suggests that to achieve competitive advantage firms should identify, seek develop, reinforce, maintain and leverage distinctive competences [14]. Grant argues that resources are not a source of competitive advantage by their own. In line with this reasoning, capabilities are the source of competitive advantage. Hamel and Prahalad use the term "core competences" to describe the central strategic capabilities of a firm to achieve competitive advantage [15]. Hence, competitive advantage can be achieved by distinctive competences. We can recognize distinctive competences as enablers of a Service Dominant strategy by answering the question "How do we enact our business relations in a Service Dominant business?" For example, we can identify the Co-creation and Co-production business competence elements from the "competing through service" research by analyzing the Service Dominant strategic statement: "Firms gain competitive advantage by engaging customers and value network partners in co-creation and co-production activities". Furthermore, we can group the business competences within value and collaboration:

The *Value group* contains the elements related with our proposition to our primary stakeholders from the value-in-use and the pricing perspectives. Firstly, *Co-creation* is about what we are enabling as value-in-use by delivering solutions with our primary stakeholders. Secondly, *Risk-based Pricing* is based on transitive risk with our primary stakeholders in our network. Moreover, the pricing mechanism should be based on the risk of actors that are participating co-producing the solution.

The *Collaboration group* contains the networked competences that we need to establish with our stakeholders for doing business. Firstly, *Co-production* is about how we create with our stakeholders in a collaborative way. This co-production is achieved by including all the stakeholders in the production of our solution-centered approach defined as value-in-use. Secondly, *Service Integration* is about how and why we integrate the business processes between all the stakeholders involved in our collaboration. This service integration is achieved by enabling the composition and orchestration of business processes to achieve the best solution that maximizes the value-in-use of all our stakeholders. Thirdly, *Knowledge Sharing* is about how and why we need to share knowledge. Moreover, knowledge sharing is achieved by capturing, processing and distributing the information related with value-in-use with all our stakeholders.

**Market Relationships.** The relational marketing strategic view suggests that to achieve competitive advantage, firms should develop a relationship portfolio with stakeholders such as customer, suppliers, employees and competitors [14]. Competitive advantage can be achieved by distinctive relational approaches. Moreover, the shift of the SDL towards "marketing with" the customer implies a relationship. We can recognize distinctive market relationships as enablers of a Service Dominant strategy by answering the question "How do we relate with our business environment in a Service Dominant business?" For example, we can identify the Empowerment relationship element from the strategic service orientation" research by analyzing the service dominant strategic statement: "Empowered interaction with an emphasis on enabling customers to shape the nature and/or content or exchange". Furthermore, we distinguish between endogenous an exogenous market relationships:

The *Endogenous group* contains the inside-out relationship elements that start from inside the company to the outside world. Firstly, *Contextually Individuated* is about how we customize our relationship with the customer. This contextualization is achieved by understanding the needs of the customer that maximize the value-in-use. Secondly, *Empowerment* is about how we enable our collaborators to participate. The firm should facilitate the active role of the customer in the co-production process by taking customer input. Moreover, this empowerment should also be established with other stakeholders of our collaborative network.

The *Exogenous group* contains the relationship elements that we need to establish with the outside world. Firstly, *Bidirectional* is about how we communicate with the external parties. This interaction facilitates conversation and dialog by co-producing and co-creating with the customer. Secondly, *Ethical Mutual Benefit* is about how we share with our collaborators. This relationship is established by a mutual gain for all the actors in the business collaboration. Thirdly, *Flexible Organizational Boundaries* is about how we establish our collaborative network. This relationship is established by being flexible through the inclusion of multiple actors for the enactment of value-in-use. This relationship minimizes the barriers between firms to co-produce service offerings.

**Business Resources.** The resource-based strategic view suggests that a firm possess resources to achieve competitive advantage and superior long-term performance [14]. The term resource is variously defined in the resource-based view literature. We take Grant's resource definition, because he distinguishes between resources and capabilities. A resource can be defined as the inputs or factors available to a company through which it performs its operations or carries out its activities [15]. We identify business resources as enablers of a Service Dominant strategy by answering the question "What ingredients do we need to enact our Service Dominant strategy?" For example, we can identify the Employees business resource element from the "competing through service" research by analyzing the Service Dominant strategic statement: "Firms that treat their employees as operant resources will be able to develop more innovative knowledge and skills and thus gain competitive advantage". Furthermore, we can group the business resources within actors and infrastructures:

The *Actors group* contains the business resources who participate in the service dominant business. Firstly, the *Customer* is an actor that meets the profile of an active customer. The customer, as an individual rather than a group, participates by determining the value-in-use and co-producing the desired solution. The customer is the main stakeholder in the determination of value-in-use, because he is the actor that will use the solution. By involving the customer we can get knowledge related with their needs in an active manner. Secondly, the *Partners* are actors that meet the profile of an active partner. The partners participate in the co-production of the solution for the established value-in-use. Moreover, engaging network partners in co-production activities enable the firm to gain competitive advantage. Thirdly, the *Employees* are actors that meet the profile of an active employee that is willing to understand what is valuable for the customer. Employees are a source of customer knowledge and understanding. They participate in the co-production of the solution for enabling value-in-use.

The *Infrastructures group* contains what resources we needed to develop a service dominant business. Firstly, the *Service Flows* are the activities that define our value-in-use proposition. Service flows, acting as cross-organizational business process oriented to the customer, are needed to enable the collaboration and co-production. Secondly, the *Information Technologies* are the enablers that facilitate the collaboration and the enactment of our value-in-use proposition. Moreover, Information Technologies increase the likelihood of cross-organizational and customer collaboration.

## 4    The Service Dominant Strategy Canvas

In this section, we present our canvas as a management tool to facilitate the design of Service Dominant strategies by using the elements and categories identified in Section 3. We use the canvas approach, inspired by the success of the Business Model Canvas, which is used by practitioners due to its rich visual approach [8].

Figure 1, shows the resulting Service Dominant Strategy Canvas that facilitates the design of a service dominant strategy by answering the questions associated for each of the fifteen elements that we have identified and categorized before. As shown in Figure 1, the three rectangular main columns named market relationships, business competences and business resources are the strategic bridges between traditional and service dominant strategic concepts. Each main column has two groups represented by rounded rectangular boxes that contain the Service Dominant elements represented by a circular icon and a rectangular label with their associated question below. These questions facilitate the interaction and communication with the participants in a structured and active manner.

As shown in Figure 1, the business competences column is located in the middle within the Service Dominant Strategy Canvas. We place this strategic pillar in the center to emphasize the value and collaboration groups. These two groups establish our strategic context for the understanding and design of a Service Dominant strategy.

We have tested our Service Dominant Strategy Canvas in three session with innovation managers and strategists within an information logistics company, an asset-based financial services provider and an international car leasing company. These industries currently are very asset oriented, making a perfect scenario to test the tool: a change in dominant logic is sought. The testing process is depicted as follows: firstly, we have presented the canvas with an explanation of all their elements using a well-known highly Service Dominant sample scenario. Secondly, we have asked the participants to design a Service Dominant strategy for their company by using the canvas. Each session was guided by a facilitator that knows the business of the company, the researcher who asked the strategic canvas questions and a senior manager for each industry setting.

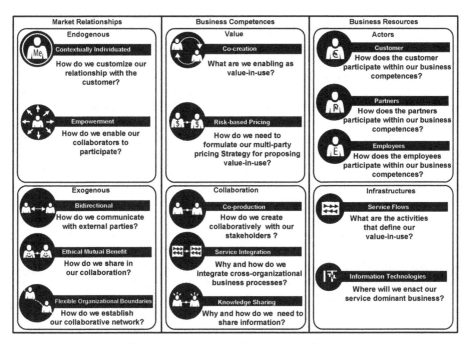

**Fig. 1.** The Service Dominant Strategy Canvas

As outcome of our qualitative research, we have three strategic canvases. From each of the sessions previously depicted we can conclude the following: in the three tested industry settings, we found that value-in-use explained by the co-creation element was an eye-opener for the participants. This element shifts the mindset from the focus of the good to the service that renders. After this mindset change, strategic canvas achieved successfully to communicate the collaboration perspective. In the case of the logistics industry, we observe that canvas facilitates the focus on a logistic experience where collaborators can participate in the transportation service. In the case of the asset-based finance industry, the mindset change is achieved by moving from asset centered activities towards the activities focused on the usage of the asset. Al last, in the car leasing industry the canvas facilitated the shift from cars toward a customer centric solution enabled by Information Technologies.

The participants were able to deal with the novel aspects of a Service Dominant Strategy. After the first session, we communicated the mindset change and we were able to guide the participants to answer the questions. However, we found out that we need more than just one session to refine the outcome of the filled canvas. This is explained due two main reasons. Firstly, the concept is new for the industry. Secondly, the numerous elements needed for conceptualization of a service dominant strategy. Furthermore, the service dominant strategy will be the basis for their future service dominant business models and service-oriented information systems empowered by collaborative networks.

## 5      Conclusions and Future Work

In this paper we present the Service Dominant Strategy Canvas as a management tool to facilitate the design of service dominant strategies. In our test sessions, the strategic tool appears to be an innovation catalyst for asset dominant companies towards service orientation. Innovation managers and strategists find the tool useful for defining future strategies.

In a nutshell, the Service Dominant Strategy Canvas facilitates the understanding that solutions require multi-stakeholder perspective enabled by collaborative networks. This strategic perspective is constructed by taking a multidisciplinary approach on service by integrating business, marketing and information systems point of views. The presented canvas is the outcome of the development of the first layer of the Service Dominant Business Logic Framework. This framework is defined by four layers. Firstly, the Strategy layer is the long-term vision that recognizes the Service Dominant strategic paradigm. Secondly, we have the Business layer that takes the networked approach on business models by following the Service Dominant Strategy. Thirdly, we have Organization layer that focuses on the networked processes on the collaborative network. Finally, we have the Systems layer that is focused on a highly modular service-oriented architecture as enabler of our approach. Currently, we are working on the business layer by developing a tool to design Service Dominant Business Models.

## References

1. Spohrer, J., Maglio, P.: The emergence of service science: Toward systematic service innovations to accelerate co-creation of value. Production and Operations Management 17(3), 238–246 (2008)
2. Chesbrough, H.: Open Services Innovation: Rethinking Your Business to Grow and Compete in a New Era. Jossey-Bass, San Francisco (2011)
3. Bettis, R.A., Prahalad, C.K.: The Dominant Logic: Retrospective and Extension. Strategic Management Journal 16(1), 5–14 (1995)
4. Vargo, S.L., Lusch, R.F.: Evolving to a new dominant logic for marketing. Journal of Marketing 68(1), 1–17 (2004)
5. Lusch, R.F., Vargo, S.L., Wessels, G.: Toward a conceptual foundation for service science: Contributions from service-dominant logic. IBM Systems Journal 47(1), 5–14 (2008)
6. Kaplan, R.S., Norton, D.P.: Linking the balanced scorecard to strategy. California Management Review 39(1), 53–79 (1996)
7. Sven, M.L., Voelpel, C., Eckhoff, R.A.: The tyranny of the balanced scorecard in the innovation economy. Journal of Intellectual Capital 7(1), 43–60 (2006)
8. Osterwalder, A., Pigneur, I.: Business Model Generation: A Handbook for Visionaries, Game Changers and Challengers. Willey, New Jersey (2010)
9. Lusch, R.F., Vargo, S.L., O'Brien, M.: Competing through service: Insights from service-dominant logic. Journal of Retailing 83(1), 5–18 (2007)
10. Karpen, I., Bove, L.: Linking S-D logic and marketing practice: Toward a strategic service orientation. In: Otago Forum 2 Proceedings, Univeristy of Otago, pp. 214–237 (2008)

11. Järvesivu, P.: Constructing a Service-Dominant Strategy: A Practice- Theoretical Study of a Start-Up Company. Ph.D thesis, Aalto University (2010)
12. Lüftenegger, E., Grefen, P., Weisleder, C.: The Service Dominant Strategy Canvas: Defining and Visualizing a Service Dominant Strategy Through the Traditional Strategic Lens. Beta Report, Eindhoven University of Technology (2012)
13. Stabell, C.B., Fjeldstad, Ø.D.: Configuring value for competitive advantage: on chains, shops, and networks. Strategic Management Journal 19(5), 413–437 (1998)
14. Hunt, S., Derozier, C.: The normative imperatives of business and marketingstrategy: grounding strategy in resource-advantage theory. Journal of Business and Industrial Marketing 19(1), 5–22 (2004)
15. Grant, R.: A resource-based theory of competitive advantage: implications for strategy formulation. California Management Review 33(3), 114–135 (1991)

# The SOAVE Platform: A Service-Oriented Architecture for Virtual Enterprises

Amihai Motro[*] and Yun Guo

Department of Computer Science
George Mason University, Virginia, USA

**Abstract.** The flexibility and reusability afforded by service-oriented architectures seems to be of singular applicability to the management of virtual enterprises. In this paper we describe the architecture of the SOAVE platform: a Service-Oriented Architecture for Virtual Enterprises. The platform provides the members of a networked community with a set of tools with which they can collaborate on the production of complex products. It allows members to perform enterprise management functions, as well as manufacture enterprise products collaboratively by means of peer-to-peer transactions.

**Keywords:** Service-oriented architecture, virtual enterprise, collaborative network, peer-to-peer transactions, production trees.

## 1    Introduction and Background

A virtual enterprise is a coalition of business entities who collaborate on the manufacturing of complex products. The collaboration is often ad hoc, for a specific product only, after which the virtual enterprise may dismantle. The members of a virtual enterprise possess complementary skills and technologies whose combination is deemed necessary for the target product at hand [2].

Web services are distributed, autonomous, platform-independent software components, often limited in their functionalities, but easily available to other applications through standard protocols, thus hiding implementation details from their consumers. Service orientation is an approach to software design that accomplishes more complex functionalities by integrating such services. In recent years, the Service-Oriented Architecture (SOA) has gained considerable popularity, notably for achieving architectural flexibility at low cost [8].

A closer look into virtual enterprises and service orientation reveals that these two approaches complement each other nicely. Service-oriented architectures are particularly attractive for virtual enterprises for several reasons:

---

[*] This paper is dedicated to the memory of Alessandro D'Atri, who introduced me to the subject of virtual enterprises.

L.M. Camarinha-Matos, L. Xu, and H. Afsarmanesh (Eds.): PRO-VE 2012, IFIP AICT 380, pp. 216–224, 2012.
© IFIP International Federation for Information Processing 2012

- **Reusability.** Virtual enterprises are typically created for specific products, and are dismantled once these products are no longer in demand, a process that potentially incurs high overhead. With a service-oriented architecture, existing services may be reused, allowing new virtual enterprises to be set up at low development cost. Cost is of particular concern to virtual enterprises, as often they involve small or medium size companies, for whom the cost of building and maintaining customized applications could be prohibitive.

- **Flexibility.** A key advantage of virtual enterprises is their *agility*: the capacity to adapt rapidly to changing market circumstances [9]. The loosely coupled nature of services in a SOA allows applications to easily evolve with the changing requirements. New services can be incorporated and old services can be dropped to achieve the desired enterprise model.

- **Interoperability.** By using standard protocols and technologies, service-oriented architectures support interoperability between clients and services. This is particularly valuable for virtual enterprises, because they bring together independent business entities possibly operating on heterogeneous platforms.

In this work, we describe the SOAVE platform: A virtual enterprise architecture built on the principles of a service-oriented architecture. There have been numerous interpretations of the virtual enterprise paradigm, and ours is derived mostly from the VirtuE model [5]. Similarly, from the numerous interpretations of service-orientation, we adopt two fundamental principles: (1) A relatively small number of services is defined; and (2) enterprise work is carried out with a set of *business processes*, where each business process "weaves" basic services into a complex task, with minimal amount of traditional programming.

Perhaps the most salient feature of SOAVE is that it provides a *formal framework* for virtual enterprises architected in accordance with the service orientation paradigm. This framework defines basic concepts, algorithms, transaction protocols, business processes and services to implement collaborative manufacturing of complex products. It formalizes concepts such as product price, product complexity, time-to-delivery, procurement risk, reliability scores, on time *vs.* late delivery, and failure.

**Related Work.** In the past five-six years there has been increased interest in implementing virtual enterprises with service-oriented architectures. Much of the work is concerned with particular industries but of more relevance to our effort here are projects that describe industry-independent architectures, and we discuss here three such projects. A model of virtual enterprises based on service composition is proposed in [10]. However, the authors interpret a virtual enterprise simply as a composition of services, and the focus is on locating and selecting the appropriate services. In contradistinction, we view a virtual enterprise as a network of business entities, and a service is a software component that assists these entities in performing their work. The virtual enterprise architecture described in [3] provides for several layers and a multitude of modules performing a variety of functionalities. But although some components are labeled "services", the architecture does not conform to the service-orientated paradigm in which complex tasks are achieved by compositions of basic services. The interpretation of both virtual organizations and service orientation assumed in [4] is more in agreement with the current literature. The authors propose a detailed framework for process management in service-oriented virtual organizations. It consists of multiple layers, and is based on common standards and protocols. In contradistinction, our work here is not concerned with massive software infrastructure as much as with the formal analysis of the fundamental concepts of setting up (and scaling down) collaborative groups, constructing complex products by procuring components from peers, and the flow of collaborative manufacturing with its aspects of risk, failure and recovery.

Section 2 reviews the virtual enterprise model: the basic concepts, the supporting information system and the workflow. Section 3 focuses on the architecture: the business processes, the shared services and the peer-to-peer communications. We conclude in Section 4 with a brief discussion of some of the remaining work.

# 2    The SOAVE Model

SOAVE provides a *formal* framework for collaborative manufacturing, in which basic concepts, algorithms, protocols and metrics can be defined and analyzed.

## 2.1    The Basic Elements: Members Making Products

A *marketplace* is a set of networked business entities that are available for participation in virtual enterprises. Any member of the marketplace can launch a new enterprise; the member then becomes the enterprise *catalyst*. The catalyst invites other members to join the enterprise; each member then becomes an *affiliate* and launches a *division*. Each marketplace member is associated with a *reliability* score that denotes its performance. This score is updated after each collaboration.

The catalyst establishes and maintains the set of *products* that the enterprise will manufacture collaboratively. These include both *end* products to be available to outside clients — the essential purpose of the enterprise — as well as interim products to be available only to affiliates to use as components in more complex products. Collaborative manufacturing implies that each product is a root of a *tree* of components: the internal nodes of the tree are *composite* components, and its leaves are *elementary* components. Each node is associated with the affiliate chosen to deliver it, and each edge indicates a procurement transaction. Only the catalyst receives and delivers external orders. Thus, it is associated with the root of every tree.

## 2.2    Product Versions and Their Properties

The same product may be offered by different affiliates, thus providing procurement alternatives. An offering of a product is called a product *version*. While versions are identical in substance, they are distinguished by six properties:

1. *Price*: This is the purchasing price of the version. It is the purchasing price paid to other affiliates for procuring the necessary components, plus a profit markup determined by the affiliate offering this version.
2. *Time*: This is the promised time to delivery (the interval between the time of ordering and the time of delivery). It is the maximal time to delivery of its components, plus time spent locally to manufacture the product.
3. *Risk*: This is the risk that the product will not be delivered as promised. It combines the risk associated with the procurement of its components and the reliability of the offering affiliate. The precise calculation of risk is elaborated later, and for now we denote it as a function $\theta$ of the underlying risks.
4. *Expiration*: This is the time when this version will expire. It is not later than the minimal (soonest) expiration time of the components.
5. *Depth*: This measures the length of the longest path (procurement chain) in the manufacturing tree of this version.
6. *Complexity*: This measures the number of nodes in the manufacturing tree.

Formally, consider a product version $P$ with components $P_1$, ..., $P_n$ which is manufactured by affiliate $A$. Then

$$
\begin{aligned}
Price(P) &\geq \sum_{i=1}^{n} Price(P_i) & (1) \\
Time(P) &\geq \max_{1 \leq i \leq n} Time(P_i) & (2) \\
Risk(P) &= \theta\,(Risk(P_1), ..., Risk(P_n), Risk(A)) & (3) \\
Expiration(P) &\leq \min_{1 \leq i \leq n} Expiration(P_i) & (4) \\
Depth(P) &= \max_{1 \leq i \leq n} Depth(P_i) + 1 & (5) \\
Complexity(P) &= \sum_{i=1}^{n} Complexity(Pi) + 1 & (6)
\end{aligned}
$$

Under this scheme, an enterprise may offer a product version that requires a long time and carries a high risk, but has a low price; another version that requires a short time and carries a low risk, but has a high price; and so on. Note that an affiliate can take advantage of new sourcing opportunities available to it, by offering a new version, and on expiration withdraw the older version. As can be seen in inequalities (1), (2) and (4), an affiliate may set *Price* higher than the cost of procurement, to include profit; it may set *Time* higher than the maximal procurement time, to include local manufacturing; and it may set *Expiration* sooner than the lowest expiration.

**Risk Calculation.** $Risk(P)$ is defined as the probability that the affiliate $A$ would not deliver the product $P$ as promised. This could happen either because $A$ did not receive any of its components $P_i$ as planned, or because $A$ itself failed. Hence, it combines $Risk(P_i)$ and $Risk(A)$ (the latter is the complement of the reliability score of $A$). In the product tree, it is convenient to view affiliate failure as *node failure* and procurement failure as *edge failure*. In general, it cannot be assumed that the $n + 1$ components of $Risk(P)$ are mutually exclusive (i.e., it may not be assumed that there is at most one failure) and, $Risk(P)$ must be calculated according to De Moivre's inclusion-exclusion principle [7]. In practice, however, unless $n$ is small, it is impossible to calculate

*Risk*(*P*) in this way, and one must settle for lower and upper bounds, such as those suggested by the Bonferroni inequalities [1]. If we assume that the $n + 1$ events are *independent* (i.e., the failure of a node and the failure of each edge are unrelated), then, using a simplified inclusion-exclusion formula [6], *Risk*(*P*) may be calculated from the risks (i.e., reliability scores) of the affiliates associated with the production of *P*. Confirming intuition, *Risk*(*P*) increases with the complexity and depth of *P*.

## 2.3    The Enterprise Information System

The virtual enterprise information system is based on nine database tables, arranged in three tiers. Tables 1 and 2 are *external*: they are the only tables available outside the enterprise. Tables 3, 4, 5 and 6 are *global*: they relate to the entire enterprise (they are mostly managed by the catalyst) and they are available to all the affiliates of the enterprise. Tables 7, 8 and 9 are *local*: they relate to individual divisions (each division stores and manages a "horizontal slice"). Database keys are underlined. The relationships among these tables are monitored by various foreign key constraints (not shown). Many of the attributes have already been discussed.

1. *Marketplace* (*Member*, *Reliability*, *Description*): The community of potential members available for participation in virtual enterprises. *Member* identifies the member and *Description* provides information on its manufacturing capabilities.
2. *Public* (*Product*, *Version*, *Price*, *Risk*, *Time*, *Expiration*): The public product catalog for placing external orders. *Product* and *Version* identify the product version. (*Public* is a view of *Availability* that shows only end products.)
3. *Catalog* (*Product*, *Description*): The products of the enterprise. *Product* identifies the product and *Description* is a textual description of the product.
4. *Directory* (*Affiliate*, *Reliability*, *Description*): The enterprise affiliates (including the enterprise catalyst). *Directory* is a subset of *Marketplace*.
5. *Availability* (*Product*, *Version*, *Affiliate*, *Price*, *Risk*, *Time*, *Depth*, *Complexity*, *Expiration*): The product versions presently available throughout the enterprise. *Affiliate* is the (unique) manufacturer of the product version.
6. *Orders* (*Order*, *Product*, *Version*, *Affiliate*, *Price*, *Risk*, *Time*, *Depth*, *Complexity*, *Expiration*, *Rtime*, *Dtime*, Status): A log of the orders received by the enterprise. *Order* is a unique identifier. *Rtime* and *Dtime* are the times the order was received and delivered. *Status* is "in progress", "completed" or "failed". The other attributes are the values published in *Availability* at the time of the order.
7. *L_Availability* (*Product*, *Version*, *Price*, *Risk*, *Time*, *Depth*, *Complexity*, *Expiration*): A view of *Availability* with versions from a particular affiliate only.
8. *Plan* (*Product*, *Version*, *CProduct*, *CVersion*): For each version offered by this affiliate, the component products it requires and the versions to be procured.
9. *L_Orders* (*Order*, *Product*, *Version*, *Price*, *Risk*, *Time*, *Depth*, *Complexity*, *Expiration*, *Rtime*, *Dtime*, *Status*): A log of the orders received by this affiliate. The attributes are similar to those of *Orders*.

## 2.4    Regular Workflow and Irregular behavior

Collaborative manufacturing begins when a client consults the *Public* table for the available product versions and their essential parameters (*Price*, *Risk*, *Time*, and *Expiration*) and sends an *Order* message to the catalyst for a particular product version. After verifying the validity of the order, the catalyst acknowledges it with an order number and sends an *Order* message to the manufacturing affiliate. The affiliate launches a production: It consults the product's *Plan*, which describes the components necessary and their chosen providers, and sends the providers *Order* messages. When all orders have been fulfilled, the affiliate assembles the product and sends a *Delivery* message to the ordering affiliate (presumably with an invoice and shipment tracking information). The ordering affiliate acknowledges (with payment information) and proceeds to assemble its own product. This continues until the catalyst receives the finished product, which it sends to the client, who responds with payment.

This workflow assumed smooth, fault-free operation. In practice, however, various things could go wrong. We identify three basic types of *irregular behavior*. The business processes are defined to manage these behaviors appropriately.

At times, an enterprise must be *scaled down*: The catalyst may want to withdraw a product, terminate an affiliate, or dismantle the enterprise altogether; similarly, an affiliate may want to withdraw a product version, or dismantle its division. The preferred way for scaling down is to perform these activities *gracefully*; for example, before quitting, an affiliate waits until all its offerings expire, and then satisfies all pending orders. However, at times, scale-down may be *abrupt* rather than graceful. For example, an affiliate may decide to quit instantly, withdraw products before expiration, refuse new orders, and cancel orders that were accepted from others or issued to others. In such cases production trees are "disconnected" at a particular node with delivery cancellations propagating up the tree all the way to the root. Another type of irregular behavior is *lack of response* during *production exchanges* among affiliates. An affiliate does not acknowledge an order, does not fulfill an order that has been acknowledged, or does not acknowledge a delivery (with payment). In these cases a similar disconnection in the production tree is detected (after a time-out period). This results in a similar wave of delivery cancellations. A third type of irregular behavior is *lack of response* during *management exchanges* between catalyst and affiliate; for example, not responding to invitation or termination notices.

# 3    The SOAVE Architecture

We describe a particular platform, yet it is important to note that the architecture allows deviation from this configuration, by customizing the business processes and the services that they deploy. SOAVE provides each marketplace member with the necessary tools to (1) launch a new enterprise as a catalyst or join other enterprises as an affiliate, (2) perform management functions, and (3) perform day-to-day operations (collaborative manufacturing of products). All members have identical configuration (clones), allowing them to function as catalysts or affiliates in different enterprises. The catalyst does not manufacture — it only supervises and leads. Possibly, a regular affiliate could be co-located with the catalyst.

The platform is based on three concepts: *business processes, services,* and *messages.* Each member has access to an identical set of business processes that perform management functions and day-to-day operations. These processes involve limited "internal logic" and most work is performed by a collection of predefined services, available from a single *service repository.* Members are able to communicate with each other as necessary, using a fixed set of message types.

### 3.1    Business Processes

Presently, SOAVE defines 13 processes for either management or production.

**Management Processes.** There are six global-level processes for catalysts and five local-level processes for affiliates. The global processes are: launch a new enterprise, dismantle an existing enterprise, invite a new affiliate, terminate a current affiliate, offer a new product, and withdraw a current product. The local processes are: launch a division, dismantle a division (quit), offer a new product version, withdraw an expired product version, and renew an expired product version.

**Production Processes.** There are only two production processes: (1) External order processing is executed by catalysts; it describes the process that begins with an *Order* message received by the catalyst from an external client, and ends with the catalyst delivering the product to the client. (2) Internal order processing is executed by affiliates; it describes the process that begins with an affiliate receiving an *Order* message from another affiliate, and ends with the affiliate delivering the product.

### 3.2    Services and Messages

The aforementioned business processes require frequent access to the enterprise information service, to look up information and to update it. Of the 13 services presently defined in SOAVE, nine are dedicated to servicing requests for each of the nine database tables. They create or destroy tables, search and retrieve information, and modify their contents. We focus here on the other four services.

**Optimization Service.** This service is called by the business process for offering a new product version. It receives a product version from the affiliate, locates the corresponding plan devised by the affiliate, and finds the best procurement options for the plan components. The optimization parameters are *cost, risk, time complexity, depth* and *expiration.* The service can perform two types of optimization. (1) The affiliate sets limits on all but one parameter, and the service finds the procurement that optimizes the remaining parameter; for example, search for the best price, while not exceeding specific risk or time. (2) The affiliate defines a weighted combination of the parameters, and the service finds the procurement that optimizes it.

**Expiration Service.** This service is called when an enterprise is launched. It monitors the *Availability* table for expirations. When a product version expires, it nullifies *Price*, *Risk*, *Time*, *Depth*, *Complexity* and *Expiration*, and notifies the affiliate. When an affiliate receives an expiration notice, it could either withdraw the version (delete the *Availability* row), or re-optimize it (update the row).

**Performance-Tracking Service**. This service is called by the catalyst upon the completion and delivery of each external order. When the values in the relevant row in *Orders* maintain *Dtime – Rtime > Time*, the order was delivered late. However, it remains to be discovered which affiliate on the production tree *introduced* lateness and which affiliate simply *propagated* lateness. By examining the global *Orders* table and local *L_Orders* and *Plan* tables, the service can assess the performance of each participant and adjust its *Reliability* scores accordingly. Recall that these scores are used in future calculations of risk.

**Failure-Tracking Service.** This service is called by the catalyst upon the receipt of a delivery cancellation (see Section 2.4). By examining the global *Orders* table and local *L_Orders* and *Plan* tables, the service can detect the affiliate responsible for the failure and adjust its *Reliability* score accordingly.

**Messages.** Finally, SOAVE provides templates for five message types. *Invite* and *Terminate* are sent by the catalyst to affiliates, and *Quit* is sent by an affiliate to the catalyst. *Order* and *Delivery* are exchanged between affiliates to launch and complete procurement transactions. The acknowledgement of *Order* includes an order identifier and the acknowledgment of *Delivery* includes payment information.

# 4     Future Work

A pilot implementation of SOAVE has been completed, showing the viability of the overall approach and pointing where the platform could be strengthened. Work is underway to extend the platform in different directions, and we mention here only two important extensions.

**Performance Indicators and Triggers.** One of the most salient features of virtual enterprises is their *agility*: The ability to adapt and transform the enterprise according to market behavior. In SOAVE this is accomplished with the help of performance indicators [5] — statistics that are collected from the information system while the enterprise is operating; for example, the average turnaround time from order placement to fulfillment; the ratio of late deliveries; the affiliates with highest failure rate; the most severe bottlenecks in the production process, and so on. These performance indicators are deployed to trigger new business processes. For example, when an affiliate receives too many orders for a product, a new member would be invited with similar manufacturing capabilities; or when an affiliate misbehaves (for example, has a high ratio of failed transactions), it would be terminated.

**Constitutional Rules.** Constitutional rules [5] are constraints that must be enforced throughout the life of the enterprise. With the use of constitutional rules, virtual enterprises of different "flavors" may be formed; for example, rules can be used to regulate the extent of affiliate autonomy or the degree of competitiveness within an enterprise. Constitutional rules can be specified as semantic constraints on the database tables (and on the performance indicators that are derived from them). Violations of these rules can be avoided by blocking the violating activity, or they may trigger a compensating business process. For example, assume a rule that a product cannot be offered in too many versions; when a business process attempts to offer a new version, it would be blocked.

# References

1. Bonferroni, C.E.: Teoria statistica delle classi e calcolo delle probabilità. Istituto Superiore di Scienze Economiche e Commerciali di Firenze 8, 1–62 (1936)
2. Camarinha-Matos, L.M., Afsarmanesh, H.: Brief historical perspective for virtual organizations. In: Virtual Organizations—Systems and Practices, pp. 3–10. Springer (2005)
3. Cui, W., Meng, X., Liu, S.: A service-oriented architecture of virtual enterprises for manufacturing industry. In: Proc. CSCWD 2010, 14th Int'l Conf. on Computer Supported Cooperative Work in Design, pp. 373–377 (2010)
4. Danesh, M.H., Raahemi, B., Kamali, M.A.: A framework for process management in service-oriented virtual organizations. In: Proc. NWeSP 2011, 7th International Conf. on Next Generation Web Services Practices, pp. 12–17 (2011)
5. D'Atri, A., Motro, A.: VirtuE: a formal model of virtual enterprises for information markets. J. Intelligent Information Systems 30(1), 33–53 (2008)
6. D'Atri, A., Motro, A.: Virtual enterprise transactions: a cost model. In: Information Systems: People, Organizations, Institutions, and Technologies, pp. 165–174. Physica-Verlag (2010)
7. De Moivre, A.: Doctrine of chances – a method for calculating the probabilities of events in plays. Pearson, London (1718)
8. Erl, A.: Service-oriented architecture: concepts, technology, and design. Prentice-Hall (2005)
9. Goranson, H.T.: The agile virtual enterprise: cases, metrics, tools. Praeger (1999)
10. Zhou, B., Tang, J., He, Z.: An adaptive model of virtual enterprise based on dynamic web service composition. In: Proc. of CIT 2005, 5th Int'l Conf. on Computer and Information Technology, pp. 284–289 (2005)

# Mappings from BPEL to PMR for Business Process Registration*

Jingwei Cheng[1], Chong Wang[1,**], Keqing He[1], Jinxu Jia[2], and Peng Liang[1]

[1] State Key Lab. of Software Engineering, Wuhan University, China
cinfiniter@gmail.com, {cwang,hekeqing}@whu.edu.cn,
pliangeng@gmail.com
[2] International School of Software, Wuhan University, China
jiajinxu89@gmail.com

**Abstract.** In order to facilitate business collaboration and interoperation in virtual enterprises, it is crucial to discover appropriate business processes modeled in different languages and stored in different repositories. For this purpose, it is more efficient to register existent process models into a common process model registry, rather than defining numerous mappings from one modeling language to another. Considering the wide acceptance of BPEL, this paper proposed a common metamodel for process model registration (PMR), and defines the mappings from BPEL to PMR with corresponding mapping rules and algorithms. In this way, BPEL process models can be registered in the process model registry based on PMR automatically, and then the essential data from their registration information can facilitate process discovery across heterogeneous process repositories.

**Keywords:** BPEL, business process, process model registration, metamodel for process model registration.

## 1    Introduction

With the rapid progress of economic globalization, business collaboration is becoming more and more popular today, demanding solutions for the exploding amount of interoperability problems [1]. Business processes are fundamental in business collaboration for virtual enterprises. To promote the interoperation among business processes from different partners, it's necessary to facilitate business knowledge sharing and business process reuse within/across enterprises.

Existent business processes are modeled by various business process modeling languages, and stored in different repositories. This situation puts obstacles in the way of cross-enterprise discovery and reuse of business processes in virtual enterprises. Therefore, it's needed to provide a uniform manner to register the selected metadata

---

* This research project was supported by the Fundamental Research Funds for the Central Universities under Grant No. 3101032.
** Corresponding author.

L.M. Camarinha-Matos, L. Xu, and H. Afsarmanesh (Eds.): PRO-VE 2012, IFIP AICT 380, pp. 225–233, 2012.
© IFIP International Federation for Information Processing 2012

and common semantics of heterogeneous business processes, promote the semantic interoperation between them, and effectively support business process reuse and collaboration. For this purpose, this paper proposes the metamodel for process model registration (PMR) as the common registration facility for business process models in different languages. Furthermore, in order to support the implementation of a PMR-based registration tool, it's necessary to provide mapping rules from process modeling languages to the PMR metamodel when performing automatic registration of these models. Considering the fact that BPEL[2] has been accepted as one of the most widely used business process modeling languages due to its best practice for process implementation in SOA[3], this paper focuses on how to register BPEL models into the common process registry by defining the corresponding mappings rules.

The rest of this paper is organized as follows: section 2 introduces the work on the transformation of BPEL process models and relevant mechanisms for process model registration; section 3 presents the main structure of PMR; section 4 defines the mapping rules from BPEL to PMR and the corresponding mapping algorithms in detail, and shows how to register BPEL models with the mapping rules. Finally, section 5 concludes our work with future work directions.

## 2     Related Work

Considerable work on mapping BPEL to the other kinds of process modeling languages has been done in the past few years. For example, [4] proposed mapping strategies to transform BPEL to OWL-S, with which the process modeling capabilities and semantic capabilities of OWL-S can be combined, and the process models can be discovered and interacted in a computer understandable way. [5] defined the mappings between BPEL and XPDL (XML Process Definition Language) to support model transformation from one to the other. Meanwhile, mappings from BPEL constructs to graphical BPMN (Business Process Modeling Notation) elements are provided in [6-7] to visualize BPEL process models using BPMN diagrams. It's obvious that those mappings are mainly used to transform BPEL models into the process models in other languages, and can support further interoperation between the corresponding process model repositories. Although one partner of the interoperation can be any repository adapting the modeling languages mentioned above, the other one is limited to BPEL model repository. In this case, it's difficult to achieve interoperation across heterogeneous process repositories.

To relieve this problem, it is common to introduce metamodels or metamodeling techniques to harmonize the differences among various process models. [8] proposed a model transformation framework based on metamodel for model conversion among various kinds of process definition languages, such as BPEL and XPDL. However, the conversion is implemented with the mapping rules from the source process definition language to the target one, which is similar to the approaches mentioned above. Differently, this paper uses PMR as the third part for the interoperation among heterogeneous process models, in which only the mappings from a modeling language to the registry metamodel are needed, rather than that between any two of those languages. Meanwhile, not all the modeling elements of a process modeling language should be mapped to that of PMR since it intends to register the selected metadata of heterogeneous process models, which is essential for further discovery and reuse of process models.

Moreover, most of the modeling languages provide no semantic information to locate requested process models in a precise and efficient way. By introducing semantic techniques into metamodeling method, PMR allows users to register semantics of process models or add semantic annotations to process components at different levels of granularity. In this way, we can promote semantic-based discovery and interoperation of process models in virtual enterprises to some degree.

# 3    Introduction of PMR Metamodel

In this paper, PMR is proposed as an extensible and flexible mechanism to register and discover process models described with a specific process modeling language. It focuses on the selected metadata and common semantics representing the function and structure of process models, rather than the information related to the details of process modeling languages or the platform for process execution, such as fault handling mechanisms[9]. The main structure of PMR is shown in Fig. 1.

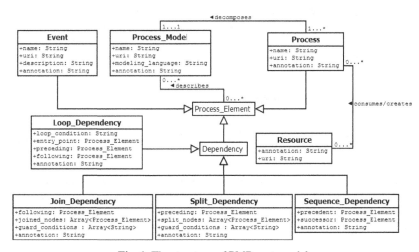

**Fig. 1.** The structure of PMR metamodel

In the PMR metamodel, *Process* is the central metaclass representing a collection of related, structured activities or tasks that achieve a particular business goal. *Process* can be related to *Resources* with the association "consumes" or "creates", which is used to indicate inputs or outputs of a process, respectively. A process can be decomposed, and *Process_Model* in a specific modeling language can describe its decomposition with *Process_Elements*. *Process_Element* is an abstract metaclass that can be instantiated as *Processes*, *Events* or *Dependencies*. More specifically, *Event* designates an occurrence or a state at a particular point of time, and *Dependency* represents the control constraints among *Process_Elements* in a *Process_Model*.

The abstract metaclass *Dependency* can be generalized as *Sequence_Dependency*, *Split_Dependency*, *Join_Dependency*, and *Loop_Dependency* in PMR. In detail, *Sequence_Dependency* connects two *Process_Elements* that comes sequentially. *Split_Dependency* accepts one *Process_Element* as its predecessor and forks into several branches. Each branch will be registered as a "split_node", and it precedes a *Process_element* and is associated with a "guard_condition". Similarly, *Join_Dependency* merges several branches into one branch. *Loop_Dependency* connects three *Process_Elements*, in which "entry_point" is the start of the loop, "preceding" node refers to the end of the loop, and "following" node is the first *Process_Element* coming after the loop.

All the *Process_Elements*, including *Processes*, *Events* and *Dependencies*, as well as *Resources* and *Process_Models*, may contain an "annotation" attribute. It refers to the URI of a concept of an ontology, and can be manually added when necessary for semantic-based discovery of business processes. Suppose two concepts are used to annotate two separate processes respectively that are stored in different repositories, and the relationship between those two concepts is defined in an ontology. If we query a process in a certain repository using one concept, the process annotated by another concept will be located and retrieved from other repositories in terms of the semantics in the ontology. In this way, the underlying relationship between distributed processes can be specified through semantic annotation provided by ontologies to promote semantic discovery of processes, and preserve recall and precision ratio of process discovery.

# 4    Mapping BPEL to PMR

This section defines the mappings from BPEL to PMR. When registering a BPEL process, the corresponding BPEL document(.bpel file) will be registered as the instance of *Process_Model* in PMR. The concrete activities and relationships between the activities described in the BPEL document will be registered as the instances of corresponding metaclasses or their attributes in PMR. Note that in this paper, not all the elements or their attributes in BPEL can be mapped to PMR accordingly. Some of the unmapped elements will be discussed in the second paragraph of section 5.

## 4.1    Mappings of the Main Process

In a BPEL document, the root element <process> is used to describe the main process, which represents the process that is described by the BPEL document as a whole and can be further decomposed. Thus, <process> and its attribute "name" in BPEL will be mapped to metaclass *Process* and its attribute "name" in PMR respectively. <variable> in <variables> in BPEL records the artifacts that are used to perform a process, so it can be mapped to metaclass *Resource* in PMR.

There are many other elements nested directly or recursively in <process> that are used to describe the decomposition of the main process. The mappings of activities are specified in the following sections.

Generally, there are two types of activities in BPEL, i.e. basic activity and structured activity. The mappings of the former will be discussed in section 4.2, and the latter will be presented in section 4.3. Each type of activity has two common attributes "name" and "suppressJoinFailure". As for the attribute "name", it will be mapped to the attribute "name" of metaclass *Process_Element* in PMR. The attribute "suppressJoinFailure" is related to fault handling, which is out of the scope of PMR and the corresponding mapping will be omitted.

## 4.2    Mappings of Basic Activities

Basic activities in BPEL describe elemental steps of the process behavior. In this paper, basic activities are mapped to *Events* or *Processes* in PMR, as Table 1 shows. Note that the elements <assign>, <empty> and <exit> are not considered in the mappings since they are used to describe the details of process execution, which is out of the scope of PMR.

The <invoke> element allows a business process to invoke an operation offered by a partner, and it is the only element that can be mapped to *Process*. Its attributes "inputVariable" (or its equivalent element <toPart>) and "outputVariable" (or its equivalent element <fromPart>) are used to designate the inputs and outputs of <invoke> activity. Therefore, "inputVariable" and <toPart> can be mapped to the association "consumes" from *Process* to *Resource* in PMR. The value of "inputVariable" and the attribute "fromVariable" of <toPart> indicate the corresponding instances of *Resources*, which have been registered as specified in section 4.1 when handling <variables> element. The attribute "outputVariable" and <fromPart> element are mapped in a similar way.

**Table 1.** Mappings of basic activity elements

| Element or attribute in BPEL | Metaclass or association in PMR |
| --- | --- |
| <invoke> | Process |
| inputVariable of <invoke> | consumes ( from Process to Resource ) |
| <toPart> in <toParts> | consumes ( from Process to Resource ) |
| outputVariable of <invoke> | creates ( from Process to Resource ) |
| <fromPart> in <fromParts> | creates ( from Process to Resource ) |
| <receive> | Event |
| <reply> | Event |
| <wait> | Event |
| <throw> | Event |
| <rethrow> | Event |

In this section, all the other basic activities in BPEL are mapped to *Event* except for <invoke>. For example, <receive> and <reply> are two essential activities for communication with other processes, such as receiving or sending a message to a specified port. So it's better to map them to *Events* rather than *Processes*. The <wait> element specifies a delay of the execution and can also be mapped to *Event*. Although <throw> and <rethrow> are used to handle faults, this paper maps them to a special kind of *Event* named "fault" to keep the consistency and integrity when registering the structured activities with these elements. Let's take <if> control flow with two branches as an example. If one branch refers to a normal activity while the other is a <throw> activity, then the <throw> activity cannot be omitted. Otherwise, this branch structure is incomplete.

## 4.3    Mappings of Structured Activities

Structured activities in BPEL prescribe the order in which a collection of activities is executed. They describe how a business process is created by composing the basic activities it performs into structures. There are three common types of structures, i.e. branch structure, loop structure and sequence structure. In this paper, they can be respectively mapped to *Split_Dependency*, *Join_Dependency*, *Loop_Dependency* and *Sequence_Dependency*, but there are still some differences when performing structure and dependency mappings due to the fact that BPEL is a block structured language [7] while PMR is not. Table 2 lists the mappings of those structured activities. Due to page limit, this paper only discusses how to map <if>, <pick> and <sequence> activities, and the mappings of other activities in Table 2 are omitted.

**Table 2.** Mappings of structured activity elements

| Element in BPEL | Metaclass in PMR |
| --- | --- |
| <flow> | Split_Dependency and Join_Dependency |
| <if> | Split_Dependency and Join_Dependency |
| <pick> | Split_Dependency and Join_Dependency |
| <repeatUntil> | Loop_Dependency |
| <while> | Split_Dependency, Join_Dependency and Loop_Dependency |
| <forEach> | Split_Dependency, Join_Dependency or Loop_Dependency (Note: The dependency type to be mapped is depended on the attributes of <forEach>) |
| <sequence> | Sequence_Dependency |

### (a)    Mapping <if> and <pick> Activities

In Table 2, <if> is mapped into a pair of *Split_Dependency* and *Join_Dependency*. Practically, it's easy to convert all the branches of <if> activity into "split_nodes" in *Split_Dependency* and "join_nodes" in *Join_Dependency*. Considering all the branches of <if> activity, one of the branches is expressed as a <condition> element with its corresponding activity, another branch is <else> element, and all the other ones are <elseif> elements. For each branch, its condition should be recorded as the "condition" attribute of the *Split_Dependency* in the pair.

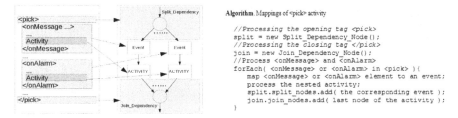

**Fig. 2.** Mappings and the corresponding algorithm of <pick> activity to PMR

The <pick> element in BPEL is used to wait for the occurrence of exactly one event from a set of events and execute the activity associated with that event. It is comprised of a set of branches, and each branch contains an event-activity pair. So <pick> can be mapped to a pair of *Split_Dependency* and *Join_Dependency*. Then, as shown in Fig.2, its sub-elements <onMessage> and <onAlarm> can be treated as sequence control flows, and each sequence control flow starts with an event that the <pick> activity waits for.

**(b)  Mapping of <sequence> Activity**

In BPEL, <sequence> activity is the simplest activity, and the contained tasks in <sequence> activity are performed sequentially. In PMR, *Sequence_Dependency* is not a container of several *Process_Elements*, but a connector between two *Process_Elements*. When mapping <sequence> activity to *Sequence_Dependency*, it's needed to attach sequence dependencies to the process elements. For instance, if there are N activities in a <sequence> activity, at most N-1 *Sequence_Dependencies* should be inserted for mapping. However, it's not necessary to attach a sequence dependency to each process element. In general, a sequence dependency should be added only when neither the preceding process element nor the following one is an instance of *Dependency*. For example, if a <receive> activity and an <invoke> activity are executed sequentially, a sequence dependency should be inserted between them. If they are <if> and <invoke> activities, no sequence dependency is required.

## 4.4    Example of Implementing the Mapping Rules

This section takes the BPEL process "PurchaseOrderProcess" from [2] a registration example to evaluate the effectiveness of PMR metamodel and show how to use the proposed mappings from BPEL to PMR in section 4.3.

If the process in the example above is taken as a whole, its nested activities will be mapped to the PMR-based skeleton in Fig.3(a), with the processes and the dependencies between them. As shown in Fig.3(b), the mapping rules of <receive> and <reply> are used to generate events named "Receive Purchase Order" and "Invoice Processing" respectively when registering the process model, while the mappings of <flow> activity is used to generate the instances of *Split_Dependency* and *Join_Dependency* as the registration information of the process. The rest of the exemplary process will be handled similarly and the trivial descriptions are omitted in this section.

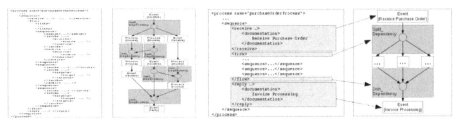

(a) PMR-based skeleton of registering process "PurchaseOrderProcess"

(b) Mappings from nested activities in BPEL to the metaclasses in PMR

**Fig. 3.** Example of implementing the mapping rules

## 5    Conclusion and Future Work

In this paper, a registration metamodel called PMR is proposed to register BPEL process models. Then, the mapping rules from BPEL to PMR with mapping algorithms are defined to transform BPEL process models to the corresponding registration information based on PMR. Next, we use an example to show that the mapping rules can facilitate automatic registration of BPEL processes effectively.

However, not all the elements in BPEL specification can be mapped to the corresponding metaclasses and associations of PMR in this paper. For example, <extensionActivity> and <scope> are not taken into account due the complexity of the mappings, and a more comprehensive mapping will be given in the next step. In addition, the mapping rules and the corresponding algorithms are incomplete due to page limit, and considerable work is needed to be done later. Finally, we plan to define the mappings from other process modeling languages to PMR, and develop a PMR-based registration tool to support automatic registration of more process models in practice.

## References

1. Jeusfeld, M., Backlund, P., Ralyté, J.: Classifying Interoperability Problems for a Method Chunk Repository. Enterprise Interoperability II, 315–326 (2007); Model registration. Master thesis. Wuhan University (2011) (in Chinese)
2. OASIS: Web Services Business Process Execution Language Version 2.0 Standard (2007), http://docs.oasis-open.org/wsbpel/2.0/wsbpel-v2.0.html
3. Khodabakchian, E., Shaffer, D., Gaur, H., Zirn, M.: SOA Best Practices: The BPEL Cookbook, http://www.oracle.com/technetwork/articles/soa/index-095969.html
4. Aslam, M.A., Auer, S., Shen, J.: From BPEL4WS Process Model to Full OWL-S Ontology. Faculty of Informatics-Papers, 433 (2006)
5. Yuan, P., Jin, H., Yuan, S., Cao, W., Jiang, L.: WFTXB: A Tool for Translating between XPDL and BPEL. In: High Performance Computing and Communications, pp. 647–652 (2008)

6. Schumm, D., Karastoyanova, D., Leymann, F., Nitzsche, J.: On Visualizing and Modeling BPEL with BPMN. In: Grid and Pervasive Computing Conference, pp. 80–87 (2009)
7. Gao, Y.: BPMN-BPEL transformation and round trip engineering. Technical report, eClarus software (2006)
8. Li, H., Lan, Y., Yang, L., Guo, S.: A Framework for Workflow Process Definition Transformation Based on Meta-Model. In: Computer Science and Software Engineering, pp. 566–569 (2008)
9. Chong, W., Keqing, H., Wen, Z., et al.: Personalized Reuse of Business Process through the Metamodel for Process Model Registration. In: The 4th International Workshop on Personalization in Grid, Service and Cloud Computing (PGSC 2010) at The 9th International Conference on Grid and Cloud Computing (GCC 2010), pp. 438–443. IEEE Computer Society, Nanjing (2010)

# Context-Specific Multi-Model-Template Retrieval

Frank Hilbert and Raimar J. Scherer

Institute of Construction Informatics, Dresden University of Technology,
Dresden, Germany
{Frank.Hilbert,Raimar.Scherer}@tu-dresden.de

**Abstract.** Although the construction industry, in contrast to the stationary industry, is characterized by One of a Kind fabrication, there can be found similarities in project, product, process and organizational structures. The focus of this paper is to identify relationships, roles and model types, which are often needed in a specific project context and summarize these similarities by the use of a collaboration ontology providing for Multi-Model logistics. Reference models on the one side and a model to describe the project context on the other side should ensure that all partners retrieve precisely situation-specific selections of the application models which are necessary for their tasks. Furthermore, a pilot scenario is presented, which evaluate this approach on an Azure Cloud collaboration platform. As a result, we obtain an approach, which allows simplified handling and reuse of complex project-, product- and collaboration-models in order to support the collaboration within a virtual Organization in Construction Industry.

**Keywords:** Context model, Multi-Model, Project Collaboration Ontology.

## 1 Introduction

In History of the construction industry, always separate independent organizations of different domains and disciplines joined together in various short-term forms of organisation to combine their core competencies for handling of large and complex construction projects [1]. To allow a collaborative partnership with cooperative aspects, it is necessary to set up transparent rules for cooperation with clearly defined competencies, rights and duties of the participants, therefore various project-specific organizational, process and product models are necessary. Organizational models have evolved from tayloristic, hierarchical organizational structures towards to new forms of organization, like Virtual Organization, Collaborative Networked Organization or VO Breeding Environments as can found in [2]. For the definition of organizational roles in the building industry, there are several classifications developed, such as IFC-Actor roles [3] and OmniClass [4]. For the modelling of processes it is essential if there are predominantly material or information-transforming processes. For both process model types a variety of methods, languages and notations have been developed, here a detailed summary is given in [5]. In our Work we focus on information transforming processes. To facilitate the representation and ex-

L.M. Camarinha-Matos, L. Xu, and H. Afsarmanesh (Eds.): PRO-VE 2012, IFIP AICT 380, pp. 234–241, 2012.
© IFIP International Federation for Information Processing 2012

change of product information, data product models are an efficient way and in the course of time, they have evolved from the pure 2D drawings with small reuse value to rich building information models (a detailed summary is given in [6]). The current trend is concerned with modeling of implicit dependencies between different and inhomogeneous elementary models in the form of so-called Multi-Models (see chapter 2.2).

Although AEC is typically characterized by an One of a Kind fabrication, there can be found similarities in organizational, process and product structures, because a construction process is a repeated but mostly not identical course of action, while a construction product is a unique composition of common construction processes [5]. Similarities can be found by comparison of model metadata. Therefore the focus of this paper is the use of such implicit similarities to support project collaboration. With the help of ontologies dynamic entity centric context models [7] (actor, process and product context) should be generated, which summarize the information obtained by crosslinking the metadata. It is expected that with the help of such a context model significantly more context-specific collaboration possibilities can be determined.

In chapter 2 the developed project collaboration ontology is described and the generation of the context model is presented in Chapter 3. The last paragraph summarizes the results and gives a short outlook.

## 2    Project Collaboration Ontology

The Fundamental idea of the Project Collaboration Ontology is a generic formal description of organisation, process and product information to enable the utilization in a framework of integrated processes. Thereby Collaboration includes all the process and product related activities between entities (actors, processes and products), whose common goal is the creation of a product (or service) [8]. Basic elements of collaboration are coordination; communication and cooperation (see also [9]). For the representation of the entities we orient on the Semantic Web approach [10] and expand all entities with descriptive, machine-readable metadata, organized in ontologies, which are defined in [11] as "a formal, explicit specification of a shared conceptualization". This allows automated interpretation, evaluation and processing of information and enables us to extract the implicit knowledge, which can represent similarities. Thereby Ontologies stores concepts as well instances [12]. The concepts consist of classes of descriptive properties with cardinality, transitivity and symmetry qualities. Each property has a definition range and a set of values, distinguishing here between data type properties, representing simple Data types and class properties, which map classes to other and can be organized in hierarchical structures. Ontology containers can be evaluated through description logic algorithms used by Reasoner, for example RACER [13] or JESS [14]. Another important advantage is the possibility to integrate other ontologies. Figure 1 illustrates the structure of the used Project Collaboration Ontology integrating various ontologies necessary for the context determination, as as described below. If several Organizations joining collaboration the same underlying concepts and terminology has to be used.

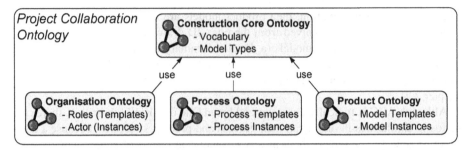

**Fig. 1.** Project Collaboration Ontology (PCO)

The Purpose of the *Construction Core Ontology* on the top is to define concepts and relationships between them, used in the construction domain. More information about this core ontology can be found in [16].

(1) The scope of the *Organisation Ontology* is describing the actors, rules of their collaboration as well as roles and permissions of a virtual Organization in an organizational model. In our approach, we use an organisational model, which closely follows the IFC standard [3] mapping the competences of involved partners to roles, which consist of permissions on product model types (e.g. multi-model types, defined in the construction core ontology). Such permissions may also be required for the execution of processes. The distinction between potential roles (competences) and current user roles, as described in [17] will be neglected here.

(2) Reusable Processes can be depicted as Configurable Reference Process Models (CRPM) as described in [5]. In our scenario we use Business Process Modelling Notation (BPMN) [18] for the representation of common reference processes, which specify used resources, produced results and necessary permissions. Such Reference Processes are stored in the *Process Ontology* and can have a large number of attributes. Important for our scenario is the description of in- and output models as well as necessary actor-permissions.

(3) The basic idea of the *Product Ontology* is the description of product model instances and templates for a better assignment of actors and processes. Eessential with the use of product models are the knowledge of their dependencies. For this requirement in the German research project Mefisto [19] the multi-model approach was developed, which provides the externalization of implicit relationship of semantically and structurally inhomogeneous models. The Multi-Model was transferred in a multi-model container (MMC) which contains a generic link model, describing the relationships between models elements together with the application models, described by metadata (more information is given by Fuchs in [20]). Reference models can be described by multi-model templates (MMT), which consist of partly filled MMC with metadata about the required application models [21]. Considering the different skills and tasks of the involved actors, it is not necessary for them to know all product models in every technical detailing. Therefore MMCs may consist of a task depending set of various application models, described as MMT. Input models, required for the instantiation of processes and their output models are specified as multi-model templates.

# 3    The Derivation of the Context Model

Entity models cannot capture all the relationships between the entities of a construction project that affect collaboration processes. Some dependencies are beyond the scope of the reference templates (e.g. process patterns or MMTs), but can help to identify exceptions or conflicts. Therefore a context model to characterize the considered project situation is necessary, as described in [22]. Several context models for every entity type can be considered. As example we show the generation of the actor-context model, which should specify the available collaboration options for an actor to instantiate processes, use existing models or create new models in the current state of all project entities. As the actor context model reflects the relationship information of this actor to other entities, their structure follows the main aspects of the derived entity ontologies. In our case, the actor context model consists of relationship information from this actor to processes, to multi-models and to other actors. The generation of the context model occurs in three steps (see Fig.2) as described below:

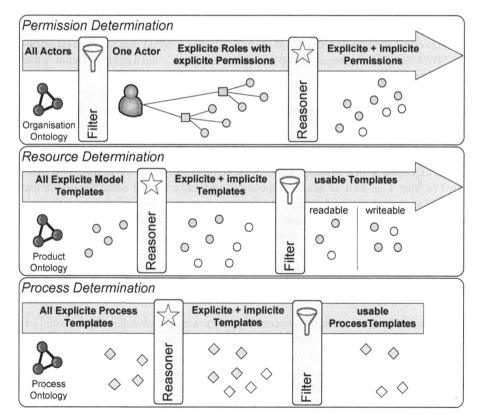

**Fig. 2.** Context model determination in three steps

(1) *Permission determination*: To determine utilizable processes and product models it is necessary in a first step, to collect actor roles with their permissions. The explicit permissions are determined from the actor instance of the organization ontology. If roles are organized hierarchic (e.g. OmniClass Organizational Roles [4]) so explicitly assigned roles (e.g. 34-251100 Space Designer) includes also implicit roles (e.g. 34-250000 Interior Designer). The same can apply for permissions: From a write permission can be derived the read permission, which can be necessary to start a process. It should be noted that the permission accumulation of roles should correspond to specific conditions (e.g. Separation of Duty [23]). To generate the extended permissions list, the organization ontology is evaluated by an ontology Reasoner who can derives further facts, either from the description of the organisation structure as well as from the instance data.

(2) *Resource determination*: In the Resource ontology explicit process templates are specified by their metadata. The semantic and structure of these metadata can be used to evaluate similarities, dependencies and inheritance structures. In our example, we limit ourselves to four class attributes: Domain, Project Phase, Level of Detail and Status, whose structure and vocabulary is defined in the construction core ontology. In step two, the structure of the metadata can now be used to inflate the object space of the product model templates (MMT). For example, a MMT has the domain attribute "BIM.BES.LBS", project phase "tender preparation", the Level of Detail value "5" (fine) and the status "beta", it can shortly described as follows: MMT(BIM.BES.LBS, tender preparation, LoD 5, status beta). This template also implicitly corresponds to even more coarsely defined templates, as e.g. MMT(BIM, Tender, LOD 1, beta). In addition we can use the information about the included application models to determined potentially compassable multi-model Templates (without linkmodel). In this manner, the object space of the product model templates can be expanded with a "implicit hull". A subsequent filter uses the permissions identified in Step 1 as well as actor competences and capacity and collect readable and writable product model templates.

(3) *Identifying usable processes*: A similar procedure is applied in the evaluation of process templates. A Reasoner generates a transitive hull by the recombination of explicit processes from the process ontology. New implicit (in this case transitive) processes can occur, which have the same input model like the first process and the same output model as the last process. The enlarged object space is reduced again by a filter using the previously determined readable (input) and writable (output) models.

If we connect in a last step, the process templates with the available input model instances, we obtain (for the current project context) all processes which can be used and all product models, which can be created. Thereby, if implicit models are potential input models for process templates, they may also increase the number of executable processes. Therefore, iterations are worthwhile.

As result a rich actor-context model is created with added further elements by the use of Ontologies. In a similar manner, the context models for the consideration of processes (collect usable actors and product models) and product models (shows authorized actors and executable processes) can be determined.

# 4    Results, Pilot and Outlook

By the use of the context model it is possible to identify similarities as well as transitivity's to determine on the basis of explicitly specified processes further implicit processes and suitable implicit models in the form of an "implicit envelope". It turns out that with the use of additional context information it is possible, to improve the selection of proportionate templates either qualitatively (by selection) and quantitatively (by the generation of the implicit envelope). So a context-dependent prediction is possible, whether a specified process can be started or a special model is available (or can be generated) in a current situation of the project. As a result, we obtain an Approach for generating rich context models, which allows the use of structural similarities and dependencies of product models within processes. Using semantically described task and model templates on the one side and a rich context model describing the project context on the other side should ensure that all partners receive a situation-specific selection of process and model templates which are necessary for their task and reflect the project situation at the current moment.

The use of the presented approach is being evaluated in the German BMBF research project Mefisto aims at overcoming client-contractor interoperability problems in construction processes based on partnership [24]. The overall architecture of the Mefisto collaboration platform is a hybrid SOA-based system on a Microsoft Azure cloud environment [25] with various platform services providing for the integration of local legacy applications, such as 3D CAD, scheduling, quantity take-off, ERP and PPM systems. So each project partner continues use its own familiar tools and environment meanwhile the communication with other partners is achieved by means of harmonised Multi-Model Containers, created and guided in process-centric manner by means of the project collaboration ontology. The use of the in Chapter 2 presented ontologies (jena framework) and Reasoner (jess Reasoner) are here encapsulated as methods of platform services for horizontal and vertical information integration. In a pilot scenario for bidding processes as described in [24] MMTs for tenders and offers are exchanged and evaluated with potential suppliers. Due to the shortness of the paper, most of the addressed themes could only be briefly highlighted. Details can be found the technical reports of the Mefisto project.

Several Approaches for collaborative Networks exist, especially for virtual enterprises, professional virtual communities or collaborative virtual laboratories [2]. Plisson present in [26] an Ontology for virtual organisation breeding environments (VBE) focused on organisational structures. He uses actor and role concept without a context-and domain-specific relation.

The focus of this paper is not the invention of a new organizational model, but rather the integration of contextual and model-structure information in a collaboration structure. In the presented approach, only a reduced set of entity attributes was considered. By using data mining techniques it is possible to consider complex dynamic attribute sets. Also, we have only used the entity ontologies to determine the context model. Here the consideration of further (Project and World) factors is necessary. This approach can also be used for optimization purposes, for example, to define model templates that satisfy reasonable process orchestration, or to create Roles which have accurately privileges identified in the transitive processes - so that as few as possible Roles are needed. In this paper, we focus on information-transforming processes in a project planning phase, but the approach can be adapted for use in subsequent phases - including material transforming processes.

**Acknowledgments.** The research described in this paper was enabled by the financial support of the German Ministry of Education and Research, Department of ICT under Contract No. 01lA09001A, which is gratefully acknowledged. Moreover, the authors would like point out that the results presented have been developed in collaboration with industry and academic partners (www.mefisto-bau.de) of the Mefisto project.

# References

1. Binding, G.: Construction in the Middle Ages. In: Wissenschaftliche Buchgesell-schaft, Darmstadt, p. 269 (1993) (in German)
2. Camarinha-Matos, L.M., Afsarmanesh, H.: A comprehensive modelling framework for collaborative networked organizations. Journal of Intelligent Manufacturing (2007)
3. buildingSMART: Specifications of the Industry Foundation Classes (IFC), Standard (2010),
   http://buildingsmart-tech.org/products/
   ifc_specification/ifc-releases
4. OmniClass – A Strategy for Classifying the Built Environment, Webside,
   http://www.omniclass.org/
5. Scherer, R., Sharmak, W.: Process Risk Management Using Configurable Process Models. In: Camarinha-Matos, L.M., Pereira-Klen, A., Afsarmanesh, H. (eds.) PRO-VE 2011. IFIP AICT, vol. 362, pp. 341–348. Springer, Heidelberg (2011)
6. Weise, M.: Ein Ansatz zur Abbildung von Änderungen in der modell-basierten Objektplanung. Dissertation, Institut für Bauinformatik, Technische Universität Dresden, Dresden (2006)
7. Abowd, G.D., Dey, A.K.: Towards a Better Understanding of Context and Context-Awareness. In: Gellersen, H.-W. (ed.) HUC 1999. LNCS, vol. 1707, pp. 304–307. Springer, Heidelberg (1999)
8. Altmann, J.: Kooperative Softwareentwicklung – Rechnerunterstützte Koordination und Kooperation in Softwareprojekten. Dissertation, Linz (1999)
9. Luczak, D., Bullinger, H.-J., Schlick, C., Ziegler, J. (Hrsg.): Unterstützung flexibler Kooperation durch Software: Methoden, Systeme, Beispiele. Springer, Heidelberg (2001)
10. Davies, J., Fensel, D., van Harmelen, F.: Towards the Semantic Web: Ontology-Driven Knowledge Management. John Wiley & Sons (2003)
11. Studer, R., Benjamins, R., Fensel, D.: Knowledge Engineering: Principles and Methods. Data & Knowledge Engineering 25(1-2), 161–198 (1998)
12. Baader, F.: The Description Logic Handbook: Theory, Implementation and Applications. Cambridge University Press, Cambridge (2003)
13. Haarslev, V., Möller, R.: RACER System Description. In: Goré, R.P., Leitsch, A., Nipkow, T. (eds.) IJCAR 2001. LNCS (LNAI), vol. 2083, pp. 701–705. Springer, Heidelberg (2001)
14. Friedman-Hill, E.J.: Jess, The Expert System Shell for the Java Platform. Sandia National Laboratories, Livermore, CA (2001)

15. Gomez-Perez, A., Fernandez-Lopez, M., Corcho, O.: Ontological Engineering. Springer, Berlin (2004)
16. Schapke, S.-E., Kadolsky, M., Scherer, R.J.: Representing project information spaces based on semantic multi-model annotations. In: Proc. CONVR 2011, International Conference on Construction Applications of Virtual Reality, Weimar, Germany (2011)
17. Hilbert, F., Araujo, L., Scherer, R.J.: Multi-model-based Access Control in Construction Projects. In: Bryans, J.W., Fitzgerald, J.S. (eds.) Proc. Formal Aspects of Virtual Organisations (FAVO 2011), Sao Paulo, Brazil (2011)
18. Object Management Group: Business Process Model and Notation (BPMN), http://www.omg.org/spec/BPMN/
19. MEFISTO: Management – Führung – Information – Simulation im Bauwesen. German BMBF research project (BMBF Project 01IA09001), Website, http://www.mefisto-bau.de
20. Fuchs, S., Kadolsky, M., Scherer, R.J.: Formal Description of a Generic Multi-Model. In: 20th IEEE International Workshops on Enabling Technologies: Infrastructure for Collaborative Enterprises (WETICE), Paris, France (2011)
21. Scherer, R.J., Schapke, S.-E., Katranuschkov, P.: Mefisto: A Model, Information and Knowledge Platform for the Construction Industry. In German: Mefisto: Eine Modell-, Informations- und Wissensplattform für das Bauwesen, Project Presentation, BMBF Project 01IA09001 (2010)
22. Hilbert, F.: Context sensitive access to multi-models. In: Proc. 23rd European Conference Forum Bauinformatik, Cork, Irland (2011) (in German)
23. Ferraiolo, D.F., Cugini, J.A., Kuhn, D.R.: Role-based access control (rbac): Features and motivations. In: Proceedings of 11th Annual Computer Security Application (1995)
24. Schapke, S.-E., Fuchs, S.: Mefisto – A multi-model-based platform for construction project management. In: Proc. 2nd Mefisto Congress MEFISTO: Management – Führung – Information – Simulation im Bauwesen, Dresden, Germany (2011)
25. Microsoft Azure, http://www.microsoft.com/windowsazure/
26. Plisson, J., Ljubic, P., Mozetic, I., Lavrac, N.: An ontology for virtual organization breeding environments. IEEE Trans. on Systems, Man, and Cybernetics 37 (2007)

# 9

## Collaborative Business Frameworks II

# Embedding Interoperability in System of Systems: Definition and Characterization of Fundamental Requirements

Nicolas Daclin

LGI2P – Laboratoire de Génie Informatique et d'Ingénierie de Production
Site de l'Ecole des Mines d'Alès – Parc scientifique G. Besse
30035 Nîmes cedex 1, France
nicolas.daclin@mines-ales.fr

**Abstract.** The main objective of this communication is to discuss the engineering of a System of Systems (SoS), including interoperability concept. More precisely, the here presented research focuses on the fundamental requirements to consider in a System of Systems Engineering (SoSE) project and that have to be maintain during the entire life cycle of a SoS. First, the concept of interoperability, according to its definition and its characteristics, is presented. Then, the concept of SoS is presented in the same manner. This leads to introduce and present the possible links between System of Systems and interoperability. These links are (1) clarified and defined, (2) re-expressed to meet requirements' definition and (3) not related to a given SoS in order to be generic.

**Keywords:** System Engineering, System of Systems, interoperability, requirements.

## 1    Introduction

Global environment, fundamental changes and fast evolution lead organizations and further, our society, to be able to adapt to these constraints (*e.g.* technological, organizational...). To handle this context, the concept of *System of Systems* (SoS) has become essential in order to create added value and to be efficient. More than anything, System of Systems Engineering (SoSE) becomes also essential in order to limit and avoid extra-cost, delay...throughout SoS life cycle *i.e.* not only for its engineering phase but also for its disassembly phase *via* its operational phase. On the other hand, *interoperability* has become a crucial issue to consider for organizations that want to interact in a common relationship. In this way, numerous researches have been initiated and performed from last years. Although System of Systems' characteristics and interoperability characteristics present possible similitude, their connections and the possible advantages to consider these two concepts as complementary are not yet highlighted. The here presented research focuses on the definition and characterization of fundamental requirements to consider in a SoSE

L.M. Camarinha-Matos, L. Xu, and H. Afsarmanesh (Eds.): PRO-VE 2012, IFIP AICT 380, pp. 245–253, 2012.
© IFIP International Federation for Information Processing 2012

project and that have to be maintain during the entire life cycle of SoS and, in compliance with interoperability paradigm.

This paper is structured as follow. After this brief introduction, the needs and issues addressed by our research are described in the second section. Section 3 and 4 present the notions of interoperability as well as SoS, according to their definitions and their characteristics. Section 5 presents a first tentative of definition and characterization of fundamental SoS requirements. The final section presents the conclusion, and the future perspectives for this research.

## 2     Problematic and Needs

Dealing with System Engineering (SE) means to be able to verify [1] requirements [2] to respect all along the life cycle of the studied system [3]. In the case of SoSE, that means (1) to identify these requirements and, (2) these requirements remain as generic as possible (not related to a specific SoS) in order to be adapted to any SoSE project. First, the concept of System of Systems is emerging from last years. Basically, a SoS can be shown as a system resulting from the interaction of its constituent systems that are themselves independent [4]. On the other hand several researches on systems interoperability [5] have been initiated from last decades to facilitate and to ensure "relationship" basically in terms of sharing and exchange. Both concepts deal with the presence of several systems to put in relation, in order to work together and to reach a final purpose. In this way, it is interesting to analyze potential similitude that can be shared by interoperability and SoS. Precisely, the two concepts deal with characteristics that they have to respect, and these characteristics seem to be closely linked. Furthermore, it is interesting to identify these relations and their related works, in order to facilitate the engineering of SoS. This work attempts to point out:

- If interoperability is a part of SoS then, what fundamental requirement(s) belonging to interoperability can be useful to design SoS;
- A definition and an adaptation of these identified requirements to the specificity of SoS.

Thus, it is necessary to analyze which requirement(s) is not clearly identified and/or defined in order to embed in SoS paradigm to evaluate it.

Secondly, once the requirements are identified, they have to be exploitable either by acquirer or prime contractor. However, requirements are often expressed with natural language giving their use difficult (omission, repetition, ambiguity, conflict) [6]. From a SE point of view, it means that requirements have to be re-expressed to meet formal requirements' definition, in order to avoid problems related to expressivity. Thus, requirements must be clearly expressed, identifiable, traceable, verifiable, unambiguous, and consistent with another requirement. The final purpose is to allow the use of formal verification techniques in order to verify the satisfaction or not of these defined SoS requirements.

# 3    Interoperability

Numerous initiatives, in different fields (crisis management, military, enterprises, health care, transport…) [7] [8], developed over the past years, have shown that systems' ability to be interoperable, is a major issue and a key factor for the success of collaboration. Regarding enterprise interoperability, it is defined as the *"ability of enterprises and entities within those enterprises to communicate and to interact effectively"* [9]. Furthermore, to study interoperability, several works have defined the fundamental characteristics to consider to develop interoperability. Thus, according to [10] [11] [12], interoperability can be characterized by the four characteristics:

- *Compatibility.* It represents the ability of partners to ensure interfacing aspect, mainly related to interoperability barriers (conceptual, technological, and organizational).
- *Interoperation.* It represents the ability of partners to achieve a performance level in terms of interactions (quality of exchange, exchange time…), over a partnership.
- *Autonomy.* It represents the ability of a partner to receive or provide services, data, product… while retaining its own operational thinking.
- *Reversibility.* It represents the ability of a partner to be still able to achieve its original objectives, after a partnership, despite adaptations or changes.

Existing approaches to measure and to evaluate interoperability are mainly focused on maturity measurement [13]. In terms of maturity models for interoperability, we can mention the important contribution such as LISI, OIM and LCIM. In manufacturing fields we can also note the MMEI. The LISI proposes a maturity model allowing to define, to measure and to assess the interoperability of Information Systems [14]. The OIM [15] is an extension of the LISI and addresses the evaluation of the interoperability maturity from an organizational point of view. The LCIM [16] considers the evaluation of the conceptual interoperability. Based on these existing maturity models, the MMEI [17] for enterprise interoperability covers all facets of interoperability, according to the conceptual, organizational and technological issues.

Last, it is to note that more formal approaches are developed for the last years. The objective of these researches is to consider interoperability from a formal point of view in order, to verify, to measure and to evaluate it. For instance, [18] defines three main quality attributes (connectivity, information flow and data latency), and their equations in order to measure the efficiency of operational interoperability. [19] takes also an interest in the measurement and the assessment of the operational interoperability. In this way, these works define height modes (directional, self, pure, contextual, time variant, constrained upper bound collaborative and confrontational) and their associated metrics. Finally, works proposed in [20] uses and offers an approach based and supported by formal verification techniques to verify interoperability requirements - according to the main characteristics of interoperability - in a public or private collaborative process. Precisely, the goal is to verify that a given collaborative process satisfies (or not) a set of properties related to interoperability in terms of compatibility, interoperation, autonomy and reversibility and according to a predefined interoperability requirements repository.

## 4    System of Systems

Basically, a SoS can be defined as *"a set of collaborative integrated systems"* [21]. Numerous definitions of SoS are existing in literature, each one with their own specificities, but the fundamental concept still remains the same [22] [23] [24]; a SoS is a collection of several systems which interact for a given purpose that an isolated system cannot achieve alone. Beyond these basic definitions, a SoS presents some characteristics that define and differentiate it from a simple system. Indeed, among the numerous definitions, [25] highlights five fundamental characteristics that define a System of Systems (known as Maier's criterion):

- *Operational independence.* It represents the ability of a given system to operate independently and efficiently if the SoS is disassembled.
- *Managerial independence.* It represents the ability of a given system to keep and to continue its operational purpose, while it is integrated to SoS.
- *Distribution.* The set of systems that compose the SoS are geographically distributed over a large extent.
- *Evolutionary.* The development and existence of SoS is evolutionary. Functions and purposes can be added/ removed/ modified.
- *Emergence.* The SoS performs functions and achieves purpose that component cannot fulfill independently.

Nowadays, the concept of SoS is widely studied and deployed in numerous fields where several systems have to interact [26] [27] [28]. As in interoperability fields, these study consider SoS paradigm under a formal point of view or not. For instance, [28] considers SoS paradigm in order to participate to the Spatial Data Infrastructure (SDI) life cycle. [27] adopts a more formal vision of the SoS applied to crisis management. Its work focuses on the definition of coupling matrix - according coupled systems - in order to ensure (and to secure) the services provided by SoS, despite its evolution. Finally, [26] proposes methods and tools based on state modeling and simulation in order to evaluate operational performance effectiveness of the SoS.

According to the previous definitions, Systems Interoperability concept and System of Systems concept share common basic characteristics. Indeed, SoS is developed when several systems (human, technological, organizational) are connected, exchange, and share, in order to work together and to reach a final purpose. Moreover, the characteristics of interoperability such as autonomy and reversibility characterize also a SoS commonly as managerial and operational independence. Despite, the fact that the word *"interoperability"* is not always mentioned in literature when we talk about SoS, interoperability seems to be a property that a SoS must fulfill. Last, SoS is a broader concept than interoperability, so, a *SoS is based (in part) on interoperable systems but interoperable systems do not constitute a SoS.* Among characteristics of SoS and interoperability someone –such as managerial and operational independence - are more or less studied due to (1) a lack of definition of these requirements (they stay often at a high level of abstraction) and (2) to the difficulties to evaluate them formally. In this way, we are taking an interest in the definition and the characterization of the two before-mentioned characteristics belonging both to interoperability and SoS.

## 5    Requirements Definition and Characterization

The objective is to clarify and to propose first definitions and formalizations of the two SoS requirements, such as *"Managerial independence"* and *"Operational independence"*. These definitions are based on the characterization of these requirements in SoS and interoperability paradigm. This formalization is not specific to any SoS and, furthermore, can act as basis to specify and precise these fundamental requirements for a specific SoS or other concepts that integrate either autonomy and/or reversibility.

Let S the set of systems that constitute the System of Systems:

$$S = \{s_i | 1 \leq i \leq N\}, N, i \in \mathbb{N}^*$$

Let $\prod$ the set of moment (time) of the System of Systems' life cycle:

$$\prod = \{\pi | \pi = post \lor per \lor pre\}$$

Where:

- *pre*: the time before the assembling of the System of Systems.
- *per*: the time when the System of Systems is existing and fulfill its purpose.
- *post*: the time when a system component of a System of Systems is disassembled at the end of the System of Systems existence.

Let F the set of functions[1] of a system at a given moment of the SoS life cycle:

$$F(\pi)_{s_i} = \{f(\pi)_i | 1 \leq i \leq N\}, N, i \in \mathbb{N}^*$$

Where:

- $f(\pi)_i \in \{executable, \overline{executable}\}$ indicates that a given function of the system is executable, *i.e.* the function is able deliver its services, products… or non executable *i.e.* the function is unable.

Let P the set of performances of a given system at a given moment of the SoS life cycle:

$$P(\pi)_{s_i} = \{p(\pi)_i | 1 \leq i \leq N\}, N, i \in \mathbb{N}^*$$

Let E the set of admissible variations of a given performance *p* of a given system:

$$E = \{\varepsilon_i | 1 \leq i \leq N\}, N, i \in \mathbb{N}^*$$

---

[1] A function is *"a task, action or activity performed to achieve a desired outcome"*.[29]

The admissible variations of the performance can be a loss of performance (*e.g.* increasing of the time of an activity) or a gain of performance (*e.g.* decreasing of the time of an activity).

**Managerial Independence (autonomy)**

We define managerial independence requirement as: "*the ability for each system, that contribute to the SoS, to satisfy its own performance[2] and integrity[3] during SoS existence*". This statement is formalized by the following equation:

$$MI = Perf\ (per) \wedge Int(per)$$

Where:

- $MI \in \{true, false\}$, is the property of the managerial independence of the SoS. Its value depends of the property of performance and the property of integrity during the existence of the SoS.
- $Int(per) \in \{true, false\}$, is the integrity of a system during the existence of the SoS such as:

$$Int(per) = \begin{cases} true\ iff\ F(per)_{s_i} = executable \\ false\ otherwise \end{cases}$$

Integrity is considered as true if and only if all the functions of a system during its participation to the SoS are executable. It means, for instance, that if a given resource of the system cannot perform its own activity because it is involved in the SoS, this activity is still executable by the system.

- $Perf(per) \in \{true, false\}$, is the performance of a system during the existence of the SoS such as:

$$Perf(per) = \begin{cases} true\ iff \begin{cases} P(per)_{s_i} = P(pre)_{s_i}\ if\ E = \emptyset \\ \vee \\ P(per)_{s_i} = P(pre)_{s_i} \pm E\ otherwise \end{cases} \\ false\ otherwise \end{cases}$$

Performance is considered as true if and only if the system can reach its own objectives during its participation to the SoS.

**Operational Independence (reversibility)**

We define operational independence requirement as: "*the ability for each system to satisfy performance and integrity after its disassembling from the SoS*". This statement is specified by the following equation:

$$OI = Perf(post) \wedge Int(post)$$

Where:

- $OI \in \{true, false\}$, is the property of operational independence of the SoS. Its value depends of the property of performance and the property of integrity of a given system components after the disassembling of the SoS.

---

[2] Performance is "*the ability of a system to reach its objectives*".[30]
[3] Integrity is "*the ability of a system to stay coherent and to be able to ensure its functions*".[30]

- $Int(post) \in \{true, false\}$, is the integrity of a system component after the SoS is disassembled, such as:

$$Int(post) = \begin{cases} true \ iff \ F(post)_{s_i} = executable \\ false \ otherwise \end{cases}$$

Integrity is considered as true if and only if all the own functions of the system after it is disassembled of the SoS, are executable. It means, for instance, that if a given resource is retrieve (or not) by the system to perform it original activity, this activity is executable by the system.

- $Perf(post) \in \{true, false\}$, is the performance of a system component after the SoS is disassembled, such as:

$$Perf(post) = \begin{cases} true \ iff \begin{cases} P(post)_{s_i} = P(pre)_{s_i} \ if \ E = \emptyset \\ \vee \\ P(post)_{s_i} = P(pre)_{s_i} \pm E \ otherwise \end{cases} \\ false \ otherwise \end{cases}$$

Performance is considered as true if and only if the system can reach its own objectives after it is disassembled of the SoS.

This first formalization considers only two requirements that defines interoperability and that are existing in SoS. From a Collaborative Network Organizations point of view, it would be interesting to decompose and specify these two requirements for Virtual Organization [31] where autonomy and reversibility take a preponderant part in consequence of its temporary aspect (creation on business opportunity, operation, disassembling). Furthermore, it will be essential, to consider other requirements. For instance, the characteristic of emergence is primordial so that the SoS performs its functions and achieves its purpose. Indeed, it is important to make sure of (and to maintain) the emergence of "good" properties (or behavior) expected or not and, to anticipate and to eradicate the emergence of "bad" properties on (1) the SoS itself and (2) on the components.

# 6    Conclusion and Prospects

In collaborative context SoS Engineering takes a preponderant part to make SoS as efficient as possible. SoS presents characteristics that have to be satisfy during all its lifecycle phases. This paper has presented a first rapprochement with another concept related to collaboration between systems *i.e.* interoperability. Common characteristics such as operational/managerial independence for SoS and autonomy/reversibility for interoperability are closely related but not yet clearly defined and studied. In this way the first goal was to precise and clarify this characteristics, beyond their basics definitions and, in order to be studied deeper, as shown in this communication. Future work is related to the definition of criteria that have to allow to fully characterize these requirements in order to be formally proven.

# References

1. ISO 8402: Quality management and quality assurance, Vocabulary, 2nd edn. International Standard Organization (April 01, 1994)
2. Scucanec, S.J., Van Gaasbeek, J.R.: A day in the life of a verification requirement. U.S. Air Force T&E Days, Los Angeles (February 2008)
3. INCOSE: System Engineering (SE) Handbook Working Group, System Engineering Handbook, A « How To ». Version 3.1, Guide For All Engineers (2007)
4. Anderson, D.J., Campbell, J.E., Chapman, L.D.: Evaluating a complex System of Systems using state modeling and simulation. In: National Defense Industrial Association Systems Engineering Conference, San Diego, USA (2003)
5. IEEE: A compilation of IEEE standard computer glossaries, Standard computer dictionary, New York (1990)
6. ISO/IEC 15288:2008(E): IEEE Standards 15288.2008 – Systems engineering – System life cycle processes, 2nd edn. (February 2008)
7. Truptil, S., Benaben, F., Pingaud, H.: Collaborative process design for Mediation Information System Engineering. In: 6th International ISCRAM Conference, Gothenburg, Sweden (May 2009)
8. Advanced Technologies for Interoperability of Heterogeneous Enterprise Networks and their Applications (ATHENA): Integrated Project Proposal – Description of work (2003)
9. ISO/DIS 11345-1: Advanced automation technologies and their applications. Part 1: Framework for enterprise interoperability (2009)
10. Panetto, H.: Meta-modèles et modèles pour l'intégration et l'interopérabilité des applications d'entreprises de production. In: Habilitation à Diriger des Recherches, Université de Nancy 1 (2006) (in French)
11. Chen, D., Dassisti, M., Elveaeter, B.: Enterprise interoperability framework and knowledge corpus – final report, Interop deliverable DI.3 (May 2007)
12. Daclin, N., Chen, D., Vallespir, B.: Methodology for enterprise interoperability. In: 17th IFAC World Congress (IFAC 2008), Seoul, South Korea, July 6-11 (2008)
13. Guedria, W., Naudet, Y., Chen, D.: Interoperability maturity models – survey and comparison. In: 3rd IFAC TC5.3 International Workshop (EI2N 2008), Monterrey, Mexico (2008)
14. C4ISR Architecture Working Group: Levels of Information Systems Interoperability (LISI). United States of America Department of Defense, Washington DC (March 30, 1998)
15. Clark, T., Moon, T.: Interoperability for joint Coalition Operations. Australian Defence Force Journal 51 (2001)
16. Tolk, A., Diallo, S.Y., Turnitsa, C.D.: Applying the Levels of Conceptual Interoperability Model in Support of Integratability, Interoperability, and Composability for System-of-Systems Engineering. In: Proceeding Systemics, Cybernetics and informatics, vol. 5(5) (2007)
17. Guédria, W., Chen, D., Naudet, Y.: A Maturity Model for Enterprise Interoperability. In: Meersman, R., Herrero, P., Dillon, T. (eds.) OTM 2009 Workshops. LNCS, vol. 5872, pp. 216–225. Springer, Heidelberg (2009)
18. Kasunic, M., Anderson, W.: Measuring systems interoperability: challenges and opportunities, Software engineering measurement and analysis initiative. Technical note CMU/SEI-2004-TN-003 (2004)
19. Ford, C.T.: Interoperability measurement. Thesis, Department of the Air Force Air University, Air Force Institute of Technology (2008)

20. Mallek, S., Daclin, N., Chapurlat, V.: Formalisation and Verification of Interoperation Requirements on Collaborative Processes. In: 18th IFAC World Congress (IFAC 2011), Milano, Italy (2011)

21. Maier, M.W.: Architecting Principles for System-of-Systems. Systems Engineering 1(4), 267–284 (1998)

22. Kotov, V.: Systems of systems as communicating structures. Hewlett Packard Computer Systems Laboratory Paper HPL-97-124, pp. 1–15 A (1997)

23. Krygiel, A.J.: Behind the wizard's curtain: An integration environment for a system of systems. C4ISR Cooperative Research Program (1999)

24. DeLaurentis, D., Callaway, R.K.: A System-of-Systems Perspective for Public Policy Decisions. Review of Policy Research 21(6), 829–837 (2004)

25. Maier, M.W.: Architecting Principles for Systems-of Systems. In: 6th Annual International Symposium of INCOSE, Boston, USA (1996)

26. Campbell, J.E., Longsine, D.E., Sirah, D., Anderson, D.J.: System of Systems modeling and Analysis. sand report sand 2005-0020 (January 2005)

27. Autran, F., Auzelle, J.P., Cattan, D., Garnier, J.L., Luzeaux, D., Mayer, F., Peyrichon, M., Ruault, J.R.: Coupling component systems towards systems of systems. In: 18th Annual International Symposium of INCOSE, Utrecht, The Netherlands (2008)

28. Bejar, R., Latre, M.A., Nogueras-Iso, J., Muro-Medrano, P.R., Zarazaga-Soria, F.J.: Systems of systems as a conceptual framework for spatial data infrastructures. Internatioanl Journal of Spatial Data Infrastructures Research 4, 201–217 (2009)

29. Electronic Industries Alliance (EIA): Processes for Engineering a System, EIA/ IS 632, version 1.0 (April 1998)

30. CEA (Commissariat à l'Energie Atomique): Méthode SAGACE: le systémographe, training manual version 1.0 (1999) (in French)

31. Camarinha-Matos, L.M., Afsarmanesh, H., Rabelo, R.J.: Infrastructure developments for agile virtual enterprises. IJCIM 16(4-5) (2003) ISSN 0951-192X

# Building Computational Grids
# Using Ubiquitous Web Technologies

Robert John Walters, Stephen Crouch, and Phillip Bennett

University of Southampton, Highfield, UK. SO17 1BJ
{rjw1,stc,pb903}@ecs.soton.ac.uk

**Abstract.** Grid computing is an exciting development which promises to be the enabling technology for many users with periodic requirements for massive computing power. There are a number of Grid computing infrastructures available which are fully featured, powerful, efficient and secure. However, for novice users, these systems are not easy to setup and use which presents a significant barrier to their adoption. M-grid offers an alternative approach which permits the creation of a computational grid able to accept tasks from any user with access to the web and distribute them to machines running standard a web browser without any security implications.

**Keywords:** Lightweight grid computing, computational grid, Applet, m-grid.

## 1    Introduction

One of the most widespread applications of grid technology is a computational grid [1-3] whereby a network of machines is organized to permit the distribution of processing power to users with computationally intense tasks. Such a system accepts tasks from users, distributes them for processing and collects the results to pass back to the users. To achieve this, software is installed on all of the machines involved. It is often also necessary to install software on users' machines to present their tasks to the system. This software [1-7] is crafted to ensure the resulting grid offers the very best performance and security but is usually quite extensive and requires considerable configuration. This is not a problem for experts using dedicated hardware but it can be an insurmountable barrier for the interested potential user who needs a light weight system which they can install and use with a minimum of initial effort.

## 2    M-Grid in Outline

The heart of a computational grid is a mechanism for tasks to be sent to other machines for execution. This is risky for the receiving machine ("node") since it involves executing code supplied by a third party (Figure 1). This code might be poor quality; or even be malicious. The traditional solution is to ensure tasks are only accepted from trustworthy users. Nodes then trust coordinating systems only to distribute safe code [8].

L.M. Camarinha-Matos, L. Xu, and H. Afsarmanesh (Eds.): PRO-VE 2012, IFIP AICT 380, pp. 254–261, 2012.
© IFIP International Federation for Information Processing 2012

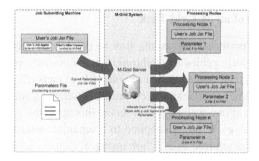

**Fig. 1.** Distribution of Applets to Nodes

M-grid avoids these issues by using a mechanism for remote execution of code which is available on nearly every machine: the sandbox used by web browsers to execute java applets [9-11]. No software needs to be installed as the sandbox is available within the web browsing software on most machines. The sandbox insulates the host from bad behaviour by applets. Preventing applets from damaging of interfering with their hosts, places some limitations on applets but it was felt that these are outweighed by the fact they can be run on virtually any machine without formality. The coordinating machine supplies tasks to nodes as applets dynamically embedded into web pages. All that is necessary for a machine to join m-grid as a computational node is a java enabled browser. Users with jobs to execute upload these (as java applets) to m-grid using a web based interface. A proof of concept system [12] was built using the ASP technology provided within the Microsoft IIS web server supplied the Windows operating system [13-15]. The system has now been completely redeveloped using JSP [11, 15, 16]. At the same time, some additional features have been added, enabling users to specify that tasks be executed many times with different parameters, some resilience to the failure of nodes to return results and optional security features.

## 3    Joining and Using M-Grid

There are three roles to a computational grid: the computation nodes, the users with tasks to execute and the coordinator who arbitrates between the other two. Since there is no software to install and no security/trust relationships to establish, joining m-grid as a computational node is trivial; almost any machine can take part. All that is required is open the m-grid page with a Java-enabled browser.

A user who wishes to use m-grid to execute a task first embeds their task into an applet (see below). They then upload this to the m-grid using their web browser.

The coordinator role is the only element which requires any effort to establish. The co-ordinating machine needs to run the Tomcat Java Application container (available free from Apache Software Foundation) [16]. All that then needs to be done is for the m-grid application files to be copied to the correct directory and the URL of the m-grid home page to be advertised.

### 3.1    The Lifecycle of an M-Grid Task

A user with task to perform follows the link to the job submission page from the m-grid home page which guides them through the submission process of specifying the jar file containing their applet and an optional file of (sets of) parameters. When a processing node becomes available, the co-ordinator selects a job from those waiting for execution, embeds it in a web page and serves this up to the node. Where a file of parameters is supplied, each line is supplied to a separate instance of the applet. An applet/parameter pair is referred to as a "job instance".

On completion, the applet returns its results to the coordinator which identifies and stores the results ready to be returned to owner upon request. The results are retained by the coordinator until they are deleted by the task owner.

### 3.2    Constructing a Task for Submission to M-Grid

In common with most computational grid infrastructures, users wishing to m-grid to execute a task for them must supply it in a form which palatable to the grid infrastructure. In the case of m-grid this means that it must be an applet in a single jar file which can execute within the sandbox of a standard browser. M-grid adds some further requirements which concerned with marshalling outputs at the co-ordinator.

The m-grid task development kit provides resources needed to create applets in the required form. The main class of the applet must inherit from the supplied "MGridApplet" class (which itself inherits from the standard applet class). This class encapsulates the various methods for the developer to read parameters and write results. For development, output methods write onto face of the applet. When submitted to m-grid these methods are substituted with others which also marshal and return the output to the task owner (via the coordinator).

### 3.3    Submitting a Task to M-Grid

A user with a task to submit to m-grid navigates to the m-grid job submission page and uploads their jar file containing the applet together with an optional text file containing the necessary parameters (if required).

Once received by the m-grid coordinator, classes relating to methods provided by the MGridApplet class are substituted with alternatives which include additional functionality required for the applet to read its parameters and return results. The jar file is also checked for all necessary class files and the class containing the main method is identified. A unique job number is allocated for each set of parameters in the file. This job number, the modified user jar file and the parameters are then stored to await execution. Where no parameters file is supplied, a single job instance is stored. This process is shown in Figure 2.

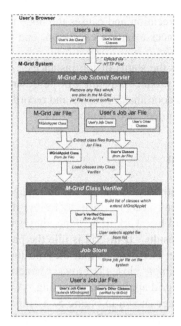

**Fig. 2.** Uploading a task to m-grid

## 3.4    Execution of a Task

When a node becomes available, the coordinator checks for job instances awaiting execution. It there are no waiting instances, a place holder page is served states that

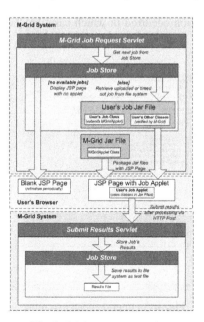

**Fig. 3.** Job instance execution

there is no work awaiting execution and causes the node to check again after a short delay. If there are job instances awaiting execution, one is selected, embedded in a page and served up to the node.

The coordinator monitors the status of job instances. Any job instance taking an excessive period of time to produce a result will be downloaded to further nodes as they become available. The coordinator accepts and records the first result it receives; repeat results arrive are discarded. See Figure 3.

## 4    M-Grid in Action

A new user's first contact with m-grid will be the homepage. If they wish to volunteer processing capability, all they need to do is to follow the link to "Volunteer your CPU". That's all. If m-grid has work to be done, they will see applets appear in the page, work and send back results. If m-grid is idle the page says so and periodically checks for tasks. When the user decides that they no longer wish to be supporting m-grid's computation they simply close the browser window or navigate to a different page. Figure 4 shows an m-grid application executing. A user with a task follows the "Submit a job" link to the page shown in Figure 5. Using this page they first name to their task for later identification. They then give m-grid the location of the jar file containing their applet and a text file of parameters, if required.

The user may then use the "View Jobs" page to see a list of their tasks. The page displays the name of the task and the status of all the job instances within the task. In the example shown in Figure , there is one task named Task 1 of three job instances, of which the second instance has been allocated (downloaded) to a node and the third is waiting. The first has completed and the link points to a text file containing the outcome, unless an exception occurred in which case details of the event will appear instead.

**Fig. 4.** An m-grid applet executing

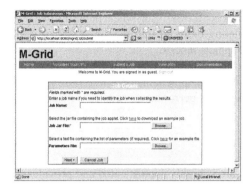

**Fig. 5.** The job submission page

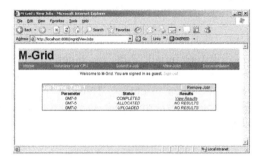

**Fig. 6.** The Results Page

# 5    Issues and Further Work

M-grid has its limitations which will prevent it from challenging more conventional grid infrastructures. Most are inherited from the applet mechanism which it uses. For example, m-grid user applications/tasks cannot use of the local file system on the machine where it is executing and an applet's communications are limited. These constraints are imposed on applets in return for being allowed the privilege to execute without formality. The implementation of m-grid described here has improved on the first implementation in a number of respects:

As m-grid is now a web application running within a container, the previous constrain that the coordinator role be executed on a machine running a Microsoft operating system has been relaxed. M-grid may now be run on any platform for which a suitable application container is available.

Users are now permitted to use any number of classes (provided they are packed into a single jar file).

This implementation is able to survive and complete tasks properly if an applet doesn't complete, for whatever reason. This same behaviour permits it to handle tasks which throw exceptions.

The new implementation permits users to execute a piece of code many times with different parameters to inject this into the system as a single task.

The requirements placed on the user when building their applet have also been simplified by encapsulating them all into the single MGridApplet pure virtual class from which all m-grid applets inherit.

One issue which hasn't been investigated in detail is the performance penalty associated with executing tasks as applets inside a web browser. However, casual observation suggests that the actual performance penalty is modest.

# 6     Conclusion

Mainstream grid software is highly sophisticated and provides the very best performance and security. These are large, complex systems which demand significant quantities of hardware, time and effort to establish. However, this is a real barrier for the potential user who is curious about the potential of grid computing and would like to know more.

Much of the difficulty associated with building grid systems arises from the need to install and configure software on all of the machines which will take part. The problem is not just the logistics of reaching the machines the software. It is also many users don't have full control of their machines. Hence a "trial" installation of a grid infrastructure can require obtaining permissions as well as the physical installation. By using the applet mechanism, m-grid avoids most of these difficulties.

The new implementation of m-grid permits a novice potential user to set up a computational grid with very little effort and minimal cooperation from others who have access to java enabled browsers. They can then experiment with the operation of a computational grid. By the time they reach the limits of the m-grid, they will be in a strong position to select, install and operate one of the "full size" grid infrastructures.

# References

1. Altair Engineering Inc: Portable Batch System (2004)
2. Litzkow, M., Livny, M.: Experience with the Condor Distributed Batch System. In: Workshop on Experimental Distributed Systems. IEEE (1990)
3. Livney, M., Basney, J., Raman, R., Tannenbaum, T.: Mechanisms for High Throughput Computing. SPEEDUP Journal 11, 36–40 (1997)
4. Erwin, D.W., Snelling, D.F.: UNICORE: A Grid Computing Environment. In: Sakellariou, R., Keane, J.A., Gurd, J.R., Freeman, L. (eds.) Euro-Par 2001. LNCS, vol. 2150, pp. 825–839. Springer, Heidelberg (2001)
5. Foster, I., Kesselman, C., Tuecke, S.: The Anatomy of the Grid: Enabling Scaleable Virtual Organization. International Journal of Supercomputer Applications and High Performance Computing 15, 200–222 (2001)
6. Frey, J., Tannenbaum, T., Livney, M., Foster, I., Tuecke, S.: Condor-G: A Computation Management Agent for Multi-Institutional Grids. Journal of Cluster Computing 5, 237–246 (2002)
7. http://gridsystems.com/pdf/IGIntro.pdf/
8. Grandison, T., Sloman, M.: A survey of Trust in Internet Applications. IEEE Communications Surveys & Tutorials 3 (2000)

9. Chen, E.: Poison Java. IEEE Spectrum 36, 38–43 (1999)
10. Flannagan, D.: Java in a Nutshell. O'Reilly and Associates (2002)
11. http://java.sun.com/
12. Walters, R.J., Crouch, S.: M-grid: Using Ubiquitous Web Technologies to create a Computational Grid. In: Sloot, P.M.A., Hoekstra, A.G., Priol, T., Reinefeld, A., Bubak, M. (eds.) EGC 2005. LNCS, vol. 3470, pp. 59–67. Springer, Heidelberg (2005)
13. Buser, D., Kaufman, J., Llibre, J.T., Francis, B., Sussman, D., Ullman, C., Duckett, J.: Beginning Active Server Pages 3.0. Wiley Publishing Inc. (2003)
14. Microsoft Corporation, http://www.microsoft.com
15. Bergsten, H.: JavaServer Pages. O'Reilly and Associates (2003)
16. The Apache Jakarta Tomcat 5.5 Servlet/JSP Container (2004)

# Supporting Collaborative Work by Preserving Model Meaning When Merging Graphical Models

Keith Phalp[1], Frank Grimm[2], and Lai Xu[1]

[1] Bournemouth University, Fern Barrow, Poole, Dorset, BH12 5BB, UK
[2] ScopeSET Technology Deutschland GmbH, Germany

**Abstract.** An important aspect of support for distributed work is to enable users at different sites to work collaboratively; models need to be accessible by more than one user at a time allowing them to modify them independently from each other supporting parallel evolution [1]. As design is a largely creative process users also use layout to convey meaning. However, tools for merging such models tend to do so from a purely structural perspective, thus losing an important aspect of the meaning conveyed by the modeller. This paper presents a novel approach to model merging which allows us to preserve such layout meaning when merging. We first present evidence from an industrial study, which demonstrates how users use layout to convey specific meanings. We then introduce an approach to merging which will allow for the preservation of meaning and finally describe a prototype tool.

**Keywords:** UML class models/diagrams, model merging, diagram merging model-driven, distributed, software engineering.

## 1 Introduction: The Need for Merging Models within Collaborative Development

This paper presents a novel approach to model merging [2] which is intended to bring gains to those working on collaborative software development. Whilst, in our case the primary objects (in the wider rather than software sense) are UML models, the lessons learned here have implications for collaboration more widely, where any shared artefact may be developed in a similar collaborative manner (based on diagrammatic modelling notations).

The rest of the paper is organised as follows: section two gives background to model merging and the industrial context, section three outlines our findings on the importance of layout and section four then discusses the need for a different approach to merging. Section five discusses our 'semi-automatic' approach to merging and finally section six offers some conclusions.

## 2 Model Merging and Context

The context for this study was the production of software for automatic gearbox controllers, using a model driven approach [3, 4]. Hence, modifying, the software was

L.M. Camarinha-Matos, L. Xu, and H. Afsarmanesh (Eds.): PRO-VE 2012, IFIP AICT 380, pp. 262–269, 2012.
© IFIP International Federation for Information Processing 2012

achieved by first modifying the model, then the respective implementation (source code) modifications followed automatically [5]. Modifications could only be carried out in a sequential manner: before starting to work on the model and realise their modifications, developers at one site had to wait for the developers at the other site to finish their modifications, which was clearly an inefficient form of collaboration [6]. Hence, the main motivation for the research presented here was to remove the limitation of only one user modifying a model at the same time [7] and to enable a genuinely collaborative approach. However, when evolved models are modified independently from each other, the same model elements might have been modified in different and potentially contradicting ways [8]. These 'merge conflicts' usually cannot be solved automatically by a merge tool, since such a tool cannot decide which element version to use in the merged model [8]. Hence, modellers (in our case software engineers) have to manually resolve conflicts and reason about conflicting changes [9, 10]. It is important to re-iterate that, for model-driven software development, models are not just a means of visualisation and communication since source code can be derived automatically. Hence, the need to understand how modellers interpret the models, so that we could understand fully the impact of merging, as this will directly impact the resultant software artefacts.

## 3     The Importance of Layout

Initial results of this analysis are presented in [11]; the results having come from examination of two substantial projects [12]. The following lists some of the ways in which we found that the software developers used layout to convey meaning (in our case for class diagrams). Notably, this, often domain-specific meaning, is neither formally defined in the model nor the diagram itself. The interested reader is referred to Grimm [12] for an exhaustive list.

- The absolute position of a class symbol was meaningless [20, 22], though the symbol's proximity (diagram context) and relation the other class symbols was important for the modellers' mental-map [13] of a diagram.
- Class symbols did not overlap (a fundamental requirement  of readability) [14], were often ordered according to their semantics in the software design domain, and UML class diagram layout guidelines  often [15] ignored. Symbols of closely related classes were then positioned in close proximity to each other; for instance in containment (whole-part) and inheritance hierarchies [16].
- Diagrams dealing with similar domain concepts, i.e., representing classes whose semantics were closely related, often exposed a similar layout structure, supporting the finding that diagram layout conveys inherent information important to modellers.
- Elements placement was based on modellers' knowledge of semantic relationships among elements and how they wanted to represent this knowledge in a diagram. For instance, sometimes two subclasses were placed on the left hand side close together, while another subclass on the

same inheritance level was placed on the right apart from its semantically related variants. This concurs with Petre [16] who found that placing unrelated elements close to each other led to the misinterpretation that they were semantically related.

- The position of class symbols was more important than being able to draw connection as straight lines. So, positioning class symbols in their semantic context overweighted the connections the class had to other classes in the respective diagram [17]. However, there was no preferred direction of connections; though if a diagram depicted classes in a clear hierarchical context, then a top-down direction of connections was preferred [18].

Moody [19] argues that the layout guidelines given by the UML standard [15] are flawed in several ways, and, as the results of our diagram analysis show, those guidelines were not followed rigorously. Hence, diagram layouts can, and do, differ and are subject to the interpretation of the modellers who create or modify them.

The main generic finding is that the layout that modellers choose for a diagram is intentional and follows informal, unspecified rules. Elements (mainly class symbols) were placed in accordance with the element's semantic (i.e., domain) meaning and the engineer's understanding of this meaning. Hence, elements that are closely related in terms of their domain semantics are likely to be positioned close together in a digram as well. Thus, adjacent diagram symbols usually reflect a close relationship of the semantic concepts and their layout in the diagram conveys this meaning visually.

## 4    Implications: A Different Approach to Merging

It was clear from our study that layout heuristics were being used in the construction of models and allocation of classes to models. These findings strengthened the conviction that merging was vital, but needed to take account of, or at least try to preserve, as much of the meaning that layout conveyed as possible.

However, having conducted a thorough analysis of existing automatic diagram layout approaches (typically based on automatic graph layout algorithms) it became clear that these did not meet our needs because they merely preserved the connections (in a topological sense) rather than dealing with the layout itself, and, similarly ignored many of the heuristics suggested above [20].

In addition, for UML, automatic layout algorithms are based on UML model elements, i.e., the semantic elements like packages, classes, and inheritance and association relations among classes [21]. Since automatic layout algorithms focus on creating aesthetically pleasing layouts, they try to optimise diagram layouts with respect to edge crossings and bends [22], but they do not take the mental map of a diagram into account. When symbols are added to or deleted from a diagram, an automatic layout approach might create a completely different layout. Hence, users working with the diagram would have to re-learn the diagram.

Given those issues related to conventional layout algorithms, the challenge was how to enable efficient model and diagram merging whilst still allowing modellers to preserve the domain-specific information. Ideally, a diagram merge approach would automatically merge diagrams in a meaningful way and burden users only with solving "real" diagram merge conflicts. The ideal scenario would be to allow modellers to create diagrams the way they want with all possible layout freedom, but still be able to rely on mental-map-preserving automatic layout. These two objectives of course contradict each other – layout freedom and automatic layout cannot be combined without one limiting the other.

The authors suggest that a certain degree of automatic layout is desirable, for creating diagrams in the first place and for merging them. When model elements depicted by diagram symbols are updated, a modelling tool has two possibilities, (1) update the diagram symbols' graphical properties (including its size) or (2) leave them as they are and let the modellers take care of manually updating the diagrams. Given the above drawbacks of fully automatic diagram layout, but also given that automatic layout is useful to some extent, and given that merging fully manual diagram layout in a meaningful way is not possible, a semi-automatic layout is described briefly in the following section.

# 5     Implementing a Merging Tool

Since a diagram can be independently modified by different modellers, in parallel, the diagrams should ideally be combined without user interaction if there are no diagram merge conflicts (and the resulting diagram layout should still be meaningful). Therefore, a semi-automatic layout approach is presented which allows modellers to make the grouping and ordering of class symbols explicit.

As discussed above, these two layout features were found to be most important with respect to defining and conveying domain-specific meaning; thus, when modellers create diagrams, they can explicitly define the order of class symbols. In our approach this is the only layout information that can be defined manually. The more layout features modellers can influence, the more diagram merge conflicts can occur because the features were conflictingly changed in parallel in both evolved diagrams. Those conflicts then have to be resolved manually. This additional diagram information is then taken into account when class  diagrams are laid out automatically. The extra information is leveraged in order to position class symbols according to the manually defined order. Thus, for example, modellers are able to explicitly define the principal horizontal and vertical ordering of class symbols – which are then automatically laid out as trees in a top-down manner. Being able to automatically re-arrange diagram symbols during the diagram merge process relieves modellers from having to deal with unimportant layout merge conflicts (e. g., symbol overlapping) and allows them to automatically create uncluttered diagrams during the merge.

Fig. 1 shows a merge example. The screen-shot shows four UML class diagrams: the initially merged diagram is shown in the upper-right corner, both evolved diagrams are in the lower half, and their common ancestor diagram is shown in the upper-left corner. The latter three diagrams are immutable, only the merged diagram and its underlying model can be modified by the modeller. Modifications are necessary to resolve merge conflicts. Both evolved diagram versions and the ancestor diagram are annotated with change and conflict information. Diagram symbols and model elements deleted in one or both evolved diagrams are highlighted and annotated in the ancestor version - since they are not part of evolved diagram (in which they got deleted). Any other changes are highlighted and annotated in the evolved diagrams. Conflicting changes are highlighted in a different colour to non-conflictingly ones.

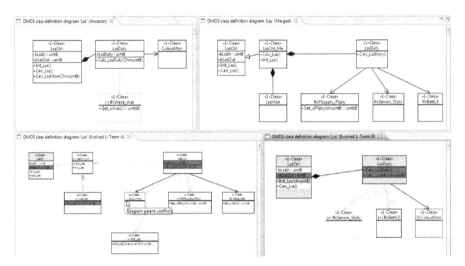

**Fig. 1.** Merged diagram example (also shown: evolved diagram versions and their common ancestor with change and conflict annotations)

A brief description of our algorithm now follows (again see Grimm [12] for a more detailed treatment). As a first step, the changes between both evolved models and the common ancestor are calculated by comparing the states of equivalent model elements. Equivalent elements in different model versions are determined by means of globally unique identifiers and it is then decided, for each change, whether or not it can be accepted. Conflicting changes are rejected. For model elements with conflicting containments this means that the model element is not part of the initially merged model. Then, so-called existence conflicts exist, and the modeller has to manually decide which parent element contains the element. If an element is not included in the initial merged model, its children elements are also omitted. Referencing any such element from other elements is not possible. Thus, such references are also marked with merge conflicts. As a second step, the actual merged model is created. Any model element which does not have an existence conflict becomes part of the merged model. Of course, these model elements might have merge conflicts, too. However, these conflicts do not prevent the element from becoming part of the merged model, though they would need to be resolved manually by the modeller.

The merge tooling also provided modellers with the possibility to resolve merge conflicts by accepting and rejecting model and diagram changes. Not only could modellers modify the merged model (diagram) by means of accepting or rejecting changes, but also they could also modify it in any way. Therefore, even model elements or symbols which were not changed at all (not even non-conflictingly) could be modified. Hence, the editing capabilities of the implemented model merge tool were those specific ones required for dealing with changes, in addition to the common editing functions provided by an ordinary modelling tool and used when models and diagrams are created in the first place. The dedicated merge tooling took care of updating the acceptance status of changes when the merged model or diagram was updated – so that modellers could learn whether a change made in one model (diagram) was (still) part of the merged model.

In contrast to other automatic UML class diagram layout approaches, no layout heuristics or iterative layout were applied for the implemented layout approach. Such approaches are used to create more aesthetically pleasing and potentially more readable diagram layouts, but they have the drawback that the resulting layout might 'look' different every time a diagram is laid out and when the model is updated (and thus the information used to calculate the layout changed). Hence, the semi-automatic layout approach implemented here is a trade-off between diagram mergablity and manually creating UML class diagrams with all the freedom with respect to positioning / laying out of diagram symbols.

Hence, in our approach, the 'freedom' of manual layout was reduced in favour of being able to efficiently merge class diagrams, while the most important layout features (regarding embedding domain-specific information into the layouts of class diagrams) can still be defined manually by modellers. That is, the layout approach implemented here has as a priority keeping a stable and predictable layout. This means that the order of class symbols is not altered so long as the modeller does not change it. The layout of connection symbols depicting relationships among classes is done completely automatically; a connection symbol's layout is not changed as long as the order of the connection's class symbols does not change.

## 6     Conclusions

This paper examines support for collaboration across multiple sites when developing automotive software, focussing on the issue and importance of model merging.

In order to understand the way developers used layout we examined two substantial industrial projects (see section four). The main generic finding was that modellers use layout to convey meaning, often in a way that is not defined by given model heuristics (such as guidance on the production of UML class diagrams). Having established the importance of layout we then wanted to enable modellers to work  independently on certain models in parallel.

Therefore, we present an approach for laying out models (class diagrams) in a semi-automatic fashion that allows modellers to manually define the order of class symbols and at the same time allows diagrams to be merge-able. This approach provided a trade-off between (1) the amount of layout freedom modellers had regarding the position of diagram symbols and (2) the ability to automatically create 'meaningful' merged diagrams whose layout was untangled - and preserved the manually defined class symbol hierarchy. In addition, an approach to visualising differences and conflicts between 'to-be-merged' UML models and class diagrams was implemented. This allowed the developers to work with merged models in the same way that modellers work with them when they create them in the first place, and crucially allowed developers to exchange partially merged models.

In summary, this paper has provided evidence for the importance of layout in models and has presented a 'semi-automatic' approach to merging which allows modellers to retain a greater recognition and understanding of their work when models across sites are merged. In addition, by allowing the exchange of partially merged models conflicts between versions can be resolved effectively. We contend that such merging is a vital cog in the support for collaborative development processes.

# References

1. Mens, T., Buckley, J., Zenger, M., Rashid, A.: Towards a taxonomy of software evolution. In: Proceedings of the Workshop on Unanticipated Software Evolution (2003)
2. Westfechtel, B.: Structure-oriented merging of revisions of software documents. In: Proceedings of the 3rd International Workshop on Software Configuration Management, pp. 68–79. ACM Press, New York (1991)
3. Hermsen, W., Neumann, K.-J.: Application of the object-oriented modeling concept OMOS for signal conditioning of vehicle control units. Technical report, SAE 2000 World Congress, Detroit, MI, USA (March 2000)
4. Schweizer, M., Benkel, M.: Development of product families - an example from the automobile industry. In: Proceedings of the 3rd Workshop on Object-oriented Modeling of Embedded Real-Time Systems, OMER3 (2005)
5. Kleppe, A.G., Warmer, J., Bast, W.: MDA Explained: The Model Driven Architecture: Practice and Promise. Addison-Wesley Longman Publishing Co., Inc., Boston (2003)
6. Harrison, W.H., Ossher, H., Sweeney, P.F.: Coordinating concurrent development. In: Proceedings of the 1990 ACM Conference on Computer-Supported Cooperative Work, CSCW 1990, pp. 157–168. ACM, New York (1990)
7. Mens, T.: A state-of-the-art survey on software merging. IEEE Trans. Softw. Eng. 28(5), 449–462 (2002)
8. Conradi, R., Westfechtel, B.: Version models for software configuration management. ACM Comput. Surv. 30, 232–282 (1998)
9. Ohst, D., Welle, M., Kelter, U.: Difference tools for analysis and design documents. In: ICSM 2003: Proceedings of the International Conference on Software Maintenance, p. 13. IEEE Computer Society, Washington, DC (2003)
10. Kelter, U., Wehren, J., Niere, J.: A generic difference algorithm for uml models. In: Proceedings of the SE 2005, Essen, Germany (March 2005)
11. Grimm, F., Phalp, K., Vincent, J.: Enabling multi-stakeholder cooperative modelling in automotive software development and implications for model driven software development. In: Ist International Workshop on Business Support and MDA (MDABIZ) a Tools 2008 Workshop, Zurich (July 2008)

12. Grimm, F.: Enabling collaborative modelling for a multi-site model-driven software development approach for electronic control units. PhD thesis, Bournemouth University (2012)

13. Misue, K., Eades, P., Lai, W., Sugiyama, K.: Layout adjustment and the mental map. Journal of Visual Languages and Computing 6(2), 183–210 (1995)

14. Tamassia, R., Di Battista, G., Batini, C.: Automatic graph drawing and readability of diagrams. IEEE Trans. Syst. Man Cybern. 18(1), 61–79 (1988)

15. UML Notation Guide. Object Management Group (2003)

16. Petre, M.: Why looking isn't always seeing: readership skills and graphical programming. Commun. ACM 38(6), 33–44 (1995)

17. Eichelberger, H.: Nice class diagrams admit good design? In: SoftVis 2003: Proceedings of the 2003 ACM Symposium on Software Visualization, pp. 159–167. ACM Press, New York (2003)

18. Purchase, H.: Evaluating graph drawing aesthetics: defining and exploring a new empirical research area. In: DiMarco, J. (ed.) Computer Graphics and Multimedia: Applications, Problems and Solutions, pp. 145–178. Ed. Idea Group Publishing (2004)

19. Moody, D.L.: The "physics" of notations: a scientific approach to designing visual notations in software engineering. In: Proceedings of the 32nd ACM/IEEE International Conference on Software Engineering, ICSE 2010, Cape Town, South Africa, May 1-8, vol. 2, pp. 485–486 (2010)

20. Eichelberger, H.: Aesthetics of class diagrams. In: Proceedings of the First IEEE International Workshop on Visualizing Software for Understanding and Analysis, pp. 23–31. IEEE (2002)

21. Eiglsperger, M., Gutwenger, C., Kaufmann, M., Kupke, J., Jünger, M., Leipert, S., Klein, K., Mutzel, P., Siebenhaller, M.: Automatic layout of UML class diagrams in orthogonal style. Information Visualization 3(3), 189–208 (2004)

22. Eichelberger, H.: On class diagrams, crossings and metrics. In: Jünger, M., Kobourov, S., Mutzel, P. (eds.) Graph Drawing, Dagstuhl Seminar Proceedings (2006)

# 10

## Services Design

# Services Design in a Collaborative Network for Multidisciplinary Research Projects

Maria Krestyaninova[1,2] and Yulia Tammisto[3]

[1] Institute for Molecular Medicine Finland, FIMM, University of Helsinki,
Biomedicum Helsinki 2U, 00014 Helsinki, Finland
{Masha}@simbioms.org
[2] Uniquer Sarl, 12 rue de la Mercerie,
Lausanne, 1003, Switzerland
[3] Aalto University School of Economics, Runeberginkatu 14,
00100 Helsinki, Finland
{Yulia.Tammisto}@aalto.fi

**Abstract.** Providing information management services for multi-disciplinary research projects presents scientific, technological and communication challenges: constant change of themes and objects of scientific studies, entangled privacy and ownership requirements along with rapidly evolving methods of analysis and ways to look at data call for a highly dynamic communication and data service. We will present a case study of a collaborative network (simbioms.org). SIMBioMS, founded in 2005, develops open source software and provides data management services in biomedical research through four academic organisations and one company.

**Keywords:** multidisciplinary project, research consortia, open data, data management, service design.

## 1    Introduction

Post-genomic era in life sciences has arrived with an unprecedented number and scale of multidisciplinary collaborative projects [1]. It is no longer sufficient to look only at one type of data in order to report a discovery in environmental or biomedical research. Translation to practical applications is imperative [2,3]. Complex studies utilizing several technological platforms to assay thousands of biological samples have become a norm. Technological and analytical advances are reinforcing this trend [4]. However, work and expertise required for such multidisciplinary research projects cannot be delivered by a single organization. Collaborative networks and research consortia are being organized and compete with each other at a remarkable rate. Communicating ideas, study designs, complex data sets and information regarding data structures is the key challenge for the success of a collaborative project [5].

L.M. Camarinha-Matos, L. Xu, and H. Afsarmanesh (Eds.): PRO-VE 2012, IFIP AICT 380, pp. 273–279, 2012.
© IFIP International Federation for Information Processing 2012

## 1.1     Central Bioinformatics Services and New Challenges

Originally, IT services in life sciences research were dedicated to collecting and preserving the data for posterity in a uniform fashion (often as a compulsory exercise precluding a publication in a peer-reviewed journal), and to making it available to the worldwide scientific community. This was delivered by large centralized archives, funded by governments [6,7].

However archives were unable to support new, collective fashion of carrying out studies by research consortia with large number of participants. Such studies often deal with data that often cannot be released to general public (population–wide human genomics), their participants need to exchange data prior to discovery (at the stage of study design), there are complex requirements regarding authorship and administration of a study. Combined, these factors have led to formation of a new type of services [8, 9]. Since 2004-2005 there has been a wave of open source and proprietary software and services initiatives that undertook a mission of supporting complex cross-organisational communications that were not provided for by large public archives in life sciences (Fig. 1).

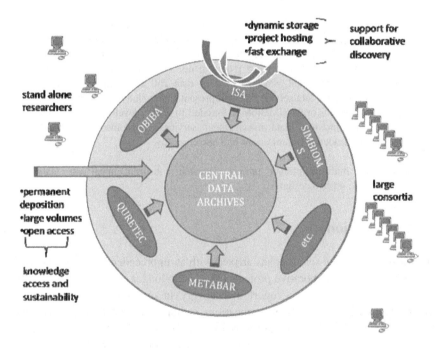

**Fig. 1.** Central archives (purple) collect all the data and make it available for everyone, open access; main mission: knowledge accumulation and dissemination for the entire scientific community. Dynamic collaborative IT platforms (green) facilitate efficient dataflow and other communications within a group of collaborators in the context of a specific study; main mission: provide means of communicating analysis-related information throughout a project; assist with data deposition upon completion of a project.

## 1.2     Solutions for Collaborative Discovery

Currently, such service providers do not serve only a specific community, as it was in the beginning. Generic use-cases, communication flow and reporting requirements in various fields of research have been formulated [10,11] and implemented in numerous instances. Often the same provider would have customers in ecology, human genetics, pharmaceutical and biomolecular fields and would implement services simply by configuring the same software. Demand for consortium services continues to grow, and, as service providers gain domain-specific expertise, competition between IT players also increases.

If one was to generalise the implications of the multidisciplinary collaboration trend on the evolution of research data management services, one could name three fast-developing directions:

1) means for fine-tuning of access rights for data owners: data can no longer be categorized into completely private or completely open
2) instruments for handling heterogeneity of data, metadata and the variety of standards
3) accessibility and suitability of the source code used in services construction

Research groups nowadays deploy tools that assist in structuring and describing their data in a way, which is most useful for the scope of their study and for the format of their communication with the collaborators. The underlying architecture and semantics of those tools is compatible with international data formatting standards [12].

## 1.3     Distributed Software Development and Services Provision

Whilst the majority of service providers for research consortia have put effort into creating generic software and, therefore, services that they provide consist of installing and configuring their own software (i.e., service and software are inseparable), we pursued a scenario in which we created a collaborative IT network with four academic institutions and one company as contributors (simbioms.org). The motivation behind such a set-up lays in avoiding a long-term dependency on a specific architecture or software platform. We aimed to develop a mechanism for building partnerships between several software suppliers and a service provider and thus to respond promptly to newly emerging needs and rapidly expand across knowledge domains without loss in sustainability or quality. One of the major challenges that we faced as a network was the absence of services design culture in bioinformatics: creating/configuring software and developing a service were one and the same.

# 2     Results

The SIMBioMS collaborative network, Systems for Information Management in BioMedical Studies, was created in 2005 when IT specialists from two academic institutions – Institute of Mathematics and Computer Science (Riga, Latvia) and European Bioinformatics Institute (Hinxton, UK) - formed a working group to provide data management services for an EU-funded large research project [13]. Since 2007, software engineers, data managers and system administrators from Karolinska Institutet (Stockholm, Sweden), Institute for Molecular Medicine Finland (Helsinki, Finland) and Uniquer (Lausanne, Switzerland) have joined the network. The establishment of SIMBioMS as a virtual enterprise included:

- web visibility: domain, website
- central code management: CVS (Concurrent Versions System), git (Distributed version control and source code management system)
- standard operation procedures (SOPs) for code release, testing and deployment for services
- single-point user support: email, ticketing and other services
- internal communications: wiki, email lists, meetings and teleconferences.

## 2.1    Software and Services

The network so far has produced 5 modules of software for data management and for administration design of complex meta-studies [14] and provided services in more than 10 EU and national collaborative projects (see Table 1).

**Table 1.** List of projects in which SIMBioMS has provided data exchange services. Contribution to various projects on strategy and design (ELIXIR, BBMRI, P3G and TaraOceans) aren't included.

| Projects | N partners | Description | N samples/data files |
|---|---|---|---|
| ENGAGE | 25 | Genome-wide association studies | >100k |
| SUMMIT | 24 | Genetic basis of diabetic complications | 65k |
| SIROCCO | 27 | siRNA research consortium | 20k |
| Biomedinfra.fi | 4 | Finnish national biobank network | 70k |
| sail.simbioms.org | 14+ | Sample availability on-line resource | 180k |
| MOLPAGE | 18 | Molecular phenotyping, 11 HT platforms, multiple tissues | 25k |
| MuTHER | 4 | SNP, RNA, methylation in multiple tissues | 1k |
| EGG | 16 | Early growth genetics | 5k |
| CAGEKID | 14 | Cancer genomics of kidney | 3k |
| ENGAGE | 25 | GWAS | >100k |
| BIOBANQUES | 70 | French national biobank network | 1mln |

The software is modularized and customizable. It is compatible with the major public archives and integrates well with other software products available in the same niche. Tutorials, guides, and documentation for installation and use are provided along with a service provision.

Services for each of the projects have been implemented using 2 or 3 modules depending on project's communication flow. For each project there is a number of configurations (up to 25 per project per module) and services blueprints. Requirements analysis, design of the services and of the release cycle were done jointly by a service providing partner and a software developing partner.

## 2.2    Partnership Formation

The network has a procedure for introducing new partners and additionally it has experience in providing services jointly with external IT players. The longevity of a partnership depends on whether it is happening within a specific project or line of funding, or beyond it. In the latter case a group is considered a part of the network, while in a project-based partnership – an external collaborator. Licensing agreements (software must be open source), code of conduct, communication set-up with the network have been put in place in order to clarify the terms of membership in the network. Issues regarding acknowledgement, IP ownership and, generally, ethical and legal settings of the network remain work in progress.

## 2.3    Collaborative Framework for IT Services Provision

Two types of intellectual value generated by the SIMBioMS network have been established: configurations (metadata structures) and services blueprints. Over 7 years, there have been over 100 configurations and over 10 blueprints created by the partners. Software developing partners capitalized on the former, while service providers benefitted from the latter. The two values are essentially the currency within the virtual enterprise. The communications and work within the network are aimed at increasing both types of intellectual value. Collaboration with external partners, e.g. large public archives, is anchored to blueprints and configurations as well. The larger the study-specific collection of use-cases and data structures the more complex the design of the tools (blueprints and configurations) for data collection, re-annotation and standardization, as well as the design of the interface that serves the data to the community.

# 3    Discussion

Multidisciplinary and cross-organisational nature of research calls for more advanced communication systems. The notion of open data is no longer as clearly defined as it used to be: in the process of discovery one does need to open data consecutively, first to collaborators, then to publishers and then to the general public. Research collaborations urgently require some dedicated virtual environment that can ease the administrative and communication burden in large collaborative projects. It is often hard to pre-define a communication structure due to numerous legal, ethical, psychological, technological and intellectual challenges. We argue that not only creation, but rather succession and sustainability of research consortia and results it produces collectively can be helped and enhanced by a well-designed communication and data exchange platform. Such a platform would allow:

-to share data selectively, and leave access control in the hands of those who are responsible for extracting value from data,
- to declare an intended study in standardized terms that later on can be tracked from the resulting publication or patent.

The main requirements for such an IT platform for collaborative discovery are data semantics services (translation between terminology, assistance in tagging, normalizations) and the means to fine-tune data access.

Designing software for a wide variety of constantly evolving research themes is a massive task, unless data generators are forced to convert data into a universal standard. The services design approach could become a suitable alternative: capturing service blueprints and corresponding configurations along different studies  can help to develop more efficientinformation management solutions for large biomedical studies. However, it requires a sustainable partnership between service providers and open source software suppliers.

Undoubtedly, it is possible to produce software and design services at the same time. In bioinformatics the two activities are not usually separated and users participating in the design of services are often unaware that they contribute significantly to the software design. The more complex the dynamics of collaboration is, the more efforts are required for crafting an IT service that mimics this complex communication.

When talking about the communication infrastructure for multidisciplinary collaboration, the focus shifts from software production to creating and capturing metadata structure and services blueprints. Information about interactions between the players of research collaborations represents the intellectual value that is equally significant to technological value of the software. Intellectual value is gathered collectively by scientists exchanging the data, software engineers and service designers.

Establishing simple ways to exchange designs among the network members would enable the players to sustain collaborative IT networks beyond one specific project, and that would yield a sustainable IT infrastructure. It remains to be seen what legal and ethical instruments can be put in place in order to strengthen partnerships required for designing bioinformatics services or even to develop a culture for exchanging of designs within the biomedical research community more effectively.

In order to provide reliable and efficient services IT groups themselves will have to gain a deeper understanding of dynamics and nature of joint work. Therefore, longevity and sustainability of collaborative links in bioinformatics services and software development are crucial for complete and comprehensive collection of requirements from the entire research ecosystem.

**Acknowledgments.** This research was supported through funds from The European Community's Seventh Framework Programme (FP7/2007-2013), ENGAGE Consortium, grant agreement HEALTH-F4-2007-201413. The authors would like to thank everyone who participated in, contributed to and funded SIMBioMS work in the course of 7 years. The full list of people would be over 100 names and over 60 institutions and organizations. Special thanks to those who  delivered services and software under SIMBioMS umbrella: Sudeshna Guha Neogi (NIHR), Teemu Perheentupa (FIMM), Jani Heikkinen (FIMM), Juha Muilu (FIMM), Joern Dietrich (Uniquer Sarl), Natalja Kurbatova (EMBL-EBI), Julio Fernandez-Banet (EMBL-EBI), Janna Hastings (EMBL-EBI), Mikhail Gostev (EMBL-EBI), Stathis Kanterakis (EMBL-EBI), Sandra Ose (IMCS), Juris Viksna (IMCS), Andris Zarins (IMCS), Edgars Celms (IMCS), Russell Vincent (Uniquer Sarl), Inga Prokopenko (OCDEM, WTCHG), Huei-Yi Shen (FIMM), Ola Spjuth (KI). We would also like personally thank Ugis Sarkans (EMBL-EBI) who beside being a valuable member of SIMBioMS network, has significantly contributed to the development of this paper by discussing our approach, suggesting ideas and commenting on the text.

# References

1. Mesko, B., et al.: The triad of success in personalised medicine: pharmacogenomics, biotechnology and regulatory issues from a Central European perspective. N. Biotechnol. (March 10, 2012)
2. Prokopenko, I., et al.: Variants in MTNR1B influence fasting glucose levels. Nature Genetics 41, 77–81 (2009)
3. Karsenti, E., et al.: A Holistic Approach to Marine Eco-Systems Biology. PLoS Biol. 9(10) e1001177
4. McConnell, P., et al.: The cancer translational research informatics platform. BMC Med. Inform. Decis. Mak. 24(8), 60 (2008)
5. Anderson, N.R., et al.: Issues in Biomedical Research Data Management and Analysis: Needs and Barriers. J. Am. Med. Inform. Assoc. 14(4), 478–488 (2007)
6. National Center for Biotechnology Information, http://www.ncbi.nlm.nih.gov
7. European Bioinformatics Institute, http://www.ebi.ac.uk
8. Rocca-Serra, P., et al.: ISA software suite: supporting standards-compliant experimental annotation and enabling curation at the community level. Bioinformatics 26(18), 2354–2356 (2010)
9. Smedley, D., et al.: BioMart – biological Queries made easy. BMC Genomics 10, 22 (2009)
10. Smith, B., et al.: The OBO Foundry: coordinated evolution of ontologies to support biomedical data integration. Nat. Biotechnol. 25, 1251–1255 (2007)
11. Quackenbush, J.: Standardizing the standards. Mol. Syst. Biol. 2, 0010 (2006)
12. Sansone, S.A., et al.: Towards interoperable bioscience data. Nat. Genet. 44(2), 121–126 (2012)
13. Nicholson, G., et al.: A genome-wide metabolic QTL analysis in Europeans implicates two loci shaped by recent positive selection. PLoS Genet. 7(9), e1002270 (2011)
14. Krestyaninova, M., et al.: A system for Information Management in BioMedical Studies-SIMBioMS. Bioinformatics 25(20), 2768–2769 (2009)

# Structure Dynamics Control-Based Service Scheduling in Collaborative Cyber-Physical Supply Networks

Dmitry Ivanov[1] and Boris Sokolov[2]

[1] Berlin School of Economics and Law, 10825 Berlin, Germany
[2] St. Petersburg Institute of Informatics and Automation RAS
Divanov@hwr-berlin.de

**Abstract.** An original model for dynamic scheduling of services in collaborative cyber-physical supply networks is stated and solved with the help of structure dynamics control approach. The proposed service-oriented description makes it possible simultaneously to (i) schedule information services according to business process execution and (ii) plan costs of information resources.

**Keywords:** Supply network, collaborative cyber-physical system, services, scheduling, reconfiguration, structure dynamics control, optimal control.

## 1 Introduction

The impact of information technologies (IT) on the material processes in collaborative value-adding networks in general and supply networks (SN) in particular becomes more and more crucial [1], [2]. Recent research indicated that an aligning of business processes and information systems (IS) may potentially provide new quality of decision-making support and an increased SN performance [3], [4], [5]. Most of the new IT share attributes of intelligence. Examples include data mining, cloud computing, physical internet, pattern recognition, knowledge discovery, to name a few. That is why it becomes a timely and crucial topic to consider SNs as *collaborative cyber-physical systems*. Such SNs are common not only in manufacturing but also in different cyber-physical systems, e.g., in networks of emergency response units, energy supply, city traffic control, and security control systems.

Cyber-physical systems incorporate elements from both information and material (physical) subsystems and processes which are integrated and decisions in them are cohesive [6]. Elements of physical processes are supported by information services. Cyber-physical systems are characterized by decentralization and autonomous behavior of their elements. In addition, such systems evolve through adaptation and reconfiguration of their structures, i.e. through *structure dynamics* [7], [8].

In these settings, two questions may be raised: (1) what is the optimal volume of information services needed to ensure operation of physical systems and (2) how these services shall be scheduled at the planning stage and adapted in dynamics at the execution control stage. It can be observed that current concepts and models for SN integration do not provide adequate decision support from intelligent information and

L.M. Camarinha-Matos, L. Xu, and H. Afsarmanesh (Eds.): PRO-VE 2012, IFIP AICT 380, pp. 280–288, 2012.
© IFIP International Federation for Information Processing 2012

product technologies; we regard this shortcoming as an opportunity for research and development, which could significantly improve the practice of SN management. On one hand, aligning of new intelligent elements of IT infrastructures, i.e., the information services, with real material flows can be achieved. On the other hand, investments into information resources can be estimated regarding real execution dynamics.

This paper faces these two decision domains on the basis of structure dynamics control (SDC) approach [7]. Conventionally, the above-described two problems have been solved step-by-step. With the help of SDC, a special dynamic representation of multi-structural networks is proposed where such problems can be solved simultaneously. In addition, due to the increasing role of information services in different forms, e.g., cloud computing, the service-based approaches to integrated planning and scheduling of both material and information flows in collaborative networks are needed [9], [10]. Such integration is also to prevent failures of IT-enabled SNs [11].

Although recent research has extensively dealt with SN scheduling ([12], [13], [14] and IT scheduling (see, e.g., works on scheduling telecommunications) in isolation, the integrated scheduling of both material and information flows still represents a research gap. In this paper, the problem of dynamic scheduling of services in SNs as cyber-physical systems is stated and solved with the help of SDC approach. In addition, specific research contributions are the considerations of IT reconfiguration in a real execution stage and monetary estimation of investments into IT.

## 2    Research Methodology

Both material and information flows are subject to structural changes. SDC approach is multi-disciplinary and reaches beyond the classical borders of control theory and mathematical optimization [15]. It is based on a combined application of optimal program control (OPC) theory and mathematical programming (MP), and extents their classical borders by their mutual integration and by decentralization of system description with help of active modelling objects (AMO). With the help of AMO, ideas of incorporating control policies into agent-based architectures can be addressed [16]. SDC approach has been previously applied to telecommunication networks, aerospace, and supply chains [7], [13], [15].

The SDC-based models are based on the dynamic interpretation of planning in accordance with the natural logic of time where the decisions on SN planning are taken for certain intervals of structural constancy and regarding problems of significantly smaller dimensionality. For each interval, a static optimization problem of a smaller dimensionality can be solved with the help of MP. The transitions between the intervals are modelled in the dynamic OPC model. As the SDC is based on control theory, it is a convenient approach to describe *intangible* services due to abstract nature of state variables which can be interpreted as abstract service volumes. The study [13] has proposed an original model to represent SN schedules as OPC. In this paper, this model is extended to service scheduling.

## 3     Problem Statement

The *problem* is to find a joint schedule taking into account the IS modernization, i.e., four schedules should be generated in a coordinated manner, i.e.,

- an OPC (schedule) for the material supply processes in the SN (model M1),
- an OPC (schedule) for information services (model M2),
- an OPC (schedule) for the information resources (IR) (model M3), and
- an OPC (schedule) for the IS modernization (model M4).

Goals are measured by the job's delivery times to customers and the volume of the delivered jobs. Jobs are to be scheduled subject to maximal customer service level, minimal backlogs, minimal idle time of services, and minimal costs of IT (including, fixed, operation, and idle cost). Customer service level is measured by a function of the times when the jobs are delivered to the customers. A simple example of the interrelations among business processes, services, functions, and IRs is presented in Fig. 1.

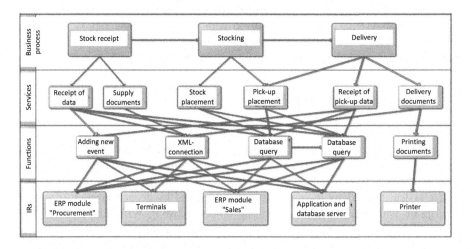

**Fig. 1.** Interrelations among business processes, service, functions, and IRs

*General assumptions and parameters*

- Consider jobs $A = \{A_v; v = 1,...,n\}$ in business processes. The jobs are independent and are not available for processing at time zero. Each of the jobs has a release date that is known in advance through the SN coordination.
- Each of the jobs $A_v$ is composed of the operations $D^{(v)} = \{D_i^{(v)}; i = 1,...,k_v\}$.
- Precedence constraints exist, i.e. the operations are logically arranged in jobs.
- $a_i$ is the planned processing volume of the operation $D_i^{(v)}$.
- The execution of operations $D^{(v)}$ is realized by different IR $B_r^{(v,i)}$.
- Denote $B^{(v,i)} = \{B_r^{(v,i)}; r = 1,...,\rho_v\}$ as a set of IRs in an IS.

- IRs have unequal rates which may also differ for various operations and therefore influence the processing time. Denote $e_r^{(i)}, V_r^{(i)}, \Phi_r^{(i)}$ as maximal processing intensity of the operation $D_i^{(v)}$ at the IR $B_r^{(v,i)}$, maximal capacity of the IR $B_r^{(v,i)}$, and maximal productivity of the IR $B_r^{(v,i)}$ before the reconfiguration correspondingly; $\overline{e}_r^{(i)}, \overline{V}_r^{(i)}, \overline{\Phi}_r^{(i)}$ are given variables characterizing the same domains but after the modernization.

- Let $t$ be current instant of time, $T = (t_0, t_f]$ the scheduling horizon, and $t_0 (t_f)$ the start (end) instant of time for the scheduling horizon respectively.

- Denote $\varepsilon(t)$ as an element of the matrix of time-spatial constraints ($\varepsilon(t) = 1$, if $t_0^k < t \le t_f^k$, $\varepsilon(t) = 0$ otherwise), where $k$ are the numbers of time windows available for operations' execution (e.g., subject to maintenance).

- Denote $S^{(v)} = \{S_l^{(v)}; l = 1,...,d_j\}$ as a set of IT services to execute operations $D^{(v)}$.

- Denote $F^{(v,l)} = \{F_\chi^{(v,l)}; \chi = 1,...,S_l\}$ as a set of functions of IR to implement the service $S_l^{(v)}$, i.e., each service is may be composed of functions $F_\chi^{(v,l)}$ from different IR and is characterized by availability time windows subject to the function $\varepsilon(t)$, productivity, i.e., the processed volume of operations at an instant of time, and costs (fixed cost $c_{il}^{(v,1)}(t)$ and operation cost $c_{il}^{(v,2)}(t)$).

- Denote $g_l^{(v)}$ as a number of operations $D_i^{(v)}$ which may be served by a service $S_l^{(v)}$.

- Denote $h_i^{(v)}$ as a given number of services $S_l^{(v)}$ which may be simultaneously used by execution the operation $D_i^{(v)}$.

- Denote $D_l^{(v,i)} = \{D_{<l,\chi>}^{(v,i)}; l = 1,...,d_j, \chi = 1,...,S_l\}$ as operations of IR (e.g., information processing, storage, transmission, and protection).

- Denote $D_r^{(p,i)} = \{D_{<r,k>}^{(p,i)}; k = 1,...,\pi_i^{(r)}\}$ as operations in the given jobs for planned reconfiguration (modernization) of the IR $B_r^{(v,i)}$.

- Denote $V_\chi^{(v)}$ as the online storage capacity of the IR $B_r^{(v,i)}$ to execute the operation $D_{<l,\chi>}^{(v,i)}$ and $\delta_{\chi r}^{(v,l)}(\tau)$ as a quality function to estimate the execution results.

- Denote $c_{\chi r}^{(l,1)}(\tau)$, $c_{\chi r}^{(l,2)}(\tau)$ as given time functions of fixed and operation cost of an IR $B_r^{(v,i)}$ used for the operation $D_{<l,\chi>}^{(v,i)}$ by realization of the function $F_\chi^{(v,l)}$.

- Setup times are independent and included in the processing time.

- Denote $\eta_{il}^{(v)}(t)$ as a given time function which characterizes the costs of idle time of services for the operation $D_i^{(v)}$;

- $y_{il}^{(v)}$ denotes the value of current idle cost due to a backlog in the operation $D_i^{(v)}$ caused by unavailability of the service $S_l^{(v)}$.

In order to describe the execution of operations, let us introduce the *state variables*:

$x_{il}^{(v)}(t)$ to characterize the execution of the $D_i^{(v)}$ with the use of the service $S_l^{(v)}$,

$x_{il}^{(v,1)}(t)$ is an auxiliary variable characterizing the current state of the operation $D_i^{(v)}$. Its value is numerically equal to the time interval that has elapsed since the beginning of the scheduling interval and the execution start of the operation $D_i^{(v)}$;

$x_{il}^{(v,2)}(t)$ is an auxiliary variable characterizing the current state of the processing operation. Its value is numerically equal to the time interval that has elapsed since the end of the execution of the operation $D_i^{(v)}$ and the end of the scheduling interval;

$x_r^{(v,l)}$ is an auxiliary variable characterizing the employment time of the IR $B_r^{(v,j)}$;

$x_\chi^{(v,l)}$ which characterizes the execution of the operation $D_{\triangleleft\chi\triangleright}^{(v,j)}$;

$x_{rS_l}^{(v,l)}(t)$ is an auxiliary variable characterizing the current state of the information processing operation. Its value is numerically equal to the time interval that has elapsed since the end of the execution of the operation $D_{\triangleleft\chi\triangleright}^{(v,j)}$ and the instant of time $t$.

*Decision variables and goals*

$u_{il}^{(v)}(t)$ is a control that is equal to 1 if the operation $D_i^{(v)}$ is assigned to the service $S_l^{(v)}$ at the moment $t$; otherwise $u_{il}^{(v)}(t) = 0$.

$\vartheta_{il}^{(v,1)}(t)(\vartheta_{il}^{(v,2)}(t))$ are auxiliary control variables that are equal to 1 if the operation $D_i^{(v)}$ has not been executed and is equal 0 otherwise.

$w_{\chi r}^{(v,l)}$ is a control that is equal to 1 if the operation $D_{\triangleleft\chi\triangleright}^{(v,j)}$ is assigned to the IR $B_r^{(v,i)}$ and is equal 0 otherwise;

$\omega_{rS_l}^{(v,l)}(t)$ is auxiliary control that is equal to 1 if all the operations $D_{\triangleleft\chi\triangleright}^{(v,j)}$ in the function $F_\chi^{(v,l)}$ are completed and is equal 0 otherwise;

$\vartheta_r^{g(p,2)}(t)$ is auxiliary control that is equal to 1 if the reconfiguration from old parameters $e_r^{(i)}, V_r^{(i)}, \Phi_r^{(i)}$ to new ones $\bar{e}_r^{(i)}, \bar{V}_r^{(i)}, \bar{\Phi}_r^{(i)}$ is completed and is 0 otherwise.

# 4    Mathematical Model

The SN is modelled as a networked controlled system described through a dynamic interpretation of the operations' execution. Control models (M1-M2) are first used to assign and sequence services to business operations. Then M2-M3 are employed to assign and schedule services to IRs. Finally, M3-M4 are launched to schedule IT modernization (reconfiguration) in compliance with the results of M1-M2. The basic interaction of these models is that after the solving the conjunctive system for M1, the found control variables are used in the constraints of the conjunctive system for M2. Analogously, M2, M3, and M4 are interconnected. In solving the main systems, the interaction of the models is organized in the reverse way, from M4 to M1. Note that in the calculation procedure, the models M1-M4 will be solved simultaneously, i.e., the supply, service, IR, and modernization scheduling will be integrated. Because of the limited size of this paper, we shortly introduce the models M2; it can be easily extrapolated on models M3-M4.

The *model of execution dynamics* of operations $D_i^{(v)}$ can be expressed as (1)-(3):

$$\frac{dx_i^{(v,l)}}{dt} = \varepsilon_{il}(t) \cdot u_{il}^{(v)}(t) \tag{1}$$

$$\frac{dy_{il}^{(v)}}{dt} = \eta_{il}(t)[1 - \vartheta_{il}^{(v,1)} - u_{il}^{(v)} - \vartheta_{il}^{(v,2)}] \tag{2}$$

$$\frac{dx_{il}^{(v,1)}}{dt} = \vartheta_{il}^{(v,1)}; \; \frac{dx_{il}^{(v,2)}}{dt} = \vartheta_{il}^{(v,2)} \tag{3}$$

Eq. (1) describes operation's execution. Eq. (2) represents idle time in the business process caused by unavailability of the service $S_l^{(v)}$. Eq. (3) represents the dynamics of operation's execution according to precedence constraints.

The control actions are *constrained* as follows:

$$\sum_{i=1}^{k_j} u_{il}^{(v)}(t) \le g_l^{(v)}; \forall l; \; \sum_{l=1}^{d_j} u_{il}^{(v)}(t) \le h_i^{(v)}; \forall i \tag{4}$$

$$\sum_{l=1}^{d_j} u_{il}^{(v)}[\sum_{\alpha \in \Gamma_{v1}}(a_\alpha^{(v,l)} - x_\alpha^{(v,l)}) + \prod_{\beta \in \Gamma_{v2}}(a_\beta^{(v,l)} - x_\beta^{(v,l)})] = 0; \forall v \tag{5}$$

$$\vartheta_{il}^{(v,1)} \cdot x_{il}^{(v,l)} = 0; \; \vartheta_{il}^{(v,2)}(a_{il}^{(v,l)} - x_{il}^{(v,l)}) = 0; \forall i; \forall l \tag{6}$$

$$u_{il}^{(v)}(t) \in \{0,1\}; \; \vartheta_{il}^{(v)}(t) \in \{0,1\} \tag{7}$$

Constraints (4) are assignment problem constraints. Constraints (5) determine the precedence relations. Constraints (6) interconnect main and auxiliary controls. Equation (7) constraints control to be Boolean variables.

The *end conditions* are defined as follows:

$$t = t_0^{(j)} : x_i^{(v)}(t_0^{(j)}) = y_{il}^{(v)}(t_0^{(j)}) = x_{il}^{(v)}(t_0^{(j)}) = 0 \tag{8}$$

$$t = t_f^{(j)} : x_i^{(v)}(t_f^{(j)}) = a_i^{(v)}; \; y_l^{(v)}(t_f^{(j)}); \; x_i^{(v)}(t_f^{(j)}) \in R^1 \tag{9}$$

Eqs. (8) and (9) define initial and end values of the variables $x_i^{(v)}(t)$, $y_{il}^{(v)}(t)$, $x_{il}^{(v)}(t)$ at the moments $t_0^{(j)}$ and $t_f^{(j)}$.

The *goals* are defined as follows:

$$\min J_1^{(v)} = \sum_{i=1}^{k_v} \sum_{l=1}^{d_j} y_{il}^{(v)}(t_f^{(j)}) \tag{10}$$

$$\max J_2 = \sum_{i=1}^{k_v} \sum_{l=1}^{d_j} \frac{1}{x_{il}^{(v,2)}(t_f^{(j)})} \int_{t_0^{(j)}}^{t_f^{(j)}} \vartheta_{il}^{(v,2)}(\tau) d\tau \tag{11}$$

$$\min J_3 = \sum_{i=1}^{k_v} \sum_{l=1}^{d_j} \int_{t_0^{(j)}}^{t_f^{(j)}} [c_{il}^{(v,1)}(\tau) + c_{il}^{(v,2)}(\tau)] \cdot u_{il}^{(v)}(\tau) d\tau \tag{12}$$

Eq. (10) minimizes idle time of services. Eq. (11) estimates the service level by the volume of completed jobs. Eq. (12) minimizes total service costs.

The models M3 and M4 are constructed analogously. They also contain some additional elements, e.g., control actions are constrained by information processing intensities. In addition, perturbations impacts $0 \le \xi_r^{(j,1)}(t) \le 1$ are introduced in the constraint system to take into account uncertainty of real execution and to estimate schedule robustness on the basis of attainable sets [18].

# 5     Discussion of Results and Conclusions

New intelligent information services result from decentralized IT infrastructures. This forces changes in decision support systems for SN which may become cyber-physical systems. If so, a new challenge of joint scheduling the material flows and information services will be faced in practice in next years. In addition to the existing models on the scheduling of material processes in SNs, this study has added models for integrated service, IR, and IS modernization scheduling. The coordinated usage of these models allows dynamic scheduling of services integrated with material and IR scheduling taking into account possible IS reconfiguration in a planned (i.e., the modernization) and perturbation-driven (i.e., adaptation) modes. This study is among first to explicitly formulate and solve in a dynamic manner the stated service scheduling problem. The proposed service-oriented concept allows explicitly incorporate material and information processes in the SN and take into account modern trends of decentralized information services, e.g., cloud computing. In doing so, this study contributes to consideration of SNs as collaborative cyber-physical systems.

With the help of SDC, problems of network design and scheduling can be solved simultaneously. In addition to the service scheduling and interconnecting each service with ISs needed for its realization, the proposed approach makes it possible simultaneously to (i) determine the volume of information services needed for physical supply processes (Eqs. (10) and (11)) and (ii) determine this volume in monetary form (Eq. (12)). In addition, the models M3-M4 allow taking into account IS dynamics and reconfiguration.

The proposed models and algorithms have been validated in a developed prototype based on C++ and XML. The OPC calculation is based on the *Hamiltonian* function. In integrating the main and the conjunctive equation systems, the values of variables in both of the systems can be obtained at each point of time. The maximum principle guarantees that the optimal solutions (i.e., the solution with maximal values) of the instantaneous problems (i.e., at each point of time) give the optimal solution to the overall problem. For these sub-problems, optimal solutions can be found, e.g., with the help of MP. Then these solutions are linked into an OPC. The optimality properties have been proved theoretically and experimentally.

Further analysis may include an explicit incorporation of AMO into scheduling model, and a detailed representation of models M3-M4. This paper can also be extended in future by application to concrete case-studies. The proposed models are implemented in software prototype where numerical experiments have already been performed to validate hybrid scheduling algorithms on the basis of OPC and MP. In future, IR modernization and adaptation can be further investigated with the developed models and algorithms.

# References

1. Camarinha-Matos, L.M., Macedo, P.: A conceptual model of value systems in collaborative networks. J. Int. Man. 21(3), 287–299 (2010)
2. Lee, J., Palekar, U.S., Qualls, W.: Supply chain efficiency and security: Coordination for collaborative investment in technology. Eur. J. Oper. Res. 210, 568–578 (2011)
3. Dedrick, J., Xu, S., Zhu, K.: How does information technology shape supply-chain structure? Evidence on the number of suppliers. J. Man. Inf. Sys. 25(2), 41–72 (2008)
4. Camarinha-Matos, L.M.: Collaborative networked organizations: Status and trends in manufacturing. Annual Rev. Control 33(2), 199–208 (2009)
5. Jain, V., Wadhwa, S., Deshmukh, S.G.: Revisiting information systems to support a dynamic supply chain: Issues and perspectives. Prod. Plan Control 20(1), 17–29 (2009)
6. Zhuge, H.: Semantic linking through spaces for cyber-physical-socio intelligence: A methodology. Artif. Intell. 175(5–6), 988–1019 (2011)
7. Ivanov, D., Sokolov, B., Kaeschel, J.: A multi-structural framework for adaptive supply chain planning and operations with structure dynamics considerations. Eur. J. Oper. Res. 200, 409–420 (2010)
8. Dekkers, R., van Luttervelt, C.A.: Industrial networks: capturing changeability? Int. J. Net. Virt. Org. 3(1), 1–24 (2006)
9. Bardhan, I.R., Demirkan, H., Kannan, P.K., Kauffman, R., Sougstad, R.: An interdisciplinary perspective on IT services management and service science. J. Man. Inf. Syst. 26(4), 13–64
10. Li, Q., Zhou, J., Peng, Q.-R., Li, C.-Q., Wang, C., Wu, J., Shao, B.-E.: Business processes oriented heterogeneous systems integration platform for networked enterprises. Comput. Ind. 61(2), 127–144 (2010)

11. Soroor, J., Tarokh, M.J., Keshtgary, M.: Preventing failure in IT-enabled systems for supply chain management. Int. J. Prod. Res. 47(23), 6543–6557 (2009)
12. Chen, Z.-L.: Integrated Production and Outbound Distribution Scheduling: Review and Extensions. Oper. Res. 58(1), 130–148 (2009)
13. Ivanov, D., Sokolov, B.: Dynamic supply chain scheduling. J. Sched. 15(2), 201–216 (2012)
14. Giard, V., Mendy, G.: Scheduling coordination in a supply chain using advance demand information. Prod. Plan. Control 19(7), 655–667 (2008)
15. Ivanov, D., Sokolov, B.: Adaptive supply chain Management. Springer, London (2010)
16. Seok, H., Nof, S.Y., Filip, F.G.: Sustainability decision support system based on collaborative control theory. Ann. Rev. Control 36(1), 85–100 (2012)
17. Surana, A., Kumara, S., Greaves, M., Raghavan, U.N.: Supply-chain networks: a complex adaptive systems perspective. Int. J. Prod. Res. 43(20), 4235–4265 (2005)
18. Ivanov, D., Dolgui, A., Sokolov, B.: On applicability of optimal control theory to adaptive supply chain planning and scheduling. Ann. Rev. Control 36(1), 73–84 (2012)

# Advanced Services for Supply Chain Design Processes in Collaborative Networks

Eva A. Coscia[1], Rosanna Fornasiero[2], João Bastos[3], Américo Azevedo[3], Domenico Rotondi[4], and Salvatore Piccione[4]

[1] TXT e-Solutions SPA, Via Frigia 27, 20126 Milano, Italy
[2] ITIA-CNR, Via Bassini 15, 20133 Milano, Italy
[3] INESC Porto, Campus da FEUP, Rua Dr Roberto Frias 378, 4200-465 Porto, Portugal
[4] TXT e-solutions SpA, c/o Tecnopolis N.O. Str. Prov. Per Casamassima Km 3, 70010 Valenzano (BA), Italy

**Abstract.** Design and production of small series for specific customer target groups in collaborative networks can help companies to increase their competitiveness. This paper aims to describe a new framework of services for collaborative networking for on-demand productions. After describing the business processes that need to be supported by innovative tools for partner search and collaborative production planning, we describe the developed services and how they are integrated to ease the communication between different activities.

**Keywords:** Partner Search, Collaborative Networks, Value Chain, Business Intelligence, Collaborative Framework.

## 1 Introduction

In recent years, the importance of collaborative strategies addressing the small series production of highly-customized products is emerging at industrial level. European companies of the Textile, Clothing and Footwear industry (TCFI) are asked to supply small series of innovative and fashionable goods having high quality, affordable prices and eco-compatibility. In order to support the design and production of such kind of products, companies need to be fast and flexible in answering to market demand. The CoReNet[1] Project provides a set of tools and services addressing those requirements.

This paper, in particular, presents some of the services developed in the CoReNet project that address the complexity of collaborative networks management able to respond to the high variability of the consumers demand and expectations. The particular case of TCFI companies producing healthy and fashionable products is taken as case study.

---

[1] CoReNet (Customer-ORiented and Eco-friendly NETworks for healthy fashionable goods: www.corenet-project.eu)

L.M. Camarinha-Matos, L. Xu, and H. Afsarmanesh (Eds.): PRO-VE 2012, IFIP AICT 380, pp. 289–298, 2012.
© IFIP International Federation for Information Processing 2012

Small series and customized products require totally different supply network management, where each company should be able to collaborate with specialized partners. In customized production, supply networks should be easily re-configurable for each covered market niche, or, even, for each customer order. In practice these scenarios are characterized by a very large number of small orders, each of them involving different partner companies, selected on the basis of their availability and capabilities. In this context, partner profiling and monitoring, as well as co-planning and control processes need to be re-engineered and supported by integrated services and based on easy to retrieve, easy to manage and reliable information.

After a short description of the business processes that are required and supported by the developed tools, the paper will shortly describe the tools and how they are integrated for a combined service to networked companies.

## 2     Collaborative Business Processes for Supply Chain Design

Supply networks should be easily reconfigured time after time according to the specific orders as expressed by target groups, for the creation of dedicated small series, or by single people, in case of customized products. Two business processes have been taken into account to support TCFI companies in small series production: Partner Profiling and Search and Collaborative Planning.

These processes start at the end of the design and development process, when all the items belonging to a specific collection and the related basic elements have been defined (e.g.: 2D/3D models, part programs for cutting, printing and any other automation step) and the products need to be prepared for sales. At this stage TCFI companies need to manage many different product variants as well as the design and production of related components.

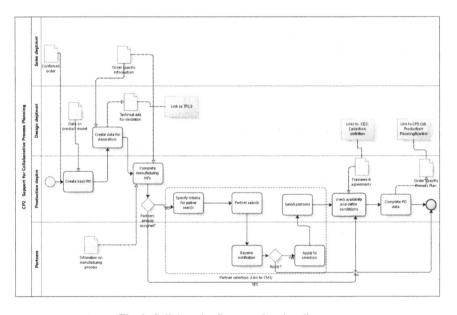

**Fig. 1.** Collaborative Process planning diagram

Beside the early phases for the design and development of the collection, once the sales start and the actual product request is defined and configured, in terms of measures, quantities and due dates, all the complete set of information required for the actual production can be finally defined (final BOM, accessories, etc.) and the production orders (PO) can be generated for a specific customer order. It is therefore possible to design and create a specific Supply Chain for the processing of the customer order, which implies to have identified all the suppliers and partners in charge of carrying out all the external activities, assigned the whole set of operations associated to a specific product and finally obtained all the information and data needed for the planning activities.

The business processes taken into consideration are depicted by BPMN diagrams and some activities are represented in Figure 1.

The process of Partner Search for supplying components and for outsourcing operations may occur both at strategic and operational level.

Many different approaches are proposed in literature on this issue and inspiration is taken from (Lambert, et al. 2001) for the application of methodologies to measure performance as a way to improve collaborative networks, from (Gunasekaran, et al. 2005) for the KPIs used as criteria to suggest supply network partners, from (Jarimo, et al. 2006) and (Crispim, et al. 2007) who introduced other criteria, like trustworthiness and risk values and from (Westphal, et al. 2007) for the utilization of KPIs related to collaboration and commitment.

During the definition of the product collection, the manufacturer needs to strategically identify partners who can support both the design and the production of the collection itself or the product customization. Strategic identification of partners is based on a partners profiling process: manufacturer assigns to each partner category some indicators based on previous performance and selects them specifying some selection criteria. From the organizational point of view, the relationship to be established is not only a pure buyer-seller relationship, but it is a more complex relationship that may require sharing data both on product quantity/quality, as well as on the company performances, machines, capacity availability, environmental performance, etc.

Once a customer order is collected, it is necessary to choose among the pre-selected partners those that will be activated for that specific order. In order to shorten the Partner search process at operational level the search is based on capacity availability for the lead time required by the manufacturer where previous agreements on quality and costs have already been taken. At this level it is mainly a matter of monitoring status of suppliers and outsourcers' availability.

The Partner search tool developed in CoReNet is based on the definition of Partner Profiles including both data provided by the supplier itself (e.g. administrative data, description of competences, provided material or process, etc.), as well as data derived from the analysis of the suppliers' past behavior based on performance indicators like the following ones:

- Collaboration degree: indicating how the supplier behaved in previous collaborations (e.g.: number of collaborations held in the previous period, number of successful negotiations, etc.).
- Products quality: reflecting the quality of the provided products (e.g.: number of defective products, etc.).
- Flexibility: describing the partner's ability to react rapidly and adapt to changes in the order or at production time.

Subsequently collaborative planning process manages the activities to support companies' plans towards each other to reach a joint optimization of the planning across departmental boundaries. Collaborative planning involves activities by means of which individuals coordinate their planning processes (Windischer, Grote et al. 2009).

When working with actual and complex business scenarios (like the textile or footwear sectors, for instance), local autonomy of each entity is an important issue.

For this reason, based on the analysis of the state-of-the-art, an innovative collaborative planning concept and approach is proposed in CoReNet for supporting decision making in supply network planning, respecting the requirements of complex products and small series production networks. The new approach is based on decentralized and cooperative actions and offers user friendly interface to the supply network stakeholders, supporting complex negotiation practices on a web-based platform. Furthermore through the use of a multi-criteria analysis, it is possible to define assessment mechanisms in order to optimize the overall supply network planning process

This approach is based on a decentralized negotiation model, which allows partners to propose new delivery dates and costs, represented graphically in Figure 2.

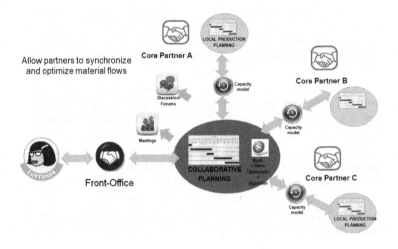

**Fig. 2.** Collaborative planning approach

# 3    The Services Supporting the Business Processes

## 3.1    The Partner Search Module

The *Partner Search* (PS) service offers partner profiling and searching capabilities and is one of the key elements of the CoReNet architecture to set-up supply chains. It is a web-based tool that allows a manufacturer to manage knowledge about its suppliers, by creating and updating Partners Profiles (a set of parameters describing competences and past performance), by visualizing data and performance indicators and by providing search features to select those partners that best match the entered criteria.

The *Partner Search* service provides an AJAX graphical user interface and a REST API. Through this REST interface, information is made available as two different, but equivalent, output formats: RDFa enriched XHTML, so that the service is accessible using a standard web browser, or RDF enriched XML, that is more suitable for automatic processing by external applications. The REST interface allows integrating the PS tool with other CoReNet tools in order to set up powerful services for the supply chain design and for the automatic detection of suppliers that best fit a set of search criteria.

Data can be both manually entered by human users, (through a GUI implemented as a *portlet*) and automatically retrieved from legacy systems (e.g. manufacturer's ERP systems).

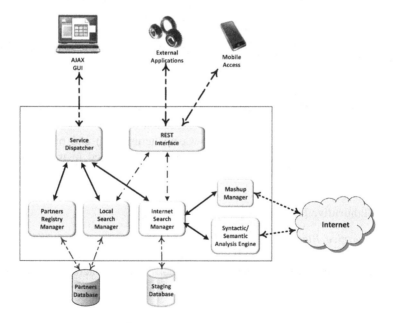

**Fig. 3.** Partner search module structure

The system consists of three main blocks:

- **Partner Registry Manager:** this functional block is in charge of providing the functionalities to add new, or revise existing, partners.

- **Local Search Manager:** this block provides all search capabilities on profiles of partners with which the manufacturer has a past work history and for which, as a consequence, has KPIs. This module provides its functionalities both via the GUI and via the REST API;

- **Internet Search Manager:** this block, finally, is in charge of performing searches for potential partners on a set of Internet sites.

## 3.2     Workflow Manager

A *Workflow Management* (WfM) solution should guarantee companies to create network flows and communicate with partners more efficiently and in an intuitive way. These issues are extremely important especially in the case of small series production, where the exchange of orders and business documents usually happens more frequently than for normal production and the time for producing and exchanging them might be very strict. Therefore it is necessary to have agile tools and services that allow SMEs to quickly react to orders and setup production.

In this context, it is very useful to define a set of basic workflow templates because small series orders come very frequently and are very similar to each other. Such templates might be directly deployed with no need of further adjustments.

The WfM architecture is actually based on an Enterprise Service Bus (ESB) that takes care of: managing the exchange of information with external applications/services (ERP, CRM, etc.), decoupling the specific way the information is transferred from an external application/service to the ESB and vice versa (the WfM offers transport protocols abstraction by using multiple *binding components* that provides in/out interoperability with the outside world), as well as routing the received information according to a set of rules or information. The CoReNet WfM platform supports the deployment and the execution of workflows using Enterprise Integration Patterns (EIP – see http://www.eaipatterns.com/) and provides a UBL Business Rules Execution Engine: both technologies are used to manage business documents exchange within a specific business process context.

## 3.3     Collaborative Planning Module

The *Collaborative Planning* (CP) module is a web-based tool deployed under the Liferay portlet container platform. It is a *portlet* that offers different web-based views accessible for specific user groups/roles supporting user interaction through the planning tool as depicted in the picture 4.

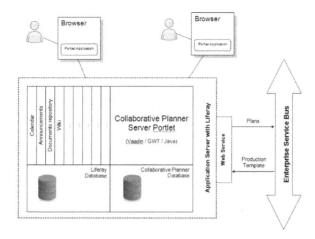

**Fig. 4.** Module architecture diagram for the Collaborative Planning module

The CP module allows each partner to directly propose new delivery dates, lead times and costs, via a web-based planning graphical tool which is available and shared by all supply network partners. Every time a partner proposes a change on a given operation, it is (actually) asking the affected partner to accept this change (and declare its cost) or to make a counter-proposal. Each negotiation round correspond to a pre-defined time period available to discuss/negotiate delivery times and costs, allowing partners to present quotations for each request-for-quotation (RfQ) performed by other partners.

Each proposed change (which "triggers" RfQs to all involved partners), actually asks the partners to present quotations, which might totally or partially meet, the asked RfQ or even suggest new changes. When a proposal has 100% agreement of all partners (i.e. "no pending notifications") it will be considered a *plan*; although it might be changed by any supply network partner, as long as the negotiation time period is not expired. This plan is serialized according to a set of criteria defined in advance by the *Front-office* and *Core* partners. For each of these criteria, it is possible to define a degree of importance, using a percentage score as a final weighting factor, which will used to calculate the best partner proposal. In this way each criterion has not got the same importance but each one has got an importance expressed by a ranking system.

The CP promotes a decentralized approach on the definition of the supply networking planning, since every *Core* partner has the same "weight" on the decision process as it is capable of proposing and participating actively on the characterization of each required operation and to request from any other partner a change on the plan. Therefore, the proposed planning approach integrated with the partner profiling and search service fits the needs of customer-oriented supply networks in achieving flexibility and responsiveness to the market demands.

## 4     Integration of the Services and Common Visualization Layer

The ability of TCFI industries to quickly adapt to new orders and to consumers' requests is the key factor in the design and set-up of supply chain for the production of small series or even single customized items. Therefore a flexible integration of services aimed at rapidly and accurately identifying partners, at communicating with them, and collaboratively agreeing on production plans would provide a great benefit on the supported business process.

Before defining a production plan, a manufacturer should identify the best candidates to become suppliers. Therefore the CP calls the PS through the REST API, providing a list of criteria and KPIs that better define the potential partners for fulfilling the small-series order.

The PS returns an XML document that contains the list of candidates that best match the searching criteria. The same REST API allows also retrieving complete profiles of the selected partners. When the CP has identified the best candidates for setting up the supply chain, some business documents are exchanged between the manufacturer and the (potential) suppliers, such as RfQs, Bills of Material (BOM) etc.

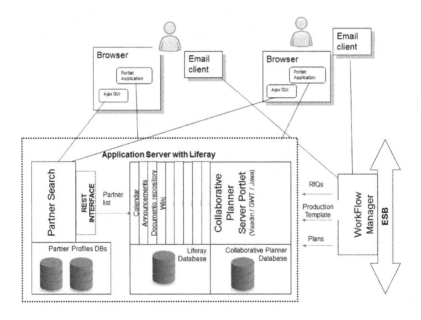

**Fig. 5.** The integration among tools for supply chain design and set-up

The management of this complex flow of information is performed through the WfM tool, which is activated by the CP in order to dispatch documents to the right parties and to check their contents and consequently apply business rules. These rules can vary from the mere check of the document structure, to more refined checks on the actual content of the document that trigger pre-defined actions (e.g.: if some values of a RfQ do not respect the defined rules, the RfQ is refused and its owner is notified about that).

The figure 5 represents the technical choices performed for integrating the CoReNet tools developed to support the Supply Chain design and set-up.

From a technical point of view, the integration between the CP and the WfM is performed by exploiting the SMTP binding component offered by the ESB underlying the WfM tool. Therefore the two tools exchange emails containing business documents on which pre-defined business rules can be applied.

The applications are made available to the end users through a unique access point, based on the Liferay portal (called the CoReNet Collaboration Portal) that enriches these services with social networking functionalities and advanced communication services for commenting, ranking, reporting bugs and asking for assistance.

The proposed approach provides several benefits for manufacturers and suppliers of the TCFI sector that are looking for agile solutions for the order management and the production plan processes supporting the production of small series. Indeed, the solution:

- is easily accessible and easy to use, as the tools provide advanced GUI and are available within a unique portal (thus no installation is required);
- supports the exchange and the automatic check of business information through well-known channels, like the emails (hiding technical details about the internal format of the exchanged documents);
- helps the selection of partners leveraging on information already owned by the manufacturer and provides an open collaborative environment where planning with the selected ones an agreed production plan.

## 5    Conclusions and Further Research

In this research, it has been studied a conceptual approach for managing supply chain set up process in collaborative networks, based on a set of services that address the network definition (partner profiling and search) and the network operation. This innovative approach presents a truthful framework for partner selection and subsequent collaborative negotiation among partners in the TCFI supply networks, providing support for the definition and organization of operations and activities relevant to fulfill customer orders of high customizable products and services.

The increase of the collaborative level in business processes is not only a matter of changing the organization of the related activities but of creating bridges among them and among involved actors. ICT technologies can play a relevant role for the improvement of business processes performance. Moreover the service orientation of the nowadays technologies allows networks of companies to deal with the complexity of fast changing customer demand and need of flexibility using IT applications which allows to collect and manage easily updated information on suppliers, products, time scheduling, etc. The innovative aspect of this work is linked to the definition of collaborative paths between suppliers and manufacturers and supporting them with services that cover different activities to exchange information and data for the configuration of collaborative networks. Nevertheless service orientation allows integrating and coordinating distribute ICT modules which can be complementary and can easily exchange information and data.

The developed services and related integration protocols are under validation with some companies from the TCFI and further development are planned to make the services fully compliant with their requirements.

**Acknowledgments.** The research leading to these results has received funding from the European Union's Seventh Framework Programme (FP7/2007-2013) under grant agreement n° [260169].

# References

1. Crispim, J.A., de Sousa, J.P.: Multiple Criteria Partner Selection in Virtual Enterprises. In: Camarinha-Matos, L., Afsarmanesh, H., Novais, P., Analide, C. (eds.) Establishing The Foundation Of Collaborative Networks. IFIP AICT, vol. 243, pp. 197–206. Springer, Boston (2007)
2. Gunasekaran, A., Williams, H.J., Mcgaughey, R.E.: Performance measurement and costing system in new enterprise. Technovation 25(5), 523–533 (2005)
3. Jarimo, T., Salkari, I., Bollhalter, S.: Partner Selection with Network Interdependencies: An Application. In: Camarinlia-Matos, L., Afsarmanesh, H., OUus, M. (eds.) Network-Centric Collaboration and Supporting Fireworks. IFIP AICT, vol. 224, pp. 389–396. Springer, Boston (2006)
4. Lambert, D.M., Pohlen, T.L.: Supply Chain Metrics. International Journal of Logistics Management 12(1), 1–19 (2001)
5. Westphal, I., Thoben, K.D., Seifert, M.: Measuring Collaboration Performance in Virtual Organizations. In: Camarinha-Matos, L., Afsarmanesh, H., Novais, P., Analide, C. (eds.) Establishing the Foundation of Collaborative Networks. IFIP AICT, vol. 243, pp. 33–42. Springer, Boston (2007)
6. Windischer, A., Grote, G., et al.: Characteristics and organizational constraints of collaborative planning. Cognition, Technology & Work 11(2), 87–101 (2009)

# 11

e-Governance

# Assessing Maturity for e-Government Services

Egidijus Ostašius

Vilnius Gediminas Technical University, Department of Fundamental Sciences, Lithuania
Egidijus.Ostasius@vgtu.lt

**Abstract.** E-service development as an integral part of e-government is growing area so the assessment of maturity of these services is becoming increasingly relevant. This paper presents more precise method for the evaluation of e-service maturity. It is based on stage model, the service division into the components – operations and the statistics of intensity of their usage in traditional and electronic space. The method is illustrated by data sample for the driver license e-service maturity evaluation. It can be applied to both the online service compared to the same at different stages of its evolution, or installed in different organizations (e.g. municipalities) or even in different countries, as well as comparing maturity among different e-services.

**Keywords:** e-government, public e-service, assessment, e-service maturity, benchmarking, sophistication.

## 1    Introduction

Electronic government (or e-government) has not a long history since the first official government sites appeared in the middle of 1990s delivering information and services. There exist a number of different definitions of e-government [1]. According to one of them e-government beside constituency participation, governance by transforming internal and external relationships is a continuous optimization of service delivery through technology, the Internet, and new media [2]. Electronic services (or e-services), the core parts of e-government are in continuous processes of improvement and evolutional changes in order to provide better services to their customers. That causes the need for the measure of how big these trends of changes are and what is the growth in such kind of evolution. A number of methods and models were proposed and applied (e.g., [3], [4], [5], [6]). Mostly they are based on stage models that describe and predict main aspects of e-government and supporting e-services.

Stage models are used for evaluating and benchmarking the level of maturity of the developed e-services [7], categorizing, evaluating the progress and guiding the directions for public service development, help in understanding the current e-service status [8], for directing where to go and assessing the developing process [9]. They are also used to rank the countries for e-government implementations and their trends (e.g., [7], [10], [11], [12]) although because of differences in assessment methods these surveys show some very different results [13]. Usually stage models are defined

L.M. Camarinha-Matos, L. Xu, and H. Afsarmanesh (Eds.): PRO-VE 2012, IFIP AICT 380, pp. 301–309, 2012.
© IFIP International Federation for Information Processing 2012

by various stages of e-government, which reflect the degree of technical sophistication and interaction with users [14] (e.g., (1) information necessary to start the procedure to obtain the service available on the website(s), (2) interaction: downloadable or printable form to start the procedure to obtain the service on the website(s), (3) two-way interaction: electronic forms to start the procedure to obtain the service on the website(s), (4) transaction: full electronic case handling of the procedure by the service provider, (5) proactive, automated service delivery [7]). But after the empirical investigation of real e-services there do not appear to be discernible steps or stages in e-government. Rather, after an initial e-government presence, governments adopt e-government slowly and incrementally [15] - development of services is not sudden jumps, but even increase. That leads to the thoughts that there is a need for developing methods and models that describe e-government and their e-services more accurate.

On the other hand these models just express the potency of examined cases of e-government services but do not consider the structure of e-services and the intensity (volumes) of their usage in real world. It's often the will "If we build it, they will come!" not come true. At the end of the day, e-government is what it is, not what it was predicted to be [15]. That prompts that evaluating the e-services we should take into account not only the potential possibilities of the provided e-service that are based on the speculations of e-government models – the 'potential maturity' of e-service but also take into consideration the empirical data of the usage of the e-services.

The investigation of the problem why the e-service with high maturity level is not used in such volumes as it was expected is far beyond the scope of this paper. In this article, we ask if the e-services with the same maturity level ('potential maturity') but different intensity of their online usage should be evaluated at the same rate.

We present more accurate assessment method for e-service maturity that is based on stage models, service decomposition into the components – operations, which are related to the total intensity of their usage, as well as intensity of online service usage. In our case we decided on the stage model [7] that was approved and used for several years by collaborating Member States for the eGovernment performance benchmarking in EU though the method can be used for any other type of stage model that were listed before. The method first of all can be used for self-assessment of trends of maturity of e-services in different time periods of e-service development evolution. It could be also useful for benchmarking, comparing different e-services with each other or indicating weak aspects of the e-service and eliminating these weaknesses by appointing directions for further development. Finally, the presented method was adopted for use with the set of evaluation criteria that are based on generic e-service model [16] when assessment is carried out in accordance with the stage model definitions for each criterion.

## 2    Case Study: Driver's License Service

We'll analyze and evaluate the maturity of the driver's license (DL) service – a standard procedure to obtain a driver's license for a personal vehicle not for professional use which is one of the 'traditional benchmark' public services [7].

In our case DL service structure is composed of service operations (marked as 1, 2, ..., 5) that are detailed by service cases (marked as 3 a, 3 b, ..., 5 b). DL service operations:

1  Issue a new driver license.
2  Change/renew driver license.
3  Change of status of driver license: 3 a. activate driver license, 3 b. reports on driver license losses.
4  Obtain information on the right to drive or driver license: 4 a. obtain information on the right to drive: granted / deprived, 4 b. obtain information on driver license: produced / sent / handed, 4 c. obtain information on driver license validity, 4 d. obtain information from driver license register, 4 e. obtain information on driver examination: statement / protocol / reference.
5  Obtain information on driver license production or expiration: 5 a. obtain information on driver license production, 5 b. obtain information on expiration of driver license.

A particular DL service may consist of one or more non contradictory operations. As the maturity level for different operations of the service may be different we'll apply the model for every separate operation individually.

Service operations number 1 and 2 may be assessed by $3^{rd}$ or $4^{th}$ stage depending on service conditions: $3^{rd}$ stage - if it is not possible to accept required data not electronically and customer must physically deliver lacking data documents to the service provider office; $4^{th}$ stage – if all required data for the service are accepted online. The service operations number 3 and 4 may be assessed by: $3^{rd}$ stage – if the request is delivered to service provider not electronically; $4^{th}$ stage – if the request is delivered online. The service operation number 5 may be assessed by $4^{th}$ or $5^{th}$ stage: $4^{th}$ stage – if the customer of the service did not provide contact data that could be used to send him information and $5^{th}$ stage – if service provider prompts the customer automatically online.

According to [7] the overall DL service maturity level would be assessed to stage 5 that correspond to the possibly highest evaluation level for this kind of service. It is because the current method is referenced to the highest evaluation of the service operation that is service operation number 5 in our case and that satisfy the model $5^{th}$ stage conditions. But such an assessment of the service for DL service does not fit for the rest operations of the service. Though the service operation number 5 would be assessed to stage level 5 is it correct to assess the whole service to $5^{th}$ stage level? It is obvious that such a method of service evaluation when the service is composed of operations with different maturity level is not precise.

## 3    E-service Maturity Level Assessment Method

E-service maturity level according to the method described in [7] is formed as follows: the maturity level evaluation $M_n$ for the online service n, (n=1, ..., N, N – number of services that participate in evaluation) is calculated in percentages using current stage model level evaluation of the service $K_n$ and highest possible stage model level $H_n$ for the service n:

$$M_n = K_n (100 / H_n) \tag{1}$$

where    n – index of the service, n=1, ..., N,

$M_n$ – maturity evaluation level for service n,

$H_n$ – possible highest stage model level for service n: $H_n \in \{1, 2, 3, 4, 5\}$ (according to recommendations for DL service [7] this level is 5),

$K_n$ – stage model level evaluation defined by the experts according to the definition of the stage model levels: $K_n \in \{0, 1, 2, 3, 4, 5\}$, when the highest evaluation level is $H_n=5$.

The overall maturity level M for the services that participate in assessment is:

$$M = 1/N \sum_{n=1}^{N} M_n \tag{2}$$

We'll apply formula (1) for the maturity level evaluation for every separate operation j of service n. In this case the maturity level evaluation $M'_{n1}$ of service n is calculated as follows:

$$M'_{n1}= 1/ P_n \sum_{j=1}^{P_n} (1/ R_{jn} \sum_{i=1}^{R_{jn}} k_{ijn} (100 / h_{jn})) \tag{3}$$

where    i – evaluation index for operation j of service n, i=1, ..., $R_{jn}$,

$R_{jn}$ – number of evaluations of operation j for service n,

$k_{ijn}$ – evaluation rate for evaluation i of operation j for service n: $k_{ijn} \in \{0, 1, 2, 3, 4, 5\}$,

$h_{jn}$ – possible highest evaluation rate for operation j of service n: $h_{jn} \in \{1, 2, 3, 4, 5\}$, $k_{ijn} \leq h_{jn}$.

Evaluation formula (3) we'll make more accurate by introducing usage coefficients $\alpha_{jn}$ for operation j of service n that correspond to the intensity of the service operation usage as a part of the intensity of the usage of all service operations. In this case maturity level evaluation $M'_{n2}$ for service n:

$$M'_{n2}= \sum_{j=1}^{P_n} \alpha_{jn} (1/ R_{jn} \sum_{i=1}^{R_{jn}} k_{ijn} (100 / h_{jn})) \tag{4}$$

where    $\alpha_{jn} = \omega_{jn} / \sum_{j=1}^{P_n} \omega_{jn}$,

$\omega_{jn}$ – total intensity of usage of operation j for service n (number of operations j for service n per time period T) via traditional and electronic (online) space,

$$\sum_{j=1}^{P_n} \alpha_{jn} = 1, \text{ for every } n.$$

After collected statistics on intensity of the usage of operation j for e-service n we can evaluate the volume $S'_n$ of the service which is delivered online:

$$S'_n = 1/ P_n \sum_{j=1}^{P_n} \beta_{jn} \, 100 \tag{5}$$

where    $\beta_{jn} = \varphi_{jn} / \omega_{jn}$,

$\varphi_{jn}$ – intensity of online operations - number of online operations j for service n per time period T,

$$1 / P_n \sum_{j=1}^{P_n} \beta_{jn} \leq 1, \text{ for every } n.$$

The statistics on intensity of the usage of operation j for e-service n we'll use for the service maturity evaluation $M'_{n3}$:

$$M'_{n3} = \sum_{j=1}^{P_n} \sum_{i=1}^{R_{jn}} (\varphi_{ijn} / \sum_{l=1}^{P_n} \omega_{ln}) \, k_{ijn} \, (100 / h_{jn}) \tag{6}$$

where    $\varphi_{ijn}$ – intensity of online operations (number of online operations j for service n per time period T) for evaluation i,

$\omega_{ln}$ – total usage intensity of operation l for service n (number of operations l for service n per time period T) in traditional and electronic (online) space.

We'll use (2) formula for the total evaluation of maturity M' for all e-government services:

$$M' = 1/N \sum_{n=1}^{N} \sum_{j=1}^{P_n} \sum_{i=1}^{R_{jn}} (\varphi_{ijn} / \sum_{l=1}^{P_n} \omega_{ln}) \, k_{ijn} \, (100 / h_{jn}) \tag{7}$$

In case, when there is a set of evaluation criteria (e.g., see [17]) that are defined by stage models, the maturity evaluation $M'_{n4}$ of every operation j (j=1,…, $P_n$) for service n (n=1,…, N) instead of one we use several criteria $k'_{njl}$ (l=1,…, $L_{nj}$) with possible highest evaluation rate $h'_{njl}$ and "weights" $w_{njl}$. Here formula (6) will be as follows:

$$M'_{n4} = 1/ P_n \sum_{j=1}^{P_n} \alpha_{jn} \sum_{l=1}^{L_{nj}} w_{njl} \, (k'_{njl} \, (100 / h'_{njl})) \tag{8}$$

where        l – evaluation criteria index for operation j of service n, l=1,…, $L_{nj}$,
$L_{nj}$ – number of evaluation criteria for operation j of service n,

k'$_{njl}$ – evaluation rate according to the criterion l of operation j for service n,

h'$_{njl}$ – possible highest evaluation rate of criterion l for operation j of service n, k'$_{njl}$ ≤h'$_{njl}$,

$w_{njl}$ – "weight" for evaluation criterion l of operation j of service n,

$$\sum_{l=1}^{L_{nj}} w_{njl} = 1, \text{ for every n and j.}$$

# 4    E-service Maturity Evaluation Sample

For the method illustration we'll use artificial data that show service maturity evaluations in different situations of evolution of DL service development. E-service maturity evaluations are presented graphically in Fig. 1. (For more detailed data refer to Electronic Table in [18]). Different cases A, B, C, D, E and F represent DL service with different usage intensity and different maturity level for the operations of the service.

In our sample every operation j for service n (DL service) is evaluated according to 2 possible maturity levels: lower and highest possible maturity evaluation rate ($R_{jn}=2$; j=1, ..., 5):

1    Issue a new driver license;
1.1   if not all data are accepted online this operation is evaluated in level 3;
1.2   if all data are accepted online this operation is evaluated in level 4.
2    Change/renew driver license;
2.1   if not all data are accepted online this operation is evaluated in level 3;
2.2   if all data are accepted online this operation is evaluated in level 4.
3    Change of status of driver license:
3.1   if the messages about the DL status is transmitted not electronically this operation is evaluated in level 3;
3.2   if the messages about the DL status are transmitted online this operation is evaluated in level 4.
4    Obtain information on the right to drive or driver license:
4.1   if the request and data are transmitted not electronically this operation is evaluated in level 3;
4.2   if the request and data are transmitted online this operation is evaluated in level 4.
5    Obtain information on driver license production or expiration:
5.1   if responding to the request of the customer information is transmitted online this operation is evaluated in level 4;
5.2   if information is transmitted online without the request of the customer (proactively) this operation is evaluated in level 5.

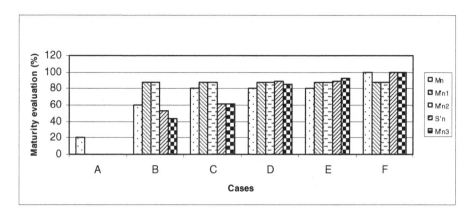

**Fig. 1.** E-service maturity evaluations

Case A presents situation when there is no online service operation though some general information is presented in official web site: maturity level 1. Case B presents situation when some service operations are online but evaluated at the lower rate: maturity level 3. Cases C, D and E represent intermediate situation when service operations are in two levels: maturity level 3 and 4. Case F represent situation when all service operations are evaluated in the highest rates that means the service has fully matured.

Comparing maturity evaluations (see Fig. 1) we'll notice that evaluation $M'_{n3}$ represents the maturity trend more accurately comparing it with $M_n$, $M'_{n1}$ and $M'_{n2}$ evaluations that ignore the usage intensity of online service operations in different levels of their maturity and that's these evaluations are not informative in this case. When the usage intensity of service operations is the same for different service operation evaluation (cases C, D and E) service maturity evaluation $M'_{n3}$ grows according to the growth of service operations: more usage intensity in higher maturity level higher maturity of the service. Evaluations $M'_{n2}$ and $M'_{n3}$ for every separate operation of the service represent its own maturity.

In real situations in order to evaluate the service maturity the experts should make a decision for every separate operation of the service on the level of the maturity and they should apply presented formulas to calculate the total service maturity using the statistics of the operation usage. It may be helpful to use Electronic Table similar to presented in [18].

## 5    Conclusions and Future Work

This article proposed a more accurate method for assessing maturity of e-services. The assessment method is based on stage models, service decomposition into the components – operations. Evaluation of maturity of e-service depends on statistics such as the total intensity of the usage of every separate operation and the intensity of the usage of online service operation. The option of the e-service maturity evaluation is presented when there is used more than one criterion for maturity evaluation of every operation of the service. The advantage of the method was illustrated by modeling evaluation of the service with artificial data.

Still, there are several requirements that should be satisfied to be able to use the method in practice. First of all the service should be accurately decomposed into separate operations. There should be collected reliable statistical information of the usage of each operation in traditional and electronic space.

The method is focused to be used for self-assessment of maturity of e-services in their development process or for benchmarking, for comparing different e-services one with each other or for comparing the same e-services that are provided by different administrations (e.g., municipalities) or even in different countries.

For the future the presented method should be tested and validated for the maturity evaluating on real data of e-services.

# References

1. Jansen, A.: Assessing E-government progress – why and what. In: Tessem, B.J., Iden og, G., Christensen, G. (eds.) NOKOBIT 2005. Department of EGovernment Studies, University of Oslo, Norway (2005), ISBN 8280330267, ISSN 15041697, http://www.uio.no/studier/emner/jus/afin/FINF4001/h05/undervisningsmateriale/AJJ-nokobit2005.pdf
2. Gartner Group: Key issues in E-Government Strategy and Management. Research Notes, Key Issues (2000)
3. Baum, C., Maio, A.D.: Gartner's Four Phases of E-Government Model. Gartner Inc. (2000)
4. Layne, K., Lee, J.: Developing fully functional E-government: A four stage model. Government Information Quarterly 18, 122–136 (2001)
5. Ronaghan, S.A.: Benchmarking E-Government: A Global Perspective. United Nations Division for Public Economics and Public Administration and American Society for Public Administration, New York (2001)
6. Hiller, J., Belanger, F.: Privacy strategies for electronic government. PricewaterhouseCoopers (2001)
7. 9th Benchmark Measurement. Digitizing Public Services in Europe: Putting ambition into action. Prepared by Capgemini, Rand Europe, IDC, Sogeti and DTI (2010)
8. ANAO. Electronic Service Delivery, including Internet use by Commonwealth Government Agencies, Australian National Auditing Office, Canberra, Australia (1999)
9. SAFAD. The 24/7 Agency: Criteria for 24/7 Agencies in the Networked Public Administration, Statskontoret, 41, Sweden (2000)
10. United Nations. E-Government Survey 2010. Leveraging e-government at a time of financial and economic crisis, p. 95 (2010)
11. West, D.M.: Improving Technology Utilization in Electronic Government around the World, 2008. Center for Public Policy, Brown University, US (2008), http://www.brookings.edu/~/media/Files/rc/reports/2008/0817_egovernment_west/0817_egovernment_west.pdf

12. The Economist. Intelligence Unit. Digital economy ranking 2010. Beyond e-readiness. IBM (2010),
    `http://graphics.eiu.com/upload/EIU_Digital_economy_rankings_2010_FINAL_WEB.pdf`
13. Vintar, M., Nograsek, J.: How much can we trust different egovernment surveys? The case of Slovenia. Information Polity 15(3), 199–213 (2010),
    `http://www.fu.uni-lj.si/iiu/Clanki/How_much_can_we_trust_different_e-government_surveys_The_case_of_Slovenia.pdf`
14. Moon, M.J.: The Evolution of E-Government among Municipalities: Rhetoric or Reality? Public Administration Review 62(4) (2002)
15. Coursey, D., Norris, D.F.: Models of E-Government: Are They Correct? An Empirical Assessment. Public Administration Review 68(3) (2008)
16. Ostasius, E., Petraviciute, Z.: Modeling e-services in public sector. INFORMACIJOS MOKSLAI 53 (2010) ISSN 1392-0561,
    `http://www.leidykla.eu/en/journals/information-sciences/information-sciences-2010-vol-53/`
17. Ostasius, E., Petraviciute, Z.: Applying e-Service Model in Assessment and Comparison of Services. In: Camarinha-Matos, L.M., Boucher, X., Afsarmanesh, H. (eds.) PRO-VE 2010. IFIP AICT, vol. 336, pp. 443–450. Springer, Heidelberg (2010)
18. DL Service Assessment: maturity evaluation data. Electronic Table (2011),
    `http://e-stud.vgtu.lt/files/dest/13822/dl_service_assessment.xls`

# Assessing Value-Based Plans in Public R&D Using the Analytic Hierarchy Process

Pawadee Meesapawong, Yacine Rezgui, and Haijiang Li

School of Engineering, Cardiff University, Queen's Buildings, The Parade, Cardiff, CF243AA,
Wales, United Kingdom
{MeesapawongP,RezguiY,LiH}@cardiff.ac.uk

**Abstract.** There is a need for research regarding how to manage public research and development (R&D) to create societal values. The paper focuses on the Analytic Hierarchy Process (AHP) in a case study, the microelectronics research center. Twenty-four factors (e.g. mission, internal R&D, collaboration and management-related factors) were constructed in a hierarchy model for assessing three innovation plans: knowledge, societal and commercial orientation. The AHP analysis reveals that commercial orientation has the highest impact score on innovation factors. However, given that the selected case study is a taxpayer-funded public R&D organisation, societal expectations have to be factored into their innovation plans. Hence, the paper provides a sensitivity analysis as a result of which a suggestion is made to increase the priority of collaboration-related factors to improve the impact of societal orientation.

**Keywords:** AHP, collaboration, innovation, public R&D, societal value.

## 1 Introduction

Managing research and development (R&D) needs more efforts to develop innovation models which span multiple dimensions such as individual, organisational, and environmental [1]. Environmental factors influencing corporate innovations involve the customer dimension, i.e. how to carry out customer-oriented innovations [1], [2]. In contrast, taxpayer-funded organisations should not only serve specific customers but also serve general citizens, thus focusing on societal-oriented innovations [3], [4]. However, many taxpayer-funded R&D organisations have failed to create values to theirs nations [1], [5].

Additionally, values can be created at different levels: individual, organisational, and societal level [6]. The individual values that employees perceive in a given situation influence the overall values of an organisation [7]. The important issue for employees is what the organisations values are. Societal values can guide expressions of individuals and organisations, however, individual perceptions to societal values are non-systematic approaches. Employees tend to respond to performance evaluations whether or not they meet such values. Organisations have to realise which functional areas are relevant to societal values and shape perception of those areas

L.M. Camarinha-Matos, L. Xu, and H. Afsarmanesh (Eds.): PRO-VE 2012, IFIP AICT 380, pp. 310–317, 2012.
© IFIP International Federation for Information Processing 2012

into systematic approaches [8]. However, value orientations within societies change over time, thus proactive organisations learn to respond to societal influences [8].

The authors identify a research gap in that there have been very few studies on how to manage innovations in public R&D [9]. Organisations may build collaborative networks in order to perform meaningful contribution [3], [4]. Hence, this paper first reviews existing collaborative networks in R&D. Next, the consolidation of the Analytic Hierarchy Process (AHP) to achieve a hierarchy model for corporate innovations in public R&D is described. The AHP findings in the selected case study, namely 'MEC', are then further discussed. The final section draws out the contribution of the paper and provides the directions for further research.

## 2    Collaboration Dimension in R&D

Innovation has become an important aspect of organisational management. It has been defined broadly in different contexts and usually the word 'new' is emphasised. Managing innovation is a process to find the proper ways involving all the activities in turning new ideas into widely used practice such as commercialisation [10].There has been a growing awareness in a crucial role of collaborative networks in innovation performance [1], [11], [12]. Private R&D organisations collaborate with others for several economic reasons, such as reducing cost, reducing time, reducing risk and achieving high novelty degrees of innovations [10], [11]. For public R&D organisations, however, the reasons to initiating collaboration may be slightly different. Some public R&D organisations have been spurred to collaborate with universities and firms because of the growth of societal expectations and factors related to national policies [13].

To achieve successful collaboration, public R&D has to communicate with internal and external players. For internal players, public R&D needs to motivate employees with clear understanding of responsibilities and clear policies for commitments such as time-limited policies [1]. For external players, budget constraints force public R&D to select potential projects and make the decision whether funding is on the basis of repayment, non-repayment or repayable if successful [5], [13]. Performance of collaboration can be assessed both in terms of tangible and intangible values. The tangible values are new products which meet societal expectations and intellectual properties for innovation competitiveness. The intangible values include, for example, that professional researchers in public R&D help industries which lack human capital [1]. An important role of collaborative R&D leads to a growing need for new perspectives on innovation management in R&D [14]. R&D should emphasis strong and strategic linkages amongst collaborating stakeholders. The model of innovation management should increase importance of societal ingredients such as having the potential to capture knowledge originating from social interactions [15]. However, a business model of an organisation should represent of what value is provided to customers [16]. In addition, innovation management encompasses all the key activities needed to develop successful products and services [10], thus the authors argue that the innovation model should not only focus on the performance of collaboration, but also the other organisational dimensions.

Meesapawong et al. [9] proposed an innovation model involving four dimensions of public R&D: the mission of public R&D, internal R&D, collaborative projects, and management. They advocated that public R&D organisations should focus on nurturing values from these four dimensions. Furthermore, Meesapawong et al. [17] employed the Delphi method, an expert-based judgment, to provide the factors associated to each dimension which are essential for applying the proposed framework in public R&D. However, the Delphi findings could not provide a clear-cut rank of the factors. Moreover, the level of importance of the collaboration-related factors is what constitutes the focus of the research?

# 3    Methodology

To address research gap of practicing collaborative projects to stimulate innovations in public R&D, the authors employ the AHP to provide a clear-cut rank of collaboration-related factors including an authoritative model to manage innovations in practice.

The AHP is a widely used tool in solving a complex problem involving tangible and intangible factors. Breaking down a decision problem into a hierarchical structure makes decisions more comfortably than rating the large number of items [18], [19], [20]. The unequal priorities by which alternatives are evaluated could be used as supporting information to describe how changes of the factors affect scores of alternatives [18], [21]. Although many studies propose that the combination of the AHP and Fuzzy theory can handle uncertainty of decision making, Saaty [22], who first introduced the AHP, states that the way in which the Fuzzy approach reduces inconsistency judgments distort the original priorities and makes the validity of the outcome worse.

The research focuses on a case study drawn from Thailand, the same country as selected in the Delphi study of Meesapawong et al. [17] because conducting research across countries may face results diversity stemmed from socio-cultural differences [23]. The AHP case study is the first integrated circuits fabrication research center in Thailand, namely MEC (the name has been disguised for confidentiality issues). MEC is fully funded by Thai government to develop commercialised products and to collaborate with local industries. The current shrinking of governmental budget forces MEC to plan a management model to deal with its complex missions. Thus, the AHP is employed to select a proper plan of managing future innovations in MEC.

The first step of adapting AHP for innovation planning in MEC is to construct a pre-determined hierarchy and then discuss it with MEC's managers. The top level of the hierarchy is the goal to evaluate innovation plans in MEC. The next levels consist of the factors verified by the Delphi study of Meesapawong et al. [17]. Alternative plans evaluated by the factors are then arranged at the lowest level. Although the factors are assumed to be influencing factors fitting to Thai public R&D, MEC's managers are expected to approve and rearrange the factors in the hierarchy. The approved hierarchy is used as the model in developing the AHP questionnaire asking the respondents to compare the importance of the factors in the hierarchy, and then evaluate the impact of alternative plans on the factors. The scale of pairwise comparison in the AHP uses integer '1' to '9'   to represent the intensity of importance over another factor ranging from equal importance to extreme importance [19]. The AHP questionnaire asks each expert to compare importance amongst factors: which factor is more important, and how much more? The answers of each expert represented in ratio scale are then transferred to a matrix. The validity of AHP is approved by '*Consistency Ratio (C.R.)*' calculated to reflect the confidence in the priorities derived from a pairwise matrix. The acceptable consistency ratio should be less than 0.10 [18], [24]. The consistency ratio is calculated from equation (1). If a consistency ratio of a matrix is unacceptable, revisions are called for.

$$C.R. = \frac{(\lambda_{max} - n)/(n-1)}{R.I.}. \tag{1}$$

where: $\lambda_{max}$ = max eigenvalue of matrix ; $n$ = matrix size ; $R.I.$ = random index [24].

Each question yields a set of matrices results from individual experts, hence the set of matrices need to be aggregated into a group's matrix by deriving geometric means. The importance priorities of each group's matrix are then derived from the principal eigenvector of the matrix [18]. The summation of local priorities in each matrix (or each hierarchical level) is equal to 1. Each local priority needs to be converted to global priority by multiplying with the priority of its parent's priority. The sum of global priorities of all factors in a hierarchy is equal to 1.

The impacts of alternative plans are rated in pairs with respect to each of the sub-factors. Similar to importance priorities, impact weights of alternative plans $(a_{mn})$ are calculated from the eigenvectors of group's matrices where total impact weight of all alternative plans is equal to 1. Basically, the alternatives are evaluated by using the composite scores which each alternative contributes to all the criteria in the hierarchy [18]. The alternative which shows the highest composite score is the most likely selected alternative. The composite scores are the product of impact multiplied by importance as shown in equation (2).

$$Cm = \sum_{n=1}^{n} a_{mn} * g_n \tag{2}$$

where:  $a_{mn}$  =  impact weight of alternative plan $m$ with respect to factor $n$
       $g_n$  =  global priority of factor $n$

## 4    Results

Discussion with top management in MEC resulted in a five-level hierarchy model (Fig. 1) the first level (H1) of which is the goal of the hierarchy model to evaluate innovation plans in MEC. The second level (H2) is constructed from four main dimensions of MEC: mission, internal R&D, collaboration and management. The third and fourth levels are composed of factors verified by the MEC's managers. The fifth level of the hierarchy is arranged for alternative plans which are hypothesised plans of innovation management that are conceived by making assumptions about current and future trends of MEC. There are 3 plans which focus on different orientations (a) knowledge orientation focusing on for academic excellence (b) societal orientation focusing on societal values and (c) commercial orientation focusing on commercial values of research products. As shown in the hierarchies (Fig. 1), there are 24 sub-factors arranged in the third (H3) and the fourth level (H4) by which alternative plans are evaluated. Group's judgments regarding unequal importance of the factors are presented in terms of *'Global priorities (G)'*. The results show that the 'Commercial orientation (Plan C)' has the highest composite score at 0.4871, while the composite score of the 'Societal orientation, (Plan S)' and the 'Knowledge orientation (Plan K)' are 0.3369 and 0.1760, respectively.

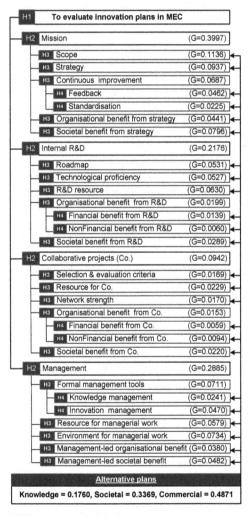

**Fig. 1.** Hierarchy model for innovation management in MEC

## 5    Discussion

The AHP study shows that the commercial orientation has the greatest impact on innovations. As a taxpayer-funded organisation, MEC cannot ignore the importance of collaboration-related factors and the innovation plan focusing on societal values. Hence, a sensitivity analysis is performed to establish whether any change in priority of any factor could make the societal orientation plan become the most impact plan on innovations. The sensitivity tests with respect each dimension shows that changes in ranks of plans are only found in the collaboration dimension (Fig. 2). The societal orientation becomes the most impact plan on innovations when the priority of collaboration is more than 43%, whereas the original value is 9.42%. There is a large gap to bring the priority of collaboration to the point that made the societal orientation plan become more important in terms of impact to the overall innovation factors. To highlight the collaboration dimension, MEC may start from understanding the sub-factors under the dimension. Fig. 3 reveals similar patterns of impact and importance of sub-factors. This means that MEC have already distributed priorities to the sub-factors corresponding to the impact. However, to increase in overall importance of collaboration-related factors by keeping the same fraction amongst them is essential for MEC to improve its innovation capability and satisfy societal aspirations.

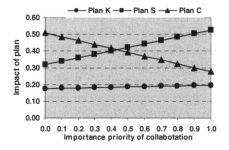

**Fig. 2.** Sensitivity of innovation plans with respect to collaboration

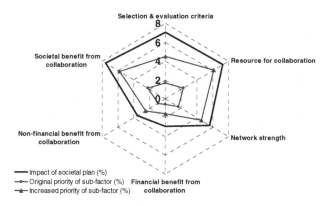

**Fig. 3.** Impact and importance of collaboration-related factors

The AHP findings in MEC can be further applied for particular activities in collaboration such as selecting collaborative projects based on the collaboration-related factors obtained from the paper (as shown in Fig. 4).

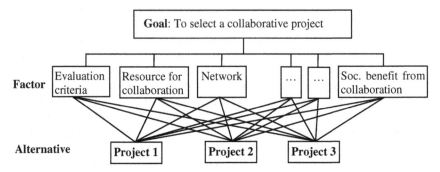

**Fig. 4.** A pre-determined hierarchy for selecting collaborative projects

# 6    Conclusions

The paper addresses the research gap for innovation management in public R&D by underling the collaboration-related factors. A public R&D case study, namely MEC, provides an innovation management model arranged by AHP. The model is established to assess three innovation plans in MEC: knowledge, societal and commercial plans. The model yields different weights of collaboration-related factors and other influencing factors on innovation. With respect to all factors, the commercial plan shows the highest impact score on innovation factors. However, the sensitivity analysis provides a view that MEC can improve its innovation capability and satisfy societal aspirations by raising the priorities of collaboration-related factors. Additionally, there is a large gap to bring the priority of collaboration to the point that made the societal orientation plan become the most impact plan.

The AHP study in MEC can be further elaborated by establishing a new AHP model, the goal of which is to implement the plan of societal orientation such as selecting collaborative projects. Nevertheless, this study is limited at the stage of innovation planning and is not extended to the implement stage such as selecting collaborative projects.

Although, the AHP model is specifically designed for MEC, other public R&D organisations could use this model as a pre-determined hierarchy model to develop hierarchy models suited to their organisational environment because the factors are originally gathered from research of public R&D in developed and developing countries before refinement by a Thai Delphi panel. The authors hope that the present paper will contribute to the ongoing improvement of innovation management in public R&D.

# References

1. Shavinina, L.V.: The international handbook on innovation. Pergamon, Oxford (2003)
2. Hoonsopon, D., Ruenrom, G.P.: The Empirical Study of the Impact of Product Innovation Factors on the Performance of New Products: Radical and Incremental Product Innovation. The Business Review 12, 155–162 (2009)
3. Denhardt, R.B., Denhardt, J.V.: The New Public Service: Serving Rather than Steering. Public Administration Review 60, 549–559 (2000)
4. Greener, I.: Public management: a critical text. Palgrave Macmillan, Basingstoke (2009)
5. Cozzarin, B.P.: Data and the measurement of R&D program impacts. Evaluation and Program Planning 31, 284–298 (2008)
6. Vorakulpipat, C., Rezgui, Y., Hopfe, C.J.: Value creating construction virtual teams: A case study in the construction sector. Automation in Construction 19, 142–147 (2010)
7. Burnes, B.: Managing change: a strategic approach to organisational dynamics, 4th edn. Financial Times, Harlow (2004)
8. Dierkes, M., Antal, A.B., Child, J., Nonaka, I.: Handbook of organizational learning and knowledge. Oxford University Press, Oxford (2001)
9. Meesapawong, P., Rezgui, Y., Li, H.: Perceiving societal value as the core of innovation management in public research and development organizations. In: The 5th International Conference on Management of Innovation and Technology, Singapore, pp. 312–317 (2010)
10. Tidd, J., Bessant, J.: Managing Innovation: Integrating Technological, Market and Organizational Change, 4th edn. John Wiley & Sons, Chichester (2009)
11. Nieto, M.J., Santamaría, L.: The importance of diverse collaborative networks for the novelty of product innovation. Technovation 27, 367–377 (2007)
12. Tsai, K.-H.: Collaborative networks and product innovation performance: Toward a contingency perspective. Research Policy 38, 765–778 (2009)
13. Mowery, D.C.: The changing structure of the US national innovation system: implications for international conflict and cooperation in R&D policy. Research Policy 27, 639–654 (1998)
14. Daniel, H.Z., Hempel, D.J., Srinivasan, N.: A model of value assessment in collaborative R&D programs. Industrial Marketing Management 31, 653–664 (2002)
15. Trott, P.: Innovation management and new product development, 3rd edn. Financial Times Prentice Hall, NJ (2005)
16. Osterwalder, A., Pigneur, Y.: Clarifying Business Models: Origins, Present, and Future of the Concept. Communications of AIS, 1–25 (2005)
17. Meesapawong, P., Rezgui, Y., Li, H.: Factors influencing innovation management in public research and development. Submitted manuscript in R&D Management Journal (2011)
18. Saaty, T.L.: The Analytic Hierarchy Process. McGraw-Hill, New York (1980)
19. Saaty, T.L., Vargas, L.G.: Models, Methods, Concepts and Applications of the Analytic Hierarchy Process. Kluwer Academic, Boston (2000)
20. Turban, E.: Decision support and expert systems: management support systems, 4th edn. Prentice-Hall, NJ (1995)
21. Chin, K.S., Pun, K.F., Xu, Y., Chan, J.S.F.: An AHP based study of critical factors for TQM implementation in Shanghai manufacturing industries. Technovation 22, 707–715 (2002)
22. Saaty, T.L., Tran, L.T.: On the invalidity of fuzzifying numerical judgments in the Analytic Hierarchy Process. Mathematical and Computer Modelling 46, 962–975 (2007)
23. Hayne, S.C., Pollard, C.E.: A comparative analysis of critical issues facing Canadian information systems personnel: a national and global perspective. Information & Management 38, 73–86 (2000)
24. Saaty, T.L., Ozdemir, M.S.: Why the magic number seven plus or minus two. Mathematical and Computer Modelling 38, 233–244 (2003)

# iSurvival: A Collaborative Mobile Network System for Disaster Management

Ali Al-Sherbaz, Rashmi Dravid, Espen Svennevik, and Phil Picton

School of Science and Technology, University of Northampton,
St. Georges Avenue, Northampton, NN2 6JD, United Kingdom

**Abstract.** When disaster strikes, optimal access to real-time information of the disaster situation during 'blind time' – the time prior to the arrival of the first responders - and during response and recovery stages is essential to improve the effectiveness of the first responders and recovery. This paper describes a disaster management system, iSurvival, which uses specialist applications on the smart phones of those affected by disaster and wireless devices of first responders, to establish Wireless Mesh Networks (WMN), to facilitate the secure exchange of information in the disaster area, when the normal GSM and 3G telephone networks are compromised or unavailable. This information is further communicated with central control centre for analysis and resource scheduling for effective mobilisation of emergency services which are involved in rescue and recovery. The research, currently under the analysis and design stage, has been awarded a 'Special Mention' from Nokia for Ideas for Development Challenge 2012.

**Keywords:** Disaster, wireless mesh networks, smart phones, Instantaneous Digital Infrastructures.

## 1    Introduction

Disasters, natural and man-made, require a timely and co-ordinated response to improve the effectiveness of the first responders and emergency organisations. Disaster Management is defined as "... range of actions and processes to control disaster and emergency situations and to provide a framework to prevent and/or lessen the effect of disaster before, during and after a disaster..." [1].

When disaster strikes, the public infrastructure and utilities, including, communications networks - terrestrial networks, voice services and cellular networks - are damaged, impaired, marginally available, intentionally shutdown or non-existent as in the case of remote areas. The need for a flexible and rapidly deployable communication infrastructure is a pre-requisite for optimal provision of real-time information between the victims in the disaster area and the first responders during the response and recovery stages of disaster management. Equally important and critical to disaster management is the access to information during the 'blind time'- the time immediately after the disaster and prior to the arrival of first responders, as it offers vital insight into the disaster situation and improves the effectiveness of the first responders and mobilisation of emergency services.

L.M. Camarinha-Matos, L. Xu, and H. Afsarmanesh (Eds.): PRO-VE 2012, IFIP AICT 380, pp. 318–326, 2012.
© IFIP International Federation for Information Processing 2012

There is a growing recognition that technology enhanced disaster management systems could help to reduce fatalities of human lives during disasters. A recent example includes the aftermath of the Haitian earthquake in January 2010, where a WiFi network was the first network to come alive to establish communication with trapped people. The evolving landscape of wireless and mobile technologies, voice and data convergence, computing and modelling capability of services, the growth trend in mobile phones and their ubiquitous uptake is driving the research to harness their potential for integrated technological solutions.

This paper describes a disaster management system, iSurvival, which utilises the resilient and self-configuring capabilities of a Wireless Mesh Networks (WMN) and the capability of smart phones to establish a P2P (peer-to-peer) network using Bluetooth or WiFi in the disaster area to facilitate phone to phone communications. The iSurvival system utilises specialist software applications, the iSurvival applications, available on victims' smart phones and first responders' wireless devices, to instantiate Instantaneous Digital Infrastructures (IDIs), which facilitate routing and forwarding of secure information in the disaster area. When temporary telecommunication infrastructures are set up by first responders at a disaster site, wireless and mobile technologies from GSM, WiFi, WiMax and others are used as backhaul networks to communicate information from the disaster area to a control centre for analysis, access to services and databases to help co-ordination between emergency services involved in rescue and recovery.

Of the many non-technical challenges faced by disaster relief systems, a critical challenge is the adoption and usability of technology in the event of a disaster. The role of the community and NGOs in disaster management solutions cannot be undermined due to their well-established experience in disaster rescue, relief and rehabilitation of victims under disaster situations. This research is conducted as a pilot study in association with external partners, the Northamptonshire Emergency Services, who would be associated throughout the system development life cycle.

The structure of the rest of the paper is as follows: following introduction, Section 2 overviews research in disaster management solutions using wireless and mobile technologies. Section 3 presents a brief overview of system functionality; Section 4 offers a logical overview of the iSurvival applications. Section 5 discusses testing and evaluation of the system. Section 6 concludes the paper with future directions in research implementation.

## 2     Literature Review

There remains a significant research gap in the field of disaster management in terms of network architecture, protocol design, application development, network interoperability and security [2].

WMNs are increasingly being incorporated in disaster management solutions with a mesh architecture providing easy configuration, resilience, quickly deployment and interoperability in a heterogeneous environment with minimum interdependencies. Raheleh and Ramesh [3], present the results from a campus trial of deploying a wireless mesh network to provide first responders with an infrastructure for local communication, with the network connected to the outside world through a wired backhaul. With disaster solutions incorporating wireless MANETs (Mobile Ad-hoc Networks) and WMNs, the potential issues in forwarding information through instant communications system include node mobility, efficient address allocation mechanisms and non-usability of wired routing protocols. While multicast streams are the most popular traffic pattern in many applications of MANET, A.K. Vatsa et. al. [4] have proposed multicast-based routing mechanism using efficient address allocation over a mesh-based and tree-based multicast through the random casting method of node selection. Another solution uses Cluster-Mesh based Multicast Routing (CMMR) methodology [5] that combines network clustering and mesh-based multicast routing to provide scalability and robustness to multicast routing by grouping nodes into link-layer clusters and forms a backbone using cluster-heads. Roc, et. al. [6], present a set of design patterns to support communication and coordination in mobile ad-hoc scenarios. With the SafeMesh, Asad, *et al.* [7], propose a routing protocol that implements modifications to AODV (AD-hoc on demand Distance Vector routing protocol) and achieves significant performance improvement in terms of the packet delivery ratio, routing overhead and latency over other contemporary routing protocols.

With the increasing trend of smart phone usage, a number of mobile application-based solutions are available using smart phones for disaster management. MyDisasterDroid [8], is a disaster management system, implemented in an Android-based mobile platform that uses genetic algorithms to facilitate the logistics for the rescue and relief operations during a disaster. Although the use of smart mobile devices and applications in disaster scenarios can improve collaboration dynamically, nevertheless, it poses interesting challenges, such as user's mental attention, small screen size, unavailability of reliable network, reduced power, and battery consumption [9]. The iSurvival system will address these challenges that would take into account technology adaptability, ease of usage and effective GUI techniques.

The paper describes characteristics of an optimum, scalable routing solution that would build on existing research to cater to heterogeneous wireless technologies and permit fast adaptation of the flow of information through a dynamically changing topology of connected wireless mesh networks in the disaster area. The research provides an integrated technological solution that not only builds and develops on existing research using smart phones, WMN and web technologies, but also offers a unique solution to capturing communication during blind time.

## 3     iSurvival System

The iSurvival system (Fig. 1) is a disaster management system that uses special applications on the smart phones of end-users in the disaster area, the victims, to create wireless mesh networks. The system design is currently being researched with regard to implementation platforms, issues on smart phone density, security and data protection with external partners. Furthermore the research is currently exploring how the iSurvival system integrates with the existing national emergency services framework.

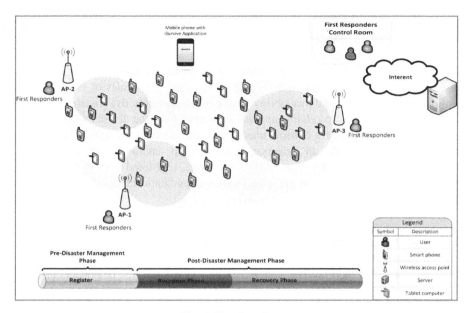

**Fig. 1.** iSurvival System

The system is designed around three main communicating entities within and outside the disaster area that include end-users in the disaster area, the *victims,* onsite specialist team, the *first responders,* and offsite specialist team, the *control centre,* using specialist applications, iSurvival, for the smart phones of victims, the wireless devices of first responders and the web based system at the control centre.

The iSurvival system addresses the preparedness, response and recovery stages of disaster management system (Fig.1). As part of the *preparedness phase* of pre-disaster management, the end-users download the application from the project website, www.isurvival.co.uk, to smart phones and register their profile to a web-based system, managed at the control centre. The communication during response and recovery phases is 'user-centric' as it relies on victims to initiate the communication process using the iSurvival application on the functioning smart phones that helps to establish wireless mesh networks, called the Instantaneous Digital Infrastructures (IDIs), in the disaster area. The IDIs, created transparently, allow co-operation and the exchange of information using smart phones between victims and are analogous to 'wireless intercoms' in the absence of cellular infrastructures in the disaster area. The iSurvival application helps to save the communication in victims' smart phones and creates a distributed knowledge base. This distributed knowledge base created during *blind time* is accessible to first responders when they connect to IDIs in the disaster area, using the iSurvival application on their wireless devices. The IDIs facilitate bidirectional communication between victims and first responders using instructions, messages, images and video.

The recovery phase relies on forwarding distributed knowledge base and real-time information to the *control centre*, using ubiquitous wireless, voice and mobile network infrastructures for analysis, data-aggregation, resource scheduling, and access to services and databases to help co-ordination between the emergency services involved in rescue and recovery. *The control centre* provides additional services for data validation, monitoring and logging as well as tracking the victim's data from the information received from a disaster area and the profile available through the initial registration on the web-based system. The issues of security - the confidentiality, integrity and availability - are essential, as effective disaster response depends on rapid access to *reliable* and *accurate* data, from the disaster situation. For example, in the context of a terrorist attack, without adequate encryption and source authentication primitives an adversary may snoop and/or insert false crisis information. The iSurvival system utilises user data, registered with the web-based system during the preparedness phase to verify and authenticate identity of victim in the disaster area.

## 4     iSurvival Implementation Technologies

The three entities in the iSurvival system are the victims, the first responders and the control centre. These get connected through the WMN using the following specialist iSurvival applications:

### 4.1     iSurvival Mobile

The Mobile App software design has two separate tasks/threads. The background thread seeks to establish and maintain itself as part of a mesh network and to establish a link with one or more first responders. The implementation of this part of the software has to take into account that the mesh network may change topology and its role as a leaf or branch node may change over the time of the disaster period. As shown in Fig. 2, the foreground task seeks information from the victim regarding the disaster and the victim's situation within the disaster. Initially, upon a mesh network having been established, victims will be able to exchange information about their circumstances. When the mesh network connects to a first responder, the victims' data will be uploaded to the first responder for further uploading to the data centre. Victims will also able to communicate outside their network through the first responder. A high level overview describing the iSurvival mobile App process in pseudo code follows:

```
if (user_response == disaster){
Gather and store user data
do {
  if (FR WiFi network present){
   Connect to FR then Upload user data
   Enter Interactive mode
  }
  else if (WiFi MESH present){
   Connect to WiFi MESH
```

```
      Exchange cooperative data (I have survived)
} while (FR not present)
 Connect to FR then Upload user data
 Enter Interactive mode
}
else if ( Bluetooth MESH present) {
   Connect to Bluetooth MESH
   Exchange cooperative data(I have survived)
   while (FR not present) {
       Connect to FR then Upload user data
       Enter Interactive mode
     }
  }
} while (not connected)}
```

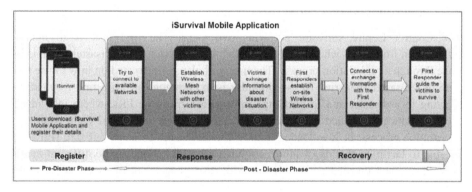

**Fig. 2.** iSurvival Application in different stages

## 4.2    iSurvival First Responder (FR)

The software for the First Responder initially attempts to link to both the Control Centre and any mesh networks created by the victims' devices. When a member of a mesh network detects a FR it will connect to it. All other nodes, on the same mesh, which are in range of the FR, will also connect directly to the FR, as shown in Fig. 1. Only devices outside the range of the FR will remain part of, potentially, a simplified mesh network or networks. When a victim connects it will upload the data to the FR and, if connected, this will be further uploaded to the control centre, as shown in Fig.2. A further complication is that both single devices and networks can connect to the FR and the FR needs to extract data from all members of a mesh network. The FR will also be capable of routing between two or more attached networks. A high level overview describing the iSurvival First Responder process in pseudo code follows:

```
        initialise FR WiFi Network // Setting SSID to
        "iSurvivalFR"
do {
            wait_for_connection
            if (connection == LEAF_NODE){
            Download user data from leaf node
            attempt to Upload user data to Control Centre
            }
            else (connection == BRANCH_NODE){
             for each LEAF on BRANCH {
             Download user data from leaf node
             attempt to Upload user data to Control Centre
             }
            }
} while (true)
```

### 4.3    iSurvival Control Centre

The Control Centre software performs two tasks. The first task is to obtain information from users who have downloaded the App prior to any disaster and this is done through a registration process. The user will also be instructed on how to use the App in a disaster scenario. The second task is to communicate with first responders reacting to a disaster and to exchange information from the FRs, where individual victims' data is uploaded to the control centre and relevant stored data, from the registration process, is downloaded to the FRs. The Control Centre software will also be able to facilitate sharing of information between FRs connected to different mesh networks. The Control Centre software will also provide an overview of disaster collated from the FRs and victims for bodies engaged in disaster relief. A high level overview describing the iSurvival Control Centre process in pseudo code follows:

```
    User registration
        do{
                if (FR connects) {
                    for each user (connected to the FR) tag as
                        disaster victim
                     return registered data on victim to FR
                    do {
                        if victim status changed update record
                        } while (!end of disaster)}
            } while (!end of disaster)
```

## 5    Testing and Evaluation

The intention is to develop iSurvival applications for both mobile and web server platforms. The proposed methodology uses agile system development to include the partner's input in drafting system requirements and specifications. The partners have been consulted to review system design and validation, field testing and the final evaluation of the complete system. Northamptonshire Emergency services have confirmed their assistance in testing of the system including facilitating the incorporation of the iSurvival system into broader emergency response exercises and explore the opportunities to further increase distribution.

## 6    Conclusion and Future Work

This paper discussed the iSurvival system that offers an efficient and cost-effective solution which benefits from using no special hardware, utilises the potential of ubiquitous mobile and wireless technologies, the growth trend of smart phone usage and end-user familiarity with the mobile phone technology. The perceived impact and uptake of the iSurvival system is anticipated to be global as it relies on a globally available, open standard and interoperating mobile and wireless technologies and smart phones and does not depend on any specialist radio equipment, which could have limitation due to radio spectrum usage. The added value offered by the system is the access to information during 'blind time' of disaster, normally untapped in available solutions. Future work may include producing an open framework for first responders to allow integration into the iSurvival system.

## References

1. WHO. Definitions for EHA - general disaster/emergency definitions. WHO (2003)
2. Legendre, F., Theus, H., Felix, S., Bernhard, P.: 30 Years of Wireless Ad Hoc Networking Research: What about Humanitarian and Disaster Relief Solutions? What are we still missing? In: ACWR 2011 Proceedings of the 1st International Conference on Wireless Technologies for Humanitarian Relief. ACM, New York (2011)
3. Dilmaghani, R.B., Rao Ramesh, R.: Hybrid Wireless Mesh Network with Application to Emergency Scenarios. Journal of Software (Academy) 3(2) (February 2008)
4. Vatsa, A.K., Prince, C., Meenakshi, C., Jyoti, S.: Routing Mechanism for MANET in Disaster Area. International Journal of Network and Mobile Technologies 2(2), 49–60 (2011)
5. Younis, M., Osama, F., Sookyoung, L.: Cluster Mesh Based Multicast Routing in MANET: An Analytical Study. In: IEEE International Conference on Communications (ICC), pp. 1–6. IEEE, Baltimore (2011)
6. Messeguer, R., Sergio, F.O., José, A.P., Leandro, N., Andrés, N.: Communication and Coordination Patterns to Support Mobile Collaboration. In: 12th International Conference on Computer Supported Cooperative Work in Design, CSCWD 2008, pp. 565–570. IEEE (2008)

7. Pirzada, A.A., Marius, P., Ryan, W., Jadwiga, I.: SafeMesh: A wireless mesh network routing protocol for incident area communications. In: Pervasive and Mobile Computing, pp. 201–221. Elsevier (2008)
8. Therese, J., Fajardo, B., Oppus Carlos, M.: A Mobile Disaster Management System Using the Android Technology. International Journal of Communications 3(3), 77–86 (2009)
9. FrontlineSMS, Communications for change: How to use text messaging as an effective behaviour change campaigning tool (2012), http://www.frontlinesms.com

# 12

## Collaboration in Traditional Sectors

# Modelling a Collaborative Network in the Agri-Food Sector Using ARCON Framework: The PROVE Case Study

Patricia Macedo[1,3], António Abreu[1,3], and Luis M. Camarinha-Matos[3]

[1] EST Setúbal, Instituto Politécnico de Setúbal, Setúbal, Portugal
[2] ISEL, Instituto Politécnico de Lisboa, Lisboa, Portugal
[3] CTS – Uninova and Faculdade de Ciências e Tecnologia, Universidade Nova de Lisboa, 2829-516 Caparica, Portugal
`patricia.macedo@estsetubal.ips.pt, ajfa@dem.isel.ipl.pt,`
`cam@uninova.pt`

**Abstract.** PROVE network is an agri-food network that aims to enable small farmers to sell their goods directly to consumers resulting from this exchange benefits to both parties. This network was selected to apply the ARCON Modelling Framework in order to evaluate its appropriateness to represent this kind of collaborative networks. Starting with a brief presentation of PROVE, this paper presents a systematic representation of the network using the ARCON framework. Furthermore a discussion about the benefits, challenges and difficulties found in our experience of applying ARCON to this kind of network is presented.

**Keywords:** Collaborative Networks, modelling framework, ARCON, agriculture sector, case study.

## 1 Introduction

In the last decade, the increasing globalization of markets has caused profound changes in global economy. Collaborative networks appeared as a way to face some of the challenges introduced by globalization. There are high expectations that collaborative networks bring clear benefits to its members (Abreu and Camarinha-Matos 2010), (Abreu, Macedo et al. 2008). These benefits include an increase of the "survival capability" in a context of market turbulence, but also the possibility to better achieve common or compatible goals. On the basis of these expectations are, among others, the following factors: joining of complementary skills and capacities, access to new / wider markets and new knowledge, etc. However, in spite of these positive expectations, it is also frequently mentioned that there is a lack of published cases that clearly shows the benefits of such organizational form, which is an obstacle for a wider acceptance of this paradigm. Therefore, this work intends to present a real collaborative network and analyze its characteristics. This case study is based on a Portuguese network in the agri-food sector, the PROVE initiative. This network can

L.M. Camarinha-Matos, L. Xu, and H. Afsarmanesh (Eds.): PRO-VE 2012, IFIP AICT 380, pp. 329–339, 2012.
© IFIP International Federation for Information Processing 2012

be framed in the scope of the alternative agri-food networks (AAFN) (Volpentesta and Ammirato 2010), and its aim is to support the development of collaborative processes enabling small farmers to sell their goods directly to consumers, and it already supported the creation of several local networks in distinct regions of Portugal.

Most of the published collaborative networks cases (Ferreira 2001; Garita 2004; Botarelli, Taticchi et al. 2008; Volpentesta and Ammirato 2008) do not follow any specific structure, what implies that: (i) some relevant aspects of networks are not explicitly identified; (ii) for the reader it is more difficult to observe a specific characteristic in the network description; (iii) it is harder to comparatively analyze two networks. In order to overcome these difficulties, the ARCON (Afsarmanesh and Camarinha-Matos 2008) modelling framework, which has been proposed to capture the various aspects involving the representation of Collaborative Networks, is adopted in this case study. There are already a few published cases of modelling collaborative networks using ARCON, such as (Beckett and Jones ; Baldo and Rabelo 2009), and all these cases suggest that ARCON is a useful modelling tool to guide the process of describing and analysing the studied collaborative networks.

The aim of this paper is to present a case study of a specific Portuguese collaborative network in the alternative agri-food sector and to discuss the appropriateness of the ARCON modelling framework to represent this kind of collaborative networks.

# 2     ARCON Overview

ARCON (Afsarmanesh and Camarinha-Matos 2008) is a modelling framework that addresses the complexity involving the representation of CNs. The modelling framework divides this complexity into three dimensions in order to cover all relevant aspects of the Collaborative Networks (CNs) in terms of life-cycle stages, environment characteristics, and modelling intent.

Vertical dimension: Life-cycle stages - This perspective captures the diversity and evolution of CNs during their entire life cycle.
Horizontal dimension: CN environment characteristics - This perspective includes two subspaces: the internal or endogenous characteristics as well as the external or exogenous interactions that are related to the logical surrounding of the CN:

- Endogenous Elements subspace represents the CN *from the inside*, four sub-dimensions are proposed: (i) the structural dimension; (ii) the componential dimension; (iii) the functional dimension; and (iv) the behavioural dimension
- Exogenous Interactions subspace represents the CN as seen from the outside, with a focus on the interactions between the CN and this environment; four sub-dimensions are defined: (i) the market dimension; (ii) the support dimension; (iii) the societal dimension; and (iv) the constituency dimension.

Diagonal dimension: Modelling intent - This perspective is related to different intents for the modelling of CNs. Three layers are considered: (i) The general representation layer that includes the most general concepts and related relations, common to all CNs regardless of the application domain; (ii) The specific modelling layer that includes more detailed models focused on different classes of CNs; and (iii) the implementation modelling layer that includes models of specific CNs.

## 3     The PROVE Network Case Study

In the last decade, the increasing globalization of markets has caused profound changes in the local farming (Feenstra 1997). The advances in the means of transport and communication, and the improvement of quality of life were the main causes of these changes. As a result, there was a greater exchange of goods and services, which allow access to almost all agricultural products. Nowadays, indeed, we easily find for sale any kind of fruits and vegetables, regardless of the month of the year or the place where we are. Consequently, the result of these changes brings a devastating effect for small local farmers, who do not have access to the market due to their lack of competitiveness in terms of market prices and accessing to distribution channels (O'Hara and Stagl 2001). This environment leads to abandonment of rural activity and in consequence the farming land. As a consequence, the region loses products and services essential to its sustainability and social and economic regeneration, creating serious imbalances in terms of population and regional resources. In order to ensure the sustainability and/or increase the "survival capability" of the region, it is necessary to stimulate farmers, entrepreneurs and service providers for new business models and ways of working (Higgins, Dibden et al. 2008). In this context, the development of collaborative processes that enable small farmers to sell their goods directly to consumers resulting from this exchange a benefit to both parties was the strategic approach that motivated the PROVE network (PROVE 2012).

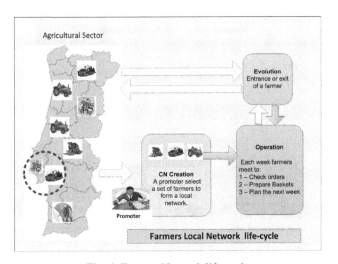

**Fig. 1.** Farmers Network life-cycle

The PROVE network initiative can be classified as being an alternative agri-food network where the business model adopted is the direct-sale based on box-schema (Bosona, Gebresenbet et al. 2011). Its main purpose is to increase the negotiation power of farmers with local actors involved directly or indirectly in the business activities of the small farmers, stimulating and reinforcing local business capability of these farmers and promoting the development of a close relationship between farmers and consumers The PROVE initiative is nowadays implemented in the following regions: Sesimbra, Palmela, Lousada, Penafiel, Paços de Ferreira, Montemor-o-Novo, and Mafra. In order to support management activities and ensure the sustainability of the network some ICT tools were developed and several rules related to governance and polices were defined. Fig. 1 shows the life-cycle of a PROVE local network. At the creation phase the local promoter select a set of farmers (such as 3 to 5 farmer) and creates a PROVE network in the target region. During the operation phase, the farmers meet weakly and plan product baskets according to customers' orders and products' season. On the delivery day, the farmers prepare the baskets and make their distribution in the selected locations. In the following week the farmers meet to divide the money from the previous week and start again the process of organizing baskets. However, during the operation phase, new farmers can join the network, and others may go out.

# 4     Modelling PROVE Using the ARCON Framework

In this section, ARCON is used in order to characterize and understand in a systematic way the main dimensions of the PROVE network. Fig. 2 shows the main perspectives of the ARCON framework, which are described below in tables. Following ARCON framework the proposed model belongs to the Specific Modelling Layer, since this layer includes detailed models focused on specific classes of CNs.

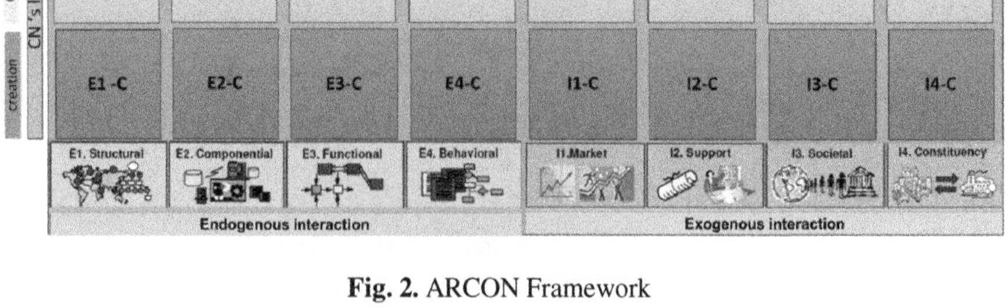

**Fig. 2.** ARCON Framework

The Endogenous Elements subspace represents the PROVE network as seen from the inside, in which four sub-dimensions are defined: (i) Structural Dimension, which addresses the structure or composition of the PROVE network constituting elements, as well as the roles performed by those elements; (ii) Componential Dimension, which focuses on the individual tangible/intangible elements of the PROVE network; (iii) Functional Dimension, which addresses the "basic functions / operations" available in the PROVE network; (iv) Behavioural Dimension, which addresses the principles, policies, and governance rules that drive or constrain the behaviour of the PROVE network and its members over time. Table 1 presents a short description of the elements identified as belonging to the ARCON's Endogenous subspace.

**Table 1.** Endogenous Elements subspace for the PROVE network

| | | Endogenous Elements subspace |
|---|---|---|
| **Structural** | C | (i) Promoters; (ii) Facilitator; and (iii) Farmers. |
| | O | (i) Facilitator; and (ii) Farmers. |
| | E | (i) Facilitator; and (ii) Farmers (members of the network and new members who join the network). |
| **Componential** | C | Network Components: (i) Human Resources: Individuals that belongs to the Promoter Organization. (ii) Knowledge: Manual of best practices to manage PROVE networks. |
| | O | Network Components: (i) Human Resources: Individuals that belongs to the Promoter's organization, Facilitators and Farmers that belong to the network. (ii) Knowledge: Manual of best practices to manage PROVE networks. (iii) Technology: G-PROVE software (supports operation). |
| | E | Network Components: (i) Human Resources: Individuals that belong to the Promoter's organization, Facilitator, Farmers that belong to the network and also potential new members (Farmers). (ii) Knowledge: Manual of best practices to manage PROVE networks. |
| **Functional** | C | **(i) Preparatory planning phase**, which includes the visit of the promoter to potential farmers and their farming land in order to identify and characterized the region in terms of: (i) type of available goods, (ii) type of production. **(ii) Consortium formation phase,** which includes: (i) farmers and mediators searching; (ii) promoting meetings in order to explain the business idea to the potential partners; (iii) farmers and mediators selection to form the network. **(iii) CN Lauching phase,** which comprises the specification of the logistic process, comprising three main activities: (i) defining the workflow to compose the baskets with fresh vegetables and fruits and assignment of responsibilities (ii) choosing what of type of basket will be used; and (iii) defining the rules to divide the profits and to contribute to the common expenses. **(iv) CN set up phase,** which includes: (i) customization of the G-PROVE software system to support the network; (ii) acquisition of the first set of empty baskets to prepare the first orders; (iii) implementation by the promoter of some marketing actions in the respective region. |

**Table 1.** (*Continued*)

| | | |
|---|---|---|
| | O | **(i) Operational functions**, which are the responsibility of farmers and are related to farming activities. <br> **(ii) Process orders functions**, which are the responsibility of farmers and are performed weekly and include calculating the quantities of each product per basket and per farmer, based on the fruits and vegetables available for this week and the existing orders. <br> **(iii)Accounting functions**, which include: (i) setting of the basket price and products price; (ii) purchasing new baskets; and (iii) dividing the money according to the agreed norms. <br> **(iv) Control Activities functions**, which are the responsibility of the Facilitator/Promoter, and include the organization of periodic meetings that serve to monitor the marketing process and to be aware of the main Farmers difficulties. |
| | E | The functions that belong to this phase are: (i) integrating new farmers (each new farmer accompanies all the operational activities for a certain period, just as an observer); (ii) re-planning the logistics weekly; (iii) updating the list of available vegetables and fruits to the consumer. |
| **Endogenous Elements (Endo-E) subspace** | | |
| | C | The policies and governance rules that drive this phase are: <br> • The Facilitators and Promoters should be aware of the region's opportunities and challenges. <br> • The Facilitators and Promoters should have complementary professional competences. <br> • Facilitators should have competences in the area of promoting the relationship between consumers and farmers. |
| Behavioural | O | *1.  Legal and Fiscal Duties of Farmers:* <br> • Each farmer has to contribute with vegetable products from its farm whenever possible. <br> • The Farmers have to use sustainable production practices. <br> • Each Farmer has to coordinate its production with the others Farmers in order to guarantee variety of products to consumers. <br> • The elaboration of the basket should follow hygienic principles, and all the products must be fresh. <br> • The Farmers should comply with the local and time agreed to deliver the baskets. <br> • Each Farmer should improve the landscape of its farm and should encourage visits from consumers. <br> • Each Farmer contributes actively to the work group, and participates in promoting activities. <br> *2.  Legal and Fiscal Duties of consumers:* <br> • The consumer buys the basket previously ordered, accepting that the products available are seasonal. <br> • The consumer should respect the local and time agreed for the delivery. |

| | | |
|---|---|---|
| | | • The consumer should pay in money the basket to the Farmer at the time of the delivery.<br>• The consumer should be sympathetic with Farmers, in respect with stock ruptures due to weather constraints.<br>*3.   Productions and Basket Preparation Rules*<br>• All the orders' sheets should be available 2 days before delivery date.<br>• All the products that compose a basket should be traceable. Farmers should keep registers from production in order to guarantee product traceability.<br>• In each basket preparation, Farmers should satisfy the preferences of the consumers. |
| | E | The principle that drive *the integration of new members is:*<br>• During two weeks each new member must join a Farmer, in order to follow the working process, from production to delivery of the baskets. |

According to the ARCON model the Exogenous Interactions subspace represents the PROVE network as seen in interaction with the outside, with a focus on the interactions between the PROVE network and its environment. Four sub-dimensions are defined: (i) Market Dimension, which covers the issues related to interactions with "customers" and "competitors"; (ii) Support Dimension, which covers the issues related to support services provided by third party institutions; (iii) Societal Dimension, which covers the issues related to interactions between the PROVE network and the society; (iv) Constituency Dimension, which focuses on the interaction with the universe of potential new members of the PROVE Network. Table 2 presents a short description of the elements identified as belonging to the ARCON's exogenous subspace.

**Table 2.** Summary of Exogenous Interaction subspace for the PROVE network

| | | |
|---|---|---|
| **Exogenous Elements (Endo-E) subspace** | | |
| Market | C | Communication strategy to customers:<br>(i) The PROVE network is represented by a logo<br>(ii) A web page which describes the process guidelines.<br>(iii) An attractive leaflet to reach the customers not covered by the Internet.<br>(iv) Advertising campaigns in newspapers and local radio stations. |
| | O | Interaction with "customers" and stakeholders:<br>(i) A web page that supports a FAQ (Frequently Asked Question) service to consumers.<br>(ii) Meetings between Farmers and consumers.<br>(iii) Weekly newsletter.<br>(iv) Demonstration activities in schools. |
| | E | Interactions related to admission of new members into the network:<br>(i) Carry out a visit to the farming land of the potential new member with the purpose of establishing an exploratory contact.<br>(ii) General meeting between the potential new member and all other members in order to identify common interests. |

**Table 2.** (*Continued*)

| | | |
|---|---|---|
| Support | C | Main third party institutions that support the network creation are:<br>• Local Authorities<br>• NGOs<br>• Local Development Associations<br>• Institute of Employment and Vocational Training |
| | O | Main third party institutions that support the network operation are:<br>• Local Authorities<br>• NGOs<br>• Local Development Associations<br>• Institute of Employment and Vocational Training |
| | E | Main third party institutions that can also support the network during evolution are:<br>• Confederations and associations of producers<br>• Cooperatives of Producers<br>• Agri-food Companies<br>• Agricultural Service Providers<br>• Consumers associations |
| Societal | C<br>O<br>E | PROVE network contributes to:<br>• Increase the competitiveness of rural communities;<br>• Provide a positive interaction between rural and urban population;<br>• Stimulate the development of new value-creating activities in the region. |
| Constituency | C<br>O<br>E | This interaction is done essentially through the promoters:<br>• Visiting farmers<br>• Promoting meetings to explain the business idea to the potential partners<br>• Following agreed norms. |

# 5    ARCON Application Assessment

One of the goals of this study is to discuss the advantages of using ARCON as a modeling framework to describe a CN with the characteristics of PROVE.

PROVE is a network with a low level of complexity and involves a low number of members. In spite of this fact, the use of ARCON, allows us to structure in a systematic way an amount of disperse and unstructured information, and to identify some hidden gaps. Fig. 3 illustrates the mapping in the ARCON framework of the gaps described below.

**A1.** The use of ARCON allowed to notice that the dissolution phase is not covered. All the formal documents provided by the PROVE network do not cover any item related to the process of disintegration of a PROVE local network. For instance it is not defined: (i) how to manage the cessation of baskets supply; (ii) how to manage the tangible (baskets, vehicles, etc.) and intangible (consumer contacts, consumer profiles, etc.) networks assets.

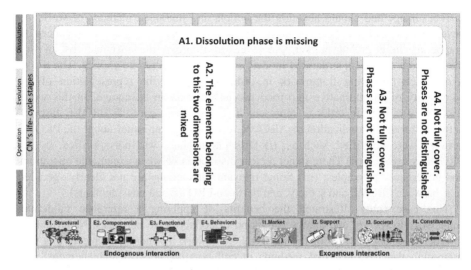

**Fig. 3.** PROVE local network gaps

**A2**. The use of ARCON allowed to make a clear distinction between executable operations and governance rules that drive PROVE's local network behavior. In fact, based on the information collected during this study we realized that members (Promoters, Facilitators and Farmers) were unaware of the difference between operation and governance rules. Furthermore, during the documentation analysis, we realized that the description of governance rules were mixed with the description of the work flows.

**A3**. The use of ARCON allowed concluding that the iteration between the network and society is not well defined for each life-cycle phase. In fact, based on the information collected during this study we realized that it is just possible to have a broad description of the relationships between the network and the local community. Several important items to characterize this issue are missing, such as: (i) types of relationships with external actors; (ii) evolution of relationships over the life-cycle; (iii) assessment of PROVE impact in society.

**A4**. The use of ARCON allowed realizing that the analysis of the potential iteration with new members is missing. In fact, based on the information collected during this study we concluded that promoters had not addressed some relevant issues of this dimension, such as: (i) definition of mechanisms to interact with local farmers in order to identify potential new members for the PROVE local network; (ii) identification of the various transactions types with public institutions over the life-cycle phases.

# 6    Conclusions

The globalization created an increasingly turbulent and competitive environment for agri-food sector. In this dynamic environment, farmers cannot afford to resist the market change and should abandon the beliefs and ingrained methods of work. As never before, today's farmers must develop new methods and competences to competing in a global market. However, to improve the sustainability of this management approach, structured models and methods should be applied. The use of a reference modelling framework in order to support the representation of the complexity of an alternative agri-food network can be an advantage. In this work, ARCON was used in order to represent in a systematic way the PROVE farmers' network. From the application of ARCON, a set of relevant issues about the PROVE network were identified, such as: (i) Dissolution phase was not specified, by the PROVE managers; (ii) There is not a clear distinction between executable operations and governance principles; (iii) Some relevant interactions are not clearly specified (e.g. between PROVE and society; and between PROVE and new members).

This case study illustrated the benefits of applying a reference modelling framework to specify and analyse this kind of collaborative networks. Nevertheless, in order to enable the use of the ARCON framework by end-users, and in this way promoting the use of formal methods in collaborative network management, it is important to develop a full practical software tool. Such software tool should aim to support the process of capturing the elements required to fill in the ARCON cells, and to provide reasoning mechanisms to analyze the obtained models.

**Acknowledgments.** This work was supported in part by the FCT-MCTES – "Fundação para a Ciência e Tecnologia" (CTS multiannual funding) through the PIDDAC Program funds.

# References

1. Abreu, A., Camarinha-Matos, L.M.: Understanding Social Capital in Collaborative Networks. In: Ortiz, Á., Franco, R.D., Gasquet, P.G. (eds.) BASYS 2010. IFIP AICT, vol. 322, pp. 109–118. Springer, Heidelberg (2010)
2. Abreu, A., Macedo, P., et al.: Towards a methodology to measure the alignment of value systems in collaborative networks. In: Azevedo, A. (ed.) Innovation in Manufacturing Network, vol. 266, pp. 37–46. Springer, Boston (2008)
3. Afsarmanesh, H., Camarinha-Matos, L.: The ARCON modeling framework. Collaborative networks: Reference modeling, pp. 67–82 (2008)
4. Baldo, F., Rabelo, R.: For a methodology to implement virtual breeding environments: a case study in the mold and die sector in Brazil. Leveraging Knowledge for Innovation in Collaborative Networks, 197–206 (2009)
5. Beckett, R., Jones, M.: Active Ageing: Using an ARCON Framework to Study U3A (University of the Third Age) in Australia. Adaptation and Value Creating Collaborative Networks, 189–196
6. Bosona, T., Gebresenbet, G., et al.: Box-Scheme Based Delivery System of Locally Produced Organic Food: Evaluation of Logistics Performance. Journal of Service Science and Management 4(3), 357–367 (2011)
7. Botarelli, M., Taticchi, P., et al.: The Virtual Development Office framework for business Networks: a case study from the Umbrian packaging district. In: Pervasive Collaborative Networks, pp. 611–618 (2008)

8. Feenstra, G.W.: Local food systems and sustainable communities. American Journal of Alternative Agriculture 12(01), 28–36 (1997)
9. Ferreira, J.J.P.: The workflow-enabled supply chain, the Civil Construction Enterprise case study. International Journal of Logistics Research and Applications: A Leading Journal of Supply Chain Management 4(3), 297–311 (2001)
10. Garita, C.: A Case Study of VO Education in Costa Rica. In: Camarinha-Matos, L. (ed.) Virtual Enterprises and Collaborative Networks. IFIP AICT, vol. 149, pp. 589–596. Springer, Boston (2004)
11. Higgins, V., Dibden, J., et al.: Building alternative agri-food networks: Certification, embeddedness and agri-environmental governance. Journal of Rural Studies 24(1), 15–27 (2008)
12. O'Hara, S.U., Stagl, S.: Global food markets and their local alternatives: a socio-ecological economic perspective. Population & Environment 22(6), 533–554 (2001)
13. PROVE. PROVE web site (2012), http://www.prove.com.pt/english (retrieved March 2012)
14. Volpentesta, A., Ammirato, S.: Networking agrifood SMEs and consumer groups in local agribusiness. Pervasive Collaborative Networks, 33–40 (2008)
15. Volpentesta, A.P., Ammirato, S.: A Collaborative Network Model for Agrifood Transactions on Regional Base. Organizational, Business, and Technological Aspects of the Knowledge Society 112, 319–325 (2010)

# Knowledge Exchange and Social Learning Opportunities in Direct Agri-Food Chains

Antonio P. Volpentesta, Salvatore Ammirato, and Marco Della Gala

Department of Electronics, Computer Science and Systems, University of Calabria
via P. Bucci, 42\C, 87036 Rende (CS), Italy
{ammirato,mdellagala,volpentesta}@deis.unical.it

**Abstract.** In direct agri-food chains (DAFCs), farmers and consumers are brought together with the aim of shortening, localizing and synergizing an agri-food chain. As food moves from the farm to the fork, all the economic activities are performed by farmers/producers or consumers, and none intermediary is required to handle an agri-food product before it is consumed. Any DAFC form provide a sort of liminal space for social learning and for local lay knowledge exchange, through face-to-face interactions. In this paper, we investigate the relationship between face-to-face interaction attributes and the learning opportunity domain of DAFCs that exhibit a same basic form. Our study is mainly based on qualitative data obtained from case studies reported in literature, field observations and informal interviews to various DAFC actors.

**Keywords:** agri-food, direct marketing, knowledge exchange, social learning.

## 1 Introduction and Backgrounds

Over recent years, agribusiness has been facing new challenges due to deregulation and globalization of markets. Mainstream agrifood systems are controlled by a small number of big organizations that monitor every transaction among millions of disconnected producers and consumers. This has led to the loss of decisional power for farmers/producers and to the 'crisis of trust' in 'placeless and faceless' mass-production for consumers [1], [2].

Agri-food SMEs are subjected to a continuous imbalance of their bargaining power; they suffer the cost-price squeeze and unfair contractual agreement, rising production costs and declining commodity prices thus reducing their profitability [1], [2]. The increasing disconnection between farming and food as well as producers and consumers, led to a widening consensus that radical changes are needed in agri-food systems. First efforts to overcome these limits are noticed since the '80s, when farmers, and other people or organizations have started organizing themselves spontaneously in order to solve their problems and those of rural communities.

In more recent years, scholars are helping farmers to develop new and alternative business models characterized by a re-connection or close communication among producers and consumers, allowing the development of new forms of relationship and governance of the actors' network and also enhancing a re-distribution of value for

L.M. Camarinha-Matos, L. Xu, and H. Afsarmanesh (Eds.): PRO-VE 2012, IFIP AICT 380, pp. 340–348, 2012.
© IFIP International Federation for Information Processing 2012

primary producers.[3] In literature, the umbrella term *alternative agrifood networks* (AAFNs) is used to indicate all these forms of collaborative development. AAFNs are alternative to the organizational logic of dominant agri-food systems based on long and multinational supply chains. They aim to shorten the physical, social and economic distance between world production and world consumption [2].

As a more specific term of AAFNs, *Direct Agri-Food Chains* (DAFCs) refer to AAFNs where all economic activities are performed by only two types of actors (namely, producers and consumers). In a DAFC, there are no intermediaries, thus a lot of commitment from farmers and consumers is required, as they have to perform activities (e.g. packaging, transportation, marketing, customer relationship management) that are often conducted by other middle-men.

In a DAFC, an agri-food product is 'embedded' with value-laden information, concerning the mode of production, provenance and distinctive quality assets of the product, when it reaches the consumer. DAFCs are configurable as learning systems where interactions and knowledge exchange, between producers and consumers, enable *learning opportunities* (shortly, LOs) and let network members benefit from shorter distances, better information flow and greater trust. LOs lie in face-to-face interactions (F2FI) between consumers and producers which happen within the social, economic, physical and environmental context of a DAFC initiative.

In our exploratory study, we investigate the relationship between F2FI attributes and the LO domain of DAFCs that exhibit a same basic form. "Learning opportunities" is a consolidated field of research since sixties, but studies have been conducted in school or educational context, and mostly focalized on how LOs impact on student achievement. Although many scholars affirm that AAFNs provide LOs, none of them deal with the identification of F2FI attributes impacting on LOs.

The paper is organized as follows. In section 2, we characterize the DAFCs as learning systems. In section 3 a brief classification of DAFC basic forms is proposed. In section 4, we present the objects (i.e. the F2FI and the LO domain elements) of the relationship we want to investigate. In section 5, we formulate our research questions and we present results obtained through a survey study.

## 2     DAFC: A Knowledge and Learning Perspective

In conventional agrifood supply chain, knowledge processes need long learning time before they can be mastered. In such chains, knowledge and information become rapidly outdated. The long physical distance from decisions to their effects and feedback heavily affect decision-making processes.

In a DAFC, the particular partnership among producers enables new learning by continuously identifying routines that need to be modified or renewed. Furthermore, direct interactions between producers and consumers allow producers to learn faster and better, thanks to rapid and not mediated feedback cycles, thus becoming an essential element of competitive advantage.

Interaction-based learning processes, carried out in an informal way, empower actors and allow them to create a non-competitive learning context that produces higher-degree knowledge processes. They allow the explicating of tacit knowledge through experience sharing (learning by doing and peer-to-peer exchange).

The learning relationships between producers and consumers in a DAFC are enabled by the exchange of local lay knowledge more than the expert or managerial ones. It can revitalize local/traditional knowledge [4] and encourage sustainable land management [5]. Moreover, it engenders trust and cooperation within a community [1], and it is also an important way to educate consumers about where their food comes from, including the environmental and social conditions of its production.

Learning interactions have two main dimensions: the process and the contextual one. The first one is represented by social practices in a learning event. The second one regards the learning event which provides the social framework within which learning can occur. The basic idea is that learning occurs in a well-defined socio-cultural context characterized by features like the societal and institutional values which prevail at any one time.

Learning happens in different ways. On one side, consumers may learn the story and background of the producer, and the cultural significance behind a product tied to specific method or place of production. Moreover, they may "recover skills and knowledge that have been lost along with the change of purchasing and eating habits. For example, knowing seasonality and variety of vegetables (there are a lot of species unknown to citizens), learning how to cook them (to make them edible and more tasty, but also less monotonous), and how to preserve them "[6]. On the other side, the interactions with consumers lead producers to face new systems of activities and new technical, managerial and marketing choices. In many DAFCs, consumers negotiate collectively with the farmer(s) the production/distribution process. In such negotiations farmers may learn about consumers' taste and culinary uses, and consumers about farmers' production/distribution constraints. Thanks to personal interactions with their regular customers, producers can learn about customer receptivity to products and services and generate ideas about new products/services.

## 3     Basic Forms of DAFCs

DAFCs have been developed in many countries shaping different organizational forms in many grassroots initiatives promoted both by producers and consumers. In what follows, we summarize main forms of DAFCs reported in literature. They are to be considered as "basic" forms that could be combined to shape different DAFCs.

*Direct (on farm) sale* - DoFS: it is based on producer–consumer face to face transactions in the place/space of production. *DoFS* includes on-farm stores (FS), or roadside stands, where a grower establishes a selling stand for agrifood products grown on his own farm; agritourisms (AT) which promote and direct sale the farm products allowing visitors to take part in agricultural activities for recreation or leisure purposes, or complementary activities like hospitality, meal provision, agricultural festivals, farm tours and educational activities [7]; pick your own operations (PYO), allowing consumers to gather products by their own directly from the field [8].

*Box schemes - BSs:* they involve local consumption groups and famers' cooperatives participating to a common agreement to ensure a regular procurement of seasonal food grown up in a sustainable way in the local community or its close surroundings [2]. Consumers agree to buy available seasonal food (fruit, vegetables, meat or cheese) from producers who are responsible to delivery periodically at the consumers' home [2]. In Community-supported agriculture (CSA), community members purchase a share of agricultural production by paying in advance, assuming the risk/benefit of a poor or very productive season with the manufacturer.

*Farmers' markets - FMs:* These are markets, generally placed in urban areas and with periodic frequency, where a group of farmers meets and where each producer direct sell his own agri-food product to single customers attending the market. Two main features characterize a FM: first, sold products are "local" (usually produced within 50 km from the market place); second, manufacturers are directly involved in sales. In some occurrence FMs evolve into collective farmer shops (CFSs), where farmers act together to set up and jointly manage a shop in a market town where products are sold (usually every day) by some of the farmers themselves [2].

*Collective buying groups - CBGs:* organized consumers that choose to commonly buy directly from selected producers. Group members are nodes of a network aimed to acquire and share information, as well as to define quality criteria for products to purchase. The interaction among producers and group members is mediated by a group leader. Consumers decide to share their "shopping lists" to create a unique cumulative order submitted, by the leader, to each producer who is charged to deliver ordered products to a unique pick up site [6].

*Collective kitchens or Community kitchens – CKs:* they are community based cooking programs where small groups of people come together at designated times (e.g., weekly, monthly) to buy in bulk and cook healthy local food that often is eaten together or is taken home to their families. CKs allow participants to share resources (kitchens, and cooking facilities), the costs of food and food preparation labor, as well as provide means for socializing with other community members [9]. In some cases, local farmers team up with CKs' participants, providing advices and support.

## 4    Face to Face Interactions and Learning Opportunities

Although the above described DAFC forms are mainly focalized on distribution/selling processes, each of them provide a sort of liminal space that subverts the normal experience of food shopping and where a variety of local lay knowledge related to agriculture, rural economy, the environment, food production, healthy eating and consumer values, may be exchanged [4].

Beyond the immediacy of the transaction between producers and consumers, the social context of any DAFCs provides an arena for social learning and knowledge exchange. As matter of fact, many multifaceted DAFC initiatives involve economic relations which transcend the boundaries of profitability and are built on F2FIs.

Here, a F2FI is regarded as the process in which two or more persons are physically co-present (in a way that allows for mutual visual and physical contact) and influence each other's actions. Face to face communication is a fundamental part of any F2FI, since it allows people to be sending and delivering messages almost simultaneously, in a cycle of interruption, feedback and possible repair the F2FI.

F2FIs enable learning processes and let both producers and consumers benefit from the shorter distances, better information flow and greater trust between them [1]. Much of the potential of development of DAFC initiatives lies in building new relations through which a large share of 'tacit knowledge' can be made explicit and shared through the activation of a learning and societal embedding process.

Any notion of social learning presupposes interactions between the social actors themselves and the social, economic, physical and environmental context where they employ (this aspect refers to the 'embeddedness' of learning, [10]). Two main assumptions underpin our LO identification framework for DAFCs:

- F2FIs have the potential to result in a learning and/or knowledge exchange process. We conceive these interactions as opportunities for communicative/instrumental learning [11], and exchange of experiences.
- Any LO is associated with attribute values of a F2FI and the context embedding it.

Under these assumptions, a LO for actors in a DAFC is provided by a F2FI in which many sensory, cognitive and social cues could allow to connect the communication content with the social, economic, physical and environmental context that embeds it. These cues are context-dependent, since they are related to things from the environment and situation where learning may occur. They may regard the F2FI location, the appearance, taste, and consistency of an agri-food product, and so on.

In this sense, a LO can be regarded as an affordance for "understanding more about the perspectives and interests of others, what others mean, and how to communicate one's own meaning, to make sense of and relate to the particular context within which the communication takes place" [11]. In our framework, we consider F2FI attributes that play a significant role in providing opportunities for learning from context during a F2FI that takes place in a DAFC:

*Communication Content Orientation* (CO): it specifies the category of topic is talked about. Categories are oriented to products ( e.g. seasonality, varieties, taste shapes, textures and aromas), actors (e.g., trustworthiness of other peers, consumers' wishes), primary and secondary activities (e.g., agricultural practices, processing methods, food preparation), organization culture (e.g. norms, values, history, experiences), social, economic and natural environment (e.g. terroir, traditions, customs, laws);

*Interaction Participants Role* (IPR): it is the DAFC role of participants to a contextualized F2FI. Factor values are "consumers with consumers", "producers with producers" and "consumers with producers";

*Interaction Timing* (IT): it is the DAFC activity stage ("production", "distribution", "consumption", and "waste management") at which the contextualized F2FI occurs;

*Interaction Place* (IP): it specifies the location of the place where the contextualized F2FI occurs. Such locations are typed as "farm site", where DAFC product is coming from, "agri-food terroir", i.e. the land bestowed upon DAFC product, "proximate area", i.e. an area (e.g. urban area) that is proximate to the agri-food terroir;

*Participant Motivation* (PM): it specifies the type of motivation for the participation to DAFC activities. Participation is seen in terms of expressing and discussing ideas, developing plans, evaluating actions, and decision-making. Motivation types are social (e.g. tighter relationship with others, social belonging.), ecological (e.g. lower environmental impact), economical (e.g. disposable income/budget impact), and personal wellbeing (e.g. physical and mental health, pleasant time).

The values of these attributes depend on the particular form of the DAFC, and they have a great importance in creating good opportunities for learning about the F2FI context. The learning opportunity domain is hierarchically structured as follows:

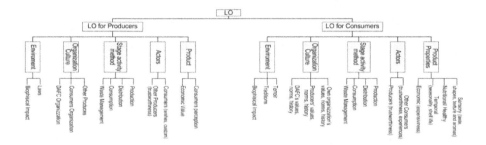

# 5     The Survey Research

Our aim is to find out: which are the main LOs arising from initiatives of DAFCs that exhibit the same basic form; which F2FI attributes values should be considered important for LOs detected in DAFCs initiatives with the same organization form.

In our study, we surveyed 330 initiatives by gathering data from three sources of information: **documentation** (scientific papers and project reports describing case studies of DAFC), **web sites** (examination of the description of F2FIs in DAFC experiences) and **direct observation** (unstructured interviews to farmers, store managers, consumers, and consumers groups leader, involved in Italian DAFC cases).

We have employed a methodology that is based on three main steps: (I) collect a relevant set of real world DAFC case studies and group them according to their organizational form type. In our study we have considered the basic forms listed in in section 3; (II) for each group, identify F2FI attributes values that are considered to be relevant for some LOs; (III) detect the most frequent LOs in the (reported or directly observed) case studies of each group, and map them onto the LO domain described in section 4 . The obtained results are summarized in table 1, table 2 and table 3. (where *cr*=consumer, *pr*=producer, *pn*=production, *dn*=distribution, *cn*=consumption, *on*=organization, *wm*=waste management, *env*=environment).

**Table 1.** F2FI attribute values in DAFC basic forms

|     | DoFS | BS | FM | CBG | CK |
|-----|------|-----|-----|------|-----|
| CO | Products; activities; *pr* history and values; *env.* | Products; activities; *pr* history and values; *cr* wishes; *env.* | Products; activities; *pr* history; *cr* wishes. | Products; activities; *cr* wishes *pr* history and values; *env.* | Products; activities. |
| IPR | *cr/pr* | *cr/pr; cr/cr; pr/pr* | *cr/pr; pr/pr;* (2) | *cr/cr; cr/pr,* (3) | *cr/cr;* |
| IT | *pn* (PYO); *dn* (FS); *cn*(AT) | *pn* (CSA); *dn* | *dn* | *dn* | *cn* |
| IP | farm site; | proximate area | proximate area; agri-food terroir | proximate area | proximate area |
| PM | Economical; personal wellbeing; (1) | Ecological; Social; personal wellbeing; | Economical; Social; | Economical; Social; Ecological | Economical Social |

**Notes for Table 1:**

(1): PYO is addressed to consumers who look for fresh and quality products at a reduced price by letting them to make direct connections with the place/space of production. In addition, consumers may enjoy the gathering as a recreational experience [8].

(2): FMs afford intensive, periodic opportunities for vendors to interact directly both with their customers and with other farmers' market vendors [12].

(3): Consumers have periodic meetings planned by the CBG; producers regularly meet with CBG leaders [6].

**Table 2.** LOs for Consumers in DAFC basic forms

|     | DoFS | BS | FM | CBG | CK |
|-----|------|-----|-----|------|-----|
| Product properties | Sensory; Temporal | Sensory; Temporal; Economic; Healthy; | Sensory; Temporal Economic; | Sensory; Temporal; Economic; Healthy | Sensory; Nutritional/ healthy; (5) |
| Actors | *pr* | *pr.; other crs.* | *pr* | other *crs;* | other *crs;* |
| activity method | *pn; dn;* | *pn; dn; cn; wm;* (3) | *pn; cn;* (4) | *dn; cn;* | *cn; wm;.* |
| Org. Culture | *pr* values, norms, history; (1) | own *on;* DAFC values, norms, history; *pr* values, norms, history; | DAFC values, norms, history *pr*, history; | own *on;* DAFC values, norms, history *pr* values, norms, history; | own *or.* |
| Enviroment | Terroir; Tradition; (2) | Terroir; Tradition; Biophisical Impact; | Tradition; | Biophisical Impact; | Tradition |

**Notes for Table 2:**

(1): DoFSs offer opportunities to better understand, the culture and values of the people involved in farming and the production methods employed [8].

(2): While consumers are travelling to the rural countryside to purchase agrifood, they may learn the original cultural, geographical and economic context linked to the food [2].

(3): In BS, consumers negotiate collectively with the farmer(s) over the process of production and distribution (e.g., the content of the box over the growing season, the choice of crop varieties, etc.). As the content of the box is imposed by food seasonality, they recover skills and knowledge on local variety of vegetables as well as they learn how to cook within the offerings of the season. In some cases, BSs and CSA subscribers are engaged in waste management and compost production.

(4): Consumers may learn about vendors and their food production practices as well as how to use the products in cooking (recipes, storage, varieties) [11].

(5): CKs offer to participants LOs about the importance of healthy eating with an increased variety of local foods in their diets through the social interaction among participants [9]

**Table 3.** LOs for Producers in DAFC basic forms

|  | DoFS | BS | FM | CBG | CK |
|---|---|---|---|---|---|
| **Product** | *cr* perception | *cr* perception; | *cr* perception; Economic Value; | *cr* perception | *cr* perception |
| **Actors** | *cr* | *cr;* other *prs* | *cr;* other *prs*; (1) | *cr;* | |
| **Activity Changes needs** | *dn* | *pn; dn* | *pn; dn;* (2) | *dn* | |
| **Org. Culture** | | *cr's on;* DAFC' *on* | other *pr;* DAFC *on;*(3) | *cr's on* | *cr's on* |
| **Enviroment** | | Biophisical Impact | Laws | Laws; Biophisical impact | |

**Notes for Table 3:**

(1): Producers may learn about consumers' demand and products offered by other vendors [12].

(2): Producers may learn about new products to be developed and new ways of marketing them. Such LOs are supported by the generation and circulation of knowledge enabled through the feedback coming from the producers-consumers interaction and from the interaction with other vendors. In CFSs, farmers have LOs about management logics typical of a distribution structure that encompasses and exceeds that of the individual producer [12].

(3): Producers adhering to FMs and CFSs share agreement to regulate the behavior of individual producers, the market/store management and the joining of new participants [12].

# 6    Conclusions

The rationale of our research was to identify the main F2FI attributes values, that can represent important factors for LOs, in each DAFC basic form. In our opinion, the obtained results can be utilized in conceiving social network services that expand LOs well beyond traditional DAFC settings. To see that, imagine a DAFC wireless community where all members are provided with access to mobile handheld devices and advanced social networking services to enhance LOs inside and outside the "space" where F2FIs take place. Such enhancement may happen through providing more accurate information to the right people, at the right time, and at the right place (e.g. giving people support to meet their social, economic and cultural needs, increasing trust in products, processes, people and experiences). Since F2FIs and LOs depend on the particular nature of a DAFC, we have highlighted important issues for effective social networking services aimed to expand LOs in each DAFC basic form.

**Acknowledgments.** This work has been conducted as part of the AGROMATER project.

# References

1. Watts, D., Ilbery, B., Maye, D.: Making reconnections in agro-food geography: alternative systems of food provision. Progress in Human Geography 29(1), 22–40 (2005)
2. Sánchez Hernández, J.L.: Alternative Food Networks: concept, typology and adaptation to the spanish context. Boletín de la A.G.E. (49), 375–380 (2009)
3. Volpentesta, A.P., Ammirato, S.: Alternative agrifood networks in a regional area: a case study. To appear in International Journal of Computer Integrated Manufacturing

4. Fonte, M.: Knowledge, Food and Place. A Way of Producing, a Way of Knowing. Sociologia Ruralis 48(3), 200–222 (2008)
5. Ilberry, B., Maye, D.: Alternative (shorter) food supply chains and specialist livestock products in the Scottish-English borders. Enviroment and Planning A 37, 823–844 (2005)
6. Rossi, A., Brunori, G.: Drivers of transformation in the agro-food system. GAS as co-production of Alternative Food Networks. In: Darnhofer, I., Grötzer, M. (ed.) Proceedings of 9th European IFSA Symposium, Vienna Au., pp. 1913–1931 (2010)
7. Tew, C., Barbieri, C.: The perceived benefits of agritourism: The provider's perspective. Tourism Management, 215–224 (2012)
8. Lloyd, R.M., Tilley, D.S., Nelson, J.R.: Pick-Your-Own Markets. In: Direct Farm Marketing and Tourism 62. In: Tronstad, R., Leones, J. (eds.) Tuscon, Arizona (1995)
9. Drake, J.: Community-Based Alternative Food Source Models; Livable New York Sustainable Communities for all ages; Cap IV.1.k, http://www.aging.ny.gov
10. Granovetter, M.: Economic Action and Social Structure: The Problem of Embeddedness. American Journal of Sociology 91(3), 481–510 (1985)
11. Milestad, R., Westberg, L., Geber, U., Bjorklund, J.: Enhancing Adaptive Capacity in Food Systems - Learning at Farmers' Markets in Sweden. Ecology & society 15(3), 29 (2010)
12. Hinrichs, C.C., Gillespie, G., Feenstra, G.: Social Learning and Innovation at Retail Farmers' Markets. Sociologia Ruralis, 31–58 (2004)

# Collaborative Networks Model for Clothing and Footwear Business Sector

João Bastos[1], Valentina Franchini[2], Américo Azevedo[1], and Rosanna Fornasiero[3]

[1] INESC TEC (formely INESC Porto) & Faculdade de Engenharia da Universidade do Porto, Rua Doutor Roberto Frias 378, 4200-465 Porto, Portugal
{joao.bastos,ala}@fe.up.pt
[2] University of Padova Enterprises, Stradella San Nicola 3, 36100 Vincenza, Italy
franchini@gest.unipd.it
[3] ITIA-CNR -Institute of Industrial Technologies and Automation -National Council of Research, Via Bassini 15, 20133 Milano, Italy
rosanna.fornasiero@itia.cnr.it

**Abstract.** In clothing and footwear business sector, consumer needs and expectations of specific target groups - such as elderly, obese, disabled, or diabetic persons - are arising as challenging opportunities for European companies that are asked to supply small series of innovative and fashionable goods of high quality, affordable price and eco-compatible. This paper aims at propose a three level (strategic, tactical, and operational) reference model to support the Textile, Clothing and Footwear (TCF) collaborative supply networks in addressing the need for Fashionable and Healthy Clothing & Footwear products.

**Keywords:** Reference Model, Supply Networks, Collaborative Networks, Clothing and Footwear.

## 1 Introduction

The recent years have stressed the need to re-invent the concept of enterprise. Since 2008, with the global financial crisis coupled with the remarkable increase of oil and energy prices, the way to make business have changed dramatically. The flow of money decreased and consequently the flow of products and services have changed dramatically. Enterprise managers are now forced to address the market and especially the individual customer with augmented care by putting more emphasis on the service levels they provide, by reducing response times and by tackling the specific needs of the diversity of customers. This confluence of trends has led managers moving from a traditional functional focus in the way they conduct business into a more holistic approach in the manner they address the supply chain. As consequence, it is emerging at industrial level an adoption of collaborative strategies addressing the small series production of high-customized complex products with increased emphasis in the service levels and the reduction of the response times. Along this vein, consumer needs and expectations of specific target groups - such as

L.M. Camarinha-Matos, L. Xu, and H. Afsarmanesh (Eds.): PRO-VE 2012, IFIP AICT 380, pp. 349–359, 2012.
© IFIP International Federation for Information Processing 2012

elderly, obese, disabled, or diabetic persons - are arising as challenging opportunities for European companies which are asked to supply small series of innovative and fashionable goods of high quality, affordable price and eco-compatible in short periods of time and with high service levels. In order to design, develop, produce and distribute such products, a new framework and related components of collaborative networking are necessary.

The main objective of this research, framed within the EU (European Union) funded project CoReNet, is to present an innovative Reference Model for the TCF SMEs (small and medium enterprises) companies in collaborative networks to support the manufacturing of small batches of products addressing the need of the special consumer target groups. The aim of this new reference model is to equip fashionable and healthy footwear & garments network managers and stakeholders with the necessary guidance to model, design and configure the combination of processes, functions, activities, relationships and pathways along which products, services and information move in and between TCF companies.

The remaining of this paper is organized as follows: first the existing related literature is shown, followed by a presentation about multiple case studies conducted within footwear companies to single out and study distinctive practices and processes. Finally, based both on literature review and within and cross case analysis, a comparison between the distinctive practices and relevant processes in the TCF industry is presented in order to highlight the best practices and add new knowledge to the sector.

## 2    Foundations and Research Topics

In order to address the new type of target groups (elderly, obese, disabled, or diabetic persons) demand, it is necessary to develop new collaborative supply chain solutions based on cost effective, social compliant and eco-efficient design and production of customized products that fully satisfy the customers, considering their health issues as well as their desire for fashionable products.

Recent research in the field addressed different forms of business networks. The literature distinguishes for example by value chain orientation (horizontal, vertical, lateral), life span (long-term vs. short-term), and degree of virtualization or hierarchical structure (hierarchical vs. non-hierarchical networks) [2]. Nevertheless, the most common business networks are formed along the value chain and for enduring purposes [3].

At the same time, the current market trends calls for flexibility at the supply network level, the processes and the product designs in order to empower the companies to quickly adapt for new business requirements and sustainability challenges. This new demands are forcing business networks to have much shorter life-time existence and take advantage of new infrastructure technologies supported in distributed information systems and knowledge [4].

The new concept of demand-driven supply networks is emerging in literature as a collaborative approach in response to consumer's needs and expectations [5,6]. In reality, many companies that embrace this paradigm transformed their operating systems from the traditional functional supply networks through a holistic approach that addresses demand in all of its dimensions. This implies different approaches to the market based not only on traditional sales channels (shops, retailers) but more and more on an Internet mediated direct contact with consumers equally for product conception, for product sales but also for after-sales services.

Simultaneously, the market increasingly values collaborative networks that endorse the sustainability challenges. These networks by seeing the world's present and future challenges seek to develop new products and processes that can be part of the solution. Namely, through a holistic view of the supply network it is possible to measure and optimize the overall impact of the "carbon footprint", to implement policies that seek recycling and waste prevention, product design for sustainability and the use of emerging clean technologies [4]. From the production viewpoint, companies from different sectors in sustainable networks need to integrate their production systems in order to offer to the customer integrated solutions and innovative services and products.

A deep analysis of some of the most important supply network reference models present in literature - among others: Value reference model, SCOR model and Y-Cim model – have shown the applicability of the SMART model proposed by Filos and Banhan [9] as starting point for the definition of the Fashionable and Healthy Clothing & Footwear reference model for supply networks. The SMART model allows the definition of practices, technological and performance models for collaborative networks according to the following three main dimensions:

1.  Knowledge dimension – to map partners' competencies to be shared within the network in terms of products and processes;

2.  Information & Communication Technologies (ICTs) dimension – to support the requirements for the implementation of ICT services at different process levels along the network;

3.  Organizational dimension– to provide specifications of the organizational changes for SMEs for structuring supply networks in small series production.

In order to make the reference model for the TCF European companies cope with the environmental consciousness, the present reference model approach used the SMART model proposed by Filos and Banhan [9] and additional presented a new dimension, coherent with eco-efficiency objective, the Sustainability dimension. This new dimension is intended to support the enterprises in the developing of an eco-compatible approach for their products and processes.

A set of companies belonging to the TCF sector has been selected to conduct multiple case studies to investigate this new research field, within textile, clothing and footwear companies in order to identify and investigate distinctive practices and processes suitable for characterising the Reference Model proposal. The sample was selected adopting theoretical sampling [10], and multiple investigators are used to reduce bias and create more reliable data [11, 12].

An "as is" business process analysis was conducted through focused interviews and BPMN (Business Process Modelling Notation) representation to collect and formalize a rich set of data, both qualitative and quantitative. Furthermore, the requirements of each company were pointed out and analysed in detail to draw the relevant characteristics, procedures and techniques along their supply constellation.

Within-case analyses allowed the study of each individual company singularly and understand their requirements in terms of the four dimensions, while a cross-case analysis among the different companies allowed the comparison of the companies' behaviour and understand their collaboration mechanisms.

# 3     Reference Model for TCFI Collaborative Networks

The research project CoReNet (Customer-Oriented and Eco-friendly Networks for Health Fashionable Goods) [13,14], intends to support textile, clothing and footwear companies in the implementation of new models for small series production for health and fashionable goods. Furthermore it follows the Competitive Sustainable Manufacturing (CSM) paradigm [15] and current initiatives of European Technological Platforms like Manufuture [16] and Footwear. The project intends to support the whole value chain to get and manage consumer data to investigate its needs; involve consumer into design and product configuration phases; exchange consumer data through adequate data models and secure systems; manage the collaboration with suppliers in order to plan and distribute on time; implement innovative manufacturing technologies; deliver timely the product to customer; and monitor the quality and sustainability of products. This approach aimed to develop a systematic strategy for the supply network configuration, coupled with a detailed definition and characterization of the operative level of processes and activities along four main dimensions (Knowledge, ICT, Organizational and Sustainability).

The Reference Model enhances the TCF companies in addressing specific target groups by enabling them in producing healthy and fashionable products in a collaborative environment. The base ground for the model was based in a comprehensive literature review and case-analysis field work.

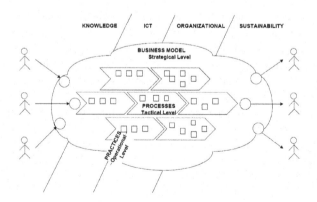

**Fig. 1.** Reference Model Context Diagram

As depicted in Fig.1 diagram the Reference Model will support TCF companies at strategic level covering the overall collaboration framework of the supply chain, at tactical level with the support to the definition of the processes which emerged as relevant for this kind of business and at the operational decision level by presenting rules and "best practices" to align the material flow to the specific market needs. In the following sections it will be detailed these three levels.

## 3.1    Strategic Level

Regarding the strategic level, the business model framework proposed by Osterwalder [17] was applied as conceptual approach. The model maps the most important building blocks that influence the definition of the value proposition. The idea is to instantiate the model to the specific case of TCF sector. Osterwalder [18] widens this concept and defines Business Models as: "…a conceptual tool that contains a set of elements and their relationships and allows a company's logic of earning money. It is a description of the value a company offers to one or several segments of customers and the architecture of the firm and its network of partners for creating marketing and delivering this value and relationship capital, in order to generate profitable and sustainable revenue streams".

In this regard, it is understood that business models should not only comprise the perspective inside organizations, but also embrace a wider perspective that includes potential partnerships, customers' requirements, revenue shares and other elements. A graphical representation merging the models presented by Ostervalder and (improved by) Romero et al. [19], as well as the empirical-based marketing approaches developed by Plantin [20] is shown in Figure 2. It is important to mention that this amalgamated representation is in accordance with Chesbrough and Rosenbloom [21] proposition, where a business model is placed as a linking ingredient between technical inputs (infrastructure management) and economical outputs (customer interface and financial aspects).

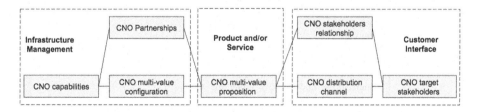

**Fig. 2.** Supply chain strategy based on building blocks

In collaborative endeavours, and therefore co-creation environments, value propositions are common ground between collaborative-networked organizations and customer communities. Collaborative networks should combine the capabilities of their members to create new abilities to better support the personalization of experiences and with customer knowledge synergies co-create real personal value propositions where the consumer is starting to play an increasingly important role in the co-construction of value offers [22].

Following this perspective, Table 1 depicts the most important features of the building blocks for the business model of healthy and fashionable SMEs. In addition the dimensions involved in each building block are identified. The most important characteristics that differentiate healthy and fashionable SMEs from the traditional footwear companies is the direct contact via web with final customers, that gives to small and medium manufacturers the possibility to understand customers needs without intermediaries and easily create best-fit configurations to fulfil their requirements. In order to allow firms to achieve this result it is fundamental to implement the right infrastructures in the companies, basing on the four dimensions of the Reference Model. In particular: knowledge on the requirements of target groups, ICT infrastructure to support the whole business model, organizational aspects to manage the supply network and sustainability to guarantee competitive advantages along the time.

**Table 1.** Building blocks for traditional SME and healthy and fashionable SME

|  | **Healthy and Fashionable SMEs** | **Dimensions involved** |
|---|---|---|
| Target stakeholders | B2C: End consumer from target groups<br>B2B: Shops | Knowledge – ICT |
| Multi-value proposition | Healthy and fashionable best fit shoes and garments produced and distributed in collaborative environment | Knowledge – ICT – Organizational – Sustainability |
| Distribution channel | B2C/B2B – e-commerce<br>B2C – traditional shops | ICT – Organizational |
| Stakeholder relationship | Periodic fit sessions to define and adjust configuration space (of variants) according target groups' needs | Knowledge – Organizational |
|  | Direct electronic communication to end-consumer using internet interface and feedback |  |
| Capabilities | Market analysis based on Data from Knowledge Management Tools (KMT) supporting the definition of the configuration space | Knowledge - Organizational |
|  | Made-To-Measure sizing technology and knowledge |  |
| Multi-value configuration | Management of Made-To-Measure products design | Knowledge – ICT |
| Partnerships | Management of the Made-to-Measure manufacturing and delivery along the CNO with:<br>Suppliers (raw materials and components)<br>Outsourcers<br>Service Providers<br>Technology providers<br>Customers belonging to Target groups<br>Communities | ICT – Organizational |

## 3.2    Tactical Level

From the case-studies analyses a set of critical processes emerged as important to satisfy collaboration business requirements at network level. These processes have been mapped and formalized in a BPMN (Business Process Model Notation) representation [13] as presented in figure 3.

The overall tactical level of the model is based on a customer-oriented approach to the supply network configuration. The starting point of the overall process is twofold according to the level of customization/configuration it is decided for the Target groups. On one side, the processes IM1 and IM2 represent the starting point from the customer. Traditional shopping as well as online configurators and customer profiling for specific customer groups are taken into consideration. IM1 and IM2 allow direct customer interaction on footwear, textiles or clothing products with special features for the consumer target groups (elderly, obese, diabetics and disabled people) with the possibility of product configuration and full visualization of products characteristics. From IM1 and IM2 it is possible to go to CD3.

On the other side, Co-design with Knowledge Management Tools (CD1) supports the identification of market needs and consumer preferences for new products and functionalities in CD2. Another important process is the Definition of Product Collection (CD2) for specific target groups based on collaborative environment where different type of users (internal and external to the company) with different roles can contribute to define a collection of suitable products for the target consumers. Regarding the small series production, it has been defined the Product Design process with CAD modelling (CD3) which is carried out by the (internal and external) designer and outcomes the CAD technical model of the product. Also includes selection of materials for both clothing and footwear.

Process planning (CD4) is related to product engineering and has the aim to decide how to manufacture the product and to generate all related information. In this phase suppliers and outsourcers are identified and defined and the costs for the different manufacturing phases are determined. Also the BOM, the working cycles and the production times of the new product model are also defined.

Customer order processing support (CP1) is based on automatic pre-processing of customer orders for administrative and pre-production checks and issues. The final output is the list of customer orders ready to be processed for production. With collaborative process planning (CP2) all standard and default data can be uploaded to the early (automatic) set of Production Orders; external activities (to be outsourced) require the identification of potential partners to be assigned. The output is the set of production orders ready to be scheduled. In Collaborative production planning and control (CP3) production orders related to the same customer's orders can be scheduled using a collaborative tool where manufacturer and partners inside the collaborative network can share a view of the production order schedules and close a "negotiation" for the definitive launch of manufacturing activities.

Last, the cross-cutting process of partner monitoring and trace support aims to monitor production orders as well as KPI related to Quality and Sustainability. The outcome includes overall status, alerts/warnings and high-level KPIs. For each of these processes a detailed description has been developed including information related to the flow of activities and related to the four dimensions of the model.

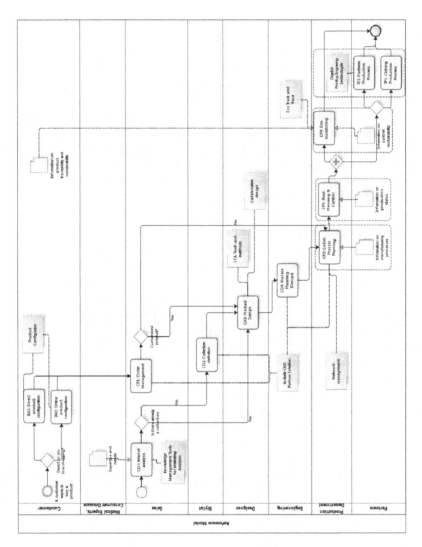

**Fig. 3.** BPMN representation of the mapped processes

### 3.3    Operational Level

Regarding the Operational Level it has been identified a set of practices that define the relationships between the tactical level and the four main dimensions and establish guidelines for the operational level decision making. An excerpt of the vast list of these Reference Model rules and operational best practices is presented in Table 2.

**Table 2.** Excerpt of Operational Level table

### SALES/CONFIGURATION PROCESS

| BUSINESS REQUIREMENTS | IM1 - Traditional shopping support for specific customer groups | IM2 - Online visualization, configuration and acquisition of leather/footwear |
|---|---|---|
| KNOWLEDGE | Customer involvement. Customer requirements management. Clinical aspect and functional requirements. | Formalized knowledge of information needed for the customer to assess the performance of the product. |
| ICT | Availability of machines like scanners, cameras, virtual mirrors, etc.. able to get images, 3D rendering of feet\bodies for product design. | It is necessary to create a clear and single access point that customers can recognize as online shop. |
| ORGANIZATIONAL | In a customer driven supply chain, end-user demand drives all activities among trading partners according to a culture that puts the customer first. | Some steps realized by downstream supply chain actors can be reduced compared to direct sales. |
| SUSTAINABILITY | Commitment with the customer to give information on sustainability. | Formalized knowledge of information needed for the customer to assess the sustainability of the products. |

### DESIGN PROCESS

| BUSINESS REQUIREMENTS | CD1 - Co-design with Knowledge Management Tools support | CD2 - Definition of Collection Support | CD3 - Product Design with CAD modeling support | CD4 - Process planning support |
|---|---|---|---|---|
| KNOWLEDGE | Need of data sharing agreements between retailers, manufacturers and designers but also the involvement of consumers through specific online communities of consumer target groups. | Knowledge on the specific functional requirements of the customers. | Modularity, Postponement, Product innovation, Open innovation | New solutions in terms of new process plans, as well as reduces the time needed to reach satisfactory solutions. |
| ICT | ... | ... | ... | ... |

### PRODUCTION PLANNING PROCESS

| BUSINESS REQUIREMENTS | CP1 - Customer order processing support | CP2 - Support for collaborative process planning | CP3 - Support for collaborative production planning and control | CP4 - Partner monitoring and trace support |
|---|---|---|---|---|
| KNOWLEDGE | (a) The analysis and translation of the product configuration information into the production article data in terms of materials and production processes (for lot size 1, and for small series). (b) Aggregation of orders. (c) Partner selection in order to collaborate with them. | Information already stored in the PDM system and related to generic BOM and working cycles for product models. Order specific information that will integrate these will have to be coherently structured according to a common framework. | Impact of the right or wrong production on the pathologies. | Ability to include in the definition of KPIs proper inputs from final customers requirements and needs, especially the ones belonging to the target groups addressed by the project as, for example in terms of an allergic and no toxic materials. |
| ICT | ... | ... | ... | ... |

## 4    Conclusions and Further Research

The ongoing European project "Customer-oriented and eco-friendly networks for healthy fashionable goods (CoReNet)" aims to provide TCFI companies with the tools and methods to face the challenge of working in demand-driven and customer oriented collaborative networks.

Until now the project research work allowed the definition of a Reference Model that set up the foundations for the development of future technologies and tools that support network operation. The following phases include the instantiation to specific companies' requirements of the reference model according to their business model in order to support them in the path to small series production of healthy products. The model is currently under evaluation and improvement in the CoReNet project together with the industry partners and the customers. The final goal is to provide a sound customer-oriented reference model suitable to collaborative network managers and stakeholders of TCF industry.

**Acknowledgments.** The research leading to these results has received funding from the European Union's Seventh Framework Programme (FP7/2007-2013) under grant agreement n° [260169].

# References

1. EU Commission: The demographic future of Europe – from challenge to opportunity (2007),
   http://europa.eu/legislation_summaries/employment_and_social_policy/situation_in_europe/c10160_en.htm
2. Camarinha-Matos, L.M., Boucher, X., Afsarmanesh, H.: Collaborative Networks for a Sustainable World 11th IFIP WG 5.5. In: Proceedings of Working Conference on VE (2010)
3. Christopher, M.: Logistics and supply chain management - Creating Value-Adding Networks, 3rd edn. Prentice Hall (2005)
4. Simchi-Levi, D.: Operations Rules – Delivering Customer Value through Flexible Operations. The MIT Press (2010)
5. Paul, C., James, A., Towill, D.R.: Analysis and design of focused demand chains. Journal of Operations Management 20(6), 675–689 (2002)
6. De Treville, S., Shapiro, R.D., Hameri, A.-P.: From supply chain to demand chain: the role of lead time reduction in improving demand chain performance. Journal of Operations Management 21(6), 613–627 (2004)
7. Adler, P.S.: Market, Hierarchy and Trust: the Knowledge Economy and the Future of Capitalism. Organization Science 12(2), 215–234 (2001)
8. Cohen, S., Roussel, J.: Strategic Supply Chain Management - The five disciplines for top performance. MacGraw-Hill, New York (2005)
9. Filos, E., Banahan, E.: Towards the smart organization: An emerging organizational paradigm and the contribution of the European RTD programs. Journal of Intelligent Manufacturing 12(2), 101–111 (2001)
10. Glaser, B., Strauss, A.: Grounded Theroy: the discovery of grounded theory. Aldine (1967)
11. Eisenhardt, K.M.: Building theories from case study research. Academy of Management Review 14(4), 532–550 (1989)
12. Pagell, M.: Understanding the factors that enable and inhibit the integration of operations, purchasing and logistics. Journal of Operation Management 22(5), 459–487 (2004)
13. Fornasiero, R., Chiodi, A., Carpanzano, E., Carneiro, L.: Research Issues on Customer-Oriented and Eco-friendly Networks for Healthy Fashionable Goods. In: Ortiz, Á., Franco, R.D., Gasquet, P.G. (eds.) BASYS 2010. IFIP AICT, vol. 322, pp. 36–44. Springer, Heidelberg (2010)

14. Azevedo, A., Bastos, J., Almeida, A., Soares, C., Magaletti, N., Del Grosso, E., Stellmach, D., Winkler, M., Fornasiero, R., Zangiacomi, A., Chiodi, A.: Customer-Oriented and Eco-friendly Networks for Health Fashionable Goods – The CoReNet Approach. In: Camarinha-Matos, L.M., Pereira-Klen, A., Afsarmanesh, H. (eds.) PRO-VE 2011. IFIP AICT, vol. 362, pp. 69–76. Springer, Heidelberg (2011)
15. FoF-PPP: Factories of the Future: Public, Private Partnership, Strategic Roadmap (2009)
16. Manufuture, Strategic Research Agenda (2006)
17. Osterwalder, A., Pigneur, Y.: Business Model Generation - A Handbook for Visionaries, Game Changers, and Challengers. John Wiley & Sons, Inc., Hoboken - New Jersey (2010)
18. Osterwalder, A.: The Business Model Ontology - A Proposition in a Design Science Approach. Phd Thesis (2004)
19. Romero, D., Galeano, N., Giraldo, J., Molina, A.: Towards The Definition Of Business Models And Governance Rules For Virtual Breeding Environments Network-Centric Collaboration and Supporting Frameworks, vol. 224, pp. 103–110. Springer, Boston (2006)
20. Plantin, S.: Orange Labs R&D internal methodology for building business models (2008)
21. Chesbrough, H., Rosenbloom, R.S.: The role of the business model in capturing value from innovation: evidence from Xerox Corporation's technology spin-off companies. Industrial and Corporate Change 11(3), 529–555 (2002)
22. Romero, D., Molina, A.: Collaborative networked organisations and customer communities: value co-creation and co-innovation in the networking era. Production Planning & Control 22(5-6), 447–472 (2011)
23. Fornasiero, R., Zangiacomi, A., Stellmach, D.: A Reference Model for Customer-Oriented and Eco-Friendly Networks for Healthy Fashionable Goods. In: Proceedings of the APMS 2010 Stavanger, Norway (2011)

# 13

## Collaboration Motivators I

# On the Paradox of Collaboration, Collaborative Systems and Collaborative Networks

Donald Neumann

Graduate School of Excellence for Advanced Manufacturing Engineering,
University of Stuttgart, Keplerstr. 17, R10.027, 70174, Stuttgart, Germany
donald.neumann@gsame.uni-stuttgart.de

**Abstract.** It has been claimed that collaborative networks are the societal structure of this century. Nonetheless, low success rates often observed in the practice of purposeful collaboration suggest that our understanding is still limited. In this paper, I advance on the theory of collaborative systems, a systems theoretical approach to interorganizational collaborative relationships, critically investigating their nature. Based on the characteristics of social systems, I suggest an explanation to the low success rates observed in practice. Furthermore, I offer an alternative definition of collaborative networks according to the theory presented and discuss some implications and challenges to the discipline of Collaborative Networks.

**Keywords:** Systems Theory, Collaborative Systems, Collaborative Networks, Interorganziational Collaborative Relationships, Social Systems.

## 1    Introduction

The history of society is the history of how individuals communicate and join forces to pursue goals in a coordinated way [13], 'collaborating' in the broadest sense of the term. Hence, the evolution to a functionally differentiated society, in which social systems (e.g. politics, law, and economy) fulfill different societal functions autonomously [13], cannot be distinguished from the evolution of collaboration among individuals. Interorganizational collaborative networks emerged from the recognition of the potential of coordination and collaboration among organizations and have been claimed to be the 'societal structure of the $21^{st.}$ century' [19].

Interorganizational collaborative relationships are not a new phenomenon though. Artisans probably worked together to increase product complexity and production capacity. Nonetheless, these relationships gained momentum in academia only in the past 50 years [19]. Thereby, interorganizational collaborative relationships, defined broadly as *"voluntary interactions among autonomous organizations that are not strictly based on economic transactions"* [16], have been studied under different labels, for example, 'Collaborative Relationships', 'Strategic Alliances' and 'Collaborative Networks'.

L.M. Camarinha-Matos, L. Xu, and H. Afsarmanesh (Eds.): PRO-VE 2012, IFIP AICT 380, pp. 363–373, 2012.
© IFIP International Federation for Information Processing 2012

Different economic benefits have been associated with collaboration [9]. Nevertheless, high failure rates have been systematically reported [10]. This fact suggests an apparent paradox of collaboration: while the success of social systems in fulfilling their function relies on the almost intuitive communication and coordination of actions among individuals, organizations strive to achieve the potential of collaboration. Thus, it seems that our understanding of interorganizational collaboration is either incomplete or incompatible with the properties of collaboration among individuals in society.

Seeking to offer an innovative explanation to this paradox, in this work I abstract from specific forms of collaborative relationships. Therefore, in section 2 I analyze existing theoretical perspectives on collaboration, highlighting their limitations. Advancing on the investigation of the nature of interorganizational collaborative relationships, in section 3 I further develop the theory of collaborative systems and offer an explanation to the high failure rates observed in practice. In section 4 I discuss the main implications of collaborative systems to the practice and the discipline of collaborative networks, offering an alternative definition of collaborative networks. Finally, in section 5, I conclude, highlighting some possible extensions of this work.

## 2     Collaborative Relationships

Interorganizational collaborative relationships have been investigated from different perspectives. Focusing on the properties of competitive markets, Neoclassical Economics interprets firms as rational agents who compete for market power. This tradition is translated in Porter's well-known Five Forces Model [18]. Collaborative relationships are described as interactions among competitors concerning prices and quantities, allowing firms to create monopoly rents. Nonetheless, rationality assumptions suggest that firms are expected to maximize individual profits at the expense of joint ones [20]. Consequently, collaborative relationships tend to be unstable, characterized by competitive and opportunistic behavior.

Transaction Costs Economics (TCE) explains a firm's choice among markets, hierarchies and hybrids as equivalent forms of coordinating transactions [24]. Markets accomplish this function through output-based rewards and hierarchies through input-based ones ruled by employment contracts. Collaborative relationships are hybrid governance mechanisms that involve both output- and input-based rewards structured by incomplete, long-term contracts [24]. Assuming that transactions differ on asset-specificity, uncertainty and frequency, TCE asserts that the choice of the governance forms is contingent on the costs resulting from the match between transactions properties and governance form. Similarly to Neoclassical Economics, TCE describes firms as rational agents that maximize individual gains. Thus, opportunistic behavior is expected and hybrids are competitive unstable governance forms [15].

The Resource-Based View of the firm (RBV) and its derivations describe the firm as a bundle of resources from which a subset, the strategic ones, allows it to sustain competitive advantage [12]. Assuming that firms interact with their environment in order to acquire resources, collaborative relationships are described either as a means to access resources or as strategic resources themselves [5]. Consequently, RBV suggests that collaborative relationships are strategies capable of generating and sustaining competitive advantage [7].

Supply Chain Management (SCM) focuses on the flows of information and goods between and among firms [23]. Collaborative relationships are characterized by the communication of decisions about demand, supply and stock. By allowing the production and flow of goods to be coordinated [6], collaborative relationships are described as the rational choice and hence cooperative behavior is expected.

Game Theory and Principal-Agent Theory focus on interactions among players, in which the outcomes depend on the decisions made by players individually [22]. Offering a set of mathematical tools to analyze strategic situations, these theories highlight the connection between decisions under a specific set of expectation structures. Based on the prediction of a partner's response, these models suggest adequate decisions, thereby absorbing decision uncertainty [2]. Collaborative relationships are thereby described as a set of repeated interactions according to known expectations structures [17]. In spite of rationality assumptions, outcomes are not restricted to (but nonetheless are mainly described as) economic ones and relationships may assume either a cooperative or competitive nature, depending on the rules of the game.

Social Network Analysis (SNA) approaches the network of actors constituted by multiple relationships [25]. Similarly to Game Theory, SNA does not constitute a theory itself, but rather a set of mathematical tools. In the realm of interorganizational networks, SNA researchers have focused mainly on the relation between the structure of the network and their benefits, i.e. social capital [25]. Thereby it is assumed that the structure of the network changes the level of access and control over information, resulting in different performance [11]. Consequently, SNA abstracts from specific collaborative relationships focusing on the totality of relationships in the network.

Each theory mentioned above offers a different model for collaborative relationship. Nonetheless, they share three common properties that affect how these relationships are understood.

1. *Incompatible goals:* each one of the mentioned theories was motivated by the explanation of phenomena other than collaborative relationships. Consequently, although these theories explain collaborative relationships, these explanations remain partial and constrained by the theories' original (mainly, if not strictly, economic) motives and goals.

2. *Incompatible unit of study:* these theories focus on units of study other than the collaborative relationship itself. For instance, while TCE approaches transactions, RBV investigates resources, Game Theory specific decisions, and networks abstract from the relationships themselves. Consequently, collaborative relationships are explained partially and in reference to the respective unit of study.

3. *Focus on content, not nature:* finally, the theories described above do not approach the nature of collaborative relationships. Rather, they approach the content and behavior of specific types of relationships (e.g. Strategic Alliances).

Consequently, the theories briefly described above seem to miss the point. They investigate the motives, consequences and properties of collaborative relationships without describing their nature, i.e. the mechanisms that allow these behaviors to emerge in the first place. Hence, they *"are often used to make predictions, yet they do not provide explanations"* [1]. Together, these properties contribute to a partial and incomplete understanding of collaboration, limiting the understanding of high failure rates observed in practice. Consequently, as highlighted by [3], an *"urgent need to establish a sound theoretical foundation for CNs"* has been already identified in the discipline of Collaborative Networks.

As proposed by [3], Collaborative Networks (CN) constitutes a discipline that covers different forms of interorganizational collaborative relationships. A research community that identifies itself with the object of study 'collaborative networks' and an already organized set of basic knowledge characterizes it as a discipline. Thereby, 'collaborative network' is defined as a network *"constituted by a variety of entities (e.g., organizations and people) that are largely autonomous, geographically distributed, and heterogeneous in terms of their: operating environment, culture, social capital, and goals. Nevertheless these entities collaborate to better achieve common or compatible goals, and whose interactions are supported by computer network."* While this ontological definition is useful for modeling purposes, it is not related with any underlying theory about the social and organizational nature of these relationships. Thus, even though it offers some guidance for researchers in the discipline of Collaborative Networks, by ignoring the fact that a structured nexus of communications, i.e. a social system, is necessarily a constitutive part of such a network, it restricts the advancement of knowledge about the social structure and organizational behavior of these networks.

# 3    Collaborative Systems

Instead of describing collaborative relationships as a rational means to an end, I follow [16] and advance on collaborative relationships from the perspective of social systems theory. Functionally, collaborative relationships provide organizations with information that [16]:

1. Can be adopted as a decision, absorbing uncertainty and thereby offering a solution to an organizational problem.
2. By functioning as a decision premise conditions further decisions.

When fulfilling these functions for every partner, collaborative relationships structurally couple partners, allowing them to co-adapt. Thus, these relationships stabilize (i.e. succeed) if and only if they contribute to absorb uncertainty and reduce complexity. This functional approach differs from the ontological definition of collaborative network. In this context, an interorganizational relationship constitutes a collaborative system only if the function of collaboration is fulfilled and recognized as being fulfilled by the relationship itself.

In order to fulfill this function, organizations 'organize their relationship', i.e. they decide about the expectations about the relationship itself. When these decisions condensate into decision premises that structure further collaborative decisions, an autopoietic network of collaborative decisions emerges and the relationship becomes a social system of the type organization: the 'Collaborative System'. Thus, generalizing the proposition offered in [16], I propose:

**Proposition 1.** *A collaborative system is an organization system that fulfills the organizational function of collaboration.*

As in the case of social systems, the basal element of collaborative systems is a specific type of communication. Furthermore, as an organization system, collaborative systems are reproduced by the communication of decisions (in this case collaborative decisions) among partners (the organizations recognized by the collaborative system as members). This definition widens and therefore includes the definition presented in [16]. Consequently, even though a collaborative system structurally couples partners allowing them to co-adapt structures (decision premises), the boundaries of partners and the boundaries of the collaborative system remain clear. For in a collaborative relationship (or, specifically, in a collaborative network) each decision is clearly identified either as a decision of the relationship or a partner's one.

Differently from organization systems in general, collaborative systems are included in the specific context of interorganizational relationships. Thereby they recognize their partners as the main source of resources. This resource dependence allows partners to influence collaborative systems by choosing specific members and by restricting topics to those of actual interest. Nonetheless, collaborative systems remain autonomous. Thus, even though a partner may try to influence the relationship in a specific direction, it cannot force the relationship to respond. This decision remains a decision of the collaborative system. This autonomy is the result of operational closure and implies that the organizational network of decisions neither generates collaborative decisions nor control them as causal function of organizational ones.

There are two direct consequences of operational closure. First, a partner cannot influence another one directly. Therefore, he needs first to influence the collaborative system through communicating about collaborative decisions. This necessarily indirect path increases the probability that influence or control attempts will fail. Second, as social systems collaborative systems cannot be controlled externally. As the experience with communism and political regulation of markets show, organizations (as any other social system) interpret their environment according to their internal structure and state. Consequently, even though environmental events influence organizations, the organizational reaction is not causal. Thus, management is an internal function of the system. Similarly, collaborative systems cannot be installed, controlled or managed [16]. In fact, the effort to control a collaborative system often relies on communication of power, breaking expectation structures such as trust, eventually destroying the relationship as a whole [26].

Collaborative systems contribute to the advancement of knowledge about collaborative relationships, hence collaborative networks, in different ways. First, collaborative systems are coherent with a theory of communication and coordination in society. Unlike the concepts presented in the previous section, it is motivated by the study of the behavior that emerges from the basal operation and structure of collaborative relationships. Therefore, organizations are not reduced to firms as production functions, bundles of resources or governance forms that emerge rationally because it is cheaper to produce than to buy. Organizations are recognized as complex societal achievements, resulting from the co-evolution of complementary social systems as forms of structural coupling among organisms in the social domain. Consequently, collaborative systems complement social systems theory by describing the communication and coordination of decisions between and among organizations.

Second, collaborative systems describe collaborative relationship as an indivisible unit of study, highlighting the nature and the specific characteristics of these relationships. Based on the organizational function of collaboration, collaborative systems explain how organizations become coupled through a structured network of communications, namely, collaborative decisions. Thereby, collaborative systems offer a clear-cut description of the nature and structure of collaborative relationships, without being restricted by content. Thus, collaborative systems complement the discipline of Collaborative Networks by specifying the social and organizational nature of collaborative networks.

Third, based on the distinction between system and environment, collaborative systems do not assume a specific context, e.g. the economic or the political one. Consequently, the theory is general and valid for any type of collaborative relationship. In fact, the context independence highlights the potential societal role of collaborative relationships. As a result of societal functional differentiation, organizations are expected to operate simultaneously according to different and potentially contradictory expectations, e.g. economic, social, political and ecological. Collaboration is a potential solution for this problem [21], allowing organizations to coordinate decisions in the context of different function systems. Thus, in order to develop the full potential of collaboration, a respective general model is necessary, including, but not exclusively, the economic context.

Fourth, collaborative systems suggest an answer to high failure rates observed in practice. As emergent, autopoietic networks of communications structured by expectations, collaborative systems constitute the social domain of organizations, in which meaning is constructed through recursive communications about collaborative decisions. Consequently, collaborative systems are dependent on history and exist only while collaborative decisions are (re-)produced. Paraphrasing [14] 'only collaborative decisions decide about collaboration.' Structure emerges as eigenvalues of the system, i.e. as stable expectation structures in the relationship, that constantly change and are changed by collaborative decisions.

Nonetheless, collaborative systems are rarely understood as autonomous systems, capable of managing themselves. Rather, the approaches mentioned in section 2 describe collaborative relationships as controllable input-output systems. Consequently, partners seek to develop management best practices and information systems in an effort to better control the relationship. Thereby organizations often constrain the evolution of the system, contributing to the emergence of conflict, hindering the fulfillment of the function of collaboration.

Even though standards and best practices fulfill a similar function as language, i.e. they constitute symbols for generalized meaning, they are not meaning itself. Consequently, collaborative systems cannot be installed and regulated through the simple use of standards and information systems. Because organizations are operationally closed systems, the meaning of these standards is a construction of the system itself that cannot be transferred from one system to another (e.g. from organization to collaboration). Nonetheless, in the quest to achieve the potential (economic) results of collaboration, organizations often rush to adopt standards, processes and key performance indicators. Thereby, they overlook the fact that standards acquire meaning through collaborative decisions in the collaborative system and not the other way around.

# 4    Implications

Underlying the theories presented in section 2 is the assumption that collaborative relationships are controllable input-output systems. As social systems instead, they tend to draw *"our attention to the very points at which an attempt to intervene will fail"* [8]. Counter-intuitively, by seeking better ways of 'managing the relationship' partners impede collaborative systems to manage themselves and, thereby, succeed. Thus, collaborative systems suggest an analogy between collaborative relationships and firms. Even though this analogy is imperfect, the metaphor is useful for better understanding collaborative systems. Thus, as firms, collaborative systems are organization systems in their own right, even though they need not be legal institutions. Furthermore, collaborative systems offer a product to a set of clients, the partners, and also have a set of suppliers, again their partners, who provide them with the necessary resources.

The firm analogy has important consequences for the practice of collaboration. Although partners have the choice of engaging in a collaborative relationship, they do not have the choice of controlling or managing it in the cybernetic sense. Collaborative relationships are evolutionary systems, whose structure, identity and management emerge from their ongoing autonomous operation. Partners can only influence this process in two ways. As their suppliers, partners influence collaborative relationships through the control of resources. As clients, partners establish the *raison d'etre* of the collaborative system expecting from them a product of (not necessarily economic) value that translates the specific function of collaboration. Last, but not least, just as in any organization, collaborative relationships are able to autonomously decide about their resources in order to provide their services. Because collaborative systems cannot be controlled, after clearly defining suppliers, clients and products, partners should let management emerge *in* the collaborative system as a function of its operation (the relationship). In fact, the one-sided imposition of decisions to the relationship highlights its lack of autonomy. The consequence may be the deterioration to game playing following an exclusively economic rationality.

In the specific context of collaborative supply chains and in accordance with the model proposed in this work, [4] highlight that *"firms' efforts to manage supply chains have often led to frustration and helplessness. Managers have struggled with the dynamic and complex nature of supply networks* [collaborative relationships] *and the inevitable lack of prediction and control."* Consequently, the firm analogy backs up the authors' conclusion that *"clearly, 'good intention' is not enough. Managers must possess a mental model of supply networks [collaborative relationship] that more accurately reflects its true underlying complexity and dynamism"* [4].

Finally, collaborative systems have an important implication to the research and discipline of Collaborative Networks. Describing the function and nature of interorganizational collaborative relationships as a specific type of organization system, collaborative systems suggest a revision of the strictly ontological definition of collaborative networks offered in [3]. Reviewing this definition according to the theory presented here, a collaborative network is properly defined as:

**Proposition 2.** *A collaborative network is a collaborative system that allows its members to achieve common or compatible goals and whose communications are supported by a computer network.*

According to social systems theory, social systems are idiosyncratic and, therefore, the members of the collaborative system are intrinsically understood as heterogeneous in terms of their structures, which include goals, organizational culture, hierarchy, etc. Furthermore, by restricting collaborative networks to collaborative systems, it is assumed that collaborative networks fulfill the function of collaboration. Thus, collaborative networks describe themselves as indivisible wholes, as a relationship among organizations that is capable of fulfilling the function of collaboration for every partner and, thus, couples them structurally. Moreover, in the specific case of collaborative networks, this function is translated into common or compatible goals and a computer network supports the interaction, i.e. the communication about collaborative decisions. Consequently, according to this definition, every collaborative network necessarily involves a collaborative system, even though a collaborative system is not necessarily a collaborative network. For instance, in price collusions among competitors the function of collaboration is fulfilled through the communication about prices, even though there is no decision about common or compatible goals and no computer network is therefore required.

In contrast to the original definition, the alternative definition proposed here maintains important ontological characteristics but explicitly includes the social nature of collaboration, highlighting collaborative networks as autonomous organization systems. Thereby it suggests an extension of research towards an organizational theory of collaborative networks, contributing to close the existent lack of theoretical foundation for collaborative networks highlighted in [3]. Thereby, collaborative systems establish a link between organizational theory and collaborative networks, allowing the latter to formally benefit from the knowledge already existent. For instance, social systems theory, theories of leadership, organizational culture, behavior, change and learning can be transported into the realm of collaborative networks, contributing to a greater understanding of the phenomenon. Furthermore, by establishing important differences between the context of organizations in general and collaborative relationships specifically, collaborative systems suggest a starting point to adapt organizational theories to the specific case of collaborative networks. Last, but not least, by being independent of a specific context (e.g. economy), collaborative systems formally include collaborative relationships between different types of organizations, for instance, political parties, NGOs, universities and firms. Thereby, it offers a general framework to study collaborative networks and their role in addressing emerging societal challenges.

## 5     Conclusions and Future Work

This work extended the concept of collaborative systems. Describing interorganizational collaborative relationships as social systems of the type organization, it was suggested that, in contrast to collaboration among individuals, firms strive to control the uncontrollable, i.e. their relationships, allowing the apparent paradox of collaboration to emerge. Drawing on the properties of social systems, an analogy between collaborative systems and firms was presented, explaining how the understanding of these systems can help increase success rates. Finally, an alternative definition for the concept of collaborative network was offered, which explicitly highlights the social nature of these networks turning the concept coherent with a theory of organizations and society.

Even though this work builds on the concept of collaborative systems presented in [16], it is only a small step towards a theory of interorganizational collaborative relationships in general and collaborative networks specifically. Consequently, several extensions of this work are possible. First, future work should be dedicated to further detail collaborative systems, relating them to and distinguishing them from organizations in general, according to existent organizational theory. Second, the role of power, contracts, trust and reputation in collaborative systems should be investigated. Third, the theory of collaborative systems should be extended to detail the evolution of these systems in contrast to the evolution of organizations in general, describing the common life cycle of collaborative relationships. Finally, existent methods and information systems to support collaboration could be evaluated and adapted according to the theoretical proposition described in the last section.

## References

1. Bacharach, S.B.: Organizational theories: some criteria for evaluation. The Academy of Management Review 14(4), 496–515 (1989)
2. Baiman, S., Rajan, M.V.: Incentive issues in inter-firm relationships. Accounting, Organizations and Society 27(3), 213–238 (2002)

3. Camarinha-Matos, L.M., Afsarmanesh, H.: Collaborative networks: a new scientific discipline. Journal of Intelligent Manufacturing 16(4-5), 439–452 (2005)
4. Choi, T.Y., Dooley, K.J., Rungtusanatham, M.: Supply networks and complex adaptive systems: control versus emergence. Journal of Operations Management 19(3), 351–366 (2001)
5. Das, T., Teng, B.: A resource-based theory of strategic alliances. Journal of Management 26(1), 31–61 (2000)
6. Datta, P.P., Christopher, M.G.: Information sharing and coordination mechanisms for managing uncertainty in supply chains: a simulation study. International Journal of Production Research 49(3), 765–803 (2011)
7. Dyer, J.H., Singh, H.: The Relational View: cooperative strategy and sources of interorganizational competitive advantage. The Academy of Management Review 23(4), 660–679 (1998)
8. Forrester, J.W.: Counterintuitive behavior of social systems. Theory and Decision 2, 109–140 (1971)
9. Gulati, R.: Managing Network Resources. Oxford University Press, Inc., New York (2007)
10. Kapmeier, F.: Common learning and opportunistic behaviour in learning alliances. Systems Research and Behavioral Science 25, 549–573 (2008)
11. Kilduff, M., Brass, D.J.: Organizational social network research: core ideas and key debates. The Academy of Management Annals 4(1), 317–357 (2010)
12. Lockett, A., Thompson, S., Morgenstern, U.: The development of the Resource-Based View of the Firm: a critical appraisal. International Journal of Management Reviews 11(1), 9–28 (2009)
13. Luhmann, N.: Die Gesellschaft der Gesellschaft, Suhrkamp, Frankfurt am Main, Germany (1998)
14. Luhmann, N.: Die Form 'Person'. In: Soziologische Aufklärung 6: Die Soziologie und der Mensch, 3rd edn., pp. 137–148. VS Verlag, Wiesbaden, Germany (2009)
15. Ménard, C.: Hybrid organizations. In: Klein, P., Sykuta, M. (eds.) The Elgar Companion to Transaction Cost Economics, pp. 176–184. E. Elgar, Cheltenham (2011)
16. Neumann, D., de Santa-Eulalia, L.A., Zahn, E.: Towards a Theory of Collaborative Systems. In: Camarinha-Matos, L.M., Pereira-Klen, A., Afsarmanesh, H. (eds.) PRO-VE 2011. IFIP AICT, vol. 362, pp. 306–313. Springer, Heidelberg (2011)
17. Parkhe, A.: Strategic alliance structuring: a game theoretic and transaction cost examination of interfirm cooperation. The Academy of Management Journal 36(4), 794–829 (1993)
18. Porter, M.E.: The five competitive forces that shape strategy. Harvard Business Review 86(1), 78–93 (2008)
19. Raab, J., Kenis, P.: Heading toward a society of networks: empirical developments and theoretical challenges. Journal of Management Inquiry 18(3), 198–210 (2009)
20. Samuelson, P.A., Nordhaus, W.D.: Economics, 18th edn. McGraw-Hill International Edition, New York (2005)
21. Senge, P., Smith, B., Kruschwitz, N., Laur, J., Schley, S.: The Necessary Revolution, 2nd edn. Nicholas Brealey Publishing, London (2010)
22. Sotomayor, M.: Introduction to game theory. In: Meyers, R.A. (ed.) Encyclopedia of Complexity and Systems Science, pp. 4095–4097. Springer (2009)
23. Stock, J.R., Boyer, S.L.: Developing a consensus definition of supply chain management: a qualitative study. International Journal of Physical Distribution & Logistics Management 39, 690–711 (2009)

24. Williamson, O.: Comparative economic organization: the analysis of discrete structural alternatives. Administrative Science Quarterly 36(2), 269–296 (1991)
25. Zaheer, A., Gözübüyük, R., Milanov, H.: It's the connections: the network perspective in interorganizational research. The Academy of Management Perspectives 24(1), 62–77 (2010)
26. Zaheer, A., McEvily, B., Perrone, V.: Does trust matter? Exploring the effects of interorganizational and interpersonal trust on performance. Organization Science 9(2), 141–159 (1998)

# What Is Collaboration? An Analytical Cut
# from the Business Processes and SaaS Perspectives

Maiara Heil Cancian[1], Ricardo J. Rabelo[1], and Christiane Gresse von Wangenheim[2]

[1] Department of Automation and Systems,
Federal University of Santa Catarina, Florianópolis, (SC) Brazil
[2] Department of Informatics and Statistics,
Federal University of Santa Catarina, Florianópolis, (SC) Brazil
{maiara,rabelo}@das.ufsc.br,
gresse@inf.ufsc.br

**Abstract.** This paper refers to how the collaboration among members of a Virtual Organization composed of software services providers can be enlarged within a SOA/SaaS scenario, maintaining partners' independence, autonomy and heterogeneity. It considers the situation where software companies work collaboratively to meet business opportunities so attending wider markets in a more agile way and with less risk, taking advantage of opportunities, capacities and capabilities that they would not have alone. Working collaboratively is not a mere wish. Companies should know and be prepared for supporting the required processes and to implement related practices. That is the goal of this article and ongoing research: to elicit the additional processes that are necessary to be supported by such a companies in the act of collaborating under the SOA/SaaS scenario.

**Keywords:** Collaboration, Business Process, Software Providers, SaaS.

## 1 Introduction

An increasing number of organizations have been investing in strategic alliances focused on larger collaboration as an alternative to increase competitiveness through innovation and productivity [1]. Collaborative Networks (CN) allow companies to keep focused on their skills and to aggregate competencies with other companies in order to offer products with higher value to meet businesses [2].

Despite turbulences in the global economy, the result was reasonably stable for the ICT (Information and Communication Technology) industry [3]. Part of this favorable scene is due to the expansion of cloud computing concept, putting these companies ahead of the technological innovations available, as the movement related to outsourcing and virtualization software [4].

Following the Cloud Computing, web applications can be developed using some approaches, like SOA (Service-Oriented Architecture). SOA provides flexibility in systems project and facilitates their integration, allowing the creation of interoperable services that can more easily be reused and shared across applications [5]. This

L.M. Camarinha-Matos, L. Xu, and H. Afsarmanesh (Eds.): PRO-VE 2012, IFIP AICT 380, pp. 374–384, 2012.
© IFIP International Federation for Information Processing 2012

scenario creates new needs and challenges. On the side of business users, they are increasingly pressured to streamline and better improve the growing investment in ICT [6]. On the side of developers, they are also pressured to provide services that can add value to companies to stay in the market. In this context, the business, architectural and availability model "Software-as-a-Service" (SaaS), combined with SOA, is ascending more and more in significance [7].

Generally, SaaS is a form of software which is available on demand via Internet and that is paid for use. In this model companies stop buying licenses and start renting specific software services. Developing their software solutions as services/SaaS puts companies ahead of the issues of innovation, bringing benefits to customers and suppliers [8]. This happens because the technologies used in this model are emerging and have the potential to leverage new sustainable models as they are loosely coupled and can be accessed from the cloud [9].

The essential issue tackled in this paper and underlying research question refer to how the collaboration among CN members within that SOA/SaaS scenario can be enlarged, maintaining partners independence, autonomy and heterogeneity. More precisely, it considers the situation where CN members are software companies that want / need to work collaboratively to meet business opportunities so attending wider markets in a more agile way and with less risk, taking advantage of opportunities, capacities and capabilities that they would not have alone [10]. In this scenario, services providers try to join their *individual* services into a composite and more valuable (SOA/SaaS-based) *solution* to be offered to the market, being it on demand or prospectively. To this model the authors of this paper have been calling as "*Collaborative SaaS*", seeing the so-called independent *software* vendors (ISV) as independent *service* providers (ISP).

Collaboration between software development companies in the SaaS model is a quite new concept and involves a number of challenges and issues. In this research, it is of interest to face two of them: i) how to select the most adequate ISP, i.e. how to trust on the others' services quality and reputation to minimize technical problems in that global solution ? ii) which actions are effectively involved in a collaboration among a CN of ISP ?

For the first question authors have already developed a reference guide for software quality devoted to SOA/SaaS, which was based on reference models for software quality improvement [11]. The second question refers to what this paper is about: which business processes are involved in such collaborative scenario?

It is important to understand what collaboration indeed means in this context as working collaboratively is not a mere wish. Companies should know and be prepared for supporting the required processes and to implement related practices. That is the goal of this article and ongoing research: to contribute to understand and to elicit the *additional* processes that are necessary to be supported by ISPs in the act of collaborating under the SOA/SaaS scenario.

This article is organized as follows: section 2 presents a general description of the main forms of collaboration in the context of this research. Section 3 presents a literature review, and section 4 presents the conclusions of this article.

## 2     Collaboration Forms

Collaborative-SaaS grounds on CN, which represents the more general theoretical foundation that characterizes the diverse manifestations of collaboration between organizations. This involves the structure, behavior and evolution dynamics of networks of autonomous entities that collaborate to better achieve common or compatible goals [12].

Regarding the envisaged collaboration between ISP, the CN manifestation called *Virtual Organization* (VO) represents quite well the scenario. A VO corresponds to a temporary and dynamic strategic alliance of autonomous, heterogeneous and usually geographically dispersed companies or professional communities that are created to attend to particular business opportunities, sharing costs, benefits and risks, acting as one single enterprise. After ending all legal obligations a VO is dismissed [13]. Under this view, a VO should be created, operated and managed regarding its intrinsic dynamics, and ended [6].

In the *Creation* phase the business is identified, the most suitable ISPs are selected for its parts (based on a variable set of criteria, including the quality of their software development processes), the governance model is instantiated, related performance indicators and metrics are settled, the software development project as a whole is designed and set up, SLAs are specified and contracts signed, and the VO is launched. In the *Operation* phase the whole development project is constantly monitored to ensure the collaboration is on the track, that the involved processes are being correctly performed and that performance metrics and SLAs are being fulfilled. In the *Evolution* phase, some actions should be planned to handle problems that happen in the Operation phase. Examples of problems include the inability of a partner to execute its task in time, the need to increase the workload, some metrics are well below to the agreed plan, etc. These problems usually lead to the addition, withdrawn or replacement of a partner (which should be selected again); to changes in specifications, contracts, agreements, etc.; or even to the business cancellation in a very serious case. The *Dissolution* phase embraces business processes involved with all technical, organizational, financial, legal and regulatory aspects related to the VO ending. This can happen either when business has been properly accomplished (i.e. VO / ISP partners delivered the services solution as contracted) or when the VO did not succeed due to major problems.

Therefore, acting collaboratively under the SaaS model to attend to business opportunities demands many other processes from the VO members than just putting pre-selected and a priori known companies to write services' code separately and to integrate and bundle them afterwards.

## 3     Literature Review

### 3.1     Methodology

Regarding the essentially exploratory characteristic of this research, the literature review procedure was considered as the most suitable for the case. Yet, considering the relatively novelty of the envisaged scenario and Collaborative-SaaS, there is not much real case scenarios upon which a rigorous analysis can be based on. Thus, and for a preliminary elicitation of the business processes involved in that form of collaboration, the revision was based on the state-of-the-art.

In order to gather a comprehensive revision of the state-of-the-art, the method SLR (*Literature Systematic Review*) [14] was chosen. SLR corresponds to a way to identify, evaluate and interpret all available research relevant to a specific research question, topic area or phenomenon of interest. It involves different activities and stages along three main phases: Planning, Conduct and Report.

In short, *Planning* phase frames the research objectives and defines the so-called protocol review. It describes the essential research question - *what are the processes involved in collaboration ?* - and how the review itself will be conducted. This was done via defining a set of keywords and acronyms which can cover that question as well as exclusion criteria. The respective search string was then drawn up. Articles written in English and published in journals and in conference proceedings between Sept 2000 and Sept 2011 have defined the search scope. As sources of information it was mainly considered the most recognized scientific repositories in the related area: *IEEExplore, ACM Digital Library, Compendex/Engineering Village,* and *ScienceDirect*.

In the *Conduct* phase the primary results from that search should be identified, evaluated and selected. The metadata (title, keywords and abstract) has to be extracted and synthesized for each retrieved/selected paper. In this work, the search returned a total of 278 articles. These articles were read and their contents were evaluated to see at which level of depth they indeed dealt with collaborative processes among enterprises. Actually it was observed that a large amount of those papers covered collaboration (in the paper's context) at a very shallow level, sometimes just pointing out the need for such processes. After a more rigorous analysis nine papers were taken as the main theoretical referential for this research: [6, 15, 16] [17-22].

The last phase, *Report*, aims at consolidating the results out of this referential. These activities were used to check aspects like redundancies (i.e. different processes' definitions dealing with equivalent concepts), synonyms (i.e. different words but with the same meaning) and semantics misleading (i.e. definitions of processes that were in fact more related to other process' definition), so to have a more precise and compiled list of collaborative processes.

## 3.2    Preliminary Results

With the processes compiled with 'standardized' names and descriptions, they were categorized according to the proper VO life cycle. This categorization also aimed to facilitate the processes organization as well as their visualization. Due to a more variety, the processes within Operation and Evolution phases were organized into subcategories, regarding their intrinsic nature and also weighing up what the authors of those referential papers stated about. Besides a comparison among such papers, a number of supporting books were taken into account for that 'standardization', [23] in particular.

Table 1 presents the elicitation of the business processes required to support the collaboration among ISP in a SOA/SaaS scenario from a VO point of view. It is important to mention that this list *complements* the other traditional processes of software development solidly covered by some reference models, like CMMI [24]. In other words, it means that this new scenario requires *additional* processes – which can be called *collaborative business processes* - besides the traditional ones, like project management, risk management, configuration management, verification and validation.

It is also important to mention that this list does not represent the processes that any 'traditional' SaaS provider should follow, but rather which processes should be taken into account when an ISP wants to collaborate with others.

**Table 1.** Processes for Collaborative SaaS

| PHASE | | PROCESSES | DESCRIPTIONS |
|---|---|---|---|
| Creation | | Business Opportunity characterization | Involves the identification and characterization of a new collaboration opportunity that will trigger the formation of a new SaaS collaboration. |
| | | Selection of performance indicators | To use the monitoring data to the partner selection. The performance indicators to be used in the monitoring must to be defined by the SaaS collaboration group. |
| | | Partner Search | Identification of potential partners, and their assessment and selection to be a SaaS provider. |
| | | Partner Selection | To select a SaaS partner are considered elements like technical, reliability indicators, preferences, consideration of collaboration history, external search and indicators based on past performance of enterprise members. |
| | | Negotiation & Risk Analysis | Set of management activities and supporting tools that will assist human actors (partners) during the negotiation processes and risk analysis assessment towards the SaaS collaboration constitution. |
| | | E-Contracting | Involves the final formulation and modeling of contracts and agreements as well as the contract signing process itself, before the SaaS collaboration can effectively be launched. |
| | | Collaboration Planning | Determination of a rough structure of the potential SaaS collaboration, identifying the required competencies and capacities, structure of the task to be performed as well as the organizational form of the SaaS collaboration and corresponding roles. |

**Table 1.** (*continued*)

| | | | |
|---|---|---|---|
| **Operation & Evolution** | **QoS Management Processes** | Trust Management | To promote the establishment of trust relationships among SaaS participants, including the assessment of the trust level among members. |
| | | Governance Management | Set of management activities and supporting tools that refer to the SaaS collaboration policy management, including internal operational rules and bylaws, for supporting the operation, regulation, and control of the network structure. |
| | | Measurement and analysis | To develop and sustain a measurement and analysis capability of the SaaS collaboration that is used to support management information needs. |
| | | Decision Support Management | Set of management activities and supporting tools for decision support, using monitoring key performance indicators in the SaaS collaboration. |
| | | Process and Product Assurance | Provides appropriate conformance guidance and objectively reviews the activities and SaaS work products of work efforts within the collaboration to ensure they comply with applicable laws, regulations, standards, organizational policies, business rules, process descriptions, and work procedures. |
| **Operation & Evolution** | **Strategic collaborative processes** | Strategic Management | Is formulating, implementing and evaluating functional decisions that will enable a SaaS collaboration to achieve its objectives, including supportive strategic programs to ensure the evolution of the collaboration. |
| | | Collaborative Customer Relationship Management | To manage the interaction of potential or actual SaaS customers with the collaboration, using enterprises data and information. |
| | | Organizational Innovation | To select and deploy incremental and innovative improvements that measurably improve the SaaS collaboration's processes and technologies |
| | | Collaborative Strategy | Investment in core strategies to improve the SaaS collaboration, develop provider competence and improve the general network. |
| | | Reconciling Individual and Collective Interests | Achieving individual organizational missions and maintaining an identity that is distinct from the collaborative and a collective interest. Achieving collaboration goals and maintaining accountability to collaborative partners. |
| | | Simulation | A simulation component should be available to generate scenarios reflecting the effects of the implementation of strategic decisions, evolving SaaS and collaboration. |

**Table 1.** (*continued*)

| | | | |
|---|---|---|---|
| **Operation & Evolution** | **Project Processes** | Collaborative Project Management | To establish and manage the project Collaborative SaaS and the involvement of the relevant stakeholders. |
| | | Requirements Management | To manage the requirements of the SaaS project's products and product components and to identify inconsistencies between those requirements and the project's plans and work products. |
| | | Requirements Development | To produce and analyze customer, product and product component requirements. |
| | | Risk Management | To identify potential problems before they occur so that risk-handling activities can be planned and invoked as needed across the life of the collaboration, product or project to mitigate adverse impacts on achieving objectives. |
| | | Quantitative Project Management | To quantitatively manage the project's defined process to achieve the project's established quality and process-performance objectives. |
| | | Partnership formation project | Negotiation of roles and responsibilities, deliverables and payments related with SaaS collaborative project |
| | | Resources Management | Plans and manages the acquisition, allocation, and reassignment of people and other resources needed to prepare, deploy, operate, and support the collaboration products and services. |
| | | Product Development Collaboration | Software product development phases. |
| **Operation & Evolution** | **Technical Processes** | Interoperability and Collaboration Technologies | To standardize the usage of a set of baseline tools, techniques and methods for interoperability and collaboration. |
| | | Technical Solutions | To design, develop, and implement solutions to the committed requirements between SaaS and collaboration. |
| | | System design and task partitioning | Modularity, interface definition and task interdependencies in a SaaS development. |
| | | Support Institutions Management | Set of management activities and supporting tools for identifying and integrating Support Institutions into the SaaS collaboration. |
| | | Performance Management | Set of management activities and supporting tools based-on a systematic procedure of planning, monitoring, rating and rewarding collaboration actors' performance based-on the definition of key performance indicators. |

Table 1. (*continued*)

| | | | |
|---|---|---|---|
| | | ICT Management | Set of management activities and supporting tools for managing a low cost, easy-to-access and operational ICT-infrastructure that will allow collaboration actors with different distributed/heterogeneous applications to communicate with each other transparently and seamlessly, in order to support collaboration (businesses) between them over the Internet. |
| Operation & Evolution | Administrative, Legal & Financial Processes | Collaboration Launching | To refine the SaaS collaboration plan and its governance principles, to formulate and model contracts and agreements and to put the collaboration into operation. |
| | | Collaboration Agreement | To set up the terms in which the collaboration within the enterprise takes place as well as the management of throughout the whole life of a collaboration. |
| | | Marketing Management | Set of management activities and supporting tools that will support the strategic formulation process, including the marketing and branding activities, for promoting the enterprise competencies among its potential SaaS members and potential SaaS customers. |
| | | Financial Management | It is about planning income and expenditure, and making decisions that will enable the enterprises survive financially. |
| | | Accounting Management | Set of management activities and supporting tools based-on accounting procedures to guarantee the enterprise financial health and ensure the effective, efficient and equitable use of the resources. |
| | | Value system Information Management | Set of management activities and supporting tools that will provide features for supporting and handling both, material and immaterial values, within the collaboration. |
| | | IPR Management | (Intellectual Property Rights) to clarify and agree the terms of the Intellectual Property Rights within the collaboration. |
| Dissolution | | Collaboration inheritance | This task comprises the management of inheritance information after collaboration dissolution. |
| | | Partners assessment | Is the final collaboration partners' assessment results. Sharing the analysis results is dependent on the network and the collaboration rules and practices. |
| | | Checking contract | Finalization the collaboration contract terms. |
| | | Security access cancellation | Finalization the access between the enterprises collaboration. |
| | | Legal issues | To finish the legal issues on the use of virtual companies (with Collaborative SaaS), since they imply cooperation agreements and might restrain concurrence between partners and or between these and third parties. |

# 4    Conclusions

This paper has described the results of an ongoing work, presenting a systematic literature review (SLR) on collaborative processes. Its essential goal was to provide a preliminary but comprehensive single and categorized list of processes to companies that are interested to collaborate to provide a more aggregated services solution within a SOA/SaaS scenario. On the other hand, and at this point of this research, it does not represent a list of "new" processes. Instead, it collects and provides some formalization of results from other isolated initiatives that somehow have tacked some forms of collaboration among companies.

This SLR about collaborative processes is part of a wider research, which aims at devising at the end, on top of existing software processes improvement reference models, one model devoted to and that can guide SaaS providers to work collaboratively.

Considering the essentially exploratory characteristic of this research and hence the relatively novelty of the envisaged collaborative scenario tackled in this paper, the SLR could only be carried out over state-of-the-art works. Very few initiatives with some equivalence with the so-called "collaborative SaaS" concept were found out in practice. In these cases, it could be observed that companies do that in an ad-hoc way, very much based on trust and on knowledge or relationships with previously known companies. Yet, they apply the same project management practices indicated in the classical reference models, and nothing grounded on a more solid foundation that considers SaaS in a more ample mode.

The collaborative processes that were elicited through this research should be taken as a *complementary* list of processes related to the other ones presented in reference models like CMMI and ISO15504. This means that such processes are additional actions that should be considered when SaaS providers want to work collaboratively to offer more valuable SOA/SaaS-based solutions instead of a mere group of individual / isolated services that should be further composed at the client side. This scenario leverages new and sustainable business models for SMEs of SOA/SaaS software providers.

Working collaboratively is not just a wish. Instead, it is a long process, of diverse natures and levels of impact. Thus, one of the most important usages of this list is to give awareness to SaaS providers about the impact on their processes. Therefore, they should be prepared for that, which is not trivial at all as this represents even still more processes to be coped with besides the 'traditional' ones.

SaaS itself and Collaborative SaaS are new areas, and more solid supporting theoretical foundations are required. For instance, it could be also realized that the elicited processes have different levels of complexity and scope if they want to be introduced in the daily life of those companies, which may even lead to think about adapting existing maturity models for that.

The provided list of processes related to collaboration has been verified only via a bibliography analysis. As such, next main short-term step refers to a validation of this close to a community of specialists (via the *Expert Panel* methodological technique). Yet, adequate practices to be associated to each process are currently being researched in order to provide a more concrete guidance to adopt the processes. ISO capability and SOA models will be used as a basis for.

# References

1. Gulati, R., Nohria, N., Zaheer, A.: Strategic Networks. In: Hahn, D., Taylor, B. (eds.) Strategische Unternehmungsplanung - Strategische Unternehmungsführung, pp. 293–309. Springer, Heidelberg (2006)
2. Camarinha-Matos, L.M., Afsarmanesh, H., Ollus, M.: Virtual Organizations - Systems and Practices, 340 pages. EUA, Springer (2005)
3. ABES, Brazilian Software Market - Overview and Trends 2010, Brazilian Association of Software Companies, p. 1–42 (2010) (in Portuguese)
4. Velte, A.T., Velte, T.J., Elsenpeter, R.: Cloud Computing - A pratical approach, 334 pages. The McGraw Hill, United States of America (2010)
5. Hongqi, L., Zhuang, W.: Research on Distributed Architecture Based on SOA. In: International Conference on Communication Software and Networks, ICCSN 2009, pp. 670–674 (2009)
6. Rabelo, R.: Advanced Collaborative Business Ict Infrastructures. In: Methods and Tools for Collaborative Networked Organizations, pp. 337–370. Springer (2008)
7. Zhiqiang, N.: Credibility evaluation of SaaS tenants. In: 2010 3rd International Conference on Advanced Computer Theory and Engineering (ICACTE), pp. V4-488–V4-491 (2010)
8. Laplante, P.A., Zhang, J., Voas, J.: What's in a Name? Distinguishing between SaaS and SOA. IT Professional 10(3), 46–50 (2008)
9. Junjie, P.: Comparison of Several Cloud Computing Platforms. In: Information Science and Engineering (ISISE), China, pp. 23–27 (2009)
10. Cancian, M.H., Hauck, J.C.R., von Wangenheim, C.G., Rabelo, R.J.: Discovering Software Process and Product Quality Criteria in Software as a Service. In: The 11th International Conf. Product Focused Software Develop. Ireland, pp. 95–103 (2010)
11. Cancian, M.H., Rabelo, R.J., von Wangenheim, C.G.: Supporting Software Services' Trustworthiness in Collaborative Networks. In: Camarinha-Matos, L.M., Boucher, X., Afsarmanesh, H. (eds.) PRO-VE 2010. IFIP AICT, vol. 336, pp. 672–684. Springer, Heidelberg (2010)
12. Camarinha-Matos, L., Afsarmanesh, H.: The Emerging Discipline of Collaborative Networks. In: Virtual Enterprises and Collaborative Networks. IFIP, vol. 149, pp. 3–16. Springer, Boston (2004)
13. Rabelo, R., Baldo, F., Tramontin, R., Pereira-Klen, A., Klen, E., Camarinha-Matos, L.: Smart Configuration of Dynamic Virtual Enterprises. In: Virtual Enterprises and Collaborative Networks, pp. 193–204. Springer, Boston (2004)
14. Kitchenham, B.: Guidelines for performing Systematic Literature Reviews in Software Engineering. EBSE Technical Report K, University, 87 pages (2007)
15. Alonso, J., Martínez de Soria, I., Orue-Echevarria, L., Vergara, M.: Enterprise Collaboration Maturity Model (ECMM): Preliminary Definition and Future Challenges. In: Enterprise Interoperability IV, pp. 429–438. Springer, London (2010)
16. Soria, I.M.d., Alonso, J., Orue-Echevarria, L., Vergara, M.: Developing an Enterprise Collaboration Maturity Model: Research Challenges and Future Directions. In: The 15th International Conference on Concurrent Enterprising 2009. The Netherlands, pp. 89–103 (2009)
17. Santanen, E., Kolfschoten, G., Golla, K.: The Collaboration Engineering Maturity Model. In: Proceedings of the 39th Annual Hawaii International Conference on System Sciences, vol. 01, pp. 16–26. IEEE Computer Society (2006)

18. Fraser, P., Farrukh, C., Gregory, M.: Managing product development collaborations—a process maturity approach. Proceedings of the Institution of Mechanical Engineers Part B Journal of Engineering Manufacture, 1499–1519 (2003)
19. Fraser, P., Gregory, M.: A maturity grid approach to the assessment of product development collaborations. In: 9th International Product Development Management Conference, Sophia Antipolis, France, pp. 28–36 (2002)
20. Magdaleno, A.M., Araujo, R.M.d., Borges, M.R.S.: Designing Collaborative Processes. In: Business Process Management Workshops, pp. 156–168 (2007)
21. Thomson, A.M., Perry, J.L.: Collaboration Processes: Inside the Black Box. Public Administration Review 66, 20–32 (2006)
22. Romero, D., Galeano, N., Molina, A.: VO breeding environments value systems, business models and governance rules. In: Methods and Tools for Collaborative Networked Organizations, pp. 69–90. Springer (2008)
23. Camarinha-Matos, L., Afsarmanesh, H., Ollus, M.: Methods and Tools for Collaborative Networked Organizations, 532 pages. Springer Publishing Company, Incorporated (2008)
24. SEI, Software Engineering Institute (SEI) - CMMI for Development (CMMI-DEV). In Technical Report CMU/SEI-2006-TR-008, V. 1.2, Editor, Carnegie Mellon University / Software Engineering Institute, Pittsburgh, 198 pages (2006)

# Identifying the Reasons Why Companies Abandon Collaborative Networks

Rolando Vargas Vallejos, Paulo Fernando Pinto Barcellos,
Margareth Rodrigues de Carvalho Borella, and Rosimeri Machado

University of Caxias do Sul, PPGA, Francisco Getúlio Vargas 1130, 95070-560,
Caxias do Sul, RS, Brazil
{rvvallej,pfpbarce,mrcborel}@ucs.br,
{rosimeri.machado}@ponzoni.com.br

**Abstract.** The present work identified possible factors that led some collaborative network organizations to close. The case study was based on experiences obtained in networks that took part of the Collaborative Network Program of the State of Rio Grande do Sul (Brazil). One of the Program creators, managers, consultants and entrepreneurs of six networks that broke down were interviewed based on a semi-structured instrument. The analysis of the Collaborative Network method indicated that important factors could motivate the failure of networks, which were validated with the integrated model of alliance failure proposed by Park and Ungson [1]. The article ends by suggesting some improvements in the Collaborative Network Program of the State of Rio Grande do Sul to become more efficient and contribute to the network success.

**Keywords:** Collaborative Network Organization, Collaborative Network Method, Network Failure.

## 1 Introduction

The collaborative network model of cooperating to compete started with the studies of Brandenburger and Stuart [2] and Brandenburger and Nalebuff [3] who popularized the term "coopetition" [4]. Porter [5] who has systemized competition strategies of individual companies, also considers the strategy of cooperation as an alternative to compete and develop a competitive advantage.

There are several studies of Collaborative Networks Organizations (CNOs) success in the State of Rio Grande do Sul [6] and [7], among others. However, few studies describe the failures of Collaborative Networks. For this reason, this paper aims at contributing to the development and/or improvement of methods and practices to be used for the success of future Collaborative Networks.

The Collaborative Network Program of the State of Rio Grande do Sul (CNPRS) is an initiative of the Government in order to stimulate small and medium enterprises to become more competitive. The Program begun in 2000 and, therefore, it is important to identify the reasons why companies, which integrate collaborative networks,

L.M. Camarinha-Matos, L. Xu, and H. Afsarmanesh (Eds.): PRO-VE 2012, IFIP AICT 380, pp. 385–394, 2012.
© IFIP International Federation for Information Processing 2012

abandon them. This identification may help to create new successful CNOs, and especially to support the existing ones. The research question therefore is: which are the reasons why enterprises that belong to CNPRS give it up?

## 2    Failures in Collaborative Network Organizations: Theoretical Background

In the last two decades, a special attention has been paid to CNOs, which are formed by several entities (e.g., organizations and specialists) that are autonomous, geographically distributed, and heterogeneous in terms of their operating environment, culture, social capital, and goals. These entities collaborate with each other to achieve common goals, and their interactions are supported by Information and Communication Technology (ICT) [8]. Under an economic perspective, a network organization may be an answer to the competitive pressure over individual enterprises to increase their competitiveness in production, new products development and launching, new technologies access, and knowledge share among suppliers, customers and competitors [9].

A large number of research projects involving CNOs are carried out worldwide, and a growing number of practical cases have been reported. Camarinha-Matos and Afsarmanesh [10] have raised the need for modeling to understand, manage, simulate, and predict the behavior of CNOs.

The concept of breeding environment has emerged as the necessary context to support the effective creation of CNOs. Shortly, Virtual organization Breeding Environment (VBE) is an association of organizations and their related supporting institutions, adhering to a long-term cooperation agreement, and adopting common operating principles and infrastructure. The target of this association is the preparation of its members and the increase of their chances to collaborate in potential Virtual Organizations [11].

All of these aspects have been discussed by studies that approach CNOs success. This study, however, refers to causes that lead to unsuccessful CNOs. According to the Park and Ungson Model [1], problems with trust, reputation and commitment among network members undermine the network desired objectives such as equity, efficiency and adaptation, leading to failure (Figure 1).

Others factors have been reported as contributors to the network failure:

- the growing number of members that increases the conflict risk, disrupting the CNO [12];
- CNO institutional consolidation problems leading to cognitive, social and political blocking, as well as attitudes that do not generate new benefits to the network members [13];
- no achievement of common objectives centered on knowledge acquisition, learning, cost reduction, gains of scale, adaptation to change, risk decreasing, assets integration, and training [14].

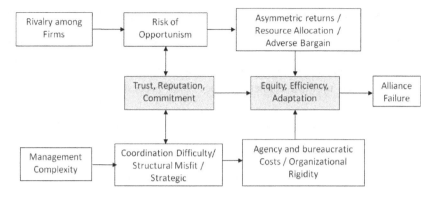

**Fig. 1.** An Integrated model of Alliance Failure

# 3    Collaborative Networks in the State of Rio Grande do Sul

The State of Rio Grande do Sul, the southernmost state in Brazil, bordering with Argentina and Uruguay, seeking to incorporate the development of small and medium size enterprises as an alternative to foster the state's economy, is encouraging the building of organizational networks since the year 2000.

The State, through the Development and International Affairs Department (SEDAI), established a Collaborative Network Program, emphasizing the associative culture among small businesses that operate in various segments such as industry, commerce, service, agribusiness, and, recently, the third sector. The program aims at "... promoting the formation of collaborative networks joining business strategies, mutual cooperation between enterprises and institutions in order to establish integration among the State and the various sectors of the society" [15].

The effective operation of the program is based on a specific method developed by SEDAI, which is transferred to universities. The universities are the partner institutions that hold the knowledge about the peculiarities of each region and play the role of liaison between the public and private sector. The university has a program coordinator and is responsible for the selection of consultants who are qualified according to the program method. These consultants are responsible for identifying networking opportunities, diagnosing the existence of common ground among business, and assisting in actions planning to build collaborative networks.

The working method is the same for any sector, and the developed networks under this design process present the same organization strategy and tools. The steps shown in Figure 2 form the SEDAI Collaborative Network method [15].

Networks formed by the Collaborative Network method are structured to allow CNO members to participate in the network activities through the board, councils, and working committees. CNO governance responsibilities are split as follows:

**General Members Meeting.** It is the forum where proposals that involve the interests of the network are approved or disapproved. The process is democratic, where every member has one vote, regardless of the company size. According to the established rules, each network requires a minimum quorum of participants to validate the decisions.

**Board.** Responsible for developing the statute, the code of ethics, operational procedures, and legal rules to represent the network interests. The board is elected by majority vote. Each network defines the succession process in accordance with its legal rules.

**Councils.** Play the role of assisting the board in order to reach network interests, and are usually formed by boards of directors, ethics and taxation. Councils are also elected by majority vote.

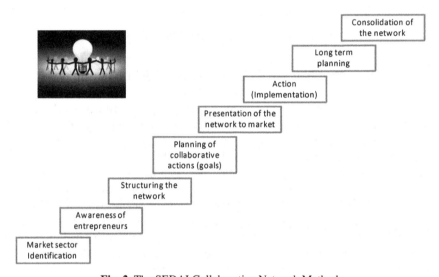

**Fig. 2.** The SEDAI Collaborative Network Method

**Manager/Executive.** (Only present in some networks) is usually a professional hired by the network to fulfil the role of reconciling members' interests, in order to implement strategies approved by general members meetings, as well as to deal with the network routines.

**Staff.** Operational issues related to the network running.

**Coordinators.** Members are responsible for strategic committees, which play an active role. The Coordinator appointment is due to member's leadership and to his identification with the area of each committee activity.

**Strategic Committees.** Are formed by members whose roles in the committee must fit their profiles. Strategic committees are the base of collaborative networks operation and performance in accordance with the SEDAI Collaborative Networks method. In general, committees are divided into four activity areas: Marketing, Innovation, Expansion and Negotiation. Committees have autonomy to develop proposals of activities to be implemented by the CNO. The general members meeting is the adequate forum where such propositions are approved.

# 4    The Research Method

This is a descriptive study based on multiple cases, where one of the program creators and managers, one senior consultant and one program coordinator of the CNPRS were interviewed, also twelve entrepreneurs of six collaborative networks located in the region of Caxias do Sul, which became extinct, were interviewed. These collaborative networks were constituted through the SEDAI Collaborative Network method. The University of Caxias do Sul (UCS) was the Program partner university.

The first phase of this study involves the analysis of the senior consultant' interview, showing the relevant and probable causes that contributed to the failure of these networks, validated with the UCS Program coordinator and one of the program creators and managers. In the second phase, those factors that contributed to the networks failure were identified from the content analysis of semi-structured interviews with twelve entrepreneurs. The respondents were the companies' owners, former members of six collaborative networks. Two companies were interviewed in each of the studied networks (Furniture, Wine and Grape, Non-Governmental Organizations, Footwear, Glazing and Electronic Security Equipment sectors).

The Collaborative Network method was analyzed, and important factors that could motivate the failure of those networks were identified. Finally, those identified factors were validated with the integrated model of alliance failure proposed by Park & Ungson [1].

# 5    Identifying the Failures Factors of Rio Grande do Sul CNO's

Factors blamed for CNOs failure in the state of Rio Grande do Sul can be divided into two groups according to: (1) consultants' point of view, and (2) entrepreneurs' point of view.

## 5.1    Consultant's Point of View

The analysis of the consultants' interviews has identified factors that may explain the reason for some failures occurred within CNPRS. These factors were validated with the UCS Program coordinator and one of the program creators and managers of the CNPRS, and can be classified in two main groups, one inside and the other outside the CNO. Factors are presented in Figure 3.

**Inside CNO Factors.** There are specific characteristics of the CNO that have proven to be relevant for the failure or success of the network itself. Among them, the following factors can be mentioned:

*The CNO president's profile.* Entrepreneurs should be trained to develop leadership and conflict management. They must be trained to develop better network governance.

*Attitudes and behaviors as an outcome of participants' mind models.* When there is a concentration of less flexible participants in the group their attitudes and behaviors tend to a radical positioning, and a group mind model is difficult to be built.

*Trust among CNO participants.* This is a mandatory factor to explain CNOs failure. Trust absence is a barrier to a joint work of the participants as a sole entity.

*The need for several professionals in the CNO.* The lack of professionals in the CNO can erode trust among participants leading to an inadequate internal environment, which will end up by the network organization failure.

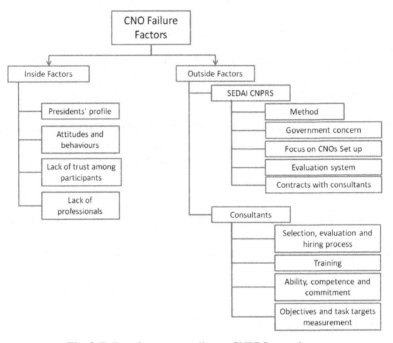

**Fig. 3.** Failure factors according to CNPRS consultants

**Outside CNO Factors.** These are factors found outside the network organization. Among important factors the following ones can be considered:

*The method adopted by SEDAI.* The SEDAI Collaborative Networks method is a robust one. However, some points call for attention according to the experience acquired along time by the consultants from the University of Caxias do Sul involved in CNOs support. Some of these concerns are referred in the following items.

*Government concern with CNPRS.* From the Government side, the CNPRS is not sustainable since the financial support from the Government to the program is subject to break offs, generating troubles to partner universities which have to maintain an operational structure to keep the project running.

*CNPRS consultants' selection, evaluation, and hiring process.* In the beginning of the CNPRS, the consultant selection process was based on interviews with several people such as the university extension program director, the CNPRS coordinator, and a psychologist. However, that process has changed along the years. Right now, it is not a rigorous process anymore.

*CNPRS consultants training.* There was a well-structured training program for the consultants but its duration time was being reduced gradually. Nowadays, that procedure is just past.

*CNPRS consultants' ability, competence, and commitment.* The consultant role is basic for the network organization start up and initial footsteps. The development of adequate attitudes and behavior by consultants is required for their commitment to the program. The consultant works in the CNPRS forefront. Thus, the personal factor is relevant for the consultant development but it is not considered by the SEDAI method.

*CNPRS consultants' main objectives and task targets measurement.* Usually consultants are measured by the quantity of CNOs, which are created without any concern with the quality of the resulting network organizations.

*Type and duration time of the CNPRS contract with consultants.* Another aspect to negatively impact on consultants' motivation is the type of the contract they are submitted to, under a clause of limited duration, and an explicit expiration date.

*CNPRS focus on CNOs set up.* The SEDAI method does not foresee the network organization follow up by consultants; the focus is on the CNO set up.

*CNPRS evaluation system.* The CNPRS evaluation is done through an executive summary made by the program supervision – the partner university – that is sent to SEDAI. The success factor is not considered.

## 5.2    Entrepreneur's Point of View

Empirical results of twelve interviewed entrepreneurs of six extinct collaborative networks located in the region of Caxias do Sul are represented in Figure 4. These aspects can be considered as possible variables to drive the decision of abandoning their networks.

Based on the content analysis, the conclusion that the entrepreneurs' decision of abandoning the collaborative network is related with the particular culture of each network member, according to his own way to conduct his business, was reached to. Structural aspects are important in providing network sustainability; however, structural discrepancies among network members make it difficult to establish a common culture in the collaborative network.

Some respondents' comments show the coexistence of individual and network iteration causes that could have influenced the decision to leave their networks, as shown below:

"... one was leaving after the other...", "... there were complaints about the travel time for the meetings ...","" ... some members were participating only to learn how other companies were working and did not share anything ...", "... when only three companies remained in the CNO, we decided to close the network, finally ..." (Respondent of the Furniture Industry Network).

"...I was the youngest member of the network, the others were older than me and they had more experience with the grape business ...", "... everyone distrusted of what I said ...", "... they thought that my ideas were too modern ...","... with the members' lack of trust, I decided to leave the network ..." (Respondent of the Wine and Grape Industry Network).

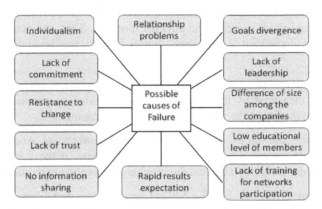

**Fig. 4.** Reasons for abandoning CNOs according to Entrepreneurs

## 6    Conclusions

The analysis of the interviews with one of the CNPRS creators and managers, consultants and entrepreneurs indicate that CNOs that are being developed in industrial districts have some advantage – as, for instance, a common business culture and a sense of community – when compared to networked organizations that are geographically spread. It is a belief that despite being geographically concentrated in a same place CNOs should be prior prepared to form alliances.

Considering the Park and Ungson Model, it is possible to say that the research shows the "rivalry among firms" and the "management complexity". It was detected from the interviews that those firms that fail to consolidate the CNO do not build trust, reputation, and commitment. For that reason, equity, efficiency and adaptation cannot be developed. To minimize this situation for the future, in the particular case of SEDAI Collaborative Network method, improvements are suggested, having in mind some method phases and activities.

In the present work, CNOs' inside and outside possible failure factors are differentiated. Among the internal factors, a lack of structure and preparation to allow network participants better prepare for developing trust, attitudes and the necessary behaviors to collaborate were detected. Even though, in the Collaborative Network method the following steps are considered: (1) network structuring, (2) long term planning (that is questioned by the consultants), and (3) network consolidation. These steps should be strengthened because the interviewed entrepreneurs have raised questions like: lack of commitment, individualism, resistance to change, lack of trust, no information sharing, and relationship problems. Other important inside CNO factor is the qualification of the CNO president and its professionals, pointed out by the consultants as preparedness of the president and lack of professionals, and by the entrepreneurs as lack of leadership and low educational level of CNO members. Furthermore, entrepreneurs should be trained to develop leadership and conflict management. Some of them will be a CNO president in the future. Network success depends on entrepreneurs' commitment and management ability. Thus, they must be trained to develop the best network governance. Therefore, the creation of a new step in the SEDAI Collaborative Network method is suggested: qualification and preparation of CNOs presidents.

Considering the outside CNO factors, other contribution of the present work is the identification of the need for investing in the preparation and qualification of the CNPRS' consultants. In the beginning, the CNPRS Program included a structured consultants training but its duration time was increasingly reduced. Furthermore, the consultant qualification must be considered as one of the criteria for selection, evaluation and hiring processes. Thus, the creation of a new step in the SEDAI Collaborative Network method is suggested: qualification and training of consultants. From the Government side, the CNPRS needs to be supported constantly. The effectiveness of the CNPRS method will assure the future success of the network.

**Acknowledgments.** The University of Caxias do Sul is supporting this work.

# References

1. Park, S.H.E., Ungson, G.R.: Interfirm Rivalry and Managerial Complexity: A Conceptual Framework of Alliance Failure. Organization Science 12(1), 37–53 (2001)
2. Brandenburger, A.M.E., Stuart Jr., H.W.: Value-based Business strategy. Journal of Economics and Management Strategy 5(1), 5–24 (1996)
3. Brandenburger, A.M.E., Nalebuff, B.J.: Coopetition. Doubleday, New York (1996)
4. Rodrigues, L.C., Maccari, E.A.E., Riscarolli, V.: Structure and cooptation in organization network. Journal of Information Systems and Technology Management 4(2) (2007)
5. Porter, M.E.: On Competition. The Harvard Business Review Book Series (1998)
6. Vallejos, R.V., Lima, C., Varvakis, G.: A framework to create a virtual organisation breeding environment for small and medium enterprises. International Journal of Services and Operations Management 6, 335–351 (2010)
7. Barcellos, P.F.P., Galelli, A., Mueller, A., Reis, Z.C., Peretti, J.L.G.: Collaborative Networks: an innovative approach to enhance competitiveness of small firms in Brazil. In: Thoben, K.D., Pawar, K.S., Gonçalves, R. (eds.) Proceedings of the 14th International Conference on Concurrent Enterprising, ICE 2008, pp. 211–216 (2008)
8. Camarinha-Matos, L.M., Afsarmanesh, H.: Collaborative Networks: A new scientific discipline. Journal of Intelligent Manufacturing 16, 439–452 (2005)

9. Balestrin, A., Vargas, L.M., Fayard, P.: Criação de Conhecimento nas Redes de Cooperação Interorganizacional. Revista de Administração de Empresas 45(3), 52–64 (2005)
10. Camarinha-Matos, L.M., Afsarmanesh, H.: A framework for virtual organization creation in a breeding environment. Annual Reviews in Control 1(31), 119–135 (2007)
11. Castells, M.: A era da informação: economia, sociedade e cultura. Paz e Terra, São Paulo (1998)
12. Messner, D., Meyer-Stamer, J.: Governance and networks. In: Oliver, A., Ebers, M. (eds.) Networking Network Studies: an Analysis of Conceptual Configurations in the Study of Interorganizational Relationships. Organization Studies, vol. 19(4), pp. 549–583 (1998)
13. Pereira, B.A.D., Venturini, J.C., Wegner, D., Braga, A.L.: Desistência da Cooperação e Encerramento de Redes Interorganizacionais: em que momento essas abordagens se encontram? Revista de Administração e Inovação 7(1), 62–83 (2010)
14. Ebers, M.: Explaining interorganizational network forming. In: Ebers (ed.) The Formation of Inter-Organization Networks, Oxford (1997)
15. Secretaria do Desenvolvimento e Assuntos Internacionais do Rio Grande do Sul – SEDAI: Manual de Orientação dos Consultores do Programa Redes de Cooperação. Porto Alegre, RS, Brazil (2004)

# 14

## Collaboration Motivators II

# A Roadmap Focused on SMEs Decided to Participate in Collaborative Non-Hierarchical Networks

Beatriz Andrés and Raúl Poler

Research Centre on Production Management and Engineering (CIGIP),
Universitat Politècnica de València (UPV). Plaza Ferrándiz y Carbonell, 2, 03801 Alcoy, Spain
{Beaanna,rpoler}@cigip.upv.es

**Abstract.** The importance of collaboration has increased in supply networks; thus, the number of so called non-hierarchical manufacturing networks (NHN) has also increased. A roadmap to help SMEs to participate and create collaborative non-hierarchical networks is developed. Specifically, the methodology carried out in the *NHNmap* is described along the paper.

**Keywords:** roadmap, collaboration, non-hierarchical networks, SMEs.

## 1 Introduction

In recent years, researchers from different disciplines have shown a growing interest study in strengths of collaborative manufacturing networks along dynamic environments. As a result the concept of Non-Hierarchical Manufacturing Network (NHN) has emerged, changing from centralised (hierarchical network, HN) to decentralised decision making approaches. Collaborative participation requires greater exchanges of information, responsibilities sharing and partners' commitment as a whole. In collaborative NHN, SMEs are actively involved in network decision-making and problems are tackled together. NHN take into account the objectives of all the partners by equally considering all networked nodes [1].

Despite the growing interest posed in NHN, so far there is no roadmap that enables SMEs following common guidelines to participate or/and create collaborative NHN (section 2). In light of this, to carry out the roadmap, presented below, we have sought inspiration in a number of examples of roadmaps [2][3][4]. However, the proposed roadmap has developed its own and innovative procedure to help SMEs to participate in collaborative environments within a NHN (section 3).

## 2 Roadmap Literature Overview

According to [5] a roadmap is defined as the view of a group of how to get where they want to go or, achieve their desired objective and helps the group to ensure that the capacities to achieve their goals are in right place and time. Another definition is the roadmapping concept as the learning process and a communication tool for the

L.M. Camarinha-Matos, L. Xu, and H. Afsarmanesh (Eds.): PRO-VE 2012, IFIP AICT 380, pp. 397–407, 2012.
© IFIP International Federation for Information Processing 2012

group. [6] attempt to bring some common definition to roadmaps and roadmapping processes to unify the broad scope of roadmap objectives and uses.

Numerous gains are derived from developing roadmaps in collaborative contexts [6]: greater product flexibility, better quality, quickly solve technical problems, identify areas with high potential promise, improve collaboration of activities and resources in complex and uncertain environments, develop long-term sustainable relationships capable of adapting to changes in broader market demands, are few examples.

Various types of roadmaps, with rather different scopes and level of generality, can be considered [2]: (i) science and research, (ii) cross-industry, (iii) industry, (iv) technology, (v) product, (vi) product-technology and (vii) project and issue roadmaps.

Different frameworks and roadmaps have been developed in order to tackle problems when establishing collaborative relationships among networked SMEs.

First records of roadmapping application date back to 1980s at Motorola, to support technology planning to integrate markets, products and technologies [7]. Technology roadmaps became popular as an approach to strategic planning for the future of technology in different sectors [2]. A multidisciplinary approach involving the perspectives of technology is provided by [8] in order to deal with collaboration-based information technology solutions. In the same research line, [9] also propose a method of technology roadmapping.

Service orientation provides an architectural pattern able to cope with the needs of integrated and distributed collaborative solutions. [10] develop a roadmap into a major adoption of SOA to support agile reconfigurable supply chains. Furthermore, [11] propose a framework based on web service system to offer interoperability among distributed participants in a collaborative network (CN), and their management information systems, and provides the appropriate support to all necessary decision-making steps towards the attainment of the network strategic common goals.

Interoperability problem in CNs is further addressed in the literature through roadmapping. A roadmap is proposed by [12] to deal with interoperability of enterprise applications and software. Another example is the roadmap developing the Unified Enterprise Modelling Language (UEML) as a result of the work of [13]. In order to allow the integration of systems and interoperability to operate in virtual enterprises, [14] design a strategic roadmap. Related with interoperability and sharing information, [15] present a preliminary version of a roadmap towards defining a standard to be used in a collaborative knowledge-based platform for information and knowledge sharing.

Furthermore, the innovation view in CNs is also addressed through roadmapping. In the research of inter-firm task partitioning, resource sharing activities and capability development behaviours, [16] contribute providing a roadmap in networked product innovation contexts. To deal with the implementation and evaluation for facilitating innovation in collaborative environments, [17] report another roadmap.

Roadmapping allows bringing together people from different parts of the CN, giving an opportunity to share information and perspectives and providing a vehicle for holistic consideration of problems, opportunities and new ideas [18]. An example of a research agenda for CNs is given by the *VOmap* roadmap for advanced virtual organizations [2]. VOmap aims at identifying the key research challenges needed to fulfil the vision for the European initiative on dynamic collaborative VOs. Thus, the Reference Model for COllaborative Networks (ARCON) [19] is focused on a modelling approach considering multiple modelling perspectives: environment characteristics, life cycle and modelling in CNs. Furthermore, [20] propose a collaborative network approach to develop an integrated business service concept in VO context. With the purpose of identifying what component capabilities possess SMEs, what system capabilities are required and what skills must be developed to establish collaboration within a network, it is also proposed a roadmap [21]. A roadmapping initiative is introduced by [22] to address a strategic research plan covering the social, organizational, and technological perspectives in CNs. In order to jointly move towards integrated business solutions as well as a culture shift towards long-term trusted relationships, [23] provides the supply chain Integration Roadmap Organization developed both in-house and among supply chain partners. Continuing with the intra-/inter-organizational research, [24] address two kinds of behaviour, Individual Collaborative Behaviour and Network Collective Behaviour, and introduce an approach to compare networked partners in order to identify conflicts, select the best-fit collaborative members and assign roles and rights in CNs.

In order to properly design organizational structures, GloNet project matches SMEs needs and emerging models identified in the disciplines of collaborative networks [25]. Finally, [26] provide a method useful for any SME who does not have advanced knowledge of groupware and who needs collaborative modelling tools.

The literature review carried out enlighten that the developed roadmaps and frameworks deal with collaborative problems focused on technology, interoperability, services oriented, VO, modelling, information and knowledge sharing, innovation, measurement of collaboration, partners identification, alignment, collaborative behaviour, etc. Consequently, it is needed to develop a specific roadmap to the deal with the collaborative situation in NHN. Contrariwise the roadmaps and frameworks provided in the literature, the roadmap proposed in this paper provides a migration path between the current state of SMEs belonging to non-collaborative networks, and the long-term vision to achieve collaborative relationships in NHN, together with the linkages between layers, in a form that is flexible enough to be updated over time.

## 3    NHNmap Vision

When SMEs decide to participate in collaborative NHN, they have to deal with a series of problems arising from inter-organizational relationships. To do this, a generic roadmap is proposed, whatever the sector to which the NHN belong, in order to allow decision makers to identify problems concerning the establishment of collaboration in decentralised decision models, what characterises NHN.

The developed roadmap –*NHNmap*– identifies the weaknesses that arise in SMEs when decide to participate in collaborative NHN. Besides, *NHNmap* help SMEs to identify proper solutions to overcome the weaknesses derived from collaborative relationships characterised by decentralised decision making. To sum up, NHNmap provides the necessary research, in SMEs, to develop collaborative solutions for dealing with problems derived from NHN participation/formation.

The provided roadmap aims to (i) identify multiple perspectives and abstraction levels of collaborative problems, (ii) identify the problem design possibilities, (iii) analyse models, guidelines and tools (M/G/T) to cope with collaboration and (iv) design integrated and aligned solutions for collaborative NHN partners.

The *NHNmap* considers two important elements: the SMEs initial features when belonging to *non-collaborative NHN* and the SME desired vision in *collaborative NHN*. Figure 1 represents the *NHNmap* goal, which develops a guide that enables SMEs to consider all transitional decisions necessary to achieve the desired future state of collaborative NHN.

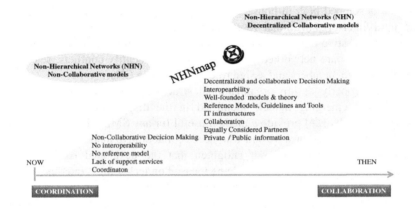

**Fig. 1.** NHNmap goal. Collaborative Non-Hierarchical Networks → TO BE and AS IS.

Collaborative NHN have been less studied due to the complexity of its structure. SMEs participation in collaborative NHN involves a change of environment, decision making and implementation processes regarding the traditional networks based on centralised decision systems. With the appearance of NHN it appears the need to lay the groundwork for new research on (i) collaborative NHN formation and (ii) SMEs needs when establishing collaborative relationships between partners belonging to a NHN, in order to make more efficient networks.

Not all the problems arising from the collaborative processes among partners of the same network are fully considered in the proposed roadmap. However, problems that significantly influence in establishing collaboration between partners are contemplated to achieve the desired collaborative NHN.

Therefore, by considering the statements above, *NHNmap* vision is expressed as:

In the future, most companies will be part of collaborative networks characterised by decentralised decision making, such as NHN, and dynamic networks capable of rapid response to change market conditions. *NHNmap* will cover:

- Decentralised and collaborative decision making.
- Training and participation of partners in order to belong to collaborative NHN.

- Interoperability in communications and collaborative infrastructures (IT/IS).
- Standardization and jointly business process.
- Distinction between private and public information.
- Well founded collaborative network models, guidelines and reference tools.
- Equally considered members.
- Management principles tailored to collaborative NHN behaviours.
- Collaboration mechanisms to deal with decentralized decision making.

Collaborative participation in NHN enables SMEs to create new opportunities, becoming more competitive and innovative, which implies greater risk-taking.

The contribution of the proposed roadmap is to allow SMEs to overcome the adaptation path for belonging to collaborative NHN.

NHNmap is structured from 4 focus areas: (i) collaboration establishment, (ii) proposition of M/G/T to overcome problems in collaborative processes, (iii) identification of IT/SI to support collaborative processes and decentralised decision models and (iv) performance evaluation of collaborative NHN participation.

Based on [5] many reasons to establish the NHNmap are provided below:

- NHNmap allows an orderly and planned evolution from *non-collaborative NHN* to *collaborative NHN*.
- NHNmap helps to establish objectives and strategies aligned with collaborative NHN partners.
- NHNmap provides a guide for NHN members, enabling partners to recognize and act on events that require changes of direction towards belonging to a collaborative NHN.
- NHNmap reveals gaps on SMEs capabilities when they want to take part in a collaborative NHN. Regarding to technology, decision making and culture.
- NHNmap allows identifying models, guidelines and tools to apply the proper solution in SMEs.
- NHNmap allows decision makers to agree and communicate research, technology and innovation plans to NHN collaborative members.
- NHNmap helps to identify priority investments in collaborative SMEs.

## 4    NHNmap Phases

Given the literature review carried out in section 2, no collaborative framework to identify the SMEs needs when deciding to participate in collaborative NHN has been already generated. In light of this, in this section the NHNmap is provided.

The developed roadmap helps SMEs, which have decided to participate in collaborative processes within a NHN, to start establishing decentralised collaborative relationships. NHNmap is multi-layered at network level and SMEs level (local level), reflecting the integration of technology, processes and collaborative perspectives among SMEs, including internal and external sources and supporting communication across partners and network boundaries. The adopted structure for defining the phases and sub-phases of the roadmap is important, reflecting fundamental aspects of the collaborative NHN and issues being considered.

Before implementing the NHNmap, all the processes that take place within the decentralised collaborative network must be identified for each SME.

*NHNmap* allow SMEs to align the businesses with collaborative networked partners and propose a set of common objectives, joint leadership, information sharing, processes adaptability to collaborative non-hierarchical networks, assessment and continuous reviewing results through a measurement system.

According to figure 2, the provided roadmap, *NHNmap*, consists of ten phases.

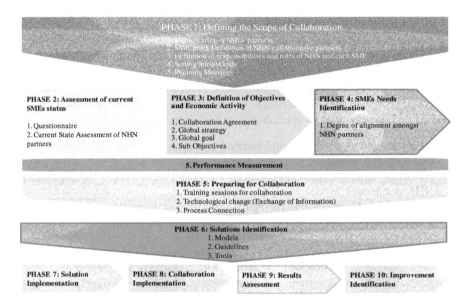

**Fig. 2.** NHNmap: roadmap to achieve collaborative non-hierarchical manufacturing networks

Each phase is briefly developed and explained next.

*PHASE 1: Defining the scope of collaboration.* The contact among SMEs, that decide to participate in collaborative NHN, is initiated. Furthermore, this phase allows networked partners to define the scope of collaboration. All NHN members are identified and defined in terms of the processes performed in the NHN: (i) procurement, (ii) production, (iii) distribution and (iv) marketing and sales. The degree of collaboration of each SME is also identified. After that, responsibilities, roles and initial objectives of each SME in the collaborative NHN are defined. A consultant manager can be designed in order to monitoring the *NHNmap* sequence. Phase 1 allows collaborative partners establishing meetings in each roadmap phase to collect information, undertake further stages and collect feedbacks from each partner.

*PHASE 2: Assessment of Current SMEs Status.* The current status of each SME, willing to participate in collaborative NHN, is evaluated. Before starting the activity in the collaborative NHN, networked partners assess their business needs, values, culture, strategies and trading partner relationships in order to implement best practices. After this phase, networked SMEs exactly know whether they are ready to link its activities in a collaborative network characterised by decentralised decision making. Thus, a questionnaire must be filled for identifying SME areas that need immediate attention, in order to participate in a collaborative NHN. Results achieved in phase 2 helps NHN partners to recognize their status and identify where change is needed to successfully implement collaborative partnerships in NHN.

*PHASE 3: Definition of Objectives and Economic Activity.* The objectives and economic activity, to carry out in the collaborative NHN, are defined. At the end of this phase, SMEs are able to define the objectives and the economic activity to perform within the collaborative NHN. The collaboration agreement is firstly defined to enable collaborative nodes following instructions and rules for governing the relationship among NHN members. After defining the collaboration agreement the global strategy is defined; then, the global objective is determined to describe the purpose of economic activity. The global objective consists of different sub-objectives that have to be achieved by SMEs in order to reach the activity at the defined network level. For better collaborative network participation, the performance measurement system (PMS) is designed. The elements of the performance measurement must be based on the objectives, strategies, critical success factors and key performance indicators (KPIs) at different levels of the network.

*PHASE 4: SMEs Needs Identification.* A methodology to identify the needs and weaknesses that arise in SMEs willing to collaborate in a collaborative NHN is provided. The methodology consists of an analysis that identifies the SMEs needs and associates them with a list of problems through a 4-dimensional analysis: (i) strategy, (ii) technology, (iii) membership and (iv) product. The given methodology identifies the weaknesses for establishing collaborative relationships with partners belonging to a collaborative NHN.

*PHASE 5: Preparing for Collaboration.* Networked partners must be able to work in an integrated way, while individually must maintain its independence and autonomy. This phase identifies the technology and additional resources required to support collaboration. Collaborative NHN are known for establishing decentralised decision making models, and NHN members must define rules for collaboration to cope with the dynamism that characterizes the network environment. Phase 5 provides training sessions to collaborate, and identifies areas that need further attention in the development of behaviour patterns. Furthermore, in this phase the technological change of view is overcome as a critical factor. Prior to technological change, there should be reviewed existing technologies and skills that organizations possess for helping partners to communicate and collaborate, taking into account the principles of interoperability (phase 3). Technological change is directly involved with information exchange. The exchange of information between companies in the same NHN is done taking into account the following aspects: (i) technology infrastructure and platforms (ii) federated information management (iii) visibility and access rights (iv) standards (v) data logging and (vi) data synchronization. Besides, process connection must be also considered through (i) process reengineering (ii) collaborative transactions and (iii) distributed platforms.

*PHASE 6: Solutions Identification.* This phase identifies solutions to overcome SMEs needs, previously identified in Phase 4. Furthermore, allows NHN partners identifying solutions to deal with concerns expressed at the phase of preparation for collaboration (Phase 5). In this phase problems arising from collaboration between SMEs when participating in collaborative networks are analysed. Those problems are the result from inter-organizational barriers such as lack of confidence, lack of knowledge exchange and flow, lack of leadership and lack of change vision. Definitely, problems and associated supporting solutions are collected and structured, determining the extent to which these solutions can be adopted to address problems in collaborative NHN. Provided solutions are classified into models, guidelines and tools (Figure 3).

**PROBLEMS** → Relevant For Collaborative Processes
↑ associated
**SOLUTIONS** → In NHN Context
↑ classified into
**MODELS / GUIDELINES / TOOLS** →

*Non-Hierarchical Networks NHN*

**Fig. 3.** Solutions identification

*PHASE 7: Solution Implementation.* A guideline to implement the solutions identified in phase 6 is provided. This step permits to identify the extent to which the considered solutions can be applied in the SMEs, taking into account the capabilities and resources they have.

*PHASE 8: Collaboration Implementation.* Collaboration within NHN partners is started in this phase. NHN members begin to collaborate and exchange information with each other. Networked partners adopt solutions to meet with collaborative conditions. In this phase, personal in charge for executing and implementing technology increase their experience in the ICT arena. Collaborative partners start to establish collaborative process and technologies. After a period of time the NHN management team meets to discuss the progress, problems and changes.

*PHASE 9: Results Assessment.* In this evaluation phase, NHN managers review the progress results. SMEs managers report the assessment results obtained from the collaborative participation in the NHN. Data recorded from the evaluation allow NHN managers to identify and generate performance improvements for SMEs (phase 10). The loop of performance measurement (phase 4) and evaluation (phase 9) will be periodically repeated. Furthermore, it is recommended to agree the review period before implementing NHN collaborative initiatives. This phase is specifically relevant to assess the collaboration results, and provides an excellent opportunity to report on the progress of collaborative NHN formation and participation.

*PHASE 10: Improvement Identification.* Future lines of action in the collaborative NHN are addressed in this stage. NHN partners must identify and decide further actions, carried out by SMEs, relating to collaboration. This phase allows decision makers to orderly capture future justified SMEs initiatives to achieve the desired collaborative environment. This stage is developed taking into account the evaluated results obtained in phase 9. Efforts to determine further SMEs actions can be aimed at improving collaborative relations either within the same NHN or forming a second NHN with different partners.

A joint report to communicate all partners the NHN collaborative decisions agreed in the collaborative process should be published at the network level. The report must give shape a common project and the potential impact of collaboration. SMEs managers are responsible of elaborating this report to record the assessment of results and further actions that must be developed to efficiently participate in collaborative relationships within NHN. NHN managers review the results of progress as regards evaluation results. The main aim of recording the evaluation results in phase 10 is to identify and apply improvements in SMEs when belonging to collaborative NHN.

# 5     Conclusions

Inter-enterprise collaboration in NHN allows SMEs to increase competitiveness, agility and dynamicity in today's global market. Empowering SMEs to establish collaborative relationships, within the network they belong, is a key question for reinforcing the necessary conditions to participate in collaborative NHN. In terms of research, collaborative NHN involve a significant activity due to the reached benefits both in network and SMEs level. Amongst problems related with NHN we find specifically interesting the initiative related with the evolution from non-collaborative NHN to collaborative ones. This paper focuses on supporting the path to be carried out by SMEs decided to participate in a collaborative NHN. As a result, it is required to start a research in collaborative NHN context. *NHNmap* provides a strategic tool focused on creating the necessary mechanisms for establishing collaborative NHN.

Research work, in collaborative NHN, has been launched only few years ago. That is to say, the most of the work has to be done in the next future, and we are in the early stage of development: SMEs as-is analysis, requirements definition, roadmaps, case studies, etc. Therefore, NHNmap is a dynamic construct that needs to be periodically revised its implementation, taking into account new trends.

Future research is aimed at implement the NHNmap in different organizations and sectors. This will be fundamental to complete the external validation of the roadmap in order to demonstrate the NHNmap potential benefits. The original contribution of this work is that NHNmap is developed at both network and SMEs levels and serves as a beginning of application to create collaborative NHN.

# References

1. Intelligent Non-Hierarchical Manufacturing Networks (iNet-IMS) (February 2012),
   http://www.ims.org/sites/default/files/iNet-
   IMS%20MTP%20Initiative%202009%20v1.3.doc

2. Camarinha-Matos, L., Afsarmanesh, H.: A RoadMap for strategic research on Virtual Organizations. In: Camarinha-Matos, L.H., Afsarmanesh, H. (eds.) Proceedings of the 4th IFIP Working Conference on Infrastructures for Virtual Enterprises (PRO-VE 2003). Kluwer Academic Publishers (2003)
3. VICS, Voluntary Interindustry Commerce Standards (2012), http://www.vics.org/committees/cpfr/, http://www.vics.org/docs/guidelines/cpfr_roadmap_case_ studies/06_3_Roadmap_To_CPFR.pdf
4. NZBCSD -New Zealand Business Council for Sustainable Development (2003), http://www.nzbcsd.org.nz/supplychain/
5. Albright, R.E.: A roadmapping perspective: Science-driven technologies (2002), http://www.albrightstrategy.com/papers/A_Roadmapping_ Perspective-Albright-09-26-02.pdf
6. Kostoff, R.N., Schaller, R.R.: Science and Technology Roadmaps. IEEE Transactions on Engineering Management 48(2), 132–143 (2001)
7. Rinne, M.: Technology roadmaps: Infrastructure for innovation. Technological Forecasting & Social Change 71(1/2), 67–80 (2004)
8. Osório, A.L., Camarinha-Matos, L.M., Afsarmanesh, H.: Cooperation Enabled Systems for Collaborative Networks. In: Camarinha-Matos, L.M., Pereira-Klen, A., Afsarmanesh, H. (eds.) PRO-VE 2011. IFIP AICT, vol. 362, pp. 400–409. Springer, Heidelberg (2011a)
9. Caetano, M., Amaral, D.C.: Roadmapping for technology push and partnership: A contribution for open innovation environments. Technovation 31, 320–335 (2011)
10. Cândido, G., Barata, J., Colombo, A.W., Jammes, F.: SOA in reconfigurable supply chains: A research roadmap. Engineering Applications of Artificial Intelligence 22, 939–949 (2009)
11. Lin, H.W., Nagalingam, S.V., Kuik, S.S., Murata, T.: Design of a Global Decision Support System for a manufacturing SME: Towards participating in Collaborative Manufacturing. Int. J. Production Economics 136, 1–12 (2012)
12. Chen, D., Doumeingts, G.: European initiatives to develop interoperability of enterprise applications-basic concepts, framework and roadmap. Annual Reviews in Control 27, 153–162 (2003)
13. Ducq, Y., Chen, D., Vallespir, B.: Interoperability in enterprise modelling: requirements and roadmap. Advanced Engineering Informatics 18, 193–203 (2004)
14. Rezgui, Y., Zarli, A.: Paving the Way to the Vision of Digital Construction: A Strategic Roadmap. J. of Construction Engineering and Management, 767–776 (2006)
15. Azouzi, R., d'Amours, S.: Standards for information and knowledge sharing in collaborative design of planning systems within the forest product industry. CILRET 46 (2011)
16. Perks, H., Moxey, S.: Market-facing innovation networks: How lead firms partition tasks, share resources and develop capabilities. Industrial Marketing Management 40, 1224–1237 (2011)
17. Budweg, S., Schaffers, H., Rulanda, R., Kristensenc, K., Prinz, W.: Enhancing collaboration in communities of professionals using a Living Lab approach. Production Planning & Control 22(5–6), 594–609 (2011)
18. Phaal, R., Farrukh, C.J.P., Probert, D.R.: Technology roadmapping - A planning framework for evolution and revolution. Technological Forecasting & Social Change 71, 5–26 (2004)
19. Camarinha-Matos, L.M., Afsarmanesh, H.: On reference models for collaborative networked organizations. Int. J. of Production Research 46(9), 2453–2469 (2008)

20. Osório, L., Afsarmanesh, H., Camarinha-Matos, L.M.: A Service Integration Platform for Collaborative Networks. Studies in Inf. and Control 20(1), 19–30 (2011b)
21. Barton, R., Thomas, A.: Implementation of intelligent systems, enabling integration of SMEs to high-value supply chain networks. Engineering Applications of Artificial Intelligence 22, 929–938 (2009)
22. Camarinha-Matos, L.M., Afsarmanesh, H.: Active Ageing Roadmap – A Collaborative Networks Contribution to Demographic Sustainability. In: Camarinha-Matos, L.M., Boucher, X., Afsarmanesh, H. (eds.) PRO-VE 2010. IFIP AICT, vol. 336, pp. 46–59. Springer, Heidelberg (2010)
23. Hvolby, H.H., Trienekens, J.H.: Challenges in business systems integration. Computers in Industry 61, 808–812 (2010)
24. Shadi, M., Afsarmanesh, H.: Addressing Behavior in Collaborative Networks. In: Camarinha-Matos, L.M., Pereira-Klen, A., Afsarmanesh, H. (eds.) PRO-VE 2011. IFIP AICT, vol. 362, pp. 263–270. Springer, Heidelberg (2011)
25. Camarinha-Matos, L.M., Afsarmanesh, H., Koelmel, B.: Collaborative Networks in Support of Service-Enhanced Products. In: Camarinha-Matos, L.M., Pereira-Klen, A., Afsarmanesh, H. (eds.) PRO-VE 2011. IFIP AICT, vol. 362, pp. 95–104. Springer, Heidelberg (2011)
26. Gallardo, J., Bravo, C., Redondo, M.A.: A model-driven development method for collaborative modeling tools. J. of Network and Computer Applications 35, 1086–1105 (2012)

# Internal and External Collaborative Technology Adoption: A Focus on a European and an Emerging Countries' Gaps Based on the Adaptive Structuration Theory

Marc Diviné[1] and Julie Stal-Le Cardinal[2]

[1] IAE-Paris, University Paris1 Panthéon-Sorbonne, 21, rue Broca, 75005 Paris
divine.iae@univ-paris1.fr
[2] Ecole Centrale Paris, Industrial Engineering Department,
Grande Voie des Vignes, 92295 Chatenay Malabry Cedex, France
julie.le-cardinal@ecp.fr

**Abstract.** This research highlights the differences of the adoption of collaborative tools between one European and one emerging country in Asia. Based on the Adaptive Structuration Theory and the Technology Spirit concept, it uses a three dimensional model focused on both internal and external collaboration. 18 tools were surveyed in a sample of 75 managers of large companies with more than 1000 employees. The results show a wider external collaboration in the emerging country, particularly in the dimensions of actor's satisfaction and flexible frontier. Internal collaboration is more developed in both countries, but mainly in the dimension of value creation. The paper illustrates and adapts the theory in a high tech web 2.0 environment. Managerial implications are suggested in collaboration practices and measurements.

**Keywords:** Collaborative networks, collaborative tools, collaborative behavior, technology adoption, community management, web 2.0.

## 1 Introduction

Assuming that the e-collaboration practices are today a key factor of management success, this paper focuses on the differences of the adoption of collaborative technologies between two countries. The adoption of collaborative tools is considered as performance indicator, as it shows the transformation of relations to the virtual mode and the capacity to adapt to its new dynamics. The research aims to achieve a step forward in understanding collaboration behavior in order to help face future societal challenges. It also tackles the problem of the usual separation of the dual management of collaboration know-how: this competence is necessary to internal virtual teams and to external customer brand communities' management and marketing managers are major contributors to both. The literature until now has proposed several measurements, but no one covers the large range of tools internal as well as external, and gives an understanding of behavior. With a metrics of the use in

L.M. Camarinha-Matos, L. Xu, and H. Afsarmanesh (Eds.): PRO-VE 2012, IFIP AICT 380, pp. 408–415, 2012.
© IFIP International Federation for Information Processing 2012

a sample of large companies and the concepts of the Adaptive Structuration Theory, we will give an insight of the difference of behavior in two countries. In the first part, this paper shows up research results concerning technology adoption in collaborative activities, and underlines theories which point out the impact of adoption of tools. In the second part, the design of the research is detailed, including the sample of large companies from one emerging and one European country, the information collect methodology and its' treatment. The last part gives the findings of the research with a gap analysis of 18 collaborative tools. It compares the close internal and very different external uses between the two countries, in favor of the emerging country. It is completed by a three dimensional local vision of virtual teams and communities, based on the Technology Spirit concept, which explains this gap. The last part lists the contributions and suggests large companies' practical implications of the research.

## 2    Current Understanding in the Literature and Research Question

Since 1995, the Gartner Group has published a report on the global adoption of emerging technologies, summarized in the Hype curve [8] (Fenn, 1995). The adoption or appropriation is the process of actions documenting the use of technology [14] (Majchrzak et al., 2000). This report includes a few collaborative tools, such as the wiki or the blog, but lacks many of them, as it is focused on new technologies only. It does not provide country comparison. In 2000 a methodology to create a technology readiness index (TRI) was proposed [19] (Parasuraman, 2000). It uses qualitative questionnaires for each technology adoption analyzed. In 2008 the European Union published an e-business adoption index which takes into account mainly online revenue and ignores the collaboration. Models of e-collaboration have been published, based on three media richness levels [10] (Heidecke, 2009), or on virtual groups' links between electronic collaboration and factors such as electronic information sharing and exploitation capability [11] (Ko, 2009) or internal factors and economic external factors [13] (Madlberger, 2009). Another model has emerged from the network pictures concept, that is the managers' surroundings representation, a distant concept to communities, but which is close to collaboration. The proposed factors of pictures which influence behaviors are mainly power, followed by dynamics, broadness and indirectness [2] (Corsaro, 2011). Closer to the tools, the cooperation model based on the efficiency of collaborative tools must be mentioned [1] (Baker, 2002). This model makes differences between tools with cognitive factors: the ability of symmetry of the roles, the members' agreement visibility, and the progress in alignment in phases. These qualitative models and their outcomes are incomplete, due to the explosion of more than 150 collaborative tools [9] (Good, 2011) and the industry dynamics. Today, the abundant web analytics information provides large volume of data from the different web 2.0 tools separately [15] (Malo, 2009), without global internal and external collaboration vision.

Another authors presents new methods to support collaboration for virtual teams. [20, 21] (Schumacher, 2009 and 2012) tool consists in the implementation of an

Aided Competence Management for Virtual Team Building System which features recommendations, guidelines and practices for virtual team building adapted at micro level to the requirements of each specific organization.

Based at macro level, the research question of this paper is "What are the differences of collaborative technology adoption in both internal and external usage between two given countries?"

This objective makes it necessary to identify the most used tools, and measure their use with a quantitative sample, which the present research did not do. While the internal collaborative practices are necessary in large multinational companies, they are a privileged field. The Adaptive Structuration Theory (AST) helps to understand the impact of technology adoption on behaviors. The AST [4] (DeSanctis, Poole, 1994) considers that there is a mutual interaction between agent's behavior and the system, which includes the technology environment. Later researches [17, 18] (Orlikowski, 1992 and 2000) [16] (Nikas, 2009) complemented it and see the adoption of tools as a key activity in the process of structuration of the virtual teams or communities. The adoption of technologies generates new behavior in specific directions, the technology spirits, which correspond to the initial intents of their designers. This research will identify, evaluate and compare the technology spirits and corresponding behavior in two countries.

In this perspective, the choice and use of tools provides information to unable the understanding of the qualitative differences of collaboration behavior between countries.

## 3     Research Design

Our research design to evaluate practices is made possible with the AST. Collaborative network projects need tools and reciprocally the collaborative tools generate innovative practices. The speed of adoption of the tools gives a measurement of the network potential capability. Applying the Adaptive Structuration Theory, the choice of the tools made by the managers of project virtual teams or customer communities reveals the type of technology spirit, and reciprocally, the present use of the tools develops the intent. The methodology is based on a comparative analysis of the use and probability of use of 18 tools by two samples of marketing managers. The tools are listed in Table 2. The Marketing Managers work in companies of more than 1000 employees: a first sample of 54 based in France and a second of 21 in Vietnam. They are in an ideal position for this research, as their job includes being members of virtual teams and knowing the tools used with their company's customers. The interviews aimed at listing the collaborative tools in use in their virtual teams and with customer communities. Interviewees were asked to say whether or not these tools were commonly used (yes-no) and their estimation of the probability of use if they were available (0-10) with comments. The information collected provides an adoption level of each tool. The weighed addition of all the tools use or probability to use gives global internal and external collaboration levels to each sample. The adoption pace measurement is then static (the use) and dynamic (the difference between use and probability to use). A correlation is calculated between the tools used in both countries, in order to measure divergences not only in intensity of use, but in choices. In a second information treatment step, we will use the model of classification of tools conducted by the authors [5, 6] (Divine, 2010 and 2012). It is a statistical analysis using principal component analysis and correlation index to identify groups of tools on the same database. It shows three classes, corresponding to three technology spirits: the value addition to the virtual team or community (VA), the actors' satisfaction (AS), and the flexible frontier (FF). The two first intents are directly linked to the Actors Theory [3] (Crozier, 1977) which demonstrates that the organization members' behavior is not only explained by their value addition to the organization, but also by their personal strategy and satisfaction. The last intent is linked to the virtuality, i. e. here distance collaboration, which allows a different perspective of virtual groups, with the wish or not to extend its frontiers. The category of value creation tools includes web conferencing, rating, commenting, sharing, wiki, remote control, pooling, posting, forum, LMS and partner's blog. The actors' satisfaction tools are the blog, rich directory, commenting, chat, tag, RSS and forum. The flexible frontier tools are the microblogging, the rich media, social networks and forum. The calculation concluded that commenting and forum are in several categories. In the tables of this paper the different tools are grouped in these categories. An interpretation of the qualitative differences between French and Vietnamese collaboration is made.

## 4    Findings

Despite a common level of interest internally as well as externally, we see in Table 1 a large gap in current use of the tools. The internal use of the collaborative tools is unequal in favor of Vietnam, whereas the external use shows an even larger difference. Large companies tend to set up worldwide internal communication modes integrated into their marketing procedures. On the opposite side, more freedom is given to local marketing customer communication patterns. Vietnam which has fewer marketing traditions and less marketing budget has taken the opportunity of this low cost customer media faster.

**Table 1.** Comparison of internal and external use and interest of Vietnam and France

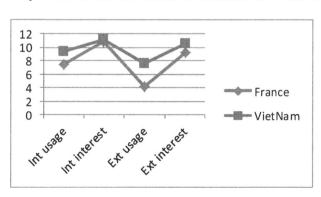

The insight into the different tools' internal use is given in Table 2. These practices which concern the management of marketing projects, show a 25% difference between the two countries in the intensity of use; 9.3 tools are used on average in Vietnam against 7.4 only in France. The correlation index is .70 in the type of tools between the two countries, showing some parallelism. Ten tools are used more than 10% in Vietnam, and one tool only in France. Web conference, social media, and document sharing are among the tools which are more commonly used internally in Vietnam. The interest level is high for 11 tools and identical for the two countries, showing room for more internal collaboration. We can conclude that in terms of collaboration practices, the internal marketing processes will become close when projects have a worldwide scope.

**Table 2.** Comparison of internal use in virtual teams of tools between Vietnam and France

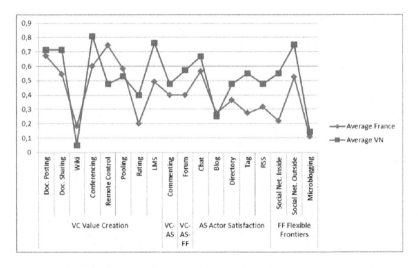

**Table 3.** Comparison of external use with customers of tools in Vietnam and France

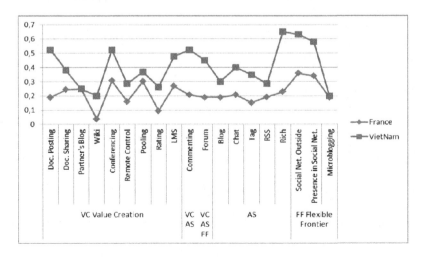

The external use of collaborative tools with customers is very different. The emerging country performs much better than the European country. This concerns all opportunities of interactive collaboration, between customers and customers with the brand. Much fewer tools are used externally, 4.1 on average in France, and 7.6 in Vietnam. The correlation between the choices of tools is .65, showing a wider gap and more different local choices. In terms of use intensity, fifteen tools are used more than 10% in Vietnam than in France. In terms of use probability, 9.2 tools are targeted in France, a huge jump compared to 4.1 today. In Vietnam 10.5 tools are targeted, a better score, but a lower jump compared to 7.6. The tools with the biggest gaps are commenting, posting, social network and rich media, which are also the most popular. Six tools are already used by more than half of the sample in Vietnam, and none in France.

We can mention that the correlation index between internal and external collaboration is .79 for the total sample: the collaboration is more developed internally, but it is correlated to external practices. It is a dual culture inside the organization as well as with customers.

The table 4 gives the split of the tools use between the three dimensions, in both internal and external use.

**Table 4.** Comparison of internal and external three dimensions: Value Creation, Actor Satisfaction and Flexible Frontier

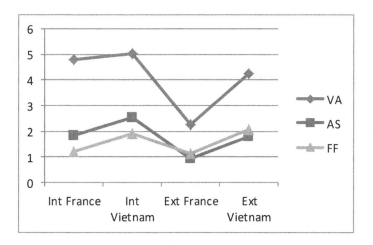

The results show a wider external collaboration in the emerging country, particularly in the dimensions of actor's satisfaction and flexible frontier. Internal collaboration is more developed in both countries, but mainly in the dimension of value creation. The most important gap is in the value creation in external usage: the perception in the emerging country of the web 2.0 contribution to the branding mechanics is stronger.

# 5    Outcomes and Discussion: Theoretical and Managerial Implications

This research reveals a specific perspective of e-collaboration based on the tools' use and a dual internal and external vision. It illustrates the AST with an identification of three technology spirits and explains the three behaviors levels in two countries. This outcome provides a model which can be extended to other countries, groups or organizations. This model is flexible to different types of tools, can accept new ones. It is can be extended from internal and external use to new mix use in virtual structures, where structures mix members from different organizations and communities [7] (Fahy, 2007).

The research demonstrates that the large companies' management should focus on some emerging countries e-collaboration with a dual vision of tools. On the one hand, Vietnam shows a collaborative intimacy with customers which will create a considerable impact on the future. The constant dialog with the brand and between customers developed by the e-collaboration is a source of good understanding, reactivity and secure innovation success [12] (MacCormack, 2008). On the other hand, due to the correlation between internal and external use, their position will accelerate their internal use and collaboration performance.

The technology adoption is the layout for new internet behavior. Large companies' Innovation Managers should gain from the following managerial propositions:

o   Use the emerging countries as the inspiring area of the collaborative tools adoption process.
o   Develop more employee and customer satisfaction and practices of frontier extension based on the tools of this class in European countries
o   Track and set a target of internal and external tools use

The pace of adoption of collaborative tools in Vietnam is due to a start-from-zero beneficial status, comparable to pure-players start-ups in old industries. The extension of the Vietnamese success result to other emerging countries can be discussed, so that other measurements and needed. This research will go further towards the directions shown by the collaborative tools evolution. New tools and new behavior will appear, and other researches at micro level to optimize choices of tools. In order to trace this evolution, our index of collaboration activity is planned to be maintained and results provided as an operational benchmark to managers.

# References

1. Baker, M.: Forms of cooperation in dyadic problem-solving. In: Salembier, P., Benchekron, T.H. (eds.) Cooperation and Complexity in Sociotechnical Systems, Lavoisier, vol. 16, pp. 587–620 (2002)
2. Corsaro, D., Ramos, C., Henneberg, S.C., Naudé, P.: Actor Network Pictures and Networking Activities in Business Networks: An Experimental Study. Industrial Marketing Management 40(6), 919–932 (2011)

3. Crozier, M., Friedberg, E.: L'acteur et le système, Le seuil, Paris (1977)
4. DeSanctis, G., Poole, M.: Capturing the Complexity in Advanced Technology Use: Adaptive Structuration Theory. Organization Science 5(2), 121–147 (1994)
5. Diviné, M., Schumacher, M., Le-Cardinal, J.: Learning Virtual Teams: How to Design a Set of Web 2.0 Tools. International Journal of Technology Management, Acceptance notice (2010)
6. Diviné, M.: Virtual Customer Communities: e-Collaboration is Not a Given. A Three-dimensional Model Based on Web 2.0 Tools; Industrial Marketing Management Journal, IMM (submitted in February 2012)
7. Fahy, M., Feller, J., Finnegan, P., Murphy, C.: Complexity and context: Emerging forms of collaborative inter-organizational systems. Journal of Information Technology Theory and Application 8(4), 1–19 (2007)
8. Fenn, J.: When to Leap on the Hype Cycle. Gartner Group publications (1995)
9. Good, R.: Best Online Collaboration Tools 2008 - The Collaborative Map (2008), http://www.masternewmedia.org/best-online-collaboration-tools-2008-the-collaborative/#ixzz1IZpWVLYU
10. Heidecke, F., Back, A.: A reference model for e-collaboration within the dispersed sales force training process in multinational companies. International Journal of e-Collaboration 5(1), 32–46 (2009)
11. Ko, I., Olfman, L., Choi, S.: The Impacts of Electronic Collaboration and Information Exploitation Capability on Firm Performance: Focusing on Suppliers using Buyer-Dominated Inter-Organizational Information Systems. International Journal of e-Collaboration 5(2), 1–17 (2009)
12. MacCormack, A., Forbath, T.: Learning the fine art of global collaboration. Harward Business Review 86(1), 24–26 (2008)
13. Madlberger, M.: What Drives Firms to Engage in Interorganizational Information Sharing in Supply Chain Management? International Journal of e-Collaboration 5(2), 18–42 (2009)
14. Majchrzak, A., Rice, R., Malhotra, E., King, N.: Technology adaptation: The case of a computer-supported inter-organizational virtual team. MIS Quarterly 24(4), 569–600 (2000)
15. Malo, N., Warren, J.: Web Analytics, Eyrolles, ed. d'Organisation (2009)
16. Nikas, A., Poulymenakou, A.: Technology Adaptation: Capturing the Appropriation Dynamics of Web-based Collaboration Support in a Project Team. International Journal of e-Collaboration 4(2) (January-March 2008)
17. Orlikowski, W.J.: The duality of technology: rethinking the concept of technology in organizations. Organization Science 3(3), 398–429 (1992)
18. Orlikowski, W.: Using technology and constituting structures: A practice lens for studying technology in organizations. Organizational Science 11(4), 404–428 (2000)
19. Parasuraman, A.: Technology readiness index (TRI): A multiple-item scale to measure readiness to embrace new technologies. Journal of Service Research 2(4), 307–320 (2000)
20. Schumacher, M., Diviné, M., Stal- Le Cardinal, J., Bocquet, J.C.: Virtual Teams Challenging Human and Technical Web 2.0 dimensions. International Journal of Networking and Virtual Organisations; Plüss, A., Huber, C.: Virtual Project Management: Collaboration and Leadership, Special Edition, accepted September 2010 (Publication scheduled for, 2012)
21. Schumacher, M., Stal-Le Cardinal, J., Bocquet, J.-C.: Towards a Methodology for Managing Competencies in Virtual Teams – A Systemic Approach. In: Camarinha-Matos, L.M., Paraskakis, I., Afsarmanesh, H. (eds.) PRO-VE 2009. IFIP AICT, vol. 307, pp. 235–244. Springer, Heidelberg (2009)

# From Groupware to Social Media -
# A Comparison of Conceptual Models

Nils Jeners[1] and Wolfgang Prinz[2]

[1] RWTH Aachen University, Informatik V, Ahornstr. 55, 52056 Aachen
nils.jeners@rwth-aachen.de
[2] Fraunhofer FIT, Schloss Birlinghoven, 53754 Sankt Augustin, Germany
wolfgang.prinz@fit.fraunhofer.de

**Abstract.** Although Groupware research has yielded a number of productive and successful systems, it appears that the current social media trend is somewhat out ruling the traditional cooperation support systems such as email or shared workspaces. In this paper we propose a conceptual model that identifies major elements and concepts of cooperative systems to provide a basis for their comparison. We will illustrate that social media systems apply the same basic concepts as other collaborative systems but with a different adoption creating a different user experience.

**Keywords:** groupware, social media, meta model, conceptual model.

## 1    Introduction

Groupware has a long history [1]. All systems belonging to this class of applications are trying to help workers to organize their work and get it done. A lot of research and developments has been made for professional scenarios. Social Network Sites which rise since 1997 [2], evolve from leisure or non-professional use cases within groups of friends or people with same interest. These systems do not try to represent business workflows or support organizational tasks. These systems try to keep leisure cooperation simple, e.g. arrange an evening with friends, or share pictures from a party.

Nowadays these systems are also used in professional environments. Not for marketing purpose only, but also for organizational communication (yammer.com) and setting project meetings (doodle.com) for example.

Big companies such as Cisco copy social network concepts of systems like Facebook and many others. Business applications like Cisco's Quad[1] and Jive[2] evolved trying to bring social systems into a professional environment.

If we anticipate that there are groupware systems on the professional side, and social media on the leisure side, we want to identify the influences each of the system has to one another. Further we want to ask whether these two types remain on each

---

[1] www.cisco.com/web/products/quad/
[2] www.jivesoftware.com/

L.M. Camarinha-Matos, L. Xu, and H. Afsarmanesh (Eds.): PRO-VE 2012, IFIP AICT 380, pp. 416–423, 2012.
© IFIP International Federation for Information Processing 2012

side or merge and evolve to one system class that is either for professional and leisure usage scenarios.

Therefore we developed a generic model which can represent all the systems and tools that we are using in daily work and private cooperation. This generic model consists of abstract classes that are instantiated with each analyzed system. With the generic model in mind we are able to compare the systems component by component and find out whether the systems are based on similar concepts with different shapes, or not.

Common underlying concepts provide the potential to transform one system in to another. Legacy groupware systems can evolve and be enhanced to social systems, keeping the same set of features with another shape or different UI. To identify the key concepts and point on possible transformations we try to apply the meta model.

In the following we first present related approaches in modeling cooperative applications. This is followed by the presentation of our conceptual model and its instantiation for two example systems. Afterwards we will compare the particular adoption of core concepts by groupware and social media systems.

## 2    Background

A lot of models help to classify groupware in general. The Space/Time matrix of Johanson [3] and the 3C-Model of Teufel [4] are the most famous of them. These models are suitable as a taxonomy, however an instantiation of these models is not possible.

The Zachman Framework is an early framework for information systems architecture [5] that can also be applied on groupware systems. Its basic concepts are roles and perspectives, which also fit on groupware and social media. The framework of Zachman is quite useful in terms of planning and developing applications. Like a pattern language it provides a mutual understanding for all stakeholders.

The basic building blocks of group communication support systems are roles, message objects, functions and rules [6]. A so called CSCW system with the above mentioned building blocks access a common underlying system which provides services to applications and user access. TOSCA [7] and MOCCA [8] understand CSCW systems as a heterogeneous collection of applications, paradigms and models and not a single system. Within this environment there are models that specify the environment. The four presented models (informational model, organizational model, workspace model, and room model) are considered as perspectives with an abstract view on the environment functionality.

Three aspects of groupware concept models defined by Ellis et al. [9] are the ontological model, the coordination model and the user-interface model. The ontological model consists of objects and the operations on these. Objects are modeled with attributes and values. Values can either be atomic or other objects. The operations are divided in four classes, namely view, create, modify, and destroy. Objects own an intended semantics or an operational semantics. The coordination model covers the dynamic aspects in terms of activities. Activities are performed by actors with a specific role. Procedures are sets of activities. The third aspect is the user interface, the appearance of the system, the user experience.

The reference architecture proposed in [10] identifies several layers as well as architectural components. Most relevant for our approach are the basic services that realize access to the underlying data structures which implement the concepts identified in this paper. The generic CSCW model, proposed by Farias et al. [11], consists of four concepts, namely activity, actor, information and service, whereas activity is the core that connects everything. An activity consists of a goal and a state. It is performed by an actor, uses information and supports services. The ARCON framework provides help in order to understand, design and implement collaborative networks [12]. A reference architecture that helps enterprises to cooperate in virtual enterprises is VERAM [13].

In summary, several approaches to identify generic architectures and building blocks exist. However, a comprehensive conceptual model that enables the modeling and comparison of different collaborative applications is yet missing. We will present our approach in the next section.

## 3    Conceptual Models

In our approach, we first defined elementary actions the user can perform at existing system like Email, Twitter, etc. We categorized these activities to generalize them in a meta model which covers these system. We instantiated the abstract classes with the applied techniques of the existing systems.

### 3.1    Meta Model

Our proposed meta model (see fig. 1) consists of abstract classes, that describe the generic system for cooperative applications. Each system implements the abstract

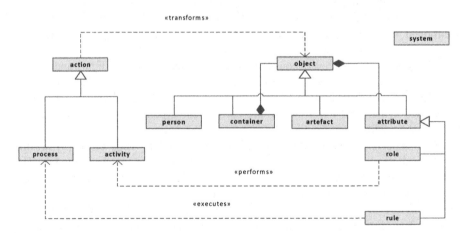

**Fig. 1.** Meta model of cooperative systems

classes and inherits from them. The three top-level classes are *action*, *object* and *system*. *Action* denotes all activities and processes performed by either users of the system or the system itself. *Object* represents all virtual entities of the system namely *person, container, artifact and attribute*. The system class contains all systems represented in the meta model. Every implemented class of the model belongs to either one or several systems.

The *action* class is specialized in the two subclasses *activity* and *process*. *Activities* can be performed by persons who have a specific role and *processes* can be executed by the system itself, controlled by a rule. Both subclasses can transform (create, modify, and destroy) specific objects, e.g. create a new container, modify an attribute, or destroy an artifact.

*Object* is the abstract parent class of *person, container, artifact* and *attribute*. *Person* stands for every humane actor in the system, i.e. user, specified by *roles*. *Containers* are collections of objects. They can contain containers itself, persons and artifacts. *Artifacts* denote the basic entities of the system such as messages, files or any other objects the users can interact with. *Attributes* belong to objects and cannot stand alone. They are always attached to other objects (person, container, and artifact. The two attributes, already implemented are *role* and *rule*. *Roles* specifies person in terms of the activities they can perform. We distinguish between four kinds of roles: Organizational roles describe people in the context of their work hierarchy, e.g. boss, colleague, and partner. Activity roles specify the activities one person can perform, e.g. author, reader. Right roles show the rights a particular person has, e.g. manager, owner. The last kind of roles is the cultural roles. *Rules* are expressions that can stick to objects and if this rule is valid, a *process* will be performed. An example for this kind of *rule* is an autoreply mechanism in email systems or a notification mechanism in shared workspaces.

## 3.2    Instantiated Systems

We instantiated the proposed meta model exemplary with two common cooperation system. We compare email (Fig. 2) on the one hand with the social media system Yammer (Fig. 3) on the other. The instantiated models of the systems are on a more generic level, to not get lost in details and fit into this paper.

Fig. 2 shows the basic building blocks of an IMAP email system like it is implemented in Outlook or Thunderbird. It has mails, contacts, folders. Mails are structured in several folders called inbox, outbox, etc., depending on their status (send, received, etc.) and have attributes e.g. from, to, subject, body, etc. There are three roles: author, sender, and receiver, which perform certain activities like write, send, and read.

Fig. 3 shows the enterprise social network called Yammer. It mainly consists of posts in certain networks (groups). Posts can contain polls, events, embedded images of videos and different other content. Posts can be liked (as in Facebook) and tagged (called topic) to be searchable. There also are three roles called admin, author, reader, which perform activities like read, write, tag, invite.

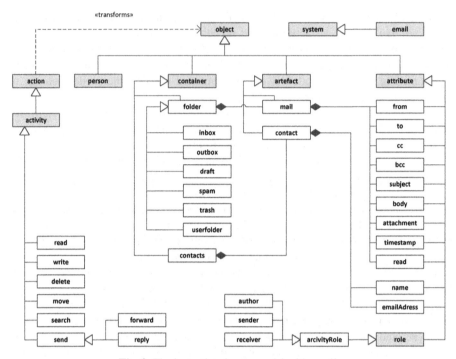

**Fig. 2.** The instantiated meta model with email

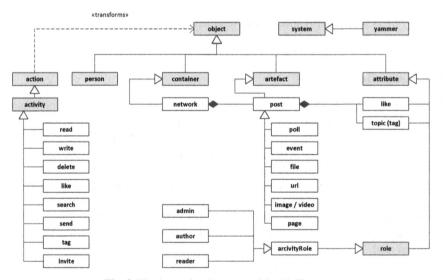

**Fig. 3.** The instantiated meta model with Yammer

The two systems are mainly used to exchange certain information with others. Email applies a sending metaphor, where the author writes a message and sends it to the desired receiver. The data (mail) is not owned by the author or the system. The author and the receiver, they both hold a copy. Yammer provides a sharing metaphor. The author writes a post, and saves it in the system. The data (post) is stored in the centralized system and everybody (with respective rights) can access the data.

While the appearance of these two systems is different, the purpose of the systems is the same. Whether it is called mail or post, does not change the entity which holds the information, but it indicates a different concept.

## 3.3    Comparison of Core Concepts

In this section we compare the particular instantiation of core concepts and their effect. First we look at the people concept group as well as the relation of people into larger sets. The following table 1 identifies four relations.

**Table 1.** Relation of people

|  | mutual | container | visibility | purpose |
|---|---|---|---|---|
| group | yes | yes | public | Access management |
| friends | yes | no | public | Notification management of sender/receiver, publicity two-way |
| follower | no | no | public | Notification management of receiver, publicity one-way |
| circle/lists | no | yes | private | Notification management of sender |

The classic group concept is primarily used in shared folder or teamroom systems, mainly for the purpose of defining access rights. Social media systems relate people by friends and follower networks or in circles (Google+). The difference is that groups are symmetric, while the networks can be asymmetric. This means that all members of a group know each other, i.e. each user knows that the information he provides is accessible to all group members. Friends and follower networks are not as transparent, since they are created individually by each user. Thus two users who belong to the same network of another user do not necessarily know each other. Thus information sharing is more directed to the personal network of a user and not to a symmetric group. In an organizational context this can cause problems as it is often not clear if important information is received by all required people in case that they did not configure their own network accordingly.

**Table 2.** Container of objects

|  | cardinality | container | visibility | purpose |
|---|---|---|---|---|
| folder, workspace | 1:m | yes | public | access management, hierarchy, group |
| tags | m:n | no | public | filtering |

Another aspect is the relation and organization of objects into container illustrated in the following table 2. Again the classic approach is the folder approach that organizes objects into a hierarchical order.

Most social media systems apply tags to organize and structure object. The advantage is an easier networking of information as long as tags are applied in a disciplined way.

This brief comparison of the implementation of relations of two core concepts indicates that social media systems apply a network-based relationship while classic applications apply a group- or folder-based approach.

Table 3 shows how information is shared among the different systems. In common shared workspace systems, a group respectively a community is the entity in which information is shared. The members of a group are known to everybody within the group. This concept is used to map existing groups, e.g. project groups. A follower network is established by people who are interested in posts from the author. This concept is applied in Twitter and can be compared to subscriber systems of newsfeeds. Walls like in Facebook often tend to be semi-public. A wall belongs to one person and everybody can write to the walls of friends which is not the same as sending a message how it is done in inbox systems. A sender actively decides who the message receives.

**Table 3.** Sharing / Messaging / Activity stream concepts

|  | responsibility | visibility | purpose |
|---|---|---|---|
| groups, communities | admin or all members | public/private | common goal/interest |
| follower | user | private | user interest |
| walls | friends | friends | public friendship |
| inbox | contacts | private | 1:1 messages |

## 4    Conclusion

This paper presents a conceptual model enabling the instantiation for different collaborative applications and thus their comparison. We have illustrated the instantiation for email as well as the social media system Yammer. The comparison has shown that most model elements are applied by both, yet in a different manner.

The comparison has shown that the two systems do not differ in a great manner, but rather in small pieces how something is called at what core concept is followed.

With believe that this paper contributes to a more systematic understanding of the core elements of collaborative applications. Our next steps will focus on further applications of the model with the aim of further refinement and validation.

# References

1. Ellis, C., Gibbs, S., Rein, G.: Groupware: some issues and experiences. Commun. ACM 34(1), 39–58 (1991)
2. Boyd, D.M., Ellison, N.B.: Social network sites: Definition, history, and scholarship. Journal of Computer-Mediated Communication 13(1), article 11 (2007)
3. Johansen, R.: Leading business teams. Addison-Wesley, Reading (1991)
4. Teufel, S., Muelherr, T., Bauknecht, K.: Computerunterstützung für die Gruppenarbeit. Addison-Wesley, Bonn (1995)
5. Zachman, J.: A framework for information systems architecture. IBM Systems Journal 26(3), 276–292 (1987), doi:10.1147/sj.263.0276
6. Prinz, W., Pennelli, P.: Relevance of the X.500 Directory to CSCW Applications. In: Marca, D., Bock, G. (eds.) Groupware: Software for Computer Supported Cooperative Work, pp. 209–225. IEEE Computer Society Press (1992)
7. Prinz, W.: TOSCA: Providing Organisational Information to CSCW applications. In: Michelis, G.d., Schmidt, K., Simone, C. (eds.) Proceedings of ECSCW 1993: Third European Conference on Computer Supported Cooperative Work, Milan, Italy, pp. 139–154. Kluwer Academic Publishers, Dordrecht (1993)
8. Benford, S., Mariani, J., Navarro, L., Prinz, W., Rodden, T.: MOCCA: An Environment for CSCW Applications. In: Kaplan, S. (ed.) Proceedings of Conference on Organizational Computing Systems, pp. 172–177. ACM Press, Milpitas - California (1993)
9. Ellis, C., Wainer, J.: A conceptual model of groupware. In: Proceedings of the 1994 ACM Conference on Computer Supported Cooperative Work (CSCW 1994), pp. 79–88. ACM, New York (1994), http://doi.acm.org/10.1145/192844.192878
10. Peristeras, V., Martinez-Carreras, M.A., Gomez-Skarmeta, A.F., Prinz, W., Nasirifard, P.: Towards a Reference Architecture for Collaborative Work Environments. International Journal of e-Collaboration 6(1) (2010)
11. Farias, C.R.G., Pires, L.F., van Sinderen, M.: A Conceptual Model for the Development of CSCW Systems. In: Designing Cooperative Systems: The Use of Theories and Models (Proceedings of COOP 2000), pp. 189–204. IOS Press, Sophia Antipolis, France (2000)
12. Camarinha-Matos, L., Afsarmanesh, H.: A Modeling Framework for Collaborative Networked Organizations. In: Network-Centric Collaboration and Supporting Frameworks, vol. 224, pp. 3–14. Springer, Boston (2006)
13. Zwegers, A., Tolle, M., Vesterager, J.: VERAM: virtual enterprise reference architecture and methodology. In: Karvonen, I., Van den Berg, R., Bernus, P., Fukuda, Y., Hannus, M. (eds.) Global Engineering and Manufacturing in Enterprise Networks, vol. 224, pp. 17–38. VTT (2003)

# 15

Virtual Organization Breeding Environments

# Green Virtual Enterprise Breeding Environments: A Sustainable Industrial Development Model for a Circular Economy

David Romero and Arturo Molina

Tecnológico de Monterrey, Mexico
david.romero.diaz@gmail.com,
armolina@itesm.mx

**Abstract.** A Green Virtual Enterprise Breeding Environment (GVBE) is a long-term strategic alliance of green enterprises and their related support institutions aimed at offering the necessary conditions to efficiently promote the sharing and recycling of resources such as: information, materials, water, energy and/or infrastructure with the intention of achieving sustainable development in a collaborative way. A GVBE can be a three-level holistic sustainable industrial development model for achieving a Circular Economy at a micro-level with its green enterprises development, at meso-level with green virtual enterprises creation and at a macro-level with the GVBE it-self as an intelligent network for competencies and resources management from different green enterprises aiming to combine their green capabilities to develop triple top-line strategies to create sustainable value. This paper provides basic concepts and general guidelines to create sustainable industrial development models for Circular Economy based-on Collaborative Networked Organisations.

**Keywords:** Collaborative Networked Organisations, Circular Economy, Green Virtual Enterprises, Breeding Environments, Industrial Ecology, Industrial Symbiosis, Sustainable Industrial Development.

## 1 Introduction

A New Economy is emerging based on sustainable design and innovation [1] [2]. *Circular Economy (CE),* also called 'material close economy' or 'lifecycle economy', is an alternative model to the one-way model of economic activities characterised by linear flows of resources → products → wastes. *CE* aims a "sustainable economy", a closed-loop model of economic activities creating feedback cycles of resources → products → renewable resources, following the 3R principles or operating rules of reduce, reuse and recycle in the processes of production, logistics and consumption in order to achieve a sustainable industrial development. *CE* aims to meet sustainable consumption and production through (a) cleaner production, (b) industrial ecology and (c) lifecycle management / assessment, seeking to create a balance between economic development and environmental protection [2].

L.M. Camarinha-Matos, L. Xu, and H. Afsarmanesh (Eds.): PRO-VE 2012, IFIP AICT 380, pp. 427–436, 2012.
© IFIP International Federation for Information Processing 2012

*Cleaner production (CP)* refers to "the continuous application of an integrated, preventative environmental strategy to processes, products and services to increase eco-efficiency and reduce risks to humans and the environment". For *processes, CP* results from conserving raw materials, water and energy; eliminating toxic and dangerous raw materials; and reducing the quantity and toxicity of all emissions and wastes at source during the production process. For *products, CP* aims to reduce the environmental, health and safety impacts of products over their entire lifecycles, from raw materials extraction, through manufacturing and use, to the disposal of the product. For *services, CP* implies incorporating environmental concerns into designing and delivering services [3].

*Industrial Ecology (IE)* aims at "the shifting of industrial processes from linear (open-loop) systems, in which resource move through the system to become waste, to a closed-loop system where wastes can become inputs for new processes". *IE* focuses on eco-restructuring the industrial processes by: optimising the use of resources; closing material loops and minimising emissions; dematerialising activities; and reducing and eliminating the dependence on non-renewable sources of energy [4].

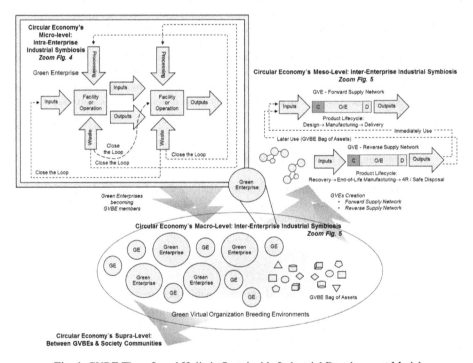

**Fig. 1.** GVBE Three-Level Holistic Sustainable Industrial Development Model

*Lifecycle Management (LM)* refers to "the process of managing the entire lifecycle of a product from its conception (imagine, specify plan, innovate), through design (define, develop, test, analyse and validate) and manufacture (make, build, procure, produce, sell and deliver) to service (use, operate, maintain, support, sustain) and disposal (phase-out, retire, recycle, safe-disposal)", while *Lifecycle Assessment (LCA)* is "a technique to assess environmental impacts associated with all the stages of a product´s life from-cradle-to-grave, from raw material extraction through materials processing, manufacture, distribution, use, repair and maintenance, and disposal or recycling". *LCA* can help avoid a narrow outlook on environmental concerns by compiling an inventory of relevant energy and material inputs and environmental releases; evaluating the potential impacts associated with identified inputs and releases; and interpreting the results to help to make more informed decisions [5].

A *Green Virtual Enterprise Breeding Environment (GVBE)* is a long-term strategic alliance of green enterprises and their related support institutions aimed at offering the necessary conditions to efficiently promote the sharing and recycling of resources such as: information, materials, water, energy and/or infrastructure with the intention of achieving sustainable development in a collaborative way [6] [7]. A *GVBE* can be a three-level holistic *sustainable industrial development model* (see Fig. 1) for achieving a *Circular Economy* at a *micro-level* with its green enterprises development, at *meso-level* with green virtual enterprises creation and at a *macro-level* with the *GVBE* it-self as an intelligent network for competencies and resources management from different green enterprises aiming to combine their green capabilities to develop triple top-line strategies to create sustainable value. This paper provides basic concepts and general guidelines to create *sustainable industrial development models* for *Circular Economy* based-on *Collaborative Networked Organisations.*

## 2    Green Enterprises: Circular Economy's Micro-level

A *Green Enterprise* is an enterprise that strives to meet the triple bottom line by ensuring that all products, processes, manufacturing and logistics activities in its business operation address the sustainable principles [6] (see Fig. 2).

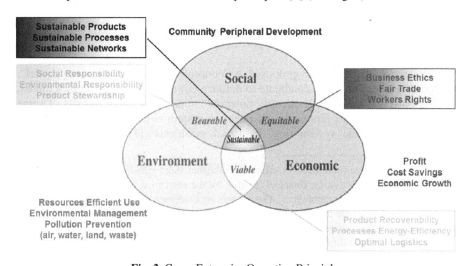

**Fig. 2.** Green Enterprise Operating Principles

According to the *Circular Economy* literature, the baseline of a strategy to develop a *Circular Economy* starts with the establishment of more *Green Enterprises* in the industrial landscape, representing the micro-level (small-cycle) of a *sustainable industrial development model*. Modern enterprises should then adopt "green enterprise systems" (see Fig. 3) [8] in their business operation in order to become *GreenEnterprises,* continuouslymonitoring,analysing,re-designingandimplementing a triple top-line[1] value production (for a product) or a triple top-line value offering (for a service) as conditions change and new opportunities emerge for achieving new sustainability levels. *Green Enterprises* aim to change the way products are manufactured and the way services are provided to the customers towards a *sustainable enterprise development model* [9].

- **Green product/service** – *refers to a product or service whose manufacturing or offering, purchase and use allows a sustainable economic development.*
- **Green design** – *refers to a product or service design that puts special consideration into its environmental impact during its whole lifecycle.*
- **Green materials** – *refers to a material that preserves natural resources and reduces the environmental impact, including those materials composed of recycled materials or can be recycled at the end of its lifespan.*
- **Green processes** – *refers to a process that eliminates the environmental burden in its resources input, energy consumption, and outputs impact.*
- **Green production** – *refers to a production system that puts a strong effort to lessen its environmental impact by conserving raw materials (using more recycled and/or renewable materials), minimising energy use and emissions, and wastes.*
- **Green packaging** – *refers to the use of green materials in packaging, comprising recycled content, or reusable or degradable packaging materials to minimise landfill waste and transportation costs.*
- **Green logistics** – *refers to any environmental friendly logistics strategy such as: commuting and shipping products together, using alternative fuel vehicles, reducing overall packaging, sharing warehouses and containers, etc.*
- **Green recycling** – *refers to any of the 5R strategies: repair, re-manufacture, recycle, re-use or re-generated to reduce environmental impact.*

**Fig. 3.** Green Enterprise Systems / Technologies

Despeisse et al. [10] have proposed a "conceptual factory ecosystem model", which can be considered as a candidate to define a *Green Enterprise* reference model, focusing on resources flows to identify potential connections where outputs of some activities can be used as inputs elsewhere in the system rather than treated as losses or wastes leaving the system (e.g. industrial symbiosis[2] [11] at *intra-enterprise*

---

[1] A triple top-line value production or offering establishes three simultaneous requirements of sustainable business activities: financial benefits for the enterprise, natural world betterment, and social advantages for employees. Though this is sometimes called the triple bottom line, triple top line stresses the importance of initial value rather than after the fact effects [9].

[2] Industrial Symbiosis can be defined as an industrial ecology strategy, based on collaboration and synergetic possibilities, aimed at sharing/exchanging information, materials, water, energy and/or infrastructure (e.g. services) among industrial actors in order to increase economic gains and achieve sustainable development in an eco-industrial network [11].

*level* – see Fig. 4). This ecosystem view of a factory, an eco-factory, can be used to build cross-disciplinary models of the material, energy and waste flows linking the manufacturing operations, the supporting facilities and the surrounding buildings [10]. Furthermore, other sustainability strategies as factory level include: *at the source,* preventive measures such as product and process design and dematerialisation to reduce the intake of resources in the technosphere; *during manufacturing,* with technical and organisational measures to increase the efficiency with which resources are transformed into economically valuable products; and *at the end of product lifecycle,* with closed-loop circulation of resources with the technosphere through reuse, remanufacturing and recycling [10] [12] [13] [14] [see also 9 for Greening the Industrial Facility] .

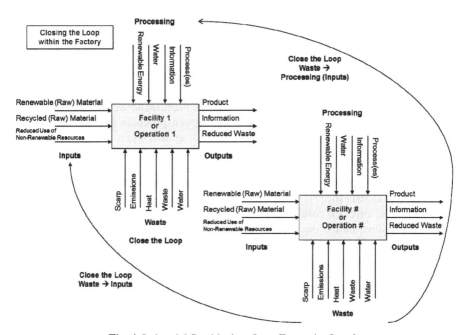

**Fig. 4.** Industrial Symbiosis at Intra-Enterprise Level

At the *Circular Economy's micro-level* [2], *Green Enterprises* are the access point to put pollution prevention in practice by seeking higher efficiency through cleaner production; reduce consumption of resources and emissions of pollutants and waste; reuse resources; and recycle by-products [15].

Within a *GVBE*, a *Green Enterprise,* as a *GVBE member,* will be able to develop "collaboratively" new green capabilities and capacities in order to re-engineer its "individual" production and distribution processes towards eliminating/recycling its wastes to maximise returns per unit of resource consumed, sharing/reducing its costs over limited natural resources (e.g. raw materials) and supporting infrastructure (e.g. logistics), and increase its green business opportunities and profit by establishing long- and short-term strategic coalitions to develop new competitive advantages (e.g.

green products, services and processes) without compromising critical resources for the future [6] [7].

Moreover, a *GVBE* can offer its *members* the "collaboration opportunity" to share lessons learned (knowledge) and other kind of tangible and intangible assets towards developing new technologies and standards in regards to the minimisation of pollution and the reuse, recycling, conversion and safe-disposal of waste, and new lifecycle frameworks to optimise the use of water, energy and materials at *intra-enterprise level* in order to minimise environmental impact.

## 3     Green Virtual Enterprises: Circular Economy's Meso-Level

*Green Virtual Enterprises (GVEs)* are short-term and dynamic coalitions of green enterprises, that may be tailored within a *GVBE,* to respond to a single collaboration opportunity, through integrating the green technology (skills or core-competencies and resources) required to meet or exceed the quality, time and cost frames expected by the customer with a low ecological footprint, and that dissolve once their mission/ goal has been accomplished, and whose cooperation is supported through computer networks. *GVEs* represent an emerging sustainable manufacturing and logistics mode focused on offering, delivering and recovering green products to/from the market, under a lifecycle thinking. *GVEs* focus on adopting lean-agile manufacturing and other sustainable engineering and logistics principles in order to enhance production, reduce wastes and improve their management, decrease energy consumption, achieve logistics efficiency and consequently reduce production and logistics costs and environmental impact [6] [7].

*GVEs* as goal-oriented collaborative networks can be designed within a *GVBE* with two different aims, on the one hand to become *dynamic forward supply networks* for delivering new green products/services to the market, and on the other hand to become *dynamic reverse supply networks* for recovering the products sold under the *GVBE* brand (e.g. product stewardship) for direct-use, repair, re-manufacture, recycle or safe-disposal. The two *GVE modalities* proposed will be crafted within a *GVBE* in where *Green Enterprises* will be prepared and ready to participate in *dynamic forward and reverse supply networks* created according to the needs and opportunities of the market, and remain operational as long as these opportunities persist, offering in this way an assertive approach towards the market dynamicity and true sustainability [6] [7].

*GVEs* as *dynamic forward supply networks (F-GVEs)* are temporary alliances of green enterprises that come together in order to better respond the market demands through the most efficient use of their complementary skills or core-competences and shared resources, for developing and delivering in a sustainable way new products (goods and services) to the customer with a minimal environmental impact [6] [7].

*GVEs* as *dynamic reverse supply networks (R-GVEs)* are temporary alliances of green enterprises that come together in order to better respond a business opportunity based on a sustainable reverse logistics and end-of-life manufacturing approach for recovering products, parts, subassemblies and/or scrap through the most efficient use of their complementary skills or core-competences and shared resources for their direct-use (re-use), repair, re-manufacture, recycle or safe disposal - within a GVBE [6] [7].

At the *Circular Economy's meso-level* [2], *GVEs* will help to respond to emerging interdependence opportunities and potential synergies between *GVBE members'* participating with their "individual" production and distribution processes (see Fig. 4) as *GVE partners* in temporary eco-value networks (the *GVEs*), so the waste and surplus of downstream operations within the *GVEs lifecycle* (creation, operation/ evolution and dissolution), through a certain degree of technical processing, return to the upstream operations of other *GVEs* and/or *GVBE members* within the *GVBE* in order to close the loop (see Fig. 5).

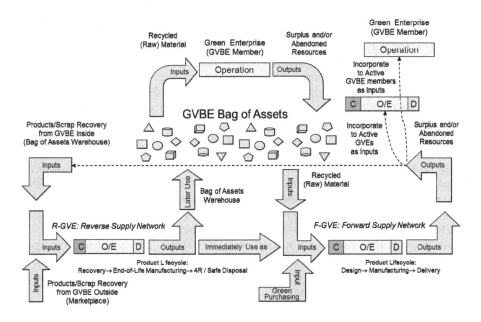

**Fig. 5.** Industrial Symbiosis at Inter-Enterprise Level

In this sense, industrial symbiosis opportunities at *inter-enterprise level* will take place within the *GVEs lifecycle* and also within the *GVBE members* individual business operations, including opportunities in where some inputs for a *GVBE member* as an individual entity and/or a *GVE* as a group entity can be collected from the waste and surplus of downstream operations of other businesses (the *GVBE members* and the running *GVEs*) in real-time and/or from the waste and surplus and/or abandoned resources stored by the *GVBE members* and *GVEs* after their dissolution in the *GVBE* bag of assets[3] [6] [15] [16].

Moreover, *R-GVEs* will support the logistics to share, reuse and recycle all potential resources (e.g. information, materials, water, energy and/or infrastructure)

---

[3] A GVBE bag of assets is a common virtual and physical warehouse to make easier the share of tangible and intangible assets between the GVBE members for different purposes [6] [7].

within the *GVBE*, so that resources will circulate fully thought the GVEs' "collaborative" production and distribution processes. Hence, *GVEs* will advocate, as a shared common operating principle of their GVE partners, to establish an industrial ecology pattern aiming to reduce resources input, extend productions lifecycle and renewable resources from scraps [6] [15] [16].

## 4     GVE Breeding Environments: Circular Economy's Macro-level

*Green Virtual Enterprise Breeding Environments (GVBEs)* have as their main goal becoming intelligent networks for competencies and resources management in order to match *GVEs* inputs and outputs (match-making) to maximise resources utility towards achieving industrial symbiosis at *inter-enterprise level* (see Fig. 4). *GVBEs* concentrate on bringing their business eco-systems as close as possible to being a closed-loop system by keeping a close interaction of material, energy, information and technology among their members towards a near complete recycle and sharing of resources for producing and delivering green products with sustainable manufacturing and logistics practices through *GVEs* creation, and by recruiting new *GVBE members* that can enhance the network capabilities and capacities to grasp new green business opportunities in time and taking into account environmental impact and resources utility. Furthermore, *GVBEs* at *intra-enterprise level* aim to enhance their members' green degree level by providing incentives to share and implement best practices that can reduce natural resources consumption, improve approaches for sustainable business operations, reduce (raw) materials costs, reduce treatment and disposal costs, etc. to meet economic gains by saving money and protecting the environment.

At the *Circular Economy's macro-level* [2], *GVBEs* aim to create synergies between enterprises and industrial networks for a more efficient and ecological use of materials, energy and other resources. *GVBEs* ultimate goal is to promote a "sustainable management" culture that oversees the sharing of information, services, utilities, by-products, and other resources among or within enterprises in order to add value, reduce costs, and improve performance in terms of sustainability [6] [15] [16].

## 5     Discussion: Collaborative Networks for a Sustainable World

Authors have introduced a *sustainable industrial development model* for a *Circular Economy* - the *GVBE model* - based on the *Collaborative Networked Organisations* and *Industrial Ecology paradigms*. The paper proposes a bottom-up approach towards *Sustainable Development* and *Circular Economy* following a "sustainable islands approach" [17]. The basic assumption of this approach is that development towards sustainability and closed-loop systems can be introduced in a more effective and efficient way to an enterprise, a value network and/or a business eco-system by starting from the achievement of small sustainable entities (e.g. green facilities or operations → green enterprises) and then building block to larger ones (e.g. → GVEs and their GVBEs) through different collaboration mechanisms [17] [18].

Moreover, the *sustainable islands approach* [17] has been used in this research work as an assisting mean and roadmap to increase *industrial symbiosis* and *collaboration activities* at *intra-* and *inter-enterprise levels* to develop in a hierarchical way a *sustainable industrial development model:* the *GVBE.* Furthermore, the strategy is to create islands of sustainability at *intra-* and *inter-enterprise levels* and then increase eco-networking activities to interconnect the sustainable entities (e.g. facilities → enterprises → networks) within a business eco-system to create a true *sustainable industrial development model* for a *Circular Economy.* Therefore, the *GVBE model strategy* is to reach sustainability in a business eco-system by starting from an *intra-enterprise level* and then move up to diverse *inter-enterprise levels* by promoting on a lower hierarchical level *Green Enterprises* creation and operation [6] [8] [10], which will allow to increase efficiency and hazardous substitution in the micro-system, and at a higher hierarchical level *GVEs* and their *GVBEs* creation and operation [6] [7] that will help to optimise the macro-system in an interactive way with the creation of *F-GVEs* and *R-GVEs,* and the recruiting, integration and enhancing of new *GVBE members* capabilities and capacities for developing triple top-line strategies to create sustainable value [17].

## 6    Conclusions and Further Research

"Eco-industrial networking" is rapidly becoming an important tool for enterprises to improve their competitiveness in a collaboratively and sustainable way [1] [2] [15] [16]. Different eco-industrial networking projects can be already found around the World, for some relevant case studies in America, Europe and Asia [please read 19].

This paper continues the exploration of potential synergies between *Industrial Ecology* [4] and *Collaborative Networked Organisations* [1] scientific disciplines to achieve more *sustainable industrial development models.* The final aim of this research work is to explore holistic and systemic strategies for seeking integrated solutions at both *intra-* and *inter-enterprise levels* for lowering resources input, enhancing resources productivity, reducing wastes and emissions, and lowering operating costs within an enterprise and between industrial networks based-on *(Sustainable) Collaborative Networked Organisations* models.

**Acknowledgments.** The research presented in this document is a contribution for the ECOLEAD Project (FP6 IP 506958), for the S-MC-S Project (FP7 NMP-ICT-FoF 260090), and for the ITESM, Campus MTY & CCM, Research Chairs.

## References

1. Camarinha-Matos, L.M., Afsarmanesh, H., Boucher, X.: The Role of Collaborative Networks in Sustainability. In: Camarinha-Matos, L.M., Boucher, X., Afsarmanesh, H. (eds.) PRO-VE 2010. IFIP AICT, vol. 336, pp. 1–16. Springer, Heidelberg (2010)
2. Shao-ping, X., Yun-jie, H.: The Research of the Development Principles and Development Model of Circular Economy. In: Proceedings of the 2010 International Conference on Challenges in Environmental Science and Computer Engineering, vol. 1, pp. 97–100. IEEE Computer Society, Washington, DC (2010)

3. United Nations Environment Program (UNEP): Definition of Cleaner Production, http://www.unep.org/

4. International Society for Industrial Ecology (IS4IE): Definition of Industrial Ecology, http://www.is4ie.org/

5. US Environmental Protection Agency: Definition of Lifecycle Assessment, http://www.gdrc.org/

6. Romero, D., Molina, A.: Green Virtual Enterprises and Their Breeding Environments. In: Camarinha-Matos, L.M., Boucher, X., Afsarmanesh, H. (eds.) PRO-VE 2010. IFIP AICT, vol. 336, pp. 25–35. Springer, Heidelberg (2010)

7. Romero, D., Molina, A.: Green Virtual Enterprise Breeding Environment Reference Framework. In: Camarinha-Matos, L.M., Pereira-Klen, A., Afsarmanesh, H. (eds.) PRO-VE 2011. IFIP AICT, vol. 362, pp. 545–555. Springer, Heidelberg (2011)

8. Graedel, T.E., Howard-Grenville, J.A.: Greening the Industrial Facility: Perspectives, Approaches, and Tools. Springer, New York (2005)

9. Tueth, M.: Fundamentals of Sustainable Business: A Guide to the Next 100 years. World Scientific Publishing Co., Hackensack (2010)

10. Despeisse, M., Ball, P.D., Evans, S., Levers, A.: Industrial Ecology at Factory Level – A Conceptual Model. Journal of Cleaner Production 31(1), 30–39 (2012)

11. Chertow, M.R.: The Eco-Industrial Park Model Reconsidered. Journal of Industrial Ecology 2(3), 8–16 (1998)

12. Lovins, A.B., Lovins, L.H., Hawken, P.: A Road Map for Natural Capitalism. Harvard Business Review 77(3), 145–158 (1999)

13. Allwood, J.M.: What is Sustainable Manufacturing? Sustainable Manufacturing Seminar Series, Cambridge University, pp. 1–32 (2005)

14. Abdul Rashid, S.H., Evans, S., Longhurst, P.: A Comparison of Four Sustainable Manufacturing Strategies. International Journal of Sustainable Energy 1(3), 214–229 (2008)

15. Wang, J.F., Li, H.M.: Circular Economy and Sustainable Development: China's Perspective. In: Proceedings of the R 2005 - 7th World Congress on Recovery, Recycling and Re-integration (2005), http://csp.eworlding.com/3r/

16. Lie, Y.: The Ideology of Sustainable Development of the Circular Economy and the Development Mode based on the point of Industrial Chains. In: Proceedings of the International Conference of E -Business and E-Government, Shanghai, China, pp. 1–6 (2011)

17. Wallner, H.P., Narodoslawsky, M.: The Concept of Sustainable Islands: Cleaner Production, Industrial Ecology and the Network Paradigm as Preconditions for Regional Sustainable Development. Journal of Cleaner Production 2(3-4), 167–171 (1994)

18. Romero, D., Galeano, N., Molina, A.: Mechanisms for Assessing and Enhancing Organisations' Readiness for Collaboration in Collaborative Networks. International Journal of Production Research 47(17), 4691–4710 (2009)

19. Fleig, A.: ECO-Industrial Parks: A Strategy towards Industrial Ecology in Developing and Newly Industrialised Countries. Deutsche Gesellschaft für Technische Zusammenarbeit (GTZ) GmbH (2000)

# A Collaborative Network Model
# for the Standards Community

Ovidiu Noran

Griffith University, Australia
O.Noran@griffith.edu.au

**Abstract.** Standards, as agreed-upon norms and requirements about systems, are essential pillars of enterprise and network operation and interoperability. However, standards themselves often display interoperability, inconsistency and overlap problems partly due to the custodian work groups' heterogeneity, the politics involved and limited communication and cooperation. This paper proposes and investigates the use of a Collaborative Network (CN) model in the standards community so as to take advantage of the wealth of knowledge accumulated in this domain, the artefacts built and the lessons learned in practice. Following an introduction and a review of the current issues in standards development, the paper presents the specific features of the CNs and the Virtual Organisations (VOs) they would create in order to tackle standards creation and revision in an integrated and synergistic way. A case study is also used to describe a possible implementation of the CN / VO model in practice and to illustrate the benefits of the proposed approach.

**Keywords:** Collaborative Networks, International Standards Organisation.

## 1    Introduction

Today's enterprises must permanently adapt to a competitive and ever-changing business environment. Continuous change processes support enterprise agility; however, they also have the potential to affect data, application and business processes interoperability at technical, syntactic, semantic and pragmatic levels. These problems can 'make or break' the affected parties and may occur within a single enterprise but also at company network level [1]. A potential solution for the conceptual and syntactic aspects of interoperability involves agreeing on and upholding standardised formats to overcome barriers (see [2], [3]). This in turn demands unambiguous, non-overlapping and interoperable standards as crucial enablers of enterprise and network agility and survival. Unfortunately however, standards are themselves often plagued by the above-mentioned problems, brought about by quasi-isolated creation and evolution. The result is low usability and end user confusion as to what standards to use and how, for a given task.

This paper proposes the use of a Collaborative Network (CN) [4] approach in order to tackle some of the root causes of the issues affecting standards - so that operational, competent and *synergic* teams can be formed to develop and revise standards in a consistent way, within an integrated and supportive environment.

L.M. Camarinha-Matos, L. Xu, and H. Afsarmanesh (Eds.): PRO-VE 2012, IFIP AICT 380, pp. 437–445, 2012.
© IFIP International Federation for Information Processing 2012

## 2    Standards Development - Some Current Issues

A simplistic image of standards is that of documented agreed-upon norms or requirements about systems of interest. The concepts discussed in this paper are widely applicable; however, the present scope is limited to technical standards developed by the International Standards Organisation (ISO) [5] (with input from other organisations such as IEEE [6] and INCOSE [7]), relevant to the proper (inter)operation of enterprises, CNs and Virtual Organisations (VOs) they form.

A large majority of the standards involve the work and consensus of experts that are typically volunteering their time and resources in the process. The use of standards is mandated by laws and many governmental and private organisations and agencies. Thus, to secure and manage projects, companies must abide by the standards specified by the clients and/or in legal documents. Standard administration and development is assigned to Work Groups (WGs) in Technical Committees (TCs) and Sub-Committees (SCs). Typically, the WGs have their own websites with access restricted to members. This results in low visibility between WGs and is likely to lead to the development of standards displaying coverage gaps, overlaps, redundancy and inconsistency.

ISO has developed a general vocabulary [5] and also usually standards have glossaries attached so as to formalise the terminology and improve interoperability; however, the vocabulary is generic and glossaries are often inconsistent across WGs working on related standards. As currently it is difficult to find and update other affected standards, changes to one standard do not automatically propagate to, or are checked for compliance with all other relevant standards.

Typically, several standards are required in order to set up and operate a project (whether cooperatively or not). While ISO maintains a website with the information relating to standards, it is often difficult for the average user to establish the standards required for a particular type of project. The free guides sometimes provided have a low usability and level of detail; in addition, they cannot cover and explain the use of every *combination* of standards as it will most likely be necessary. Terminology inconsistency, gaps, overlaps and interoperability deficiency of the standards that may have been selected using a guide add to the users' confusion and end up affecting all levels of enterprise(s) and network operation. There is some literature that explains the use of standards in more depth, albeit scarce and specialised (see the case of software development standards [8]).

There are currently several mechanisms within ISO to promote cooperative work and improve WG organisational interoperability. Thus, SCs hold yearly and half-yearly Plenary and Interim Meetings, where WG members meet to work but also socialise in events and ceremonies [9]. Study Groups (SWGs) recruit members across WGs in order to work on issues perceived as having common areas and 'liaisons' (members that belong to several WGs) are also used in order to facilitate information exchange. These approaches are a good baseline; however, they can be improved. For example, the meetings are too few to promote trust and cultural interoperability, especially in an environment where politics and lobbying for different agendas (other standards organisations, national bodies, major government contractors, etc) are an inherent part of decision-making. The SWGs creation occurs in a rather ad-hoc manner and the liaisons, while well-intended and hard-working, in the author's experience are often constrained by limited resources and authority.

As each standard has its own lifecycle, the mandatory review processes occur in an asynchronous way across ISO. Ideally, all other interested WGs should be aware of the proposed revisions to a standard and participate if necessary. Currently however, this is rather occurring on an irregular and anecdotal basis.

It also appears that currently, many TCs and SCs do not have a holistic view of the standards they develop and maintain and their potential impact on other standards. To the knowledge of the author, to date such views have only been attempted in an isolated and ad-hoc way. This lack of a 'big picture' further hinders the proper cooperation and consistency within and across SCs and TCs.

To summarise, the main problems are that a) members of various groups need to properly interoperate and *collaborate* in developing and revising standards and b) all *relevant* groups need to be involved in a project so that gaps, scattering and overlap is avoided so that the resulting standards are consistent in structure, vocabulary etc.

An analogy can be made here with commercial enterprises that come together in order to tackle projects requiring resources and knowledge beyond their own. Such enterprises typically set up (or join) CNs that allow them to get to know and trust each other. CNs act as 'breeding environments' who can promptly create VOs that successfully bid for projects, complete them and subsequently dissolve.

The following section attempts to explain how the CN concept can be applied to the universe of discourse of standards development.

## 3    The Suitability of a Collaborative Network Model

The CN paradigm, brought about by globalisation and ICT infrastructure progress, has evolved to become a scientific discipline [10]. The application of the CN principles nowadays is wide – in industry, aged care, medicine, education, defence, but also in areas such as social networking [11], or environmental sustainability and disaster management [12, 13]. Interoperability (the lack of which is one of the root causes of standards development inconsistency and overlap problems) is paramount in the efficiency and survival of a CN – therefore it has been extensively researched (see [14] and many others). The intricate area of organisation and culture interoperability, very relevant to the standards community, has also been tackled (see e.g. [15]).

Adopting a CN approach for standards development would allow using all this wealth of CN and related interoperability knowledge. For example, to address the technical (such as infrastructure) and syntactic interoperability aspects, a shared 'on-line' intelligent repository (see e.g. [16]), capable of representing the standards-related information in various ways (including the life cycle context and interactive / 3D views as argued by Cleveland [17] and Gomes et al. [18]) would significantly benefit every type of group involved. The participants in a so-called 'CN for standards development' would also have the opportunity to address the organisational culture interoperability aspect by getting to know, *understand* (i.e. achieve semantic interoperability) each other and thus build trust and synergy.

### 3.1    Specific Features of the Collaborative Network and Virtual Organisations

In order to be applied to standards development, the CN paradigm needs to be tailored to its specific requirements so it can effectively address the problems outlined in the previous sections. Thus, the commercial and competitive motivations of the typical CN participants are less present (perhaps in the companies that must use the standards produced and who seek to yield the standards to their advantage by lobbying WGs' members). Rather, the main motivation to enter what could be called a 'Standards Development Collaborative Network' (SDCN) would be to improve interoperability and efficiency of the WGs and other groups that must come together to create / revise standards. Such an SDCN could be formed at TC or SC level, comprising WGs, SWGs and other relevant external bodies (including individual experts - see Fig. 1).

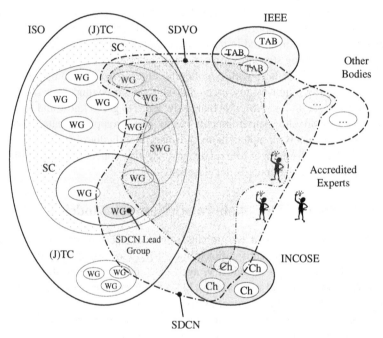

*Legend:* ISO: International Standards Organisation; IEEE = Institute of Electrical and Electronics Engineers; INCOSE = International Council on Systems Engineering; (J)TC = (Joint) Technical Committee; SC=SubCommittee; WG = Work Group; SWG = Study Group; TAB = IEEE Technical Activities Board; SDCN= Standards Development Collab. Network; SDVO = Standards Development Virtual Org.; Ch = (INCOSE) Chapter; —·—·· = SDCN Boundary;    —···—· = SDVO Boundary

**Fig. 1.** Possible SDCN and SDVO structures

In a SDCN, the typical create / join / remain / leave the network decisions would be left at WG level with some guidance from the SC conveners and the ISO directives. Lessons learned from past activities are currently not effectively reused; they could be abstracted and stored in reference models contained in a structured repository made available to the entire SDCN and integrated into an ISO-wide expert system [16].

The 'Standards Development Virtual Organisations' (SDVOs) created would be similar to their commercial VO counterparts, except that they would not bid for a project but rather be assigned one such as a New Work Item (NWI) of standard creation, or a revision. The operating guidelines of the SDCN and SDVO would be set by the ISO rules. The 'lead partner', customary in commercial CNs, could be represented here by the WG custodian of the new / revised standard.

Fig. 1 shows a simplistic view of an example SDCN and SDVO created by it. The network in this case reaches across several SCs and includes one SWG, WGs and structures from other interested organisations (in whole or in part according to the resources committed for the network) as well as individual experts accredited with ISO. The SDCN shown also has a 'lead group' that may be elected based on size, knowledge, resources, standards custody, etc. The SDVO is created as a subset of the SDCN with the mission to develop or revise one or several related standards.

# 4    Case Study: Integrated Standard Development and Revision

Systems and software systems engineering make use of two important standards, namely ISO 15288: Systems Life Cycle Processes [19] and ISO 12207: Software Life Cycle Processes [20]. The names suggest that ISO12207 is the specialisation of ISO15288 for the software domain. If that was true, ISO12207 should inherit and specialise the content of ISO15288, having identical shared definitions and inherited concepts such as life cycle phases, aspects, etc. Unfortunately, this is not the case as the two standards were developed by different WGs, at different times, with limited cross-consultation and input.

A harmonisation project was started to address these problems; however, it had a rather limited and erratic WG involvement and was beset by lobbying and politics. Work was discontinued after several years of efforts yielding disappointing results. Despite this outcome, valuable insight has been gained regarding a) the lack of a holistic image of the standards within the parent SC and b) the serious technical and organisational problems involved in the reconciliation of existing standards.

During the harmonisation efforts, a parallel attempt was made to use a framework [21] that was generic in nature, hence neutral and acceptable to 'mediate' between the two standards and identify gaps, overlaps and terminology inconsistency. This effort has led to the unsettling conclusions that c) the mediating framework itself and several related standards also displayed terminology inconsistencies with the two standards in question and d) the custodian WGs were not fully aware of the problem.

## 4.1    Application of the Proposed Collaborative Network Approach

In order to address the above-mentioned conclusions and problems, it is proposed to create an SDCN as shown in Fig. 1, supported by an intelligent shared repository such as described in [16]. The call for SDCN creation can be broadcast at Plenary / Interim Meetings. WGs and other bodies (IEEE, INCOSE, etc) shall identify themselves as stakeholders / custodians of the standards and start working together to achieve proper interoperability in all relevant aspects (semantic in particular). The SDCN will allocate members for the SDVO that will tackle the envisaged project. In this case, the SDCN members may be WG7, WG10, SWG5 from JTC1/SC7, WG1 from TC184/SC5, Technical Activities Board (TAB) members from IEEE and US / EU Chapter members from INCOSE. The SDVO members would be members of WG7, WG10, all SWG5 and interested IEEE TAB and INCOSE US Chapter.

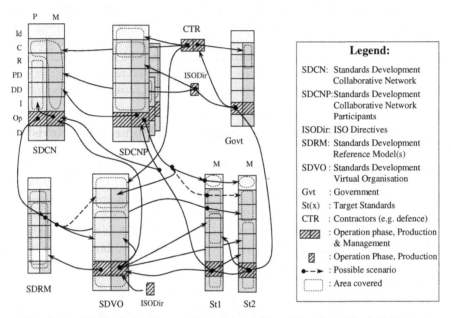

*Life cycle phases:* **Id** = Identification; **C** = concept; **R** = requirements, **PD** = preliminary design, **DD** = detailed design, **I** = implementation, **Op** = operation, **D** = decommissioning. *Other aspects:* **P** = Production / Service, **M** = management

**Fig. 2.** Life cycle-based model of SDCN and SDVO creation / operation

As all participant groups, organisations and entities evolve, the interactions that take place between the participants must be considered and represented in a life cycle context. In this paper, we use a modelling formalism derived from the reference used to mediate between the standards within the cased study, namely ISO15704 Annex A. This artefact contains a framework whose modelling framework (MF), called the Generalised Enterprise Reference Architecture (GERA), contains a rich repository of aspects including life cycle, management, organisation, human, decision, etc (see [21] for details). Fig. 2 shows the interactions between the participants in the proposed CN model using a GERA MF-based formalism featuring only the life cycle and management/operations viewpoints. The arrows represent the interactions between the participants in the context of their life cycles. Details have been omitted in the attempt to emphasize the most important features of the proposed model, as further described.

As shown in the figure, the SDCN is created by participants (the arrows from SDNCP to SDCN's Concept to Implementation life cycle phases). The SDCN then creates SDVOs as required in order to create or revise standards (St) (the arrows from SDCN to SDVO's Requirements to Decommissioning life cycle phases).

Beyond this basic interpretation however, this kind of representation also allows to show more intricate and essential facts that help stakeholders understand, adapt and better manage the standard development endeavour. Thus, it can be seen (arrows from CTR to one of the SDCNPs) that SDCN participants are lobbied or even created by some end users (e.g. larger companies that are required to use the standards by government (Govt) and laws, or other bodies who are interested in influencing and/or adopting the standards) and operate in accordance to the ISO Directives.

The SDCN and the SDVO created by it have a certain level of agility (arrows in SDCN and SDVO from Operation phase to their *own* upper life cycle phases) – i.e. they can 'redesign themselves' to a certain degree to achieve some stability in the face of changes in the environment (laws, other standards, WGs, etc). The figure also shows that the extent of the standards designed by the SDVO can vary. Some phases, e.g. identifying the need for a standard and defining the concepts underlying the standards may come straight from the SDCN participants (arrows from SDCNP to upper phases of St1 and St2). The same applies for the SDVO itself.

Importantly, standards influence each other's development (arrows from St1 to St2 and vice versa). This aspect must be detailed in additional models and implemented in the supporting structured repository so that changes to a standard can propagate to all related standards via their respective custodian WGs and any other SDVOs in charge.

The artefacts built and lessons learned during SDCN and SDVO creation and operation can be abstracted in reference models stored in a structured repository as previously described (arrows from SDCN, SDVO to SDRM).

# 5 Conclusions and Further Work

Standards development is a complex endeavour that is made possible by volunteers having a large variety of backgrounds and cultures. While notable results have been achieved, the standards community could further benefit from adopting a holistic and life cycle-based view of the standards and groups involved, addressing the politics and lack of trust and bridging organisational and geographical culture gaps that trigger counter-productive semantic barriers between participants.

The proposed model is based on SDCNs (supported by an integrated repository) who can timely and optimally select participants and build a SDVO for the required task. The work accomplished by SDVOs is broadcast and visible to *all* relevant stakeholders. Importantly, in this model the principles and vocabulary reflecting the SDCN participants' knowledge is inherently consistent across all products created or revised by the SDVOs. Redundant work is avoided, inconsistencies are eliminated, conflict and politics are minimised and efficiency and cooperation are improved.

There are also a number of caveats to this proposal. Firstly, the proposed CN model implies changes to ISO's organisational culture. Secondly, the creation and operation of the SDCNs and SDVOs must be regulated in the ISO directives to allocate proper authority and responsibility. And thirdly, a supporting infrastructure mirroring and enabling the proposed model must be implemented and accepted (and thus, actually *used*) by the work groups. Facilitating and modelling these change processes and artefacts constitutes the focus of further research and work in this area.

# References

1. EI2N & CoopIS. Interoperability Issues in Collaborative Information Systems (Presentation to the Plenary) (2010),
   `http://tc.ifac-control.org/5/3/events/ei2n2010-folder/ei2n2010-presentations-reports-and-conclusions/EI2N_2010_Interoperability_Issues_in_Collaborative_Information_Systems.pdf/at_download/file`
2. Chen, D.: Framework for Enterprise Interoperability (2006),
   `http://www.fines-cluster.eu/fines/jm/Download-document/53-Framework-for-Enterprise-Interoperability-Chen.html`
   (cited July 2011)
3. Noran, O., Bernus, P.: Effective Disaster Management: An Interoperability Perspective. In: Meersman, R., Dillon, T., Herrero, P. (eds.) OTM-WS 2011. LNCS, vol. 7046, pp. 112–121. Springer, Heidelberg (2011)
4. Camarinha-Matos, L., Afsarmanesh, H.: Collaborative Networks: A new scientific discipline. Journal of Intelligent Manufacturing 16, 439–452 (2005)
5. ISO. ISO/IEC Guide 2:Standardization and related activities — General vocabulary (2004),
   `http://www.iso.org/iso/iso_iec_guide_2_2004.pdf` (cited 2011)
6. IEEE. Institute of Electrical and Electronics Engineers - Technical Activities Board Ops Manual (2012),
   `http://www.ieee.org/about/volunteers/tab_operations_manual.pdf`
7. INCOSE. International Council on Systems Engineering - About INCOSE (2012),
   `http://www.incose.org/about/index.aspx` (cited 2012)
8. Moore, J.M.: The Road Map to Software Engineering: A Standards-Based Guide, 1st edn. Software Engineering Standards 2006. Wiley-IEEE Computer Society Pr (2006)
9. Portes, A.: Social Capital: Its Origins and Applications in Modern Sociology. Annual Review of Sociology 24, 1–24 (1998)
10. Camarinha-Matos, L., et al.: Collaborative networked organizations - Concepts and practice in manufacturing enterprises. Computers and Industrial Engineering 57(1), 46–60 (2009)
11. Badr, Y., Faci, N., Maamar, Z., Biennier, F.: Multi-level Social Networking to Enable and Foster Collaborative Organizations. In: Camarinha-Matos, L.M., Pereira-Klen, A., Afsarmanesh, H. (eds.) PRO-VE 2011. IFIP AICT, vol. 362, pp. 3–10. Springer, Heidelberg (2011)
12. Noran, O.: Towards an Environmental Management Approach for Collaborative Networks. In: Camarinha-Matos, L., Boucher, X., Afsarmanesh, H. (eds.) Collaborative Networks for a Sustainable World, pp. 17–24. Springer, Berlin (2010)
13. Noran, O.: Towards a Collaborative Network Paradigm for Emergency Services. In: Camarinha-Matos, L.M., Pereira-Klen, A., Afsarmanesh, H. (eds.) PRO-VE 2011. IFIP AICT, vol. 362, pp. 477–485. Springer, Heidelberg (2011)

14. ATHENA State of the art of Enterprise Modelling Techniques and Technologies to Support Enterprise Interoperability. Deliv D.A1.1.1 2(004), http://www.athena-ip.org (cited March 30, 2011)

15. Whitman, L., Panetto, H.: The Missing Link: Culture and Language Barriers to Interoperability. Annual Reviews in Control 30(2), 233–241 (2006)

16. Noran, O.: Towards a Sustainable Interoperability of Standards. In: 14th IFAC Symposium on Information Control Problems in Manufacturing, Bucharest, Romania (2012)

17. Cleveland, W.S.: Visualizing Data. Hobart Press (2008)

18. Gomes, A., Maneschy, M.C.: Communication and Power in Collaborative Networks: The Hypothesis of Technology as Confidence Enhancer. In: Camarinha-Matos, L.M., Pereira-Klen, A., Afsarmanesh, H. (eds.) PRO-VE 2011. IFIP AICT, vol. 362, pp. 19–26. Springer, Heidelberg (2011)

19. ISO/JTC1/SC7, ISO/IEC15288: Information Technology - Life Cycle Management - System Life Cycle Processes (2008)

20. ISO/JTC1/SC7, ISO/IEC12207 (Amd2): Standard for Information Technology - Software life cycle processes (2008)

21. ISO/IEC, Annex A: GERAM, in ISO/IS 15704:2000/Amd1:2005: Industrial automation systems - Requirements for enterprise-reference architectures and methodologies (2005)

# Systematic Analysis of Information Management Challenges within Long-Term Collaborative Networks

Ekaterina Ermilova and Hamideh Afsarmanesh

University of Amsterdam, FCN group,
Science Park 107, 1098 XG Amsterdam, The Netherlands
{e.ermilova,h.afsarmanesh}@uva.nl

**Abstract.** Long-term strategic networks – the so called Virtual organizations Breeding Environments (VBEs) – support their members with formation of virtual organizations (VOs), aimed to address opportunities in market/society. But, both establishment and management of these networks are challenging. On one hand, VBE aims at guiding its member organizations to accumulate/share their abilities and resources and work together as one strong virtual company. On the other hand, attempts to aggregate their competencies and resources to both identify what they can jointly achieve and to represent them as a single strong entity in the market/society. These in turn require support for strong interaction and interoperability among VBE members, as well as preserving interdependencies among their variety of information. This paper systematically analyses the base requirements and describes foundational criteria for modeling and management of information in VBEs. Particularly, it justifies the need for development of a generic unified VBE ontology-based system, in response to the identified VBE information management challenges. Finally, it specifies the main research problem areas and questions. Forthcoming publications will focus on the next steps of this research and how the raised research questions are addressed by our designed mechanisms and developed systems.

**Keywords:** Virtual organizations breeding environments, virtual organizations, information management, ontologies.

## 1    Introduction

Last decades have shown that the SMEs' chances of remaining competitive increase when they join forces and work together, e.g. within some new form of organisations called Virtual Organisations (VOs) [1]. As members of the VOs, organisations benefit from combining their resources, capacities and expertise in order to together create a larger / stronger entity in the market/society, and while agreeing to also share their profits and losses. For instance, in the manufacturing sector, SMEs establish VOs so that together they can produce more complex and cost/quality effective products, which they cannot produce individually.

Furthermore, both research and practice in the area of VOs have shown [2] a large number of cases where pre-establishing some form of longer-term networks among

L.M. Camarinha-Matos, L. Xu, and H. Afsarmanesh (Eds.): PRO-VE 2012, IFIP AICT 380, pp. 446–456, 2012.
© IFIP International Federation for Information Processing 2012

the SMEs, the so called Virtual organisations Breeding Environments (VBEs), can optimise and facilitate the effective / agile formation and setup of the VOs. VBEs primarily aim to provide a set of required functionalities which on one hand can increase the discovery of suitable market opportunities, identify best-fit partners to address the opportunity, and support the VO formation and establishment, and on the other hand prepare their member organisations in advance of the VO formation, in order to support effective collaboration among them within the established VOs.

In this research [3], we collaborated with a number of existing 1st generation VBEs from Europe and Latin America. Namely, we studied their current practices, identified their requirements, and deployed and validated our developments in their environments to bring them towards their 2nd generation.

This article presents the results of our systematic requirement analysis in this problem area. In section 2, the paper describes the variety of knowledge, information, and data that needs to be structured and managed in VBEs, as well as the list of related challenges that prevent VBEs from successful establishment and operation. Section 3 justifies the need for ColOnto - an ontology-based system, designed for responding to the identified VBE's information management challenges. Section 4 addresses the background on ontologies for VBEs. Section 5 lists the main problem areas for research that need to be tackled prior to development of ColOnto, as well as the research questions that are addressed by this research. Section 6 presents the research and development methodology that was followed in this research. Finally, section 7 concludes this paper.

## 2     Research Challenges and Justification for VBE-Ontology

Rooted in [4], we define the data, information and knowledge of VBEs as follows: *VBE data* represent some sets of symbols, which are typically held in the cells of the VBE database. As such, these data have no significance beyond their existence and do not have meaning on their own. *VBE information* represents data that have been given meaning by way of expressing their relational connections, e.g. within the relational database that we develop for VBEs, however this "meaning" does not have to be necessarily useful for the VBE stakeholders. *VBE knowledge*, on the other hand, represents an appropriate set of collected information and its related context within the VBE, intended to facilitate VBE functionality and its stakeholders. Knowledge accumulated in VBEs should be commonly understood by all its stakeholders, as well as properly formatted and stored in the form of information and data so that it can be effectively processed and analysed.

The data, information and knowledge about VBEs will be gathered from the following two sources: (1) from the generic VBE specification and VBE reference model, which is shared by all VBE instantiations and (2) from the specific domains of activities for this VBE (e.g. metalworking, health-care, etc.). These three types of information/knowledge are illustrated in Fig. 1, and further defined and characterised in this section.

The **generic VBE data, information and knowledge** addresses the VBE aspects and characteristics that are common to all VBEs. Here, the main types are defined as they already specified by the ARCON reference model [5]. The main features characterising these knowledge sources include their: (i) *Heterogeneity* – the ARCON reference model addresses a wide variety of heterogeneous concepts and aspects which comprehensively define VBEs, including the set of eight complementary dimensions of knowledge represented in Fig. 1. (ii) *Innovativeness* - The generic VBE knowledge specifications addressed in the thesis are new and still need to pass the test of time through their application to different VBEs. (iii) *Dynamism* - The generic VBE knowledge constantly evolves, caused by the inherent dynamism in the nature of VBE research and development area.

The data, **information and knowledge about activity domains** address the main processes, products, services, expertise and competencies which are available within a specific VBE domain of activity or business area. The main characteristics of these elements include their: (a) *Domain variety* - A large number of activity domains already exist, ranging from manufacturing to service provision. (b) *Specificity* – Knowledge within every domain has a wide variety of distinct elements. (c) *Dynamism* – VBE domain knowledge goes through a continuous dynamic evolution typically caused by innovation in technology.

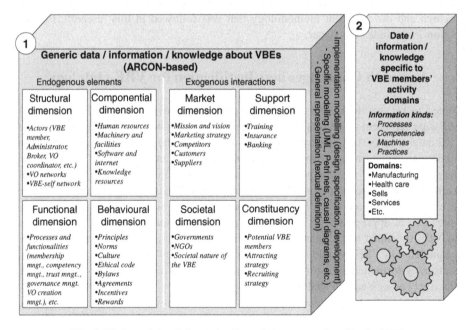

**Fig. 1.** Variety of data/information/knowledge accumulated in the VBE

The above characteristics entail a number of information-handling-related challenges for the management of VBEs. Our research focuses on four specific high-level challenges, described below and illustrated in Fig. 2. For each challenge, this figure shows relevant types of VBE knowledge (with solid arrows connecting them), which characterise this challenge and briefly defines a number of aspects related to each challenge.

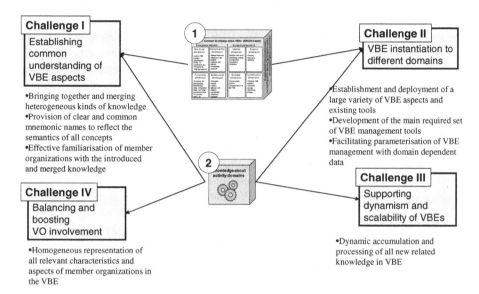

**Fig. 2.** VBE management challenges

**Challenge I - Establishing Common Understanding of VBE Aspects.** Due to innovativeness concepts introduced for 2$^{nd}$ generation VBEs, there is still a lack of common definition for the generic VBE concepts, which in turn causes the lack of understanding and effective communication within the VBEs [6]. In practice, this problem becomes even more severe due to both: (i) the need for merging and interrelation of different types of generic within the VBE and (ii) the continuous and dynamic joining of new members/actors to the VBE, each bringing their own new domain-dependent knowledge to the VBE.

**Challenge II - VBE Instantiation to Different Domains.** Heterogeneity and dynamism of the VBE knowledge poses obstacles to its instantiation and further extension, since it makes the development, parameterisation and interoperability creation among different VBE software systems more challenging.

**Challenge III - Supporting Dynamism and Scalability of VBEs.** Evolving of VBE knowledge also creates obstacles dynamism and scalability, since it requires continuous and fast acquisition, integration and processing of large amounts of new VBE information.

**Challenge IV - Balancing and Boosting VO Involvement.** The variety of representation and dynamism in character knowledge related to VBE member organisations pose challenges to their involvement in potential VOs. At present, the lack of homogeneity in organisations' representation in 1$^{st}$ generation VBEs causes the lack of homogeneity in their chances of being involved in configured VOs.

To address the information-handling-related challenges described in the previous section, we suggest the development and management of an ontology for VBEs. Considering the traditional definition of ontology [7] as: *"a specification of a representational vocabulary for a shared domain of discourse"*, the use of ontology lies at the heart of developing the management system functionalities for the emerging VBEs (2nd generation VBEs). The VBE ontology can therefore serve as the shared conceptualisation, which needs to be communicated between people and application subsystems. Furthermore, it can provide a base for common understanding among different stakeholders at the VBEs, as well as for creating interoperability among different VBE management tools.

Our research addresses the development of the **VBE-ontology** a generic and unified ontology for VBEs, called to specifically address Challenges I, II and III. Furthermore, a main part of this ontology focuses on specification of **profiles and competencies** of the VBE member organisations, which have to be stored in VBEs to support the match-making process for VO configuration. This specific aspect of VBE-ontology specifically addresses challenge IV mentioned above.

Namely, the VBE-ontology responds to Challenge I through its representation of the VBE related general concepts and domain-related terminology/standards in a detailed and uniform format, so that it can be shared, learned, and commonly understood by a variety of autonomous VBE stakeholders. It responds to Challenge II by serving as a formalized and standardized VBE data model that is useful for development of the VBE databases, and specification of a VBE data classification, also useful for parameterising VBE management tools. Furthermore, it responds to Challenge III through provision of semantics and formalism that support semi-automated management of VBE information (i.e. information extraction from texts and semantic search), and which in turn accelerates the information management processes of the VBEs. Finally, it responds to Challenge IV by providing means for formal and uniform representation of character information related to VBE members, such as their profiles and competencies, which provide similar opportunities for being automatically suggested for selection for VOs, and support balanced involvement of organisations into potential VOs.

In addition to development of the VBE-ontology, we developed the development of a system, called the **ColOnto** (Collaborative networks Ontology), which is built on top of this ontology. The ColOnto system consists of two main modules, namely:

(1)    a conceptual part, consisting of the VBE-ontology and
(2)    the functional part consisting of the set of functionalities required for the VBE-ontology maintenance and management.

# 3    Research Background, Problem Areas, and Research Questions

Although the need for **ontology** development and management to support Collaborative Networks and VBEs is identified in previous research [8] [9], in 2005 area of research was still at its early stages. A small number of existing publications in this area, which are closer to our work, have mainly focused on the following three topics:

- *An empirical development of an ontology for VBEs.* An early attempt to address an ontology for VBEs is presented in [10]. This ontology is developed empirically and includes a narrow sub-set of the VBE related top-level concepts.
- *A sub-ontology for specific VBE management subsystem.* An ontology for VBEs' Performance Indicators (PIs) and VBEs' Collaborative Opportunities (COs) called "PI and CO Ontology" is presented by [11]. The main concepts of this ontology include: "PI", "CO", "Organisation", "VBE", "VO", "Performance requirement" and "Measurement objective".
- *Ontology library for VBEs.* In [12] the concept of an Ontology Library System (OLS) addressed by [13] is adapted for VBEs. The OLS is defined as "an important tool in grouping and re-organising ontologies for reuse, integration, maintenance, mapping and versioning".

In relation to our **profile and competency** partition of the VBE-ontology, while there was a  significant number of research publications addressing the general topic of competencies of people, mainly within the human resources management area, there was a limited number of research addressing competencies of organisations, especially within the context of organisations' networking, including:

- *Organisation "competency models" for VBE members.* In [14] a competency model for "clusters of manufacturing organisations" is addressed, which aims to support the automation of the VO formation from this cluster. The introduction of this model was the first step towards competency-based supporting for boosting VO creation, but the model is not generic enough to be adapted to the variety of different VBEs.
- *Requirements for "competency management" in VBEs.* In a number of past research [15] [16] [17] the need for competency management functionalities for VBEs is identified. However, while some of these functionalities are identified in previous research, they are not further specified or developed.
- *Profile and competency management in existing VBEs.* A few existing VBEs handle digitised profiles and competencies of their members [3]. Furthermore, while every VBE stores profiles of their members, which represent a variety of characteristics about their member organisations, only a few of them store some details about competencies of their members.

The overview of the research background demonstrates the significant gaps existed in areas of **ontology management for VBEs**. Particularly, we have identified a number of open problem areas, including:

*1. Systematic design and development of the VBE-ontology.* A systematic approach to design and further development of the VBE-ontology needs to be defined and applied while answering the following questions:  Should there be one VBE-ontology or a set of ontologies? Which areas of VBE related knowledge and information should be addressed by ontologies? Should the VBE ontologies be formal or informal? Etc.

*2. Maintenance and evolution functionalities for VBE-ontology.* The VBE-ontology needs to continuously evolve, reflecting the new findings in the VBE area of research and well as the changes in existing VBEs due to market and society changes. Four specific functionalities have been already defined for this purpose as follows: Ontologies library; Collective development of ontologies; Semi-automated ontology discovery; and Semi-automated integration of related ontologies.

*3. VBE ontology-based management functionalities.* A number of ontology-based functionalities need to be developed to support the VBE through its entire life cycle from its creation stage to its dissolution stage, aimed mainly at coping with the large amounts of information to process, and at accelerating the VBE management operations. The following main functionalities are already identified as required for VBEs: Establishing of common understanding; Instantiating VBE to different domains; and Supporting dynamism in VBEs.

*4. Ontology visualisation.* Most ontology interfaces typically locate ontology classes through their hierarchical (i.e. subclass-superclass) relationships with other classes. However, such location is often not convenient or user-friendly for the human VBE actors who want to learn about the entire network of VBE concepts and the relationships among them (e.g. including part-of relationships).

In relation to the **profile and competency partition of the VBE-ontology**, open problem areas of research include the following:

*a. Establishing unified/generic models.* The profile and competency models included in the VBE-ontology need to be generic in order to suit every VBE, regardless of its application area.

*b. Continuous update of profile data.* In today's dynamic market, a large number of an organisation's characteristics, such as their resources (human, machinery, etc.), position in the market, financial status, organisation's aim/strategy, details of its products, associated partners etc, are also not static and are subject to changes at different times during the life time of the organisation.

*c. Maintenance and management of VBE profiles.* The profile and competency models should satisfy their purposes, namely supporting the VBE management functionalities/operations, which are mainly aimed at boosting VO creation.

*d. Generic competency naming.* With the lack of standards for naming the competencies in different domains, it is clearly challenging for VBEs to specify and describe their competencies. Nevertheless, the problem of naming and developing taxonomy for the existing and emerging competency names in different domains and applications is outside the scope of our research and remains an open area.

*e. Cataloguing competencies.* Classification of the wide variety of existing competencies in the world, even if limited to a specific domain and application area is still challenging. So far, there are no standards defined for classification of competencies, and every day new competencies emerge in many domains and application areas.

Based on the analysis of the research problem areas described above, we state the main general research question (GRQ) as follows:

***GRQ.*** *Can we effectively specify an ontology for Virtual organisations Breeding Environments (VBE), as well as develop semi-automated ontology-based support functionalities for VBEs such that they respond to the challenges of: (1) establishing common understanding of aspects for all VBE stakeholders, (2) creating VBEs in different domains, (3) handling VBE dynamism and scalability and (4) facilitating the boosting and balancing of organisations' involvement in potential VOs?*

This research question is further refined into three more specific questions RQ1 to RQ3. In the RQ1, we address the definition task of VBE-ontology and particularly introduce the definition of the profile and competency models within the VBE-ontology.

***RQ1.*** *Can we identify the scope and the elements of ontology encompassing the wide variety of VBE related entities and concepts so that it represents the diversity of its subspaces, addressing all endogenous elements and exogenous interactions, and specifically the subspace of profile and competency management?*

In RQ2, we address both the logical and the physical organisation of the VBE-ontology. Particularly we introduce the way in which this organisation responds to identified challenges for VBE-ontology development. Furthermore, we exemplify the specification of the VBE profile and competency models within it.

***RQ2.*** *Can we capture, organise and specify the large set of diverse but interrelated aspects identified in RQ1 in the VBE-ontology, considering both their evolutionary nature and the heterogeneity of their sources?*

In RQ3 we address the required ontology management functionalities to be developed on top of the VBE-ontology. These functionalities are mainly divided into two main groups. Namely the functionalities for maintaining the VBE-ontology itself, and VBE-ontology-based support functionalities. The second group of functionalities is specifically aimed at supporting profile and competency management in VBEs.

***RQ3.*** *Which set of functionalities are needed to maintain (e.g. discover, engineer and integrate) the continuously evolving VBE-ontology, as well as the semi-automated management needed of the information supported through the VBE-ontology?*

# 4    Research and Development Methodology and Achievements

The methodology followed to design and develop the ColOnto system for VBEs consists of six main steps divided into three main groups of "Input", "Approach & Development" and "Validation":

**Input – complete background analysis needed for development of ColOnto:**
- *Step 1: State of the art research.* In order to develop the ColOnto system for VBEs beyond the state of the art, and to position ColOnto among the past and present research and practices, the state of the art research is studied and analysed.
- *Step 2: State of the art practice.* This step is conducted through contacting a number of existing 1st generation VBEs, and collecting their responses through a set of questionnaires.
- *Step 3: Requirements analysis.* This step is mainly aimed at analysis of the VBE stakeholders' requirements for the ColOnlo system. Requirements were collected from different VBE stakeholders and some general requirements were also obtained from the literature.

**Approach & Development – designing & prototypical development of ColOnto:**
- *Step 4: Conceptual design of ColOnto.* This step is aimed at the development of the conceptual part of the ColOnto system, namely at the definition, design and specification of the VBE-ontology.
- *Step 5: Functional specification and development of ColOnto.* This step is aimed at the development of the functional part of the ColOnto system, namely at the development of functionalities for management of the VBE-ontology.

**Validation – validating correctness of the ColOnto system:**
*Step 6: Validation of the ColOnto system.* The ColOnto system for VBEs, addressed in this thesis, is validated through a number of empirical and rational approaches.

Both the conceptual and the functional parts of ColOnto introduced in section 3 of this article are developed. The VBE-ontology is built up in OWL. Currently it is represented by: (1) the complete meta-level, (2) the complete core level, and (3) domain level for the metalworking sector. The concepts for the domain level are provided from the existing 1st generation VBE from Mexico called IECOS (www.iecos.com). On the physical level the VBE-ontology represents set of files – one for every developed sub-ontology. Two software applications are developed to serve as prototypes of the VBE-ontology management system – Ontology Discovery and management System (ODMS) and Profile and Competency Management System (PCMS). PCMS focuses of management of a specific part of the VBE-ontology devoted to VBE member organizations' profiles and competencies. One screen-shot from the PCMS is illustrated in Fig. 3. It demonstrates a user interface for viewing profile model, which is based on the profile and competency sub-ontology.

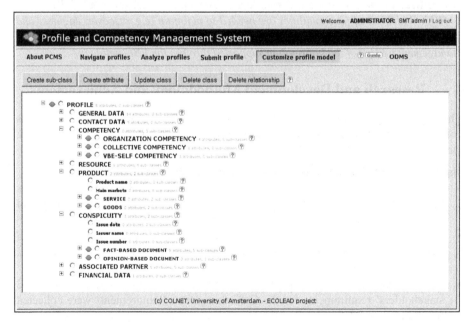

**Fig. 3.** Screen-shot from the PCMS's user interface for viewing VBE profile model

# 5    Conclusions

This paper motivates the need for applying ontologies to the  design and management of information in running Virtual Organizations Breeding Environments (VBEs), as well as those VBEs that are currently passing through their establishing phases. Particularly, it aims at consolidation of motivation for development of an ontology-based system called ColOnto for information management in VBEs. Therefore, it first addresses the main challenges for information management in VBEs that can be solved by using ontologies. It further addresses research on management of ontology in VBEs, and the main research questions that need to be tackled for development of ColOnto.

As such, this paper describes the results of a systematic analysis of the base requirements and the foundational criteria for modeling and management of information in virtual organizations breeding environments (VBEs). While some specific aspects of the raised research questions are addressed in our earlier publications [18], other forthcoming publications focus on systematic addressing of all specified research questions..

# References

1. Camarinha-Matos, L.M.: Virtual organizations in manufacturing: trends and challenges. In: Proceedings of FAIM 2002 (2002)
2. Camarinha-Matos, L.M., Afsarmanesh, H.: Elements of a base VE infrastructure. J. Computers in Industry 51(2), 139–163 (2003)
3. Ermilova, E., Afsarmanesh, H.: Modeling and management of Profiles and Competencies in VBEs. International Journal of Intelligent Manufacturing (JIM) 18(5), 561–586 (2007) ISSN: 0956-5515
4. Ackoff, R.L.: From Data to Wisdom. Journal of Applies Systems Analysis 16, 3–9 (1989)
5. Camarinha-Matos, L.M., Afsarmanesh, H.: A comprehensive modeling framework for collaborative networked organizations. At the Journal of Intelligent Manufacturing (2007)
6. Ollus, M.: Towards structuring the research on virtual organizations. In: Virtual Organizations: Systems and Practices. Springer Science, Berlin (2005)
7. Gruber, T.R.: A translation approach to portable ontology specifications. Knowledge Acquisition 5, 199–220 (1993)
8. Franke, U.L.: The Competence-Based View on the Management of Virtual Web Organizations. In: Managing Virtual Web Organizations in the 21st Century: Issues and Challenges. Idea Group Inc, (IGI) (2002)
9. Camarinha-Matos, L.M., Afsarmanesh, H.: The emerging discipline of collaborative networks. In: Proceedings of PRO-VE 2004 - Virtual Enterprises and Collaborative Networks, pp. 3–16, 23–26. Kluwer Academic Publishers (2004) ISBN 1-4020-8138-3
10. Plisson, J., Ljubic, P.: The CNO Ontology Page (2005), http://kt.ijs.si/software/CNOntology
11. Baldo, F., Rabelo, R.J., Vallejos, R.V.: An Ontology- Based Approach for Selecting Performance Indicators for Partners Suggestion. In: Camarinha-Matos, L., Afsarmanesh, H., Novais, P., Analide, C. (eds.) Establishing the Foundation of Collaborative Networks. IFIP, vol. 243, pp. 187–196. Springer, Boston (2007)

12. Simões, D., Ferreira, H., Soares, A.L.: Ontology Engineering in Virtual Breeding Environments. In: Camarinha-Matos, L., Afsarmanesh, H., Novais, P., Analide, C. (eds.) Establishing the Foundation of Collaborative Networks. IFIP, vol. 243, pp. 137–146. Springer, Boston (2007)
13. Ding, Y., Fensel, D.: Ontology Library Systems: The key to successful Ontology Re-use. In: Proceedings of the First Semantic Web Working Symposium (2001)
14. Molina, A., Flores, M.: A Virtual Enterprise in Mexico: From Concepts to Practice. Journal of Intelligent and Robotics Systems 26, 289–302 (1999)
15. Afsarmanesh, H., Camarinha-Matos, L.M.: A framework for management of virtual organizations breeding environments. In: Proceedings of 6th PRO-VE 2005 - Collaborative Networks and their Breeding Environments, Valencia, Spai, pp. 35–48. Springer (2005)
16. Galeano, N., Molina, A.: Core competence management in virtual industry clusters, in CD preprints. In: Horacek, P., Simandl, M., Zitek, P. (eds.) 16th IFAC World Congress, pp. 4–8. Czech Republic, Prague (2005)
17. Vallejos, R.V., Lima, C., Varvakis, G.: A Framework to Create a Virtual Organisation Breeding Environment in the Mould and Die Sector. In: Centric Colabaration and Supporting Fireworks. IFIP, vol. 224, pp. 599–608. Springer, Boston (2006)
18. Ermilova, E., Afsarmanesh, H.: Competency modelling targeted on boosting configuration of Virtual Organizations. In the International Journal of Production Planning & Control, Special Issue on Engagement in Collaborative Networks 21(2) (2010)

# 16

Collaboration Spaces

# Collaborative Spaces as Mediators for Information Sharing in Collaborative Networks

António Lucas Soares[2] and Fábio Alves[1,2]

[1] INESC Porto, Campus da FEUP, Rua Dr. Roberto Frias, 378, 4200-465 Porto, Portugal
[2] DEI, FEUP, University of Porto, Rua Dr. Roberto Frias, sn 4200-465 Porto, Portugal
[3] ESTGF-IPP, Apartado 205 4610 - 156, Felgueiras, Portugal
{Asoares,fabio.j.alves}@inescporto.pt

**Abstract.** Information and knowledge sharing within collaborative networks stills being a challenging problem. Particularly in self governed or mediated networks the information/collaboration deadlock is likely to occur if there are not instrumental methods, socially accepted, that foster usable and useful patterns of collaborative information management. This paper describes how the vision for a solution to this problem was developed using the design science frameworks and the concept of technological rules. The result is materialised in the concept collaborative spaces as pivoting collaborative structures in the network enabling locally shared information to feed the network global level.

**Keywords:** collaborative spaces, design science, technological rules.

## 1   Introduction

Collaboration, social networking, information and knowledge management are common places nowadays when the subject is collaborative networks of organisations for example for business applications. In the last decade thousands of research pages have been written about this, be it addressing the study of real world phenomena or proposing unforeseen strategies and tools. Nevertheless, no one dares to claim that there are enough models, architectures, theories, empirical knowledge, IT platforms, that don't justify more research on those subjects. The technological, economic, social, cultural, political context is always evolving, bringing new problems and opportunities to collaboration and networking. In spite of this, companies still need to cooperate, not just to compete, still need to work together with others, not just to develop their own products and services, still need to share knowledge, not just to increase their competitive edge. In an internet of services the need for belonging to collaborative networks is even more pressing, as the value added for the customers passes more and more for the provision of integrated, combined services. The research reported in this paper, addresses both the design of a collaborative network as a socio-technical artefact, and its outcome in a form of an information/ knowledge collaborative portal based in a social network platform. Section 2 of the paper describes the design science framework for the visioning of the platform features,

L.M. Camarinha-Matos, L. Xu, and H. Afsarmanesh (Eds.): PRO-VE 2012, IFIP AICT 380, pp. 459–466, 2012.
© IFIP International Federation for Information Processing 2012

while the section 3 details the connections between technological rules and the platform's innovative features. This research carried out during the h-know EU project[1].

# 2     The Socio-technical Design of a Collaborative Network

## 2.1     The Design Science Research Framework

The design of a collaborative platform aiming to support a collaborative network of organisations is unquestionably a socio-technical process. It requires a comprehensive visioning and methodological approach addressing the business, technology, management and people dimensions. If the socio-technical artefact is being developed as part of a research and development project, or within an innovation process, its vision is normally centred around two aspects: (i) Recognised and community validated business needs (for problem solving or for grabbing a business opportunity) encompassing technology as well as social and organisational development; (ii) Informed arguments justifying a new idea or web of ideas that hopefully will end up in an original and innovative socio-technical system (with varying degrees of novelty in each of the sub-systems).

Although these aspects are intertwined, this paper addresses the later, considering, in this case, the socio-technical artefact as composed by an IT based collaborative platform, a set of procedures and methods for the network formation, operation and dissolution, as well as community (virtual breeding environment) management, and a set of relationships between the individuals, groups and organisations using the platform.

Within the Design Science paradigm, as defined by [1] for research in management, "the mission of a design science is to develop knowledge for the design and realisation of artefacts, i.e. to solve construction problems, or to be used in the improvement of the performance of existing entities, i.e. to solve improvement problems". Both the collaborative networks and the information systems (IS) engineering disciplines can be, to a certain extent, considered design science disciplines.

There are several theoretical and methodological perspectives regarding the use of design science principles in IS design [2]. In this paper the general framework proposed by [3] will be used, together with the concept of technological rules as interpreted by [1]. The goal is to show how research results from explanatory sciences research - social networks modelling and simulation in this case - can be used to inform and inspire the design.

## 2.2     Getting Inspiration and Guidance

[3] Information Systems Research Framework (ISRF) proposes that IS research (i) develops/builds theory and artifacts and (ii) justifies/evaluates the outcomes of (i) by analytical, case study, experimental, field study and simulation means. Research in IS

---

[1] http://www.h-know.eu

must be relevant for a business environment and rigourous for a scientific community. As for the relevance, ISRF aggregates in "business needs" the requirements of the business "environment" composed by people, organizations and technology. In terms of rigour, research activities are to be informed by a knowledge base of foundations (theories, frameworks, models, instruments, etc.) and methodologies (formalisms, validation criteria, data analysis, etc.). At the end of a research, its results are to be applied in the business environment and contributions are made to enrich the knowledge base.

The h-know research was guided by the above framework (eventhough sometimes not explicitly). A socio-technical artefact was developed and theory about collaboration and information/knowledge management was built. A subset of the above results will be analysed below: the architecture of the h-know collaborative platform and a theory on the relationship between information/knowledge sharing and social networking based collaboration.

For the detailed development of the informed argument leading to a web of innovative ideas (see previous section) the concept of technological rule was used. [1] defines a technological rule (after the original concept coined by the philosopher Mario Bunge) as "a chunk of general knowledge, linking an intervention or artefact with a desired outcome or performance in a certain field of application". In the case of the h-know research, the desired outcome or performance was, in general terms, the successful formation and operation of a collaborative network of SMEs and research centres, and, more specifically, to achieve effective sharing of information and knowledge in the network through effective collaboration processes.

Technological rules can be derived from explanatory sciences such as sociology, cognitive sciences, or organizational science. For the design of socio-technical solutions for business problems involving organizational work, the more useful technological rules are likely to be derived from empirical studies. For example, [4] in their study of knowledge sharing barriers in complex, multi-national RTD projects, found that one the barriers most mentioned by project managers was the lack of initiative and strategy by the workers in what concerns to organising and disseminating non-operational information, e.g., lessons learnt. The reasons that were pointed out had to do basically with lack culture of collaborative work and knowledge sharing. It is then possible to derive technological rules from this study such as: "if you want to achieve effective information sharing in a collaborative network, select the most autonomous and collaboration prone employees" or "if there is a need to control and track information effectively in a collaborative network, procedures and workflows must be put in place to prevent document exchange through email". In this paper, rules derived from empirical studies or similar are named type 1 technological rules.

However, when looking for innovative ideas to incorporate in a socio-technical artefact, besides empirical studies it might be interesting to look at experimental studies, for instance modelling and simulation studies of social structures (social networks). For example, [5] in their network models for social influences processes hypothesise that various networks may be involved in the transmission of influence in different ways, and that influence might occur not only through public knowledge but also through private dyadic interactions. This can lead to a technological rule stating that "the existence of private spaces for collaboration in a collaborative platform are likely to result in the global spread of collaborative practices in the network". Such a derivation of technological rules is exploratory and speculative, but it can be inspirational for discovering innovative solutions. Rules derived from non-empirical studies such the ones referred above are called here type 2 technological rules.

## 3     h-know: A Socio-Semantic Collaborative Platform

### 3.1     Business Requirements and Scientific Objectives

h-know research aimed to develop a collaborative network artefact (an IT based collaborative platform and a methodology for its management) responding to specific business needs from the rehabilitation, restoration and maintenance areas in the construction industry. Furthermore, as part of an EU RTD research project, there was a strong requirement for developing a solution that is placed beyond the state-of-the-art, i.e., with an high degree of originality and innovativeness. Only short summary of the business needs or requirements is given next, as the focus of this paper is on the innovative requirements and solution features specification.

The increasing number of complex works in construction industry, particularly for the retrofitting, refurbishment and maintenance of old buildings or construction complexes, are urgently requesting an new solutions to enable a systematic and effective access to the construction knowledge related to this area, and to the state-of-the-art processes and materials to be applied. In the complex world of the restoration works there is still a sub-optimality of the information flow between different actors taking a role in the processes, such as the final users of the building, the administration responsible for the restoration works and other administration involved, the architects, the bodies in charge of the diagnosis of the building, the construction companies, and the SME's in charge of specific works. This is even more complex if multi-disciplinarity required for restoration works (including archaeologists, architects, engineers, etc) is considered. For this reason, innovative solutions to support new forms of collaborative knowledge and business networks of groups of SMEs and RTD centres, experts for restoration/maintenance, are needed. There is thus a need for a solution which will provide (i) innovative competitive knowledge and training providing services, and (ii) an advanced support for realisation of new forms for SME-RTD networking through their specific knowledge/competence integration, within a new collaboration structure.

### 3.2     Building a Vision for h-know

A set of type 2 technological rules were derived during the problem definition and requirements elicitation phase. Here follow three examples:

> TR_T2_03: "If the achievement of high levels of information creation and sharing in the collaborative network is fundamental, private interaction spaces should be provided for specific and situation dependent activities";

TR_T2_04: "If we want to increase the participation of individuals and organizations in the collaborative network, then promote the participation of influential actors (high centrality) in more than one collaboration space;

TR_T2_05: "If effective results are required from collaboration mediated by the platform, then information management support tools must be tightly coupled with social networking features";

TR_T2_06: "If we want to achieve and maintain a critical mass of members in the collaborative network, then the platform must represent an "obligatory passage point" for individuals and organisations, either by means of providing authoritative information or state-of-the art tools".

Next, some examples of explanatory results conveying the knowledge that enabled the derivation of the above rules are given. This derivation is not a systematic process, but requires interpretation and ingenuity as well as the skills to know and access relevant scientific and technical information sources.

To the socio-technical approach purposes, [6] agree that "social interaction ties are regarded as one of the antecedents in motivating knowledge sharing behaviors. The social interaction ties among individuals lead to creating trust, and wider communication, producing positive effects on sharing knowledge" and add, "The stronger social interaction ties become, the more frequent knowledge exchange behaviors as well as communication are observed" (quoted in Chai and Kim, 2011a).

[5] Social influence occurs when an individual adapts his or her behavior, attitudes or beliefs to the behavior, attitudes or beliefs of others in the social system. Influence does not necessarily require face-to-face interaction, but is based on information about other people. Social influence may arise when individuals affect others' behaviors, or when individuals imitate the behaviors of others, irrespective of the intention of the behavior's originator.

From the business requirements and the technological rules, the visioning process in the h-know research developed the concept of information and knowledge supported collaboration adopting a social network paradigm. In simple terms, h-know provides contained and private working spaces for the development of joint activities (seen as inter-organisational collaboration), strongly levered on information/knowledge management, built upon a social network platform for the interconnection of individuals and organisations.

### 3.3     Collaborative Spaces: Fostering Collaboration and Information Sharing

The concept of "collaborative space" emerged as the central structure in the platform, both in terms of collaboration tools and context and in terms of information/knowledge management. It provides content, document and event management, information organisation and classification based on domain ontologies, as well as the usual tools for communication and debate (such as foruns and blogs). It is a rich structure as it incorporates privacy schemes for all the informational objects and a life-cycle based on the collaboration status (see figure 1 for the overall concept and figure 2 for the life-cycle).

Despite the central role of the collaborative spaces, h-know would not respond to the initial requirements if information (and knowledge in some extent) could not be shared at the level of the business community (virtual breeding environment). This is done through a an hybrid process of publishing/collection of the public content available in each of the collaborative spaces. In fact, this is one of the distinctive features of the h-know platform: a process from local to global sharing that is likely to improve the quantity and utility of the shared information.

The h-know platform has a semantic structure for its content description implemented through the integration of social and domain ontologies. The social component uses FOAF (Friend of a Friend) and SIOC (Semantically-Interlinked Online Communities) ontologies that enable a description of the users, spaces and their relationships. The domain ontology implements a global/local approach to ontology management, and it is used to classify the content and actors according to the work and technical domains. This approach to the semantic structure of the platform enables to obtain answers to searches such as "who wrote something about subject s in the form of content c". A complete account of the development of the semantic structure of h-know is given by [7].

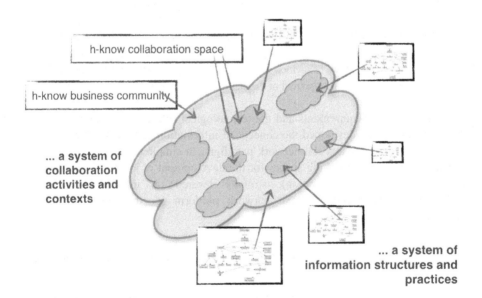

**Fig. 1.** The overall concept of a collaborative network structured upon collaborative spaces

problem-solving **ColSpace** life-cycle
**scenario:** looking for a problem solution
**pre-conditions:** user is logged in the portal; the user searched for a solution and didn't find one

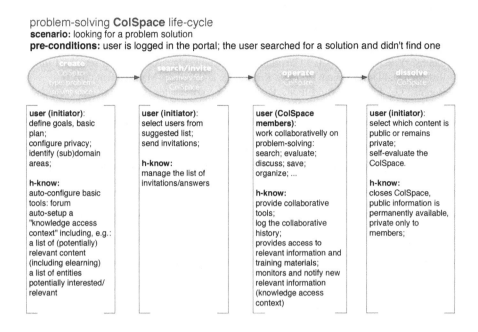

| user (initiator): | user (initiator): | user (ColSpace | user (initiator): |
|---|---|---|---|
| define goals, basic plan; configure privacy; identify (sub)domain areas; | select users from suggested list; send invitations; | members): work collaborativelly on problem-solving: search; evaluate; discuss; save; organize; ... | select which content is public or remains private; self-evaluate the ColSpace. |
| **h-know:** auto-configure basic tools: forum auto-setup a "knowledge access context" including, e.g.: a list of (potentially) relevant content (including elearning) a list of entities potentially interested/ relevant | **h-know:** manage the list of invitations/answers | **h-know:** provide collaborative tools; log the collaborative history; provides access to relevant information and training materials; monitors and notify new relevant information (knowledge access context) | **h-know:** closes ColSpace, public information is permanently available, private only to members; |

**Fig. 2.** An example of the life cycle of a "Problem solving type of collaborative space"

## 4    Conclusions and Further Work

h-know three years research resulted in a fully working platform ready to be used in establishing collaborative networks in a variety of domains, besides the rehabilitation, restoration and maintenance of buildings defined in the original project. In a great extent, the authors believe that this was due to the technological rules approach and the ISR framework adopted for the design of the socio-technical artefact. In this paper we did not present an evaluation/validation of the visioning process neither of the resulting h-know collaborative platform, due to space limitations. For this, the design evaluation methods proposed by [3] are the most appropriate. An informed argument and a scenario are the more adequate options in this situation, and a first approach can be found in a former paper [7]. The h-know platform is now being deployed in some real applications. There are three practical implementations planned: the implementation of a collaborative platform to support a national association of small companies in the construction sector in France, the support to a local community of small companies in the rehabilitation area in Italy (implemented through a local association) and the support to a big R&D project in Portugal.

## References

1. Van Aken, J.: Management research based on the paradigm of the design sciences: The quest for field-tested and Grounded Technological Rules. Journal of Management Studies (2004)

2. Winter, R.: Design science research in Europe. Eur. J. Inform. Syst. (2008)
3. Hevner, A., March, S., Park, J., Ram, S.: Design Science in Information Systems Research. Mis. Quart. (2004)
4. Santos, V.R., Soares, A.L., Carvalho, J.Á.: Knowledge Sharing Barriers in Complex Research and Development Projects. Knowledge and Process Management (2012)
5. Robins, G., Pattison, P., Elliott, P.: Network models for social influence processes. Psychometrika 66, 161–189 (2001)
6. Cheng, J.-H.: Inter-organizational relationships and information sharing in supply chains. International Journal of Information Management 31, 374–384 (2011)
7. Carneiro, L.C., Sousa, C., Soares, A.L.: Integration of Domain and Social Ontologies in a CMS Based Collaborative Platform. In: Meersman, R., Dillon, T., Herrero, P. (eds.) OTM 2010 Workshops. LNCS, vol. 6428, pp. 414–423. Springer, Heidelberg (2010)

# Towards Collaborative Alignment
# of Engineering Networks

Kim Jansson, Iris Karvonen, and Mikko Uoti

VTT, Technical Research Centre of Finland
Tekniikantie 2, Espoo, P.O.Box 1000, FI-2044 Finland,
{Kim.Jansson,Iris.Karvonen,Mikko.Uoti}@VTT.fi

**Abstract.** This paper reports further development of competence management in engineering networks through the consolidation of two different approaches for competence management; the Innovation and Engineering Maturity Model and the Project Alignment concept. To support the proactive competence management in collaborative networks the paper proposes first, further development of the IEMM into a more dynamic and networked structure and second, extension of the project alignment concept from the temporary project level to the more continuous organization, network level.

**Keywords:** Collaborative alignment, maturity model, competence management, project alignment model.

## 1 Introduction

Networking is a reality within the Finnish marine industry. Outsourcing of activities has resulted in permanent restructuring of the industry. The change is characterized by increased competition from Asia, dynamic company rearrangements and need for fast adaptation to customer requirements. The flexibility can be supported by creating collaboration preparedness in the marine networks. One component of the preparedness is the management of the network competencies and being able to align them with what is needed in customer deliveries.

VTT and a number of industrial organizations in the marine sector are carrying out a collaborative research program, which has defined and developed an Innovation and Engineering Maturity Model for Marine Industry Networks (IEMM). The results and usage experiences are reported in [1].

Recently the COIN project (Collaboration and Interoperability in Networked Enterprises) [2] was carried out to develop innovative solutions and services for Enterprise Collaboration and Interoperability. One focus area was collaborative project management. One-of-a-kind products, like ships or large machines in marine industry, are often engineered and manufactured in projects distributed both by organization and by geographic location. Solutions to support collaborative management of collaborative projects were developed in [3, 4]. One of the implemented solutions is the Project Alignment process and the Project Alignment Model (PAM), supported by the Project Alignment Booster software [3, 5].

L.M. Camarinha-Matos, L. Xu, and H. Afsarmanesh (Eds.): PRO-VE 2012, IFIP AICT 380, pp. 467–474, 2012.
© IFIP International Federation for Information Processing 2012

This paper reports further development of competence management in engineering networks through the consolidation of the IEMM and the Project Alignment concept. The objective is "Collaborative Alignment of Engineering Networks". Chapter 2 describes the current challenges and trends of marine industry and chapter 3 presents the background research and the methodology. The development towards advanced collaborative alignment is described in chapter 4 and chapter 5 gives the conclusions.

## 2     Challenges in the Marine Engineering Ecosystem

According to the project "Performance Monitoring of and Industry Foresight for the Finnish Maritime Industry" [6, 7] the global trends in the marine industries are:

- Globalisation – The centre of gravity for global trade moves further away from Europe. The developing markets need foreign skills.
- Greenness – Alternative fuels and energy forms are developed. Emission is reduced using various technologies. Products are moving from using hydraulics to electricity.
- Energy economy – Life cycle costs and in particular energy consumption is in the focus. Fuels and electricity consumption are reduced by different means.
- Cost-efficiency – Due to the general cost pressure, all on-board processes are optimised e.g. efficient design of spaces usage.

In addition to challenges also important market opportunities were identified: energy- and environmental innovations, arctic knowledge, newbuildings on the growing offshore and cruise markets, retrofits and conversions of aging ro-ro and cruise fleets due to tighter environmental requirement.

To response to the market opportunities the industry needs proper knowledge, capabilities and skills available when needed. This requires that the needed competencies exist in the ecosystem and that they can be found fast when needed. Currently one major challenge for organisations, due to the demographic change because of retirements, is lost knowledge which will be difficult to replace. [8, 9, 10]. Only a fraction of this knowledge is documented and shared, which results in employees leaving without passing on enough of their valuable expertise.

As a conclusion from the current trends (networking, market and aging) there is a need to better manage the competencies, identify the gaps and take care of the knowledge transfer in collaborative networks on all levels of activity – individuals, company internal, networks, national and international. Engineering organisations need to align their skills and collaboration potential.

## 3     Background Research and Methodology

Competence management can be considered as one part of preparedness. Preparedness in general expresses how much effort has been performed to prepare for a certain task before the actual task is carried out [11]. Competence management is a large research area that can be studied from different points of view: physiological, managerial, educational etc. Due to limited space available only a small set of previous work is referred to, from the aspects of networking and modelling.

### 3.1 Profiling and Competency Management System

The research in the area of Collaborative Networked Organisations (CNO) has a long tradition in the European research environment. The creation and management of Virtual Organisations (VO) together with the related concept of Virtual Organisations Breeding Environment (VBE), has been studied in several projects [12].

Organisations' competencies refer to capabilities to exploit its resources. The ECOLEAD project [13] has developed a Profiling and Competency Management System for VBEs. A competency of an organisation is defined as the "organisation's capability to perform (business) processes (with partners), having the necessary resources (human, technological, physical) available, and applying certain practices, with the final aim to offer products (services, goods) to the customers".

### 3.2 Maturity Models

A maturity model is a framework that describes a number of levels at which an organization can carry out activities for a specific area of interest. Maturity models focus on different disciplines that an organization can address to improve its business. A maturity model defines a structured collection of elements that describes the characteristics of processes. There are several well established maturity models, of which the CMMI [14] is the most known and used. The models are often used to achieve two objectives: 1) to help to set process improvement objectives and priorities, 2) to appraise organisations for the sake of improvement and competence development. The COIN project developed an Enterprise Collaboration Maturity Model (ECMM) that focuses on collaboration and interoperability capabilities [2].

### 3.3 Innovation and Engineering Maturity Model for Marine Industry Networks

The IEMM model, mentioned in the introduction section, is focused on the particular needs of the marine industry sector. The success factors of tomorrow are grouped into six dimensions (Innovation, Technology, Project Management, Collaboration Internationalisation and Knowledge Management/PDM)

The six dimensions are then further divided into four to six process areas per dimension, Fig. 1. For each dimension and process area, five levels of maturity have been defined.

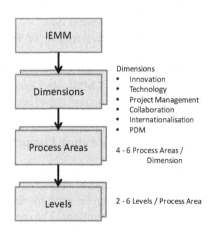

Fig. 1. First maturity model

### 3.4     Project Alignment Model

The PAM model [5] describes the main objects or elements that need to be aligned between project demand and project partners' offering in the collaborative environment. For example, the customer may have requested that mechanical engineering in a project must be done using certain software. The partners' competences have to be aligned with this requirement; visualising the partners' competences with this software and the availability of resources. If not aligned, corrective actions may have to be taken.

The PAM model is a flexible, modular and configurable framework that consists of Alignment Elements – configurable independent entities that describe different things that need to be aligned to ensure successful completion of a project, Fig. 2. Alignment element can for example be:

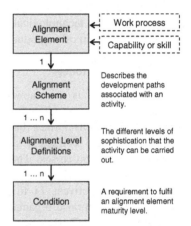

- A project management task that has to be performed (e.g. define the communication management plan),
- A process that is executed during the course of the project (e.g. using local engineering standards),
- A competence (e.g. experience in using certain 3D CAD-tool), or
- A feature, attitude or cultural attribute of a project partner (e.g. openness towards new ideas).

It should be noticed that an alignment element is not part of the project work break down structure. Each alignment element may be described on different qualitative or quantitative levels. The number of levels may vary depending on the element type.

**Fig. 2.** Description of an Alignment Element

Although the development of the model uses structures from existing maturity models, there are some important differences. The PAM is configurable for any number of elements and levels, does not support the calculation of an overall maturity index as in e.g. CMMI, and involves non-quantitative levels, e.g. level 3 is not "better" or "more mature" than level 2, it is just different.

### 3.5     Forecasting Future Competence Needs

A recent report [15] from the "Osaameri" project forecasts knowhow and training needs within the marine industry. The purpose of the report is to produce forecasting information that can be used by occupational, vocational high school and university level education institutions. The report is based on a large number of interviews, web-questionnaire and workshops. The identified important future marine knowledge sub-domains are:

- Ship newbuildings (in particular special-purpose ships, cruise liners and ferries),
- Repair and retrofit,
- Off shore and arctic marine engineering,
- Ship services and maintenance,
- Equipment and systems, and
- Ship operation.

A question is how these future requirements should be considered in companies and networks. Should they be made visible when defining competencies and maturity models in the marine field? Could the concept of alignment be applied to align the future needs and the network capabilities, to identify the capability gaps?

### 3.6    Research Progress and Steps

In the used research methodology, the results from previous work have been deployed as far as possible (see Fig. 3). Achievements from the work by the authors, in the development of the IEMM and project alignment approach, have been consolidated with results from the external Osaameri results.

The research includes the following steps: 1) identification of IEMM development needs, 2) evaluation of the project alignment approach and 3)

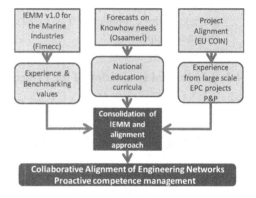

**Fig. 3.** Used research approach

consolidation of IEMM and alignment approach, extending the methodology from project alignment to proactive competence management.

## 4    Consolidation of IEMM and Alignment Approach

The objective is to develop an industrially viable approach for proactive competence management in marine industry innovation and engineering networks. The approach can afterwards be extended to cover also other engineering sectors. The following steps have been completed.

### 4.1    Identification of IEMM needs

The IEMM model was evaluated by a number of Finnish marine companies. Based on the company feedback, the development potential was identified:

- New abstraction levels: The current model is designed to be used on a company or department level. In order to apply the concepts in CNOs, there is a need to include additional "abstraction levels" e.g. domain-, company- and project-levels. There are no features to merge maturity levels from different organisations to get a combined "networked" maturity.

- From static to dynamic structure: The maturity analysis is based on static predefined structure. The structure corresponds to the needs of "today", but in the future the marine industry needs will change. The users should be allowed to modify and extend the model, by adding and modifying the dimensions and process areas. For example the high importance of explicit and tacit knowledge transfer due to the expected demographic.
- Support specialisation in certain niches. The needed competencies of important future marine sub-domains can be incorporated, e.g. the off-shore domain.
- Continuous updating the benchmarking data: The graphical user interface, to benchmark a company against the average within the industry is based on average values collected two years ago. The benchmarking values need continuous updating.

### 4.2     Industrial Evaluation of the Project Alignment Approach

The project alignment approach and the PAM were evaluated in a large distributed engineering project environment. The following benefits were identified:

- Shared and unified views on how to reach project objectives.
- Shared and aligned working methods and processes, including agreement on how to conduct and perform engineering work and how to use engineering software tools, and identification of learning needs.
- Identification of required external skills and knowledge.
- Providing a checklist for project management collaboration activities.
- Raised awareness of potential risks and scheduling weakness.
- Positioning and comparing project partners' attitudes and organizational cultures.

The experience and future development grand vision for collaborative project alignment were presented in [5].

### 4.3     Vision for Proactive Collaborative Alignment of Engineering Networks

This section outlines the development path towards "Collaborative Alignment of Engineering Networks". By consolidation of IEMM and alignment approach, the methodology can be extending from project alignment to proactive competence management. The development needs identified in Section 4.1 are combined with the following development potential coming from the PAM evaluation. To meet this grand vision, some new features should be included, for example:

- A knowledge base consisting of project alignment elements suitable for different domains collected into templates and instantiated into domain specific alignment models. The model can then "socially evolve" through sharing and enhancing it among the partners in a real project.

- Links to legacy systems. Basic project information could be imported from standard project management systems using interoperability standards.
- To get a more reliable assessment of partners' capability and skills, some kind of peer review or single partner's self-assessment could be established. As an example, a grading system (one to five stars, "I like" / "I don't like") or free text comments could be used.
- Using partners' ontology to retrieve capabilities and skills semi-automatically. Industrial companies and organizations do not yet today issue any partner (or company) ontology. However in the future this could be the case. The availability of a reliable and up-to-date ontology would then remove the need for project partners to do self-assessment of their alignments status.

## 5    Conclusions

This paper reviews different approaches relating to maturity and alignment within or between organizations. Maturity models have traditionally been applied at the level of a single enterprise. This is the case also with the IEMM and ECMM approaches even if collaboration preparedness is one of their focus areas. The project alignment model is a step towards the network level assessment: it focuses on the identification of competence and preparedness gaps in a collaborative project, creating a collective view of identified gaps within the project consortium (or Virtual organization).

One of the companies' drivers for collaboration is to focus on core competencies and to be able to utilize the partners' knowledge to serve customers. To be able to successfully respond to customer requests, the network or VBE should have the needed capabilities available when needed. This requires that 1) the needed competencies exist in the network and 2) the most suitable competencies can be identified in the network.

For the latter task different partner search and selection methods can be used if there is information available about the partners' capabilities. The maturity models and alignment models can support the task if the information is available throughout all the partners for the network level.

Currently the information regarding companies' competencies, knowledge and capabilities are typically dispersed in different systems. The competencies may be managed in companies' human resource management systems at the employee level and are not as such available for the network level. The maturity models look at the process area capabilities on a company level and cannot directly use the employee level information. The alignment model extends the competence and capability aspect to cover also other types of preparedness items.  Currently the methods for the definition of the data are typically different and it is not straightforward to exchange it between the different models and to make it usable at the network level.

The first condition above (availability of needed competencies) requires not only knowing and assessment of the current competencies in the network. Additionally it is important in the current dynamic environment to be able to foresee and prepare for the competencies available and needed in future. In the marine industry there is a risk to lose existing knowledge because of ageing and a need to extend the current knowledge to new areas as described above in Section 3.5. To support the proactive competence management in collaborative networks this paper proposes first, the extension of the project alignment concept from the temporary project level to the more continuous organization, network level and second, the forecasting and inclusion of future needs for the alignment; that is alignment between the future competence status and future competence needs at the network level.

# References

1. Jansson, K.: An Innovation and Engineering Maturity Model for Marine Industry Networks. In: Camarinha-Matos, L.M., Pereira-Klen, A., Afsarmanesh, H. (eds.) PRO-VE 2011. IFIP AICT, vol. 362, pp. 253–260. Springer, Heidelberg (2011)
2. IST FP7 IP Project 216256, Collaboration and Interoperability in Networked Enterprises (COIN), http://www.coin-ip.eu/
3. Ollus, M., Jansson, K., Karvonen, I., Uoti, M., Riikonen, H.: On Services for Collaborative Project Management. In: Camarinha-Matos, L.M., Paraskakis, I., Afsarmanesh, H. (eds.) PRO-VE 2009. IFIP AICT, vol. 307, pp. 451–462. Springer, Heidelberg (2009)
4. Ollus, M., Jansson, K., Karvonen, I., Uoti, M., Riikonen, H.: Supporting collaborative project management. Production Planning & Control 22(5-6), 538–553 (2011)
5. Uoti, M., Jansson, K., Karvonen, I., Ollus, M., Gusmeroli, S.: Project alignment: A configurable model and tool for managing critical shared processes in collaborative projects. In: 15th IEEE International Enterprise Distributed Object Computing Conference 2011 (EDOC), Helsinki, Finland, pp. 87–96. IEEE (2011)
6. Fimecc Innovations & Networks Programme, http://www.fimecc.com
7. PROBE Performance Monitoring of and Industry Foresight for the Finnish Marine Industry. Fimecc
8. Myerson, J., Bichard, J., Erlich, A.: New demographics, new workspace: office design for the changing workforce. Gower, Surrey (2010)
9. DeLong, D.W.: Lost Knowledge – Confronting the threat of an ageing workforce. Oxford University Press, New York (2004)
10. Määttä, H.: The Challenge of the Retiring Workforce - An Overview of Knowledge Transfer Methods. In: 2011 FIMECC Innovations and Networks Research Programme (2011)
11. Tolle, M., Vesterager, J.: Virtual Enterprise Methodology. In: Karvonen, et al. (eds.) Global Engineering and Manufacturing in Enterprise Networks (GLOBEMEN), VTT Symposium, vol. 224, pp. 53–70 (2003)
12. Ermilova, E., Afsarmanesh, H.: Profiling and Competency Management in VO Breeding Environment. In: PRO-VE 2006 Conference, Helsinki - Finland, September 25-27 (2006)
13. Camarinha-Matos, L.M., Afsarmanesh (eds.): Collaborative Networks: Reference Modeling. Springer, New York (2008) ISBN-13: 978-0-387-79425-9
14. The Carnegie Mellon Software Engineering Institute, Pittsburgh, the United States. CMMI® for Development, CMU/SEI-2006-TR-008, ESC-TR-2006-008, Improving processes for better products
15. Osaamisen ennakointi meriteollisuudessa 2025 – Osameri Project (2012), Meriteollisuuden Osaamistarveraportti, http://www.osaameri.fi/

# The Challenge of Learning for Networked SMEs to Increase Competitiveness in Virtual Enterprises

Heiko Duin[1], Manuel Oliveira[2], Sobah Abbas Petersen[2], and Klaus-Dieter Thoben[1]

[1] BIBA – Bremer Institut für Produktion und Logistik GmbH,
Hochschulring 20, D-28359 Bremen, Germany
{du,tho}@biba.uni-bremen.de
[2] SINTEF Technology and Society,
S.P. Andersens vei 5, 7465 Trondheim, Norway
{manuel.oliveira,sobah.petersen}@sintef.no

**Abstract.** Collaborative Networked Organisations (CNO) face the same if not even harder problems when trying to transform towards a learning organisation. Small and medium sized organisations - which still represent the motor for job creation in Europe - often respond to market turbulence by engaging in non-hierarchical CNOs such as Virtual Enterprises. A proven method to support learning in distributed set-ups is Serious Gaming, but the question remains whether the application of such tools is equally effective in SMEs compared with monolithic large organisations. In SMEs and networks of SMEs learning needs to move towards contextualised learning and a serious gaming based transformative environments such as TARGET can be used to achieve learning goals and competence development in distributed set-ups. This paper introduces such a transformative environment and highlights the background, its usage, benefits and limitations.

**Keywords:** Learning, Collaborative Networked Organisations, SMEs, Serious Gaming, Transformative Environments.

## 1    Introduction

In the global market, with the emergent economies, European enterprises have serious difficulties in surviving, let alone excelling, unless they are capable to leverage successfully their capacity to learn and to innovate. Especially, within the knowledge economy, a key survival factor for organizations facing an uncertain turbulent business environment is their ability to change, adapt and evolve, exploring new opportunities as they emerge and drive the organization towards the realization of its full potential. Often, enterprises - and more specific small and medium sized enterprises (SMEs) - address emerging business opportunities in Collaborative Networked Organisations (CNOs) such as Virtual Organisation Breeding Environments (VBEs) and Virtual Organisations (VOs) (Camarinha-Matos et al., 2009).

However, the willingness to cooperate and the installation of management procedures for the networked organisation alone is not a key for being successful.

L.M. Camarinha-Matos, L. Xu, and H. Afsarmanesh (Eds.): PRO-VE 2012, IFIP AICT 380, pp. 475–482, 2012.
© IFIP International Federation for Information Processing 2012

According to Senge, the only way for organizations to maintain market competiveness is when *"people continually expand their capacity to create the results they truly desire, where new and expansive patterns of thinking are nurtured, where collective aspiration is set free, and where people are continually learning to see the whole together"* (Senge, 1990).

This implied agility and holistic approach requires collaborative design, innovation and learning at all levels of the networked organization, but also converting learning into collaborative action. While being anchored in individual learning, organizational learning means much more than just the sum of the parts of individual learning. Of course, learning as the cognitive process takes place at the individual level, but there is clearly an organizational phenomenon connected with it. Individual learning can be considered organizational when it is done to achieve organization purposes or the learning outcome is shared or among members of the organization and/or network or learning outcomes are somehow embedded in the organizations' systems, structures, and culture (Snyder & Cummings, 1998).

Organisational Learning in a Network of SMES faces different challenges coming from being a SME and from being engaged in a Collaborative Network. SMEs often don't have a formalised competence development process. Daily business is in the foreground and learning takes place on-the-job or when there is some time left (which is never planned, but occur occasional). In almost all cases SMEs do not have an explicit budget for learning and competence development. Employees are highly specialised and enterprise culture (including language) can be very specific. If these SMEs are involved in a Collaborative Network additional challenges show up: while all the individuals involved in a Virtual Organisation are specialists in their specific area they may have just a little knowledge and understanding of other areas or the general objectives of their involvement in collaboration. In such a context, collaboration is an essential dimension of the learning process. Working and learning should be interleaved processes in a networked organization. The reduction of cost of learning and to potentially increase work quality makes it necessary to have a smooth transition between work and learning - on individual, organizational and network level.

Besides collaborative learning a participative approach to learning, called also "learner-centred", "constructivism", or "problem-based" is necessary. Such an approach implies active exploration, construction, and active learning rather than the passive attendance at lectures or the reading of textbooks (Cristea & Florea, 1999).

Serious Gaming has proven to support learners in acquiring new and complex knowledge and is ideally suited to support problem based learning by creating engaging experiences around a contextual problem where users must apply competences to solve specific challenges (e.g. Duin et al., 2012). The advent of serious games has given rise to the possibility of enhancing the learning (Freitas, 2006) with an increasing number of advocates promoting the use of serious games as a delivery platform (Aldrich, 2005) for education and competence development. This effort has been hampered by the perceived lack of concrete evidence concerning the effectiveness of learning and the fragmentation of the research community raises difficult challenges (Hauge et al, 2010). However, gradual well-designed studies begin to emerge demonstrating that learning does take place, albeit it remains debatable if the results can be expounded to cover other learning domains, or even applications, since context plays a key role in how well a person performs a particular activity.

For cases where it is recognized that learning outcomes have been achieved, some argue the result was not derived from intentional pedagogical design (Gee, 2003). A special difficulty with the development of entertainment games, the design of serious games is very much a craft, which in the case of serious games is compounded by the challenge of making an engaging game that is "fun", but at the same time, it needs to be "serious" to support situated learning contexts where learners can acquire knowledge, abilities and skills.

The objective of this paper is create awareness for transformative environments as personalized and collaborative learning systems to support competence development of team members which are typically geographically distributed when considering collaborative networked organisations. Such a transformative environment is developed by the EU project TARGET and trialled with three different end user scenarios concerning complex project management, social composition and management of (distributed) teams and the ability to perform a Lifecycle Assessment (LCA) for the whole life cycle of a consumer product. All these scenarios contain the potential to be executed collaboratively in a networked context.

## 2    Related Research

Early research in learning in Virtual Organisations focussed on the creation and management of tacit and explicit knowledge assets (Steil, Barcia, and Pacheco, 1999). With moving focus from knowledge management related aspects towards the management of individual and organisational competences, CNO related research focussed on competence management like recent publications from the Pro-VE community show (e.g. Klamma & Petrushyna, 2010, Fazel-Zarandi & Fox, 2010, and Moreira et al, 2010).

Klamma and Petrushyna (2010) used a pattern-oriented approach to manage and develop competences in networked organisations. Pattern recognition is done by applying techniques from Social Network Analysis (SNA). Communities of Practice in an academic environment were the test cases from which a new modelling approach called i* modelling technique has been developed supporting competence development and management tasks.

Fazel-Zarandi and Fox (2010) address the problem of competence development through the view of Human Resource Management (HRM). A formal ontology has been developed which allows formal reasoning about competence development problems. Special focus has been set to the problems of identifying the set of skills of individuals, conducting competence gap analysis and testing whether a selected individual matches a given set of competence requirements.

Moreira et al (2010) developed a conceptual framework for the management of organisational competences to contribute to the evolution of business model of an enterprise. Results of their study involving automotive and furniture industry showed that the framework has high potential for ex-ante strategy formulation (strategic planning) and ex-post strategy explanation. "Soft" concepts such as leadership were identified as important with further research needs.

A high-level architecture for personalised learning in CNOs has been presented by Afsarmanesh and Tanha (2010). The authors point out that in collaborative networks the involved individuals are not typical learners compared to academic environments, and therefore it is even more important to make the learning time/cost effective. The personalized learning approach suggested in their paper aims to carefully apply both the learner's and the environment's characteristics into the customization of the most suitable reduced list of Learning Objects, as well as the near optimal learning path.

The efforts presented by these researches mainly focus on the identification of competence gaps on either individual or (inter-)organisational level and how to manage the closing of these gaps. Specific SME related challenges have not been addressed and the acquisition of "soft" skills through a Serious Gaming based approach is not considered in above mentioned research.

There is a need to capture the situation or the work context and to support learning in the workplace or situated learning (Lave & Wenger 1991). As Fig. 1 says, there is a need to capture context and transform our perceptions of the environment. Working contexts, or work-spaces, can be developed as a set of models which can enable common and role-specific views to be derived and shared, and hence our perceptions will change, and we will learn as work and collaboration progresses (Lillehagen, Krogstie, 2008).

SME's often do not have the time or the resources to invest in learning. However, there sustainability is dependent on their ability to adapt to the changing face of business and the needs of their customers in a timely manner. SMEs can benefit enormously from peer learning by having access to the experiences of others either from other SMEs or larger organisations, The ideas of Communities of Interest of Communities of Practice (Wenger, 2002) can be a powerful tools in designing learning support for SMEs.

## 3    Innovative Transformative Environments

In TARGET, the learning process draws heavily from Problem Based Learning (PBL) and Action Learning (AL), resulting in the use of digital interactive stories in a serious game environment that provide situated rich contexts where a learner is required to apply and develop competences to achieve successful outcomes.

The situated contexts captured by Stories represent a scoped business environment where multiple characters are defined with specific roles and responsibilities. Since the paradigm of emergent storytelling is adopted, some of the characters are strategically controlled by Non-Player Characters (NPC) to ensure the Story unfolds with the aim of developing the associated competences. The aim is for the Project Manager to improve his/her competences, such as conflict management, negotiation and communication, through the experiences in the game. So for example, with conflict management, the NPC will control the anti-protagonist to oppose the learner's (e.g. the Project Manager's) goals. However, taking aside these strategic characters assumed by NPCs, the learner may choose which one of the remainder characters to assume in the Story. In the cases where there is more than a single character available for the learner to choose, then it is possible to have multiple learners engaged in the same Story. The fact that a few learners may simultaneously engage with the same Story does not change that learning continues to be individual irrespective of the possibility of learners exhibiting behaviours out-of-character, communicating with one another.

In addition to the virtual business environment provided in TARGET, it also includes an arena for the learners and other users to socialise virtually, called the Lounge". Learners are able to meet other users in the Lounge and access "experiences" (the capture of a learner's experience through the game) of other learners. Capabilities supported in the Lounge support peer learning as well as the social aspects of learning, through ideas such as Communities of Practice and Communities of Interests.

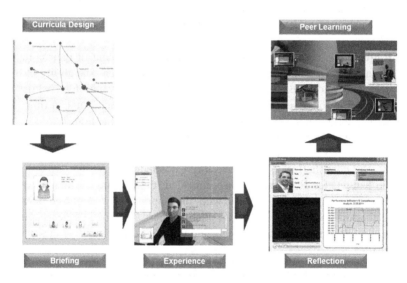

**Fig. 1.** Overview of the TARGET Learning Process

The instantiation of the TARGET Learning Process, which is supported by a componentized platform, is illustrated in the diagram of Fig. 1. Each of the stages in that diagram can be characterized as follows:

- **Curricula Design.** The TARGET Learning Process begins with the learner deciding on what competences to develop. This is done in one of two ways, either goal-oriented or self-directed learning. In the case of goal-oriented learning, the learner defines their current competence profile and their desired learning outcome in the form of outlining their target competence profile. The result of profiling leads to the creation of a learning plan based on custom stories tailored to the particular needs of the learner. Each story captures a business context, which may also involve defined characters with particular roles. The process of creating the learning plan is governed and shaped by a learning strategy that is chosen by the learner. In the case of self-directed learning, the learner builds their learning plan from the experiences of others within the community and these are stored in the knowledge ecosystem.

- **Briefing.** The learner is provided a background to a Story, which gives insight into the context, including the various characters available and their role in the Story. Some of the characters are available to the learner to be played by them, but in many cases the characters are only manipulated by NPCs.

- **Experience.** Whilst engaged with the Story, the system provides an environment where the learner engages with other characters (either controlled by another learner or a NPC) and the environment, enacting their decisions. These decisions will have an impact which will affect and change the situated context of the Story. By monitoring the actions of the learner and taking into account the desired learning outcomes, the TARGET platform makes changes to the Story if necessary. As examples, these changes may be modifying the personality of a NPC to be more confrontational or delaying tasks within a project.

- **Reflection.** The learner is presented with the assessment of their competence during the experience in the form of a timeline manner. The ability of looking back on their decisions by reviewing how the story unfolded whilst cross-referencing the assessment of their competence at each point in time, allows the learner to evaluate their performance leading to reflection.

- **Peer Learning.** The TARGET learning process supports the learner in externalizing the tacit knowledge acquired after their experience of a Story, thereby contributing to the creation of knowledge assets that are uploaded to the Knowledge Ecosystem. Once uploaded, the learning community plays an important role in the process with the support of recognized mentors as facilitators and in discussion with other learners. The social aspects address the need of an ability to deal with flux and instability, and to thrive in situations of flux.

Each of the five phases of the TARGET learning process is supported by a set of well-defined services embodied into components that are event driven, thus loosely decoupled from one another with some sharing functional dependencies. This means that the TARGET platform need not be entirely deployed as an integrated solution, but only subsets of the supported functionality. However, one needs to ensure that those components sharing functional dependencies are deployed together otherwise they may be operational at run-time but not work as required.

One of challenges of this approach is to enrich the set of stories or game scenarios that are available for the learners in the TARGET environment. Similarly, to support peer learning, learners or other users need to annotate the experiences that are captured in the system. This is perhaps one of the important aspects of learning support for SMEs where they are able to capitalise on the experiences of their peers, thus saving time and effort that is used in learning.

## 4     Conclusions

This paper addresses the challenges of learning and competence development in CNOs, in particular, SMEs. Initiatives to support formalised learning for employees in an organisation have been mostly conducted by larger organisations, while SMEs often do not have the means or the time to engage in such activities. The objective of this paper is to create awareness for transformative environments as personalized learning systems to support competence development of team members which are typically geographically distributed. Serious gaming has proven to be an effective means of supporting situated and contextualised learning within a work environment. We believe that serious gaming will meet the learning needs of SMEs, supporting experiences based learning that is focused to the situation at hand, thus reducing the time and effort that is required to rapidly gain competences in relevant areas. In SMEs and networks of SMEs, learning needs to move towards contextualised learning and a serious gaming based transformative environments such as TARGET can be used to achieve learning goals and competence development in distributed set-ups. This paper introduces such a transformative environment and highlights the background, its usage, benefits and limitations.

**Acknowledgements.** This work has been partly funded by the European Commission through ICT Project TARGET: Transformative, Adaptive, Responsive and enGaging Environment (No. ICT-231717). The authors wish to acknowledge the Commission for their support. We also wish to acknowledge our gratitude to all TARGET project partners for their contribution.

## References

1. Afsarmanesh, H., Tanha, J.: A High Level Architecture for Personalized Learning in Collaborative Networks. In: Camarinha-Matos, L.M., Boucher, X., Afsarmanesh, H. (eds.) PRO-VE 2010. IFIP AICT, vol. 336, pp. 601–608. Springer, Heidelberg (2010)
2. Aldrich, C.: Learning by doing: a comprehensive guide to simulations, computer games, and pedagogy in e-learning and other educational experiences. Pfeiffer (2005)
3. Baldwin, J.: Social Institutions: the School, the State, the Church. In: Badger (ed.) The Individual and Society or Psychology and Sociology, Boston, pp. 118–144 (1911)
4. Camarinha-Matos, L.M., Afsarmanesh, H., Galeano, N., Molina, A.: Collaborative Networked Organizations - Concepts and Practice in Manufacturing Enterprises. Computers and Industrial Engineering 57, 46–60 (2009)
5. Cristea, V., Florea, A.: Concurrent learning in virtual organisations. In: Proceedings of ICE 1999, The 5th International Conference on Concurrent Enterprising, Hague, The Netherlands, March 15-17, pp. 385–392 (1999)
6. Duin, H., Oliveira, M., Thoben, K.-D.: A Methodology for Developing Serious Gaming Stories for Sustainable Manufacturing. In: 18th International ICE-Conference on Engineering, Technology and Innovation (accepted paper 2012)

7. Fazel-Zarandi, M., Fox, M.S.: Reasoning about Skills and Competencies. In: Camarinha-Matos, L.M., Boucher, X., Afsarmanesh, H. (eds.) PRO-VE 2010. IFIP AICT, vol. 336, pp. 372–379. Springer, Heidelberg (2010)

8. Flanagan, M., Taylor, P., Meyer, J.: Compounded Thresholds in Electrical Engineering. In: Land, R., Meyer, J.H.F., Baillie, C. (eds.) Threshold Concepts and Transformational Learning. Sense Publishers, Rotterdam (2010)

9. de Freitas, S.: Using games and simulations for supporting learning, Learning. Media and Technology 31, 343–358 (2006)

10. Gee, J.: What video games have to teach us about learning and literacy. Palgrave Macmillan, New York (2003)

11. Hauge, J.B., Riedel, J., Fradinho, M., Westra, W.: Addressing Research Fragmentation in Serious Gaming for Manufacturing. In: 13th International Workshop of the Special Interest Group on Experimental Interactive Learning (2010)

12. Klamma, R., Petrushyna, Z.: Pattern-Based Competence Management: On the Gap between Intentions and Reality. In: Camarinha-Matos, L.M., Boucher, X., Afsarmanesh, H. (eds.) PRO-VE 2010. IFIP AICT, vol. 336, pp. 364–371. Springer, Heidelberg (2010)

13. Lave, J., Wenger, E.: Situated Learning: Legitimate Peripheral Participation. University Press, Cambridge (1991)

14. Lillehagen, Krogstie: Active Knowledge Modelling of Enterprises. Springer, Heidelberg (2008)

15. Moreira, M.P., D'Amours, S., Beauregard, R., Azouzi, R.: The Role of Organizational Competences in the Evolution of Business Models. In: Camarinha-Matos, L.M., Boucher, X., Afsarmanesh, H. (eds.) PRO-VE 2010. IFIP AICT, vol. 336, pp. 396–403. Springer, Heidelberg (2010)

16. Senge, P.: The Fifth Discipline. The Art and Practice of the Learning Organization, New York (1990)

17. Snyder, W., Cummings, T.: Organizational Learning Disorders: Conceptual Model and Intervention Hypotheses. Human Relations 51(7), 873–895 (1998)

18. Steil, A.V., Barcia, R.M., Pacheco, C.S.: An approach to learning in virtual organizations. Electronic Journal of Organizational Virtualness (eJOV) 1(1), 69–88 (1999)

19. Wenger, E., McDermott, R., et al.: Cultivating Communities of Practice: A Guide to Managing Knowledge. Harvard Business School Press (2002)

# 17

Designing Collaborative Networks

# Towards a Cybernetic Theory and Reference Model of Self-designing Complex Collaborative Networks

Hadi Kandjani and Peter Bernus

Centre for Enterprise Architecture Research and Management (CEARM)
School of ICT, Griffith University, Brisbane, Australia
{H.Kandjani,P.Bernus}@griffith.edu.au

**Abstract.** The multi-disciplinary and inter-disciplinary movement studying Collaborative Networks (CNs) introduced terminologies, reference architectures, methodologies and models, with the aim of helping the design, creation, operation and maintenance of CNs, and its virtual organisations (VOs). Almost a decade ago, the IST European VOMap project reported a lack of 'well founded theory and models' for sustainable collaborative networks, and this article is an attempt into this direction. The article defines and introduces 'Cybernetics of Collaborative Networks' (C2N) as a field of CN-research intended as a unified theory of CNs, formalising, synthesising, harmonising and systematising individual CN-related results addressing management and control problems in CNs. Through this envisaged synthesis, the paper invokes a number of relevant reference models and corresponding theories to outline a possible reference model and theory for self-designing CNs.

**Keywords:** Collaborative Networks, Cybernetics, Enterprise Reference Architecture and Methodology, Self-designing systems, Self-evolving systems.

## 1    Introduction

For the study of Collaborative Networks, like for any other developing discipline, there is a need for a roadmap [1,2,3,4,5,6,7,8] attempting to facilitate the integration of previous results into a theoretical foundation (including terminology, axioms, models, methodologies). The study of complex CNs requires a theory that allows the analysis and modeling of properties such as complexity, emergence, self-organization, dynamics, etc. E.g., while the study of emergence started a rapidly developing trend in CNs, the new types of CNs, and ways of collaboration are not well understood yet. Camarinha-Matos and Afsarmanesh (2008a) argue that the required theoretical foundation must consolidate the existing body of knowledge, and provide grounding to define how to invoke results of other relevant disciplines.

There can be various theories of CNs, depending on what relevant questions we intend to answer. Almost a decade ago, the IST European VOMap project reported [1] a lack of 'well founded theory and models' for sustainable collaborative networks, and this article is an attempt into this direction. The theory of which a possible initial formulation is presented here is intended to explain the structure of processes (and thereby create

L.M. Camarinha-Matos, L. Xu, and H. Afsarmanesh (Eds.): PRO-VE 2012, IFIP AICT 380, pp. 485–493, 2012.
© IFIP International Federation for Information Processing 2012

predictive models) of how collaborative activity creates controllable, sustainable and evolving enterprise networks (and their 'offspring' VEs / VOs).

Cybernetics, Management Cybernetics and General Systems Theory (GST) have already previously attacked the problem of designing, creating and managing and sustaining complex systems [9,10,11]. Cybernetic thinking provides a method to unify (and relate) the apport of multiple disciplines: it can be used to represent the essence of multiple theories using abstract functions and processes, meta-processes, and their relationships, and governing axioms (likely to be expressed using a suitable logic).

A relevant field of study called 'Enterprise Architecture Cybernetics (EAC)' [12,13] has a similar purpose and level of abstraction to this intended theory, however EAC has a different scope and genericity (namely its scope encompasses all socio-technical systems of systems in the broadest sense, including social, economic and ecological systems, and aggregates thereof). In order to formulate a specific enough (and practically usable) theory, Cybernetics of CNs (C2N) could follow EAC, but elaborate it with CN-specific detail, and illustrate the theory with relevant examples. For the purpose of theory development we need to harmonise the terminology of a number of relevant reference models and corresponding sub-theories – see Section 4.

Norbert Wiener defined cybernetics as "the science of control and communication in the animal and machine" [14]. According to Ashby [9] "truths of cybernetics are not conditional on their being derived from some other branch of science", therefore the field embraces a set of self-contained groundings and foundations, which he tried to describe in his book [9]. Ashby proposed that the study of the complexity of systems is one of the peculiarities of cybernetics. Stafford Beer [10] believed that the dynamics of enterprises is "the manipulation of men, material, machinery and money" and the "management of complexity". He coined the term 'management cybernetics' and believed that over the last two centuries, the whole of science has been based on reductionism however cybernetics uses a holistic paradigm [15].

Using this holistic paradigm for CNs and VOs, they can be thought of as intrinsically complex adaptive living systems instead of 'designed systems': deliberate design processes are mixed with emergent change. This mix may create a situation where CNs/VOs maintain (for some stretch of time) a dynamic equilibrium – a property studied in General Systems Theory [11,16]. As the evolution of the CNs includes emergent as well as the deliberate aspects of change, and we believe that the CNs discipline needs to interpret previous research in both.

## 2     Design Concerns in CN-Design and Evolution

Introducing a theoretical foundation for CNs requires two directions [7]: 1) Consolidation (structuring of the body of existing empirical knowledge), and 2) Adoption (extension of theories and modeling tools developed elsewhere, to understand and explore emerging forms of collaborative networks/ their behavioral patterns), but also the study of new forms of CNs as complex systems needs the contribution of several disciplines (computer science/engineering, management, economy, sociology, industrial engineering, law). EAC [12] as a new field of EA research has the same level of abstraction and purpose: to invoke relevant disciplines when studying enterprises as complex systems. Kandjani and Bernus argued and demonstrated in case studies that to study and explore CNs and VOs as complex systems, researchers not only apply models, methods and theories of management and control, but those of engineering, linguistics, cognitive science, environmental science, biology, social science, law, AI, systems thinking and cybernetics [12,13]. Using EAC, they demonstrated the application of Axiomatic Design and Complexity theory to measure, calculate and reduce the structural complexity of CNs [12, 17].

A unified theory of CNs and VOs must take into account the list of concerns different disciplines that studied the design and evolution of complex systems. A way to express these concerns [13] is through metaphors, i.e. 'design' or 'architecture' as:

- Conversation Process between the system's operations, the system's controller, and the environment (using Conversation Theory [18],
- Decisional Process in the management and control system [19, 20],
- Design Process as viewed by Axiomatic Design Theory [21],
- an Emergent and Evolutionary Process in Complex Adaptive Systems [22,23],
- Planning & Prediction process shaped by negotiation among designer agents (using theories of Multi-Agent Systems and other AI theories [24,25]),
- Participatory Process, using Participatory Design Approach [26],
- Learning Process, using Systems thinking and Cybernetics theories [9,27,28].

To ensure that the unified theory has sufficient breadth and depth, not only is this review useful to understand underlying concerns, it could extend the CN Body of Knowledge. Cybernetics formulated laws and theories of complex systems, but presented them on various levels of formality, generality and abstraction, so their application in the CN discipline lacks harmony: there is a need for a 'Cybernetics of CNs' (C2N) a field on its own (a special case of EAC) to (using systems thinking and cybernetics) select, harmonise, formalise, synthesise, and systematise previous results applicable to the field. C2N is to re-interpret old and new theories, and point at the need for new results for designing / creating complex CNs. Cybernetic thinking is able to provide a method of unifying (and relating) the apport of multiple disciplines, and the synthesis could be the source of a new, unified reference model for CNs.

## 3    Cybernetics of Collaborative Networks (C2N) as an Evolving Discipline

The CNs discipline, like any other developing discipline, needs a model for theory development/ testing/ knowledge creation [7]. Anderton and Checkland [29,30] developed a model of developing disciplines to demonstrate the cyclic interaction between theory development, problem formulation, and theory testing. For C2N (Fig.1) we consider the real world CN problem domains as the source of the discipline development process a source of issues to be addressed by the theory, its models / methods, and by related disciplines. The issues shape ideas to develop two types of theories [30] a) substantive theories derived from related disciplines applying them in the CN domain, and b) methodological theories (about how to invoke CN/VO related disciplines in the CN domain). Once we have such theories, we can state problems – not only existing problems in the concrete CN domain, but also more abstract problems within the new theory. Finally, such a new theory of CNs may be used to develop an interdisciplinary methodology to be used in CNs practice.

Results of the synthesis must be used in practice to create 'case records', to provide the source of criticism to improve the theory being formulated (and as a result, the models, techniques, and methodologies). This should be documented in case records to provide feedback to improve the individual- and the unified theories.

This article is only treating a first step, the enumeration of *theories that address issues arising from network complexity.* The second step would be to clarify the issues addressed, terminologies used, and the set of axioms (for theories that are formalised). The third step would be to map the above against a common model of management and control processes. The common model could serve as a 'terminological grounding' and could be the basis of a reference model accompanying a unified theory (in a way staking out the domain of the theory's applicability).

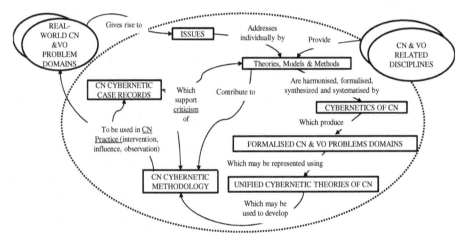

**Fig. 1.** Cybernetics of the CNs as a Developing Discipline – relationship between discipline development activities and results (based on [29] and [30])

## 4     Towards a Reference Model of Self-designing Complex Collaborative Networked Enterprises

This section's purpose is to create a shortlist of theories that addressed the complexity of large scale systems' management and control. The hallmark of these theories is that issues addressed by them re-appear in the CN research context, thus their relevance is established. The result of an extensive scan is summarised below.

**Beer's Viable System Model (VSM)** [31] views every system as consisting of three main interacting components: Management, Operation and Environment. Each entity in a CN business model has its management and operations. From every entity's point of view, the other entities are the environment. In VSM, every system needs a 'meta-system' (management of management) to be viable. From a VO's point of view, the other entities are not part of the environment but parts of the operations each with its own management, thus the VO *may* be considered a meta-system. There are communication channels ('variety attenuators and amplifiers') between these components to keep the operation in homeostasis [31,32,33]. The VSM model is to ensure that the Operation has enough 'variety' (relative to needs).

Beer's *Recursive Systems Theorem* [31] states that in the organisational structure "any viable system contains, and is contained in, a viable system." The theorem applied to CNs means a viable economy, industry, CNs, VOs, and partners all need to be considered as viable systems abiding by the axioms and principles of the VSM.

**Ashby's Law of Requisite Variety** [9] requires that to achieve dynamic stability under change, the variety of the Operation(s) should be equal to its relevant environment, and, the variety of management must be at least equal to that of Operations. A CN must maintain its requisite variety and communication channels to manage its complexity / maintain dynamic equilibrium with the environment[17]. These channels are the CN's self-perpetuating mechanisms.

**Combining Ashby and Beer's theories**. Consider the system and its environment as coupled entities. If one component is perturbed, the perturbation on the other is either amplified (positive feedback), or attenuated (negative feedback). The role of the negative feedback is to reverse the effect of perturbations and restore homeostasis (in which so-called 'critical variables' are stable), while positive feedback can create unstable states [34]. Variety amplifiers in CNs are change mechanisms for the network manager to control the change to structure or architecture of the network, to increase the Operation's variety. (NB variety amplifiers in enterprise architecture terminology are *decision frameworks* [19].) E.g., the network manager initiates a project to re-design the CN or to create a VO so as to *create new variety*.

CNs and VOs as live systems have a number of variables characterising essential survival properties. Ashby (1960) calls these 'essential variables' and defines survival as: "… a line of behaviour [that] takes no essential variable outside given limits" [27,35]. By definition, a line of behaviour outside these limits is on the non-viable system path and is fatal to the system.   For a system to be adaptive, and viable, Ashby introduces two amplifier feedback loops [27,35,36]. The *first* makes small (e.g. parametric) corrections to the system, while the *second* changes the architecture of the system, and if the second loop does not respond to / anticipates changes in environment complexity, the system is on a non-viable path.   Based on Ashby's theory of adaptation [27] and Umpleby [36] the first loop makes the system learn new behaviour for the present environment, and the second loop makes the system change, creating new behaviour for the future. As opposed to amplifiers, variety attenuators in CNs are simple feedback mechanisms (e.g. a network manager can see what the operations are doing at any one moment in time). Operational and tactical network managers do not instill change to the Operations: they control it by invoking established functions of resources and monitoring defined KPIs. Strategic network managers use control to *change* resources, structures, and network architecture. All of these are controls, but strategic controls include *design and change mechanisms*.

**Change in Complexity and Co-evolution in CNs.** We observe that both a system and its environment evolve, potentially creating imbalance between the actual variety of our system of interest and the requisite variety to maintain homeostasis: systems that want to live long must co-evolve with their environment. Formally: the environment is an entity with a set of possible observable states; if two states require different response from the system then the system must differentiate them (thus they are different *relevant states*). The complexity of a system ($C_S$) is defined to be the complexity of the model that the controller of the system maintains (appears to maintain) for managing the operations. The complexity of the system's environment ($C_E$) is a relative notion and is defined to be the complexity of the model *of the environment* the controller of the system needs / appears to maintain in the system's homeostasis. E.g., in a CN, network managers, brokers and VO management use models to understand and *control the operations* and *to interact with the environment*, and *to identify the need to change* (re-structure, re-design, re-architect).

The controllers of these entities in CNs use a model to understand and predict the environment. E.g. in a CN, the network manager and broker must have a model of what network partners do (the operations) and a model to understand and predict the environment (market and customer requirements). Based on the theorem of the 'Good Regulator' [37], the 'environment model' must have predictive capability, so that the system can maintain a homeostatic trajectory in time (and space). This environment model would include *models of external systems* with which our system interacts, and *a model of the rest of the environment*.

This ever evolving nature of the CNs needs mechanisms to control organisational learning. In the context of CNs, we propose to use Conversation Theory (CT) [18], a cybernetic model of learning processes, as CT defines process-patterns of aware management and learning situations.

According to **Aulin's Law of Requisite Hierarchy and Controllability** an unstructured CN has the largest potential to create requisite variety, but the 'setup costs' can potentially outweigh the benefits [17]. An architectural solution is to create brokerages that create VOs. Adding a *layer* of virtual brokerages can eliminate excess complexity [17], which result confirms Aulin's law of requisite hierarchy "... the required number of control levels depends on the regulatory ability of the individual control loops: the weaker that ability, the more hierarchy is needed" [38]. Heylighen and Joslyn [38] propose that the best possible solution is to maximise the regulatory ability of a single layer and minimise the number of hierarchical layers of control. In other words, it is a desirable state for systems (e.g. CNs) to be able to design themselves out of the same subsystems which recursively have the same self-design properties. The current trend towards flattening organizational hierarchies can be described by maximising regulatory abilities of personnel and organizations, using better education and empowerment, management and technological support [38].

**Heylighen's Law of Requisite Knowledge and Self-designing CNs.** Self-designing CNs be understood through the law of requisite hierarchy, but also based on the law of the 'requisite knowledge'. The management of a CN must have the knowledge of what actions to take in which states of the change in the environment so as to be ready to respond to the change in variety of the environment [38,39].

Requisite knowledge refers to the designer's ability to discern the 'relevant sates' of the environment. If the designer is *part* of the system the designer's tacit knowledge enhances the designer's ability to discern among relevant states [40].

**Extended Axiomatic Design for Lowering the Design Complexity of CNs.** An important problem facing viability and evolvability of CNs and resulting VOs is complexity, because uncontrolled complexity can cause undesired CN- and VO characteristics [12]. Axiomatic Design (AD) Theory [21] explains reasons of emerging complexity, and offers a formal design theory with two design axioms that system designs must satisfy to minimise complexity. Using AD Theory and its extension [40] it is possible to measure the complexity of the CN and of its VOs operations (so-called 'System 1s' in VSM), and measure / reduce the complexity of VO creation ('Systems 4 and 5 in VSM) [31,32,33]).

# 5    Conclusion

The article defined 'Cybernetics of CNs' as a field of research intended to develop a unified cybernetic theory of CNs, addressing complexity management and control problems in CNs. The paper briefly discussed significant models that could provide ingredients for a synthesised reference model for self-designing complex CNs. Future work will focus on harmonising the terminologies used, and proposing axioms to formalise a unified theory.   The synthesised reference model could serve as a 'terminological grounding' of the theory.

# References

1. Camarinha-Matos, L.M., Afsarmanesh, H.: A roadmap for strategic research on virtual organizations. In: Processes and Foundations for Virtual Organizations. Kluwer Academic Publishers, Boston (2003)
2. Camarinha-Matos, L.M., Afsarmanesh, H. (eds.): Collaborative Networked Organizations. A Research Agenda for Emerging Business Models. Kluwer Academic Publishers, Boston (2004a)
3. Camarinha-Matos, L.M., Afsarmanesh, H.: The emerging discipline of collaborative networks. In: Virtual Enterprises and Collaborative Networks. Kluwer Academic Publishers, Boston (2004)
4. Camarinha-Matos, L.M., Afsarmanesh, H.: Collaborative networks: A new scientific discipline. Journal of Intelligent Manufacturing 16(4), 439–452 (2005a)
5. Camarinha-Matos, L.M., Afsarmanesh, H., Ollus, M.: ECOLEAD: A holistic approach to creation and management of dynamic virtual organizations. In: Collaborative Networks and their Breeding Environments, pp. 3–16. Springer (2005)
6. Camarinha-Matos, L., Afsarmanesh, H.: Towards a reference model for collaborative networked organizations. In: Information Technology for Balanced Manufacturing Systems, pp. 193–202 (2006)
7. Camarinha-Matos, L., Afsarmanesh, H.: Motivation for a theoretical foundation for collaborative networks. In: Collaborative Networks: Reference Modeling, pp. 5–14. Springer, Berlin (2008a)

8. Camarinha-Matos, L.M., Afsarmanesh, H.: On reference models for collaborative networked organizations. Int. J. of Production Research 46(9), 2453–2469 (2008)
9. Ashby, W.R.: An introduction to cybernetics. Chapman & Hall, London (1956)
10. Beer, S.: Decision and Control: The Meaning of Operational Research and Management Cybernetics. Wiley, New York (1966)
11. Bertalanffy, L.: General System Theory-Foundations and Developments. George Braziller, New York (1968)
12. Kandjani, H., Bernus, P.: Capability Maturity Model for Collaborative Networks Based on Extended Axiomatic Design Theory. In: Camarinha-Matos, L.M., Pereira-Klen, A., Afsarmanesh, H. (eds.) PRO-VE 2011. IFIP AICT, vol. 362, pp. 421–427. Springer, Heidelberg (2011a)
13. Kandjani, H., Bernus, P.: Evolution of the Enterprise Architecture Discipline: Towards a Unified Developing Theory of EA. In: Proc. ICEIS 2012, Warsaw (to appear, 2012a)
14. Wiener, N.: Cybernetics or Control and Communication in the Animal and the Machine. MIT Press, Cambridge (1948) (2nd rev. edn., 1961)
15. Beer, S.: Cybernetics and management. Wiley, New York (1959)
16. Boulding, K.E.: General systems theory-the skeleton of science. Management Science 2(3), 197–208 (1956)
17. Kandjani, H., Wen, L., Bernus, P.: Enterprise Architecture Cybernetics for Collaborative Networks: Reducing the Structural Complexity and Transaction Cost via Virtual Brokerage. In: Proc. INCOM 2012, Bucharest, Romania (to appear, 2012)
18. Pask, G.: Conversation, Cognition and Learning. Elsevier, Amsterdam (1975)
19. Doumeingts, G.: La Methode GRAI (PhD Thesis). U Bordeaux I, Bordeaux, France (1984)
20. Doumeingts, G.: GIM, Grai Integrated Methodology. In: Molina, A., Kusiak, A., Sanchez, J. (eds.) Handbook of Life Cycle Engineering, Models and Methodologies, pp. 227–288. Kluwer, Dordrecht (1998)
21. Suh, N.P.: The Principles of Design. Oxford University Press, New York (1990)
22. Gell-Mann, M.: Complex adaptive systems. in Complexity: Metaphors, models, and reality. In: Cowan, G.A., Pines, D., Meltzer, D. (eds.), pp. 17–45. Addison-Wesley, Reading (1994)
23. Holland, J.H.: Complex adaptive systems. Daedalus 121(1), 17–30 (1992)
24. Wooldridge, M.J.: An introduction to multiagent systems. Wiley, New York (2002)
25. Wooldridge, M.J., Jennings, N.R.: Intelligent Agents: Theory and Practice. Knowledge Engineering Review 10(2), 105–112 (1995)
26. Bødker, K., Kensing, F., Simonsen, J.: Participatory IT design: designing for business and workplace realities. The MIT Press (2004)
27. Ashby, W.R.: Design for a brain; the origin of adaptive behavior. Wiley, New York (1960)
28. Senge, P.M.: The Fifth Discipline: The Art and Practice of the Learning Organization. Doubleday, New York (1990)
29. Anderton, R.H., Checkland, P.B.: On learning our lessons. Internal Discussion Paper. Department of Systems, University of Lancaster. Lancaster, 2/77 (1977)
30. Checkland, P.: Systems Thinking, Systems Practice. Wiley & Sons, Chichester (1996)
31. Beer, S.: The Heart of Enterprise: the Managerial Cybernetics of Organization. Wiley, New York (1979)
32. Beer, S.: Brain of the Firm, 2nd edn. Wiley, New York (1981)
33. Beer, S.: Diagnosing the system for organizations. Wiley, New York (1985)
34. Ashby, W.R.: Adaptiveness and equilibrium. British J. of Psychiatry 86(362), 478–483 (1940)

35. Geoghegan, M.C., Pangaro, P.: Design for a self-regenerating organisation. Int. J. of General Systems 38(2), 155–173 (2009)
36. Umpleby, S.A.: Ross Ashby's general theory of adaptive systems. Int. J. of General Systems 38(2), 231–238 (2009)
37. Conant, R.C., Ashby, W.R.: Every Good Regulator of a System Must be a Model of That System. Int. J. of Systems Science 1(2), 89–97 (1970)
38. Heylighen, F., Joslyn, C.: Cybernetics and second order cybernetics. Encyclopedia of Physical Science & Technology 4, 155–170 (2001)
39. Heylighen, F.: Principles of Systems and Cybernetics: an evolutionary perspective. Cybernetics and Systems 92, 3–10 (1992)
40. Kandjani, H., Bernus, P.: Engineering Self-Designing Enterprises as Complex Systems Using Extended Axiomatic Design Theory. In: IFAC Papers On Line, vol. 18(1), pp. 11943–11948. Elsevier, Amsterdam (2011)

# Integrated Engineering – A SME-Suitable Model for Business and Information Systems Engineering (BISE) towards the Smart Factory

Günther Würtz and Bernhard Kölmel

Steinbeis University Berlin, Gürtelstraße 29A/30, 10247 Berlin
Steinbeis-Stiftung für Wirtschaftsförderung, Willi-Bleicher-Str. 19, 70174 Stuttgart, Germany

**Abstract.** Integrated Engineering is a BISE-model and combines the following dimensions within an network-oriented SME:

- Cooperation engineering: networking of product features, process features and project parameters (internal Relationship Management);
- Collaborative networking: initiation, management, controlling of business relationships along the value chain (external RM);
- Corporate range: adaptation of the xRM-principles to the product development process (project engineering), to the complexity management (variants engineering) and to the life cycle engineering.

Integrated Engineering consists of 3 modules:

- *my*PEP_cube: customized integration of product features, process features and engineering rules based on the specific product development process (PEP);
- *my*Variants_cube: customized integration of the value-added system, the variants life cycle and the variants design rules based on the complexity management system;
- *my*xRM_cube: customized integration of the corporate know-how, the collective competence and the collaborative guide lines based on the product- and technology life cycle process within the production network.

## 1    Introduction: Increasing Complexity - Requirements for SMEs

There is a growing trend in manufacturing to move towards highly customized products, ultimately one-of-a-kind, which is reflected in the term mass customization. Important challenges in such manufacturing contexts can be elicited from the requirements of complex technical infrastructures, like security infrastructures, alternative energy, or illumination systems in large public buildings or urban equipments, but also in more traditional complex products such as customized kitchens:

- These products typically require a variety of competencies and resources, hardly available in a single enterprise, which calls for collaboration among several companies and individuals.

L.M. Camarinha-Matos, L. Xu, and H. Afsarmanesh (Eds.): PRO-VE 2012, IFIP AICT 380, pp. 494–502, 2012.
© IFIP International Federation for Information Processing 2012

- A complex multi-supplier product with a high degree of customization would benefit from associated services (e.g. maintenance support, assistance wizard, etc.), which are more difficult to plan and arrange as with standardized mass products.
- Customization demands that the recipients of the customized goods transfer their specific needs and desires into a concrete product specification. This calls for customers' integration into value creation to detailed defining, configuring, matching, and/or modifying an individual solution.

These requirements cannot be fulfilled by centrally managed organisations or systems any more – a new approach for organisations and enterprises is necessary. [1]

## 2    Cyber Physical Systems: The Smart Factory

Cyber-physical systems (CPS) are engineered systems that are built from and depend upon the synergy of computational and physical components. Examples can be found in smart electric grid, smart transportation, smart buildings, smart medical technologies, next-generation air traffic management, and advanced manufacturing. Recent efforts were focused on connecting objects (devices, sensors, sub-systems) to Internet, which led to the term Internet of Things; the challenge is now how to organize "communities" or "societies" ("ecosystems") of cyber-physical artifacts where flat organizational structures are not appropriate [2].

CPS may be equipped with intelligent sensors and actors which allow them to interact with the environment. This enables CPS on the one hand to adopt its behaviour to the environment and on the other hand to learn new ways of reaction - and even the strategy to optimize this. These "smart" abilities belong to machines but also to products and modules – even in the phase of early development. This means that these smart products can control the whole production system in an early phase of development and can interact between machine and user [3].

## 3    Important Requirements for Smart Factories

Concerning the presented BISE model mainly developed for advanced manufacturing companies, the main requirements are:

*Smart Products:* standardization of mechatronical interfaces (mechanical, electronical, software-architectural) in order to realize the interoperability between different enterprise systems using and following design rules for standardized product development.

*Smart Processes*: design of innovative process chains capable to react and control the interdependencies within the processes inside the factory and even outside the factory within the value chain or the collaborative network.

*Smart IT-Systems*: integration of heterogeneous IT-Systems by realizing a consistent (business/software as a) service-model taking into account different systems as e.g. Product Lifecycle Management (PLM), Enterprise Ressource Planning (ERP), Management Execution System (MES), etc.

As a conclusion: in order to make the Smart Factory approach happen, an integrated (engineering) approach of product-process-organization level is needed [3]

## 4     Current Achievements and Goals towards the Smart Factory

CPS in advanced manufacturing and producing companies mainly tackle with the two key processes *order fulfillment* and *product(ion) development*. To improve these 2 key processes, more and more the system of the new product development process is going to be installed, combining well known aspects of simultaneous engineering, concurrent engineering and value stream designing. But to achieve the goals of the smart factory, there still the following main issues concerning these 2 main processes have to be solved [4], [5]:

- Interoperability between the production units of different suppliers
- Adaptivity of product features and processes of the whole value chain
- Integrated engineering of mechanical, electronical and software functions.

Conclusion: current gaps towards the smart factory.

CPS in producing companies therefore require on the one hand the aspects of collaboration engineering and on the other hand a cooperative networking approach, based on a life cycle engineering system to ensure the future development of the company (corporate range).

## 5     Our Approach for Smart Factories: Model of Integrated Engineering

The Business and Information System Engineering model of "*Integrated Engineering*" combines the following three dimensions within an innovative SME:

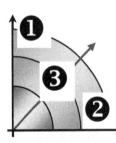

1. *Collaboration engineering*: the networking of product features, process features and project parameters in order to achieve product and process excellence;

2. *Cooperative networking*: the initiation, management and controlling of business relationships along the value chain in order to achieve business excellence;

3. *Corporate range*: the value-integrated integration of product development process (*my*PEP), complexity management system (*my*Variants) and the life cycle (*my*xRM) engineering.

The business model hereby is based on

1. The concept of *integrated engineering* which attempts to transfer the subject oriented product development process (mechanical, electronical, software)

towards a systems integrated approach (concerning collaboration engineering approach) [6].

2. The concept of *anything Relationship Management* (xRM) which attempts to design and optimize the growing complexity of relationship structures towards the smart factory (concerning cooperative networking approach) [7].

# 6    Our Solution for Collaborative Networks

The business model *Integrated Engineering* consists of 3 modules to be developed as a customized solution for each SME, identifying the relevant parameters for each module:

1. *my*PEP_cube: the customized integration of product features, process features and engineering rules based on the specific product development process (PEP)
2. *my*Variants_cube: the customized integration of the value-added system, the variants life cycle and the variants design rules based on the complexity management system
3. *my*xRM_cube: the customized integration of the corporate know-how, the collective competence and the collaborative guide lines based on the product- and technology life cycle process within the production network

**Use Case 1:** *myPEP@Feinmetall*
*Feinmetall is a SME in the testing area and has plenty of experience in safely bonding electronic components in the test room.* The number of test card and test adapter projects and their level of complexity rose so sharply over the last few years at Feinmetall, that something had to be done to take control of the situation again. The next step:introduce a standardized process for completing engineering projects. This process needed to do three things: help staff meet stipulated project completion deadlines, reduce the number of rounds of changes and in doing so, improve productivity among the project team. For years, Feinmetall has used a project management system that organizes the scope of projects as well as timings. So the mandate for the project was clear. From now on, engineering projects needed to follow one standardized process – from the first stage of development to the production handover – and include defined work packages to help staff accurately assess costs and necessary resources.

Joining forces with the Steinbeis experts, the Feinmetall team embarked on the project using an engineering method called *my*PEP. This links

- product engineering with
- process engineering and
- project engineering (rules),

uniting the seasoned approaches of simultaneous engineering with project management to create an *integrated project engineering system*. Designed around each company individually, *my*PEP integrates and synchronizes three core components:

- work packages that outline the PEP;
- working guidelines (consisting of checklists and design rules) that govern how products and production must be designed;
- a kit of ready-to-use tools for fully functional products and processes within budget.

*Work packages* needed to create two things: product development based on established routines and carefully coordinated production procedures. One important resource in this phase was a classification covering three types of projects: standard; application/change; one-of-a-kind. One-of-a-kind-projects are the only ones that require engineers to work through the work packages according to plan. For application/change and standard projects, engineers agreed to use a streamlined, shortened version to make the best use of limited resources and man-hours.

Spanning *checklists and design guidelines*, the set of rules outlines standards drawn from best practice. The biggest task lay in clearing up. Nearly half of the 50 applicable procedures and checklists were eliminated entirely;those that remained were revised, shortened and tailored to each particular application.

The greatest gains in efficiency were made when the teams structured *the methods.* Over the years, employees at Feinmetall had amassed an arsenal of product development and process planning methods. Here again, a cleanup was the order of the day. The methods that were kept in place were trimmed down to an easy-to-use "light version" and assigned to individual work packages. When it came to what is known at Feinmetall as a "specialist project", the decision maker stook a much different tack.

The outcome: a standardized product engineering process *myPEP@Feinmetall* that primarily allows Feinmetall to offer a greater sense of security to all of the project stakeholders. This means that senior managers can manage the right projects with the right priority, thus minimizing risk. Heads of specialist departments will also have fewer fires to put out as they will be able to take other departmental needs into account earlier. Project managers will spend less time checking up on things internally. And project team members will see their productivity rise – now that they know precisely what needs to be delivered, by when, and what that will require. This tailor-made PEP affords everyone involved in the project more time to come up with solutions to the real technical and business challenges they are faced with. The supposed drain on creativity has been transformed into a catalyst for creativity!

myPEP@Feinmetall now builds the basis for work within the network of customers and suppliers of Feinmetall. [8]

**Use case 2: *myVariants@ZF***
*ZF Lemförder, a member of the ZF Friedrichshafen AG group of companies, makes products such as tie rods, steering rods, suspension components and suspension modules.* The concept for the solution of *my*Variants being used in this specific use case is based on a meta-modell, consisting of principles of method engineering and built of

- a 3 step model of phases which are organized within a process model;
- a set of techniques and tools (design rules) within each phase with defined input and output data which are directly linked together;

- a framework of objects and tools for product, process and project description (value-added system) combining all necessary information to create a variant systems.

*The 3 step model: phases to install a customized variant system: the variants life cycle*

• Step 1 – clearing the decks: stripping down products by removing overlaps, items gathering dust and profit killers

• Step 2 – design: designing products by laying down standard products and "specials" based on standard templates

• Step 3 – taking control: sustainable implementation and adherence to defined product structures by adapting standard processes in sales, D&D, logistics and production

In recent years, the number of different steering tie rods, axle rods and ball joints has risen sharply. The aim was therefore threefold: to slash the time needed for D&D to issue a detailed offer; to reduce prototype delivery times once quote were given the go-ahead; and to shorten delivery lead times for serial products. All of this should be achieved by standardizing products and processes, as part of on-going plant development projects. Even as the project got underway, ZF knew it would be necessary to address many issues. All processes are integrated, so sales is involved through actively selling product standards, production is involved with standardized manufacturing processes, and financial accounts are involved with fixed calculation models for standardized products. The scope of the project was therefore clear: a new end-to-end variant management system was needed, involving standard processes that make it possible to shorten lead-times by more than 50% – from the first point of contact with the customer to final delivery – without reducing the deliverable scope of products or raising prices. The aim was to map customer solutions by using components and assemblies made from defined (standard) "building blocks." To define standard products, consensus was needed with all departments as to which standards should be used.

*Toolset for product and process design rules and the framework (value-added system)*

An important tool in this respect was the use of a software program for product configuration. This made it possible to significantly reduce the time taken to submit offers, draft designs and prepare work processes. Equally important was the task of dividing the entire job handling process into standard product processes and special product processes. A major help in this respect turned out to be a lean production system (LPS) which had already been in place at ZF for a number of years. Because of the underlying principles it is based on, an LPS makes it possible to make variants quite late in the production process. This makes it easier to reconcile the goals of maximizing capacity use while keeping batch sizes and variants flexible. Extending LPS principles to the entire job handling process – based on similar methods – made a significant contribution to achieving overall goals. Instruction covered the theory underlying the new system as well as knowledge-sharing by learning "on the job" as part of live project work.

In the three areas looked at – ball joints, axle rods and steering/tie rods – laying down standards based on pre-defined building blocks resulted in different levels of standardization. In some areas, this was as high as 65%. In combination with process optimizations, the resulting throughput times were reduced down to 50%, which was even better than planned. But for the top management, the change in attitude among co-workers was more important than bare numbers. [9]

**Use case 3:** *myxRM@2E*
*2E mechatronic, is a specialist in the development of innovative mechatronics products in the fields of sensors, precision injection molding and microelectromechanical systems.* The project scope was clearly defined: the second generation of the inclination sensor should be based on a clear design principle – similar to the architecture of a house. Preplanned, combinable product and process elements should be used to generate new customer-specific solutions quickly and reliably. The entire life cycle of the product, from initial brainstorming to follow-on products, should be taken into account, and all engineering processes should be set up accordingly. For functions and processes beyond 2E's core competences, value creation partners should be identified and successfully integrated into company networks.

The team used the Steinbeis Transfer Center's three-phase model:

1.  Phase 1: Customer requirements and system development: Systematically classify customer and market needs and develop suitable integrated technology and functional modules.
2.  Phase 2: Product classification/configuration: Draw up a product catalog of basic functionalities, standard (catalog) options and customer versions.
3.  Phase 3: Process evaluation and value creation partners: Optimize core processes (internal) for core functions; evaluate special processes (external) for special functions, network processes efficiently, adapt regularly.

Especially in phase 3, the principle of xRM was used in order to organize and control the relevant process relations within the collaborative network 2E being member of. xRM describes a management concept in which all levels of relationships are coordinated and transparent, interactive processes are created. The implementation is based on platforms and modular, domain specific applications building upon these platforms.There are two application areas: internal organizational RM uses xRM platforms e.g. for documentation within the organization; organization-wide RM supports the management and controlling of business relationships.

*Step 3.1: self-assessment (corporate wiki):* highlighted where the core competences of 2E lie within the engineering processes. However, certain key figures highlighted that there was still plenty of potential to standardize and optimize the inclination sensor product architecture. To avoid adapting products to each new customer, the team systematically analyzed selected target groups in the chosen markets, and implemented their requirements in appropriate product modules. This massively reduces the time-to-market for each order – and the freed-up development capacity can now be used for customer projects that really do match company goals. For the catalog modules, the team determined and optimized corresponding engineering processes.

*Step 3.2: network-assessment (collective competence):* 2E no longer develops special processes for tailored solutions, but buys them from reliable network partners. This requires on the one hand the identification of all required competences within the whole life-cycle-process and on the other hand an evaluation scheme to assess potential network partners due to these requirements. The matching of requirements and competences can be supported by suitable software services.

*Step 3.3: process integration (collaborative know-how):* 2E is designing an entire product portfolio for each application area – after all, they have the technological expertise to do this. But it takes careful planning to integrate this sensibly into the existing business fields (automotive industry, medical industry, process industry) without customer projects getting in each other's way. This has to be done by taking into consideration the whole process landscape of all network partners in order to reach a maximum of synergy between the different processes inside the company (each business field) and outside the company (each network partner). This will result in a maximum of efficiency and therefore profit. [10]

# 7    Conclusions

The business model *Integrated Engineering* helps to create the customized company system *"my_smartfactory"* and therefore enables the company to contribute successfully within its collaborative network, being capable to adapt on the one hand to changing customers requirements and on the other hand to changing business and process relations within the collaborative network.

The presented "customized cube solutions" are all based on a common structure including the relations between the different aspects of the cubes and can therefore be used as a basic tooling to create the company-specific, customized solution for successful collaborative and cooperative networking *"my_smartfactory"*. Nevertheless, the identification of the specific parameters of each company which form the basis for the creation of the customized solutions have to be developed for any use case separately. This effort should be reduced by using basic business scenarios which is one of the main aspects of the EC-funded research project GloNet [1]. Within the EU research project GloNet (Glocal enterprise network focusing on customer-centric collaboration), the xRM plus the Integrated Engineering approach is applied in real life settings. GloNet aims at designing, developing, and deploying an agile virtual enterprise environment for networks of SMEs involved in highly customized and service-enhanced products through end-to-end collaboration with customers and local suppliers (co-creation).

Main issues to be developed for the Integrated Engineering@xRM approach are:

- Creation of a framework and of business scenarios in order to identify the "global space" for companies acting in collaborative networks;
- Identification of key performance indicators in order to create the scenario for defining the my_IntegratedEngineering@smartfactory solution;
- Development of guidelines for mainly SMEs how to build up or improve their collaborative network for the whole life cycle of their products.

**Acknowledgements.** The authors would like to thank the European Commission for the financial support of the R&D project **GloNet** within the FinES cluster.

# References

[1] Camarinha-Matos, L.M., Afsarmanesh, H., Koelmel, B.: Collaborative Networks in Support of Service-Enhanced Products. In: Camarinha-Matos, L.M., Pereira-Klen, A., Afsarmanesh, H. (eds.) PRO-VE 2011. IFIP AICT, vol. 362, pp. 95–104. Springer, Heidelberg (2011)

[2] Camarinha-Matos, L.M., Afsarmanesh, A.: Taxonomy of Collaborative Network Forms; GloNet project, Draft Working Document; FinES – Task Force on Collaborative Networks (2012)

[3] Broy, M. (Hrsg.): Cyber Physical Systems –Innovation durch SW-intensive eingebettete Systeme (acatech diskutiert). Springer, Heidelberg (2010)

[4] Broy, M. (Hrsg.): Cyber Physical Systems –Integrierte Forschungsagenda (acatech Studie). Springer, Heidelberg (2012)

[5] Passiante, G.: Evolving towards the Internetworked Enterprise. Springer Science and Business Media (2010)

[6] Anderl, R. (Hrsg.): Smart Engineering – Interdisziplinäre Produktentstehung (acatech Diskussion). Springer, Heidelberg (2012)

[7] Britsch, J., Kölmel, B.: Anything Relationship Management as Basis for Global Process Management in Networked Enterprises. In: 6th International Conference on the Proceedings of I-ESA 2012, Valencia (2012)

[8] Würtz, G.: The art of getting everthing done – seeing engineering projects through to completion. Transfer – The Steinbeis Magazine, 20–21 (2011)

[9] Würtz, G.: Combining customer-orientation with standardization. Transfer – The Steinbeis Magazine, 25–26 (2011)

[10] Würtz, G.: Life Cycle Engineering – Thinking about tomorrow- today. Transfer – The Steinbeis Magazine, 29–30 (2011)

# A Genetic Algorithm Approach for Collaborative Networked Organizations Partners Selection

Lorenzo Tiacci[1] and Andrea Cardoni[2]

[1] Università degli Studi di Perugia - Dipartimento di Ingegneria Industriale
Via Duranti, 67 – 06125 Perugia - Italy
[2] Università degli Studi di Perugia - Dipartimento di Discipline Giuridiche e Aziendali
Via Pascoli, 20 – 06123 Perugia – Italy
{lorenzo.tiacci,acardoni}@unipg.it

**Abstract.** In the paper a genetic algorithm approach to form potential Collaborative Networked Organizations (CNOs) is presented. When analyzing a set of companies that are potential partners of a CNO, it is possible to collect specific data from each company through which evaluate, once aggregated, for which Strategic Objective (SO) the potential aggregation is most suited. At this purpose a metric, consisting in a set of performance parameters related to different SO types, has been created. Given a large number of companies, through a genetic algorithm approach is then possible to set a specific objective function related to a particular SO (eg. maximize potential creation of new Business Opportunities), and to find the cluster (or clusters) of companies that maximizes the objective function.

**Keywords:** Business Networks Formation, Genetic Algorithm, Strategic Objectives.

## 1    Introduction

In the paper a genetic algorithm approach for collaborative networked organizations partner selection is presented. The perspective adopted in this paper is related to the framework described and applied by authors in two preceding works [1][2].

In these studies authors defined and applied a framework to analyse a potential pool of partners and to identify the most appropriate CNOs form that should be adopted. The choice of the Strategic Objectives (SOs) of the collaborative network is a crucial analytical phase that determines the most appropriate form of alliance. In general, when analyzing a pool of companies that want to collaborate, strategic network objectives are not defined 'a priori', but should be the result of an assessment of the possible opportunities deriving from the collaboration. This assessment is conducted by gathering information on several aspects of each company (the so called 'Analysis Dimensions'). By evaluating and consolidating all the information gathered from a network perspective it is possible to define which type of Strategic Objective is achievable by the group, and in turn to identify the most appropriate strategic mission for the CNO, and the most appropriate strategic form among VBE[4], VDO[1] and T-Holding[1]. In [2] authors applied the proposed framework to a case

L.M. Camarinha-Matos, L. Xu, and H. Afsarmanesh (Eds.): PRO-VE 2012, IFIP AICT 380, pp. 503–512, 2012.
© IFIP International Federation for Information Processing 2012

study commissioned by the ICE (the Italian Institute for Foreign Trade) and by a local industrial association (Confartigianato Terni), whose aim was to investigate how the companies belonging to an industrial cluster of the metal-mechanic industry in Italy could be aggregated in an innovative way. A questionnaire through which investigate the analysis dimensions of each company has been defined. Data provided by this tool and by economic and financial statements of the companies have been analysed in a network perspective in a semi-quantitative way. The analysis of the consolidated data allowed clearly identifying which type of SO was at same time desirable and achievable by the alliance. This in turn allowed determining the most appropriate type of CNO. In this paper the above mentioned framework is completed through the definition of a 'metric' that allow to measure in a *quantitative* way which type of SO is most suitable for a group of companies that wants to join together. For this purpose, the metric takes mainly into consideration the so called 'hard' factors [5] (e.g. matching competence, technological fit, etc.), because its scope is limited to the selection of the SO's type. An appropriate pattern of the so called 'soft' factors (e.g. reputation, ethical issues, norms, values, trust, etc.) is considered in this context to be a necessary prerequisite. Thanks to this metric it is possible to extend the usage of the proposed framework to another interesting context: the selection, from a large number of companies, of a cluster (or more clusters, here intended as generic business networks of companies) able to achieve a specific SO. At this scope, a genetic algorithm approach is presented. The perspective adopted in our work is different from many interesting studies presented in literature related to partners selection and evaluation processes [6] that specifically address Virtual Organizations (VOs) creation process, but not the long term CNO formation process.

The paper is organized as follows: in section 2 the classification of SOs is reported; in section 3 the metric for measuring which SO is achievable by a group of companies is presented; in section 4 the genetic algorithm approach is presented.

## 2    Strategic Objectives of Primary and Secondary Type

How illustrated in [1], the strategic objectives (SOs) a generic CNO can pursue have been classified in SOs of "primary" type and SOs of "secondary" type.

The strategic goals of Primary type represent the ability of the network to permanently increase the value added related to its business core competencies. To achieve these goals it is necessary that the alliance is able to create new Business Opportunities (BOs) and Core Process Opportunities (CPOs):

- Business Opportunities: are related to new markets and new products development, able to increase the network turnover;
- Core Process Opportunities: are related to the increase of effectiveness and efficiency of the core operational activities, able to reduce the network costs.

In the strategic goals of Secondary type we can include all the other synergies that brings to new Supporting Process Opportunities (SPOs), that are related to increase the efficiency and effectiveness of all the supporting activities, such as finance, control, quality, research, administration, education, etc., that are able to emphasize the benefits of Primary type.

Figure 1 show the companies' analysis dimensions that have to be investigated in order to evaluate if a potential CNO is able to generate new BOs, CPOs and SPOs, that is, to fulfill the strategic goals that have been defined in the previous step. The dimensions identified are: Segments of Business [8], Primary and Supporting Activities [9], Critical Resources [10], Financial statements analysis [11].

As reported in [2] the proposed framework has been applied to a case study. The questionnaire is the survey tool that has been utilized to collect information on qualitative and quantitative variables from each company, and consists of three distinct sections, each one related to one of the analysis dimensions defined. Data provided by the questionnaires have then been integrated trough economical and financial data provided by the companies' balance sheets.

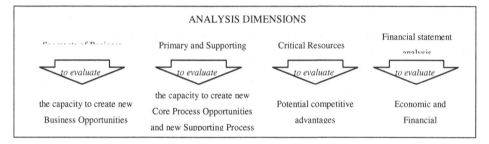

**Fig. 1.** Analysis dimensions

# 3     A Metric for Measuring Strategic Objectives Achievability

The metric proposed herein is applicable to a determined group of company. Data provided by the questionnaire and balance sheets of each company are used in this section to calculate a series of performance parameters through which asses the ability of the potential network to achieve a specific SO.

There are three set of parameters, each one related to one of the three types of strategic objectives achievable: *BOs*, *CPOs* and *SPOs* parameters. A higher value of a parameter will indicate that the group has a high probability of achieving the strategic objective to which the parameter is referred. Due to space limitation, only a part of the *CPOs* and *BOs* parameters that have been defined will be described in the following paragraphs. The remaining *CPOs*, *BOs* and *SPOs* parameters will be presented in an extended version of the paper. Each parameter $P_k$ is associated to a weight $WP_k$ and to two vectors of ordered values $\{x_1, ..., x_n\}$ and $\{y_1, ..., y_n\}$ used to discretize and normalize the parameter value through the following function:

$$f(P_k) \begin{cases} 0 & if \quad P_k \le x_1 \\ y_i & if \quad x_{i-1} < P_k < x_i \quad i = 2,...,n-1 \\ y_n & if \quad P_k \ge x_n \end{cases} \tag{1}$$

The weighted, discretized and normalized value of the parameter is equal to $WP_k \cdot f(P_k)$. The weights and vectors values for some of the $BOs$ and $CPOs$ parameters are shown in Table 1 and Table 2.

**Notation**

| | | |
|---|---|---|
| $N$ | $=$ | Number of companies in the group |
| $T_i$ | $=$ | Turnover of company $i$ |
| $E_i$ | $=$ | total external costs (purchases and closing stock + production, commercial and administrative services) |
| $S_{TOT}$ | $=$ | total number of industrial sectors (covered by at least one company) |
| $S_{ij}$ | $=$ | turnover fraction made in industrial sector $j$ by company $i$ |
| $Sb_{ij}$ | $=$ | 1 if $S_{ij} > 0$; $= 0$ otherwise (=1 if industrial sector $j$ is covered by company $i$) |
| $T_{INi}$ | $=$ | total expenditures for inbound transportations |
| $T_{OUTi}$ | $=$ | total expenditures for outbound transportations |
| $A_{ij}$ | $=$ | expenditure fraction on total purchases of company $i$ for product $j$ |
| $Ab_{ij}$ | $=$ | 1 if $A_{ij} > 0$; $= 0$ otherwise |
| $A_{(2\text{-}4)j}$ | $=$ | 1 if $2 \leq \sum_i Ab_{ij} \leq 4$; $= 0$ otherwise (=1 if product $j$ is purchased by a number of company between 2 and 4) |
| $A_{(\geq 5)j}$ | $=$ | 1 if $\sum_i Ab_{ij} \geq 5$; $= 0$ otherwise (=1 if product $j$ is purchased by more than 5 companies) |
| $C_{ij}$ | $=$ | Turnover fraction of company $i$ made with client $j$ |
| $Cb_{ij}$ | $=$ | 1 if $CL_{ij} > 0$; $= 0$ otherwise |
| $C_{(2\text{-}4)j}$ | $=$ | 1 if $2 \leq \sum_i Cb_{ij} \leq 4$; $= 0$ otherwise (=1 if client $j$ is common to a number of companies between 2 and 4) |
| $C_{(\geq 5)j}$ | $=$ | 1 if $\sum_i Cb_{ij} \geq 5$; $= 0$ otherwise (=1 if client $j$ is common to more than 5 companies) |
| $MAC_{TOT}$ | $=$ | total number of machines typologies (used in at least one company) |
| $MAC_{ij}$ | $=$ | number of machines $j$ owned by company $i$ |
| $MACb_{ij}$ | $=$ | 1 if $MAC_{ij} > 0$; $= 0$ otherwise |
| $TEC_{TOT}$ | $=$ | Total number of different technologies (adopted by at least one company) |
| $TECb_{ij}$ | $=$ | 1 if tecnology $j$ is adopted by company $i$; $= 0$ otherwise |

**Performance Parameters: CPOs, BOs, and SPOs Parameters**

$CPOs$ parameters measures the potential ability of the group of $N$ companies to achieve new Core Process Opportunities as a network. The Parameters reported in Table 1 are the following:

$CPO_1 =$ incidence of total inbound transportation costs on total turnover;

$CPO_2 =$ incidence of total outbound transportation costs on total turnover;

$CPO_3 =$ number of product types purchased by a number of companies between 2 and 4;

$CPO_4$ = incidence on total turnover of purchasing costs related to products purchased by a number of companies between 2 and 4;

$CPO_5$ = number of product types purchased by a more than 5 companies;

$CPO_6$ = incidence on total turnover of purchasing costs related to products purchased by more than 5 companies.

The higher the value of these parameters, the higher the possibility to achieve some core process opportunities such as synergies in transportations activities ($CPO_1$ and $CPO_2$) or collaborative procurement opportunities ($CPO_3$ to $CPO_6$). In order to evaluate through a unique parameter the ability to achieve generic $CPOs$, an overall parameter, $F_{CPO}$, is defined by summing the discretized, weighted and normalized values of all the considered $CPOs$ parameters:

$$F_{CPO} = \sum_{p} W_{CPOp} \cdot f(CPO_p) \tag{2}$$

**Table 1.** CPOs Parameters

| $CPO_p$ Parameter | $W_{CPOp}$ | $\{x_1, ..., x_n\}$ | $\{y_1, ..., y_n\}$ |
|---|---|---|---|
| $CPO_1 = \sum_i T_{INi} / \sum_i T_i$ | 3 | $\{0.33, 0.66\}$ | $\{5, 10\}$ |
| $CPO_2 = \sum_i T_{OUTi} / \sum_i T_i$ | 3 | $\{0.05, 0.2, 0.3\}$ | $\{2, 5, 10\}$ |
| $CPO_3 = \sum_j A_{(2-4)j}$ | 2 | $\{2, 5, 10\}$ | $\{2, 5, 10\}$ |
| $CPO_4 = \sum_i \sum_j A_{ij} A_{(2-4)j} E_i / \sum_i T_i$ | 2 | $\{0.05, 0.1, 0.2\}$ | $\{2, 5, 10\}$ |
| $CPO_5 = \sum_j A_{(\geq 5)j}$ | 5 | $\{2, 5, 10\}$ | $\{2, 5, 10\}$ |
| $CPO_6 = \sum_i \sum_j A_{ij} A_{(\geq 5)j} E_i / \sum_i T_i$ | 5 | $\{0.05, 0.1, 0.2\}$ | $\{2, 5, 10\}$ |

$BOs$ parameters measure the potential ability of the group to find new Business Opportunities as a network. The parameters reported in Table 2 the following:

$BO_1$ = degree of diversification of industrial technologies;

$BO_2$ = degree of diversification of machines types;

$BO_3$ = degree of diversification of industrial sectors;

$BO_4$ = number of clients common to a number of companies between 2 and 4;

$BO_5$ = incidence on total turnover of clients common to a number between 2 and 4 companies;

$BO_6$ = number of clients common to more than 5 companies;

$BO_7$ = incidence on total turnover of clients common to more than 5 companies.

The higher the value of this parameters, the higher the possibility to create new Business Opportunities by exploiting complementarities in technologies, machines, and industrial sectors ($BO_1$ to $BO_3$) or by supplying integrated products/services to common clients ($BO_4$ to $BO_7$). As in the previous case, to evaluate through a unique parameter the ability to achieve generic $BOs$, an overall parameter, $F_{BO}$, is defined by summing the discretized, weighted and normalized values of all the considered $BOs$ parameters:

$$F_{BO} = \sum_p W_{BOp} \cdot f(BO_p) \tag{3}$$

In an analogous way, a series of $SPOs$ parameters are defined (not reported due to space limitation), and the ability to achieve generic $SPOs$ can be measured by a unique parameter $F_{SPO}$ obtained by weighting, discretizing, normalizing and finally summing all the $SPOs$ parameters.

**Table 2.** BOs Parameters

| $BO_p$ Parameter | $W_{BOp}$ | $\{x_1,...,x_n\}$ | $\{y_1, ..., y_n\}$ |
|---|---|---|---|
| $BO_1 = 1 - \dfrac{\sum_{i=1}^{N} \sum_{j=1}^{TEC_{TOT}} TECb_{ij}}{N \cdot TEC_{TOT}}$ | 5 | $\{0.6, 0.8\}$ | $\{5, 10\}$ |
| $BO_2 = 1 - \dfrac{\sum_{i=1}^{N} \sum_{j=1}^{MAC_{TOT}} MACb_{ij}}{N \cdot MAC_{TOT}}$ | 5 | $\{0.6, 0.8\}$ | $\{5, 10\}$ |
| $BO_3 = 1 - \left( \sum_{i=1}^{N} \sum_{j=1}^{S_{TOT}} Sb_{ij} \bigg/ N \cdot S_{TOT} \right)$ | 5 | $\{0.6, 0.8\}$ | $\{5, 10\}$ |
| $BO_4 = \sum_j C_{(2-4)j}$ | 2 | $\{2, 5\}$ | $\{5, 10\}$ |
| $BO_5 = \sum_i \sum_j C_{ij} C_{(2-4)j} T_i \bigg/ \sum_i T_i$ | 2 | $\{0.05, 0.1\}$ | $\{4, 10\}$ |
| $BO_6 = \sum_j C_{(\geq 5)j}$ | 5 | $\{2, 5\}$ | $\{5, 10\}$ |
| $BO_7 = \sum_i \sum_j C_{ij} C_{(\geq 5)j} T_i \bigg/ \sum_i T_i$ | 5 | $\{0.05, 0.1\}$ | $\{4, 10\}$ |

# 4    A Genetic Algorithm Approach

The proposed metric can be applied to a group of potential partners. Given a large number of companies, the metric makes also possible to set a specific objective function related to a particular SO (eg. maximize potential creation of new Business Opportunities), and to find the cluster (or more clusters) of companies that maximizes the objective function. In order to define the desired solution features, three possible input parameters, that define the constraints that a feasible solution must respect, are taken into consideration:

$NC$    =   the desired number of clusters that has to be find;
$minC$ =   minimum number of companies in each cluster;
$maxC$ =   maximum number of companies in each cluster.

From an initial set of $M$ companies, the algorithm will give as output $NC$ clusters of companies, each containing a number of companies between $minC$ and $maxC$. The genetic algorithm approach seems to be particular suited to explore the space of this combinatorial problem, in which companies cannot be evaluated singularly. In fact, the contribution of each company to many of the performance parameters above described is dependent by which other companies are in the same cluster.

**Representation, Decoding and Fitness Functions.** In a genetic algorithm approach, each Individual represents a possible solution of the problem. Thus, the individual is formed by one or more clusters of companies. The algorithm has been implemented in Java, and the representation of an individual has been made using an object oriented approach. Each Individual $k$ contains a List of $I_k$ clusters $C_{ki}$, $i = 1,\ldots,I_k$. Each cluster $C_{ki}$ contains a certain number of companies $n_i$, so that the total number of companies contained in all the clusters $C_{ki}$ is equal to the initial set of $M$ companies. However, when decoding an individual, only the feasible clusters (i.e. respecting the relation $minC \leq n_i \leq maxC$) have to be taken into consideration for calculating the fitness function. So $F_k$, the set of feasible clusters of individual $I_k$, is sorted in descending order with respect to the selected fitness function, and only its first $NC$ clusters are considered when decoding the individual. Thus the individual fitness is calculated by considering only $C_{ki} \in F_k$ for $i \leq NC$. This set of clusters is the output of the decoding phase of an individual. It is noteworthy that, depending from the number of clusters to find and the minimum and maximum number of companies per cluster, one or more companies of the initial set of $M$ companies could not be selected to be part of this final set of clusters generated by the individual decoding. Four possible fitness functions, shown in Table 3, can be selected. By selecting one of the fitness functions defined in Table 3, it is possible to search for potential cluster(s) able to achieve specific SOs. Through the $F_{ALLO}$ fitness function the type of SO is not specified 'a priori' for all the clusters, but the algorithm will search for the best combination of clusters able to achieve different SOs.

**Initial Population.** An initial population is created by randomly generating a number P of individual. Each individual is created by iteratively forming clusters; each cluster has number of companies, randomly chosen from the initial set, between minC and maxC. Each time a cluster is formed, the set of companies belonging to the cluster is removed from the initial set. The procedure continues until the initial set is empty or it contains less than minC companies. In the latter case, the last cluster is formed including the remaining companies, although their number is out of the feasibility range.

**Table 3.** Fitness functions

| Find clusters that maximize: | Fitness function |
|---|---|
| CPOs | $F_{CPO} = \sum_{i=1}^{NC} F_{CPOi}$ |
| BOs | $F_{BO} = \sum_{i=1}^{NC} F_{BOi}$ |
| SPOs | $F_{SPO} = \sum_{i=1}^{NC} F_{SPOi}$ |
| indifferently CPOs, BOs, or SPOs: | $F_{ALLO} = \sum_{k=i}^{NC} \max\{F_{CPOi}, F_{BOi}, F_{SPOi}\}$ |

**Reproduction and Mutation.** Each generation of the genetic algorithm provides reproduction and mutation phases. In the reproduction phase, all the individuals of the population are coupled through a binary tournament selection procedure[12]. Then each couple of parents $p_1$ and $p_2$ generates two children, $c_1$ and $c_2$. For example, child $c_1$ is generated in this way: a cluster $C$ belonging to $p_1$ is randomly chosen; then the companies belonging to $C$ are removed from clusters belonging to $p_2$; finally $C$ is added to $p_2$. The resulting individual is $c_1$. Child $c_2$ is obtained inverting $p_1$ and $p_2$ roles. In this way, after the reproduction phase, the population size is equal to $2P$. Each individual of this population has now a certain probability $m$ to undergo the mutation phase. Each mutated individual is added to the population, but the original one is also maintained in the population. There are three possible types of mutation, randomly selected with probability $m_1$, $m_2$, and $m_3$ respectively. In the first type of mutation two clusters are randomly selected and are joint together. In the second type a cluster, randomly selected among clusters with a number of companies higher than $2 \cdot minC$, is halved, generating 2 clusters. In the third type, two companies, belonging to different clusters, are swapped. Note that the first type of mutation can generate clusters with a number of companies out of the feasible range. The mutation phase is responsible (together with the initial population creation phase) of the heterogeneity of the number of clusters $I_k$ in each individual $k$. The population now is sorted, following one of the four fitness function proposed, and only the first $P$ individuals survive and pass to the next generation. After a number of generation $G$, the algorithm stops, and the individual with the highest fitness is considered the final solution.

## 5 Discussion and Conclusions

The proposed metric has been validated by calculating the three performance parameters $F_{BO}$, $F_{CPO}$ and $F_{SPO}$ for the cluster of companies considered in the case study described in [2]. The study was commissioned by 'Confartigianato Terni', a local agency of 'Confartigianato', the main Italian industrial Association of SMEs, with about 700000 associated companies, and 120 local agencies spread over the territory. The resulting values ($F_{BO}$=265, $F_{CPO}$=45, $F_{SPO}$=35) are consistent with the qualitative analysis of results described in [2], that indicated the creation of new BOs as the most suited SO for the cluster. They are also consistent with the evolution of the cluster that, after the understanding of the basic characteristic of the proposed network model and the strategic logic of the collaboration, manifested a successfully capability to explore and catch new BOs, f.e. providing integrated products/services in the renewable energies plants sector. Confartigianato is currently considering the development of a software based on the metric and the algorithm presented in the paper, that, after a testing and validating phase through real data from the field, could be used by the local agencies as a decision supporting tool for networks formation. The genetic algorithm approach presented here in is a supporting decision tool to individuate, among an extensive number of companies, potential clusters of companies that can achieve specific strategic objectives. Through the proposed approach it is be possible to find out which companies, among the associated partners, could joint together to fulfill a specific mission. In particular the associations could suggest not only the cluster(s) composition, but also the type of strategic objective the cluster(s) should/could pursue. Furthermore, by analyzing the values of each performance parameters related to a determined cluster, and selecting the parameters that give the major contribute to the total fitness, it is also possible to indicate the particular opportunity that can be caught. For example, a high value of $BO_6$ indicates that there are some clients common to more than 5 companies. This suggests the possibility, for a network, to offer a new integrated product/service to that clients, given by the combination of products/services provided by the single companies.

# References

1. Cardoni, A., Saetta, S., Tiacci, L.: Evaluating How Potential Pool of Partners Can Join Together in Different Types of Long Term Collaborative Networked Organizations. In: Camarinha-Matos, L.M., Boucher, X., Afsarmanesh, H. (eds.) PRO-VE 2010. IFIP AICT, vol. 336, pp. 312–321. Springer, Heidelberg (2010)
2. Tiacci, L., Cardoni, A.: How to Move from Traditional to Innovative Models of Networked Organizations: A Methodology and a Case Study in the Metal-Mechanic Industry. In: Camarinha-Matos, L.M., Pereira-Klen, A., Afsarmanesh, H. (eds.) PRO-VE 2011. IFIP AICT, vol. 362, pp. 413–420. Springer, Heidelberg (2011)
3. Saetta, S., Tiacci, L., Cagnazzo, L.: The innovative model of the Virtual Development Office for collaborative networked enterprises: the GPT network case study. International Journal of Computer Integrated Manufacturing (2012), doi:10.1080/0951192X.2012.681909
4. Afsarmanesh, H., Camarinha-Matos, L.M., Msanjila, S.S.: On management of 2nd generation Virtual Organizations Breeding Environments. Annual Reviews in Control 22, 209–219 (2009)
5. Rosas, J., Camarinha-Matos, L.M.: An approach to assess collaboration readiness. International Journal of Production Research 47(17), 4711–4735 (2009)
6. Baldo, F., Rabelo, R.J., Vallejos, R.V.: A framework for selecting performance indicators for virtual organisation partners' search and selection. International Journal of Production Research 47(17), 4737–4755 (2009)

7. Paszkiewicz, Z., Picard, W.: MAPSS, aMulti Aspect Partner and Service Selection Method. In: Camarinha-Matos, L.M., Boucher, X., Afsarmanesh, H. (eds.) PRO-VE 2010. IFIP Advances in Information and Communication Technology, vol. 336, pp. 329–337. Springer, Heidelberg (2010)

8. Abell, D.F.: Defining the business: the starting point of strategic planning. Prentice-Hall (1980)

9. Porter, M.: Competitive Advantage: creating and sustaining superior Performance. Free Press, New York (1985)

10. Rugmann, A.M., Verbeke, A.: Edit Penrose's contribution to the resource based view of strategic management. Strategic Management Journal 23(8), 769–780 (2002)

11. Hakansson, H., Kraus, K., Lind, J.: Accounting in network. Routledge, New York (2010)

12. Goldberg, D.E., Deb, K.: A comparative analysis of selection schemes used in genetic algorithms. In: Rawlins, G.J.E. (ed.) Foundations of Genetic Algorithms, pp. 69–93. Morgan Kaufmann, Los Altos (1991)

# Pooling Supply Chain:
# Literature Review of Collaborative Strategies

Abdelhamid Moutaoukil[1], Ridha Derrouiche[2], and Gilles Neubert[2]

[1] Institut Fayol, EMSE, 158 Cours Fauriel, Saint-Etienne,
42000 Saint-Etienne, France
[2] Institut Fayol, ESC Saint-Etienne 51-53 Cours Fauriel BP29 - 42000
Saint-Etienne, France

**Abstract.** To support companies in collaborative supply chain, new strategies have been set up and developed in the past years. In this context, the first aspect of this paper is to provide an overview of these different collaborative strategies either in vertical or horizontal level. We further develop literature-based constructs for both types of collaboration. After this large-scale survey this paper proposes a conceptual framework for pooling supply chain as an horizontal collaborative logistic strategy. Moreover, our objective is to highlight the link between horizontal collaborative logistic and sustainable development, to show that the strategy of pooling supply chain can achieve the goals of sustainable development, namely, the environmental, economic and societal objectives.

**Keywords:** Pooling Supply Chain, Horizontal collaborative logistic systems, Sustainable development.

## 1 Introduction

In recent years, globalization has made customers increasingly demanding in terms of rate of service, responsiveness and flexibility. The market has become more dynamic and continuously changing. Competitive pressure causes rapid technological advances and introduction of products with shorter life cycles. Consequently, relations between the companies are based more than ever on competitiveness [1]. The current economic context characterized by the financial crisis and declining purchasing power are forcing companies to reorganize their processes and rethink their organizations, to enable them to respond quickly and cost effectively to fast and changing demands.

On the other hand, logistics has gained much attention by significantly increasing the efficiency and flexibility of organizations. The current logistics schemes favor the emergence of new forms of governance and rationalization of logistics systems. Companies now seek to create synergies with other organizations and begin to create value chains through horizontal and / or vertical collaboration with logistics partners. Increasingly, independent firms work together to reduce their operating costs and increase revenues. In collaborative logistics, parties in the supply chain (SC) aimed at reducing logistics costs through better use of their resources ([2] and [3]).

L.M. Camarinha-Matos, L. Xu, and H. Afsarmanesh (Eds.): PRO-VE 2012, IFIP AICT 380, pp. 513–525, 2012.
© IFIP International Federation for Information Processing 2012

## 2    Concepts and Definitions: Pooling SC

The literature shows that the efficiency of logistics systems is still inadequate and there is a large potential for improvement in this sector. The inconclusive results of traditional logistics schemes explain the need to develop other strategies to create new logistics systems, more efficient such as the collaborative logistics [4].

Collaborative strategies concern mainly concerted actions between different actors. Competitive advantage is created on the basis of a consensus reached through collaborative relationships. According to Audy and al., collaboration occurs when at least two structures decide to exchange and share physical and/or information resources to make decisions or achieve activities to generate profit [5]. Depending on the degree of commitment and involvement of partners, the collaboration can range from simple information sharing to a true partnership, which may include cultural and organizational changes. Inter-firm collaboration includes other concepts such as cooperation, coordination or co-decision [6].

### 2.1    Different Types of Collaborative Logistics

The literature contains much work on collaborative logistics. For a good overview, see the literature review done by Nagati and al. [7], about collaborative concepts in supply chains.

Nevertheless, the logistical collaboration today takes place primarily at vertical level. Cruijssen reports that supply chain management is the term usually describing vertical collaboration [4], a topic that has led to an abundant scientific literature. Simchi-Levi and al. define management of supply chain as "*all of the approaches used to efficiently integrate suppliers, manufacturers, warehouses and stores in way that merchandise is produced and distributed in the right quantities, to right places at the right time, in order to minimize system wide costs while satisfying service level requirements*" [8]. This definition indicates that vertical collaboration occurs between partners that operate at different levels of supply network, where the benefits of collaboration include lower supply cost due to synchronization effect by sharing information. Among the main practices of vertical collaboration, we mention: VMI (Vendor Managed Inventory), ECR (Efficient Consumer Response), CPFR (Collaborative Planning Forecasting Replenishment), and CTM (Collaborative Transportation Management).

However, collaboration can also be horizontal [9]. Horizontal collaboration in logistics consists of having collaboration between actors of the same level (between providers, between manufacturers, between distributors, etc) in a supply network. A supply network is considered as non-serial structure and therefore a structure consisting of vertical and horizontal collaboration [2] (Fig. 1). The important benefits of Horizontal collaboration in logistics are: lower prices due to aggregated purchasing quantities, reduced supply risk, reduction of administration cost due to centralized purchasing activities, reduction of inventory and transportation costs, logistics facilities through a rationalization of equipment and better sharing of manpower and information [10].

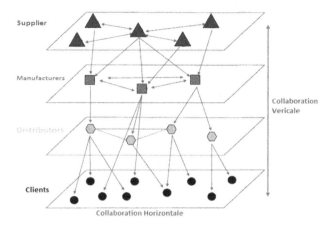

**Fig. 1.** Types of collaborative logistics

In general, horizontal collaboration in logistics concerns companies that can provide complementary goods or services, competing or not. According to European Commission [11], collaboration is described as "horizontal" if it is the subject of an agreement between companies that are at the same level in the market. It often refers to collaboration between competitors.

Some practices of horizontal collaboration in logistics are: the implantation of the Collaborative Consolidation Centers (CCC), Pooled Procurement Management (PPM), and Collaborative Transportation Management (CTM). We note that the latter practice is common between vertical and horizontal collaboration in logistics, because it involves collaboration in transport that is essential for both types of collaboration.

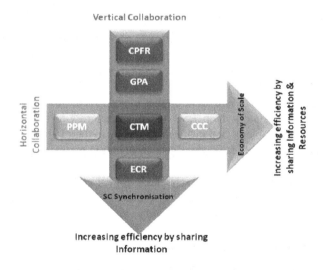

**Fig. 2.** Practices of collaborative supply network

In the literature, significant work was done by Cruijssen and Derrouiche in order to identify previous work on this topic ([4] and [12]). For its part, the "Interministerial Pole of Prospective and Anticipating Economic Change" has recently led a study on the various projects in the context of horizontal collaboration in logistics [3]. The study was designed to increase knowledge of new collaborative practices among professional actors in the logistics field. This study has identified challenges and opportunities for collaboration through concrete examples of collaborative supply, and suggested ways accompanied by a summary of good practices observed.

## 2.2  Definition of Pooling SC

Through collaboration, logistics companies in a partnership aim to increase productivity and competitiveness of their logistics networks, by optimizing the use of their means of transport and reducing costs of support activities. In practice, pooling supply chain proved to be an especially useful option for manufacturers and logistics service providers to achieve these objectives and improve their efficiency and competitiveness.

To understand the concept of pooling SC, we refer to the work of Pan [13]. He focuses on the pooled logistics schemes and, more specifically, their impact on $CO_2$ emissions in the supply chains of mass distribution sector. Pan says that the pooling SC, is the co-design, by actors with a common objective, of a logistics network where resources are pooled (warehouses, platforms, transport, etc..) to share logistical structures, and making available data needed for management to a third party. They add that pooled supply chain effectiveness can meet the concerns of sustainable development.

On the basis of different definitions from the literature such as [13] and [14], we made a detailed definition of pooling supply chain:

*"Pooling supply chain is pooling logistics services between several entities to optimize the use and operation of the logistics function or to access a service unavailable individually (example: Multimodal Transport). This requires co-design a common global supply chain. This co-design gives rise to a shared network logistics where different entities share and jointly manage their skills (logistics service manpower, materials handling manpower ...), their structures (distribution warehouses, offices ...) and their means (handling equipment, transport vehicles and fleets, information systems ...)"*

The pooling supply chain is a strategy that is not expensive to establish and can, when managed appropriately, help LSP and manufacturers to solve and overcome their chains logistics problems and increase efficiency of their logistics systems [4].

Therefore, the pooling objective consists in integrating partners with the aim of co-designing a logistics network. Such a pooled network allows actors to overcome the constraints of conventional logistics schemes (vertical collaboration). This strategy allows the development of synergies with partners competitor or not, in order to improve economic, environmental and societal performance.

## 2.3  Pooling SC and Sustainable Development

To compete, manufacturers must optimize their Supply Chain (SC). This chain has several links, from the supply of basic raw materials to end use of the product, and even beyond to also include its recovery and treatment. But this optimization, long based on an economic approach, happen today through the integration of environmental and social concerns, in line with the objectives of sustainable development. Societal and environmental degradation that go together with economic development calls for serious action from all stakeholders, including regulators such as government, business operators and consumers. Indeed, a constant pressure of European regulations pushes manufacturers to integrate sustainability concerns into their supply chains.

In addition to the requirements of economic efficiency, logistics systems must meet the requirements of sustainable development, namely:

- *At the economic level:* Reduce logistics costs.
- *At the ecological level*: Decrease both $CO_2$ emissions and energy consumption, with an incentive to proceed with more recycling and waste treatment [15].
- *At the societal level:* Consider the expectations of different stakeholders in decision-making process of companies [16].

These requirements are more difficult for SMEs to achieve rather than others, because their logistics performance level does not allow them to engage in a sustainable approach ([17] and [18]). In parallel, a just in time logistics policy has been set up in most sectors: deliver faster, more frequently, in smaller quantities. This evolution in flow management explodes SMEs logistics costs, which endangers the entire implementation of sustainable development. In this context of accelerating flow and inventory reduction, pooling supply chain between retailers, manufacturers and logistics providers is more than ever in the core of priorities.

Indeed, it is widely expected that the increased economies of scale are required to mitigate the rise in transportation costs and increased congestion and $CO_2$ emissions. Hence the importance of a pooling SC strategy between logistics systems, because such a strategy allows them to improve their logistics performance, to monitor the evolution of logistics schemes and initiate sustainable approaches.

## 3     Literature Review: Pooling SC

Relevant literature on pooling logistics remains relatively rare. The most relevant scientific works deal with the horizontal collaboration logistics practice. (Table 1) shows a short overview of the literature review we have made.

### 3.1     Related Concepts

Consolidation of flows, horizontal collaboration in logistics and urban mutualization remains the most related concepts to the notion of pooling SC.

Indeed, urban or rural logistics remains an area related to the pooling supply chain as a form of horizontal collaboration in logistics. In this context, Hageback and Segerstedt study the gains and interest of the principle of "codistribution" for rural areas in Pajala in Northern Sweden, where only a third of residents live in the city center while the rest of the population is dispersed over the countryside, making the higher costs of delivery to sparsely populated areas, because the delivery distance is longer in these areas and empty runs are more important [19]. Based on a collaborative distribution strategy, co-distribution would ensure the competitiveness of suppliers who are located in rural areas, increase service quality, reduce distribution costs, which would also a positive impact on the environment.

Regarding to distribution networks, Groothedde and al. talk about the concept of "collaborative hub" for many shippers to consolidate flows [20]. The goal is that once the flow massified, can reach sizes needed to be transported by modes of transport at high volume (rail or waterway). Access to this kind of transport can realize economic and ecological benefits.

On the other hand, Cruijssen and al. study the potential benefits and impediments for horizontal collaboration between LSPs in Flanders, Belgium [21]. Possible savings are estimated and the problems of launching co-distribution are stated.

Kale and al. study the collaborative transportation networks where only shippers collaborate; only carriers collaborate and both shippers and carriers collaborate [22]. The authors analyze the benefit of such networks for shippers.

Yilmaz and al. study the coalition formation between shippers of small sizes in a transport market characterized by uncertain demand [23]. They analyze the decisions taken by the coalition and the effect of shippers characteristics on the benefits of collaboration. The analysis shows that shippers continue to benefit from the coalition, but concerning the distribution of costs and gains, the coalition cannot always guarantee a balanced budget that is elementary for the sustainability of any coalition. Using an approach based on game theory, they offer mechanisms for allocating gains and discuss the conditions that carry a balanced budget.

## 3.2    Characteristics of Pooling SC Strategy

As mentioned above, the literature on pooling logistics is rare. However, the theoretical support of its characteristics can be found in the literature of horizontal collaboration in logistics. Moreover, we found through the literature review that there is some similarity between the notion of horizontal collaboration in logistics and pooling supply chain strategy. For that, we relied on works such as [3], [4] and [24], which identified various characteristics of horizontal collaboration logistics.

*a)    Benefits, disadvantages and impediments of pooling SC*

Benefits that can lead partners to engage in a pooling supply chain strategy can be divided into three groups: Costs and Productivity, Customer Service and Position in the market (Table 2). However, such an initiative may be subject to a number of disadvantages, such as (a) loss of flexibility, as the products purchased must have a strong similarity between the group members, (b) loss of control by individual supply chain, (c) high coordination costs (d) anti-trust problems.

Moreover, the success of this initiative depends on the quality of leadership in the group, since the ability to negotiate contracts and coordinate the interests of its

**Table 1.** Literature Review of Pooling Supply Chain

| Paper | Title | Issue | Attributes | Results | Dimensions | Decisional Level | Setting-up activities |
|---|---|---|---|---|---|---|---|
| Cruijssen [4] | Horizontal cooperation in transport and logistics | This thesis provides an analysis of horizontal cooperation in transport and logistics. From a literature review, try to show the importance of horizontal cooperation in logistics. Then, determine the different characteristics (advantages, disadvantages, obstacles ...) before quantifying its economic gains. | - Comparable logistics function. - Knowledge-sharing routines - Complementary resource endowments - Effective governance - Geographical proximity - Organizational structures of the partners need to be harmonized | - Horizontal cooperation in logistics by joint route planning can savings up to 30.7% of total distribution costs. - Horizontal cooperation increases a company's productivity for core activities and reduces the costs of non-core activities. ...... | Economic | Operational Tactic Strategic | - Planification des itinéraires - Planification conjointe - Coordination and Information sharing |
| Lehmer and al. [25] | Structural concepts for horizontal cooperation to increase efficiency in logistics | Conceptual design and a organizational aspects of horizontal cooperation. Illustration and determination of the various possibilities in the field of horizontal logistics for individual companies and the identification, design and operation of the optimal cooperation for the networking partners. | - Interoperability of Flexibility - Distribution structure of costs and benefits - Trust & Sufficient target - Companies' ability to adjust the own structures and processes in benefit of the whole network. - Similar source and sink regions ...... | - Costs could be reduced by 15% - Reducing the $CO_2$ emissions by 40%. - Sensitivity analysis: the full functionality of the model even with fluctuation of volumes and prices. - Reduction the number of journeys by 14% without any negative impacts on the logistics performance. | Economic Ecological | Tactic Strategic | - Pooled network design - Optimisation of transport network - Coalition building - Definition of management rules - Identifying compatible partners ...... |
| Naesens and al. [26] | A swift response framework for measuring the strategic fit for a horizontal collaborative initiative | Design a strategic framework to assist the decision of the implementation of horizontal collaboration, by developing a practical tool for checking the strategic fit between companies willing to initiate resource pooling in inventory management. | Trust | Development of a practical tool for checking the strategic fit between companies willing to initiate resource pooling in inventory management | Economic | Strategic | - Defining the objectives of pooling - Identifying compatible partners - Coalition building and sustaining |
| PAN [13] | Contribution to the definition and evaluation of the pooling of supply chains to reduce emissions of CO2 transport | Test the environmental (and economic) impact of the pooling of logistics in mass distribution sector. | - Choice of compatible partners - Geographical proximity - Product and flow compatibility | - The pooling SC very significantly reduced (20% and -50% )CO2 emissions for fret transport. - Economic performance is less remarkable | Economic Ecological | Operational Tactic Strategic | - Identifying compatible partners - Pooled network design - Optimisation of transport network - Localization & building of warehouses and platforms |
| ... | ... | ... | ... | ... | ... | ... | ... |
| Yilmaz and al. [23] | Collaboration among small shippers in a transportation market | - Study the coalition formation among small shippers in a transportation market characterized by uncertain demand. - Analyze the decisions taken by the coalition and study the effect of shipper characteristics on the benefit of collaboration - Propose saving allocation mechanisms -Discuss the conditions to a balanced budget | - Allocation mechanisms (the budget balance). - Geographic proximity - Shared customer(s) | Shippers always benefit from the coalition. In the absence of the coalition the shippers follow non-optimal policies. | Economic | Tactic & Operational | - Pooled network design Coalition building |

**Table 2.**  Benefits and Impediments of pooling supply chain ([3] and [4])

| Pooling SC Advantages | | Pooling SC Impediments | |
|---|---|---|---|
| **Costs and productivity** | Cost reduction | **Partners** | Difference in interests, opportunistic behavior |
| | Learning and internalisation of tacit, collective and embedded knowledge and skills | | Difficulty in finding fit partners |
| | More skilled (or more efficient use of) manpower | | Difficulty in finding a trusted party/person to lead the cooperation |
| **Customer service** | Complementary goods and services | | |
| | Ability to comply to strict customer requirements / Improved service | | Differences in operating procedures |
| | Specialisation | **Determining and dividing the gains** | Difficulty in determining the benefits |
| **Market position** | Penetrating new markets | | |
| | New product development/R&D | | Difficulty in establishing a fair allocation of the benefits |
| | Serving larger customers | | |
| | Protecting market share | **Negotiation** | Disagreement over the domain of decisions |
| | Faster speed to market | | Unequal bargaining positions (e.g. due to size differences) |
| **Other** | Developing technical standards | | |
| | Accessing superior technology | **Coordination and ICT (Information &Communication Technology)** | High indispensable ICT costs |
| | Overcoming legal/regulatory barriers | | High additional coordinating and controlling costs |
| | Enhancing public image | | Loss of control |

members is essential [10]. In addition, several barriers may hinder a strategy of pooling supply chain (table 2).

*b)    Pooling SC attributes*

Pecqueur and Zimmermann introduced the concept of "dynamic proximity" as the global attribute that query the terms of the coordination of economic and social activities by integrating their explicit spatial dimension [27]. The notion of proximity can be understood as:

- Geographical proximity, which refers to the separation of actors in space;
- Organizational proximity, concerning economic interactions between actors with complementary resources and participants completed the same activity;
- Institutional proximity, which relies on the support of players in a common system of representations.
- Product Proximity, which refers to the compatibility between products and between pooled physical flows.

Through the literature review that we conducted (Table 1), we have compiled the most important attributes that are required for a successful pooling supply chain strategy:

- Transparency and Trust
- Strategic fit: Common interest and commitment and clear expectations

- Choice of sustainable and compatible partners which have comparable logistics function: flows and product compatibility, Shared customer(s)
- Leadership and coordination.
- Geographic proximity
- Interoperability / Flexibility: Companies' ability to adjust the own structures and processes in benefit of the whole network

## 4    Towards a Framework for Implementing Pooling SC Strategy

Literature lacks a general conceptual framework to guide practitioners in implementing pooling supply chain strategy. From literature review, we provide a framework for implementing pooling supply chain strategy.

The establishment of logistics strategies involves sharing and pooling different activities on different decision levels of the company. Naesens and al. give a practical tool for checking the strategic fit between companies willing to initiate resource pooling in inventory management [26]. Activities at the operational level focus on daily operations within companies or logistics departments. They are practical operations and can be described as "joint execution" or the "sharing of operational information." Activities at the tactical level refer to achieving medium term objectives and involve more intensive planning and investment. They formalize "the common organization", or "sharing of logistics resources." Activities at strategic level aimed at achieving the strategic objectives of the coalition in the long term. Strategic collaboration at this level can be described as the "co-development".

Blanquart states that any collaboration passes through a life cycle that involves four steps: the engagement process, the management of interdependencies, the effective implementation of operations, and the evaluation process [28].

From literature review (Table 2), we have selected and compiled the various activities necessary to implementing a pooling supply chain strategy. We mention these various activities in (Fig. 3.). We develop some of these activities:

- Pooled network design: the definition of an optimal logistic concept is the main requirement to create synergies between partners. Therefore, the definition and the design of new structures and processes form the basis of a successful pooling supply chain strategy.
- The location and building of warehouses are of great importance for the efficiency of transport processes. By means of warehouse sharing, manufacturers can reduce their warehousing costs (investments, handling, conditioning, etc.).
- Optimization of transport network: the aim of increasing efficiency within a pooling supply chain can be achieved by means of reducing waste within the transportation network. Joint route planning is essential to estimate the potential savings and their sensitivity to various market characteristics.

- Supply and distribution planning: depending on production planning of each partner and the number of shipments and the complexity caused by various recipients with different delivery restrictions. This planning requires increasing effort for scheduling within the network and needs to invest in infrastructure and personnel.
- Designing an adequate information system and sharing information: coordination and communication are important catalysts of collaboration. In an economy that strongly depends on information flows, obtaining the most accurate and real-time information offers the key to success. To realize this, the organizational structures of the partners need to be harmonized, which also requires far-reaching ICT integration [29]. Besides of transport structures and transport processes, sharing information and coordinating the planning processes are also relevant for the design of pooling supply chain concept.
- Establishment of an organizational structure: both the design and operations of the network require a coordinator that ensures the overall partners satisfaction and improvement of the logistics network. This organizational structure acts as a managing and coordinating entity, it must ensure [25]:
  - ✓ Neutrality in handling or priority of jobs
  - ✓ Confidentiality regarding the given data
  - ✓ Joint definition of rules and regulations and processes
  - ✓ Definition and implementation of interfaces (IT requirements)
  - ✓ Availability of contact person or local contact point
  - ✓ Planning, executing and controlling the logistic performance for partners
  - ✓ Fair cost-benefit distribution

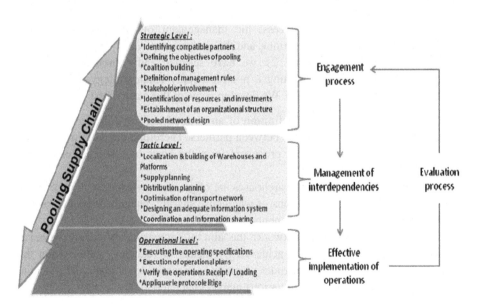

**Fig. 3.** Framework of implementation the pooling supply chain

# 5    Conclusion

Business networking strategies and especially collaboration in logistics are gaining momentum for individual companies in order to survive in competitive markets. As pooling supply chain is a new and powerful strategy to maximize benefits structures, this publication present an overview of collaborative logistics. A literature survey indicates that the pooling supply chain is a new concept which requires a deep scientific research to assimilate its various aspects. Special attention is further dedicated to understand the principle of horizontal collaboration in logistics as well as the specifications of pooling supply chain strategy, which are both considered as a form of collaborative logistics. Despite persuasive research, a major theoretical and practical shortcoming is the lack of a framework that gathers the activities necessary to implementing pooling supply chain strategy. The identification of this framework is one of the major strengths of this research.

However, this work is merely a starting point for future research on the pooling supply chain design in practice. More research is needed in order to make the given framework exhaustive and robust.

**Acknowledgments.** Authors would like to thank Region Rhône-Alpes for its financial support (Research Cluster GOSPI).

# References

1. Zigmas, L., Benas, A.: Cooperation among the Competitors in International Cargo Transportation Sector: Key Factors to Success. Engineering Economics 51(1), 80–90 (2007)
2. Mason, R., Lalwani, L., Boughton, R.: Combining vertical and horizontal collaboration for transport optimisation. Supply Chain Management: An International Journal 12(3), 187–199 (2007)
3. PIPAME: Pratiques de logistique collaborative: Quelles opportunités pour les PME/ETI? Le pôle interministériel de prospective et d'anticipation des mutations économiques, Paris (2011)
4. Cruijssen, F.: Horizontal cooperation in transport and logistics. PhD thesis. Tilburg, Nederland (2006)
5. Audy, J.-F., Lehoux, N., D'Amours, S., Ronnqvist, M.: A framework for an efficient implementation of logistics collaborations. International Transactions in Operational Research 18 (2011)
6. Camalot, J.-P.: Aide à la décision et à la coopération en gestion du temps et des ressources. PhD thesis, INSA Toulouse (2000)
7. Nagati, H., Rebolledo, C., Jobin, M.H.: Analyse de la collaboration entre industriels et distributeurs: le cas de la grande distribution française. In: 7èmes rencontres internationales de la recherche en logistique, Avignon, pp. 24–26 (2008)
8. Simchi-Levi, D., Kaminsky, P., Simchi-Levi, E.: Designing and managing the supply chain: Concepts, strategies, and cases. McGraw-Hill (2000)

9. Van Lier, T., et al.: Internal and external co-loading of outbound flows to increase the sustainability of transport: a case study. In: 12th WCTR, Lisbon-Portugal, July 11-15 (2010)
10. Bahinipati, B.K., Kanda, A., Deshmukh, S.-G.: Horizontal collaboration in semiconductor manufacturing industry supply chain: An evaluation of collaboration intensity index. Computers & Industrial Engineering, 880–895 (2009)
11. European Union: Guidelines on the applicability of Article 81 of the EC Treaty to horizontal cooperation agreements. Official Journal of the European Communities 2001/C 3/02 (2001)
12. Derrouiche, R.: Analyse et caractérisation des relations dynamiques entre partenaires d'une chaine logistique. PhD thesis. Université Lumière – Lyon II, Frence (2007)
13. Pan, S.: Contribution à la définition et à l'évaluation de la mutualisation de chaînes logistiques pour réduire les émissions de $CO_2$ du transport: application au cas de la grande distribution. PhD thesis. Mines Paris Tech., Paris (2010)
14. Ballot, E., Fontane, F.: Reducing transportation $CO_2$ emissions through pooling of supply networks: perspectives from a case study in French retail chains. Production Planning & Control: The Management of Operations 21(6), 640–650 (2010)
15. Ülkü, M.-A.: Dare to care: Shipment consolidation reduces not only costs, but also environmental damage. International Journal of Production Economics (2011)
16. Belin-Munier, C.: Logistique, SCM, et développement durable: Une revue de la littérature. Environmental Management (2009)
17. Conservatoire National des Arts et Métiers (CNAM): Enquête Nationale : La logistique dans les PME-PMI de l'agroalimentaire, synthese des resultats. Chaire de Logistique, Transport, Tourisme (2007)
18. Pôle Agroalimentaire Loire: Organisation logistique du secteur agroalimentaire dans la Loire. Saint-Etienne (2011)
19. Hageback, C., Segerstedt, A.: The need for co-distribution in rural areas—a study of Pajala in Sweden. International Journal of Production Economics 89(2), 153–163 (2004)
20. Groothedde, B., Ruijgrok, C., Tavasszy, L.: Towards collaborative, intermodal hub networks: a case study in the fast moving consumer goods market. Transportation Research Part E: Logistics and Transportation Review 41(6), 567–583 (2005)
21. Cruijssen, F., Cools, M., Dullaert, W.: Horizontal cooperation in logistics: Opportunities and Impediments. Transportation Research Part E: Logistics and Transportation Review 43(2), 129–142 (2007)
22. Kale, R., Evers, P.-T., Dresner, M.-E.: Analyzing private communities on internet- based collaborative transportation networks. Transportation Research Part E 43, 21–38 (2007)
23. Yilmaz, O., Savasaneril, S.: Collaboration among small shippers in a transportation market. European Journal of Operational Research 218(2), 408–415 (2011)
24. Derrouiche, R., Neubert, G., Bouras, A., Savino, M.: B2B Relationship Management: A Framework to Explore Impact of Collaboration. International Journal of Production Planning & Control (IJPPC) 21(6), 528–546 (2010)
25. Leitner, R., Meizer, F., Prochazka, M., Sihn, W.: Structural concepts for horizontal cooperation to increase efficiency in logistics. CIRP Journal of Manufacturing Science and Technology 4(3), 332–337 (2011)
26. Naesens, K., Gelders, L., Pintelon, L.: A swift response framework for measuring the strategic fit for a horizontal collaborative initiative. International Journal of Production Economics 121(2), 550–561 (2009)

27. Pecqueur, B., Zimmermann, J.-B.: L'économie de proximités, 264 p. Hermes- Lavoisier, Paris (2004)
28. Blanquart, C., Carbone, V.: Pratiques collaboratives et demarche environnementale dans la supply chain: mythe ou réalité?. In: 8th International Meeting on Logistics Research, BEM-Bordeaux Management School (2010)
29. Gunnarsson, C., Jonsson, S.: Charge the relationship and gain loyalty effects: Turning the supply link alert to IT opportunities. European Journal of Operational Research 144(2), 257–269 (2003)

# 18

## Cost, Benefits and Performance

# Using Value Models to Improve the Cost/Benefit Analysis of Inter-Organizational System Implementations

Silja Mareike Eckartz[*], Christiaan Katsma, and Roel Wieringa

University of Twente, The Netherlands

**Abstract.** Jointly developing a business case for inter-organizational information systems (IOS) is difficult as: (1) in a business network there are benefits that may not appear at the site where costs occur, and (2) the involved stakeholders often have different or even conflicting organizational goals. This paper analyzes the use of value modeling as a way to address these two challenges and support business case development in a network. We carried out a case study to explore the usefulness of the value modeling logic during an IOS implementation project and conclude that the integration of value modeling into business case development can help to improve the quality of the business case. The value model allows business partners to get insights into the way value is exchanged in the network and check the distribution of costs and benefits, yet doing so without having to reveal confidential details about internal business processes.

**Keywords:** Value modeling, Business case development, Inter-organizational system implementation.

## 1    Introduction

Decision makers in the current practice of IS implementations develop or receive a business case in which costs, benefits and risks of the project are estimated [1]. However, current business case development methods are expected to be of limited applicability in inter-organizational projects due to their complex nature. Cash and Konsynski [2] define an inter-organizational information system (IOS) as *"an automated information system shared by two or more companies"*. It enables joint service delivery to customers and coordination between profit-and-loss responsible business units, or between independent companies [3]. We refer to these as stakeholders in the remainder of this paper.

One of the main challenges in IOS implementations is to address different or even conflicting organizational goals of the involved stakeholders. In the case that some or all business goals are conflicting, the partners in this cooperation are not likely to reveal sensitive information [4]. A second challenge is that the costs do not occur at the same point in the network where the benefits of the implementation are gained.

---

[*] This research project was part of the NWO VITAL project (Project nr. 638.003.407).

L.M. Camarinha-Matos, L. Xu, and H. Afsarmanesh (Eds.): PRO-VE 2012, IFIP AICT 380, pp. 529–538, 2012.
© IFIP International Federation for Information Processing 2012

This paper analyzes the use of value modeling as a way to address these challenges and support business case development between different stakeholders in a network. We follow a design science approach and extend current value modeling logic to the domain of inter-organizational business case development. Business case development is already supported by a variety of tools and methods. Therefore, our research objective is a focused contribution to the value definition and knowledge sharing on the value distribution in an inter-organizational setting. We do so by developing a method called value modeling for inter-organizational projects (VM4IOP). In this paper we will specify the typical challenges for inter-organizational business case development in the background section §2 and proceed by illustrating the deployment of the VM4IOP method, using the example of a case study at the harbor of Rotterdam in §4. Our design science research approach is explained in §3.

## 2     Background

The implementation of IOS to support inter-organizational coordination is essentially a joint effort: Stakeholders first jointly need to agree on the prospective (business) goals, and then investigate and implement the information system solutions that fit these objectives. In the beginning stages of such an implementation this is supported by the development of a business case.

'Business case' is an ambiguous term often used by practitioners to refer to the relatively simple cost-benefit calculation being done for many management decisions. The business case describes and guides the evaluation of different implementation options, based on the expected costs, benefits and risks of each option. It is often used to support top management in deciding into which projects they want to invest, and it also is the highest-level requirements specification of a project. The business case is often accompanied with net present value, total cost of ownership or similar methods to support and specify cost benefit calculations.

In an inter-organizational IS implementation, the traditional business case approach does not make clear which partners get which part of the benefits and which partners incur which part of the costs, and if the costs and benefits balance per partner. Often, in a network, benefits accrued by one partner depend on costs incurred by another. These differences in the distribution of cost versus benefits may not even be the critical element, but the involved stakeholders require that costs and benefits would be distributed fairly across the business network during and after this implementation. This opens up the discussion between stakeholders on the fairness distribution. With fair we refer to a situation where (i) the stakeholders that has the most value from the IS implementation also pays the largest share of the cost and (ii) all individual stakeholders are profitable as well as the entire network. The perception of an unequal cost-benefit distribution among partners can lead to mistrust and in some situations might even then end the implementation effort.

We analyzed the combination of value models and business case development to address the problem of investment decision-making in a network. Value models can assist to explicate how value is exchanged within each organization, but also between the actors in a network of separate organizations.

A value model contains a set of objects, concepts and their relationships with the objective to express the business logic of a specific firm [5,6]. It provides powerful ways to understand, analyze, communicate, and manage strategic-oriented choices among business and technology stakeholders [6]. The origins of value models stem from the business modeling literature [7] specifying e-commerce applications. The current value modeling literature provides several methods, such as e3value [8], that are specifically designed for network settings [9].

Combining the challenges of inter-organizational business case development and the contributions of value modeling we conclude a value model allows business partners to:

(i)     get insights into the way value is exchanged both within the organization as well as in the current network [10];

(ii)    compare and assess the impact of different solutions on the business situation of each individual stakeholder as well as the entire network;

(iii)   discuss and check that a business idea will be implemented fairly, i.e. balancing costs and benefits, share the mutual perceptions between the stakeholders yet doing so without having to reveal confidential details about internal IT investments or business processes.

We acknowledge the existing business case methods and tools [11,12] and also the contributions from the domain of decision support, trust and the negotiation process [13,14], but we see an opportunity for value modeling as method to contribute to networked business case development. We expect that the use of value models in the beginning of an IS implementation project helps the stakeholders to get better insights into their network. Open communication helps to initiate the group discussion by disclosing information step by step [15], which in turn increases the development of trust between the stakeholders of a project.

# 3     Research Method

Using design science [16] we developed a method (VM4IOP) that addresses some of the problems, identified in earlier research, concerning the development of a business case in inter-organizational projects [17]. Using an iterative design setup we discussed the method with several experts and academics. The method was deployed during a case study at the port of Rotterdam in The Netherlands. We will use this case as an example in this paper. However, we make the note that the value models presented in this paper were only discussed with the members of the research project and not yet with all practitioners normally involved in such a project.

The case study at the port of Rotterdam involves multiple actors in a network that are engaged in the process of making a joint decision on an IT investment. More specifically, barge operators, terminal operators and the harbor authority discussed how a multi-agent system could support logistic planning in the port of Rotterdam.

Our case study was part of a bigger research effort: Transumo (www.transumo.nl), a platform where 150 parties from industry, government and academia jointly develop knowledge about sustainable mobility. We were involved in a business case work package of a larger project [18] that aimed at the design and implementation of a multi-agent system for the port of Rotterdam. Our role in this case study was inquisitive as well as advisory. In total, three researchers were involved alternately during our 7-month long participation in the case study. All researchers were familiar with business case approaches; two of them had practical experience in applying them in real life settings. We took both expert-based as well as participant-observation-based approaches and conducted various unstructured qualitative interviews to gather information about the business case development process. While collecting and analyzing the observations and the interviews, we focused on findings related to the business case development process as well as its outcomes. In our design effort specifically aimed to validate the value models we involved 5 researchers. We thus did not validate the models with all practitioners involved in the project, but based on the findings of Pijpers et al. [19], we expect business professionals will not be confronted with substantial impediments to work with these models.

Figure 1 presents the relations between the actors in our case setting. The figure represents both the contract relations between the actors as well as the container flow in the network. One can see that containers are transported from the line shipper via several terminal barge and truck operators to the merchant and vice versa. Barges are used to transport containers from the harbor, in our case study the port of Rotterdam to the hinterland and vice versa. Whenever a barge visits the port, it has to call on several terminals to load and unload containers. To guarantee short sojourn times in the port, the barge operator schedules convenient arrival times at the concerning terminals. The terminal operators want to operate efficiently and have to decide when a barge can be processed, taking into account all kinds of restrictions, e.g. specific times at which containers need to be at the terminal. For our project the actors jointly needed to come to an agreement about their shared business case.

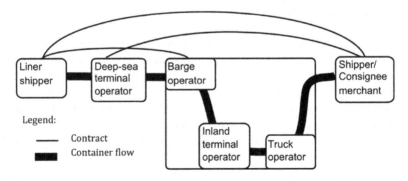

**Fig. 1.** Contract model, harbor case study setting

# 4     The VM4IOP Method

The VM4IOP method uses value models as main tool to provide insights into the network structure in an inter-organizational project. It does so by:

- Explicating the relations between stakeholders in a network.
- Providing a structured approach that helps to specify the value distribution in a network. This structured approach fits the dynamics of the business case development process.

The method treats the business case development process as project in the beginning of the entire IS implementation project. The deployment process consists out of the following three main steps. Some of the steps require individual activities of all involved stakeholder others are a group effort.

- o Step 1: Assess the entire network with the help of a value model to recognize that there is a problem (*group effort*).
- o Step 2: Assess the value model of each *individual* actor to investigate the problem in more detail.
- o Step 3: Assessment of solution options. For each solution option clarify the changes in the network when a certain solution is implemented with the help of the value model (*group effort*).

We will now describe each of the three deployment steps in more detail and give an illustration for its deployment using the harbor case.

## 4.1     Step 1: Assessment of the Current Network Constellation

Before the start of the business case development project the VM4IOP method is deployed to assess the profitability of the entire network. This activity results in a value model of the entire network, showing from a holistic point of view how the different actors are interacting with each other and how value is exchanged. Value models help the stakeholders to share their understanding regarding the collaboration and enable them to analyze the economic sustainability of the network. The main goal of value modeling is to reach agreement amongst profit-and-loss responsible units in a network regarding the question "Who is offering what value to whom and expects what value in return?" Once it is understood how different actors exchange value in a network, problems in the current network situation can be identified and located. Value objects can be money, products, services, or even experiences. Especially this aspect is important as it offers the involved practitioners a way to discuss the concept of value, explain it to each other and specify it [10].

**Illustration:** When we started our case study in the harbor there was no common understanding how the different actors currently create value in the network they are involved in. However, it was know how goods are flowing through the network and which actors have a contractual relation with each other. The contract model presented in Figure 1 was used as a basis for drawing the value model of the current network situation, shown in Figure 3.

The analysis of the models explicates where in the current network constellation a problem exists and why it might difficult to be solved. In this case we find that the shipper (upper left corner in Figure 3), as the customer of this network, has a need that can be fulfilled by executing two value streams of shipping service (the continuous lines). We also observe the value transactions are connected by the dashed lines, called dependency paths. The dependency path says nothing about the order in which these transactions must be performed. Rather, it expresses only the economic transactions that must be performed to satisfy a consumer need. We further find that all value exchanges happen via the shipper and the carrier. Although the container flow between barge operators and terminal operators describes the core of the network (Figure 1), there is no contractual relation or value exchange between these two important actors. As they might have conflicting goals they might tend to act selfish, as there is no contract with consequences specified.

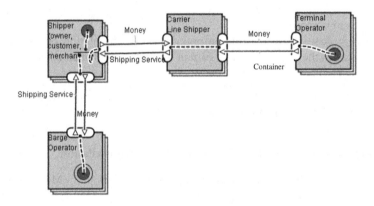

**Fig. 2.** Value model harbor network – current situation

## 4.2     Step 2: Individual Assessment of Current Network Situation

Once the problems with the current network constellation are identified and the project is started, each individual actor is encouraged to zoom in on the collaborative value model and, as extension to it, develop their own value model. This activity should happen in the problem investigation phase when the as-is business situation is analyzed in terms of organizational mission, vision and goals. In this phase each actor can analyze how he exchanges value with other actors in the network. Based on this analysis each actor should decide if a change in his current situation is needed and if this change incorporates better alignment, collaboration or information transfer with other actors in the network. The resulting "actor specific value model" (as shown in Figure 4) can be used to identify problems with current business situation and support the stakeholder to decide if he wants to continue to participate in the project at hand.

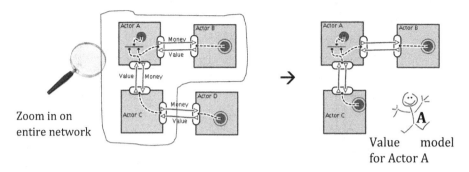

**Fig. 3.** Actor level value model of current situation

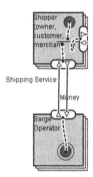

**Fig. 4.** Value model from the perspective of the barge operator in harbor case

**Illustration:** When zooming in on the network from the perspective of the barge operator, we arrive at the value model shown in Figure 5. This value model shows all actors that the barge operator has a transaction with, given the focus of the project. This figure shows us that in the current value network the barge operator exchanges value with the shipper, in terms of shipping service for money. Even though the barge operator and the terminal operator physically meet in the harbor no value exchange is depicted in their current value model. Not having a specified exchange of value makes the problem at hand very complex.

## 4.3    Step 3: Assessment of Solution Options – Link Costs and Benefits to the Value Models

Following the problem investigation, the next steps in the business case development process are executed: solution options are identified and assessed first by each stakeholder individually, afterwards collaboratively. Depending on the complexity of the implementation options, the actors might find it useful to construct a value model for each solution option that can be used as input to clarify the business case. The value model allows the actors to specify for each solution option how their network changes once a solution is implemented e.g. it might be that the actors with which an actor does business change and that new actors enter the network.

With respect to the linkage between the business case and the value model we require that all costs listed in the business case be translated into cash outflows, be it expenses or one-time investments. Cash outflows are represented as value exchanges in the e3value-modeling notation and can further be specified in the properties of actors (expenses and one time investments) or value ports (only expenses).

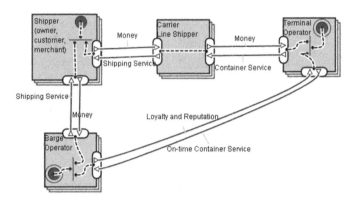

**Fig. 5.** Value model solution option 1 for the harbor case

Inclusion of the benefits in the value model seems to be more difficult. Financial benefits can be shown as cash inflows related to a particular value exchange. Adding all financial benefits as value exchanges in the value model may result in a very complex value model. The idea of value modeling (in the e3value sense) is to translate everything into financial numbers based on which the profitability analysis can be run. Thus, including intangible benefits as value streams (e.g. loyalty, reputation) in the value model is only useful when a financial value can be assigned to it. This is often a challenging task which is based on many assumptions as some of the benefits can only be expressed through indirect effects e.g. on the overall profitability. However, it is the only way that benefits can be made visible at a network level [10].

**Illustration:** Two example value models from our harbor case are shown in Figure 6 and Figure 7. The first value model introduces a solution that is based on a "loyalty and reputation in return for on-time container service" relation between the barge and terminal operators. Compared with the original value model, this is the only change; no new actors enter the network.

The second value model specifies a solution where an IOS (in this case called PAT) is implemented that is operated by a 3rd party. Figure 7 shows how the network constellation and value exchanges in the network change, e.g. by adding a new actor to the network. Other solution options one can think of can be assessed using the value models in a similar way.

The developed value models provide useful insights for each individual actor, but also for the entire network that can be used during the cost distribution and agreement making process. This process can be supported by the use of discussion support systems or negotiation interventions, but the value models deliver a valuable input to support these methods with knowledge and content. Knowing how value is currently distributed in the network and how the different implementation options change this value distribution serves as a solid basis for discussing which actor pays what part of the total investment costs.

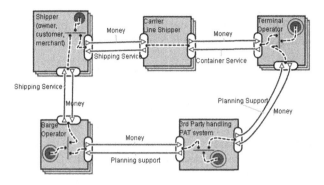

**Fig. 6.** Value model solution option 2 for the harbor case

# 5     Conclusions

Networked businesses have been leading to an increase in inter-organizational IS implementations. These implementations include some specific challenges that not always are completely supported by existing business case development approaches. Value modeling itself has been maturing and lately we have seen the first results from its application in inter-organizational settings. In this paper we have shown the results from an iterative design study in an extensive research project with scientists and practitioners. We apply value models in an inter-organizational business case development context. Our results show our VM4IOP method especially contributes to challenges often encountered in making the business case in an inter-organizational project. First, it specifies value streams -and mechanisms between the different actors and by doing so shows the involved actors the differences between cost and benefits and their location in the network. This is possible without having to reveal confidential details about internal IT investments or business processes for individual actors. Secondly, VM4IOP initiates and facilitates the group discussion and knowledge sharing in a setting where participants have conflicting goals by differentiating between private and public value streams and information.

Value modeling by no means is the only necessary improvement of business case development in inter-organizational settings. The addition of a value model to a business case improves the quality of the business case because the various options relevant to the network's actors are presented explicitly and, in turn, are understood better. Value exchanges are well reasoned about regarding the level of fairness they imply for the distribution of the costs and benefits among stakeholders in an IOS project. But our illustration also indicates the complexity of IOS implementations requires more than the mere addition of one specific modeling approach, like value modeling. We have strong indications that the addition of interventions or tools to support negotiation and discussion as well as decision support methods dedicated for the inter-organizational situation can be helpful. We recommend further research in that domain. Our results also show professionals are able to deploy the VM4IOP method in an applied research project. Another next logical step is to validate and analyze the VM4IOP method in a commercial real life project and specify the requirements for negotiation support in IOS projects.

## References

[1] Remenyi, D.: IT Investment: Making a Business Case. Butterworth-Heinemann, Oxford (1999)

[2] Cash Jr., J.I., Konsynski, B.R.: IS redraws competitive boundaries. Harvard Business Review 63(2), 134–142 (1985)

[3] Bakos, J.: A strategic analysis of electronic marketplaces. MIS Quarterly, 295–310 (1991)

[4] Daneva, M., Wieringa, R.J.: A Requirements Engineering Framework for Cross-organizational ERP systems. Requirements Engineering 11(3), 194–204 (2006)

[5] Magretta, J.: Why business models matter. Harvard Business Review 80(5), 86–92 (2002)

[6] Osterwalder, A., Pigneur, Y., Tucci, C.L.: Clarifying Business Models: Origins, Present, and Future of the Concept. Communications of AIS 15 (2005)

[7] Timmers, P.: Business models for electronic markets. Journal on Electronic Markets 8(2), 3–8 (1998)

[8] Gordijn, J.: Value-Based Requirements Engineering: Exploring Innovatie E-commerce Ideas. Vrije Universiteit Amsterdam, Amsterdam (2002)

[9] Osterwalder, A., Pigneur, Y.: An e-Business Model Ontology for Modelling e-Business. In: Proceedings of 15th Bled Electronic Commerce Conference – e-Reality: Constructing the e-Economy, Bled, Slowenien (2002)

[10] Ilayperuma, T., Zdravkovic, J.: Exploring business value models from the inter-organizational collaboration perspective. In: Proceedings of the 2010 ACM Symposium on Applied Computing (SAC 2010). ACM, New York (2010)

[11] Ward, J., Daniel, E., Peppard, J.: Building Better Business Cases for IT Investments. MIS Quarterly Executive 7(1), 1–15 (2008)

[12] Ross, J.W., Beath, C.M.: Beyond the Business Case: New Approaches to IT Investment. MIT Sloan Management Review 43(2), 51–59 (2002)

[13] DeSanctis, G., Poole, M.S., Zigurs, I.: The Minnesota GDSS Research Project: Group Support Systems, Group Processes, and Outcomes. Journal of the Association for Information Systems 9(10), 551–608 (2008)

[14] Edelenbos, J., Klijn, E.-H.: Trust in Complex Decision-Making Networks: A Theoretical and Empirical Exploration. Administration & Society 39, 25–50 (2007)

[15] Camarinha-Matos, L.M., Macedo, P.: A conceptual model of value systems in collaborative networks. Journal of Intelligent Manufacturing 21(3), 287–299 (2008)

[16] Wieringa, R.J.: Design Science as Nested Problem Solving. In: International Conference on Design Science Research in Information Systems and Technology (DESRIST). ACM, Malvern (2009)

[17] Eckartz, S., Katsma, C., Daneva, M.: Exploring the Business Case Development Process in Inter-Organizational Enterprise System Implementations. Information Resources Management Journal (IRMJ) 25(2), 85–102 (2012)

[18] Douma, A., Schuur, P., Jagerman, R.: Degrees of terminal cooperativeness and the efficiency of the barge handling process. Expert Systems with Applications 38, 3580–3589 (2010)

[19] Pijpers, V., de Leenheer, P., Gordijn, J., Akkermans, H.: Using conceptual models to explore business-ICT alignment in networked value constellations. Requirements Engineering, 1–24 (2010)

# Fundamentals for the Allocation of Financial Benefits in Virtual Enterprises

Hendrik Jähn and Thomas Burghardt

Chemnitz University of Technology, Dept. of Economic Sciences, Thüringer Weg 7
09126 Chemnitz, Germany
{hendrik.jaehn,thomas.burghardt}@wirtschaft.tu-chemnitz.de

**Abstract.** In the following fundamentals for the allocation of financial benefits such as profit are introduced. The content is based on the concept of value-adding process-related virtual enterprises. Before applying exact rules for the calculation and allocation of the financial benefits some initial process steps need to be completed. That is indispensable for the success of virtual enterprises because financial benefits are the main target of economic activities. The development of relevant approaches is based on the framework of the new institutional economics. Thereby, informational asymmetries, opportunistic behaviour, a limited rationality and an individual maximisation of utility are the basic assumptions. Considering the fundamentals of profit allocation forms an integral component of the operative management of cooperations.

**Keywords:** Allocation, Value Creation, Trust Modeling, Virtual Enterprise.

## 1    Motivation

Over the last two decades the intensified academic focus on the management of enterprise networks and virtual enterprises has led to a vast number of academic publications describing innovative approaches that are used to shape processes and solve problems more effectively from various view points and with different objectives. The research within this subject area is characterized by a great variety of concepts and a heterogeneous terminology as well as by the handling of issues based on very specific foundations and assumptions. The network management concept "Extended Value Chain Management" (EVCM) [1] was developed as one part of specific research projects that focussed enterprise networks. EVCM is an extensive approach for the generation and operation of order-specifically configured production networks and virtual enterprises focussing especially on small and medium-sized enterprises (SME). Enterprises in EVCM-coordinated value-added networks retain their legal and economic independence and also act as equal partners and compete for customer orders. In that context many processes have to be modelled and implemented. Apart from procedures concerning the generation and operation of the cooperation, there are others that have to be considered as well, for instance, procedures focussing on the delivery of the finished product to the customer. Against

L.M. Camarinha-Matos, L. Xu, and H. Afsarmanesh (Eds.): PRO-VE 2012, IFIP AICT 380, pp. 539–547, 2012.
© IFIP International Federation for Information Processing 2012

this backdrop, the allocation of profit or loss acquires a special importance. For that reason, an extensive study has been conducted dealing with possibilities of profit allocation within order-specifically configured production networks and virtual enterprises. Profit allocation in virtual enterprises is a very specific task because several economic independent enterprises cooperate on one project or order but the amount paid by the customer needs to allocated in a justified manner. This contribution focuses that problem by considering mainly the foundations.

## 2     Possibilities of a Profit Allocation

Possibilities for allocating financial benefits in cooperations are divided in a practical perspective focussing some experiences from different areas of application and a theoretical perspective represented by a literature review. In most cooperations, regardless of what particular type, it is common that the partaking enterprises calculate their profit as part of their offer. In such cases there is no need for an explicit mechanism for profit distribution. However, it is still unclear how to handle outstanding customer payments, deficit complaints, or product liability claims. At this point, it becomes apparent how important it is to look at these problems.

According to a study of the economy institute of the trade chamber Bozen, Italy from the year 2000, there are clearly defined rules concerning the profit distribution in 77% of all industrial co-operations. This is contrasted by only 13% in handy craft businesses. Since it can be assumed that the participation of enterprises in co-operations is based on their agreement to the corresponding terms and conditions, it follows that many enterprises are likely to underestimate the significance of precise regulations concerning the allocation of financial benefits. Such deficits, however, may have a negative effect on the success of cooperations. For this reason, it was recommended to establish fixed regulations based on a contract e.g. concerning the profit and loss distribution during enterprise cooperations. It is advisable to reach a consensus concerning all regulations before the value-added process starts.

Berg et al. [2] presented an empirical investigation focusing on operating companies in the agrarian sector. In the context of a review representatives of 24 companies from the North Rhine Westphalian area in Germany were interviewed. Interviews focussed the profit determination and distribution (factor remuneration and distribution solutions). It was found out that the remuneration is based on the production factors that enter the total profit of the joint venture. This could consist out of beneficial interests for real estate, and to a minor extend soil and contingents. Live stock, machines, and supplies are considered as well during remuneration. Later on, the profit which is left after the completion of the remuneration is to be distributed. With respect to the invested capital, most companies use a distribution-key for this matter. Since the factor remuneration has a higher priority, it is common to distribute the profit at this particular stage. The distribution-key may range from a ratio of 90:10 up to 50:50. In case of a loss, two thirds of all co-operations have fixed rules concerning the loss distribution which work similar to the profit distribution.

Approaches from game theory have a different take on the problem. In a concrete case, three enterprises form the area of Karlsruhe, Germany were trying to reduce the costs for their energy supply through the building of an energy supply plant. The profit in this case assumes the form of the reduced costs made visible through a reference case without an energy conservation plan [3]. Depending on the particular approach, different solutions are possible in this case.

The problem of profit distribution is addressed mostly superficially in academic literature. Schuh and Strack recommend a profit distribution which is based on the participation during the value-creation process. This can be accomplished through negotiations or through the application of solution principles that are typical for the market and that are ultimately all based on pre-defined parameters [4]. The remuneration should at least correspond to the opportunity costs of the missed utilization of the resources either in or for once own enterprise, plus, a corresponding profit share [5]. According to Borchardt, it is advisable for the cooperation partners of a Virtual Enterprise to clarify all questions concerning the profit distribution and the coordination costs already during negotiation phase [6]. In that context, transfer prices on the basis of full costs in addition to profit shares offer the best solution.

Krajewska and Kopfer consider a concrete field of application by focussing on the logistics sector [7]. The available approaches to this problem all assume similar power relations and similar market positions of the involved partners. Most of these approaches are designed for a short-term application and they are based on ideas from Operations Research, game theory, and combinational auctions. Every co-operation partner has to disclose the lowest possible fulfilment costs. Through an aggregation of the presented offers, a portfolio is created for the sake of maximizing the profit of the whole cooperation. The whole model is of a theoretic nature.

A simple proposal is introduced by Schönsleben and Hieber [8]. They suggest an equal division of the additional profit which results from the co-operation-based value-added process (e.g. the profit from a cost reduction or increased earnings) because this particular profit is not merely the result of an individual effort, but that of an effective partnership.

Jin and Wu [9] present an approach which puts the mechanisms for the development of co-operations of suppliers at the centre of their work. Hereby auctions are the preferred tool because of their simplicity and efficiency that made them a very popular form of price fixing in eCommerce. The two components of a specific co-operation mechanism are the development of a coalition through the search for suitable members and the profit distribution among these members. The profit distribution which is based on the individual profit expectations is a key function for the development of a cooperation since it is possible to start the auction mechanism with this knowledge. Additionally there are further approaches that can be found in academic literature which are rather rudimental and therefore are not included here.

## 3    A Framework for the Allocation Model

In the following basic information about the framework for the allocation model is introduced. In addition basic assumptions and its interdependencies are considered.

The operator concept EVCM for the coordination of value-added processes presents a phase model which describes the typical life cycle phases of a cooperation. Depending on the situation, EVCM can work automatically, so that a high degree of self-organization is achieved. One objective of the EVCM is to select those enterprises that are most suitable for cooperation. Following the reception of a customer request the value-added process is decomposed into its individual process steps. For every step at least one enterprise has to be selected. It has to possess not only the required resources, but also the necessary competencies. The result of this work planning is a process variants plan which includes several options for manufacturing of the product. In the following, an inquiry is sent to the selected enterprises inquiring the capability of providing the necessary resources by considering their capacity situation. Additionally soft-facts, such as co-operation and communication abilities as well as reliability, are considered as well. When the ideal network configuration is found the production process starts. After its completion and delivery, every partaking enterprise is assessed in terms of the produced effort and the obtained profit (or loss) is distributed among the involved enterprises.

As already mentioned there are several options to allocate financial benefits in networked structures. In order to account for the large number of cooperation scenarios, several approaches, which can be applied depending on the particular circumstances, have already been developed [10]. In some cases enterprises have to reveal their profit expectations. Another important point to be considered is the enterprise-related costs during the planned value-added process. It must be differentiated in fixed and variable costs. The variable costs are directly allocable to the product. The fixed costs arise independently from a specific order. They are added to the particular order or to the product through the application of some cost-accounting approaches. The extent to which the enterprises add costs to the customer order is to be determined only by the enterprises. The mechanisms of price formation have to be observed carefully. In the beginning, the revenue matches the accumulated costs since the profit is determined separately. There is an option to establish a lower price limit in the form of a contribution margin that equals zero by determining the variable costs as the total costs of an enterprise, that is, the revenue would equal the variable costs. The standard case, however, presents an appropriate contribution margin in order to cover the fixed costs of an enterprise as well.

In the following, some possibilities of how to determine the obtained net profit will be examined closer. The starting point is that a customer places an order on the basis of an enterprise offer to manufacture a product. The basis for all this is a mutual declaration of intent concerning the quality of the product, the amount and price as well as further relevant criteria. It is also assumed that all required competencies that are necessary for the manufacturing of the product can be provided by the enterprises from the resource pool. After the completion of the value-added process and the delivery of the final product, the customer pays the agreed price. Subsequently, a performance analysis and the profit allocation are realized.

In principle, it is not necessary to have the enterprises calculate their individual profit directly in the offer price. It must also be assumed that several resource pool enterprises share the same core competencies and, therefore, compete for the same customer orders. This constellation is explicitly welcomed since this guarantees that some enterprises do not work overpriced due to the competition. Obviously, this would drastically reduce their chances for being selected. If an enterprise secretly calculates profits into its offers, it is doing this at its own risk. The most important information in all allocation approaches to production nets with $n$ enterprises is $c_j$. That is the costs related to the value-added process. The fixing of $c_j$ occurs during the assignation of the individual offers to the corresponding process steps. These costs can be calculated into the value-added process either directly or indirectly. The sum of all enterprise-specific costs $c_i$ is $C$. The total costs are the basis for the offer that is submitted to the customer by the network. During that phase EVCM has to add a network-related calculative offer profit $G^{offer}$ before the final offer price $P^{offer}$ for a product can be calculated. The offer price $P^{offer}$ is the amount that the customer has to pay after the delivery of the product. To determine the offer price, cf. equation 1.

$$P^{offer} = C + G^{offer}. \tag{1}$$

The net profit $G^{offer}$ that was determined by EVCM is calculated on the basis of an algorithm and, if necessary, through the application of negotiation mechanisms. The algorithm that is used in order to determine the offer profit is presented extensively in section 4. It is apparent that the enterprises costs $c_i$, which were calculated into the purchase price, can now be safely assigned. The difference between the selling price $P^{sell}$ and the sum of the individual cost shares of the total costs $C$ results in profit $G$.

# 4    Determination of Profit

In the following the basic procedure and an algorithm for the determination of the allocable financial benefit of a production process in a Virtual Enterprise is introduced. During the request process the enterprises have to reveal a variety of data to the EVCM. One of the most important variables is the enterprise-related cost $c_i$. Another relevant variable is the fixed cost share $c_i^{fix}$ relating to a particular value-added process. In addition, it is expected that an enterprise that is being requested by the EVCM also reveals its individual profit expectation $g_i^e$. It can be expressed in different ways and is deposited as a master data record of the particular enterprise. The individual profit expectation is independent from a value-added process.

A central component of the network offer is the offer price $P^{offer}$. That variable is the sum of the total costs $C$ related to the order and the offer profit $G^{offer}$. While the total costs represent all value added process-related costs of an enterprise $c_i$, the offer profit has to be calculated seperately. Thus, a characteristic organization procedure occurs: In order to allocate a profit, a value-added process has to be fulfilled. Here for a customer order has to be initiated. This, however, presupposes an active offer. In order to create an offer, the offer profit $G^{offer}$ is required, which must be determined according to a allocation approach. Therefore, it is necessary to clarify which of the available profit allocation approaches is to be applied. The enterprise-specific profit expectation $g_i^e$ are important for determining the offer profit $G^{offer}$. This value can be expressed in the form of a percentage of the value-added process of an enterprise $g_i^{ep}$.

Absolute values $g_i^e$ that depend on the specific cost shares of an enterprise $c_i$ are an option as well. Both of these variables can be set in relation, cf. equation 2.

$$g_i^e = g_i^{ep} \cdot c_i. \tag{2}$$

A principal procedure for determining the offer profit is illustrated in fig. 1. The algorithm is presented next by utilizing calculation formulas for individual variables.

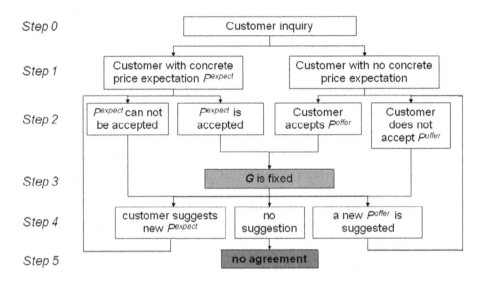

**Fig. 1.** Diagram depicting the determination of important figures

After the reception of the customer inquiry, it must be differentiated whether the customer presents an expected price $P^{expect}$ or not. In case of a concrete purchase price $P^{expect}$, it is possible to calculate the realizable profit $G^r$ of the order straight away without any further preconditions. This can be done by subtracting the total costs of the network $C$ from the expected price $P^{expect}$, cf. equation 3.

$$G^r = P^{expect} - C. \tag{3}$$

Subsequently, it must be clarified whether the individual enterprises are satisfied with their calculative profit shares. For this, the realizable profit $G^r$ from equation 3 has to be divided among the enterprises partaking in the value-added process based on the chosen profit allocation model. The resulting variable is expressed as $g_i^r$ and should at least correspond with the individual profit expectation $g_i^e$. It may occur that not all enterprises are satisfied with their calculative profit share because it is lower than expected. In order to solve this problem, a majority decision should be found. This procedure, however, could be very dissatisfying, particularly in the case of ambiguous results. Therefore, an alternative could be to sum-up all individual absolute profit expectations $g_i^e$ to $G^e$. Adding the complete profit expectations $G^e$ to the total costs $C$

results in the offer price $P^{offer}$ (see equation 1). It must be noted, however, that at this point $G^e$ is not the same as $G^{offer}$.

Now, the expected price of the customer $P^{expect}$ (including the realizable profit $G^r$) and the preliminary realizable offer price $P^{offer}$ (including the sum of the profit expectation of the enterprise $G^e$) can be laid out. A comparison of these two variables leads to two possible options. If the preliminary offer price of the complete network $P^{offer}$ exceeds the expected price of the customer $P^{expect}$ (the sum of the individual profit expectations $G^e$ is higher than the realizable profit $G^r$), it can assumed that the enterprises will not accept the expected price $P^{expect}$ because they cannot attain their expected profits. In this case, EVCM will take appropriate measures, for instance, further negotiations between EVCM and the potential customer. These kinds of mechanisms represent step four of the algorithm. Overall, some parameters may be altered in order to reach a contract agreement. If the realizable offer price of the net $P^{offer}$ is lower than the expected price of the customer $P^{expect}$ or corresponds to it, then this expected price $P^{expect}$ will be accepted. An additional profit can be obtained. The customer will accept this offer because the realizable profit $G^r$ exceeds the sum of the profit expectations $G^e$. The difference $G^d$ occurs:

$$G^d = G^r - G^e . \tag{4}$$

This difference profit $G^d$ represents a back-up or incentive payments as well as shared among the enterprises based on an extended profit distribution model. At this point, $G^{offer}$, which was calculated into $P^{offer}$, is determined conclusively.

$$G^{offer} = P^{offer} - C . \tag{5}$$

Alternatively, there is also the possibility when the customer suggests a concrete price expectation. In this case, the customer is presented an offer. The following procedure appears adequate in this respect: Starting with an individual profit expectation for the enterprise $g_i^e$, it is possible to determine the sum of the profit expectations of the entire network $G_e$. $G_e$ is then added to the total costs of the net $C$ which results in a preliminary offer price $P^{offer}$ which is presented to the customer.

$$P^{offer} = C + G^e . \tag{6}$$

Then, if the offer suits the customer, he will accept it. With this, the offer profit $G^{offer}$ corresponds to the sum of the profit expectations $G_e$ and is now fixed. It follows:

$$G^{offer} := G^e . \tag{7}$$

The situation becomes more complicated, if the customer rejects the offer. In this case it has is assumed that despite the non-existence of a concrete price expectation $P^{expect}$, the customer still has a concrete price expectation. The offer apparently exceeds this secret price expectation $P^{expect}$. This requires the start of negotiations.

Three different alternatives for a further proceeding appear after completing the negotiation process. The first option is that the customer presents a new higher price expectation $P^{expect}$. That means, the customer is willing to pay more than at the previous stage. At this stage the algorithm leads to the two already discussed alternatives. The second option is an alteration of the offer price by EVCM. Through the partial or complete disclaimer of the offer profit $G^{offer}$ the offer price can be further reduced. Here again, step two follows: The customer can either accept the offer or not - this would trigger the corresponding consequences. It is also possible that the two parties are not willing to make any further suggestions. Consequently, no agreement can be reached meaning that there can be no conclusion of a contract.

Under a careful analysis, it becomes apparent that the first two options are related to one another. The main aim of these activities is to reach an agreement concerning the purchase price. If the price expectation of the customer is below the offer price of the network, then either the price expectation has to be increased or the offer price has to be reduced. The presented algorithm allows executing several iteration steps before an agreement is reached or the negations are aborted. It is, however, open which side takes over the initiative.

# 5    Conclusion

In this contribution the fundamentals for modeling approaches for a direct allocation of financial benefits such as profit or loss in order-specifically configured production nets and virtual enterprises were introduced. This primarily theoretic research work is required if decentralized distribution of financial figures, which is related to the value-added process, is to be carried out in a as far as possible automated manner. It is fact that the research concerning the common practices has given little insights, so that a theoretical analysis was required at first. It became apparent that the problem has to be approached on a theoretical way which has to be further refined by the application of economically-relevant methods in order to arrive at an appropriate solution approach. An appropriate model has been presented in general terms. The big advantage of this model is that it is adaptable to a high degree and it is therefore suited as a general reference model. Future works will include a validation of the model. Then the focus is laid on modeling precise calculation approaches for the allocation of financial benefits in networks and its evaluation in a real-world environment.

# References

1. Teich, T.: Extended Value Chain Management - Ein Konzept zur Koordination von Wertschöpfungsnetzen. Verlag der GUC, Chemnitz (2003)
2. Berg, E., Trenkel, H., Lüttgens, B., Grienberger, R., Möller, K., Reinders, M.: Motivation, Zielsetzung und innere Organisation von Betriebsgesellschaften in der Landwirtschaft. Betriebsgesellschaften in der Landwirtschaft - Chancen und Grenzen im Strukturwandel, 141–178 (2001)
3. Frank, M.: Entwicklung und Anwendung einer integrierten Methode zur Analyse von betriebsübergreifenden Energieversorgungskonzepten. Dissertation, University Karlsruhe, TH (2003)
4. Schuh, G., Strack, J.: Virtualität in der produzierenden Industrie. Technologie und Management 48(1), 10–14 (1999)

5. Steven, M.: Produktionsmanagement in virtuellen Unternehmen. ZFO 70(2), 86–92 (2001)
6. Borchardt, A.: Koordinationsinstrumente in virtuellen Unternehmen. Deutscher Universitäts-Verlag, Wiesbaden (2006)
7. Krajewska, M.A., Kopfer, H.: Profit sharing approaches for freight forwarders: An overview. In: Lukinsky, V.S., Uvarov, S.A., Koroleva, E.A. (eds.) Proceedings of the 5th International Scientific-Practical Conference Logistics: Modern Trends of Development, April 20-21, pp. 157–161. SPSUEE, Saint Petersburg, Russia (2006)
8. Schönsleben, P., Hieber, R.: Gestaltung von effizienten Wertschöpfungspartnerschaften im Supply Chain Management. In: Busch, A., Dangelmaier, W. (eds.) Integriertes Supply Chain Management, 2nd edn., pp. 47–64. Gabler, Wiesbaden (2004)
9. Jin, M., Wu, S.D.: Supplier coalitions in on-line reverse auctions: Validity requirements and profit distribution scheme. Int. Journal of Production Economics 100, 183–194 (2006)
10. Jähn, H., Fischer, M., Teich, T.: Distribution of Network Generated Profit by Considering Individual Profit Expectations. In: Camarinha-Matos, L.M., et al. (eds.) Establishing the Foundation of Collaborative Networks. IFIP, vol. 243, pp. 337–344. Springer, Boston (2007)

# A Cost Model for Services

Jürgen Dorn and Wolfgang Seiringer

Vienna University of Technology, Institute for Software Technology and Interactive Systems,
Favoritenstr. 16, A-1040 Vienna, Austria
juergen.dorn@ec.tuwien.ac.at, wolfgang@seiringer.info

**Abstract.** Typically, services are co-created by service provider and customer. This paper describes an approach to account the full costs of a service considering costs at the provider side as well as on the customer side resulting in a more accurate cost model. Depending on the level of integration of provider and customer, explicit modeling of uncertainty is used to reflect the uncertainty about customer's competences. This model may help to improve the efficiency of services and whole service systems. We evaluate the model in a scenario derived from an industrial application.

**Keywords:** service science, service costs, accounting, cost modeling.

## 1 Introduction

The share of the service sector in most economies is growing, however, the productivity is typically much lower than in the first two economic sectors (i.e. agriculture and manufacturing). Service science tries to understand and to address services to improve the productivity in this sector and to facilitate the innovation of services [1]. A service system is the main abstraction in service science to investigate phenomena in service science [2].

Motivated by the growing importance of services, Vargo and Lusch propose Service-Dominant logic in contrast to traditional goods logic [3]. Regardless of the economic importance of services, a goods-centered view (Goods-Dominant (G-D) Logic) was the predominant concept when thinking about economic exchange. In G-D Logic goods are playing the central role of economic exchange while services are just a special form of goods; but services are more than this. This fact is considered in the concept of Service-Dominant (S-D) Logic where every company is seen as a service company and where always services are exchanged [2]. In the goods-centered view, the production of goods is separated from the consumption of goods to maximize the production output [4]. Such a separation is contrary to customer-oriented marketing as well as the S-D Logic [5]. This means that the service consumer is actively participating in the process of service co-creation by providing external activities [6]. The traditional logic is based on the exchange of goods or respectively the exchange of goods for money. If a good is sold from a provider to a customer it is already produced, potentially stored in a warehouse and, conceptually, the transaction of exchanging good and money can take place at single points of time. Such a

L.M. Camarinha-Matos, L. Xu, and H. Afsarmanesh (Eds.): PRO-VE 2012, IFIP AICT 380, pp. 548–558, 2012.
© IFIP International Federation for Information Processing 2012

transaction can be modeled easily in a state-based knowledge representation. If we do not assume the two actions to occur at the same time, we have three states and two state changes as illustrated by Fig. 1.

In a conceptual accounting framework such as REA (Resources, Events and Agents) [7] two events (in Fig 1 deliver and pay) are modeled when two agents exchange resources. If this accounting is done in real-time, an agent can determine at any time the amount of its resources (money and goods) by a simple database operation. Proponents of REA claim that with such a computational model, traditional financial balance computation is obsolete because no double entry accounting is necessary [8].

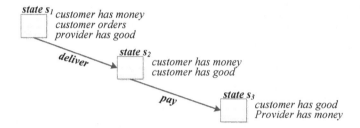

**Fig. 1.** State-based Representation

However, services are different to goods in several aspects. Service exchange is not occurring in a single point of time, but is a process that takes some time. Services are co-created by provider and customer. Thus, also the customer has to invest at least time and effort in its production. If the customer is a company with employees of different degree of competences and an employee is needed for the service consumption, the success and the efficiency of a service provision is also dependent on the selected employee at the customer side.

The provider makes only a value offering to the customer. If we account costs of services, we have to consider costs at both sides: at the provider and the customer side. If we only want to estimate at which price a provider shall offer a service, we might consider only costs at the provider side. However, if we want to sell services we have to compare different value offerings on the market and then we have to compare full prices including the cost for the customer, because the customer has to consider the offered price and its own costs in co-creation of the service.

S-D Logic claims competences to be the most important resources in services. Thus, we especially have to account the costs of human resources and need a cost model for levels of competences. If an expert is required for a service, the service is more expensive than a service for which only a novice is required.

Our research goal is a model to estimate service costs before service provision (pre-calculation) as well as for computing the real costs afterwards (post-calculation). The model enables:

- more accurate modeling of costs resulting in a better control of the efficiency of services and a comparable rating of service costs for customers and services.
- measuring true costs for customers, and
- measuring true costs in a complex service system where agents work together to provide services to customers outside of the system.

To evaluate our model we have to compare cost estimations of existing costing systems $c_t$ with our approach $c_s$ and both of course have to be compared with real costs $c_r$.

In the next section we present current theory about services and service cost modeling. In the third section we present a scenario for a typical service. In the fourth section we introduce our model. In the fifth section we describe our evaluation results derived from the application of the CMFS to existing services. Finally we summarize and conclude.

## 2     State of the Art

As mentioned in the introduction compared to goods it is said that services have some special characteristics. These are inseparability, perishability, heterogeneity and uncertainty [9]. Inseparability describes the simultaneous production or as we call it co-creation and consumption of services. The customer defines when the process of service co-creation starts and when the customer is needed by the provider during the co-creation process. The term co-creation is more suited to characterize the process-oriented service concept that the value of a service is co-created between the service consumer und the service provider. Perishability describes the fact that a service is not storable. This implies complications to plan resources for the service production. Human resources are the most important resource and cost factor in the context of services. The heterogeneous nature of services makes it difficult to standardize the process of service co-creation because services are often demanded only once.

The process of service co-creation depends on the factors *customer integration* and *external factor* and reflects the integrative nature of services. The service co-creation can be separated into the areas of *production factors, factor combination* and *output*. The production factors are all the 'objects' which are necessary to produce a service. A production factor can be something tangible or intangible, for example a defective device, information or even the customer himself. The *internal production factors* are those factors that are provided by the service provider and the *external production factor* is supplied by the service consumer. It is not possible for the service producer to produce or buy the external factor. Consequently, the external factor and the associated knowledge are under control by the customer. The service provider is forced to integrate it into the service co-creation in form of external activities. During the co-creation, the internal and external production factors are combined (factor combination) to form the tangible or intangible service output [10], [11].

In SMEs in manufacturing typically surcharge calculation is common practice to calculate costs. Fixed or variable percentages are added to the costs of materials and labor to determine the production costs [12]. The costs of services as part of a physical product like a product service system (PSS) are often only estimated [13].

A well known costing method is Activity-Based Costing (ABC) which is also used for the cost calculation of services and has its origin in the manufacturing sector. Based on the activities performed in a company, the activities and business processes are identified and analyzed. The total costs for the selected activities are computed by considering the required personnel resources and the salaries. Due to the similarity between overhead costs and service costs, ABC is also applicable for the service cost calculation. [14].

The implementation and operation of a conventional ABC System is very complex and time-consuming. Thus the Time-Driven Activity-Based Costing (TDABC) was developed. The basic idea underlying this concept is the analysis of the activities performed by the employees and is the same as in the traditional ABC concept. But to make the implementation and operation of such a costing method easier, time equations are playing a major role. Time is regarded as the leading cost driver because most of the supplied and consumed resources like employees and machines can be measured using the factor time [15]. However, neither ABC nor TDABC cover the external activities (i.e. the activities performed by the customer) and the uncertainty in their performance. The amount of the required human resources depends directly on the external activities. This implies that without the integration of them, a major cost-influencing factor is not being taken into account. This decreases the reliability and the value of service cost information.

## 3    Scenario Maintenance Service

We have applied and evaluated our approach in two scenarios derived from a manufacturing company and a software company. In this paper we present only the first scenario due to space limitations. The manufacturing company produces medical machines and equipment mainly on demand. Today, they have to provide more product-enhancing services then before due to a strong competition. However, the sales department has problems in forecasting costs for these services. Due to specific characteristics of services, the usage of costing methods designed for the usage with materials and goods require a dedicated model. If a service, such as maintenance is offered, the service provision is highly dependent on the customer. If a customer can specify problems accurately and may provide his own experts during maintenance work, the effort for a provider is smaller than for the case that the customer cannot support the service. In the following we model an abstract maintenance process for the manufacturer. The two lanes in the BPMN-diagram represent the two agents (customer and service provider). Both agents exchange information and knowledge at certain points of time. In marketing management these contact points are called touch points. They will be parameterized in our approach to calculate costs.

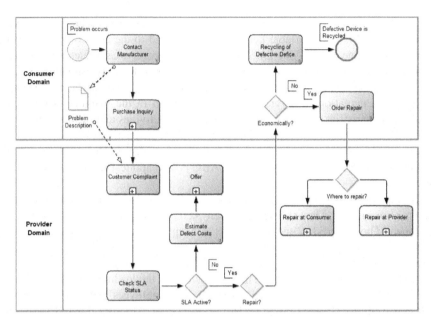

**Fig. 2.** Prototypical Maintenance Process – Step Check Status of Service Level Agreement (SLA)

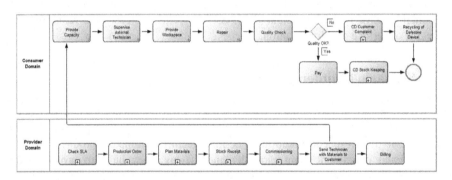

**Fig. 3.** Prototypical Maintenance Process – Variant Repair at Consumer Domain

The maintenance process starts with the step of checking the Service Level Agreement (SLA). Based on the result of the SLA check step the consumer or provider has to pay for the maintenance service, see also Fig. 2. During the maintenance process different activities carried out on the customer side are e.g. "provide capacity", "supervise external technician", "prepare workspace", "repair", "quality check", "customer complaint", "recycling of defective device", "pay" and "stock keeping". When the customer has to pay for the maintenance two decisions are made on the customer's side. First, the offer of the provider has to be accepted and secondly, the repair must be accepted. The provider activities consist of "check SLA", "production order", "plan materials", "stock receipt", "commissioning", "send technician with materials to customer" and "billing", see also Fig. 3. All these activities are dependent on the involvement of the customer. If the customer has not specified the problem correctly much more effort is required at the provider side. The repair can require much more time then estimated, an activity can be carried out several times or can also be skipped. Some activities consist of different sub-activities e.g. "production order" or "stock keeping".

# 4    The Model

A service (S) is produced by a business process (BP) consisting of a set of activities ($A_i$) carried out to fulfill customer satisfaction with a tangible or intangible output. Certain activities depend on the customer. These external activities are not under control of the provider and thus uncertainty about the performance and the service costs has to be considered. Compared to our maintenance scenario the customer provides the defective device, information about the defect and different employees with different competencies. The service provider must integrate these costs influencing external activities during the service co-creation.

Using the activities as the smallest unit, allows the identification of service costs. To calculate the costs for an activity, a time equation is created estimating the time required to carry out this activity. This step is analog to TDABC where the time equation for a service is the sum of all activities of the process realizing the service: $A_1+...+A_m$. Time is used because it is possible and relatively easy to calculate the consumed resources of humans and machines. For services, human resources are the most important cost factor [15].

Our Cost Model for Services (CMFS) integrates the external activities of the customer by a Customer Integration Factor (CIF) classifying and expressing the uncertainty of the external activities during the process of service co-creation. A central point of the CMFS is the correlation between the CIF and the service activities, see Fig. 4. The value of the CIF parameter is designed to be independent from an activity but is related to it and is used to measure the customer influence on the activity utilization. The pre-calculated activity utilization represents the expected resource consumption and consequently the costs for an activity. The sum of the involved activities corresponds to the pre-calculated service costs. During service co-creation, data about the performed activities are recorded from which the real value of

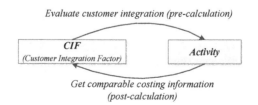

**Fig. 4.** Correlation between the CIF and service activities

the CIF parameter and activity utilization can be derived. The recorded data are used to make a post-calculation of the real service costs. The results of the pre- and post-calculation can then be compared and represent valuable costing information, see Fig. 5.

The CIF consists of the parameters *influence depth* (Idep), *influence intensity* (Iint), *influence frequency* (Ifre) and *influence duration* (Idur). *Influence depth* (Idep) measures how deep external activities are integrated into the value chain of the service provider. Iint quantifies how intensive a resource will be utilized. The Idep and Iint parameters of the CIF are combined to the Customer Utilization Factor (CUF) to get a special parameter which characterizes the potential capacity utilization for an activity. The influence frequency Ifre indicates how often external activities are part of the service production. The influence duration is used to evaluate how long additional external activities are part of the service co-creation. Resource costs are mainly the costs of the human resources depending on the type of the resource (i.e. expert or novice). The CMFS extends the basic TBABC formula to integrate the CIF parameter and we consider that the knowledge about the external activities is often vague and not precise. This assumption is based on service characteristics which complicate the standardization of the process of service co-creation and the dependency on the external factor which is not under full control of the service provider. As a consequence and to simplify the CIF rating simple linguistic variables are used to classify the four cost effecting parameters of the CIF. In the CMFS a *LinguisticVarialbe* $Lv_i, i = 1,...,o$ maps values like very low, low, medium, high,... to double values. The central formula of the CMFS is:

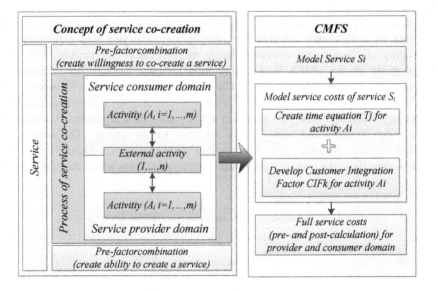

**Fig. 5.** Concept and components of the Cost Model for Services (CMFS)

$$S_i = \sum_{i=1}^{m} (A_{0A_i} + A_i) * ((Idep_{A_i} * Iint_{A_i}) * Ifre_{A_i}) + Idur_{A_i}$$

where the variables have the following meaning:

$$StandardActivityTime : A_{0A_i}, \quad Services\ S_i, i = 1,...,m\ , \quad Activies\ A_i, i = 1,...,n$$

**Formula 1:** Basic formula and variables of the CMFS to calculate the activity time

The same formula is used for the pre- and post-calculation of the service costs which allows the comparison of the results for the purpose of cost accounting. For the post-calculation, the real amount of consumed resources is accounted during the service co-creation. The required data are service process, activity, start time, end time and employee type. This data can then be assigned to the co-created service and a post-calculation using the same cost model is possible.

# 5     Evaluation

To evaluate the costing method we analyzed the maintenance service of a manufacturing company and the concept development service of a software company. For both examples we have analyzed over 60 different activities, 60 different time equations and over 100 different cost drivers. The amount of activities, cost drivers and time equations depends on the modeled service. For example in the maintenance service, the check SLA step consists of five activities and sub-processes. For each time equation per activity at least one cost driver is necessary. The first evaluation objective is the applicability to different types of business domains, services, business processes and activities. With the second evaluation point we want to find out if the application of the CMFS leads to "realistic" and useful results. The third objective is whether the CMFS parameters can be used to control a complete business process and whether the effects are measurable. The fourth objective treats the traceability of the difference between the CMFS approach and standard TDABC.

## 5.1     Result Discussion

The positive application of the CMFS to services of a manufacturer and a software company show that our approach is not only applicable for a specific business domain. We can argue this with realistic service cost results for each service and company and the CMFS provides new and valuable costing information. For the concept development service which consists of the process steps and activity times "create concept" 2.94 hours, , "document requirements" 3.30 hours, "check and estimate concept" 0.08 hours, "release concept" 0.93 hours, "create offer" 0.25 hours, "create sales order" 0.17 hours, "create forecast" 0.17 hours and "customer domain document requirements" 3.60 hours the service time is 11.43 hours. This is a reasonable result for the investigated company. Also for the maintenance/repair service the application of the CMFS leads to realistic and reasonable results, see Fig. 6. With these results our first two evaluation objectives are answered positive. An exemplary time equation for the sales process activity "create offer" as part of the maintenance service is shown in Table 1. This example illustrates the application of the CMFS on a single activity as part of a business process and that it is also possible to influence and the costs of the related business process. It is also possible to trace the costs to its origin. This allows us to answer the third evaluation objective positive. Please note that in the formula of Table 1 the linguistic variables for the CMFS parameters are substituted by real numbers used for computation. The fourth evaluation objective can also be answered positive because the CMFS is a completely independent addition to the TDABC concept which allows tracing and calculating the difference between the CMFS and TDABC results, see also Fig. 6.

**Table 1.** Example for pre- and post-calculation formula (m = minutes, u = units)

| pre-calculation formula |
|---|
| $(15\ m + (500\ u*0,05\ m)/400\ u)\ *CIF((CUF(Idep(0,75)*Iint(1))*Ifre(0,5))+Idur(0) = 5.65$ Minutes |
| **post-calculation formula** |
| $54\ m*CIF(CUF(Idep(0,1)*Iint(0,057))*Ifre(3))+Idur(30) = 30.92$ Minutes |

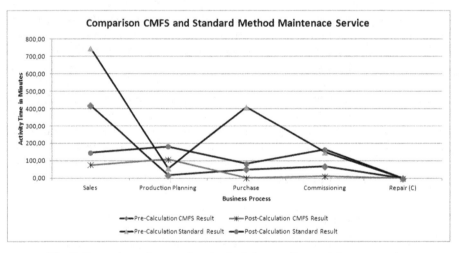

**Fig. 6.** Comparison of pre- and post-calculation results – maintenance service

# 6     Conclusions

Service systems are system configurations where actors cooperate in order to provide services to other service systems. On one side the cooperation in the service system demands win-win relations between providers and customers and on the other side service marketing demands a similar relation between provider and customer. Consequently, we ask for a cost modeling approach that takes into account costs at both sides. Especially for services the most important cost driving factor are personal costs. The competence of both actors in the service provision process is most important for the quality and efficiency of a service. Additionally, the uncertainty about the customer's behavior is a relevant factor in any cost model applied by a provider.

We have analyzed the service costs at real companies and made computations with a new model that considers these problems. Computations for prototypical services have shown that we can reach in average a higher accuracy (about 10-30%) in forecasting of service costs than with the current cost models at these companies. This first evaluation must, however, be repeated in the actual practice with more historical data and compared with actual costs. Here we have to evaluate whether the difference between forecasted and actual costs are really smaller than our first evaluation has shown. We conclude from our evaluations that it is possible to parameterize the CMFS from complex services to a single activity and that the CMFS is easily adaptable for different service scenarios and business domains. The standard activity time $A_i$ has strong influence on the results and the entire model depends on many different parameters especially from the TDABC approach.

A next step in our research is to investigate how our approach can be integrated most efficiently in an enterprise resource planning (ERP) system. Here additional information about customers has to be managed and the integration with human resources data has to be realized. We also plan to carry out additional statistical analysis of evaluation results to refine our approach.

# References

1. Spohrer, J., Maglio, P., Bailey, J., Gruhl, D.: Steps Toward a Science of Service Systems. IEEE Computer, 71–77 (January 2007)
2. Vargo, S.L., Lusch, R.F.: Evolving to a new Dominant Logic for Marketing. Journal of Marketing 68, 1–17 (2004)
3. Spohrer, J., Vargo, S., Caswell, N., Maglio: The Service System is the Basic Abstraction of Service Science. In: Proceedings of the 41st Hawaii International Conference on System Sciences (2008)
4. Lusch, R., Vargo, S.: Service-Dominant Logic: What It Is, What It Is Not, What It Might Be. In: The Service-Dominant Logic of Marketing: Dialog, Debate, and Directions, pp. 43–56. M.E. Sharp, New York (2006) ISBN 0-7656-1490-1
5. Lusch, R., Vargo, S.: Service-dominant logic: reactions, reflections and refinements. Marketing Theory 6(3), 281–288 (2006)
6. Wattanakamolchai, S.: Managing Customer Participation in the Service Production Process (2009)
7. Geerts, G.L., McCarthy, W.E.: An Ontological Analysis of the Economic Primitives of the Extended-REA Enterprise Information Architecture. International Journal of Accounting Information Systems 3, 1–16 (2002)
8. McCarthy, W.E.: The REA Accounting Model: A Generalized Framework for Accounting Systems in A Shared Data Environment. The Accounting Review, 554–578 (1982)

9. de Vries, W., Kasper, H., van Helsdingen, P.: Service Marketing Management – An International Perpective, pp. 8–20. John Wiley & Sons, West Sussex (1999) ISBN 0-471-98490-6

10. Frisch, R.: Theory of Production, pp. 3–5. Springer, Netherlands (2009) ISBN 978-9048183340

11. Flandel, G., Blaga, S.: Elements of the production of services. In: Modern Concepts of the Theory of the Firm – Managing Enterprises of the New Economy, pp. 175–189. Springer, Heidelberg (2004)

12. Myers, J.: Traditional versus activity-based product costing methods: a field study in a defense electronics manufacturing company. Proceedings of ASBBS 16(1) (2009)

13. Mont, O.K.: Clarifying the concept of product-service system. Journal of Cleaner Production 10, 234–245 (2002)

14. Cooper, R., Kaplan, R.S.: Measure Costs Right: Make the Right Decisions. Harvard Business Review (1988)

15. Anderson, S.R., Kaplan, R.S.: Time-Driven Activity-Based Costing: A Simpler and More Powerful Path to Higher Profits. Mcgraw-Hill Professional (2007) ISBN 978-1422101711

# Performance Analysis of the Quality of Products for Value-Adding Processes in Virtual Enterprises

Hendrik Jähn and Thomas Burghardt

Chemnitz University of Technology, Dept. of Economic Sciences, Thüringer Weg 7
09126 Chemnitz, Germany
hendrik.jaehn@wirtschaft.tu-chemnitz.de

**Abstract.** This contribution introduces one integral part of a comprehensive approach for the performance management in virtual enterprises by focusing the influencing factor "product quality" as one major performance parameter. This approach introduced as a meta-model is based on a value-adding process-related perspective and implies a sophisticated analysis regarding the origin of quality level deviations. In order to apply the approach, it is necessary to consider the specific structure of the cooperation. In this paper at first some important details on the conditional circumstances are explained. This includes the performance analysis approach and a short literature review. This is followed by a description of general requirements for modeling the approach. In the main section, the approach is explained in detail.

**Keywords:** Performance Analysis, Quality, Value-Added Process, Virtual Enterprise.

## 1    Introduction

In most cases, the agreement of a well-defined quality level represents an integral part of a contract between supplier and customer. Adherence to the agreed quality level should have the highest priority as deviations often entail far-reaching consequences. It may result in negative consequences for the supplier, e.g. in form of contractual penalties or loss of reliance and thus loss of customers. With regard to virtual enterprises, adherence to a quality level of a product takes on even greater significance when there is a particularly close and time-referenced cooperation. Here, deviations from the agreed product quality represents a serious problem area as reworking time can hardly be planned and can, thus, often lead to a delayed delivery.

The performance analysis of quality represents a valuable tool for an operative analysis. The performance parameter "quality" is based on different criteria that are evaluated separately. The findings are integrated into the overall result according to their relevance by applying specific weightings. Special attention is paid due to the fact that hardly any practicable quantitative-oriented approaches exist in theory or practice. However, this form of modeling represents an essential precondition for the value-added related performance analysis. Therefore, this subject matter is seized on and a solution approach is introduced in detail in the next sections of this contribution.

L.M. Camarinha-Matos, L. Xu, and H. Afsarmanesh (Eds.): PRO-VE 2012, IFIP AICT 380, pp. 559–567, 2012.
© IFIP International Federation for Information Processing 2012

## 2    Surrounding Conditions

The quantitative analysis of the influencing factor "product quality" within networked production structures such as virtual enterprises is embedded into a specific framework. In the following an approach here for is introduced. That comprehensive framework has been developed for the realization of a comprehensive performance analysis based on quantitative data [1]. It both includes value-adding process neutral and value-adding process-related process steps. The structure of the approach and the interdependencies of the components and process steps are displayed in fig.1.

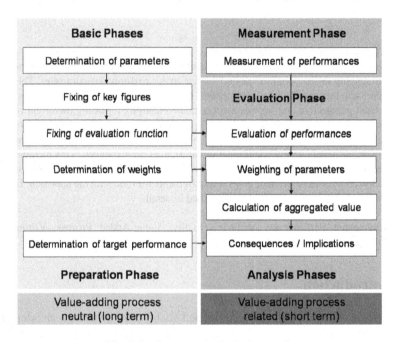

**Fig. 1.** Performance Analysis Approach

The performance analysis approach includes the measurement, evaluation and analysis of selected performance parameters identified by a modified Balanced Scorecard [2]. Herein, special attention is paid to aspects related to one specific selected value-adding process. This operational perspective allows acquiring cognitions about the degree the performance by an enterprise after finishing a specific value-adding process. Hereby, consequences, e.g. concerning the allocation of profit shares, can be deduced in case of an unsatisfactory performance of an enterprise [1]. The primary task of the performance analysis approach is to determine the degree of services performed by an enterprise. For this purpose, primarily quantitative methods are applied. The result is accounted for by the implementation of incentive and sanction mechanisms [2].

The determination of performance parameters is realized by the involvement of an adapted Balanced Scorecard approach. Performance parameters considered within the performance analysis are price, date of delivery, response time, product quality, reliance and cooperation climate [1],[2]. The last two parameters constitute soft-facts whose perceptions primarily have to be quantified through appropriate methods. Each of these performance parameters is characterized by a specific key figure. For the evaluation of the services performed, specific evaluation functions, similar to utility functions, are applied. In order to regard their different relevancies, the evaluations are weighted individually. By multiplying weighting and level of utility, aggregated utility values are calculated. The sum of the aggregated utilities of all performance parameters represents the actual performance. This can be compared to the target performance. Hereof, an enterprise-specific degree of target fulfillment is calculated. This allows a deviation of consequences. Next, the procedural method of the performance analysis approach is demonstrated in detail by considering the performance parameter "product quality".

Within the framework of a comprehensive approach for the enterprise-related performance analysis, the aim is to quantitatively analyze the degree of service provision. This means that a deviation of the realized from the agreed quality level needs to be recorded correctly and under consideration of the origin. Within networked production structures the problem is even more complex because there exists more than one upstream or downstream company. Here, monitoring and workflow management instruments need to be applied. Subsequently, the evaluation and the analysis are implemented by an adapted form of the value benefit analysis in combination with selected mathematical methods.

Approaches for the evaluation of performances within networked organization structures or supply chains exist in vast numbers and have been published in quite an uncountable quantity. It is impossible to mention all relevant publications. For that reason only a few publications are introduced which had a higher relevancy on the development of the approach. One forerunner is Neely, who deals with questions concerning the performance measurement in supply chains and networks [3]. Also Lynons et al. focus methodologies of the performance measurement in supply chains [4]. Herein, analyses can be made out of several perspectives [5]. In general, however, it has been observed that primarily medium- and long-term approaches are suggested. The background for this is the financial focus with regard to external effects of an enterprise. The development of these approaches is often reverted to the adoption of the Balanced Scorecard considering supply chains or networks [6],[7],[8]. A different perspective is introduced by Westphal et al. by investigating methodologies of measuring the performance in virtual enterprises [9]. However, this primarily represents a soft-fact and is, therefore, less relevant here. One of the few publications considering quality explicitly as one part of performance management is composed by Lockamy [10]. He stresses the necessity to research in this area by introducing a model for the development of quality-focused performance measurement systems.

# 3    The Performance Parameter "Product Quality"

In order to consider the performance parameter "product quality" at first an appropriate key figure must be determined. This allows an evaluation according to the principle structure of the approach considering a model for quantification.

### 3.1    Derivation of the Key Figure "Adherence to Quality Level"

In view of networked value-adding, the performance parameter "product quality" can only focus on the quality of one (sub)product, i.e. the quality of the product in each value-adding step or the quality of the realized value added can be evaluated. This is in each case accomplished by independent organization units that are part of the value-adding process. Formulating an appropriate key figure for the quantification of the performance parameter "product quality" appears to be comparatively complicated. Although the quality of a product is a quantifiable characteristic, a problem arises for the specific consideration in the context of the performance analysis, which results from the definition of the term "quality" according to ISO 9000: *Quality is the entirety of properties and characteristics of a given product or activity relating to its fitness to fulfill certain requirements.* This definition illustrates that for the quality evaluation of a product or subproduct a clarification regarding the product's purpose and the requirements to be fulfilled is obligatory. This is the prerequisite for the features and characteristics of the product that are included in the quality evaluation. It quickly becomes clear that this situation represents a classic use case of the value benefit analysis since the utility value (quality) of an object (product) can ultimately be determined with weighted characteristics (features and characteristics) in an multi-criteria target system (fitness to fulfill given requirements). Hereinafter, the problem for the application field at hand is the necessity to perform a separate value benefit analysis for each value-adding step of a product since each product status has to fulfill certain requirements and, therefore, shows specific characteristics. This results in a significant effort, especially because determining the associated quality criteria weights requires an interaction with the evaluator or decision maker. Furthermore, the weighting function for the characteristics has to be determined, and an independence examination of the characteristics needs to be performed, which is not at all less time-consuming. Still, for the time being this approach comes in handy as it offers the possibility to conduct different weightings of single characteristics and to determine a rooted key figure for the quality on a wide base. However, in the context of the performance analysis of a value-adding process-related production network, the effort associated with a value benefit analysis seems reasonable.

In this case, the weightings and utility value functions of the single quality characteristics are determined once and beforehand for each value-adding step and are always available for future use. A further simplification can be achieved by consolidating similar products in product groups and, thus, performing the value benefit analysis only with due regard to the appropriate product group. However, this approach limits the quality of the evaluation since certain characteristics are neglected due to the subordination in a group. If the groups and the composition of their characteristics are selected skillfully, reliable conclusions regarding the quality in the particular status should, nevertheless, be determinable. Consequently, for the key figure "adherence to quality level" the following mathematical relationship is relevant:

$$q_i = \sum w_k \cdot e_{ik} \qquad (1)$$

The degree of the quality performance of a product $q_i$ results from the sum of all of this product's degrees of criteria fulfillment $e_{ik}$ multiplied with the corresponding weight of criterion $w_k$. Index $i$ represents the producing enterprise and index $k$ the respective criterion. That approach is universally applicable however it has to be evaluated in detail whether it is suitable for the situation. Alternatively there is the possibility of using a binary evaluation as a simplification. When using a binary quality evaluation, criteria weighting and utility value function can be omitted, there is only a differentiation between criterion meets required level (1) or not (0). However this option will not discussed in a detailed way. It is obvious that quality can only be analyzed to a relatively exact degree by investing comparatively high effort. Building groups of single criteria offers an excellent possibility to reduce effort. In many cases, a mixed strategy will ultimately turn out to be the most meaningful approach. If the quality evaluation has to be performed with only a few and/or very inconsistently weighted criteria in all value-adding steps, a value benefit analysis should be used.

The evaluation method to be used should be determined by a basic agreement either before a cooperation is materialized or at the beginning of the cooperation at the latest. If the value benefit analysis is applied, it is important that the weights and the utility value functions for the single criteria per product and the independence of the criteria are considered beforehand. To verify the utility value functions, these mid-term reviews should afterwards be checked for plausibility. Only when there are satisfactory evaluation results, it can be assumed that the utility value function really comes close to the actual process of the overall objective and can be used as the basis for the weights determination. To avoid an opportunistic behavior of the enterprise during the determination of the weights and the utility value function, all members of the network or the resource pool should be involved in the process. This opens up the possibility to generate the weights of the criteria from the average value of a wealth of weighting proposals and to, thus, get an evaluation that is supported by all actors.

### 3.2 Measurement of the Key Figure "Adherence to Quality Level"

The quality evaluation has to be performed by the ingoing quality inspection of the receiving enterprise. The result of this evaluation must then be stored in a central repository. However, if this is done by the network management, the respective enterprise gains a certain authority, i.e. only this enterprise decides about the rating that the delivering enterprise gets with regard to quality. To handle possible manipulation tendencies from the beginning on, it is recommended to let the delivering company perform their own outgoing quality inspection with their own data. In doing so, a second quality value can be generated for comparison purposes. If the values of the delivering and the receiving company vary significantly, there is most likely an error within the evaluation process. This can be the result of inaccurate data used for the evaluation or a conscious falsification of the results. In such cases, it is the network management's responsibility to demand the exact single values for the evaluation criteria from all enterprises that are involved in the evaluation. This provides the possibility to subsequently identify the reason for the differences in the evaluation. As a downside of this approach it must be mentioned that in case of a non-conformance of the evaluation results a manual intervention is necessary which requires the investment of time and money.

The enterprises involved must dissolve possible differences by mutual agreement and offer a common and consistent evaluation based on the insights and results gained. This in turn facilitates the communication between the decision makers of the enterprises and delivers numerous insights for the evaluation of the cooperation which have an influence on other performance parameters such as "quality of the collaboration and cooperation". If the problem cannot be resolved through communication and agreements, the network management might, if applicable, initiate a revaluation by a neutral authority which then makes a binding decision in form of an evaluation. Should this approach not lead to a decision either – because an appropriate arbitration would take too long or cannot be conducted due to a lack of data – there is finally the possibility to not include quality in the evaluation or to choose an average value as empirical value as an exception.

### 3.3    Evaluation of the Key Figure "Adherence to Quality Level"

The performance parameter "quality" with its key figure "adherence to delivery quality" has a result interval that is mostly precisely predefined and often very limited since it has already been determined with the utility benefit analysis and usually presents ratings between 0 and 10. Subsequently, it must only be determined if the quality is linked linearly to the degree of target fulfillment or if an alternative curve shape in form of an appropriate mathematical function seems to be more reasonable. This also depends in large part on the strategic decisions of the entire network and the enterprises involved. Independent from the selected correlation between the work performed and the score evaluation an adequate function must be designed. In general, this is expressed as follows:

$$f_i^Q(q_i) = x_i^q \tag{2}$$

Thus, a specific aggregated weighted score evaluation $q_i$ for the performance parameter "quality" leads to a precisely defined evaluation score $x_i^q$ which is afterwards included in the overall evaluation in form of the performance analysis. In detail, the modeling of this mathematical function also depends on the strategic direction of the network and its members.

If the network, for example, defines quality leadership as their main target, a high number of points has to be deducted from the maximum score, even when there are only minor quality defects present, to ensure target fulfillment. However, if the network aims to achieve price leadership, it can be assumed that the quality has to meet only certain minimum requirements. In this case, (minor) quality defects do not have to be followed by major score deductions. Thus, high degrees of target fulfillment can be given even if there are relatively low quality values present. When using the utility benefit analysis for the quality evaluation, already a medium-level degree of target fulfillment (e.g. a score of 6 or 7) can, depending on the evaluation function, lead to the assumption that, for example, many less important or a few important criteria were not adhered to with regard to their tolerance values.

For simplification purposes it can be assumed that for the usage of the value benefit analysis all degrees of target fulfillment up to a certain value (e.g. 7) indicate the adherence to the tolerance values, i.e. up to a degree of target fulfillment of 7 the binary method still provides an "OK" rating (1), below that the rating is 0. In this case, a score around 7 would, thus, be the critical degree of fulfillment. This results in a 3 point maximum overvaluation of the binary method if all values are rated with 7 in the value benefit analysis. With the binary method this would add up to a 10 point degree of target fulfillment. On the other hand, if all criteria are rated with 6 points in the value benefit analysis, this results in a 0 rating in the binary method. If notably high (good) or low (bad) ratings are achieved with the binary method, the result should be validated in any case since there might exist falsifications in the rating scale.

### 3.4    Analysis of the Key Figure "Adherence to Quality Level"

The examples outlined above illustrate that the evaluation of the performance parameter "quality" based on the two possibilities presented can result in significantly different results. Several random ratings of 10 criteria demonstrated that the results achieved with the binary method can in favorable cases vary by 0.5 points from the result of the value benefit analysis. Unfortunately due to the limited space an example cannot be given in this contribution.

If for the quality rating the value benefit analysis is preferred, the subsequent application of Lagrange interpolation might be appropriate to determine an adequate utility value function and hence a weighting function. Finally, it should be noted that a utility value function can be determined more precisely if more points are included in the interpolation. However, their degree also rises to the same extend which leads to a rapid increase of complexity. Furthermore, care must be taken to ensure that the function in the interval in question does not assign negative degrees of target fulfillment. Nevertheless, in case of an unfavorable choice of points this cannot be eliminated entirely. This problem can be solved by zeroing in negative degrees of fulfillment.

Consequently, as an interim result, an appropriate weighting function is created that makes it possible to deliver a score evaluation for the entire value spectrum of possible aggregated degrees of fulfillment for the performance parameter "quality". This score evaluation is included in the performance analysis of all performance parameters to be considered and will in turn be weighted for this purpose. The reduction to one single value for the rating of a performance parameter on the basis of a predefined key figure presents the core element of the value-adding process-related performance analysis. In this context, it must be ensured that in the modeling process possible minimum degrees of fulfillment are always taken into consideration. Furthermore, if a quality criterion is not met, this cannot be offset by the above-average fulfillment of another quality criterion. That fact is important to avoid tendencies for substitution of lacking quality to one criterion with outstanding quality of another criterion. It must be ensured that every criterion representing product quality reaches a certain level.

## 4    Conclusions

This contribution introduces a framework for an approach for the measurement, evaluation and analysis of the performance parameter "product quality" by the application of the key figure "adherence to product quality". Under consideration of two different models for possible cases, a specific evaluation function can be determined by the application of Lagrange interpolation. These allow for the modeling of a calculation scheme depending on the degree to which the agreed quality level is met. With the inclusion of that framework, a major step towards a sustainable success of a network is accomplished because a very short-term analysis is possible. This allows for countermeasures in case of an unsatisfactory performance. The approach presented in this contribution is a theoretical model. Unfortunately an example cannot be given to provide a general understanding because lack of space. This approach represents a universal concept for a performance analysis that relates to the value-adding process and can be applied for enterprises operating in enterprise networks. It allows for a comprehensive analysis of the service performed by an enterprise based on selected performance measures. Efforts regarding the testing and realization from an IT point of view are being made currently and represent the actual challenge. In this context, the aim is the continuous improvement of the approach.

## References

1. Jähn, H.: Value-adding process-related performance analysis of enterprises acting in cooperative production structures. Production Planning & Control 20(2), 178–190 (2009)
2. Jähn, H.: Leistungsanalyse und Gewinnverteilung in vernetzten Produktionsstrukturen - Möglichkeiten im Rahmen des Extended Value Chain Management-Ansatzes. Dr. Kovac, Hamburg (2008)
3. Neely, A. (ed.): Business Performance Measurement, 2nd edn. Cambridge University Press, Cambridge (2007)
4. Lyons, A.C., Coronado Mondragon, A.E., Piller, F., Poler, R.: Customer-Driven Supply Chains From Glass Pipelines to Open Innovation Networks. Springer, London (2012)
5. Chendall, R.H., Langfield-Smitz, K.: Multiple Perspectives of Performance Measures. European Management Journal 25(4), 266–282 (2007)
6. Brewer, P., Speh, T.: Using the balanced scorecard to measure supply chain performance. Journal of Business Logistics 22(1), 75–93 (2000)
7. Gunasekaran, A., Patel, C., McGaughey, R.E.: A framework for supply chain performance measurement. Int. J. Production Economics 87, 333–347 (2004)

8. Bhagwat, R., Sharma, M.H.: An application of the integrated AHP-PGP model for performance measurement of supply chain management. Production Planning & Control 20(8), 678–690 (2009)
9. Westphal, I., Thoben, K.-D., Seifert, M.: Measuring Collaboration Performance in Virtual Organizations. In: Camarinha-Matos, L.M., et al. (eds.) Establishing the Foundation of Collaborative Networks. IFIP, vol. 243, pp. 33–42. Springer, Boston (2007)
10. Lockamy III, A.: Quality-focused performance measurement systems: a normative model. International Journal of Operations & Production Management 18(8), 740–766 (1998)

# 19

## Identification of Patterns

# Identifying Opinion Leaders in Time-Dependent Commercial Social Networks

Antonio P. Volpentesta and Alberto M. Felicetti

Department of Electronics, Computer Science and Systems,
University of Calabria, via P. Bucci, 42\C, 87036 Rende (CS), Italy
{volpentesta,afelicetti}@deis.unical.it

**Abstract.** The increasing amount of information flowing through commercial social networks offers clear advantages for companies who can take a valuable feedback from community actions. In particular, the identification of influential users in on-line social network can support companies in designing and targeting marketing campaigns, as influential gate-keepers and diffusers of information can ignite epidemics through word-of-mouth. In this paper, we model a time-dependent commercial social network as a time-varying weighted directed graph. Moreover, we propose an approach to determine opinion leaders and their contributions to a temporal business value, by taking into account behavioural and structural aspects of the commercial social network.

**Keywords:** Opinion leaders, Social Networks, Social Network Centrality, Viral Marketing.

## 1 Introduction

Nowadays, internet based technologies, and in particular Web 2.0 technologies, provide a multitude of platforms, such as blogs, wikis, social networks and forums where users can disseminate an abundance of information on personal experiences and opinions about products and manufacturers [1]. The advent of participatory web enables users to produce and share on-line content, radically changing the traditional communication paradigms and turning the former mass information consumers to the present information producers [2]. Hence, from a company point of view, the consumer role shifts from a pure consumer of products to a partner in the value creation process [3].

There are several motivations that drive users to share online-content within their own network of social relationships:

- The need to be part of a group, as well as to establish and maintain a certain number of social relationships [4].
- The need to affirm their own individuality: users, as consumers, "identify with products or brands to the degree that the product actually becomes part of the consumer's extended self" and they "communicate something important about themselves to others", [5].

L.M. Camarinha-Matos, L. Xu, and H. Afsarmanesh (Eds.): PRO-VE 2012, IFIP AICT 380, pp. 571–581, 2012.
© IFIP International Federation for Information Processing 2012

- Curiosity and fun: users are encouraged to share entertainment based contents, which attract their curiosity by leveraging on their passions [6].

It is widely accepted that word-of-mouth communication, both in real life and in on-line social networks, plays an important role in shaping users' attitudes and behavior [7]. Daily, our own decisions are heavily influenced by the opinions of the people around us and this influence increases with the strength of the relationship. In fact, seeing actions performed by our friends may make us curious and may sometimes tempt us to perform those actions ourselves, [8]. According to [2] and [9], the majority of people prefer consulting family, friends or colleagues over traditional advertising before buying a new product or experiencing a new service. In other words, before people make decisions, they talk, and they listen to other's experience, opinions, and suggestions.

Actually, when people perform an action, they may be influenced by what they have heard of it outside of the online social network (and have decided it is worthwhile) or they may be genuinely influenced by seeing their social contacts performing that action [10]. In what follows, when we talk about influence, we only refer to on-line genuine influence. Even in this case, users of a social networks, do not exert the same level of influence over the other participants. In fact, community members differ widely in terms of the frequency, volume, type, and quality of digital content generated and consumed [11]. Besides, some community members are more influent than other users. Through their own opinions, they guide perceptions and actions of others with respect to specific topics (eg. politics, sports, culture but also products / services / brands).

On one hand, a user may have practical and emotional benefits when participating in online discussions and content sharing processes; on the other hand it appears evident how these conversations have profound commercial implications as well [9]. In fact, in recent years consumers have shown a growing resistance to traditional forms of advertising like television commercials or newspaper [12], becoming more aware of their needs and expectations. Therefore, in addition to relying upon traditional media, many companies advertise their products and services, through new marketing strategies (e.g. "Viral Marketing") that leverage Web 2.0 technologies .

The Viral Marketing concept is based on promoting products and services through the exploitation of internet word-of-mouth, in order to achieve widespread promotional message among users [13]. The message diffusion follows an exponential model, similarly to a virus within a population.

The "social environment" enables mechanisms of interaction, cooperation and "social experience" among users, and between consumers and companies who can take a valuable feedback from the overall community. According to this perspective, the identification of most influential users (also called "opinion leaders") in a web community is a valuable problem to be studied.

Such a problem is still more important in the case of a time-dependent commercial social network (CSN). A CSN is a social network "designed to support business transaction and to build a trust between an individual and a brand, which relies on opinion of product, ideas to make the product better, enabling customers to participate with the brands in promoting development, service delivery and a better customer experience" [14].

In a CSN, opinion leaders are individuals who, through their actions and opinions, guide the perceptions of other CSN members towards products or services provided by some companies. In particular, each of them exerts a certain degree of influence on the behavior of customers in the various stages of their purchasing process. These influences may vary with time and have a relevant impact on the CSN business value. Broadly speaking, CSN business value comprises all intangible benefits deriving from social interactions that occur within a CSN in given interval times.

In this paper, we model the influence relationship in a CSN as a time-varying weighted direct graph, and we propose an approach to determine opinion leaders and their contributions to the business value of a time-dependent CSN.

## 2    Related Works

In the last decade, social platforms have radically changed the way users interact and share information. Social networks are usually modeled through a mathematical formalism based on graph theory, where the nodes represent individuals and edges (or arcs) represent the relationships and interactions between individuals [15]. Identifying influencer people through social network analysis (SNA) is gaining prominence in many application areas [16].

In order to identify the roles of individuals in the network, SNA evaluates the importance (also called centrality) of actors in the network as well as analyzes their behaviors and their interactions. In particular, two types of network analysis are studied in literature, [17]: Structural Analysis (which concentrates on measuring centrality taking into account the structure of a network) and  Behavioral Analysis (which focuses on the interactions between users rather than the structure of the network, identifying followers who propagate or share contents, and users who are engaged in conversations).

From a structural perspective, several authors have proposed different ways to measure the "importance" of a node in a network: Closeness centrality and Graph centrality [18] are based on the distances with the rest of nodes, while Betweeness centrality and Stress centrality [19] emphasize the medium mediating between a pair of nodes. Another centrality measure that is often used in network analysis is eigenvector centrality [20]. Eigenvector centrality analysis is based on the idea that a node is "more central" if it is in relation with nodes that are themselves central, so the centrality of a node does not only depend on the number of its adjacent nodes, but also on their value of centrality.

More specifically, several studies have highlighted how the structure of a social network can affect the dynamics of user influence in social activities. In [21] and [22] authors measure influence in terms of messages propagation and forwarding activities. Cha et al. [23] use Spearman's rank correlation coefficient in order to measure users' influence in Twitter, while in [24] Rad and Benyoucef study influence in terms of link strength and incoming/ outgoing activities for each node in the network. In [25], two basic diffusion models are investigated: Linear Thresholds Model and Independent cascade Model. Kundu et al. [26] propose an independent cascade model and a centrality measure in order to find top $k$ influential nodes in large scale directed social networks. In [2] authors propose a frequent pattern mining approach to discover leaders in social networks, studying the propagation of their "influence", while in [11] authors develop an approach to determine "influencing users" based on a nonstandard form of Bayesian shrinkage.

The implicit assumption that underpins the above mentioned researches is that the social network is substantially static, i.e. it has time invariance. As a consequence, most of the proposed approaches are not always well suited to evolving social networks, whose topology changes either at discrete time points or continuously over time [27], [28]. This is the reason why new approaches for the identification of opinion leaders in complex time-dependent networks have been investigated [29], [30]. However, such approaches lack in considering the relevance of the business value impact factor in ranking opinion leaders.

## 3    An Approach for Opinion Leaders Identification

The identification of opinion leaders and their contribution to a CSN business value constitute an important problem for the CSN company and also all the stakeholders. In a CSN, users are considered to be "potential consumers" of some products or services, and their social interactions are revealed by analyzing their actions on time-varying digital objects on the CSN platform.

Three main assumptions underpin our approach:

1.  Opinion leaders centrality can be measured by taking into account users' actions that are performed on digital objects on the CSN platform, during time intervals in which the CSN is observed.
2.  The CSN business value can be decomposed in chunks, each of which is due to actions that are performed on a certain digital object in a given time interval.
3.  The higher is a business value chunk, referred to an object and to an interval time, the more valuable is the centrality of an opinion leader in the CSN restricted to actions performed on that object in that time interval.

Under these assumptions we propose an approach to rank opinion leaders with respect to both their influence degree in a time-dependent CSN and a decomposition of the CSN business value.

Such approach is essentially based on a measure of the dynamic centrality of nodes in a time-varying weighted directed graph. In such graph, the weight associated to an arc $(x,y)$ represents a measure of influence of x on y, and varies at discrete times.

Main steps in our approach are the following:

1.  Model the evolution of the influence relationship in a CSN as sequences of weighted directed graphs $G^1(o)$, $G^2(o)$, ..., $G^k(o)$, where the generic $G^i(o)$ is the model of influence relationship derived from actions on an object $o$ in time interval $T^i$.

2. Compute the eigenvector centrality of any vertex in any graph $G^i(o)$.
3. Compute temporal (business) valued centrality in the CSN.

## 3.1   Modeling Influence Relationship in a CSN

In order to present the model we need to clarify some basic terms: *temporal object, user* and *action*.

An *object* consists of a pair (data, metadata), called *object state*, and an identifier, called *object identifier*. For instance, an object may represent a post (containing text, weblinks or digital media) published on a SN platform, a post with some comments, a list of members in a thematic group, and so on.

Depending on the type of the object, a certain number of types of actions can be performed on the object state. An *action* is what determines the transition from one object state to another (a special action is the "object creation" which determines the transition from the *null object state* to an *initial object state*). For instance, if the object represents a post, a user may view this post, may add a comment, may rate it (i.e. "I like" or other rate scale), or may share the post. Here, a *user* is an entity (individual, organization, ...) identified by an account that allows him/her to access the SN platform and to perform some type of actions on an object state.

A *temporal* ( or equivalently, *time-varying*) *object* is defined by an object identifier and a temporal sequence of object states, where a generic element (except the first one) is obtained by performing a suitable action on the previous one. A temporal object is used to represent the object evolution that has been happened on a SN platform in a certain interval time.

Formally, given an object identifier $o$, we consider the temporal object $s(o)=(s_1, s_2,..., s_n)$, where $s_1$ represents the null object state, $s_2$ the initial object state, and the generic element $s_i$ , i $>1$, represents the object state at time $t_i$, after a user $u_{i-1}$ has performed an action $a_{i-1}$ on the object state $s_{i-1}$. The four sequences $s(o)$, $a(o)=(a_1, a_2,..., a_{n-1})$, $u(o)=(u_1, u_2,..., u_{n-1})$, $t(o)= (t_1, t_2,..., t_{n-1})$, describe the evolution story of the object identified by $o$ in terms of what, how, who and when.

Given a set $N$ of users of the SN platform, the influence relationship, due to actions on temporal object $s(o)$, can be modeled by a weighted directed $G(o)= \{N, E(o), w(o)\}$, where:

- $E(o)=\{(x,y) \in N \times N: C(o)_{x,y} \neq \emptyset\}$, where $C(o)_{x,y}=\{(i,j) \in \{1,...,n-2\} \times \{2,...,n-1\}: x = u_i, y = u_j, i < j,\}$, for $x, y \in N$, $x \neq y$, and $C(o)_{x,x} = \emptyset, x \in N$.
  In other words, a user $y$ performing an action on $o$ at a certain time is influenced by another user $x$ that has previously performed an action on the same object.

- $w(o): E(o) \rightarrow \mathbb{N}$. $w(o)_{(x,y)}$ is a nonnegative integer that represents the weight of the influence exerted by $x$ on $y$, with respect to actions performed on a given object $o$. In order to specify $w(o)$ we need to introduce some further notations:

  - Let $AT_1, AT_{2,...,} AT_k$ the types of action that can be performed on $o$.

- Let D=(d$ij$), i,j=1,...k, a nonnegative integer matrix, where d$_{ij}$ is the degree of influence that is exerted on a user performing an action of type $AT_j$, by a user who has previously performed an action of type $AT_i$.
- Given $(i, j) \in C(o)_{x,y}$, let $AT_{h_i}$ be the action type of $a_i$, and $AT_{l_j}$ the action type of $a_j$

The weight function $w(o)$ is defined as follows:

$$w(o)_{x,y} = \sum_{(i,j) \in C(o)_{x,y}} d_{h_i l_j}$$

## 3.2     Centrality in an Influence Graph

In order to determine centrality vector in an influence graph, we can use the eigenvector centrality, based on the he well known *mutually reinforcing relationship* assumption [31]: "*a node is important if it is connected with other important nodes.*

Eigenvector centrality, also called rank prestige [32] is a measure in which the centralities or statuses of positions are recursively related to the centralities or statuses of the positions to which they are connected. We assume that if a user is recognized as influential by someone seen in turn as influential by others, this may contribute to the influence measure of the first one.

Let $F=(f_{ij})$ be an adjacency matrix of an influence graph, where $f_{ij}$ represents a measure of the influence exerted by a user $i$ on a user $j$, and let $x$ be a vector of centrality scores. Importance of a generic user $i$ is proportional to the influence exerted on other users. Numerically, it is natural to express this mutually reinforcing relationship as follows:

$$x_i = c \left( f_{i1}x_1 + f_{i2}x_2 + \cdots + f_{in}x_n \right) \tag{1}$$

In matrix notation with x=$(x_1, x_2, ..., x_n)$ this yields

$$F^T x = \lambda x \quad \text{where } \lambda = 1/c \tag{2}$$

Standards results of linear algebra lead to state that (2) is a solvable system of equations. If $F$ is an $n \times n$ matrix, Eq. (2) has $n$ solutions corresponding to $n$ values of $\lambda$. More precisely, a solution is given by setting $\lambda=\lambda^*$, the dominant $F^T$ eigenvalue, and $x=x^*$, a nonnegative eigenvector of $F^T$ in the eigenspace associated with $\lambda^*$. A normalization of $x^*$ gives a measure of the *eigenvector-centrality* of the nodes in an influence graph. The effect that different normalizations have on the interpretation of eigenvector-centrality within a graph is investigated in [33]. In order to calculate eigenvector centrality many algorithms have proposed in literature. Most of them are based on adaptations of the Hits (Hyperlink-Induced Topics Search) algorithm, introduced by Kleinberg, [32], [34].

## 3.3     Temporal Valued Centrality in a CSN

In order to define and compute the temporal (business) valued centrality we consider a sequence of time intervals $T^1, T^2, ... T^k$, and a given set $O$ of objects. Let us consider the subsets $C^i(o)_{x,y} = \{(p,q) \in C(o)_{x,y} : t_p, t_q \in T^i\}$, $i=1,2...,k$. The $i$-th footprint $G^i(o) = \{N, E^i(o), w^i(o)\}$ of the graph $G(o) = \{N, E(o), w(o)\}$, is defined by:

- $E^i(o) = \{(x,y) \in E(o) : C^i(o)_{x,y} \neq \emptyset\}$
- $w^i(o) : E^i(o) \to \mathbb{N}$. $w^i(x,y)$ represents the weight of the influence exerted by $x$ on $y$ in a given time interval $T^i$, with respect to actions performed on an object $o$.

$$w^i(o)_{x,y} = \Sigma_{(p,q) \in c^i(o)_{x,y}} d_{h_p l_q},$$

Let $evc^i(o)_x$, $x \in N$, be the eigenvector centrality of $x$ in the i-th footprint $G^i(o)$. Let $v^i(o)$ be the nonnegative real number that represents the part of CSN business value $v$, due to social interactions occurring when actions are performed on $o$ in $T^i$.

Set $\lambda^i(o) = \frac{v^i(o)}{v}$. The temporal (business) valued centrality of $x$, is defined by:

$$tvc_x = \Sigma_{o \in O} \Sigma_{i=1}^k \lambda^i(o) * evc^i(o)_x$$

### 3.4    An Example

Let $T^1 = [1, 10)$, $T^2 = [10, 20)$, $T^3 = [20, 30)$; $N = \{x, y, v, z\}$; $O = \{o\}$, where $o$ is the identifier of a post that evolves as time varies.

The types of action that can be performed on $o$ are:

- $AT_1$ = create a post.
- $AT_2$ = view a post.
- $AT_3$ = share a post.
- $AT_4$ = add a comment to a post.
- $AT_5$ = rate a post (i.e. "this post was helpful to me", "I like")

In our example, we may consider the following entries of matrix D:

**Table 1.** Example of action influence matrix

|        | $AT_1$ | $AT_2$  | $AT_3$   | $AT_4$   | $AT_5$   |
|--------|--------|---------|----------|----------|----------|
| $AT_1$ | 0      | 5/100   | 18/100   | 18/100   | 10/100   |
| $AT_2$ | 0      | 0       | 0        | 0        | 0        |
| $AT_3$ | 0      | 1/100   | 4/100    | 6/100    | 4/100    |
| $AT_4$ | 0      | 3/100   | 6/100    | 10/100   | 6/100    |
| $AT_5$ | 0      | 1/100   | 2/100    | 4/100    | 2/100    |

and the following sequences describing temporal evolution of object $o$.

**Table 2.** Example of temporal evolution of an object $o$

| $s(o)$ | $s_1$ | $s_2$ | $s_3$ | $s_4$ | $s_5$ | $s_6$ | $s_7$ | $s_7$ | $s_8$ | $s_9$ | $s_{10}$ | $s_{11}$ | $s_{12}$ |
|--------|-------|-------|-------|-------|-------|-------|-------|-------|-------|-------|----------|----------|----------|
| $a(o)$ | $a_1=AT_1$ | $a_2=AT_2$ | $a_3=AT_4$ | $a_4=AT_2$ | $a_5=AT_3$ | $a_6=AT_4$ | $a_7=AT_2$ | $a_8=AT_5$ | $a_9=AT_4$ | $A_1=AT_4$ | $a_{11}=AT_3$ | $a_{12}=AT_4$ | $a_{12}=AT_4$ |
| $u(o)$ | $u_1=x$ | $u_2=z$ | $u_3=z$ | $u_4=v$ | $u_5=v$ | $u_6=x$ | $u_7=y$ | $u_8=y$ | $u_9=x$ | $u_{10}=y$ | $u_{11}=z$ | $u_{12}=v$ | $u_{13}=z$ |
| $t(o)$ | $t_1=1$ | $t_2=3$ | $t_3=7$ | $t_4=8$ | $t_5=10$ | $t_6=12$ | $t_7=13$ | $t_8=16$ | $t_9=18$ | $t_{10}=21$ | $t_{11}=25$ | $t_{12}=26$ | $t_{12}=28$ |

The following footprints represent the  influence relationship evolution:

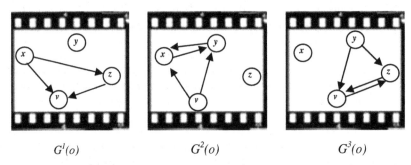

$G^1(o)$          $G^2(o)$          $G^3(o)$

**Fig. 1.** i-th"Footprints" of the overall weighted directed G(o)

The overall graph G(o) represents the influence relationship exerted through actions performed on the object $o$, in $T = T^1 \cup T^2 \cup T^3$

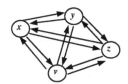

**Fig. 2.** the overall weighted directed G(o)

*Alternative 1.* ("static" eigenvector centrality). The weighted adjacency matrix of G(o) is:

| W | x | y | v | z |
|---|---|---|---|---|
| x | 0 | 0,15 | 0,51 | 0,39 |
| y | 0,04 | 0 | 0,14 | 0,22 |
| v | 0,16 | 0,3 | 0 | 0,42 |
| z | 0,1 | 0,19 | 0,25 | 0 |

The eigenvector centrality (with respect a sum normalization) is:

| | X | y | V | z |
|---|---|---|---|---|
| evc | 0,402139 | 0,1631016 | 0,2572193 | 0,1775401 |

*Alternative 2.* (Temporal valued centrality). Let $\lambda^1(o) = 0,2$; $\lambda^2(o) = 0,5$; $\lambda^3(o) = 0,3$. The weighted adjacency matrices of the three footprints of G(o) are:

| $W^1$ | x | Y | v | z |
|---|---|---|---|---|
| x | 0 | 0 | 0,05 | 0,23 |
| y | 0 | 0 | 0 | 0 |
| v | 0 | 0 | 0 | 0 |
| z | 0 | 0 | 0,06 | 0 |

| $W^2$ | x | y | v | z |
|---|---|---|---|---|
| x | 0 | 0,09 | 0 | 0 |
| y | 0,04 | 0 | 0 | 0 |
| v | 0,12 | 0,05 | 0 | 0 |
| z | 0 | 0 | 0 | 0 |

| $W^3$ | x | y | v | z |
|---|---|---|---|---|
| x | 0 | 0 | 0 | 0 |
| y | 0 | 0 | 0,1 | 0,16 |
| v | 0 | 0 | 0 | 0,1 |
| z | 0 | 0 | 0,06 | 0 |

The temporal valued centrality (with respect a sum normalization) is:

|     | $x$ | $y$ | $v$ | $z$ |
|-----|-----|-----|-----|-----|
| tvc | 0,318395 | 0,32692 | 0,317751 | 0,036935 |

In alternative 1, the temporal evolution of the network has not been taken into account. As a consequence, the user $x$ is regarded as the "most important" opinion leader, even if he/she has been active only in the initial phase of temporal evolution of the object $o$. On the contrary, our approach (in alternative 2) gives the temporal (business) valued centrality of network users; $x,y$ and $v$ are almost equally ranked as opinion leaders. This is due to the fact that we have considered different CSN business values chinks, for each time interval, and the users have participated in a discontinuous way to the "CSN's life".

## 4    Conclusions and Future Works

Social networks have a strong impact on the way users interact and share information. The individuation of influential people can help companies, advertisers and marketing professionals in designing more effective campaigns. In particular, online opinion leaders should be targeted as a high priority group in viral marketing campaigns, as they can ignite epidemics like influential gate-keepers and diffusers of information on the Internet [35].

In this paper we have introduced an approach aimed to determine opinion leaders and their contributions to the business value of a time-dependent commercial social network (CSN). More specifically, our approach takes into account both behavioural aspects (actions users perform on the CSN platform in different time intervals) and structural aspects (eigenvector centrality) of a CSN. Future steps should be addressed to the validation and experimentation of the underlying model, as well as to further extensions where trust aspects of the relationship between users are considered.

Of course, individuals may interact with people inside and outside their CSN. A limitation of the model lies in that it does not consider interactions occurring through other web platforms or digital media (instant messaging, SMS, e-mails, and so on) as well as offline interactions. Besides, present features of today's advanced platforms of social commerce make also available data on the influence that opinion leaders exert on customers in persuading them and conditioning their purchasing behavior. These remarks suggest new research directions aimed to overcome current shortages of the approach presented in our work.

## References

1. Bodendorf, F., Kaiser, C.: Detecting Opinion Leaders and Trends in Online Communities. In: Fourth International Conference on Digital Society (2010)
2. Agarwal, N., Liu, H., Tang, L., Yu, P.S.: Identifying the Influential Bloggers in a Community. In: WSDM 2008, Palo Alto, California, USA (2008)

3. Romero, D., Molina, A.: Value Co-creation and Co-innovation: Linking Networked Organisations and Customer Communities. In: Camarinha-Matos, L.M., Paraskakis, I., Afsarmanesh, H. (eds.) PRO-VE 2009. IFIP AICT, vol. 307, pp. 401–412. Springer, Heidelberg (2009)
4. Ho, J.Y.C., Dempsey, M.: Viral marketing: Motivations to forward online content. Journal of Business Research 63, 1000–1006 (2010)
5. Chung, C., Darke, P.: The consumer as advocate: self-relevance, culture, and word-of-mouth. Marketing Letters 17(4), 269–279 (2006)
6. Ramaswamy, V.: Co-creating value through customers' experiences: the Nike case. Strategy & Leadership 36(5), 9–14 (2008)
7. Vilpponen, A., Winter, S., Sundqvist, S.: Electronic word-of-mouth in online environments: exploring referral network structure and adoption behavior. Journal of Interactive Advertising 6(2), 63–77 (2006)
8. Kim, Y.A., Srivastava, J.: Impact of Social Influence in E-Commerce Decision Making. In: Proceedings of ICEC 2007, Minneapolis, Minnesota, USA, August 19–22 (2007)
9. Riegner, C.: Word of Mouth on the Web: The Impact of Web 2.0 on Consumer Purchase Decisions. Journal of Advertising Research (2007)
10. Goyal, A., Bonchi, F., Lakshmanan, L.V.S.: Learning Influence Probabilities In Social Networks. In: WSDM 2010, New York City, New York, USA (2010)
11. Trusov, M., Bodapati, A.V., Bucklin, R.E.: Determining Influential Users in Internet Social Networks. Journal of Marketing Research XLVII, 643–658 (2010)
12. Leskovec, J., Adamic, L.A., Huberman, B.A.: The dynamics of viral marketing. ACM Transactions on the Web 1, 1 (2007)
13. Dobelea, A., Tolemanb, D., Beverland, M.: Controlled infection! Spreading the brand message through viral marketing. Business Horizons 48(2), 143–149 (2005)
14. Crebolder, J., Pronovost, S., Lai, G.: Investigating Virtual Social Networking in the Military Domain. In: 14th International Command and Control Research and Technology Symposium - ICCRTS "C2 and Agility", Washington, DC, June 15-17 (2009)
15. Carrington, P.J., Scott, J., Wasserman, S.: Models and Methods in Social Network Analysis. Canadian Journal of Sociology Online (September-October 2005)
16. Jonnalagadda, S., Peeler, R., Topham, P.: Discovering opinion leaders for medical topics using news articles. Journal of Biomedical Semantics 3, 2 (2012)
17. Hajian, B., White, T.: Modelling inuence in a social network: Metrics and evaluation. In: IEEE Third International Conference on Social Computing (SocialCom) (2011)
18. Bonacich, P.: Factoring and weighting approaches to clique identification. Journal of Mathematical Sociology 2, 113–120 (1972)
19. Freeman, L.C.: A set of measures of centrality based on betweenness. Sociometry 40, 35–41 (1977)
20. Bonacich, P.: Factoring and weighting approaches to clique identification. Journal of Mathematical Sociology 2, 113–120 (1972)
21. Kwak, H., Lee, C., Park, H., Moon, S.: Finding influentials based on the temporal order of information adoption in Twitter. In: Proceedings of the 19th International World Wide Web Conference, pp. 1137–1138. ACM (2010)
22. Aus, S., Galuba, W., Huberman, B.A., Romero, D.M.: Influence and passivity in social media. In: ACM Proceedings (2010)
23. Cha, M., Haddadi, H., Benevenuto, F., Gummadi, K.: Measuring user influence in twitter: The million follower fallacy. In: Proceedings of the 4th International Conference on Weblogs and Social Media (2010)

24. Afrasiabi Rad, A., Benyoucef, M.: Towards Detecting Influential Users in Social Networks. In: Babin, G., Stanoevska-Slabeva, K., Kropf, P. (eds.) MCETECH 2011. LNBIP, vol. 78, pp. 227–240. Springer, Heidelberg (2011)
25. Kempe, D., Kleinberg, J., Tardos, É.: Maximizing the spread of influence through a social network. In: Proceedings of the Ninth ACM SIGKDD International Conference on Knowledge Discovery and Data Mining, pp. 137–146. ACM (2003)
26. Kundu, S., Murthy, C.A., Pal, S.K.: A New Centrality Measure for Influence Maximization in Social Networks. In: Kuznetsov, S.O., Mandal, D.P., Kundu, M.K., Pal, S.K. (eds.) PReMI 2011. LNCS, vol. 6744, pp. 242–247. Springer, Heidelberg (2011)
27. Lerman, K., Ghosh, R., Kang, J.H.: Centrality Metric for Dynamic Networks Analysis. In: Proceedings of KDD Workshop on Mining and Learning with Graphs (MLG), (2010)
28. Juszczyszyn, K., Budka, M., Musial, K.: The Dynamic Structural Patterns of Social Networks Based on Triad Transitions. In: Advances in Social Networks Analysis and Mining (ASONAM) (2011)
29. Braha, D., Bar-Yam, Y.: From Centrality to Temporary Fame: Dynamic Centrality in Complex Networks. Complexity 12(2) (2006)
30. Hill, S.A., Braha, D.: A dynamic model of time-dependent complex networks. Phys. Rev. E 82, 046105 (2010)
31. Wasserman, S., Faust, K.: Social Network Analysis: Methods and Applications. Cambridge University Press, Cambridge (1994)
32. Kleinberg, J.: Authoritative sources in a hyperlinked environment. Journal of the ACM 46(5), 604–632 (1999)
33. Ruhnau, B.: Eigenvector-centrality: a node-centrality? Social Networks 22, 357–365 (2000)
34. Volpentesta, A.P., Felicetti, A.M.: Eigenvector Centrality Based on Shared Research Topics in a Scientific Community. In: Camarinha-Matos, L.M., Boucher, X., Afsarmanesh, H. (eds.) PRO-VE 2010. IFIP AICT, vol. 336, pp. 626–633. Springer, Heidelberg (2010)
35. Kirby, J., Mardsen, P.: Connected marketing: The viral, buzz and word of mouth revolution. Elsevier Ltd (2006)

# Extracting the Dynamic Popularity of Concepts from a Corpus of Short-Sentence Documents

Willy Picard

Department of Information Technology, Poznań University of Economics,
al. Niepodległości 10, 61-875, Poznań, Poland
picard@kti.ue.poznan.pl

**Abstract.** The decomposition of information into smaller bunches of data is a commonly observed process on the Web, Twitter and RSS being manifestations of this process. As a consequence, a shift may be observed from an information world in which information comes in large bunches of data, to a world of short-sentence documents. This shrinking of information chunks goes along with an explosion of the number of these chunks. Therefore, information may often be aggregated in corpuses of documents consisting of many short sentences. The identification of important concepts in corpuses of short-sentence documents is a difficult, but necessary, task to understand the whole information. Understanding the dynamics of the popularity of important concepts is necessary to capture the evolution of the corpus in time. In this paper, a method to extract the important concepts from a corpus of short-sentence documents is proposed. A model of the popularity of concepts and its dynamics is proposed, together with an algorithm to analyze the dynamics of important concepts. Finally, the proposed method is validated with an analysis of the titles of the articles published at eleven IFIP Working Conferences on Virtual Enterprises, from PROVE'99 to PROVE'10.

**Keywords:** text mining, context extraction, collaborative network, virtual enterprise, virtual organization, dynamic popularity.

## 1 Introduction

A major shift in the way information is designed, produced, sold, and consumed may currently be observed. Information is currently decomposed in smaller bits of data. Instead of newspapers, single articles are written, published, sold, and read. Instead of CDs containing a list of songs, music is produced, sold, and composed in form of individual songs, as MP3 files.

The decomposition of information goes together with the production of very short bunches of data. Some websites, such as Twitter, enforce the production of small bunches of data. Twitter [1] limits the length of messages, referred to as "tweets", to 140 characters. Similarly, all major social networking websites, such as Facebook [2] and Google+ [3], provide their users with the possibility to provide a short information concerning their "status". Additionally, the graphical user interface used

L.M. Camarinha-Matos, L. Xu, and H. Afsarmanesh (Eds.): PRO-VE 2012, IFIP AICT 380, pp. 582–591, 2012.
© IFIP International Federation for Information Processing 2012

to enter data or posts is usually limited to a small input text field. As a consequence, most posts submitted to social networking websites are short.

Finally, the trend towards shorter, decomposed information goes further with the mechanism of information summarizing. Technologies such as RSS [4] and Atom [5, 6] provide a means to summarize information, usually to a few dozens or hundreds words. Although the original purpose of these technologies was the possibility to annotate websites, providing semantic meta-data for a further computer processing, RSS and Atom feeds are currently used mainly to syndicate and aggregate information for humans, especially with the rise of mobile computing.

Structuring information in small bunches of data goes together with a drastic rise of the number of bunches of data associated with a given topic. As a consequence, information is organized as set of very numerous and short bunches of data, often consisting of single sentences. In this paper, such sets of bunches of data are referred to as Corpus of Short-Sentence Documents.

> A *Corpus of Short-Sentence Documents (CSSD)* is defined as a time-indexed list of sets of documents, with each document limited to a high number of short sentences.

Examples of CSSDs may be the results of a Twitter search on a given topic, the list of email subjects in a given folder, and a list of lecture subjects offered by a university grouped by years.

The decomposition of information in CSSD leads to important challenges for their consumers. A first challenge is the identification of key concepts in the CSSD. In a world of not-decomposed information, the key concepts are explicit in the structure itself: the titles of chapters in books are usually focusing on the key concepts presented in the contents of the chapters. In newspapers, various sections and the titles of the articles emphasize the key concepts. In CSSD, no structural entity is available: no title or sections are presented. Therefore, the identification of key concepts requires the whole corpus to be analyzed, which is challenging because of the number of documents it contains.

A second challenge is the understanding of the dynamics of the popularity of concepts in the CSSD. CSSDs should be considered as streams, with new documents continuously enriching the corpus. Therefore, the popularity of a concept usually evolves in time, as new documents are added to the corpus. The popularity of concepts is a dynamic variable, having various values in time.

In this paper, a method to extract the important concepts from a corpus of short-sentence documents is proposed. A model of the popularity of concepts and its dynamics is proposed, together with an algorithm to analyze the dynamics of important concepts.

The rest of this paper is organized as follows: in Section 2, the concepts of CSSD and popularity are defined, followed by the presentation of our research goal. In Section 3, the proposed method is presented, In Section 4, the proposed method is validated with an analysis of the titles of the articles published at eleven IFIP Working Conferences on Virtual Enterprises, from PROVE'99 to PROVE'10 [7-17]. Finally, Section 6 concludes the paper.

# 2    Research Goal

## 2.1    Fundamental Definitions

The presentation of our research goal requires a precise definition of CSSDs and dynamic popularity.

A *CSSD*, further denoted as $\gamma$, is a list of time-indexed documents, i.e.,

$$\gamma = \{d_t\},$$

where $d_t$ is a document indexed by time $t$.

A *time-indexed document* $d_t$ consists of a set of sentences $S_t$ and a time index $t$, i.e.,

$$d_t = \; <S_t = \{s_{t,n}\}, t>,$$

where $s_{t,n}$ is the $n$-th sentence of the document indexed by time index $t$.

A *sentence* $s_{t,n}$ is a limited list of characters. The maximal number of characters of sentences depends on the type of CSSD. For instance, in CSSDs containing RSS 0.91 item titles (resp. item descriptions), the maximal number of characters of sentences is 100 (resp. 500) characters. In CSSDs containing Twitter "tweets", the maximal number of characters of sentences is 140 characters.

A *concept* $c$ is defined as a non-stop word stem. Stop words are most common words, such as "and", "the", and "for" in English. Stems are the base of inflected and derived words. For instance, the words "cooperate", "cooperation", and "cooperating" share the same stem "cooper".

The *static popularity* of a concept $c$ in time-indexed document $d_t$, further denoted as $p_{c,t}$, is defined as the index of the concept $c$ in the popularity ranking of $d_t$. The popularity ranking of $d_t$, further denoted as $p_{d,t}$, is the list of concepts of $d_t$ ordered by the number of their occurrences.

The *dynamic popularity* of a concept $c$ in the corpus $\gamma$, further denoted as $\pi_c$, is defined as a vector containing the indexes of the concept $c$ in the popularity global rankings of $d_t$ ordered by time. The popularity global ranking of $d_t$, further denoted as $\pi_{d,t}$, is the list of concepts of $\gamma$ ordered by the number of their occurrences in $d_t$.

## 2.2    Research Goal

Our research goal is to develop a method to extract the dynamic popularity of concepts from a CSSD. The considered CSSD are monolingual, i.e., all the sentences of all the time-indexed documents are written in the same language. The method should be independent of the language of the CSSD. The method should be fully automatic and should not require any human action. An appropriate graphical representation should provide a means for a better understanding of the results of the method.

# 3    A Method to Extract Dynamic Popularity of Concepts in a CSSD

The proposed method to extract dynamic popularity of concepts in a CSSD consists of three steps: data preparation, extraction of popular concepts, and extraction of dynamic popularity.

## 3.1    Data Preparation

The first step of the proposed method aims at preparing the data for further text mining. It is assumed that a CSSD has been formerly gathered and compiled in an appropriate digital form. The preparation phase starts by the lower case conversion of all the sentences of all the documents in the CSSD. Next, white space is removed, together with punctuation marks. Then, stop words are removed, based on a formerly prepared list of stop words for the language of the CSSD. Different lists of stop words have to be used to prepare CSSDs written in different languages. Finally, all the sentences are stemmed, i.e., all lowercase, whitespace-free non-stop words are replaced by their stems. The widely used algorithm for stemming proposed by Porter [18] is suggested as a method for the stemming of CSSD, but any other stemming algorithm may be integrated to the method.

The result of the first step of the method is a cleaned concept corpus $\gamma'$, that consists of cleaned time-indexed documents containing cleaned sentences. A *cleaned sentence s'* is a list of concepts {c'}.

## 3.2    Extraction of Popular Concepts

The next step aims at identifying the most popular concepts. The extraction of popular concepts is proposed as a bottom-up process, i.e. popular concepts are first identified for each time-indexed document, and next, all the identified popular concepts are merged into one common set of popular concepts.

The identification of popular concepts for a given time-indexed document $d_t$ consists in selecting the first elements of the popularity ranking of $d_t$. A term-document matrix of the CSSD is computed to establish the popular ranking of $d_t$. A term-document matrix *tdm* is a matrix whose values are the number of occurrences of a given concept (given in columns) in a given document (given in rows), i.e.,

$$tdm_{t,c} = \sum_{s' \in s'_t} |\{c' \in s' : c' = c\}|$$

The number of occurrences of concepts in a given time-indexed document are given is the associated row of the term-document matrix. The popularity ranking of $d_t$ is therefore the values of the sorted row associated with $d_t$ in the term-document matrix. The establishment of the set of most popular concepts is based on the popularity rankings for all the time-indexed documents: the most popular concepts of each popularity ranking are merged together to create the set of most popular concepts. An important parameter of the method is the number of popular concepts to be kept from each popularity ranking in the set of the most popular concepts. This parameter is further denoted $\alpha$.

Formally, the set of most popular concepts $C_{pop}$ for a given value of $\alpha$ is such that,

$$c \in C_{pop} \Longleftrightarrow \exists t: tdm_{t,c} \geq \alpha.$$

### 3.3    Extraction of Dynamic Popularity

The extraction of dynamic popularity is based on the processing of the *popularity matrix* from the term-document matrix. The popularity matrix *pm* is a matrix whose values are the ranking of a given popular concept (given in columns) in a given document (given in rows). The ranking of a popular concept $c$ in a document $d_t$ is the index of the concept in the sorted row associated with $d_t$ in the term-document matrix. Therefore the most popular concept of a given document, i.e., the concept that has the larger number of occurrences in this document, has a ranking equals to 1. The second most popular concept has a ranking equals to 2, etc. Therefore, each column of the popularity matrix contains the ranking of concepts in a given document, while each row of the popularity matrix contains the various ranking values of a given concept across documents. Rows of the popularity matrix are dynamic popularity of the associated concept.

### 3.4    Summarizing the Proposed Method in Pseudo-code

The proposed solution may be summarized in pseudo-code as follows:

```
corpus <- Read(corpusSource)

lowercase(corpus)
removeWhiteSpaces(corpus)
removePunctuation(corpus)
removeStopWords(corpus)
stem(corpus)

tdm <- processTermDocumentMatrix(corpus)
popularConcepts <- emptySet()
foreach row in tdm
  sort(row)
  foreach concept in row
    if (tdm(row,concept) •   )
      popularConcepts.add(concept)

pm <- emptyMatrix()
foreach row in tdm
  sort(row)
```

```
foreach concept in popularConcepts
    pm(row,concept) = row.indexOf(concept)
```

The dynamic popularity of a given concept is the row of the matrix *pm* associated with this concept.

## 4    Validation of the Proposed Method

The proposed solution has been applied to a corpus containing the titles of the articles published in the proceedings of the eleventh first editions of the IFIP Working Conferences on Virtual Enterprises, from PROVE'99 to PROVE'10 [7-17]. The PROVE CSSD contains 721 articles, with an average number of 65.6 articles per conference edition. The CSSD contains 6620 words. The proposed method has been implemented with the *R* software environment for statistical computing and graphics [19]. The associated package *tm* [20] provides support for most required functions, such as stop words removal, stemming, term-document matrix processing.

After the preparation step, the set of concepts is reduced to 1031. Next, the 20 most popular concepts for each edition have been identified, leading to a set of 68 popular concepts. The 5 most popular concepts for PROVE'99, PROVE'05, and PROVE'10 are presented in Table 1.

**Table 1.** Five most popular concepts in articles published in the proceedings of PROVE'99, PROVE'05, and PROVE'10

| Popularity | PROVE'99 | PROVE'05 | PROVE'10 |
|:---:|:---|:---|:---|
| 1 | enterpris | Virtual | collabor |
| 2 | virtual | Collabor | network |
| 3 | manag | Network | service |
| 4 | prodnet | Organ | support |
| 5 | infrastructure | Model | system |

Next, the dynamic popularity of the 68 identified popular concepts has been processed. The dynamic popularity of the chosen concepts "servic", "collabor", "network", "approach", "infrastructur" is presented in Table 2.

**Table 2.** Dynamic popularity of five popular concepts

| Concept | '99 | '00 | '02 | '03 | '04 | '05 | '06 | '07 | '08 | '09 | '10 |
|:---|:---:|:---:|:---:|:---:|:---:|:---:|:---:|:---:|:---:|:---:|:---:|
| service | 20 | 20 | 20 | 20 | 20 | 10 | 10 | 9 | 9 | 10 | 3 |
| collabor | 20 | 20 | 15 | 11 | 3 | 2 | 2 | 1 | 1 | 1 | 1 |
| network | 20 | 8 | 9 | 9 | 2 | 3 | 1 | 3 | 2 | 2 | 2 |
| approach | 20 | 20 | 20 | 6 | 11 | 6 | 15 | 20 | 6 | 8 | 7 |
| infrastructur | 5 | 5 | 6 | 20 | 20 | 20 | 20 | 20 | 20 | 20 | 20 |

The dynamic popularity of these concepts is presented graphically in Figure 1.

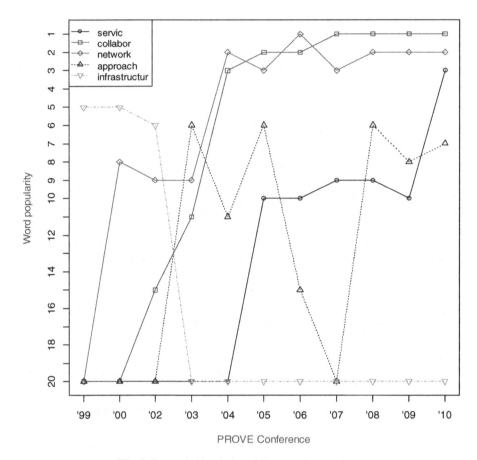

**Fig. 1.** Dynamic popularity of five popular concepts

A map of all the identified popular concepts is presented in Figure 2. Concepts are located on the x axis according to the difference between their popularity in PROVE'10 and PROVE'99. On the y axis, concepts are plotted according to the variance of the differences of their popularity between two consecutive PROVE editions. The emerging concepts, whose emergence is stable are on the top-right quadrant, e.g., concepts "servic", "collabor", "network". Extinguishing (in some case extinguished) concepts are on the left side of the figure, e.g., concept "infrastructure". The dynamics of concepts represented in the lower part of the figure is turbulent, e.g., the dynamics of the concepts "approach".

The map of concepts presented in Figure 2 illustrated the shift in core concepts used in the community attending PROVE conferences, from "virtual" "enterpris", to "collabor" "network". An additional remark concerns the identified important increase of the popularity of the concept "service", confirming the pertinence of the main topics of the PROVE'12 conference.

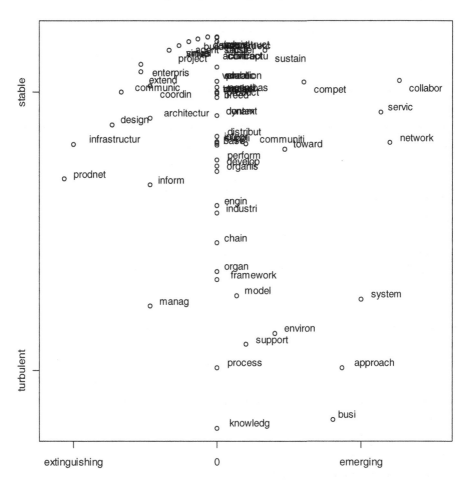

**Fig. 2.** A map of concepts according to their popularity

## 5   Conclusion

In this paper, a method is proposed for the extraction of dynamic popularity of concepts in CSSDs. It has been demonstrated that the application of the proposed method to the CSSD consisting of the titles of the papers published in the proceedings of the consecutive editions of the PROVE conferences leads to the identification of trends concerning the concepts used by the community attending these conferences. The shift from "virtual enterprises" to "collaborative networks" appears clearly in the results of the proposed method.

The proposed method may be applied not only to the title of other conference series, but also to other CSSDs. An example may be the identification of trends in the results of Twitter searches, or RSS channels.

It should also be noted that the proposed method is independent of the language of the given CSSD. The only requirement for the method to support a given language is the existence of a list of associated stop words and appropriated stemming algorithms.

A main limitation of the proposed method is its limitation to single-term concepts, e.g., "cooper". The extension to multi-term concepts, e.g., "cooperative network" is an area that should be further studied.

In future works, dynamic popularity should be normalize as regards the number of sentences or the number of concepts in a given document. Currently only the number of occurrences of a given concept in a given document is taken for the dynamic popularity.

Finally, it would be interesting to consider additional information, such as the abstract or the keywords in the identification of the dynamic popularity of concepts in a CSSD.

**Acknowledgments.** The author wishes to thank Luis Camarinha-Matos for providing the list of papers published in the proceedings of the eleven PROVE editions and studied with the proposed method.

# References

1. Twitter, http://www.twitter.com/
2. Facebook, http://www.facebook.com/
3. Google+, http://plus.google.com/
4. Libby, D.: RSS 0.91 Spec, revision 3, Netscape Communications, July 10 (1999), http://www.rssboard.org/rss-0-9-1-netscape
5. Nottingham, M., Sayre, R. (eds.): Internet Engineering Task Force (IETF): The Atom Syndication Format, RFC 4287 (2005), http://tools.ietf.org/html/rfc4287
6. Gregorio, J., de hOra, B. (eds.): Internet Engineering Task Force (IETF): The Atom Publication Protocol, RFC 5023 (2007), http://tools.ietf.org/html/rfc5023
7. Camarinha-Matos, L.M., Afsarmanesh, H. (eds.): PRO-VE 1999: Proceedings of the IFIP TC5 WG5.3 / PRODNET Working Conference on Infrastructures for Virtual Enterprises: Networking Industrial Enterprises. Kluwer, B.V. Deventer (1999)
8. Camarinha-Matos, L.M., Afsarmanesh, H., Rabelo, R. (eds.): RO-VE 2000: Proceedings of the IFIP TC5/WG5.3 Second IFIP Working Conference on Infrastructures for Virtual Organizations: Managing Cooperation in Virtual Organizations and Electronic Business towards Smart Organizations: E-Business and Virtual Enterprises: Managing Business-to-Business Cooperation: Networking Industrial Enterprises. Kluwer, B.V. Deventer (2000)
9. Camarinha-Matos, L.M. (ed.): PRO-VE 2002: Proceedings of the IFIP TC5/WG5.5 Third Working Conference on Infrastructures for Virtual Enterprises: Collaborative Business Ecosystems and Virtual Enterprises. Kluwer, B.V. Deventer (2002)
10. Camarinha-Matos, L.M., Afsarmanesh, H. (eds.): PROVE 2003: Processes and Foundations for Virtual Organizations, IFIP TC5/WG5.5 Fourth Working Conference on Virtual Enterprises, PRO-VE 2003. Kluwer (2003)
11. Camarinha-Matos, L.M. (eds.): Virtual Enterprises and Collaborative Networks, IFIP 18th World Computer Congress: IFIP TC5/WG5.5 5th Working Conference on Virtual Enterprises, PRO-VE 2004. Kluwer (2004)

12. Camarinha-Matos, L.M., Afsarmanesh, H., Ortiz, A. (eds.): Collaborative Networks and Their Breeding Environments: IFIP TC 5 WG 5. 5 Sixth IFIP Working Conference on Virtual Enterprises, PRO-VE 2005. Springer (2005)
13. Camarinha-Matos, L.M., Afsarmanesh, H., Ollus, M. (eds.): Network-Centric Collaboration and Supporting Frameworks: IFIP TC 5 WG 5.5, Seventh IFIP Working Conference on Virtual Enterprises, PRO-VE 2006. Springer (2006)
14. Camarinha-Matos, L.M., Afsarmanesh, H., Novais, P., Analide, C. (eds.): Establishing the Foundation of Collaborative Networks: IFIP TC 5 Working Group 5.5 Eighth IFIP Working Conference on Virtual Enterprises, PRO-VE 2007. Springer (2007)
15. Camarinha-Matos, L.M., Picard, W. (eds.): Pervasive Collaborative Networks: IFIP TC 5 WG 5.5 Ninth Working Conference on Virtual Enterprises, PRO-VE 2008. Springer (2008)
16. Camarinha-Matos, L.M., Paraskakis, I., Afsarmanesh, H. (eds.): PRO-VE 2009. IFIP AICT, vol. 307. Springer, Heidelberg (2009)
17. Camarinha-Matos, L.M., Boucher, X., Afsarmanesh, H. (eds.): PRO-VE 2010. IFIP AICT, vol. 336. Springer, Heidelberg (2010)
18. Porter, M.F.: An algorithm for suffix stripping. Program 14, 130–137 (1980)
19. The R Project for Statistical Computing, http://www.r-project.org/
20. CRAN - Package tm, http://cran.r-project.org/web/packages/tm/

# Identification of the Virtual Organization Breeding Environment Based on the Cooperation Network

Yun Liu[1,2], Hua Yuan[1], and Peiji Shao[1]

[1] School of Management and Economics,
University of Electronic Science and Technology of China, Chengdu, China
[2] Computer Engineering Department,
Sichuan Vocational and Technical College of Communications, Chengdu, China
liuyunuestc@163.com, {yuanhua,shaopj}@uestc.edu.cn

**Abstract.** Current studies argue that through building the virtual organization breeding environment one can quickly find partners and create a virtual enterprise. The creation of the virtual organization breeding environment requires its own social capital to satisfy some social requirements, but such researches are few This paper, based on complex network theory, proposes a new method to identify the virtual organization breeding environment, which consists of four steps: first is to build the cooperation network from the history of cooperation between enterprises, then is to translate social requirements of the virtual organization breeding environment into structural characteristics, next is to establish the problem model, and final is to design the algorithm of searching for sub-networks (namely virtual organization breeding environments) in the cooperation network, which must meet specific structural characteristics. The proposed method in this paper is based on practical cooperation networks, and therefore is a good guidance to the creation of the virtual organization breeding environment.

**Keywords:** Cooperation Network, Virtual Organization Breeding Environment, Complex Network, Community Identification.

## 1 Introduction

Afsamanesh et al. argued that in a virtual organization breeding environment (VBE) it was far less costly and much more effective to quickly build a virtual enterprise (VE) [1]. According to their theories, the planner could select its partners primarily from VBE members; only when there is a lack of skills or capacity inside the VBE, enterprises can be recruited from outside [2].

Swierzowicz et al. introduced the concept of social requirements for VBEs and utilized it in a case study to check if it was feasible to create a VBE among 10 steel manufacturers [3]. They concluded that some future work should be done, including developing algorithms to identify sub-networks that fulfill a given set of social requirements, within a given network of organizations [3].

L.M. Camarinha-Matos, L. Xu, and H. Afsarmanesh (Eds.): PRO-VE 2012, IFIP AICT 380, pp. 592–601, 2012.
© IFIP International Federation for Information Processing 2012

This paper assumes that the emergence of the VBE is the result of the voluntary, participatory gathering of some enterprises [3]. In the past these enterprises have ever cooperated with each other for a long time, so the history of cooperation between them can provide a clue to identify the VBE. This paper proposes a method based on practical cooperation networks in which there are some enterprises that tie together closely and may consist of VBEs.

This paper modifies social requirements put forward by Swierzowicz et al. and translates them into structural characteristics which VBE members should satisfy. Then based on complex network theory, this paper suggests that the problem of identifying virtual organization breeding environments can be changed to the problem of detecting communities in the complex network.

The paper is organized as follows. In section 2, the method based on the cooperation network is presented in detail. In section 3, this method is applied to a case to demonstrate its value. Section 4 is a discussion and section 5 concludes the paper.

# 2     A New Method Based on the Cooperation Network

## 2.1     Building the Cooperation Network

The cooperation network can be depicted as a graph $G = (V, E)$, which consists of a set of nodes, denoted as V, and a set of links (also called arcs or edges), denoted as E [4]. In the social science field, a node is often referred to as an actor (that is an enterprise), and a link, is an ordered pair (i,j) representing a relationship from node i to node j.

A graph can be represented by a matrix M = ( $w_{ij}$ ). If there is a link from node i to node j, $w_{ij}$ is equal to 1; otherwise 0. In this paper, the matrix M is symmetrical (that is $w_{ij} = w_{ji}$ ) and there is a reciprocal relationship between node i and node j. In this situation, the value of wij or wji means the times of actor (enterprise) i and actor (enterprise) j cooperates.

The first step to build the cooperation network is to investigate the history of cooperation between enterprises from newspaper and websites. Such data should be collected as project names, years, participating enterprises and activities undertaken by them.

Then, data can be represented by a matrix in which the rows are all projects and the columns are all enterprises. Each cell of the matrix describes if an enterprise participated a project. If yes, this cell equals 1; otherwise 0. Enterprises are categorized by their primary activities in the cooperation (that are their core competences) and coded. For example, enterprises usually undertaking design are coded as G1, G2, and G3 ...

It is often the case that network researchers, who see the world in "relational" terms, turn above matrix into an actor-by-actor relational matrix [5]. In this actor-by-actor matrix, each cell measures how many times pairs of actors were co-present at the same event [5].

Next is to turn such matrix to the cooperation network and Fig. 1 shows one sample. In this cooperation network, types of nodes represent enterprises' categories, for example rectangles for designers. Size of nodes indicates strength of enterprises' core competences, and thickness (also known as weights) of links indicates times of cooperation.

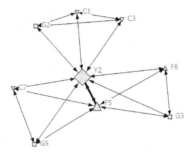

**Fig. 1.** The cooperation network

Structural characteristics to measure networks offer as follows:

The Degree $\deg(v)$ is the number of nodes that the node v is connected to [6]. High degrees usually indicate high levels of being active and wide social influence [7]. In Fig. 1, nodes with high degrees have large size.

The distances between nodes in a network may be an important macro-characteristic of the network as a whole [5]. In this paper, the (geodesic) distance $d_G(s,t)$ is the number of links in the shortest possible walk from node s to node t [5].

The diameter of a network is the largest (geodesic) distance in the (connected) network.

$$diam = \max_{s,t \in G}\{d_G(s,t)\} \tag{1}$$

## 2.2 Social Requirements and Corresponding Structural Characteristics of the Network

According to Camarinha-Matos et al., the VBE is an association of organizations and their related supporting institutions that have both the potential and the will to cooperate with each other through the establishment of a "base" long-term cooperation agreement and interoperable infrastructure [8]. When one of its members identifies a business opportunity, this member selects a subset of organizations to form a VE/VO [8].

A VBE is regulated open and have a controlled boarder, namely at any time new members can join the VBE by complying with its general operating principles [1]. Afsamanesh et al. argued that there may be different levels of membership, but in this paper, the VBE specifies tight members.

Swierzowicz et al. suggested that social requirements be used to define structural characteristics of a network and then be used to check its social capital [3]. They also noticed that social requirements are usually at a higher level of abstraction, and therefore, a "translation" between social requirements and structural characteristics of the network is usually required [3].

Swierzowicz et al. proposed a set of social requirements that are common to all VBEs, such as the size, the interconnectedness of members, and the distance between members for fast and least mediated communication while forming VO [3]. This paper assumes that the emergence of the VBE is the result of the voluntary, participatory gathering of some enterprises [3]. Under this situation, social requirements can be modified to:

- Core competences of members complement each other, and the number of members owning the same core competence is more than one;
- Members have ever cooperated with each other;
- Times of cooperation is larger than a specific value.

The VBE in the cooperation network G can be depicted as a sub-network $VBE = (V_{vbe}, E_{vbe)}) \subset G$, in which $V_{vbe}$ represents all members in the VBE and $E_{vbe}$ represents relationships between members.

In the cooperation network, all participating enterprises in a project form a clique in which each node is the neighboring node of others. So this paper argues that, if a node is one member of the VBE, its neighbors in this clique may also be members of the VBE. Table 1 shows above social requirements and corresponding structural characteristics of the network.

**Table 1.** Social requirements and corresponding structural characteristics of the network

|  | Social requirements | Structural characteristics |
|---|---|---|
| Size | Core competences of members complement each other, and the number of members owning the same core competence is more than one | $size(VBE) \geq m$ and $$\sum_{x \in VBE} type(x) = m$$ |
| Distance | Members have ever cooperated with each other | $diam(VBE) = \min\{ \max_{s,t \in VBE} d_{VBE}(s,t)\}$ $=1$ |
| Interconnectedness | Times of cooperation is larger than a specific value | $w_{st} > f$ $s,t \in VBE$ |

- The size of VBE is greater than or equal to m if types of required nodes (namely required core competences) equal to m.
- The diameter of VBE is 1 because members in the VBE form a clique.
- The weights of all links are larger than a specific value.

The specific value f is computed as the following:

First is to sort weights of all links in the cooperation network from large to small, next is to select the specific weight, that is, the sum of weights locating before it and itself is larger than 80% of the total.

## 2.3    The Problem Model

In the cooperation network $G = (V, E)$, the node $u \in V$ is designated as the start node, then subsets (sub-network) $X \subset G$ satisfying the following structural characteristics can be searched from it.

$$\begin{cases} size(X) \geq m, \sum_{x \in X} type(x) = m \\ \underset{s,t \in VBE}{W_{st}} > f \\ diam(X) = \min\{\underset{s,t \in X}{\max} d_X(s, t)\} = 1 \end{cases} \tag{2}$$

If X exists, it would be the VBE.

If an enterprise participates many projects, the degree of the node representing this enterprise in the cooperation network would be very high. While a VBE exists, it can be concluded that this enterprise must be one member of the VBE. So this paper searches the subsets X from such node.

## 2.4    Algorithm

The identification of the VBE is very similar to community detection in complex networks. Communities within the network can loosely be defined as subsets of nodes which are more densely linked, when compared to the rest of the network [9].

The problem of community detection has been the subject of discussion in various disciplines [9, 10]. Costa reported a simple and powerful hub-based community finding methodology, especially aiming at those networks in which nodes organized around hubs into communities [11]. Here, a hub referred to a node in a network exhibiting high degree [11].

The identification of the VBE does not need to partition the cooperation network into communities, but rather search for subsets that satisfy structural characteristics in (2). However, Costa's methodology is still a good reference.

While identifying the VBE, first is to get nodes $\{u_i \mid u_i \in V\}$ in the cooperation network that have high degrees, next is to check iteratively if there is subsets X that includes $u_i$ and satisfies structural characteristics in (2). Above algorithm is shown as the following:

```
program
    put the nodes that have higher degrees than the average
in {uᵢ |uᵢ ∈ V}
    compute the specific value f;
    begin traversing uᵢ
```

$$Y = \phi$$

```
    put the nodes that are neighbors of uᵢ in Y = {yⱼ}
        begin traversing yⱼ

        remove those nodes from Y whose links with uᵢ are
lower than f
        end
        begin searching cliques Xi in uᵢ ∪ Y
```

$$\text{if } \sum_{x \in Xi} type(x) = m_i$$

```
            X = Xi
            output X
        end
    end
end
```

## 3    Case Study

The production mode in the heavy equipment manufacturing industry is usually order-to-make, and in order to respond to business opportunities agilely the system integrator must unite some independent enterprises to form a temporary alliance (that is the VE).

Fig. 2 shows the value chain of the heavy equipment manufacturing industry. In this value chain there are system integrators, industry design & research institutes, heavy equipment manufacturers, logistics service providers, industrial equipment installation companies and users, which have different core competences. After a period of cooperation, some of them linked very closely and may have the potential and the will to establish the VBE.

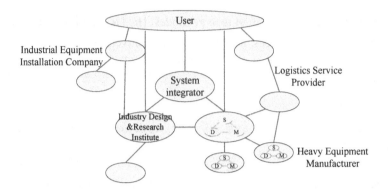

**Fig. 2.** The value chain

### 3.1    Data Collection and Processing

CDCM is one kind of products of the heavy equipment manufacturing industry, and authors in this paper collected data of 11 products manufactured from 2006 to 2009 in China, which included 29 units (each product may have more than one unit). Such data is collected as project names, years, participating enterprises and activities undertaken by them.

Because these projects attract many enterprises to participate, their cooperation usually be reported in the newspaper and they also advertise their work in their own websites. Thus, it is not difficult for the authors to collect data from the Internet.

The cooperation network generated from above data is shown in Fig. 3, which has 42 nodes. Weights of links between nodes represent times of cooperation.

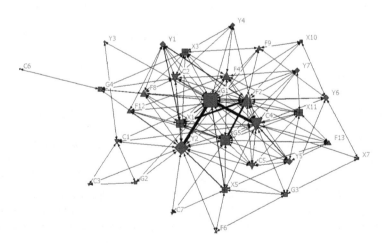

**Fig. 3.** The generated cooperation network

System integrator: X1, X3, X5, X7, X10, X11
Industry design & research institute: G1, G2, G3, G4, G5
Industrial equipment Installation Company:   Y1, Y2, Y3, Y4, Y5, Y6, Y7
Heavy equipment manufacturer (China): C1, C2, C3, C4, C5, C6, C7
Heavy equipment manufacturer (Other countries): F2, F4, F6, F8, F9, F12, F13

## 3.2    Results

In Fig. 3, nodes that have degrees above the average are G1, Y2, F2, C4, G5, X1, F4, C2, X5, Y1(from large to small). Putting them in $\{u_i \mid u_i \in V\}$ and computing with the algorithm in 2.4, results show that there is not a sub-network (subsets) that satisfies structural characteristics in (2). But there exist 6 would-be VBEs.

Fig. 4 shows these 6 would-be VBEs, and the reason why they cannot satisfies structural characteristics in (2) is that the number of types of nodes in them do not achieve m. These 6 would-be VBEs overlap, and G1, X1 and F2 are the nodes that are shared the most. The authors compare these 6 would-be VBEs through computing their densities, which are 2.8333, 3.1667, 3.6667, 3.1667, 3.1667 and 3.5 separately. It is found that the possibility of 3 to develop into a true VBE is greatest.

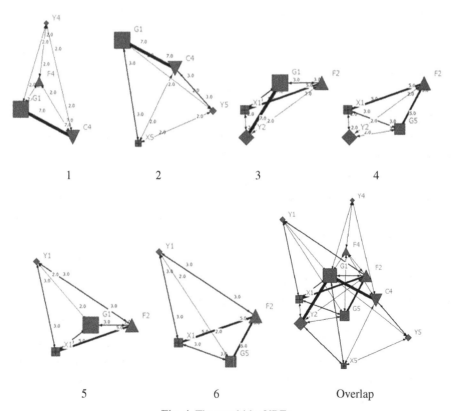

**Fig. 4.** The would-be VBEs

## 4    Discussion

In the case study, no sub-networks satisfy all social requirements; this is because Chinese companies are taking place foreign companies to become system integrator gradually. At first, users ran fast in this competition. Because of user preference and the limitation of the location, there is little possibility that enterprises cooperated again in the next project, thus resulted in that enterprises could not aggregate.

Under this situation, the requirement of the size can be relaxed, and sub-networks that satisfy other requirements can be found and they form original VBE. Then enterprises that enable the VBE to satisfy all social requirements should be attracted to join the VBE.

In this paper, the VBE specifies tight members. That is, tight members must be found first, and they form original VBE, then loose members can be attracted into the VBE. When there is a lack of skills or capacity inside the VBE, enterprises can be recruited from outside [2]. After that, if they want, they can join the VBE.

In the case study, Industry design & research institutes and large Chinese heavy equipment manufacturers grow up slowly and compete with users, so enterprises aggregate around these hubs. In the cooperation network in Fig. 3, because the node of G1 is large than others due to stronger core competences, it is suggested that it can lead the VBE to recruit new members.

## 5    Conclusion

This paper proposes a method based on the cooperation network, which can help the VBE planner identify sub-networks so that it develops the VBE. Now this method is applied only to the situation that VBE is the result of the participatory gathering of voluntary enterprises [3], other situations such as the creation of a VBE by a third authority [3] needs future study.

**Acknowledgments.** The work was partly supported by the Specialized Research Fund for the Doctoral Program of Higher Education (20100185120024).

## References

1. Afsarmanesh, H., Camarinha-Matos, L.M.: A Framework for Management of Virtual Organization Breeding Environments. In: Camarinha-Matos, L.M., et al. (eds.) Collaborative Networks and Their Breeding Environments. IFIP, vol. 186, pp. 35–48. Springer, Heidelberg (2005)
2. Camarinha-Matos, L.M., Silveri, I., Afsarmanesh, H., Oliveira, A.I.: Towards a Framework for Creation of Dynamic Virtual Organizations. In: Camarinha-Matos, L.M., et al. (eds.) Collaborative Networks and Their Breeding Environments. IFIP, vol. 186, pp. 69–80. Springer, Heidelberg (2005)

3. Świerzowicz, J., Picard, W.: Social Requirements for Virtual Organization Breeding Environments. In: Camarinha-Matos, L.M., Paraskakis, I., Afsarmanesh, H., et al. (eds.) PRO-VE 2009. IFIP AICT, vol. 307, pp. 614–622. Springer, Heidelberg (2009)
4. Otte, E., Rousseau, R.: Social Network Analysis: A Powerful Strategy, also for the Information Sciences. Journal of Information Science 28(6), 441–453 (2002)
5. Hanneman, R.A., Riddle, M.: Introduction to Social Network Methods (2005), http://faculty.ucr.edu/~hanneman
6. Hershkop, S., Wang, K., Lee, W., Nimeskern, O., Creamer, G., Rowe, R.: Email Mining Toolkit Technical Manual. Department of Computer Science, Columbia University, New York (2006)
7. Hu, D.N., Zhao, J.L.: A Comparison of Evaluation Networks and Collaboration Networks in Open Source Software Communities. In: The Fourteenth Americas Conference on Information Systems, p. 277. AIS, Toronto (2008)
8. Camarinha-Matos, L.M., Afsarmanesh, H.: Collaborative Networks: a New Scientific Discipline. Journal of Intelligent Manufacturing 16(4-5), 439–452 (2005)
9. Newman, M.E.J.: Detecting Community Structure in Networks. The European Physical Journal B - Condensed Matter and Complex Systems 38(2), 321–330 (2004)
10. Danon, L., Diaz-Guilera, A., Duch, J., Arenas, A.: Comparing Community Structure Identification. Journal of Statistical Mechanics: Theory and Experiment, 1–27 (2005)
11. Costa, L.D.F.: Hub-Based Community Finding, http://arxiv.org/abs/cond-mat/0405022v1

# 20

## Co-innovation and Competitiveness

# Knowledge Transfer Assessment in a Co-innovation Network

Paula Urze[1] and António Abreu[2]

[1] FCT/UNL – Faculdade de Ciências e Tecnologia, Universidade Nova de Lisboa, Portugal
SOCIUS _ Centro de Investigação em Sociologia Económica e das Organizações
[2] ISEL, Instituto Politécnico de Lisboa, Portugal
CTS – Uninova, Faculdade de Ciências e Tecnologia, Universidade Nova de Lisboa, Portugal
pcu@fct.unl.pt, ajfa@dem.isel.ipl.pt

**Abstract.** Frequently, the innovation processes require knowledge in several domains that enterprises do not usually hold. In order to address this problem, the issue of the knowledge transfer in collaborative environments started to attract attention. In this context, the characterization and assessment of the knowledge transfer among members within a network is an important element for the wide adoption of the networked organizations paradigm. However, models for understanding the knowledge transfer in a collaborative environment are lacking. Starting with some discussion about the nature of knowledge production and transfer, this paper introduces an approach for analysing the level of maturity in terms of knowledge transfer in a collaborative network. Finally, based on experimental results from a Portuguese collaborative network, the Brisa case study, the benefits, challenges and difficulties found are presented and discussed.

**Keywords:** Knowledge Transfer, Collaborative Networks, Case Study.

## 1    Introduction

Nowadays, enterprises in global markets have to achieve high levels of performance and competitiveness to stay "alive" [1]. In order to be competitive, enterprises must develop capabilities that will enable them to respond quickly to market needs. According to several authors, one of the most relevant sources of competitive advantage is the innovation capacity [2]. However, the innovation capacity requires access to new knowledge that enterprises do not usually hold. As a result, the enterprises can improve their knowledge either from their own assets, making sometimes high investments, or from the knowledge that may be mobilized through other enterprises based on a collaborative process.

However, despite the collaboration among enterprises has been considered unusual and indeed suspicious by many SME managers until a few years ago, nowadays it is commonly assumed that the participation in a collaborative process is a common trend for many enterprises. Literature in the field has pointed out that the participation in a collaborative process brings benefits to the involved entities. On the basis of these

L.M. Camarinha-Matos, L. Xu, and H. Afsarmanesh (Eds.): PRO-VE 2012, IFIP AICT 380, pp. 605–615, 2012.
© IFIP International Federation for Information Processing 2012

expectations are, amongst others, the following factors: sharing of risks and resources, joining of complementary skills and capacities, access to new / wider markets and new knowledge, etc [3].

In fact, there is an intuitive assumption that, when an enterprise is a member of a long-term networked structure, the existence of a collaborative environment enables the increase of knowledge production as well as the transfer of knowledge, and thus the enterprises may operate more effectively in pursuit of their goals.

However, in spite of this assumption, it has been difficult to prove its relevance due to the lack of models that support mechanisms that explain the production and transfer of knowledge in collaborative environment. Furthermore, the absence of indicators related to knowledge transfer – clearly showing the amount of knowledge transferred and the impact of this knowledge at a member level, for instance, in terms of capacity for generating new ideas, processes and products, organizational improvement through the combination of the existent resources, and diversity of cultures and experiences of other enterprises – might be an additional obstacle for a wider acceptance of this paradigm.

This paper discusses the nature of knowledge transfer as a contribution to a future identification of a set of indicators that are suitable for collaborative networks. This work aims at contributing to answer the following main questions:

- How is knowledge transferred from one network member to another?
- What are the factors that facilitate or constrain knowledge transfer in collaborative environment?

## 2     Knowledge Production and Transfer in Collaborative Networks

Upon reviewing the international literature, we find many studies highlighting the societal importance of innovation and knowledge within modern economies. CASTELL's [4]. "Network Society" or SOETE's [5]. "Knowledge Economy" are highly regarded concepts, but we could mention other interesting works from Toffler [6], Bell [7], or Giddens [8].

Knowledge always played an important role in the economy. But only over the last few years has its relative importance been recognised, just as that importance is growing. However, the stock of knowledge upon which economic activity is based today is definitely much larger than in previous eras. In the emergent economy and society, the accumulation of knowledge becomes the main motivational strength towards growth and development [9], [10], [13].

Actually, the last decades have shown a generalised concern about the study on how companies create knowledge and, particularly, on how they operate this transference. Knowledge is recognised as a principal source of economic rent, and the effective management of organizational knowledge has increasingly been linked to competitive advantage and is considered critical to the success of the business firm. One of the distinctive features of the knowledge-based economy is the recognition that the diffusion of knowledge is just as significant as its production, leading to increased attention to "*knowledge distribution networks*" and "*national systems of innovation*". These are the agents and structures which support the advance and use of knowledge in the economy and the linkages between them.

In this line of thought, Gibbons et al. [11] introduce a distinction between *Mode 1* knowledge production, which has always existed, and *Mode 2* knowledge production, a new mode that is emerging alongside it and which is becoming more and more relevant. While knowledge production used to be located primarily at scientific institutions (universities, government institutes and industrial research labs) and structured by scientific disciplines, its new locations, practices and principles are becoming much more heterogeneous. *Mode 2* knowledge is produced in different organizations, resulting in a *heterogeneous* practice. The potential sites for knowledge production include not only the traditional universities, institutes and industrial labs, but also research centres, government agencies, think-tanks, and high-tech spin-offs.

*Mode 2* refers to a production of knowledge which is not exclusively reserved for qualified academic research but focuses on the different actors integrated in a contextualised problem-solving oriented process. The importance of knowledge is then assessed by its social value and interest to stakeholders engaged in the process of production.

Five main features of *Mode 2* summarise how it differs from *Mode 1*. First, *Mode 2* knowledge is generated in a *context of application*; *Mode 1* knowledge can also result in practical applications, but these are always separated from the actual knowledge production in space and time. A second characteristic of *Mode 2* is *transdisciplinarity*, which refers to the mobilisation of a range of theoretical perspectives and practical methodologies to solve problems. Transdisciplinarity goes further than interdisciplinarity in the sense that the interaction of scientific disciplines is much more dynamic. Theoretical consensus cannot easily be reduced to specific scientific parts. Thirdly, *Mode 2* knowledge is produced in a diverse variety of organisations, resulting in a very *heterogeneous* practice. The potential sites for knowledge generation include not only the traditional universities, institutes and industrial labs, but also research centres, government agencies, think-tanks, high-tech spin-off companies and consultancies. These sites are linked through networks of communication, and research is conducted in dynamic interaction. The fourth feature is *reflexivity*. It means that researchers become more aware of the societal consequences of their work ('social accountability'). Sensitivity to the impact of the research is built in from the start. Novel forms of *quality control* constitute the fifth characteristic of the new production of knowledge. Traditional discipline-based peer review systems are replaced by additional criteria of economic, political, social or cultural nature.

In *Mode 2*, research is carried out in the context of application in which there is a continuing dialogue between interested parties – including producers and users of knowledge – from the beginning. Thus, the concept of knowledge transfer has to be reconsidered. It cannot be understood as a simple transmission of knowledge from the university to the receiver. The participants may include business people, venture capital, industry, research centres and many others in addition to the university. In short, all need to become actively engaged in the process of knowledge production and its transfer.

Figure 1 illustrates the two modes (I, II) of knowledge production and its transfer taking as environment the collaborative networks.

The purpose of the next section is to define a knowledge transfer model to be used in the context of collaborative networks.

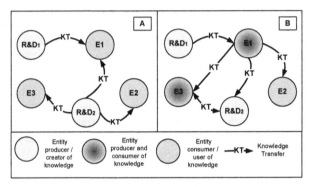

**Fig. 1.** Production of knowledge environment 1A) Mode I and 2B) Mode II

## 3    A Model to Assess the Knowledge Transfer

In order to analyse and understand the processes and mechanisms of knowledge transfer in a systematic way, it is necessary to develop a model that deals with the complexity inherent to this kind of phenomena. As starting point, the aims of the proposed model are: To understand the running of an active collaborative network; to create a common reference framework; to serve as a basis for "what-if" analyses; and to motivate changes in the operation process of the network.

Based on the literature [11,12], and taking into account the context of collaborative networks, as a first approach, the model proposed includes the following perspectives:

- **Transfer mechanisms** – This perspective focuses on the identification and characterisation of distinct ways of "physical" interrelationship that support the process of knowledge transfer between enterprises within a network, such as internal publications, external publications, reports, patents, exchange of resources between organizations, log of good practices (lessons learned), repository of information (infrastructure dedicated), e-mail, videoconferencing, infrastructure to support collaborative processes (e.g. workgroup tool), telephone / mobile phone, informal meetings, and periodic meetings.
- **Competences Management** - This perspective addresses the principles, policies, and governance rules that may facilitate or constrain the processes of creating the competence and searching for competences by the members of the network. Therefore, general issues such as definition of accessibility levels (e.g. public, internal to network members or private), definition of policies in terms of

competence dissemination among members of the network, definition of principles to assure the transparency and traceability of the competences in the network, definition of a competence taxonomy (e.g. market , ICT , management, manufacturing), levels of importance (e.g. central or marginal), time aspects (e.g. historical or current), and definition of rules in terms of Intellectual Property rights (IPR) (e.g. confidential or non-confidential) are considered here.

- **Nature of the relationships** - The nature of the relationships determines the way collaborative space enables or facilitates the flow of knowledge among enterprises. Thus, this perspective focuses on the identification and characterisation of the various types of relationships that enterprises may have with other enterprises within the network: the relationships with new enterprises created from existing enterprises that belong to the network (e.g. spin-offs and start-ups) and also the relationships between the network as a whole and external entities (e.g. suppliers, customers, end-users, competitors, external institutions, and potential new partners).

Figure 2 illustrates the proposed model for the analysis of knowledge transfer in the context of network organizations.

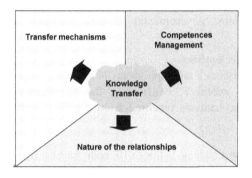

**Fig. 2.** Knowledge transfer model

# 4    Knowledge Transfer Assessment Using the Proposed Model

*Methodology*

The research is based on one case study pointed to the largest Portuguese motorway[1] is based on two main projects developed by Brisa, namely E_TOLL – *Electronic Tolling System*, a self-service toll lane where it is possible to pay by bank card or cash, and ALPR – *Advanced License Plat Recognition*, an enforcement system based on the automatic license plate recognition for situations where the vehicle is not equipped with an on-board-unit (OBU) or the OBU fails to electronically identify the vehicle.

---

[1] The present results are based on research work developed under the ongoing project – CoRe - Competências de I&D para a Criação de Valor na Rede Brisa, FCT/UNL, BRISA, ISEL/IPL, 2011-2012.

Brisa identified E_TOLL and ALPR as the projects that contribute the most to the return on investments. It means that they were relevant in terms of innovation and created value to the company. These were the criteria for choosing E_TOLL and ALPR as pilot projects. On a first stage, companies and other institutions (technology centres, universities) involved in the projects were contacted and invited to cooperate with our research. Empirical data stems from two main sources: in-depth interviews (the basic tool for qualitative research on social systems) conducted with key participants belonging to the network, and a brief survey (for quantitative data) applied to participants by using a social network analysis. The involvement of various partners in the network is critical in order to foster a spirit of openness and cooperation in this fundamental process.

*Brisa Case Study*
The Brisa company currently operates, on a concession basis, a network of eleven motorways, with a total length of around 1096 km, constituting the main Portuguese road links. Given its importance and dimension, Brisa owns several companies specialising in motoring services aimed at improving the quality of the service provided to customers and increasing its own operating efficiency. The Brisa co-innovation network is a long-term collaborative network (a VBE) that has more than 30 members from several domains and business activities (e.g. research institutions, universities, associations, governmental entities, start-ups, business angels, and suppliers).

*Knowledge transfer mechanisms*
This section aims to discuss a main question: "*how is knowledge transferred from one enterprise/partner to another?*" considering the preliminary data related to the knowledge transfer mechanisms resulting from a survey applied (table I) to Brisa network partners.

**Table 1.** Mean (based on a scale of 1- low to 10- high) for each type of transfer mechanisms identified

| *Transfer mechanisms* | *Mean* |
|---|---|
| Internal publications | 3.8 |
| External publications | 2.9 |
| Reports | 3.8 |
| Patents | 2.6 |
| Exchange of resources between organizations | 6.1 |
| Log of good practices (lessons learned) | 5.1 |
| Repository of information (infrastructure dedicated) | 4.0 |
| E-mail | 7.0 |
| Videoconferencing | 1.3 |
| Infrastructure to support collaborative processes (e.g. workgroup tool) | 1.3 |
| Telephone / mobile phone | 6.5 |
| Informal meetings | 6.9 |
| Periodic meetings | 6.5 |
| Other | 4.5 |

From the results, one can observe that the mechanisms most used by the Brisa network are the e-mail followed by the informal meetings, formal periodic meetings, telephone and exchange of human resources between organisations. The exchange of human resources in particular, when coming from industry and integrating research groups, was mentioned as a valuable collaboration strategy. On the other hand, the least used mechanisms are the video conference and other specialised infrastructures to support the collaborative processes (e.g. workgroup tool).

According to the results, the knowledge exchange among the enterprise members of the studied network is not based on much too sophisticated technologies. As argued by the manager of one enterprise partner, the Brisa network could improve the sharing of knowledge by using technologies specifically oriented for collaborative networks. In general, the interviewed partners were unanimous about the idea of an existing open network in terms of knowledge sharing, although some of them referred that the knowledge transfer process could be enriched by the use of advanced tools.

*Competences Management*

This section addresses the competences identified within E-TOLL and ALPR projects based on the information gathered through questionnaires.

From the sub-areas mentioned by the partners, a set of categories were created in order to structure a range of competences (from C1 to C25), making up this collaborative network within the projects under study. The resulting map shows that the partners hold a broad number of competences ranging from computer vision (C1), integration of systems (C5), software development (C14), Remote Monitoring (C18) and Electronic Toll Collection (ETC) systems (C20) to Plastic Injection (Industrial Design, (C8) and   Development of Moulds (C9).

The following figure shows the competences used by each partner in the collaborative projects.

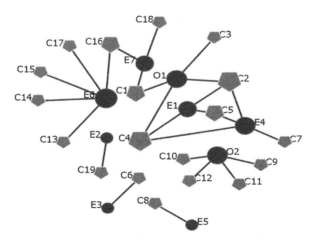

**Fig. 3 a.** Competences used by each partner in the collaborative projects

The adoption of a graphical visualisation of competences provides a tool to analyse in detail the 'sub-structures' that may be present in a collaborative network.

In Figure 3a, the node size of the enterprises/organizations represents the sum of competences used in collaborative projects (E_TOLL – *Electronic Tolling System*, and ALPR – *Advanced License Plat Recognition*), and the node size of the competences represents the level of abundance of each competence in the network during the execution of collaborative projects.

Hence, during the execution phase of the projects, for instance, the most versatile enterprise is E6, as it is the one with the greatest number of distinct competences, followed by E4 and O1. On the contrary, E5 and E3 are the institutions that individually contribute with only one specific competence to the project. On the other hand, according to the competences perspective, it is possible to confirm that competences C2 and C4 are the most common in this network. Additionally, there are some partners that are the only ones to hold unique competences, which give them a powerful position inside the network.

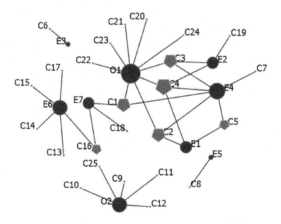

**Fig. 3b.** Competences held by each partner in the end of the collaborative projects

The node size of the enterprises/organization in Figure 3b represents the sum of competences used in the projects and the new competences achieved resulting from the collaborative project. The node size of the competences represents the level of abundance of each competence in the network at the end of the projects. Therefore, at a macro level, by looking at competence nodes it is possible to identify the emergence of new competences, such as: C21, C22, C23, C24 and C25. In addition, at a member level, it is also possible to identify the dissemination of competences among members of the network, for instance enterprise E2 owns two new competences: C3 and C4.

One can observe that almost all organisations and companies held more competences after being involved in the projects, for instance: the E2 increased the number of competencies, as depicted in figure 3a. The gains of organizations and companies are visible by comparing the two scenarios (figure 3a and 3b). When considering the *Mode 2* knowledge production features, another interesting result is related to the competences held by universities (O1 and O2) in the sense that production and knowledge transfer involves all partners and universities receive competences from companies and *vice-versa*. It is a positive sum game. The collaborative work seems to be a privileged way of combining competences and integrate specific knowledge from different sources. Knowledge results from a great variety of organizations and institutions, and is heterogeneous in terms of the skills and experience people bring to it.

*Nature of the relationships*
In order to analyse the nature of the relationships, as illustrated in Figure 4a, 4b, on a scale from 1 to 10, the following aspects were assessed:

- Frequency of contacts – measuring the number of business contacts between network members over time.
- Intensity of contacts – measuring the strength of business contacts in terms of lifespan (time) over time.

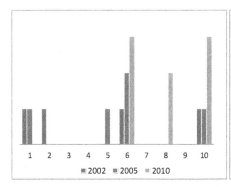 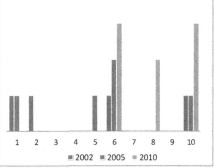

**Fig. 4a.** Frequency of business contacts over time (1- low and 10- high frequency)    **Fig. 4b.** Intensity of business contacts over time (1 – spot and 10 - long-term)

Upon analysing these charts, we identify the existence of an increase in terms of both the frequency of contacts and the intensity of contacts over time among different members of the network.

Considering this, those two variables can be viewed as a measure of the involvement capacity of network members; also, in a co-innovation network, the collaborative processes are mainly based on knowledge transfer, and thus it is possible to infer that the knowledge transferred between partners has increased over time.

Furthermore, since in a co-innovation network the pattern of linkages (knowledge transfer) between network members determines the configuration of the network structure, the position of enterprises within the network might be relevant to understand the role of each enterprise in the process of knowledge transfer. Based on this approach, a useful tool to analyse the knowledge transfer in detail can be obtained by applying several concepts from the Social Network Analysis area and relating these to mechanisms / processes of knowledge transfer.

However, the development of indicators related to knowledge transfer based on concepts from Social Network Analysis, to clearly show the amount of knowledge transferred and the impact of this knowledge at a member level, requires further research and development.

# 5    Conclusions

Summing up, it is referred by partners that knowledge transfer mechanisms could be improved by the use of more sophisticated technologies. Furthermore, the interview narratives point out that it will be important to promote useful tools to manage knowledge sharing among member partners. On the other hand, the results show increasing frequency of contacts as well as its intensity over time. Additionally, the network incorporates an extended list of competences that are shared within the work projects. One important aspect in terms of competence transfer is the mobility of people among partners. Participating partners valued the exchange of people as strategy to improve competences. As argued by the CEO of BIT (Brisa Innovation and Technology), this mobility is a relevant added value in terms of knowledge and competence transfer.

Reaching a better characterisation of the nature of knowledge production and transfer in co-innovation networks is an important element for a better understanding of the behavioural aspects and also for improving the sustainability of this organizational form.

The development of a set of indicators to capture and measure the knowledge transfer can be a useful instrument to the manager of this network, as a way to support the promotion of collaborative behaviours, and for a member to extract the advantages of belonging to a network. However, the development of practical indicators to analyse the knowledge transfer requires further work.

**Acknowledgments.** This work was partially supported by BRISA Innovation and Technology (BIT) through a research and development project.

# References

1. Tidd, J., Bessant, J., Pavitt, K.: Managing Innovation: Integrating Technological, Market and Organizational Change. John Wiley & Sons, Ltd, Hong Kong (2005)
2. Argote, L., et al.: Knowledge Transfer in Organizations: Learning from the Experience of Others. Organizational Behavior and Human Decision Processes 82(1) (2000)
3. Abreu, A., Camarinha-Matos, L.M.: Understanding Social Capital in Collaborative Networks. In: Ortiz, Á., Franco, R.D., Gasquet, P.G. (eds.) BASYS 2010. IFIP AICT, vol. 322, pp. 109–118. Springer, Heidelberg (2010)
4. Castells, M.: A era da informação: economia, sociedade e cultura, vol. I. A sociedade em rede, Lisboa, Fundação Calouste Gulbenkian (2005)
5. Soete, L.: A Knowledge Economy Paradigm and its Consequences Giddens. In: Giddens, A., Diamond, P., Liddle, R. (eds.) Global Europe, Social Europe, pp. 193–214. Polity Press, Cambridge (2006)

6. Toffler, A.: A terceira vaga, Lisboa, Edições livros do Brasil (2003)
7. Bell, D.: The coming of postindustrial society. Harmondsworth, Penguin (1974)
8. Giddens, A.: The Consequences of Modernity, Cambridge (1990)
9. Gosman, G., Helpman, E.: Innovation and Growth in the Global Economy. MIT Press, Cambridge (1991)
10. Maskel, P., Malmberg, A.: Localized learning and industrial competitiveness. Cambridge Jorunal of Regions, Economy and Society (1999)
11. Gibbons, et al.: The New Production of Knowledge: The Dynamics of Science and Research in Contemporary Societies. Sage, London (1994)
12. Forzi, T., Peters, M., Winkelmann, K.: A Framework for the Analysis of Knowledge Management within Distributed Value-creating Networks. In: Proceedings of I-KNOW 2004, Graz, Austria (2004)
13. Urze, P.: Networked R&D Units: Case Studies on Knowledge Transfer Processes. In: Camarinha-Matos, L.M., Pereira-Klen, A., Afsarmanesh, H. (eds.) PRO-VE 2011. IFIP AICT, vol. 362, pp. 215–224. Springer, Heidelberg (2011)

# Virtual Enterprise Environments (VEEs) to Enable Innovation in Collaborative Networks – Initial Modelling Approach

Benjamin Knoke and Jens Eschenbächer

BIBA - Bremer Institut für Produktion und Logistik GmbH,
Hochschulring 20 28359 Bremen, Germany
{kno,esc}@biba.uni-bremen.de

**Abstract.** This paper describes the terminology of Virtual Enterprise Environments as a construct to enable the combination of spaces for open innovation and Virtual Enterprises. This shall contribute towards better management of innovation processes in collaborative networks. Consequently this includes the Business Innovation Space and the Value Production Space, which are shared by the collaborating enterprises. Initial attempts are made to characterize the schematics of these spaces and their interactions.

**Keywords:** Virtual Enterprise Environment, Open Innovation, Innovation Space, Value Production Space, modelling innovation processes.

## 1 Introduction

While Business Innovation itself is a widely used and unclear term [1], only few accepted models, approaches and tools have been developed [2]. Innovation in Collaborative Networks has been discussed in publications, such as [3], [4], [1] or [5]. However, yet there is no research work that focuses specifically on Virtual Enterprise Environments. BIVEE

Virtual Enterprise Environments (VEEs) are a term that was proposed by the BIVEE[1] project (Business Innovation in a Virtual Enterprise Environment). VEEs can be seen as new approach to tackle innovation processes in collaborative networks. It also contains the concept of open spaces like the Value Production Space and the Business Innovation Space, which allow the integration of external resources into the collaborative network.

Companies with direct end-user connection need to be one step ahead regarding the developments of new products, due to the shortening of product life cycles. Therefore being innovative has become one of the main objectives for most of these enterprises. A prominent example of this dilemma can be found within the mobile phone market, as its market dynamics change and product life cycles shrink rapidly [6]. Until the middle of the last decade, it was commonly believed that the key competence of a

---

[1] http://www.bivee.eu

L.M. Camarinha-Matos, L. Xu, and H. Afsarmanesh (Eds.): PRO-VE 2012, IFIP AICT 380, pp. 616–623, 2012.
© IFIP International Federation for Information Processing 2012

mobile phone manufacturer is to integrate standardized components into a dominant design [7], [8], [9].

Conceptualising the business processes taking place in product development (area of the Business Innovation Space) and production (Value Production Space) is a interesting challenge. The modelling of business process in VO has been discussed in many publications (e.g. Camarinha-Matos [10]). What is missing so far is a strong focus on innovation processes. This forces the question of how this concept of open innovation can be successfully implemented and modelled within a value chain or a collaborative network. A possible approach can be identified with the concept of the Virtual Enterprise Environment, which will be explained within this paper.

## 2     Terminology and Characteristics towards Innovation in Virtual Enterprise Environments

### 2.1     Leading Practical Example

A practical example illustrates the dilemma of manufacturing companies, when improving business processes in contrast to invest in new products and services. The example will draw attention to strategy options with focus on innovation, while at the same time optimising factories is very difficult. Therefore most OEMs (e.g. Sony-Ericsson, Motorola) have focused on process improvement and low cost production. This belief has become obsolete when Apple released the iPhone in 2007. Its multi-touchscreen can be characterized as a radical innovation that revolutionized the smart phone market [11]. This new and fast-growing market has significantly decreased the revenue of high and medium quality mobile phones, as smartphones gained higher market share [12].

**Table 1.** Global Smartphone Vendor Marketshare % [13], [14]

|               | 2008   | 2009   | 2010   | 2011   |
|---------------|--------|--------|--------|--------|
| Nokia         | 40,00% | 38,80% | 33,40% | 15,80% |
| Apple         | 9,10%  | 14,40% | 15,90% | 19,00% |
| Others        | 50,90% | 46,80% | 50,70% | 65,10% |
| Market Growth | 23,1%  | 15,6%  | 71,4%  | 63,1%  |

The development of the global Smartphone vendor market share (**Table 1**) begs the question: What ia the reason for Nokia's decrease and Apple's success? This can be explained through the iPhone not only representing a product innovation (with its touchscreen and the possibility to display the World Wide Web and not a mobile version in 2007), but a service innovation as well, due to the combination with the Appstore [15]. This combination of the iPhone and the Appstore can be described as an intangible product and shows Apple's innovative advance. Unlike Nokia, Apple did not focus on a maximum efficient manufacturing of a broad array of products, but instead on a single innovative high class product. The development of the iPhone and its apps takes place within an environment, which includes contributing users. With this approach the Appstore developed far more apps, than Apple could have created on its own. The Apple App Store is a prominent example for the successful integration of an external technology base into a company's innovation process.

This business model represents a form of open innovation, which has been described by Chesborough [16]. It can be characterized as a viable option to expand innovative potential and to speed up the innovation processes [17], [18].

The topic of innovation in virtual organisations and the BIVEE project have created a few terms in the area of Virtual Enterprise Environments, which will be described within this chapter.

## 2.2     Virtual Enterprise Environments

The idea of networking is based on the collaboration of independent enterprises aiming at taking different advantages, while maintaining their individual independency [19]. The rising challenges for concurring enterprises to maintain their ability to compete have led towards a broad field of research concerning collaborations and a significant amount of terms to describe the structure of a collaborative network.

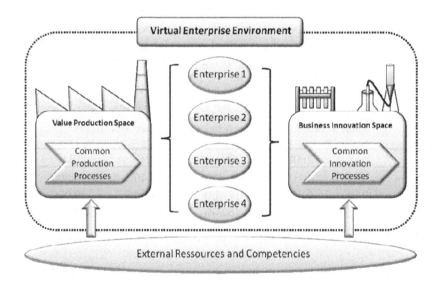

**Fig. 1.** Basic Structure of a Virtual Enterprise Environment

The term Virtual Enterprise Environments (VEEs) has been selected for the use within innovation networks, because it combines the inter-organisational structure of virtual enterprises with the concept of spaces, as sketched in **Fig. 1**. These spaces exist in the environment of a virtual enterprise. Regarding the improvement and innovation processes, two key spaces can be identified: The Value Production Space (VPS) and the Business Innovation Space (BIS), which will be described below.

### 2.2.1  Value Production Space (VPS)

A Value Production Space (VPS) can be described as an open system, which elements can be internal or external production units that share connections with each other. It is a real existing space in an production factory or similar, which contains the value production of the VEE. Therefore it contains added competencies and resources, which can be described as production units of the collaborating enterprises or external elements. Its openness carries the need of securing and protecting members, production units and innovations created within the VPS.

### 2.2.2    Business Innovation Space (BIS)

Compared to the VPS, the Business Innovation Space (BIS) contains highly diversified elements and processes. Instead of processing raw materials into products or elementary services into complex services, the BIS targets to create new processes and organizations based on their predecessors. Through this approach, another difference appears regarding the development of innovations. The added competencies and resources of the collaborating enterprises and external elements within the BIS can be described as creative units.

While the structured use of methods, principles and tools may support the innovation process, creativity, intuition and 'lateral thinking' are not to be put into repetitive tasks. Instead, these innovation processes can be supported by environments that allow a high level of creativity, by avoiding pressure of time and providing a comfortable and innovative environment. Especially within the IT-branch, this issue gains a significant value to successful enterprises.

## 3    Discussion on the Modelling of the Virtual Enterprise Environment Spaces

This chapter seeks to discuss the modelling of the Virtual Enterprise Environment spaces. Since these spaces are not independent, but tightly interwoven, initial attempts to map their connections are made.

### 3.1    Mapping the Value Production Space (VPS)

The processes within a VPS follow a predetermined path with defined production links and production units. These production units (modelled as circle-shaped nodes, **Fig. 2**) can be small- or medium-sized enterprises or parts of a single, large enterprise. Production units are connected with production links. **Fig. 2** represents a drafted version of a production map. These production maps consist of the previously described production units and links as well as other elements, which represent additional infrastructure e.g. storage warehouses. Their purpose is to picture the flow of goods, services, financials and information, as well as providing an easy comprehension to people, not directly involved in the process.

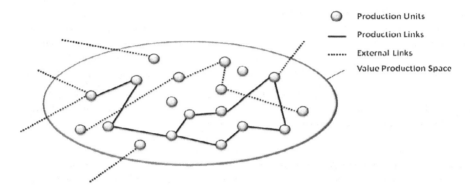

**Fig. 2.** First Drafted Production Map to Visualize the Value Production Space

### 3.2    Mapping the Business Innovation Space (BIS)

As well as the VPS, the BIS can also be visualised with connection and nodes. The nodes represent creative units, which are connected through cooperative interactions. These cooperative interactions are enabled by communication links and comprise the exchange of ideas and their supportive information. Using these elements, an innovation map can be made, as drafted in **Fig. 3**. It aims to provide an overview on the flow of knowledge, which may be created within the production process, emerges by passing through different creative units and finally leads into innovative solutions.

Radical innovations may lead into the replacement of existing elements, according to destructive innovation, as described by Schumpeter [20]. Additionally, the possibility of failure has to be taken into account, when dealing with innovation processes. Concerning this issue, it is the task of forecasting methods to determine the chances of the innovation process. This can imply the need of testing as many innovative solutions as possible; in order to achieve an optimal result.

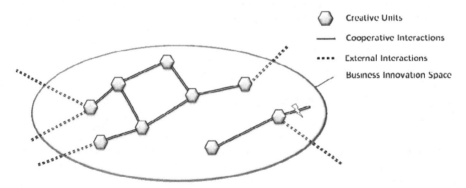

**Fig. 3.** First drafted Innovation Map to Visualize the Business Innovation Space (BIS)

### 3.3    Discussion towards an Integrated Model of BIS and VIS

Following the idea of a strong connection between BIS and VPS, the mapping of these spaces and their connections into a single innovative production map is one of the key problems in the BIVEE project. The integration of the value production map and the innovation map into a combined overview becomes a challenging task regarding the differing characteristics, roles and objectives of these tightly interwoven areas. The basic approach to complete this task is to use the value production map (including the supporting organization) as substructure and to add the innovation process report to build an innovative production map, forming an integrated meta-space.

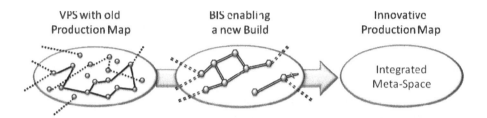

**Fig. 4.** Towards the Integrated Meta-Space

This process of creating such an integrated view is drafted in **Fig. 4**. The creation of an Innovative Production Map, framing an integrated meta-space, requires a high level of communication within the collaborating network. To cope with this challenge, the most innovative knowledge representation methods and notations need to be applied.

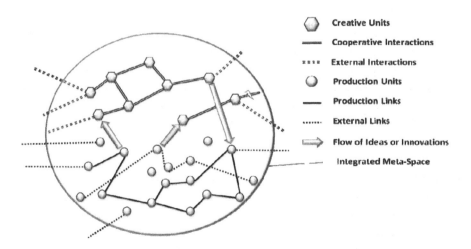

**Fig. 5.** Schematic Draft of the Integrated Meta-Space

A schematic view of this Integrated Meta-Space is drafted in **Fig. 5**. It illustrates the combination of the Production Map and the Innovation Map. Ideas that are generated within the Value Production Space are injected into the Business Innovation Space, where they start the innovation process. Following the innovation process, these ideas circulate between the creative units of the BIS. After their elaboration, these and other external ideas or innovations are injected into the VPS and applied to the value production.

In addition to the flow of innovations or ideas, the connection between the production units and the creative units can be modelled. These connections can be highly diverging depending on the modelled level of detail. A creative unit can be either a machine operator generating an idea, while operating a production unit, or a research department which requires a production unit for the creation of a prototype.

## 4     Conclusions

Scientifically the discussion of innovation in combination with the optimisation of production processes is in its infancy. This especially applies for concepts such as VEE. We believe that there are no methodologies which are helping companies to decide whether to invest in optimisation of business processes or going for new innovative products (certainly more risky and costly).

The notion of Virtual Enterprise Environments has been created to enable the combination of open spaces with Virtual Enterprises. The Value Production Space (VPS) is comprised of the internal and external production units and processes for value production connected to the Virtual Enterprise. The Business Innovation Space (BIS) is an open system, comprised of creative units and innovation processes, which allows the integration of external competencies and resources into the networks innovation process.

Initial attempts were made to characterize both spaces and to map their internal processes. In addition to their direct connections (e.g. between human resources and manufacturing tools) the flow of ideas and innovations can be mapped. Ideas generated within the VPS can be elaborated within the BIS and re-injected into the VPS to generate innovations.

Further research is needed regarding the elaboration of their structure and the connection of their elements. This shall led in the development or application of a modelling language. This research will continue during the progress of the BIVEE project.

## References

1. Eschenbecher, J.: Gestaltung von Innovationsprozessen. Mainz GmbH, Aachen (2009)
2. Chesbrough, H.: Managing Open Innovation. Research & Technology Management 47(1), 23–26 (2004)
3. Eschenbaecher, J., Graser, F.: Managing and Optimizing Innovation Processes in Collaborative and Value creating Networks. International Journal of Innovation and Technology Management 8(3), 373–391 (2009)

4. Borchert, J.-E.: Operatives Innovationsmanagement in Unternehmensnetzwerken: Gestaltung von Instrumenten für Innovationsprojekte. Cuvillier, Göttingen (2006)
5. O'Sullivan, D., Cormican, K.: A Collaborative Knowledge Management Tool for Product Innovation Management. International Journal of Technology Management 26(1), 53–67 (2003)
6. Giachetti, C., Marchi, G.: Evolution of firms' product strategy over the life cycle of technology-based industries: A case study of the global mobile phone industry, 1980–2009. Business History 52(7), 1123–1150 (2010)
7. Funk, J.L.: The Product Life Cycle Theory and Product Line Management: The Case of Mobile Phones. IEEE Transactions on Engineering Management 51(2), 142–152 (2004)
8. Abernathy, W., Clark, K.: Innovation: Mapping the winds of creative destruction. Res. Pol. 14, 3–22 (1985)
9. Ulrich, K., Eppinger, S.: Product Design and Development. McGraw-Hill, New York (1995)
10. Camarinha-Matos, L.M., Afsarmanesh, H.: A comprehensive modelling framework for collaborative networked organizations. Journal of Intelligent Manufacturing 18, 529–542 (2007)
11. Cheng, J.: iPhone in depth: The Ars review,
    http://arstechnica.com/apple/reviews/2007/07/iphone-review.ars/6
12. STL Partners Ltd.: Apple vs. Nokia: strategic lessons from the Smartphone / Appstore Wars,
    http://www.telco2research.com/articles/AN_Apple-vs-Nokia-smartphone-appstore-wars_Summary
13. Strategy Analytics: Q1 2010 Global Smartphone Market Share Update report,
    http://www.strategyanalytics.com
14. Strategy Analytics: Global Smartphone Vendor Market Share: Q2 2011,
    http://www.strategyanalytics.com
15. West, J., Mace, M.: Browsing as the killer app: Explaining the rapid success of Apple's iPhone. Telecommunications Policy 34, 270–286 (2010)
16. Chesbrough, H.: Open Innovation: The new Imperative for Creating and Profiting from Technology. Boston Harvard Business School Press, Boston (2003)
17. Chesbrough, H.: Open Business Models: How to Thrive in the New Innovation Landscape. Harvard Business School Press, Boston (2006)
18. Rai, A., Sambamurthy, V.: Editorial Notes – The Growth of Interest in Service Management: Opportunites for Information Systems Scholars. Information Systems Research 17(4), 327–331 (2006)
19. Schierenbeck, H.: Grundzüge der Betriebswirtschaftslehre, 12th edn., Munich, pp. 49–52 (1995)
20. Schumpeter, J.A.: The theory of economic development: An Inquiry into Profits, Capital, Credit, Interest, and the Business Cycle. Transaction Publishers, USA (1931)

# Business Model Development for Virtual Enterprises

Evelyn Paola Soto Rojas[1], Ana Cristina Barros[2],
Américo Lopes de Azevedo[2,3], and Antonio Batocchio[1]

[1] Faculdade de Engenharia Mecânica-UNICAMP, Rua Mendeleyev, 200-CEP 13083-860
Cidade Universitária "Zeferino Vaz" Barão Geraldo, Campinas, São Paulo – Brasil
[2] INESC TEC - INESC Technology and Science (formerly INESC Porto), Campus da FEUP,
Rua Dr. Roberto Frias, 378,4200-465 Porto – Portugal
[3] FEUP - Faculty of Engineering, University of Porto,
Rua Doutor Roberto Frias S/N, 4200-465 Porto, Portugal
{Paolasoto,batocchi}@fem.unicamp.br,
acbarros@inescporto.pt, ala@fe.up.pt

**Abstract.** Virtual Enterprise is one form of collaborative networks that allows partners to exploit emerging business opportunities in a flexible way. Moreover, in the competitive landscape of the twenty-first century, the business model innovation has become increasingly a key element for companies' positioning in the market. Consequently, this paper aims at proposing a set of business model elements to be used by a virtual enterprise in order to explore a new business opportunity for its network. Literature review is used to identify the business model elements and evidence from a pilot case study confirms that these elements are considered in practice.

**Keywords:** Virtual Enterprise, Business Model, Collaboration, Competitiveness.

## 1 Introduction

The global economy is driven by or revolves around constant innovations. Therefore, many organizations seek today to create and capture innovations by systematically collaborating with outside partners [1]. One form of collaboration is the use of virtual enterprises and organizations are motivated to create them in order to perceive business goals they cannot achieve alone. These business goals may vary from the exploration of new market segments and opportunities to the reduction of costs or risk sharing [2], [3]. This main purpose for the formation of a virtual enterprise sets out its objective and will be the basis to establish its strategy, namely to define how it will achieve high levels of performance in the markets and industries it wants to operate [4].

The interest in business model development is not a recent topic. According to Magretta [5] "A successful business model represents a better way than the existing alternatives. It may offer more value to a discrete group of customers. Or it may completely replace the old way of doing things and become the standard for the next generation of entrepreneurs to beat". Given the importance of innovation on the

L.M. Camarinha-Matos, L. Xu, and H. Afsarmanesh (Eds.): PRO-VE 2012, IFIP AICT 380, pp. 624–634, 2012.
© IFIP International Federation for Information Processing 2012

business model, this paper aims at identifying key business model elements necessary to build a business model for virtual enterprises. It features an in-depth literature study spanning various definitions, taxonomies, and ontologies about the business model and virtual enterprises themes. Subsequently, evidence from a pilot case study confirms its applicability in practice.

This paper is organized as follows. Section 2 reviews the literature about business model definition and Virtual Enterprise (VE) characteristics in order to build a theoretical background that supports the identified business model elements for a VE. Section 3 presents the research methodology and section 4 the paper's theoretical contribution by describing the sixteen business model elements identified for the development of a business model for a VE. Evidence from the pilot case study is presented and discussed in Section 5. Finally, section 6 concludes the paper.

## 2     Literature Review

### 2.1     Business Model Definition

An organization's business model is its driver for success, because it operationalizes the entrepreneurial opportunity that creates competitive advantages for the organization in its market [6], [7]. The success of many companies, e.g. Groupon, Ryanair, Amazon and Dell, can be attributed to the way they innovated their business models, challenging established industries and changing the rules of competition [8]. However, consensus about the definition of a business model has not been achieved among academics. Looking into the literature, we find several different constructs of the concept.

Amit and Zott [9] point out that "...The business model depicts the content, structure, and governance of transactions designed so as to create value through the exploitation of business opportunities". The framework proposed by these authors contains three-design elements - content, structure and governance - and four design themes - novelty, lock-in, complementarities and efficiency. This business model definition is flexible enough to be applied it to different industries and stages of venture maturity.

For Osterwalder et al. [1] "...Business model is a conceptual tool that contains a big set of elements and their relationships and allows expressing the business logic of a specific firm. It is a description of the value a company offers to one or several segments of customers and of the architecture of the firm and its network of partners for creating, marketing, and delivering this value and relationship capital, to generate profitable and sustainable revenue streams".

Morris et al. [10] propose the following definition "...A business model is a concise representation of how an interrelated set of decision variables in the areas of venture strategy, architecture, and economics are addressed to create sustainable competitive advantage in defined markets". These authors value the relationship between business model and strategy, and argue that a good business model captures the core logic and dominant strategy of a venture.

Chesbrough [11] argue that "...The business model is the heuristic logic that connects technical potential with the realization of economic value". The authors go beyond the creation of value by taking organizational aspects into consideration.

These various definitions are distinct, but complementary. Other points of view to define the business model have focused on: value creation [12], organizational aspects of the business model definition [13], [14], [15], and performance and sustainability [16], [17].

Based on the definitions from the literature reviewed, for the purpose of this paper, we define business model as follows: A business model explains how the logic of the organization is, the way it operates, and how it creates value for its stakeholders.

Previous works exist that have studied business model development in the context of business networks. Palo and Tähtinen [18] developed an empirically grounded conceptualization of a networked business model. The authors identified the generic elements of a business model in the field of technology-based services and propose to use these elements to build a networked business model.

Helander and Rissanen [19] developed a theoretical study in which they highlighted that in a network context the business model of a company must be linked to the business model of the other companies involved in the partnership. In addition, Komulainen et al. [20] identified three core elements for a network business model: product/service, business actors and their roles, and value-creating exchanges among the actors. And yet, among the existing research literature, we do not find works oriented to the context of virtual enterprises. Therefore, this paper contributes to this body of literature by proposing a set of business model elements to be used by virtual enterprises.

## 2.2 Virtual Enterprise: Relevant Characteristics and Key Issues of Competitiveness

In an attempt to increase the global competitiveness of firms, in recent years a variety of new organizational structures based on collaboration have emerged. These structures are alliances between companies, created to overcome the various limitations and challenges of the market. Thus, companies that specialize in certain knowledge, which is focused on its core competencies, seek to align themselves with other companies to fully meet the requirements of new products and services demanded by the market. Virtual Enterprise is one form of collaborative networks that allows partners to exploit emerging business opportunities in a flexible way.

Virtual enterprises have been widely discussed over the past decade. The definition of virtual enterprise used in this paper is based on the definition proposed by Camarinha-Matos et al. [21]: "...Virtual Enterprise represents a temporary alliance of organizations that come together to share skills or core competencies and resources", in order to answer to a specific business opportunity.

The concept of Virtual Enterprise (VE) is proposed as a competitiveness strategy that provides the features needed for companies to compete in the market and meet consumer needs, by means of shortening the time-to-market of their products and services. In addition, through the collaborative partnerships formed within the virtual enterprise, companies profit from further advantages, such as the division of costs, resources, and market expansion. An organization can play various roles within a VE during the different stages of the VE lifecycle. Indeed, various types of agents can be found inside and around a VE, acting in roles such as Broker of the VE, VE Coordinator, and Member of the VE. According to Molina et al. [22] the broker is the key player in the formation of the VE, as it performs the process of partner search and selection by setting up appropriate infrastructure (considering physical, legal, social, cultural, and informational) for the formation of the VE.

The creation of a VE is triggered by the identification of a new business opportunity. Subsequently, partners with the skills needed for product development and manufacturing are selected. After the negotiation of contracts for signature, the virtual enterprise is ready to start its operations. Temporality is an important characteristic of virtual enterprises because it seeks to operate in the short run, and aims to achieve business opportunities in the short and medium term. Virtual enterprises are expected to overcome enormous spatial and temporal barriers, bringing together geographically dispersed resources.

**Table 1.** Virtual Enterprise and Competitiveness

| | Characteristics | Effects on Competitiveness | Source |
|---|---|---|---|
| **Driven by opportunity** | Explore specific business opportunities | The structure of the virtual enterprise allows it to respond quickly and effectively to a particular market demand, due to its high capacity for innovation and customer orientation. | [22], [24], [25], [26] |
| | Network dynamics and temporary | Permeate organizational boundaries, through partnerships, allows the virtual enterprise to explore new competitive advantages, extracting the maximum value from its partners. | [22], [24], [25], [26] |
| **Mutual** | Sharing core competencies among partners | The combination of skills provides synergy and greater flexibility to meet customer requirements. | [22], [24], [25], [26] |
| | Integration of business processes | Sharing resources, information, and knowledge enables the network to gain competitive advantages by sharing available individual capacity. | [22], [24], [25], [26], [27] |
| **Flexibility** | Companies can participate in multiple networks simultaneously | Resources can be easily reallocated to respond the opportunities of the constantly changing global market. | [22], [24] [25], [26], [27] |
| | An organization may easily enter or leave the network | | |

The central feature of the virtual enterprise is the complementarity of skills between partners, i.e. each network partner dominates a sub-process or has a critical knowledge about a specific process, product, or market. All partners have to contribute directly or indirectly in creating customer value. Thus, the combination of skills provides synergy and greater flexibility to meet customer requirements. According to Larson [23] one of the potential success factors in this kind of collaboration is the ability to effectively and seamlessly assemble and utilize a pool of resources, derived from the various combinations of specific capabilities of the VE partners. Using this approach, partners can together achieve competitive advantages with minimum investment in permanent staff, fixed assets, and working capital.

Another feature of a virtual enterprise is its high flexibility. An organization can easily, join and leave at any time during the operation of the virtual enterprise. In a competitive environmental, the virtual enterprise is able to provide solutions that allow the replacement of partners, thus responding quickly to changing business needs. Table 1 summarizes the main characteristics of VE and some effects on competitiveness.

## 3     Research Methodology

This work aims at identifying the key business model elements necessary to build a business model for virtual enterprises. Consequently, we formulate our research question as follows: What are the relevant elements for the business model development of a virtual enterprise? This study followed two steps. First, we reviewed the literature on both areas of business model development (section 2.1) and virtual enterprises (section 2.2), in order to identify the business model elements suitable for virtual enterprises. Second, we carried out a pilot case study to verify if the business model elements identified are considered in practice [28]. The case study selected is a virtual enterprise of five members formed in the Northern Region of Portugal to explore a customer need. The unit of analysis is the VE and the data collection method used was two semi-structured interviews, one with the VE broker and the other with a VE member. Interviewer bias was countered with the use of an interview guide, the presence of two interviewers, and tape recording of the interviews. In next sections we introduce the business model elements proposed and present the pilot case study.

## 4     Business Model Elements for Virtual Enterprises

From the business model components shown by several authors in the literature and the virtual enterprise characteristics identified in section 2.1, we present in Table 2 the sixteen business model elements for VE's proposed in this paper.

This business model elements identified for the context of virtual enterprises are showed in Figure 1. Starting with the identification of the customer's needs, a virtual enterprise defines its value offer to a customer through an innovative solution. This innovation is the basis for developing the value proposition. The Value Network is further characterized by the VE key activities; Partners evaluation criteria definition; the organizational actors, their roles and core competences. Here the VE defines how the access to the complementary skills between organizations and the different types of knowledge exchange in a network will influence the network value [19].

**Table 2.** VE features and Business Model Elements

| VE Characteristics | Business Model Components | | Source |
|---|---|---|---|
| • Driving by Business Opportunity | *CUSTOMERS* | *Customer needs* | [22], [24], [25], [26] |
| | | *Value proposition* | [1], [10], [11], [29], [30], [31] |
| • Complementarity<br>• Adaptation<br>• Dynamic participation | *VALUE NETWORK* | *Key Activities* | [1], [24], [26] |
| | | *Partners Evaluation Criteria Definition* | [32], [33] |
| | | *Actors* | [9], [13], [18], [20], [34], [35], [36] |
| | | *Roles* | [18], [20], [35] |
| | | *Core competences* | [18], [24], [26] |
| • Sharing resources and processes<br>• Automation<br>• Polymorphism<br>• Flexibility | *VALUE EXCHANGE* | *Shared Resources/Activities* | [18], [19], [24] |
| | | *Shared Information* | |
| | | *Technology Supporting* | [11], [37], [38] |
| | *VALUE CAPTURE* | *Cost* | [1], [17], [39], [40] |
| | | *Revenues* | [1], [10], [13], [37], [40] [41], [42], [43], [44], [45] |
| | *NETWORK GOVERNANCE* | *Flows of information* | [9], [13] |
| | | *Security policies* | [9] |
| | | *KPI network performance* | [46], [47] |
| | | *Benefits Sharing* | [9], [13] |

Value Exchange deals with the transfer and transformation of the various resources, the effective combination of resources and capabilities of all actors in the network and how they create value, not only for the network's end customer but also for the network's partners [20]. The important elements to be considered are: technology requirements, shared resources, and shared information.

Value Capture or value appropriation, according to West [45], explain how the value creation is captured in order to sustain the business activity. The Value Capture elements identified were: Cost structure and Revenues source.

Network Governance refers to the different instruments that assess the performance level of the network, maintain a strict control of information, resources and capabilities of all actors in the network. The Network Governance elements identified were: flows of information, security policies, KPI network performance and benefits sharing.

## 5     Case Study

The Virtual Enterprise in study is located in the Northern Region of Portugal and was conceived due to the vision of Firm A (network broker) to develop a new industrial equipment in collaboration with other organizations, following a network approach. Firm A is a market-leading company that provides solutions for surface adhesion, dry lubrication, and corrosion. Firm A considers the production technology and the level

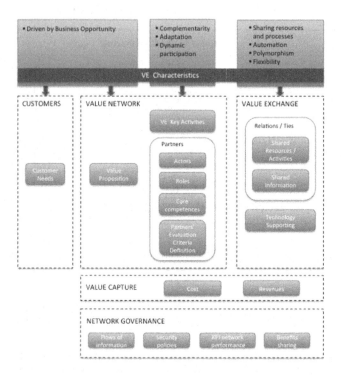

**Fig. 1.** Business Model Elements for Virtual Enterprise

of training and knowledge of the painting line operators as core capabilities and driving factors of its quality. Therefore, since the operators' training process requires approximately two years for the worker to achieve a high level of expertise, Firm A decided to create a synergetic partnership to develop a robotic cell that would learn the operator's movements and recreate them. In this way, a virtual enterprise was created with five actors: Firm A as the network broker, two research laboratories providing knowledge on robotic technology (members B and C), Firm D as the equipment manufacturer, and Firm E providing software solutions. Previous experience of one respondent specifically emphasized that it is very difficult to work in a collaborative network environment without a leading company. In our case study Firm A is the leading member, responsible for assuring that the VE accomplishes its objective and for the negotiations within the VE members.

Our focus when conducting the semi-structured interviews was to explore whether the sixteen business model elements proposed in this paper through literature review, were in line with practice. The interviews were structured around themes. First, we focused on the customer needs (explained in the preceding paragraph) and the requirements for developing the robotic solution. When asked about the VE Value Network and its covering topics - VE key activities, partners' evaluation criteria definition, actors, roles, and core competences - the respondents were easily able to describe in great detail all these components. Respondents showed detailed understanding of the definition process of roles and responsibilities of each partner, and how the cost structure under contract was defined. A strong contributor to the increase of the level of trust among parties was the real-time information sharing with full visibility and transparency for all VE members. The information exchange is performed through a web-based platform provided by the research laboratory B, which includes mechanisms for monitoring and controlling the flow of information between organizations. Benefits sharing were perceived as cornerstones of the VE's business model. Through the cooperation and close relationships, each member of the virtual enterprise brings its expertise in the development of new industrial equipment creating a competitive differentiator in the market. Finally, the broker emphasized that in terms of evaluating the performance of the virtual enterprise, the most important aspect is the timely fulfillment of the activities planned. Evidence from the case study shows, that the defined business model elements are present in this case. However, further research is needed to validate these elements in other types and more complexes networks.

## 6    Conclusions and Further Research

The fast changing market has established new standards of competitiveness for all types of organizations and has required fundamental changes in their business strategies. Thus, business model innovations have gained strength in recent years, appearing as a great opportunity that brings benefits for organizations.

This paper contributes to both fields of business model development and virtual enterprises by proposing a set of elements for the development of a business model for virtual enterprises. We were able to identify sixteen elements needed to define the business model of a virtual enterprise: Customer needs; Value Proposition; VE Key Activities; Partners (Partners Evaluation Criteria Definition, actors, roles, core competences); Relations/Ties (shared resources and shared information); Technology Requirements; Cost, Revenues; and Network Governance (Flows of information, Security policies, KPI network performance and benefits sharing).

Through the development of a pilot case study we were able to collect evidence, that the defined business model elements are present in virtual enterprises. However, further research is needed to validate these elements in other types of networks.

**Acknowledgments.** The research leading to these results has received funding from the European Union Seventh Framework Programme (FP7/2007-2013) under grant agreement n° FoF-ICT-2011.7.3 - 285220 (Adventure Project - ADaptive Virtual ENterprise ManufacTURing Environment). The authors would like to thank INESC Porto for its support and the Adventure Project for their input and contributions.

# References

1. Osterwalder, A., Pigneur, Y., Tucci, C.L.: Clarifying Business Models: Origins, Present and Future of the Concept. Communications of the Association for Information Systems 16, 1–29 (2005)
2. Camarinha-Matos, L., Afsarmanesh, H.: Collaborative networks: value creation in a knowledge society. Knowledge Enterprise: Intelligent Strategies in Product Design, Manufacturing and Management. In: Proceedings of PROLAMAT 2006, IFIP TC5 International Conference, Shanghai, China, pp. 26–40 (2006)
3. Lambert, D.M., Knemeyer, A.M., Gardner, J.T.: Supply chain partnerships: model validation and implementation. Journal of Business Logistics 25(2), 21–42 (2004)
4. Barney, J.B., Clark, D.N.: Resource-based theory: Creating and sustaining competitive advantage. Oxford University Press, New York (2007); Sirmon, D.G., Hitt, M.A., Ireland, R.D.
5. Magretta, J.: Why business models matter. Harvard Business Review (May 2002)
6. Franke, N., Gruber, M., Harhoff, D., Henkel, J.: Venture capitalists' evaluations of start-up teams: Trade-offs, knock-out criteria, and the impact of VC experience. Entrepreneurship Theory and Practice 32(3), 459–483 (2008)
7. Markides, C.: Game-changing strategies: How to create new market space in established industries by breaking the rules. Jossey-Bass, New York (2008)
8. Kumar, N., Scheer, L., Kotler, P.: From Market Driven to Market Driving. European Management Journal 18(2), 129–142 (2000)
9. Amit, R., Zott, C.: Value Creation in E-Business. Strategic Management Journal 22(6/7), 493–520 (2001)
10. Morris, M., Schindehutte, M., Allen, J.: The entrepreneur's business model: toward a unified perspective. Journal of Business Research 58, 726–735 (2005)
11. Chesbrough, H.W.: Business model innovation: it's not just about technology anymore. Strategy & Leadership 35(6), 12–17 (2007)
12. Klueber, R.: Business model design and implementation for e-services. In: Proceedings of the Americas Conference on Information Systems (AMCIS 2000), vol. 6, pp. 10–13. AIS, Long Beach (2000)
13. Timmers, P.: Business Models for Electronic Markets. Journal of Electronics Markets VIII(2), 3–8 (1998)
14. Lechner, U., Hummel, J.: Business models and system architectures of virtual communities: from a sociological phenomenon to peer-to-peer architectures. International Journal of Electronic Commerce 6(3), 41–53 (2002)
15. Gangakhedkar, K., Kevlani, S., Bist, G.: Business Models for Electronic Commerce. IETE Technical Review 17(4), 171–176 (2000)
16. Afuah, A., Tucci, C.: Internet business models and strategies. McGraw-Hill, New York (2001)
17. Rappa, M.A.: The utility business model and the future of computing services. IBM Systems Journal 43(1), 32–42 (2004)
18. Palo, T., Tähtinen, J.: A network perspective on business models for emerging technology-based services. Journal of Business & Industrial Marketing 26(5), 377–388 (2011)
19. Helander, N., Rissanen, T.: Value-creating networks approach to open source software business models. Frontiers of E-Business Research, 840–854 (2005)
20. Komulainen, H., Mainela, T., Sinisalo, J., Tähtinen, J., Ulkuniemi, P.: Business model scenarios in mobile advertising. International Journal of Internet Marketing and Advertising 3(3), 254–270 (2006)

21. Camarinha-Matos, L.M., Afsarmanesh, H., Galeano, N., Molina, A.: Collaborative Networked Organizations – Concepts and practice in manufacturing enterprise. Computers & Industrial Engineering (2008)
22. Molina, A., Velandia, M., Galeano, N.: Virtual Enterprise Brokerage: A Structure-driven Strategy to Achieve Build to Order Supply Chains. International Journal of Production Research 45(17), 3853–3880 (2007)
23. Larsson, A., et al.: Engineering 2.0 – Exploring Lightweight Technologies for the Virtual Enterprise. In: Randall, D., Salembier, P. (eds.) From CSCW to Web 2.0: European Developments in Collaborative Design, pp. 173–191. Springer (2011)
24. Camarinha-Matos, L.M., Afsarmanesh, H.: The Virtual Enterprise Concept. In: Working Conference on Infrastructures For Virtual Enterprises (PRO-VE 1999), Porto, Portugal, October 27-28, pp. 3–14 (1999)
25. Azevedo, A.L.: A emergência da empresa virtual e os requerimentos para os sistemas de informação. Gestão & Produção 7(3) (dezembro 2000)
26. Bremer, C.F., Molina, A., Ortega, L.M.: Virtual organization models: Brazil and Mexico. In: Encontro Nacional de Engenharia de Produção, São Paulo, USP, vol. 20 (2000)
27. Amato Neto, J.: As tecnologias da informação e comunicação (TICs) e as redes dinâmicas de cooperação: um novo paradigma de produção. Journal of Technology Management & Innovation 1(4) (2006)
28. Yin, R.K.: Case Study Research: Design and Methods, 3rd edn. Applied Social Research Methods Series, vol. 5. Sage Publications, Thousand Oaks (2003)
29. Dubosson-Torbay, M., Osterwalder, A., Pigneur, Y.E.: business model design, classification, and measurements. Thunderbird International Business Review 44(1), 5 (2002)
30. Lehmann-Ortega, L., Schoettl, J.: From buzzword to managerial tool: the role of business model in strategic innovation. In: CLADEA, Santiago de Chile, Santiago, pp. 1–14 (2005)
31. Casadesus-Masanell, R., Ricart, J.E.: From Strategy to Business Models and onto Tactics. Long Range Planning 43(2-3), 195–215 (2010)
32. Baldo, F., Rabelo, R.J., Vallejos, R.V.: In: Azevedo, A. (ed.) Innovation in Manufacturing Networks. IFIP International Federation for Information Processing, vol. 266, pp. 67–76. Springer, Boston (2008)
33. Che Mat, N.A., Cheung, Y., Scheepers, H.: Partner Selection: Criteria for Successful Collaborative Network. In: ACIS 2009 Proceedings. Paper 43 (2009)
34. Hedman, J., Kalling, T.: The Business model: A means to comprehend the Management and Business Context of Information and Communication Technology. In: ECIS Proceedings, Gdansk, Poland, pp. 148–162 (2002)
35. Weill, P., Vitale, M.: Place to Space: Migrating to E-business Models. Harvard Business School Press, Boston (2001)
36. Westerlund, M., Rajala, R., Leminen, S.: SME business models in global competition: a network perspective. International Journal of Globalisation and Small Business 2(3), 342–358 (2008)
37. Alt, R., Zimmerman, H.D.: Introduction to special section on business models. Electron Markets 11(1), 3–9 (2001)
38. Mason, K., Spring, M.: The practice of business models. In: Proceedings of the 26th IMP Conference, Budapest, Hungary, September 2-4 (2010)
39. Brousseau, E., Penard, T.: The economics of digital business models: A framework for analysing the economics of platforms. Review of Network Economics 6(2), 81–110 (2006)
40. Stewart, D.W., Zhao, Q.: Internet marketing, business models and public policy. Journal of Public Policy and Marketing 19, 287–296 (2000)

41. Yip, G.S.: Using Strategy to Change Your Business Model. Business Strategy Review 15(2), 17–24 (2004)
42. Wikström, K., Artto, K., Kujala, J., Söderlund, J.: Business models in project business. International Journal of Project Management 28(8), 832–841 (2010)
43. Teece, D.J.: Business models, business strategy and innovation. Long Range Planning 43, 172–194 (2010)
44. Westerlund, M., Rajala, R., Leminen, S.: SME business models in global competition: a network perspective. International Journal of Globalisation and Small Business 2(3), 342–358 (2008)
45. West, J.: Value Capture and Value Networks in Open Source Vendor Strategies. In: Proceedings of the 40th Annua Hawaii International Conference on System Sciences (HICSS 2007), Hawaii, pp. 176–186 (2007)
46. Camarinha-Matos, L.M., Abreu, A.: Performance indicators for collaborative networks based on collaboration benefits. Production Planning & Control: The Management of Operations 18(7), 592–609 (2007)
47. Romero, D.: Mechanisms for assessing and enhancing organisations' readiness for collaboration in collaborative networks. International Journal of Production Research 47(17) (2009)

# 21

## Collaborative Behavior Models

# Choose What to Feel: Emotional Labour in Space of Classic Organizations and Virtual Collaborations

Kseniya Navazhylava

HEC Paris. 1, rue de la Liberation, 78350 Jouy-en-Josas, France
navazhylava.kseniya@hec.edu

**Abstract.** Technological progress infiltrated physical space of the organizations with cables, wires, monitors, landlines, blackberries, cameras, tablets up to the point, when we happened to witness the birth of the new, virtual, space. Here control and monitoring seems non-existent and unnecessary. But in fact, it is ingrained in the structure of the virtual space by means of technology which makes virtual reality real. Ingrained control triggers changes in series of organizational life phenomena. This work aims to look at the interplay between the use of technology and organizational space, as well as at the change that occurs in frameworks of emotional processes in organizations with growth of technological entanglement. Specifically, in the virtual space communication is due to the technology which compels people to choose between available sets of emotional cues. However, it enforces reducing, mitigating and channeling the emotions with the help of limited variants of expression – and, therefore, appraisal.

**Keywords:** Technology, space, virtuality, organizational behavior, emotional labour, appraisal, ingrained control, sociomateriality.

## 1    Introduction

21th century opened a door into a new realm: the realm of unsteady space and organizations without a clear structure. Those types of organizations are known as collaborative networks – "networks of organizations that are largely autonomous, geographically distributed, and heterogeneous in terms of their: operating environment, culture, social capital and goals; nevertheless these organizations collaborate to better achieve common or compatible goals, and their interactions are supported by computer networks" [7]. Being the intersection of human agency and technology, collaborative networks materialized the claim of Bruno Latour to treat humans as things and materialize them [27]: all the objects without discrimination: humans, cats, roads, air, wires, screens, trees – became included into the imaginary and at the same time feasible network, in the form of light flashes, pixels and bits of code... At the same time, this kind of the environment requires attention to the human relationships as a base of social networks. However, the role of affect and emotion in individual and group processes has not been much recognized in attempts to understand the dynamics of collaborative research settings [4]. Emotions proved to

L.M. Camarinha-Matos, L. Xu, and H. Afsarmanesh (Eds.): PRO-VE 2012, IFIP AICT 380, pp. 637–644, 2012.
© IFIP International Federation for Information Processing 2012

have different impacts on the quality of e-learning [14]. Filipa Ferrada noted, that despite of significant benefits of the collaborations, namely innovations boosting and creating values, collaborative networks tend to fail [13]. One of the reasons she sees for that is the lack of specific systems to monitor the emotional state of the network. Hence, the research question, proposed in this paper, is: what is the way to manage the emotions in collaborative networks?

## 2    Building vs. Constructing Space in Organizations

Collaborative culture comprises all organizations' beliefs, knowledge, attitudes, and customs towards a supportive and positive behaviour to enhance the capabilities of others and the willingness to adapt for the benefit of all [35]. One of the primary requirements for the collaborative networks is effective communication, which is maintained by means of the technology in the virtual space. Being physically dispersed, but joined into the collaborative networks, people and organizations surrender to the illusion of total freedom of virtuality. But are the emotional processes in physical and virtual spaces really different? The answer to this question would play an important role in maintaining and improving the organizational culture and building the sustainable collaboration network.

From early organizational studies, architecture of buildings and other material issues is considered to have an impact on the behaviour of workers. Now this idea of technological "impact" has been deepened to the extent of inevitable "constitutive intertwining and reciprocal interdefinition of human and material agency" [42].

There are several approaches to conceptualize the notion of space in connection with organizations, from geographic space as location of business entities on the geographical map, to work space as individual area where one person works [40]. The concept of organizational space appears to be the most enveloping one, as it includes all types of influences of the environment on people within organizations. For the sake of preserving the purity of those concepts, the author finds it necessary to introduce a new nomination which is *labour space*. Labour space is defined as the intra-organizational physical emptiness at hand that may or may not be filled with objects, people, signs and senses.

There is no common view on the nature of space. Built space in the primary sense is nothing more that transformed matter, marking fixed things on maps [41]. Organizational space here is restricted to geographical boundaries of an organization. The other approach addresses space as a constant becoming [10]. Gilles Deleuze was the first to propose the concept of the virtual as a system of relations which creates actual spaces and possibilities, being modified by (here – by the worker) and constantly modifying (him or her) in its change.

When organizations started to use blackberries and iPhones, emails and internet chats, networks for data transfer and internet profiles of the co-workers, interactive maps of the departments to construct organizational space, they entered virtuality, where functions were unreadable and purposes were often obscure. Technology expanded the space into new horizons, those of collaborative networks as preordained parts of virtuality.

# 3    Emotions in Organizations: From Downplay to Appraisal

Newly constructed virtual organizational space of collaborative networks brought new challenges to understanding of emotions in the life of institutions. Although even now scientific management concepts, representing emotion as irrational, personal, and feminine [30], [43], sometimes find support within organizations, organizational studies moved to encompassing positive influence of emotions on performance on different levels [12]. The theories of emotion are still much divided, but emotion is no longer treated as a poor relation in the philosophy of mind [11]. By contrast, authors continue to argue for the importance of including analyses of emotional and unconscious processes in the study of institutional work [44].

21[th] century brought along an attempt to reconcile the theory of emotion with technological invasion. Although studies had been primarily based on cognitive models, emotions were also argued to be important drivers of behaviors. As minds are nor purely cognitive nor purely emotional - they are both and even more [28], emotions had to be concerned in management studies. Affects proved to be connected to the activity of different brain areas and amygdala [1] and therefore inevitable. Human brain is able to sense fear even before one can think of it [20]. So, treating the emotions and affects presented a new challenge for the managers. In the virtual space of the collaborative networks management of affects became one of the crucial questions. It occurred, that mere environmental possibility to communicate does not mean people would involve in Human-Computer networks [12], before they start to offer warmth, trust and affectivity of natural relationship. As a consequence, researchers claimed to consider not only user preferences, but also users emotional\affective states [33]. Beaudry and Pinsonneault [3] showed that emotions felt by users early in the implementation of a new IT have important effects on IT use. The attempts to stop ignoring emotions for the sake of the society health materialized in developing the collaborative system approach to create the networks for professionally active aging [8], and emotion-aware strategies to detect learner's affective state [13]. Some authors propose to use standard as cameras to capture subjective, unconscious motor behaviour which would encourage student's positive attitude towards learning, assure student's emotional safety and foster their meta-cognitive and meta-affective skills [14].

Hillary Anger Elfenbein's Integrated Interpersonal Process Framework for emotion in organizations [12] opens the "black box" of emotions experience. It encompasses both process and structural understandings of the emotions, by breaking the path between stimuli and emotional expression into several, cognitive and psychological, steps. The paths for the adressant and adresat of the emotion are linked into interpersonal roundabout, where the emotional cue of one functions as the emotional stimuli of the other. Coupled together with the appraisal theory of emotions, this framework casts some light on interesting new phenomena in the life of virtual organizations that hadn't been present before, like reducing, mitigating and channeling the emotions with the help of limited variants of its appraisals.

# 4    Emotions in Three Types of Spatio-technological Forms of Organizations

There are three types of organizational spaces – integrated, limited (cubicle) and virtual – that are considered within this study. Every type has its own intensity of technological infiltration and emotion control on the workplace. Development of the labour space of the organization follows its complexity, which the author witnessed on the example of the newspaper (firm B.) in Belarus where she had been working for 10 years. This example is offered as an illustration for the interplay of the labour space and emotional labour management in one given organization (Table 1).

**Table 1.** The interplay of the labour space and emotional labour management in one given organization

| Types of labour space | -big common room, the rows of desks not clustered or differentiated by belonging to a certain group. | -cubicle spaces: more privacy + lag between emotional experience of one worker and emotional registration of the other. | -geographical dispersion: technological border between worker's emotional experience and other's registration. |
|---|---|---|---|
| Function of the technology | -strictly functional; computers as printing machines, mobile phones not published on the visit cards, the exchange of information occurred in a simple meeting in a face to face | -communicational: internal network to exchange the files, inside ICQ messenger to reach the administrators or colleagues. -monitoring: surveillance by closed-circuit television cameras (CCTV) (would be impossible in the countries with a different legal system - *Author*); calls recording system | -constructional and absolutely (?) free: ICQ, Skype, internet browsers, software for editing the websites installed on their computers, contacts with help of different devices -social networks as monitoring system -ISPs able to track activities. |
| Emotional labour peculiarities | -regulation of displays of emotions instant and immediate. -constant emotion suppression -limited private places (toilet, closet or server room). -control implemented by one or more supervisors overlooking the rows of desks: modern Panopticon [17] | -fewer possibilities to observe the behaviour of the workers -freedom to choose how and when to express the emotional cues to the others (via natural communication channels, as the space of the cubicles is not totally divided from the rest of the equip, or with the means of technology). -still expected to suppress their emotional displays to meet the feeling rules of the company [37], [11] | -possibilities of monitoring ingrained into the technology -limited number of emotional cues |

As a start-up in mid-90s, B. used a bullpen open office system of labour space, where the use of technology was limited to the mere functionalist tool. Hence, emotional framework presented by Hillary Elfenbein existed in an unchanged form: stimuli->motional registration->emotional experience->emotional expression->expressive cues

[12]. Automatic components were controlled to some possible extent under the omnipresent gaze to produce an emotional cue. This cue served directly as stimuli to the other workers: for instance, the fruitless phone talk with the expert caused internal rush that is appraised as anger, experienced as the difference in the emotional state, and displayed due to the emotional style of the adresant (for instance, throwing the phone receiver on the table). This type of behaviour serves as a stimuli for the colleagues to react emotionally. In cubicles the link between emotional displays of one employee and emotional registration of the other became way weaker. In recent past, with collaborative networks of people who could work from their own locations without being observed by the supervisors, restrictions as for the software or modes of information exchange became impossible. However, virtual labour space with its deceptive freedom appeared to have the opportunity of absolute control ingrained in it (see Table 1). This control seemed not to encompass the field of emotional labour. Although free-lancers were expected to share corporate culture with the company they work for, it was no longer the supervisor responsible for it. It was material agency of technology that remained the ultimate source of constructing the labour space [6], [26]. Being functional to the communication within the organization and closely connected to the type of organizational space, technology helps to objectify the emotions and appraise them in a different way [19].

As a means of emotional control, technology gives a way to conceal inappropriate emotions because of changing direct communication between workers to indirect. The lag, which exists between emotional stimuli and display of emotion, gives an opportunity to suppress and even totally change emotional cues. Surveillance over emotions in collaborative network is no longer included, and it seems that displaying the emotions is left on behalf of the employees. This situation is quite novel, as a vast body of research shows omnipresence of emotional labour. It is not restricted just to the low-paid jobs, but also exists in the work of doctors, top-managers and academic professors [5], [30], [34], [2], [15], [22]. Accordingly, although workplace is an inevitable cauldron of repressed thoughts, fantasies and desires [24], [18], the behaviour of the personnel is put under „feeling rules" [38], [21]. Technology and geographical dispersion break the framework by giving the worker opportunity not to suppress bodily display, but to program the virtual self-reaction according to the corporate rules.

However, the ways to display emotions virtual space are limited. To express emotions, users invented special symbols - emoticons, which shortly started to prevail in communication. The choice of emoticons is restricted to less than dozen variants available. Having to choose the appropriate artificial cue from limited categories of emoticons, users have to comprehend the emotion and analyze it. Thus they move the priority in the emotional process to its cognitive phase, where they direct the emotion into proposed channel. As the appraisal theory states, "we feel sorry because we cry, angry because we strike, afraid because we tremble, and [it is] not that we cry, strike, or tremble, because we are sorry, angry, or fearful, as the case may be" [23]... It was proved with the experiment that people are incapable to differentiate emotions in lack of context. Cannon claimed back in 1929 [9], that the visceral reactions characteristic of distinct emotions such as fear and anger are identical, and so these reactions cannot be what allow us to tell emotions apart. The experiment performed by Stanley Schacter and Jerome Singer [37] bolstered this observation. Being injected with epinephrine, a stimulant of the sympathetic system, people tended to interpret the arousal they experienced either as anger or as euphoria, depending on the type of situation they found themselves in.

So, it is appraisal what predicts what is felt [2]. Technology channels the emotional feeling and changes the recognition of the emotion on the stage of primary appraisal [26] by proposing limited ways of its further displaying. Thereby seeming freedom of virtual space leaves us with a big question whether it does not present just another variant of control ingrained in it – this time, with no limits.

## 5     Conclusions

Recent organizational studies show how organization structures, controls and prescribes the emotions. But in new types of labour spaces which are provided by the collaborative networks, the nature of control is different. While in integrated space of bullpen offices the control over displays of emotions is instant, immediate and subjectivised (in the figure of supervisor), infiltration of technology into the structure of labour space changes the framework of emotion in organization. First, it creates the lag between the registration and experiencing the emotion and displaying the emotional cue, creating the agency component in the question whether to show or not the registered emotion and through which channel. It dissolves the interpersonal link between the emotional cue of the adressant and adressat in the organizational communication, as the cues might transfer just the appropriate emotions. In the virtual organizational space of collaborative networks the artificial component in the framework makes the choice of emotional cue more pronounced and limited to the number of proposed emoticons, channeling the appraisal of emotion and thus the emotional experience on the stage of primary appraisal. This theoretical proposition opens new horizons for monitoring and managing the affects in the collaborative networks. Finding means for supervising the emotions in these kinds of networks and developing the emotions-oriented system is extremely important for the health of the community [13]. As well, it would give the possibility to create effectively the affective network based on dialog and supportive and positive behaviour, which is key for to partnership renewal [36], [35]. Also it could play the crucial role in building of trust in the collaborative networks, as Istvan Mezgar proposes that demonstration of interest and commitments, being polite and positive are vital for building connections in the virtual space [32]. Therefore, the author claims for more research on emotions appraisal in collaborative network setting. Propositions, presented in the paper, are empirically testable with the help of both qualitative and quantitative tools. Experimental study would test whether use of the emoticons really changes the emotion reported by the collaborators, while comparative case-study would allow clarifying the process framework of the emotions in the collaborative networks.

# References

1. Afzal, S., Robinson, P.A.: Study of Affect in Intelligent Tutoring. In: Proceedings of the Workshop on Modelling and Scaffolding Affective Experiences to Impact Learning, International Conference on Artificial Intelligence in Education, Los Angeles (2007)
2. Ashforth, B.E., Humphrey, R.H.: Emotion in the Workplace: A Reappraisal. Human Relations 48(2), 97–125 (1995)
3. Beaudry, A., Pinsonneault, A.: Understanding User Responses to Information Technology: A Coping Model of User Adaptation. MIS Quarterly 29, 493–524 (2005)
4. Beesley, L.: The Management of Emotion in Collaborative Tourism Research Settings. Tourism Management 26(2), 261–275 (2005)
5. Brown, A.D.: Narcissism, Identity, and Legitimacy. Academy of Management Review 22, 643–686 (1997)
6. Callon, M.: Society in the Making: The Study of Technology as a Tool for Sociological Analysis. In: Bijker, W.E., Hughes, T.P., Pinch, T.J. (eds.) The Social Construction of Technical Systems: New Directions in the Sociology and History of Technology, pp. 83–103. MIT Press, Cambridge (1987)
7. Camarinha-Matos, L.M., Afsarmanesh, H.: Collaborative Networks: Value Creation in a Knowledge Society. In: Wang, K., et al. (eds.) Knowledge Enterprise: Intelligent Strategies in Product Design, Manufacturing and Management, PROLAMAT 2006. IFIP AICT, vol. 207, pp. 26–40. Springer, New York (2006)
8. Camarinha-Matos, L.M., Afsarmanesh, H.: Collaborative mechanisms for a new perspective on active ageing. In: Proceedings of DEST 2009 - 3rd IEEE Int. Conference on Digital Ecosystems and Technologies, Istanbul, Turkey, June 1-3 (2009)
9. Cannon, W.: Bodily Changes in Pain, Hunger, Fear and Rage. Appleton, New York (1929)
10. Deleuze, G.: Spinoza: Practical Philosophy. City Lights Books, San Fransisco (1988)
11. Goldie, P.: The Emotions: A Philosophical Exploration. Clarendon Press, Oxford (2000)
12. Elfenbein, H.A.: Chapter 7: Emotion in Organizations. The Academy of Management Annals 1, 315–386 (2007)
13. Ferrada, F., Camarinha-Matos, L.M.: Emotions in Collaborative Networks: A Monitoring System. In: Camarinha-Matos, L.M., Shahamatnia, E., Nunes, G. (eds.) DoCEIS 2012. IFIP AICT, vol. 372, pp. 9–20. Springer, Heidelberg (2012)
14. Feidakis, M.: Emotional scaffolding with respect to time factors in Networking Collaborative Learning Environments. eLC Research Paper Series 3, 26–36 (2011)
15. Fineman, S.: Emotion and Organizing. In: Clegg, S.R., Hardy, C., Nord, W.R. (eds.) Handbook of Organization Studies, pp. 543–564. Sage Publications, London (1996)
16. Fineman, S.: Emotion in Organisations. Sage Publications, London (2000)
17. Foucault, M.: Discipline and Punish: The Birth of the Prison. Random House, New York (1975)
18. Gabriel, Y.: Organisations in Depth: The Psychoanalysis of Organizations. Sage Publications, London (1999)
19. Gagliardi, P.: Exploring the Aesthetic Side of Organizational Life. Studying Organization: Theory & Method (1999)
20. Goleman, D.: Emotional Intelligence. Bantam Books, New York (1995)
21. Hochschild, A.: The Managed Heart. University of California Press, Berkeley (1983)
22. Jones, L.: Smiling Lessons and Service with a Scowl in Greenland. The Guardian (October 23, 1999), Cited in Fineman (2000) op. cit.
23. James, W.: What is an Emotion? Mind 9, 188–205 (1884)

24. Jacques, E.: Why the Psychoanalytic Approach to Organisations is Dysfunctional. Human Relations 48(4), 343–349 (1995)
25. Lacan, J.: The Four Fundamental Concepts of Psychoanalysis. Hogarth Press, London (1977)
26. Latour, B.: Technology is Society Made Durable. In: Law, J. (ed.) A Sociology of Monsters: Essays on Power, Technology and Domination. Sociological Review Monograph, pp. 103–131. Routledge, London (1991)
27. Latour, B.: Reassembling the Social: An Introduction to Actor-Network Theory. Oxford University Press, Oxford (2005)
28. LeDoux, J.E.: Emotion Circuits in the Brain. Annual Review of Neuroscience 23, 155–184 (2000)
29. LeDoux, J.E.: The Emotional Brain: The Mysterious Underpinnings of Emotional Life. Simon & Schuster, New York (1996)
30. Leidner, R.: Emotional Labor in Service Work. The ANNALS of the American Academy of Political and Social Science 561, 181–195 (1999)
31. Mumby, D.K., Putnam, L.L.: The Politics of Emotion: A Feminist Reading of Bounded Rationality. Academy of Management Review 17, 465–486 (1992)
32. Mezgár, I.: Trust Building in Virtual Communities. In: Camarinha-Matos, L.M., Paraskakis, I., Afsarmanesh, H. (eds.) PRO-VE 2009. IFIP AICT, vol. 307, pp. 393–400. Springer, Heidelberg (2009)
33. Picard, R.: Affective Computing. MIT Press, Cambridge (1997)
34. Pierce, J.L.: Emotional Labor Among Paralegals. Annals of the American Academy of Political and Social Science 561, 127–142 (1999)
35. Romero, D., Galeano, N., Molina, A.: Readiness for Collaboration Assessment Approach in Collaborative Networked Organisations. In: Azevedo, A. (ed.) Innovation in Manufacturing Networks. IFIP, vol. 266, pp. 47–56. Springer, Boston (2008)
36. Ståhle, P., Laento, K.: Strategic Partnership: Key to Continuous Renewal. In: WSOY, Economy, Helsinki (2000)
37. Schacter, S., Singer, J.: Cognitive, Social and Physiological Determinants of Emotional States. Psychological Review 69, 379–399 (1962)
38. Scheff, T.J.: Microsociology: Discourse, Emotion, and Social Structure. University of Chicago Press, Chicago (1990)
39. Scherer, K.R., Shorr, A., Johnstone, T. (eds.): Appraisal Processes in Emotion: Theory, Methods, Research. Oxford University Press, Canary (2001)
40. Smith, P., Kearny, L.: Creating Workplaces Where People Can Think. Jossey-Bass, San Francisco (1994)
41. Straus, E.: The Primary World of Senses: A Vindication of Sensory Experience (1963)
42. Suchman, L.: Plans and Situated Actions: The Problem of Human-Machine Communication. Cambridge University Press, New York (1987)
43. Taylor, F.W.: The Principles of Scientific Management. Harper, New York (1911)
44. Voronov, M., Wince, R.: Integrating Emotions into the Analysis of Institutional Work. Academy of Management Review 37(1), 58–81 (2012)

# MISE 3.0: An Agile Support for Collaborative Situation

Frederick Benaben, Matthieu Lauras, Sébastien Truptil, and Jacques Lamothe

Ecole des Mines d'Albi-Carmaux, Campus Jarlard,
Route de Teillet, 81000 Albi, France
{frederick.benaben,Matthieu.lauras,Sebastien.Truptil,
Jacques.Lamothe}@mines-albi.fr

**Abstract.** Mediation Information System Engineering project is starting its third iteration (MISE 3.0). The main objective of this paper is to introduce that version. MISE 3.0 aims at defining and designing a platform, dedicated to detect, initiate and support any collaboration opportunity among potential partners (obviously based on results inherited from MISE 1.0 and MISE 2.0). This MISE 3.0 platform implements the same model-driven engineering approach than MISE 1.0 and MISE 2.0. This approach is structured according to four layers: (i) gathering of individual and collaborative knowledge, (ii) design of potential collaborative behavior, (iii) deployment of accurate collaborative behavior and (iv) management and adaptation of collaborative behavior. However, this new platform is dedicated to provide improvements such as continuous working, performance measurement, smart monitoring and cloud deployment, which are the scientific backbone of this paper.

**Keywords:** Model-Driven Engineering, Interoperability, Key Performance Indicator, Decision Support System.

## 1 Introduction

Organizations (of any kind) embedded in today's economic environment are deeply dependent from their ability to take part into collaborations. Consequently, it is strongly required for them to assume the needed interoperability functions: exchange of information, coordination of functions and orchestration of processes. Furthermore, inside these organizations, Information Systems (IS) and computerized systems are assuming both the roles of interface (external and internal exchanges) and functional engine (driving processes and business activities). Therefore, IS, must be supporting the previously listed interoperability functions. The issue is to ensure that partners' IS will be able to work altogether (thanks to these interoperability functions) in order to constitute a coherent and homogeneous set of IS (the IS of the collaborative situation). Providing organizations with methods, tools and platforms able to ensure these interoperability functions makes therefore sound sense.

The MISE project (Mediation Information System Engineering) has been launched in 2004 and is dedicated to provide an approach (and the associated tools) for Mediation Information System (MIS) design. The so obtained MIS should ensure the

L.M. Camarinha-Matos, L. Xu, and H. Afsarmanesh (Eds.): PRO-VE 2012, IFIP AICT 380, pp. 645–654, 2012.
© IFIP International Federation for Information Processing 2012

interoperability functions (translation of data, sharing of services and orchestration of workflows) in an agile manner. Actually, collaborations are very unstable situations requiring adaptation: context can change (new opportunity, modification of objectives, etc.), network of partners can change (withdrawal or arrival of partner, lack of resource, etc.) or dysfunction during the collaborative behavior can occur (even if context and partners are still the same, something may not happen as expected). Therefore, the MIS should remain well adapted to the potentially changing needs of the collaboration. Two iterations of the MIS project have already been performed. MISE 1.0 is presented in [1] and [2] while MISE 2.0 is presented in [3] and [4]. The third iteration, MISE 3.0, is ongoing and this article aims at presenting how this version intends to support collaborative networks in the Internet of services.

Second section of this article provides an overview of the three iterations of MISE projects, their links, their specificities and their logical structure. Third section presents specifically the MISE 3.0 iteration and the associated features for each step of MISE structure. Fourth section concerns conclusion and perspectives about MISE.

## 2     MISE Iterations

### 2.1     General Overview of MISE Approach

This overall MISE design approach might be seen as a dive into abstraction layers based on model-driven engineering [5]. The general principle of the MISE approach (whatever the iteration considered) is structured according to three steps:

1. Design of collaboration model: this level concerns the gathering of knowledge about the considered collaborative situation in order to instantiate concepts of the so-called collaborative metamodel (concerning mainly *environment* of the collaboration, *objectives* of the collaboration, *partners* and services of the collaboration).
2. Deduction of collaborative behavior model: the second step deals with the automated deduction of collaborative processes, based on the knowledge collected at the previous level. Schematically, the aim is to select and organize *partners' services* according to *objectives* and *environment* of the collaboration.
3. Deployment of the appropriate MIS: the previously deduced *business* behavior (processes) is translated in a technical behavior (workflows) in order to be implemented. The goal is mainly to match *services* with *activities* and *data* with *information*.

Furthermore, these three steps are used in an agile framework, which deal with *detection of evolution* and *adaptation of behavior*. Performing agility of MIS is based on event analysis (according to the received event, is the situation in line with what is expected) and on behavior adaptation (by invoking step 1, step 2 or step 3 depending on the nature of the event analysis). On a technical point of view, MISE project is based on a Service Oriented Architecture (SOA) paradigm and MISE tools are deployed as web-services on an Enterprise Service Bus (ESB). Even if there are some differences and specific features, each of the three iterations of MISE project is structured according to the three previously presented steps and the associated agile framework. Furthermore, on a technical point of view, these iterations are all centered on SOA principles and on web-services. The following picture illustrates the global MISE approach (three steps in an agile framework) and underlines schematically the specificities of first and second iterations:

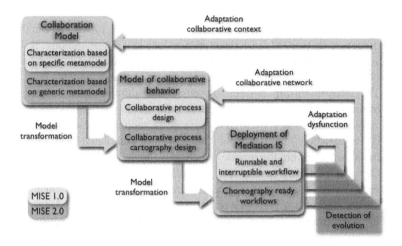

**Fig. 1.** MISE project overall structure including MISE 1.0 and MISE 2.0 iterations

On the previous figure, the three steps of MISE approach are represented from MISE 1.0 and MISE 2.0 perspectives. The *three steps* of MISE structure are presented in a waterfall sequence together with *detection* mechanism and *adaptation* loops. For every step, both first MISE iterations specificities are mentioned. It is crucial to notice that there are in fact four "so-called" steps in MISE approach, but, in the previous big picture, the first three steps (dedicated to design-time) are presented as boxes while the last one (dedicated to run-time) is represented through the three looping arrows.

## 2.2    MISE 1.0 and MISE 2.0 Articulation

MISE 1.0 uses domain specific metamodels (crisis management, manufacturing, etc.) to gather the knowledge in a meaningful collaborative situation model. That knowledge is extracted and transformed (according to [2] and [7]) to provide one single appropriate collaborative process dedicated to support the characterized (thanks to the gathered knowledge) collaborative situation. An additional knowledge concerning information about technical services (applications or functions) is then imported to define how activities of this collaborative process model may be concretely achieved and orchestrated. Once that additional knowledge integrated, the process model is transformed into a workflow model that can be run (thanks to an

ESB and its workflow engine). There are several drawbacks with that first version of MISE. Most important ones are the following:

- The use of domain specific metamodels does not allow the approach to be relevant for any kind of collaborative situation. Furthermore, there are several associated knowledge bases (one per metamodel), which cannot be used conjointly. Consequently, the concerned knowledge elements and the embedded behavioral schemes should be duplicated (or abandoned).
- Deducing one single collaborative process is not very relevant. First, most organizations are structured according to *decisional*, *operational* and *support* processes (ISO 9000-2001 recommendations [9]). Consequently, it would be significant to structure the deduced behavior according to that schema and to obtain processes covering *decisional*, *operational* and *support* views.
- The transition from business process (embedding business activities and business information) to technical workflows (concerning technical services and technical data) is quite raw: the way the technical description of services is integrated in workflow models is automated (through model transformation) but the precise selection is manual.
- Concerning agility (defined as "*detection + adaptation*"), if the adaptation functionality is assumed by the service-oriented structure, which allows to invoke design-time services at any required moment (in order to re-define the appropriate behavior), the detection functionality is fully manual, based on human analysis of reports and information coming from the situation.

Considering the previous elements, MISE 2.0 aims at reusing MISE 1.0 results and adding some new features. Therefore, one single metamodel (representative of collaborative situations has been defined [4]). This metamodel, the instances of the associated ontology (*i.e* the ontology structured according to this metamodel) and associated deduction rules (defined from concepts of the considered metamodel and dedicated to deal with instances of the associated ontology) can hence be used in any collaborative situation. This structural improvement reduces the first listed drawback. In addition, MISE 2.0 uses an objective typology to deduce a complete collaborative process cartography including several processes, which are typed as *decisional*, *operational* and *support* processes. This point tackles the second drawback. Besides, semantic reconciliation mechanisms have been injected (as described in [3]) in order to deal with the transition from business processes to technical workflow (*i.e.* the third drawback of the previous list). This improvement uses semantic annotations of business activities on the one hand and of technical services on the other hand, in order to select the most appropriate subset of technical services to ensure the behavior described by the considered business activities. Based on semantic annotations of information, these research results also provide on-the-fly data translation in order to assume correct orchestration of the selected technical services. Finally, an event-driven architecture (including a complex-event processing tool [10]) is added to the service-oriented structure of the MIS. This improved technological platform provides two main interests. The first one concerns choreography of multi-processes. Deducing a collaborative process cartography implies to be able to orchestrate each workflow but also to manage the coordination of these workflows. Workflow orchestration is assumed by the SOA structure while coordinating several workflows is assumed by the EDA structure (through choreography). The second one concerns the detection part of agility. Services (but also other devices or sensors) are able to send events. These events might be used by the system to detect any unexpected situation. This diagnosis mechanism is a solution to reduce the fourth identified drawback [11]. The following table summarizes the specificities of MISE 1.0 and MISE 2.0.

MISE 1.0 and MISE 2.0 are associated with some concrete application fields. For instance, ISyCri project concerns MISE 1.0 in crisis management context [6], while ISTA3 project concerns MISE 2.0 in manufacturing scope [12].

**Table 1.** Specificities of first and second iterations according to steps of MISE approach

|  | **MISE 1.0** | **MISE 2.0** |
|---|---|---|
| **Collaboration Model** | Domain specific metamodels have been defined, depending on considered business fields (crisis management [6], manufacturing context [7]) | One generic metamodel, dedicated to all types of collaborative situations has been defined (including external layers, enclosing domain specific concepts) |
| **Model of Collaborative behavior** | One single collaborative process has been deduced from the gathered knowledge. | Decisional, Operational and Support processes have been deduced from the gathered knowledge. |
| **Deployment of Mediation Information System** | After manual identification of technical services (or user-interfaces) that would assume identified business activities of the deduced collaborative process, the process is translated in BPEL language in order to be computerizable. | Automatic semantic reconciliation allows selecting subsets of technical services that will be invoked to assume business activities of collaborative processes on a technical point of view. Furthermore, ontological tools ensure "on-the-fly" data conversion [3]. |
| **Agility (detection + adaptation)** | Detection is a manual task based on the way situation evolves. Once detected a need of adaptation, design-time tools (model editor, process deducing tool, workflow translator) may be invoked on purpose in order to (re)define the collaborative behavior appropriate for the "new" situation. | Detection is based on an EDA. Sensors and services publish their events (reporting on the situation and on workflow progress) that can be used to update situational models. If the current model differs from the expected model, then adaptation must be started based on the same principle than MISE 1.0. |

However and obviously, there are still drawbacks in the MISE approach. First, MISE 2.0 only focuses on some main drawbacks. Consequently, there are still "second order" problems. Second, new features potentially bring new drawbacks that should also be considered. Following section presents these complementary drawbacks and introduces MISE 3.0 as a potential way to reduce them.

## 3  Specific Improvements of MISE 3.0

MISE 1.0 and MISE 2.0 did provide an improved solution for collaborative situation support by deploying a MIS between heterogeneous organizations. However, even if

MISE 1.0 provides a first conceptual backbone and a full suit of tools, even if MISE 2.0 provides some tangible improvements and fixes some critical problems, there are still some concrete research avenues to explore.

### 3.1    Knowledge Gathering: Collaboration Model

In MISE 1.0 and MISE 2.0, knowledge gathering is based on a specific filling (by the user) of the instantaneous information available concerning the collaborative situation (its objectives, its specificities and the means available to achieve these objectives). In MISE 3.0, the ambition is to use Event Driven Architecture (EDA) to continuously gather the knowledge (about organizations and situation) and continuously update the models (describing organizations and situation). The principle is to use an *event market place*, where each service and each device of the considered ecosystem publish its own events (*i.e.* reports, messages and information describing its status). By watching this *event market place* the system obtains a continuous *image* of the considered ecosystem. Moreover, the collected *events* are used to instantiate the collaboration metamodel and to create the specific instances of the *model* of the courant situation. By observing this *model* the system can diagnose any collaboration opportunity (for instance by checking some specific variables or detecting some significant patterns). Furthermore, when diagnosing any collaboration opportunity, the required *collaboration model* is already fulfilled, available and operational, thanks to this event-based principle.

### 3.2    Behavior Design: Model of Collaborative Behavior

In MISE 1.0 and MISE 2.0 the collaborative process(es) deduction is "binary": the apparently most appropriate structure of activities is built and is the result of the deduction step. However, MISE 3.0 includes a more soft principle, which (i) provides several models of potential behavior (depending on different options, different priorities and different layouts of relevant activities) and (ii) integrates decision support system to assist the user in selecting the most suitable one.

Regarding the decision support system, an important feature concerns Key-Performance Indicators (KPI). Because, the idea is to deduce not only the adequate collaborative behavior but also the associated indicators we propose to define two sets of KPI. The first one (inspired by [12]) allows comparing objectively the different scenarios of collaboration (on business and technical points of view) during second and third steps of MISE. The second one consists in designing a performance measurement system able to support the control of the most relevant collaborative workflows (inspired by [8]) during the fourth step of MISE.

Finally, second step of MISE 3.0 deduces several potential business behaviors (collaborative process cartography), the "design-time" decision support system and its associated KPI (to be used to select the appropriate business behavior, but also the appropriate technical behavior) and the "run-time" KPI (to support decision-makers to control "manually" the business and technical behaviors).

At the end of this second step, the user obtains (i) a set of "design-time" indicators defining expected performances, (ii) the adequate collaborative behavior to support the considered situation (collaborative processes selected among the deduced ones thanks to "design-time" KPI) and (iii) a set of "run-time" indicators (performance measurement system) to control this collaborative behavior during execution.

### 3.3     Implementation: Deployment of Mediation IS

Similarly to second step, in MISE 1.0 and particularly in MISE 2.0, the translation of collaborative workflows (from deduced collaborative processes) is a "binary" task: semantic reconciliation (information/data and activities/services) select the most fitting technical elements to implement the deduced business collaborative behavior. In MISE 3.0, the idea is also to use non-functional requirements extracted from previously deduced "design-time" indicators during the semantic reconciliation step. By this way, the design of technical workflows (based on services and data) to implement business processes (based on activities and information) rests on functional and non-functional requirements. Concretely, instead of selecting technical services only on the basis of expected function (for instance "weather measurement"), non-functional requirements (such as *response time*, *reliability*, *security*, etc.) are also taken into account (for instance "weather measurement within 2s with encoded data).

### 3.4     Agility: Detection and Adaptation

This step is really based on the MISE 1.0 and particularly MISE 2.0 principles: detection through EDA system and adaptation through a new run of one of the design-time steps (function of the nature of the problem detected). But in the previous versions of MISE, the detection was based only on a comparison of models (current model differs from expected one). In MISE 3.0, we propose to add to this, a way that allows to the decision-maker to detect himself an abnormal situation through the use of the performance measurement system defined in step 2 ("run-time" KPI). Actually, the interpretation of such system is quite "human" and very difficult to automatize due to the interdependency between KPI. In other words, MISE 3.0 proposes a combination of automatic detection and human detection in order to improve responsiveness (and consequently agility) of the overall collaborative system.

### 3.5     MISE 3.0 Synthesis

According to the previous points, the third iteration of MISE provides improvements that may be summarized according to the following table:

**Table 2.** Specificities of the third iteration according to steps of MISE approach

| | MISE 1.0 | MISE 2.0 | MISE 3.0 |
|---|---|---|---|
| **Collaboration Model** | *Domain specific metamodels have been defined, depending on considered business fields (crisis management [6], manufacturing context [7])* | *One generic metamodel, dedicated to all types of collaborative situations has been defined (including external layers, enclosing domain specific concepts)* | Based on an event-driven architecture one (or many) systems may be supervised in order (i) to detect any collaboration opportunity and (ii) to be immediately informed of all potential partners status (thanks to a continuous watching of the overall system) |
| **Model of Collaborative behavior** | *One single collaborative process has been deduced from the gathered knowledge.* | *Decisional, Operational and Support processes have been deduced from the gathered knowledge.* | Deducing several process cartographies (and associated sets of KPI) is a first improvement. Besides, associating a decision-support system (in order to assist the user in selecting the right one) is a second improvement. |
| **Deployment of Mediation Information System** | *After manual identification of technical services (or user-interfaces) that would assume identified business activities of the deduced collaborative process, the process is translated in BPEL language in order to be computerizable.* | *Automatic semantic reconciliation allows selecting subsets of technical services that will be invoked to assume business activities of collaborative processes on a technical point of view. Furthermore, ontological tools ensure "on-the-fly" data conversion [3].* | The main feature at this step is to include non-functional requirements in the semantic reconciliation step. Characteristics such as reliability, latency or security might then be taken into account in the workflow definition process in order to improve the quality of the selected technical services. Furthermore, decision-support system should also be integrated in that step in order to support efficiently the final selection. |
| **Agility (detection + adaptation)** | *Detection is a manual task based on the way situation evolves. Once detected a need of adaptation, design-time tools (model editor, process deducing tool, workflow translator) may be invoked on purpose in order to (re)define the collaborative behavior appropriate for the "new" situation.* | *Detection is based on an EDA. Sensors and services publish their events (reporting on the situation and on workflow progress) that can be used to update situational models. If the current model differs from the expected model, then adaptation must be started based on the same principle than MISE 1.0.* | The most important feature concerns the automated detection of evolution on the base of performance indicators (i.e. not only on the base of expected functions but also on the quality of these functions). |

## 3.6 Application Domains

MISE project, is dedicated to provide a support framework for collaborative situation by deploying an agile mediation information among partners. Currently, there are mainly three application domains (but there might me really more): support of logistics systems, support of health care systems, support of crisis management systems. We can illustrate concretely the way MISE 3.0 might be used thanks to the last domain mentioned (crisis management): a geographical area may be watched through an EDA platform, in order to gather all events (from sensors, services, people, devices, etc.) in order to build and maintain a global picture of that area. According to some unexpected (or expected) negative changes (such as a lot of tweets mentioning the same problem, a lot of GPS data showing that a lot of vehicles are stopped, some abnormal values of temperature sensors, etc.), the MISE 3.0 platform could start the behavior deduction based on (i) information concerning the situation (risk, facts, etc.) and (ii) information concerning rescue means (resource, potential actors, etc.) both extracted from the global picture. Thanks to the implementation step a MIS may be deployed among the potential partners. Agility of this MIS could be performed thanks to models based on the global picture.

## 4    Conclusion

MISE project, through its three iterations provide a way to concretely connect *Internet of Things* (sensors, devices and any event providers) with *Internet of Knowledge* (ontologies and knowledge management systems) to run *Internet of Services* (technical services connected on the ESB). MISE principle is the following: any organization may be connected to the MIS, thus giving an access to its "public part" (mainly business capabilities and information). Thanks to EDA, all "public parts" of all connected organizations may publish events on the platform. Detecting any collaboration opportunity (thanks to events), the platform could push to potential partners a suggested collective business behavior (as an automatically deduced and selected collaborative process cartography). Once accepted or modified (through a dedicated decision support system), that collaborative behavior could be run onto the MIS (as an automatically generated set of workflows associated with a set of relevant

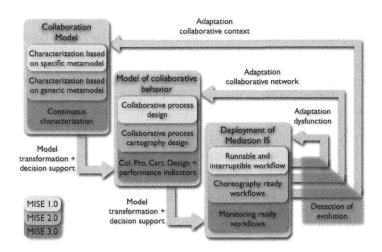

**Fig. 2.** MISE project overall structure including MISE 1.0, MISE 2.0 and MISE 3.0 iterations

KPI in charge of controlling the collaborative behavior) through orchestration and choreography. During that run-time, events (that are continuously sent to the EDA platform by invoked services and performance monitoring tool) update a permanent "picture" of the collaborative situation. That "picture" and KPI monitoring provide status knowledge useful to detect any adaptation need. If such a requirement appears, the orchestrated/choreographed workflows may be adapted on the fly by invoking design-time tools. The following picture illustrates this principle:

Similarly with figure 1, it is important to notice that there are in fact four "so-called" steps in MISE approach (whatever the selected iteration), however, the first three steps (dedicated to design-time) are presented as boxes while the last one (dedicated to run-time) is represented through three looping arrows.

# References

1. Touzi, J., Bénaben, F., Pingaud, H., Lorré, J.-P.: A Model-Driven approach for Collaborative Service-Oriented Architecture design. International Journal of Production Economics (IJPE) 121(1), 5–20 (2009)
2. Rajsiri, V., Lorré, J.-P., Bénaben, F., Pingaud, H.: Knowledge-based system for collaborative process specification. Computers in Industry (CII) 61(2), 161–175 (2010)
3. Bénaben, F., Boissel-Dallier, N., Pingaud, H., Lorré, J.-P.: Semantic issues in model-driven management of IS interoperability. International Journal of Computer Integrated Manufacturing, IJCIM (2011), doi:10.1080/0951192X.2012.684712
4. Mu, W., Bénaben, F., Pingaud, H., Boissel-Dallier, N., Lorré, J.-P.: A model-driven BPM approach for SOA mediation information system design in a collaborative context. In: IEEE International Conference on Service Computing (SCC), pp. 747–748. IEEE Press, Washington, USA (2011)
5. OMG, MDA Guide Version 1.0.1, omg/2003-06-01 (2003)
6. Truptil, S., Bénaben, F., Pingaud, H.: A Mediation Information System to Help to Coordinate the Response to a Crisis. In: Camarinha-Matos, L.M., Boucher, X., Afsarmanesh, H. (eds.) PRO-VE 2010. IFIP AICT, vol. 336, pp. 173–180. Springer, Heidelberg (2010)
7. Rajsiri, V., Lorré, J.-P., Bénaben, F., Pingaud, H.: Collaborative Process Definition Using An Ontology-Based Approach. In: Camarinha-Matos, L.M., Picard, W. (eds.) Pervasive Collaborative Networks. IFIP, vol. 283, pp. 205–212. Springer, Boston (2008)
8. Rongier, C., Gourc, D., Lauras, M., Galasso, F.: Towards a Performance Measurement System to Control Disaster Response. In: Camarinha-Matos, L.M., Boucher, X., Afsarmanesh, H. (eds.) PRO-VE 2010. IFIP AICT, vol. 336, pp. 189–196. Springer, Heidelberg (2010)
9. NF EN ISO 9000 X50-130 Systèmes de management de la qualité (2005)
10. Etzion, O., Niblett, P.: Event Processing in Action. Manning Publications Company (2010)
11. Truptil, S., Barthe, A.-M., Benaben, F., Stuehmer, R.: Nuclear Crisis Use-Case Management in an Event-Driven Architecture. In: Daniel, F., Barkaoui, K., Dustdar, S. (eds.) BPM Workshops 2011, Part I. Lecture Notes in Business Information Processing, vol. 99, pp. 464–472. Springer, Heidelberg (2012)
12. Lauras, M., Galasso, F., Rongier, C., Gourc, D., Ducq, Y.: Towards a More Effective Interoperable Solution through an A-Priori Performance Measurement System. In: Camarinha-Matos, L.M., Pereira-Klen, A., Afsarmanesh, H. (eds.) PRO-VE 2011. IFIP AICT, vol. 362, pp. 125–132. Springer, Heidelberg (2011)

# A Model for Collaborative Decision-Making for the Evolution of Virtual Enterprises

Marcus Vinicius Drissen-Silva[1] and Ricardo J. Rabelo[2]

[1] Department of Informatics, Federal Technological University of Paraná, Brazil
[2] Department of Automation and Systems, Federal University of Santa Catarina, Brazil
mvsilva@utfpr.edu.br, rabelo@das.ufsc.br

**Abstract.** Grounded on Project Management and Decision Support Systems foundations, this paper presents a distributed environment to support collaborative discussion and decision-making for managing the evolution phase of a Virtual Enterprise (VE). VE evolution deals with problems during the VE operation and that put its goals on risk. The main rationale of this work is that VE members are autonomous and hence that all the affected partners should discuss about the necessary changes on the current VE's plan in order to generate a feasible new plan. In the presented approach this discussion is guided by a flexible decision protocol and the impact of decisions can be evaluated. Final results of a prototype implementation are discussed in the end.

**Keywords:** Collaborative discussion, Decentralized Decision-making, Project Management, Change Management, Virtual Enterprises.

## 1 Introduction

Collaborative Networks (CN) have been considered one of the most prominent business strategies to face global competition. Collaboration between companies offers conditions to reduce expenses, increase capacity, broaden markets and improve themselves with knowledge acquired in business [1]. There are several manifestations of CN. This paper focuses on Virtual Enterprises (VE).

A Virtual Enterprise (VE) can be generally defined as a temporary alliance of autonomous and heterogeneous enterprises that dynamically joint together to cope with a given business opportunity, acting as one single enterprise. A VE dismiss itself after accomplishing its goal [2].

Managing the VE life cycle efficiently is crucial for the business realization, so involving the creation, operation, evolution and the dissolution of a VE. This paper focuses on the VE evolution phase. In general, the VE evolution phase comprises activities related to the management of changes and adaptations in the VE's plan in order to achieve its goals and duties. This comprehends actions like modifications in some technical specification, changes or negotiations in the VE's schedule, replacement of some members, among others [3].

L.M. Camarinha-Matos, L. Xu, and H. Afsarmanesh (Eds.): PRO-VE 2012, IFIP AICT 380, pp. 655–663, 2012.
© IFIP International Federation for Information Processing 2012

VEs impose, however, respecting a number of requirements in decision making. The most important one is that decisions should be performed in a collaborative, decentralized, distributed and transparent way, considering that VE members are partners, autonomous, independent and geographically dispersed. Besides that, the fact that each VE is per definition completely different from one to another (in terms of number of partners, their skills, culture, local regulations, specificities determined by given clients, etc.) the solution of some problems is not necessarily deterministic and the usage of previous decisions for equivalent problems is not necessarily useful [3].

Within this wide context, this paper presents very final results of previous and so far ongoing research of the authors, providing a collaborative, flexible and human-centered decision support framework to help VE members in the management of problems that cause changes in the VE operation, considering those mentioned requirements. The underlying research hypothesis is that an environment like that can significantly enhance the agility, quality and trustworthiness in the VE decision-making. It assumes that VE members come from a long-term alliance of VBE (Virtual organization Breeding Environment) type, so having some level of preparedness and sharing some common working principles [4].

This research was developed under an applied, partially exploratory, research-action and qualitative scientific methodological basis. The essential value proposition of this work compared to related works on decision-making for VE is to offer a supporting framework and methodology that systematize, guide and assist VE managers in the discussions about a specific problem within the VE evolution phase towards its resolution.

This paper is organized as follows: Section 1 has presented the general requirements for VE management in the evolution phase. Section 2 discusses the problem related to collaborative decision-making. Section 3 presents the developed framework for managing the VE evolution. Section 4 presents the prototype. Section 5 discusses the results and conclusions of this work.

## 2     Collaborative Decision Making

Distributed decision-making is not a new research topic. A number of works have been developed along the last decade on this matter, especially in the form of distributed decision support systems [5]. Actually, the work presented in this paper follows the same line but it adds diverse elements and requirements from the VE area.

Developing a comprehensive and flexible environment that can cope with those basic requirements for managing the VE evolution phase is very challenging, both in terms of managerial methods and models, and from the IT point of view. Some authors have approached this problem (including the operation phase) in different ways. Rabelo and Pereira-Klen [6] have introduced a fixed decision protocol to deal with changes in the VE. Hodík and Stach [7] have developed a multi-agent-based decision support system to simulate the impact of decisions in a VE.

Negretto *et al.* [8] have created a distributed supervision system to monitor the VE plan. Noran [9] has developed a decision support framework to help managers in the partners' selection in the VE creation. In spite of their values, they are limited in properly coping with two key requirements in the VE evolution: the need for decentralized decision-making and the consideration of partners' autonomy. They assume that the so-called VE coordinator is the only one who has the rights to access all information and to take / impose related decisions, i.e. a centralized approach. The fact is that there are so many particular details to be considered about all the involved partners that it is even dangerous to leave the decision only up to the VE coordinator, regarding that the ultimate goal is to reach a feasible solution and not just another theoretical VE plan. Partners should discuss about the problem, and the solution should emerge from this respecting their autonomies and current governance model.

In order to cope with this scenario, five basic aspects have to be supported for a comprehensive decision-making environment for the VE evolution [3]: Partners' Discussion, Methodological guidance, Decision Protocols, Performance evaluation, ICT Infrastructure. Actually there are several works that handles these issues but in an isolated way. None of the works analyzed in the literature presented a comprehensive decision model and environment that cope with those requirements in an integrated way and that are devoted to the VE evolution phase, which is the case of the this presented work.

## 3    Distributed Decision Support Framework

In order to cope with the requirements previously mentioned and to transform them into more concrete artifacts and integrated model, a framework has been conceived. It considers such requirements, transform and groups them into four pillars: *Human, Organizational, Knowledge* and *Technological*. The rationale is to enable (empowered) *people* to discuss and to decide about a problem related to a given *organizational* process, applying a set of *organizational* procedures and methods, using information and *knowledge* available in the VBE's data repositories, all this supported by ICT (*technological*) [3]. The *Human* pillar represents VE companies' managers who use their tacit knowledge and collaborative attitude to help solving the problem come from the VE operation. The *Organizational* pillar comprises intra and inter-enterprises processes, ontologies, working methods, techniques and procedures that should be involved in the distributed and collaborative decision-making process. The *Knowledge* pillar comprises explicit information and knowledge available in the VBE's data repositories. The *Technological* pillar refers to all kind of ICT tools, platforms and security artifacts available that help managers accessing organizational methods.

Those pillars are 'operated' through three concrete elements: the *Decision Protocol,* the *Distributed and Collaborative Decision Support environment,* and the *ICT Toolbox.* They all form the *Distributed Collaborative Decision Support System for the Management of VE Evolution (DDSS-VE).* Based on the classification proposed by Turban and Aronson [10], the DDSS-VE is classified as a negotiation-based, decentralized, partially hierarchical, semi-structured, multi-participant and team-based system. Figure 1 presents the framework's architecture, also illustrating the relation of these elements with those pillars.

VE operation services & systems represent the activities responsible for monitoring and detecting problems in the current VE's plan. Once a problem is detected, the control flow is passed to the DDSS-VE in order to manage the problem resolution. There are three main modules in the DDSS-VE architecture. The *Decision Protocol* (Figure 2) is responsible for guiding and coordinating the discussions among partners, also considering the set of (configured) particularities of the VE, depending on each case offering the required flexibility and adaptability. The *Discussion Environment* is responsible for supporting discussions among VE partners (VE Coordinator, the VE members and, optionally, helped by an invited expert). It is composed of an instant message module (a *Chat*), a forum module and a file exchange module, where partners can discuss, argument and exchange information during the problem resolution. The *Tool Box* contains a set of tools and software services that help partners in the discussions and evaluations. It is composed of performance monitoring and evaluation tools and other supporting services. ICT infrastructure acts as the 'bus' that integrates all these modules, tools and services as well as that grants access to the VBE database.

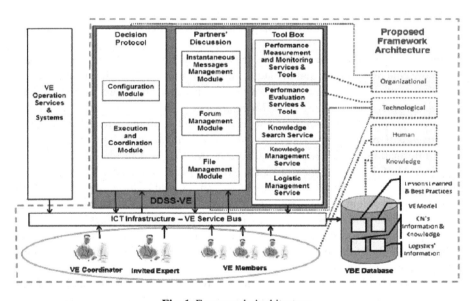

**Fig. 1.** Framework Architecture

The decision protocol reflects the vision that sees a VE as a *project*, regarding that a project consists of a temporary effort to create a product or a unique service [11]. As such, managers can have a support from project management reference models.

A number of project reference models were deeply evaluated and it was realized that most of them are not adequate at all to cope with the intrinsic dynamics of VEs, where changes and uniqueness are a routine and not an exception, besides the fact that VEs are often short-term projects. ECM (*Engineering Change Management*) [12] was the one considered as the most adequate model, defining the phases of identification of a need of change, the proposal of a change, its planning and its effective final implementation.

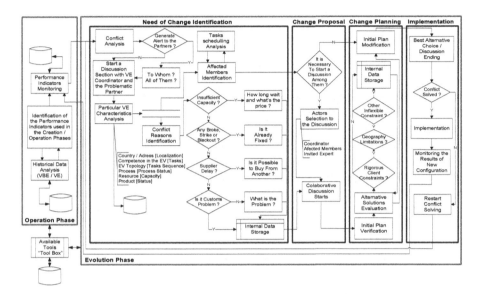

**Fig. 2.** Basis Protocol for the VE Evolution Management

## 4    Prototype Implementation

Partners Discussion Environment supports functionalities for argumentation, which were adapted from HERMES system [13]. Yet, it helps partners in finding consensus on topics of discussion (essentially via comparing alternatives to solve problems, checking the impact of proposed solutions at each member, and voting), whose functionalities were adapted from DELPHI method [14]. In general, these adaptations had the aim of supporting partners' autonomy and transparency as well as of providing a more structured way of deciding (via the decision protocol).

The decision protocol helps managers to follow general actions (according the ECM model) at the right moment in the decision making process.

The Toolbox was populated with a tool for capacity planning, which uses dashboards to support performance evaluation. The protocol was modeled in BPMN / BPM environment and its 'decision blocks' (based on ECM) were implemented as *web services*. The whole decision support environment was implemented in a web portal, on top of *Liferay* web application server (www.liferay.com).

## 4.1    Decision Protocol

Once started the decision-making environment (i.e. once a problem is detected at VE operation phase), the decision protocol appears to each invited participant as a sequence of instructions to be done. These instruction are general steps (from ECM) to guide a more or less free discussion about a problem among the affected VE members. The protocol can be customized for particular cases when a VE is created or can be generally instantiated for the whole VBE, i.e. valid for all VEs.

## 4.2    Partners' Discussion

Considering that the decision protocol has already passed through the phase "Need of Change Identification" (see Figure 2), figure 3 generally illustrates how the discussion would proceed when trying to solve a conflict from the protocol's phase "Change Proposal" on. In this example, four partners from different countries would be involved: the VE Coordinator (*Mr. Ricardo*) has concluded that it is necessary to start a discussion with two members (*Mr. Marcus* and *Mr. Rui*) due to a problem detected in the specification of the  first  allotment related to  the  development of a new helmet style for racing. After starting the collaborative discussion, the protocol enters in the "Changing Planning" phase of the protocol (Figure 2) where different scenarios are evaluated using tools from the toolbox. "Changing Planning" phase ends when the most suitable alternative is chosen in the "Implementation" phase, where the new VE plan is settled and then the VE goes back to the Operation phase.

**Fig. 3.** Some snapshots of the Partner's Discussion Environment

### 4.3    Evaluation Tool for Decision Making

In order to offer a tool for previous evaluation of the decision impact using performance evaluation methods, a specific module was developed. The performance indicators were mostly based on the SCOR model [15]. This tool uses different spreadsheets, containing dashboards that offer the possibility to see each partner's competence, production scheduling, available resources, amount of resources, etc., to consider each partner's task schedule to calculate scenarios for solving the problem under discussion within the DDSS-VE. Figure 4 shows the developed *dashboard.*

For the decision model evaluation and considering the exploratory nature of this research, the system was tested within a controlled environment (in a lab-scale), where some near-real problems were introduced related to some hypothetical VEs using reference information models. Discussions were then simulated in an asynchronous way, with a number of invited users distributed over a set of computers in a local network. The prototype and protocol were executed properly and users could realize the more agility the whole framework provided. Besides that, the system and model were carefully presented to a group of experts in the area, both from academia and companies. After this, an evaluation questionnaire was distributed to them. In general, they all agreed that the proposal has the potential to provide more transparency, quality, agility and confidence in decision-making in a VE scenario.

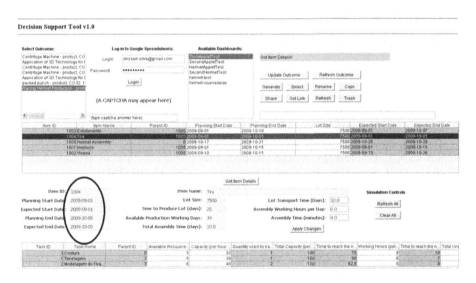

**Fig. 4.** Evaluation Scenarios Tool using Dashboards for Tasks Rescheduling

## 5    Conclusions

This paper has presented final results of a research on an integrated model to support collaborative decision-making among VE members for solving problems during the VE evolution phase. The model combines a decision protocol and a distributed and collaborative decision support framework and system. It has been designed to cope with VE requirements, in particular in what members' autonomy and decision transparency is concerned, including some governance and impact analysis.

Discussions are driven by a decision protocol and it is semi-automated by a system. This means that managers' experience and knowledge are preserved in order to reach a feasible solution for the given problem while their macro actions are guided by a protocol that help them to keep focused on the main issues about the problem, having the ECM project management model as the basis for.

The results have showed that supporting partners' autonomy, Internet-based decentralized decision-making, voting and transparency have effectively worked out in a controlled environment. During the discussions, selected partners could have access to the problem, could freely exchange opinions about how to solve it, and could express their preferences via voting. This guaranteed that the solution emerged from the collaboration and trust among partners. The decision protocol drove participants to take actions at the right moment.

Considering the limitations and assumptions applied to this research, it was possible to conclude that a framework like that has the potential to enhance: the agility in decision-making (discussions tends to flow more straight-forwarded as they are guided by a protocol that is based on project management models); the quality in the decisions (as information is obtained on-line and partners can check the impact of possible solutions at their companies); and that partners were more confident in sharing information about problems as long as the environment preserved their autonomy and they could expose their opinions and further voting.

# References

1. Camarinha-Matos, L.M., Afsarmanesh, H., Ollus, M.: ECOLEAD: A Holistic Approach to Creation and Management of Dynamic Virtual Organizations. In: Collab. Networks and Their Breeding Environments, pp. 3–16. Springer (2005)
2. Rabelo, R.J., Pereira-Klen, A.A., Klen, E.R.: Effective management of dynamic supply chains. Int. J. Networking and Virtual Organisations 2(3), 193–208 (2004)
3. Drissen-Silva, M.V., Rabelo, R.J.: A Collaborative Decision Support Framework for Managing the Evolution of Virtual Enterprises. International Journal of Production Research 47(17), 4833–4854 (2009)
4. Camarinha-Matos, L.M., Afsarmanesh, H.: Collaborative Networked Organizations – A Research Agenda for Emerging Business Models, pp. 3–16. Kluwer, United States (2004)
5. Bostrom, R., Anson, R., Clawson, V.: Group facilitation and group support systems. Group Support Systems: New Perspectives. Ed. Macmillan (2003)
6. Rabelo, R.J., Pereira-Klen, A.A.: A Multi-agent System for Smart Co-ordination of Dynamic Supply Chains. In: Proceedings PRO-VE 2002, pp. 312–319 (2002)
7. Hodík, J., Stach, J.: Virtual Organization Simulation for Operational Management. In: IEEE CSM Int. Conf. on Distributed Human-Machine Systems (2008) ISBN 978-80-01-04027
8. Negretto, H., Hodik, J., Král, L., Mulder, W., Ollus, M., Pondrelli, L., Westphal, I.: VO Management Solutions: VO Management e-Services. In: Methods and Tools for Collaboration, pp. 257–274. Springer, Boston (2008)

9. Noran, O.: A Decision Support Framework for Collaborative Networks. In: Establishing the Foundation of Collaborative Networks, pp. 83–90. Springer (2007)
10. Turban, E., Aronson, J.: Decision support systems and intelligent systems. A Simon and Schuster Company, Upper Saddle River (1998)
11. PMBOK.: A Guide to the Project Management Body of Knowledge (2004).
12. Tavčar, J., Duhovnik, J.: Engineering change management in individual and mass production. Robotics and Computer-Integrated Manufacturing 21(3), 205–215 (2005)
13. Karacapilidis, N., Papadias, D.: Computer supported argumentation and collaborative decision making: the HERMES system. Information Systems 26(4), 259–277 (2001)
14. Dalkey, N.C., Helmer, O.: An experimental application of the Delphi method to the case of experts. Management Science 9, 458–467 (1963)
15. SCOR, http://supply-chain.org/

# 22

## Risk, Governance, Trust

# A Governance Framework for Mitigating Risks and Uncertainty in Collaborative Business Processes[*]

Ziyi Su, Frédérique Biennier, and Wendpanga Francis Ouedraogo

LIRIS, CNRS, INSA-Lyon, University of Lyon, 20, Avenue Albert Einstein,
69621 cedex Lyon, France
{ziyi.su,frederique.biennier,
wendpanga-francis.ouedraogo}@insa-lyon.fr

**Abstract.** The development of collaborative business process relies mostly on software services spanning multiple organizations. Therefore, uncertainty related to the shared assets and risks of Intellectual Property infringement form major concerns and hamper the development of inter-enterprise collaboration. This paper proposes a governance framework to enhance trust and assurance in such collaborative context, coping with the impacts of Cloud infrastructure. First, a collaborative security requirements engineering approach analyzes assets sharing relations in business process, to identify risks and uncertainties and, therefore, elicits partners' security requirements and profiles. Then, a 'due usage' aware policy model supports negotiation between asset provider's requirements and consumer's profiles. The enforcement mechanism adapts to dynamic business processes and Cloud infrastructures to provide end-to-end protection on shared assets.

**Keywords:** End-to-end security, governance, framework, policy, risk and uncertainty, collaborative business process.

## 1 Introduction

With the development of knowledge and service economy, enterprises focus more on their core business while building business federation strategy to provide a better service for their clients. Accordingly, corporate Information Systems are developing toward collaborative paradigm, using different software components. This allows new opportunities for business development, taking advantage of new computing paradigm as Service Oriented Architecture and Cloud Computing. These phenomena suggest a collaborative IT-based service ecosystem trend, where enterprises use the dynamic organization offered by service composition to set flexible business processes and enhance enterprise assets value.

Nevertheless, security risks and uncertainty related to the intellectual property due to shared assets are seen as a major challenge for enterprises to participate in

---

[*] This work was partially supported by ANR project 'semeuse' and GDCIS project 'process 2.0'.

L.M. Camarinha-Matos, L. Xu, and H. Afsarmanesh (Eds.): PRO-VE 2012, IFIP AICT 380, pp. 667–674, 2012.
© IFIP International Federation for Information Processing 2012

collaborative business process [1]. Security engineering in such complex and dynamic collaborative contexts should offer end-to-end security governance concerning partners' shared assets value. This involves a multi-layered viewpoint ranging from security requirements engineering phase to security configuration and enforcement phases, paying attention to the challenges of interoperability and virtualization which stem from collaborative IT infrastructure.

After presenting the context and related work in section 2, we present our security governance framework (section 3). Built as a security policy generation and combination, our solution can enhance trust and assurance in the virtual-enterprise level collaboration context as security requirements and usage control can be used to select the convenient partners. Moreover, the 'due usage control' monitoring module [2] continuously regulates consumers operations upon assets so that shared assets (data or services) can get a life-long consistent protection in a dynamic environment.

## 2     Context and Related Work

Security engineering in a collaborative context is a multi-folded task among business process model and analysis, risks assessment and management, collaborative authorization and virtualization-aware security auditing. After presenting the IS context and risk analysis and management methods, we focus on the implementation level, paying attention to security policy and to cloud security particular models.

### 2.1     Security Requirements Identification

Recent years have seen the development of many Information System-based business process engineering methods, such as the activity-oriented, product-oriented, decision-oriented, context-oriented and strategy-oriented process meta-models that can be selected and combined [3]. To cope with interoperability constraints involved by collaborative / federated business development, standardized modeling languages can also be used [4]. However, few attentions are paid on the risks related to information assets (i.e. service and information) shared beyond security administrative domains, which are major barriers for the development of collaborative business process [1].

Of course, several methods and standards have been defined since the 1980s to capture security requirements / identify vulnerabilities and risks:

- Evaluation criteria used to certify software / hardware components have been defined as the DoD Rainbow series in the 80s or the EEC ITSEC standard in the 90s, both of them integrated in the international Common Criteria standard.
- Risks analysis can be guided by different methodologies either focusing on "standard criteria" (as the French Information System Security Agency for the EBIOS method), on particular infrastructure vulnerabilities (for example the CERT OCTAVE method focuses on the network elements) or by integrating Business Process and resources organizations (as the CERT SNA or the french

CLUSIF (federation of IS managers) MEHARI methods which pay attention on the BP organization as identified as major risks by the ISO/IEC 17799, ISO/IEC27002.

Table 1 presents a comparison of these methods used to identify risk and countermeasures in a rather "fixed" environment. Nevertheless, the dynamic context of service based collaborative organization involves an end-to-end protection on shared asset value and re-funding this security evaluation according to usage and protection agreement signed between partners. In former work, we have proposed an asset sharing relation analysis method to deal with such security concerns, i.e. extract enterprises' security requirements adapted to business federation strategy [5]. Other researchers focus more on the collaborative security engineering thoughts and explore toward secured business processes [6].

**Table 1.** Comparison of some security methods

|        | Requirements analysis | Design | Implementation |
|--------|------------------------|--------|----------------|
| EBIOS  | Text risk and objectives Identifications | Protection pattern | |
| OCTAVE | Structured information access identification | Objectives prioritization Best practices | Audit and implementation project management |
| SNA    | Process and resources workflow identification | "Survival process" design | CERT attacks information and knowledge base |
| MEHARI | Shortened risk analysis | Best practices | Implementation project management |

Based on such thoughts, we propose a structured approach to identify enterprises' security requirements on asset sharing process in business federation. The requirements can then be expressed by a flexible policy model [7] and be used to support security negotiation between enterprises, given that interoperability is achieved using shared domain knowledge reference.

## 2.2   Implementing a Secured Environment

As far as collaborative organizations are concerned, interoperability constraints often lead to use de-facto IS standards as web services. Many researchers use policy-based models to protect information assets originators' intellectual property in collaborative context [8] [9]. Based on this strategy, we use an expressive policy model that accommodates the factors related to the asset 'usage' operations and security profiles of the consumer, the shared asset, the IT-infrastructure, context and environment [7]. Such model allows a peer-to-peer security configuration of the collaborative context. Furthermore, extensions can still be made to use it to govern the QoS and QoP (quality of protection) of the collaborative context. The enforcement of such policy decisions ensures the end-to-end protection of shared assets. Nevertheless, the monitoring mechanism must cope with the software / hardware infrastructure. software virtualizations in cloud-based collaborative computing systems.

To cope with the scalability, interoperability and agility required in federated collaborative organizations, Cloud computing based solutions are more and more used. Cloud computing relies on software virtualizations to offer flexible service outsourcing models, i.e. IaaS, PaaS, SaaS, etc. The benefits are mostly related to the reduced costs for IS investment for enterprises and scalable IS upgrading, as well as dynamic choosing of service providers. As to security, the impacts are two-pronged. Positive impacts are mostly due to that the Cloud providers more visible security profiles for customers [10]. Nevertheless, more concerns are related to the negative impacts [11]. Therefore, most recently researchers start to investigate the end-to-end security and have brought forward some solution for trustworthy Cloud virtualizations [12] and auditing [13]. Although very few, these achievements shed light on how transparent security across virtualizations can be achieved. Following this track, we can build a security monitoring and auditing framework adapting to collaborative cloud infrastructure.

## 3     Security Governance Framework Organisation

The foundation of our framework (see fig. 1) includes a collaboration-oriented security requirements engineering method and a domain knowledge base to define partners' security policies and profiles with. Coupled with a negotiation strategy between the policies and profiles, as well as enforcement of decisions, end-to-end protection for assets can be achieved.

**Fig. 1.** Framework overview

Fig. 2 shows detail information of our framework. Collaboration-oriented security requirements engineering includes the security requirement/profile identification and common business goal extraction methods. According to these methods, enterprises' 'RoP' and QoP are extracted. These protection level information (regarding both requirements and protection offer profiles) can be used to define a security-aware business process. Interoperability among enterprises knowledge references is supported thanks to a domain knowledge base. Dedicated information repositories maintain the knowledge base and RoPs/QoPs policies. Negotiation between partners' RoPs and QoPs ensures that providers' requirements must be fulfilled by consumers' security profiles for a collaborative business process to succeed. Enforcement mechanism assures that asset 'due usage control' [2] is achieved, even on a cloud infrastructure.

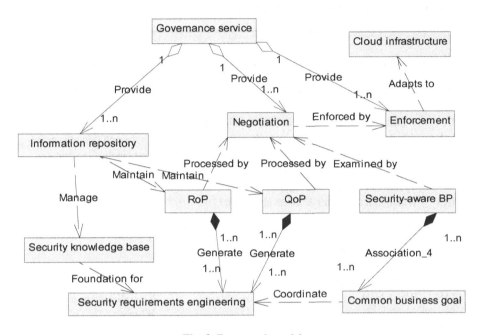

**Fig. 2.** Framework model

### 3.1    Collaboration-Oriented Security Requirements Engineering

Security engineering in collaborative context can be done in either a top-down or bottom-up way. The former suits the scenarios where one checks whether a business process can be carried out or not, w.r.t. the security aspects of participants and the context. The later is adapted to more dynamic scenarios where enterprises want to firstly define their RoPs and QoPs before leveraging this information to select partners for business federation. The engineering process focuses on the assets value of each enterprise that are going to be shared, with an iterative spiral process, as in SNA and GEM [14], to achieve more precise extraction of security factors. In each iteration, we focus on the enterprise IS infrastructure and internal business process, the assets involved, the exposed functionalities and shared assets as the enterprise opens its IS. This leads to paying attention on the risks and uncertainties brought or made grave by such openness. Table 2 shows examples of some questions that are used for the risk assessment and what security factors the answers should declare.

These questions are generic and used to guide a cycle of the iterative assessment. Some question are decomposed into more detailed question lists or forms for the information officer and personnel to be investigated with (detail discussion will be give in separate paper). In this way, risks of information compromise or misuse associated to each software stack layer of the virtual-enterprise IS infrastructure, as well as lost due to the uncertainty related to dynamic business process are identified.

**Table 2.** Comparison of some security methods

| Security goal | Questions | Answers |
|---|---|---|
| | *IS & assets questions* | |
| - | Which functionalities & assets? | List of information assets and functionalities |
| CIAN | Which security goal on these functionalities & assets? | CIAN |
| CIAN | Which security/assurance mechanisms on these functionalities & assets? | Hardware/OS/platform/network/application/human level mechanisms |
| | *Openness & assets sharing questions* | |
| CIAN | Which functionalities & assets are shared? | List of information assets and functionalities |
| N | Shared with which partners? | 'pre-difined'/ random |
| | *Risks & compensation questions* | |
| CIAN | Which security/assurance mechanisms negatively affected by the openness? | List of mechanisms |
| CIAN | Which level the negative effects have achieve? | Neutralize/damage/ineffect at times |
| CIAN | Which level of compensentation you want to have? | Total restore/partial restore |
| CIAN | Whaich security level should be achieved after the compensentation? | C/I/A/N |
| CIAN | Should these security level be maintained by partners or collaboration system? | Partner/system |
| - | Any other requirements on partners? | - |
| - | Any other requirements for the collaboration system? | - |

*Legend:    C (Confidentiality), I (integrity), A (Availability), N (Non repudiation)*

## 3.2    Policy-Based Security Configuration

The RoP and QoP can be expressed by a 'usage control' policy model (see fig. 3), which expresses the 'usage' rights upon the assets, obligations and conditions which includes security factors related to the assets (i.e. OAT), consumers (i.e. SAT) and collaboration context (i.e. CNAT).

Security configuration of the context is done by assuring that partners related by asset sharing relations have compatible security profiles. Furthermore, a 'standardized' knowledge based can be built to collect the most common security factors, whereas

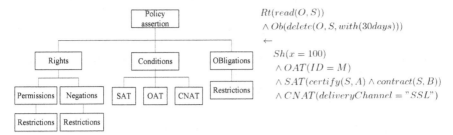

**Fig. 3.** The context-aware security policy model and a sample policy in concise syntax

enterprises can develop from it their domain knowledge references. A 'consensus based voting' [15] protocol can be used to ensure that, for the enterprises in a same context, the developed knowledge references are compatible among them.

### 3.3    'Usage' Aware Monitoring

The monitoring mechanism inspects consumers 'usage' operations on assets and make sure that providers RoPs are respected. It must be adapted to the Cloud virtualization environments enterprises are moving towards. Positive impact of the Cloud computing paradigm is that enterprises security profiles, to a great extent decided by the security profile of Cloud providers, are more visible to partners. Nevertheless the virtualization segregation between software stack layers makes the task of auditing system events more tricky. To fit with the multi-tenancy scenarios (e.g. a combined Cloud infrastructure with IaaS, PaaS, SaaS from different providers), 'usage' monitors are set at each layer.

The inspection of asset usage operations on consumer system is usually achieved by auditing systems calls or by having a closer look into the system processes, which are conventionally deemed arduous tasks. Nevertheless, very recent research has explored some possible approaches, such as enhanced JAVA runtime platform allowing the auditing of information flows [13], Trust Platform Modula-based attestation [12] for platform integrity. Whereas a great gap still exists between the security concerns for Clouds, we can expect more security-aware Cloud systems, as well as explore toward this goal. Possible approaches will close rely on Trusted Computing technology for trust root of software stack and information flow control technologies for the in-detail auditing. Such auditing, however, might compromise the privacy of Cloud providers. Therefore, trusted third parties, or privacy preserving protocols, should be used, to ensure a security policy compliance examination method without disclosure of partners' inner operations, therefore protecting their trade secrets.

## 4    Conclusion

This paper proposes a governance framework to enhance trust and assurance in virtual-enterprise, coping with the complex and dynamic collaborative business process. Our security governance framework aims at providing comprehensively management on the business operations of organizations in a collaborative process, helping them to clearly identify the risks of intellectual property infringement when their business value flows through the whole virtual-enterprise architecture. In sum, designed in a layered and modular way, our framework could be used in a wide range of industrial inter-organizational business contexts, giving enterprises more grasp of the risks related to the assets they provide, promoting the successes of business federation.

# References

[1] Linda, B.B., Richard, C., Kristin, L., Ric, T., Mark, E.:The evolving role of IT managers and CIOs–findings from the 2010 IBM global IT risk study. Technical report, IBM (2010)

[2] Su, Z., Biennier, F.: An architecture for implementing 'collaborative usage control' policy -toward end-to-end security management in collaborative computing. In: ICEIS 2012 (submitted, 2012)

[3] Hug, C., Front, A., Rieu, D., Henderson-Sellers, B.: A method to build information systems engineering process metamodels. J. Syst. Software. 82(10), 1730–1742 (2009)

[4] Ducq, Y., Chen, D., Vallespir, B.: Interoperability in enterprise modelling: requirements and roadmap. Adv. Eng. Inf. 18(4), 193–203 (2004)

[5] Su, Z., Biennier, F.: Toward comprehensive security policy governance in collaborative enterprise. In: APMS 2011, IFIP WG5.7 (2011)

[6] Maamar, Z., Benslimane, D., Thiran, P., Ghedira, C., Dustdar, S., Sattanathan, S.: Towards a context-based multi-type policy approach for web services composition. Data & Knowledge Engineering 62(2), 327–351 (2007)

[7] Su, Z., Biennier, F.: A collaborative-context oriented policy model for usage-control in business federation. In: 2011 IEEE International Conference on Uncertainty Reasoning and Knowledge Engineering, pp. 201–204 (2011)

[8] Bussard, L., Neven, G., Preiss, F.-S.: Downstream usage control. In: Proc. 11th IEEE International Symposium on Policies for Distributed Systems and Networks, pp. 22–29. IEEE Computer Society, Washington (2010)

[9] Ma, C., Lu, G., Qiu, J.: An authorization model for collaborative access control. Journal of Zhejiang University - Science C 11(9), 699–717 (2010)

[10] Wilson, P.: Positive perspectives on cloud security. Information Security Technical Report 16(3-4), 97–101 (2011)

[11] Jay, H., Mark, N.: Assessing the security risks of Cloud Computing. Technical report, G00157782, Gartner Inc. (2008)

[12] Brown, A., Chase, J.S.: Trusted platform-as-a-service: a foundation for trustworthy cloud-hosted applications. In: Proc. 3rd ACM Workshop on Cloud Computing Security Workshop, pp. 15–20. ACM, New York (2011)

[13] Bacon, J., Evans, D., Eyers, D.M., Migliavacca, M., Pietzuch, P., Shand, B.: Enforcing End-to-End Application Security in the Cloud (Big Ideas Paper). In: Gupta, I., Mascolo, C. (eds.) Middleware 2010. LNCS, vol. 6452, pp. 293–312. Springer, Heidelberg (2010)

[14] Blanc, S., Ducq, Y., Vallespir, B.: Evolution management towards interoperable supply chains using performance measurement. Computers in Industry 58(7), 720–732 (2007)

[15] Rao, P., Lin, D., Bertino, E., Li, N., Lobo, J.: Fine-grained integration of access control policies. Computers & Security 30(2-3), 91–107 (2011)

# Modeling the Trustworthiness of a Supplier Agent in a B2B Relationship

Patrícia Alves[1], Pedro Campos[1,2], and Eugénio Oliveira[3]

[1] LIAAD – Laboratório de Inteligência Artificial e Apoio à Decisão – INESC TEC,
Porto, Portugal
[2] Faculdade de Economia da Universidade do Porto, Portugal
`pcampos@fep.up.pt`
[3] DEI-LIACC – Faculdade de Engenharia da Universidade do Porto, Portugal
`{patricia.alves,eco}@fe.up.pt`

**Abstract.** In life, trust is considered the base of all relationships, including Business-to-Business (B2B) relationships. The selection of a supplier depends not only on its reputation and the costs involved, but also on its trustworthiness and other factors. But how can the trustworthiness of a supplier be measured? What are the factors that influence the supplier's trustworthiness, i.e., what are the relevant factors of trust in the selection of a supplier in a B2B relationship? Answers to these questions will help model the supplier agents' behavior in the multi-agent ANTE platform. In this paper we propose to consider fifteen attributes to measure the trustworthiness of a supplier as a conceptual model of trust, coming out of a combination of several determinants gathered from the literature review. Raw data was gathered by sending a questionnaire to a set of firms from different industrial sectors. The results support part of the proposed determinants, introducing new determinants of trust that resulted from exploratory factor analysis and a new model obtained from confirmatory factor analysis. With this, two possible multi-attribute supplier agents can be modeled. This paper discusses the results and limitations of this study and proposes suggestions for future work.

**Keywords:** B2B relationships, Trust, Trustworthiness, Trustworthiness determinants/attributes.

## 1    Introduction

To engage on a B2B relationship it is important to know the other party, or the risks involved and vulnerability can be quite high. What can be important for the relationship to work successfully and to both parties be satisfied with the contracts made? These questions arise in the sequence of the multi-agent ANTE[1] platform described in [1], that works as an Electronic Institution, where interactions between the buyers and suppliers arise, leading to the emergence of collaborative networks. In

---

[1] Agreement Negotiation in Normative and Trust-enabled Environments.

L.M. Camarinha-Matos, L. Xu, and H. Afsarmanesh (Eds.): PRO-VE 2012, IFIP AICT 380, pp. 675–686, 2012.
© IFIP International Federation for Information Processing 2012

this platform the buyer agents select the best proposals by weighting up the utility associated to each proposal with the trustworthiness of the supplier agent [2]. But what is trustworthiness? How can the trustworthiness of a supplier agent be determined and measured? What are the factors that determine if a supplier is trustworthy or not? These questions led to the need for researching and determining the attributes that can measure the trustworthiness of a supplier and help model the agent's behavior in the system.

Why focus on interorganizational trust? In life, trust is considered the base of all relationships and as Pavlou [3] says, has been associated with successful buyer-supplier relationships [4, 5, 6, 7, 8, 9] and desirable outcomes such as competitive advantage [4, 9], performance, conflict and opportunism reduction [8, 9], and satisfaction [7, 9], leading to the continuity of the relationship [3]. Furthermore, trusting relationships are likely to have lower transaction costs because incomplete contracts are sufficient for running the exchange relationship [9]. Like Doney et al. [10] say, "trust takes on even greater importance in the arena of B2B services as buyers face the complexity of examining many intangible aspects of a service firm's offering". Thus, undoubtedly trust has an important role in the B2B relationships (interorganizational trust) and therefore, in the selection of the suppliers.

So, what is trust? There is no consensus on an universal definition of trust since the relevant context affects its actual meaning, resulting in a large number of definitions [3, 11]. But like Castelfranchi and Falcone [12] say, all definitions go back to the "same layered notion, used to refer to several different (although interrelated) meanings". Given two individuals X and Y: (a) "in its basic sense, trust is just a mental and affective attitude or disposition towards Y involving two basic types of beliefs: evaluations and expectations"; (b) "in its richer use, trust is a decision and intention based on that disposition"; (c) "as well as the act of relying upon Y's expected behavior"; (d) "and the consequent social relation established between X and Y". Ganesan [9] also supported this definition earlier. Therefore the basic concept of trust is cognitive related. But for interorganizational trust, the cognitive part of trust is not enough. Considering X the buyer, X cannot just rely upon his beliefs[2] on Y (the supplier) to make a transaction, which would be very naïve and risky. Thus, some characteristics of Y need to be known by X, so he can say that he trusts Y, i.e., that Y is trustworthy. So, we decided to find these characteristics and engage on a quest for the determinants of the trustworthiness of a supplier in B2B relationship, so the computational agent, whose role is a supplier, can be modeled in the multi-agent system more accurately, providing better and more solid contracts and transactions, making the system more realistic. Exploratory and Confirmatory Factor Analysis (EFA and CFA, respectively) were used in order to confirm the adequacy of the conceptual model of trust.

The rest of this paper is organized as follows: the next section provides a review on the most relevant literature on trust in a B2B relationship and describes the proposed

---

[2] Or familiarity, because as stated by [3], "e-commerce brings together a massive number of parties with no familiarity and cultural similarities".

model. Section 3 exposes the research methodology and reports the results. In Section 4 some conclusions and suggestions for future work are taken.

## 2     Literature Review and Proposed Conceptual Model

There is a wide variety of papers on trust and in many areas that as far as we can tell, go back to the 1950s [13]: psychology, sociology, economics and marketing, and a lot of research has been made on trust in a B2B relationship. Many of the papers found are of great relevance and many can complement each other giving their contribution for the determinants of trust, but unfortunately, not all can be referenced here. So, only the ones considered more relevant are reviewed in this paper.

In 1994, Ganesan [9] affirmed that so far, researchers in marketing have wrongly treated trust as an unidimensional variable, stating that research in interpersonal trust has shown that trust is a multidimensional variable, identifying two distinct dimensions: credibility and benevolence. "Simply put, the credibility dimension refers to intentions of cooperative behavior that results from making opportunism costly or irrational, while the benevolence dimension is a trust expectation that results from goodwill that firms will not act opportunistically, even given the chance" [3]. Therefore, Ganesan proposed a model suggesting the reputation of the vendor, the retailer's satisfaction with previous outcomes, the retailer's experience with a vendor and the retailer's perception of vendor transaction-specific investments, as the antecedents of trust.

In 1997, Doney and Cannon [6] concluded that the supplier's size, the supplier's willingness to customize and trust on the supplier's salesperson have a positive impact on the buyer's trust, but that the supplier's willingness to share confidential information and length of the relationship are unrelated to the buyer's trust on the supplier.

A year after, Sako and Helper [14] also conducted a study to find the determinants of trust in supplier relations: "The conditions which facilitated the creation and sustenance of trust - and the containing of opportunism - were found to include long-term commitment, information exchange, technical assistance, and customer reputation."

Later in 2002, and according to his revision on several authors, including [6, 9, 14, 15, 16, 17], Pavlou [3] also summarized interorganizational trust in two great dimensions: credibility and benevolence. These two dimensions cannot be measured directly (latent or unobserved variables) and so they depend on other variables that can be measured directly (observed variables, factors or constructs). Therefore, [3] proposes five constructs that can positively influence the trust in the suppliers: perceived monitoring, perceived accreditation, perceived legal bonds, perceived feedback and cooperative norms.

Some years after, in 2005, Gounaris [18] suggests that the degree of trust between the supplier and the buyer is directly influenced by the quality of the service and by the bonding strategy and techniques of the provider.

So, with all this information and because of limitations in previous works, we decided to propose a different and more complete model that gathers the determinants we considered more important from all the analyzed papers, and that is described next.

## 2.1    The Trustworthiness of a Supplier: Conceptual Model

Considering the reviewed literature, we found that the papers by themselves were somehow incomplete, but that together, they could complement each other, giving a better insight of the possible attributes (or constructs, determinants) for modeling the trustworthiness of a supplier agent. Therefore, we propose the following model, depicted in Figure 1.

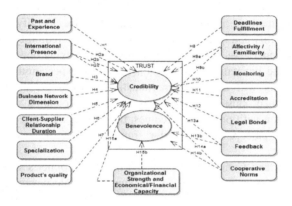

**Fig. 1.** Determinants of the trustworthiness of a supplier: conceptual model

Next, we shortly describe the proposed attributes and the several hypotheses to be tested in order to verify their impact on trust formation.

**Past and Experience (*PastExpX*[3]).** Trustworthiness is related to the supplier's role and behavior at present, and actions it has performed and events it has caused in the past [19], portfolio [20] and prior experience [3, 21]. Formally stated:

H1: Past and experience positively influences the supplier's trustworthiness in terms of credibility.

**International Presence (*InterX*).** Sako [14] shows that interorganizational trust varies according to the continent and country. Formally stated:

H2a: The production country of the supplier influences the supplier's trustworthiness in terms of credibility.

---

[3] Item name, where X is the number of the corresponding question in the questionnaire (section 3.1).

H2b: The origin country of the supplier influences the supplier's trustworthiness in terms of credibility.

H2c: The presence of the supplier in several countries positively influences the supplier's trustworthiness in terms of credibility.

**Brand (*BrandX*).** Consumers try to reduce risks by using well-known brands, and that brands provide guarantees about quality and security [22, 23, 24]. According to [25], [26] "demonstrate that trust plays an important role in the brand domain in that they link (brand) trust to brand performance through brand loyalty" [27]. Formally stated:

H3: The supplier product's brand positively influences the supplier's trustworthiness in terms of credibility.

**Business Network Dimension (*DimX*).** Several enterprises, specially small and medium enterprises, decide to get involved in a larger business network in order to increase their own opportunities of business. This was suggested by several researchers in our research lab, and so, we decided to test if this is an influent factor. Formally stated:

H4: The supplier's business network dimension positively influences the supplier's trustworthiness in terms of credibility.

**Buyer-Supplier Relationships Duration (*DurX*).** The historical duration and experience of a relationship is considered of great importance [14, 28]. "Most researchers agree that trust develops and builds over time" [6]. Satisfied buyers stay with the same supplier [25]. Formally stated:

H5: The buyer-supplier relationships duration positively influences the supplier's trustworthiness in terms of credibility.

**Specialization (*SpecX*).** The adaptation of the supplier's production processes to meet the buyer's needs and the use of specialized equipment are considered investments in the relationship [6]. Formally stated:

H6: The supplier's specialization positively influences the supplier's trustworthiness in terms of credibility.

**Product's Quality (*QualityX*).** The quality of the produced products can be a measure of the suppliers' credibility, since they dedicate more effort in the production of better products to satisfy the buyers and sell more [19]. Formally stated:

H7: The products' quality positively influences the supplier's trustworthiness in terms of credibility.

**Deadlines Fulfillment (*DFullX*).** A higher trustworthiness is associated to all the suppliers that were capable of increasing the deliveries frequency without additional costs [14]. It is also important to know when the product will be delivered [20], and [19] propose the adherence to delivery dates to evaluate trust. Formally stated:

H8: The deadlines fulfillment positively influences the supplier's trustworthiness in terms of credibility.

**Affectivity/Familiarity** (*AfectX*). Familiarity and repeated interaction create trust [3, 29, 30, 31]. Zucker [21] argues that trust generated through familiarity and prior experience is probably the most important way of building trust. Formally stated:

H9a: Familiarity with the supplier positively influences the supplier's trustworthiness in terms of benevolence.

H9b: Affectivity towards the supplier positively influences the supplier's trustworthiness in terms of benevolence.

**Monitoring** (*MonitX*). According to [3, 19, 32], monitoring encourages responsible behaviors, and is used to confirm if the transactions are taken according to the quality, delivery and performance standards. Formally stated:

H10: Monitoring processes positively influences the supplier's trustworthiness in terms of credibility.

**Accreditation** (*AccreditX*). When carried out by an independent authority, accreditation can be a reliable way of assessing the competence of an organization [3]. Formally stated:

H11: Supplier's accreditation positively influences the supplier's trustworthiness in terms of credibility.

**Legal Bonds** (*VinculX*). Legal bonds are defined as legitimate contracts that manage the economical activity and have been widely proposed as a mechanism to reduce opportunism and promote trust [3, 14]. Formally stated:

H12: Legal bonds positively influence the supplier's trustworthiness in terms of credibility.

**Feedback** (*FbX*). Feedback mechanisms collect and disseminate information about the organizations behavior in past transactions [3], and have been represented as structural assurances that discourage opportunism and engender credibility in online marketplaces [33], providing a signal of good reputation [34], and information about the suppliers' "values, principles and signs of benevolent intentions through buyers' feedback comments" [20, 35]. Formally stated:

H13a: Feedback positively influences the supplier's trustworthiness in terms of credibility.

H13b: Feedback positively influences the supplier's trustworthiness in terms of benevolence.

**Cooperative Norms** (*CoopX*). "Cooperative norms are defined as values, standards and principles to which a population of organizations adheres" [3]. Values and norms discourage opportunism, facilitate cooperation, promote joint problem solving [19, 36] and reduce costs and innovate production and management methods [14]. Formally stated:

H14a: Cooperative norms positively influence the supplier's trustworthiness in terms of credibility.

H14b: Cooperative norms positively influence the supplier's trustworthiness in terms of benevolence.

**Organizational Strength and Economical/Financial Capacity (*StCapacX*).** [19] consider the size, coverage, competences and personnel expertise, its physical, social and operational capital, and the cash in/cash out as base criteria for the evaluation of trust. The overall size of the supplier and its market share position indicate that many other businesses trust this supplier enough to do business with it [6]. Formally stated:

H15a: Organizational strength positively influences the supplier's trustworthiness in terms of credibility.

H15b: Economical/Financial capacity positively influences the supplier's trustworthiness in terms of credibility.

# 3    Methodology and Results

## 3.1    Sample Definition and Data Collection

In Management and Economics, empirical data is frequently used as a way to measure the validity of theoretical hypothesis. Therefore, to adequate the proposed model to reality, we conducted a questionnaire to determine which attributes are most important for the trustworthiness of the suppliers in a B2B relationship. The questionnaire was sent to 1126 firms in Portugal (from different industrial sectors), selected from the SABI (Iberian Balances Analysis System) firms database [37]. The number of obtained (and valid) responses was 127 (a 13% response rate).

The questionnaire was composed of a set of questions (31 items) to help measure the importance of each one of the proposed determinants, based on a five-point Likert scale. Some of the questions were adapted from [3, 9, 14, 18]. Another question was also made, where the respondents were asked to select a set of terms that they considered most important for the business regarding the suppliers.

## 3.2    Results

In order to analyze the collected data in terms of descriptive statistics, IBM® SPSS® Statistics 20 was used. As a first analysis, the determinants that correspond to the items with a high response rate are shown in Table 1, column A. Column B represents the terms the respondents selected as the most important for the selection of their suppliers. As can be seen in Table 1, all the chosen terms (B) are part of the most scored determinants (A).

**Exploratory Factor Analysis.** As a first step for the hypothesis testing and determinants validation, an EFA was conducted. This is a traditional and the most

**Table 1.** A - Determinants that correspond to ~67% or more of the answers. B - Terms the respondents selected as the most important for the selection of their suppliers (response rate equal or superior to 50%).

| | A | | B | |
|---|---|---|---|---|
| | Determinant | Response rate, % | Determinant | Response rate, % |
| 1 | Feedback | 97 | Delivery deadlines fulfillment | 92 |
| 2 | Credibility | 95 | Honesty | 82 |
| 3 | Benevolence | 95 | Cooperation | 82 |
| 4 | Cooperation | 85 | Professionalism | 76 |
| 5 | Accreditation | 84 | Quality control of end product | 70 |
| 6 | Duration of buyer-supplier relationship | 80 | Promises fulfillment | 65 |
| 7 | Past and experience | 75 | Compliance with ISO standards | 54 |
| 8 | Quality | 64 | Accreditation | 52 |

frequent kind of analysis [38], aiming to reduce the number of variables, where all the unobserved variables (attributes) can reflect in all the observed variables (items). Table 2 shows the rotation matrix obtained after the last run, resulting in 15 items (from the initial 31). As expected, the EFA showed the existence of a correlation between items from different determinants, as can be seen in Table 2. With this analysis, only five components (C1 to C5) could be extracted, two of which (C1 and C2) did not correspond to the proposed attributes, i.e., the 15 proposed attributes, referred in section 2.1, were significantly reduced to five. This brought a new vision of the model and the need to define a name for the two new attributes. Table 3 shows the names proposed for the five components (based on the corresponding items in the matrix) and Figure 2 the new proposed model (based on the EFA carried out).

**Confirmatory Factor Analysis.** To confirm if the five components were responsible for the behavior of the 15 items, a CFA was conducted on the extracted items and components (using IBM® SPSS® Amos20). The model revealed a tolerable goodness of fit ($X^2/df = 1.925$; CFI = 0.901; GFI = 0.864; RMSEA = 0.086; P[rmsea$\leq$0.05] < 0.003), suggesting that the items provide a reasonable fit with the new proposed model (Figure 2). Therefore, the global score (based on the factor score weights[4] calculated by Amos) for the Trustworthiness of the Supplier Agent ($T_{AgS}$), for the analyzed sample, can be calculated according to the following expression:

$$T_{AgS} = 0.036*Coop37 + 0.072*Coop38 + 0.013*Benev42 + 0.008*Fb31 + 0.006*Coop32 + 0.156*Vincul26 + 0.003*Credi40 + 0.049*Fb30 + 0.057*Fb29 + 0.116*Monit22 + 0.061*Monit23 + 0.196*Vincul28 + 0.069*Inter7 + 0.022*Inter8 + 0.005*Dim11 . \tag{1}$$

The items that most contribute for $T_{AgS}$ are the items Vincul26, Monit22 and Vincul28. As can be seen in Figure 2, the amount of information (made) available (C1) has an extreme positive impact on the buyers' trust formation (b = 0.87, p < 0.003), largely supporting part of the initially proposed H12 (legal bonds) and H13 (feedback). The effect of professionalism and commitment (C2) on trust is insignificant, not supporting any of the proposed hypotheses, contrary to the expected. The international presence (C3) has a significant positive impact on the buyer's trust

---

[4] Regression weights for predicting the unobserved variables from the observed variables.

**Table 2.** Rotated component matrix obtained with the exploratory factor analysis

| Item | Vincul28 | Vincul26 | Fb30 | Fb29 | Benev42 | Fb31 | Coop32 | Credi40 | Inter7 | Inter8 | Dim11 | Coop37 | Coop38 | Monit23 | Monit22 |
|---|---|---|---|---|---|---|---|---|---|---|---|---|---|---|---|
| C1 | 0,840 | 0,809 | 0,673 | 0,634 | | | | 0,336 | | | | | | | 0,318 |
| C2 | | | | | 0,855 | 0,810 | 0,800 | 0,613 | | | | | | | |
| C3 | | | | | | | | | 0,895 | 0,874 | 0,636 | | | | |
| C4 | | | 0,315 | | | | | | | | | 0,908 | 0,889 | | |
| C5 | | 0,387 | | | | | | | | | | | | 0,847 | 0,812 |

(leftmost label: Component)

**Table 3.** The proposed new attributes to measure the trustworthiness of a supplier agent

| Extracted Component | New Attribute |
|---|---|
| C1 | Amount of information (made) available |
| C2 | Professionalism and commitment |
| C3 | International presence |
| C4 | Cooperative norms |
| C5 | Audits (monitoring) |

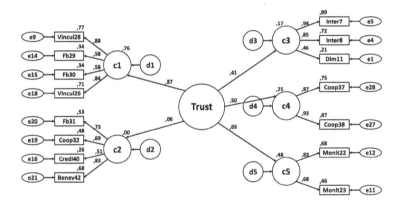

**Fig. 2.** The new proposed model for the determinants of the trustworthiness of a supplier agent, obtained after the exploratory factor analysis

formation, supporting H2. Similarly, the effect of cooperative norms (C4) on trust is significant, greatly supporting H14. Lastly, monitoring (or audits, C5) largely supports H10, having a positive influence on trust.

The implications of the obtained results are discussed in the following section.

## 4    Conclusions and Future Work

With the descriptive statistics analysis of the results, several trends could be derived from the responses, where the majority met the expectations. As a result, the most important attributes that are considered by the firms to determine the trustworthiness of a supplier are: feedback, deadlines fulfillment, cooperative norms, accreditation, buyer-supplier relationship duration (contrary to the results obtained by [6]), past and experience, and product's quality, supporting the hypothesis H13, H8, H14, H11, H5, H1 and H7, respectively. The two greater dimensions of trust, credibility and benevolence, are also supported. Thus, this would allow the modeling of a multi-attribute supplier agent $AgS_x$ (corresponding to the referred supported hypothesis), which is of great relevance for making the ANTE platform more precise and realistic.

The EFA allied to the CFA slightly altered the results, leading to the extraction of only five attributes, two of them different from the originally proposed: amount of information (made) available (C1), professionalism and commitment (C2), international presence (C3), cooperative norms (C4) and monitoring (C5). In spite of the difference, they can be associated to the most important attributes supported by the descriptive statistic analysis and to some of the originally suggested: amount of information (made) available corresponds to the feedback and legal bonds; and professionalism and commitment corresponds to deadlines fulfillment, and also feedback (but these were not supported by the CFA). The international presence extracted attribute suggests that the presence of the supplier in different countries is important for the selection of the supplier. The existence of suppliers in several countries is a signal that they are requested for business by many buyers. The hypothesis H12, H13, H2, H14 and H10, respectively, were therefore supported by the CFA, also allowing the modeling of a multi-attribute supplier agent, $AgS_y$, but with less attributes than $AgS_x$. The $AgS_y$ attributes would therefore be: feedback, legal bonds, international presence, monitoring and cooperative norms, being only the feedback and cooperative norms common to the descriptive statistics supplier agent $AgS_x$.

As future work, and to try to validate the original proposed model directly using CFA, we are going to apply the same questionnaire to a larger sample (the 5000 most selling firms from the manufacturing industry and civil construction subsidized in Portugal) expecting a five-fold increase in the number of responses, and the possibility to better model a multi-attribute supplier agent on the system. It would also be interesting to conduct the questionnaire in other cultures.

As for the multi-agent ANTE platform, after finding the attributes to help model the trustworthiness of a supplier, it would be interesting if the user could model his buyer agent by choosing the weights he would give to each attribute, according to his preferences, in a Visual Analogue Scale (from 0 to 1).

**Acknowledgments.** We would like to thank the important comments of A. P. Rocha, H. L. Cardoso, J. Urbano and H. Martins. This work is financed by the ERDF – European Regional Development Fund ˙ through the COMPETE Programme (operational programme for competitiveness) and by National Funds through the FCT – Fundação para a Ciência e a Tecnologia (Portuguese Foundation for Science and Technology) within project CRN / PTDC/EIA-EIA/104420/2008(FCOMP-01-0124-FEDER-010120).

# References

1. Cardoso, H.L., Urbano, J., Brandão, P., Rocha, A.P., Oliveira, E.: ANTE: Agreement Negotiation in Normative and Trust-Enabled Environments. In: Demazeau, Y., Müller, J.P., Rodríguez, J.M.C., Pérez, J.B., et al. (eds.) Advances on PAAMS. AISC, vol. 155, pp. 261–264. Springer, Heidelberg (2012)

2.  Urbano, J., Rocha, A.P., Oliveira, E.: A Dynamic Agents' Behavior Model for Computational Trust. In: Antunes, L., Pinto, H.S. (eds.) EPIA 2011. LNCS (LNAI), vol. 7026, pp. 536–550. Springer, Heidelberg (2011)
3.  Pavlou, P.A.: Institution-based trust in interorganizational exchange relationships: the role of online B2B marketplaces on trust formation. Journal of Strategic Information Systems 11, 215–243 (2002)
4.  Barney, J.B., Hansen, M.H.: Trustworthiness as a source of competitive advantage. Strategic Management Journal 15, 175–190 (1994)
5.  Bromiley, P., Cummings, L.L.: Transaction Costs in Organizations with Trust. In: Bies, R., Sheppard, B., Lewicki, R. (eds.) Research on Negotiation in Organizations. JAI Press, Greenwich (1995)
6.  Doney, P.M., Cannon, J.P.: An examination of the nature of trust in buyer–seller relationships. Journal of Marketing 61(1), 35–51 (1997)
7.  Geyskens, I., Steenkamp, J.B., Kumar, N.: Generalizations about trust in marketing channel relationships using meta-analysis. International Journal in Marketing 15, 223–248 (1998)
8.  Zaheer, A., McEvily, B., Perrone, V.: Does trust matter? Exploring the effects of interorganizational and interpersonal trust on performance. Organization Science 9(2), 141–159 (1998)
9.  Ganesan, S.: Determinants of long-term orientation in buyer–seller relationships. Journal of Marketing 58(1), 1–19 (1994)
10. Doney, P.M., Barry, J.M., Abratt, R.: Trust determinants and outcomes in global B2B services. European Journal of Marketing 41(9/10), 1096–1116 (2007)
11. Palmer, J.W., Bailey, J.P., Faraj, S.: The role of intermediaries in the development of trust on the www: the use and effectiveness of trusted third parties and privacy statements. Journal of Computer Mediated Communication 5(3) (2000) (online)
12. Castelfranchi, C., Falcone, R.: Trust theory – A Socio-Cognitive and Computational Model. Wiley, United Kingdom (2010)
13. Deutsch, M.: Trust and suspicion. Conflict Resolution 2(4), 265–279 (1958)
14. Sako, M., Helper, S.: Determinants of trust in supplier relations: evidence from the automotive industry in Japan and the United States. Journal of Economic Behavior and Organization 34, 387–417 (1998)
15. Ring, P.S., Van de Ven, A.H.: Structuring cooperative relationships between organizations. Strategic Management Journal 13, 483–498 (1992)
16. Mayer, R.C., Davis, J.H., Schoorman, F.D.: An integrative model of organizational trust. Academy of Management Review 20(3), 709–734 (1995)
17. McKnight, D.H., Chervany, N.L.: What trust means in e-commerce customer relationships: an interdisciplinary conceptual typology. International Journal of Electronic Commerce 6(2), 35–53 (2002)
18. Gounaris, S.P.: Trust and commitment influences on customer retention: insights from business-to-business services. Journal of Business Research 58, 126–140 (2005)
19. Msanjila, S.S., Afsarmanesh, H.: Assessment and Creation of Trust in VBEs. In: Camarinha-Matos, L., Afsarmanesh, H., Ollus, M. (eds.) Network-Centric Collaboration and Supporting Fireworks. IFIP, vol. 224, pp. 161–172. Springer, Boston (2006)
20. Elance Blog: How to review a provider profile (2009), http://www.elance.com/p/blog/how_to_review_a_provider_profile.html[5]

---

[5] Elance is the world's leading platform for online employment that offers instant access to qualified professionals who work online.

21. Zucker, L.: Production of trust: institutional sources of economic structure 1840–1920. Research in Organization Behavior 8(1), 53–111 (1986)
22. Elliott, R., Yannopoulou, N.: The nature of trust in brands: a psychosocial model. European Journal of Marketing 41(9/10), 988–998 (2007)
23. Ring, A., Schriber, M., Horton, R.L.: Some effects of perceived risk on consumer information processing. Journal of Academy of Marketing Science 8(3), 255–263 (1980)
24. Aaker, D.A.: Managing Brand Equity: Capitalizing on the Value of a Brand Name. Free Press, New York (1991)
25. Rauyruen, P., Miller, K.E.: Relationship quality as a predictor of B2B customer loyalty. Journal of Business Research 60, 21–31 (2007)
26. Chaudhuri, A., Holbrook, B.M.: The chain of effects from brand trust and brand affect to brand performance: The role of brand loyalty. Journal of Marketing 65(2), 81–93 (2001)
27. Aaker, D.A.: Building strong brands. Free Press, New York (1996)
28. Sabel, C.F.: Studied trust: building new forms of co-operation in a volatile economy. In: Pyke, F., Sengenberger, W. (eds.) Industrial Districts and Local Economic Regeneration. International Institute for Labour Studies, Geneva (1992)
29. Luhmann, N.: Trust and Power. Wiley, London (1979)
30. Gefen, D.: E-commerce: the role of familiarity and trust. OMEGA 28(6), 725–737 (2000)
31. Gulati, R.: Does familiarity breed trust? The implications of repeated ties for contractual choice in alliances. Academy of Management Journal 38(1), 85–112 (1995)
32. Williamson, O.E.: The economic institutions of capitalism. Free Press, New York (1985)
33. Ba, S., Pavlou, P.A.: Evidence of the effect of trust building technology in electronic markets: price premiums and buyer behavior. MIS Quarterly 26(3), 243–268 (2002)
34. Pavlou, P.A., Ba, S.: Does online reputation matter? An empirical investigation of reputation and trust in online auction markets. In: Proceedings of the 6th Americas Conference in Information Systems, Long Beach, CA, August 3-5 (2000)
35. Pavlou, P.A.: Trustworthiness as a source of competitive advantage in online auction markets. Best Paper Proceedings of the Academy of Management Conference, Denver, Colorado, pp. 9–14 (2002)
36. Axelrod, R.: The Evolution of Cooperation. Basic Books, New York (1984)
37. Dijk, B. v.: Bureau van Dijk Electronic Publishing, Company information in an instant. Nortel Networks, United Kingdom, Westacott Way (2003)
38. Marôco, J.: Análise de Equações Estruturais: Fundamentos teóricos, Software & Aplicações. ReportNumber, Pêro Pinheiro (2010)

# Governance as a Service for Collaborative Environment

Juan Li[1,2], Frédérique Biennier[1,2], and Youssef Amghar[1,2]

[1] Université de Lyon. CNRS
[2] INSA-Lyon. LIRIS. UMR5205, F-69621. France
{juan.li,frederique.biennier,youssef.amghar}@insa-lyon.fr

**Abstract.** In a highly competitive and collaborative network environment, enterprises have to focus on their core competencies and to increase internal and external collaboration to provide more efficient services to meet various needs of markets. However, governance is still one of the most important challenges for collaborative enterprises. Some studies on collaborative networks just focus on technological aspects, often neglecting other business related issues. Business process management, performance management and business process alignment are key questions to be solved to increase the global synergy of the Collaborative Organization. In this paper, we propose to extend the traditional XaaS model to the Business Layer and propose a flexible, efficient collaborative governance framework: Governance as a Service framework (GaaS) which supports dashboard mashups and autonomous strategy to govern globally the collaborative environment.

**Keywords:** collaborative environment, SOA, autonomic computing, mashups.

## 1    Introduction

In a highly competitive, globalized economies and collaborative network environment, the business landscape has changed dramatically and technologies are rapidly improved. To meet the new requirements of users and to survive in today's turbulent market conditions, comprising various heterogeneous entities with different competences, enterprises have to focus on their core competencies and to set collaborative strategies to provide more complex services and outstanding products fitting the markets needs. Developing Collaborative Networked Organizations (CNOs) is a way to achieve agility and increase operation efficiency and resources productivity and as a consequence increases the call for adapted governance environments to measure the success of these collaborative environments.

Some studies on business efficiency lack of paying attention neither to collaborative networks nor to the implementation layers whereas other studies focus on technological Quality of Service issues, neglecting other issues, such as business aspects within collaborative networks. To overcome this limit, our Business performance management and technical performance management framework is based on a multi-dimension approach on CNO (technological, social, semantic and business perspective).

L.M. Camarinha-Matos, L. Xu, and H. Afsarmanesh (Eds.): PRO-VE 2012, IFIP AICT 380, pp. 687–694, 2012.
© IFIP International Federation for Information Processing 2012

This paper is organized as follow: after presenting the context and the related works (section 2), we extend the traditional XaaS model to the Business layer and propose a flexible, efficient, low cost collaborative Governance as a Service (GaaS) framework, taking advantage of autonomic computing and mashups technology to support agile and adaptive dashboards management (section 3).

## 2    State of the Art

As a result of globalization, CNOs are strengthening their internal and external cooperation ability, look for improving their performance in different aspects such as increased inventory turnover, increased revenues, cost reductions, product availability, and economic value added [1]. Despite their economical interest, several factors (such as lack of top management support, cross-functional conflicts, lack of trust, etc) still limit effective collaboration [2] and may lead collaborative initiatives to fail [3], [4].

As CNOs performance level depends on both its internal organization and on each partner own performance level, it is necessary to identify and measure the inner-enterprise and external-enterprise performance elements and being able to manage effectively collaborative relationships [5]. Most of the existing Performance Measurement Systems (PMSs) are not designed to manage and improve enterprises' activities. Various barriers (decentralized organization, uncertainty, dispersed IT infrastructure, etc) obstruct collaborative governance development [6], [7]. In their survey, [2] gave an extensive literature review on monitor and control performance of Virtual Enterprises (VE) and Extended Enterprises (EE). They pointed out there was not a framework fully accomplished to monitor VE and EE and their proposal (a PMS for VE and EE (PMS-EVE)) lacks of ability to control business activities. Even if [8] presents a model and a performance measurement system for collaborative supply chain (CSC), it does not to fit complex collaborative environment nor improves the CSC performance. According to a rather technical point of view, the DMTF new Architecture for Managing Cloud takes service as a black box for managing and does not pay attention on the business perspective nor address how to build management function in a cloud [9].

This review shows that most of PMS do not support a dynamic management organization. Only few of them integrate Management Information System (MIS) features but without considering the links between top management organization and specific IT infrastructure [10]. To overcome these limits [11]. combine change management and MIS specialists in the context of globalization, servitization and networking in multi-cultural environment. Using efficiently distributed data, it still lacks of reactive abilities.

These limits are quite similar to those encountered in a biological system [12] (having to face efficiently the changing environment, being self-adaptive, self-organized, robust and allowing distributed and parallel computation as well as self-learning). Immunologically inspired strategies have been successfully used in computer and internet security [13] as it helps to answer automatically, to resolve problems, security threads and system failures in collaborative environment [14].

To overcome existing PMSs limits, we propose a flexible and agile Governance as a Service framework extending the traditional XaaS model to the Business Layer. Fitting the CNOs performance requirements (dynamicity, management of multiple dimensions…) it takes advantage of mashups to define adaptive dashboard.

# 3    Contribution

Our governance framework aims to meet the needs of collaborative enterprises, to improve the culture of openness, sharing ideas thus enhancing flexibility in business processes and innate ability to embrace innovation both inside and outside the organization. Due to the geographical distribution of collaborative enterprises, our Governance as a Service framework deploys local key performance indicator to govern performance of each participant organization and activates local action engines to reduce wastes and errors. We also build a cross-platform virtual resources repository to share governance information and make full use of existing resources to establish mashup-based dashboards and improve the efficiency of display governance reports. It consists in 4 components: Interaction Window; Mediator Component; Govern & Act Component; Resource Repository. Even if each component can be geographically distributed according to users' needs, they all closely collaborate with each other to comprehensively monitor the performance of collaborative environment. (See figure 1)

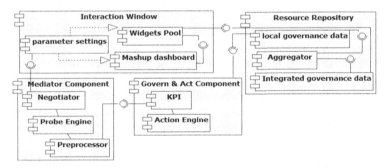

**Fig. 1.** Overview structure of Governance as a Service framework

## 3.1    Components and Working Principle of GaaS

As said previously, our framework consists in 4 main components:

- **Interaction Window (IW).** It includes Parameter Settings (IW-PS), widgets Pool (IW-WP) and Mashups Dashboard (IW-MD). The Widget pool (WP) includes all widgets that can be chosen by users to be displayed in their mashup-based dashboard. Widgets pick data from shared data repository.

- **Mediator Component (MC).** It includes Negotiator (MC-N), Probe Engine (MC-PE) and Preprocessor (MC-P). This component extends the adaptability of GaaS to make it can fit any enterprises without technical and organizational limits. MC-N negotiates with the monitored organizations to establish specific agreements. Then the mediator Probe Engine (MC-PE) establishes a governance connection with collaborative enterprise. MC-P synchronizes business processes and converts data format for follow-up governance processes.
- **Govern & Act Component (G&A).** It includes KPIs and Action Engines (AEs). According to the feature of collaborative enterprise, as business participants could be geographically distributed, KPIs are deployed into each participant organization and information system to govern its performance and activate AEs to improve enterprise's ability of self-optimizing. After that, all governance and action information is stored into a shared data pool.
- **Resource Repository (RR).** It is a geographically distributed resource repository. All resources in it closely collaborate. It includes local data from KPIs and AEs, Aggregators (RR-A) aggregate scattered governance results into comprehensive results, and save them to the integrated data pool. All shared data and resources can be used to build customized governance result displayed by the widgets.

**The working principle** of our collaborative governance architecture is shown figure 2:

- Users set parameters for governance;
- Mediator Component negotiates with monitoring participants to establish governance connecting and sign agreements for each participant, then preprocess business information for follow-up governance processes;
- Deploy KPIs and AEs to govern and act for each monitoring participant, save results to shared data pool;
- Aggregators analyze and aggregate scattered data into comprehensive governance results and save to integrated data pool;
- According to users' requirements, widgets pool picks useful resources from resource repository to build widgets can be chosen by users. Mashups dashboard can be flexibly organized by users.

### 3.2    KPI and AE Self-management

KPIs are associated with Non-functional Properties' (NFPs) definition. Our governance framework can assign and deploy KPIs to collect performance information in a cross-platform organization. Due to the complexity and dynamicity of collaborative environments, KPIs and AEs should be updated continuously to make governance framework works efficiently.

We design this KPIs' self-evolution and self-management strategies, according to the principles taken from the artificial immunity system. This self-management system aims at improving governance framework's intelligence and flexibility by:

$$\text{Self } \cup \text{ Ag} = \text{AP}; \quad \text{Self } \cap \text{ Ag} = \phi . \tag{2}$$

Action Engines as antibodies in our autonomous strategies. They are activated by KPIs to eliminate antigens. The population of KPI and AE are changed by the population of detected antigen. KPI is given by the Local Governance component (each participant in collaborative environment has efficient local KPIs), NFP (each KPI governs specific non-functional properties), Age (KPI's lifecycle phase) and AE (each KPI activates relevant action engine). AE is given by the Local Governance component (each participant in collaborative environment has its antibodies), KPI (this antibody is activated by relevant KPI), Age (antibody's lifecycle phase) and Action (antibody's action to eliminate antigens) as shown in equations (3) and (4).

$$\text{KPI} = \{<\text{Local, NFP, Age, AE}> | \text{Local} \in (\text{A, B, C}) \wedge \text{NFP} \wedge \text{Age} \in \text{KPI} \tag{3}$$
(lifecycle) $\wedge$ AE} .

$$\text{AE} = \{<\text{Local, KPI, Age, Action}> | \text{Level} \in (\text{A, B, C}) \wedge \text{KPI} \wedge \text{Age} \in \text{AE} \quad v(4)$$
(lifecycle) $\wedge$ Action} .

**Aggregator Selection Strategies.** In order to give comprehensive governance results for collaborative enterprises, aggregators analyze business processes and NFP classification to integrate scattered KPIs and AEs' results, and to aggregate global collaborative results.

$$\text{Aggregator's result} = \sum \text{ relevant KPIs' measure results} + \text{relevant AE's} \tag{5}$$
results

## 4    Conclusion

This paper proposes a distributed Governance as a Service framework with immune-inspired strategy. It has self-adaptability and can seamlessly collaborate with various enterprises. It overcomes existing collaborative enterprise governance limits; comprehensively govern collaborative networks' performance and increase the flexibility and intelligence from business processes to infrastructure operations. It optimizes enterprises' ability to quickly and efficiently set-up, maintain, develop, chose best services and collaborate with partners to reinforce external and internal collaborative work of enterprises. It also improves ability of enterprises to cope with changes from both technical and organizational points of view, and makes sure enterprises get benefits from collaboration. This collaborative and immune-inspired Governance as a Service framework that makes collaborative enterprises can remix information from inside and outside the enterprise to solve problems, reduce wastes and enhance agility flexibility and ability of self-optimization quickly.

# References

1. Fawcett, S.E., Magnan, G.M., et al.: Benefits, barriers, and bridges to effective supply chain management. J. Supply Chain Management. 13(1), 35–48 (2008)
2. Saiz, J.J.A., Rodriguez, R.R., Bas, A.O.: A Performance Measurement System for Virtual and Extended Enterprises. In: Camarinha-Matos, L.M., Afsarmanesh, H., Ortiz, A. (eds.) Collaborative Networks and Their Breeding Environments. IFIP, vol. 186, pp. 285–292. Springer, Boston (2005)
3. Burton, T.T., Boeder, S.M.: The Lean Extended Enterprise: Moving Beyond the Four Walls to Value Stream Excellence. J. Ross Publishing, Inc., Florida (2003)
4. Bullinger, H.J., Kuhner, M., Hoof, A.V.: Analysing supply chain performance using a balanced measurement method. J. Production Research 40(15), 3533–3543 (2002)
5. Architecture for Managing Clouds (v1.0.0), DMTF white paper (2010)
6. Folan, P., Browne, J.: A review of performance measurement: Towards performance management. Computers in Industry 56(7), 663–680 (2005)
7. Lohman, C., Fortuin, L., Wouters, M.: Designing a performance measurement system: a case study. European Journal of Operational Research, 267–286 (2004)
8. Angerhofer, B.J., Angelides, M.C.: A model and a performance measurement system for collaborative supply chains. J. Decision Support Systems 42(1), 283–301 (2006)
9. Simatupang, T.M., Sridharan, R.: An integrative framework for supply chain collaboration. J. Logistics Management 16(2), 257–274 (2005)
10. Nudurupati, S.S., Bititci, U.S., Kumar, V., Chan, F.T.S.: State of the art literature review on performance measurement. J. Computers & Industrial Engineering 60(2), 279–290 (2011)
11. Durdik, Z., Drawehn, J., Herbert, M.: Towards automated service quality prediction for development of enterprise mashups. In: Proceedings of the 5th International Workshop on Web APIs and Service Mashups, NY, USA (2011)
12. Lee, C., Suzuki, J.: An immunologically-inspired autonomic framework for self-organizing and evolvable network applications. ACM Trans. Auton. Adapt. Syst. 4(4), Article 22 (November 2009)
13. Li, T., Liu, X.J., Li, H.B.: A New Model for Dynamic Intrusion Detection. In: Desmedt, Y.G., Wang, H., Mu, Y., Li, Y. (eds.) CANS 2005. LNCS, vol. 3810, pp. 72–84. Springer, Heidelberg (2005)
14. An architecture blueprint for autonomic computing, IBM white paper, 3rd edn. (June 2005)

# Author Index